Biologically–Inspired Computing for the Arts:

Scientific Data through Graphics

Anna Ursyn
University of Northern Colorado, USA

Managing Director: Lindsay Johnston
Senior Editorial Director: Heather Probst
Book Production Manager: Sean Woznicki
Development Manager: Joel Gamon
Development Editor: Michael Killian
Acquisitions Editor: Erika Gallagher
Typesetter: Lisandro Gonzalez
Cover Design: Nick Newcomer, Lisandro Gonzalez

Published in the United States of America by
    Information Science Reference (an imprint of IGI Global)
    701 E. Chocolate Avenue
    Hershey PA 17033
    Tel: 717-533-8845
    Fax: 717-533-8661
    E-mail: cust@igi-global.com
    Web site: http://www.igi-global.com

Artwork within the cover image © 1999, by Anna Ursyn." Change of Matter", Ursyn.com. Used with permission.

Library of Congress Cataloging-in-Publication Data

Biologically-inspired computing for the arts: scientific data through graphics / Anna Ursyn, Editor.
      p. cm.
   Includes bibliographical references and index.
   Summary: "This book comprises a collection of authors' individual approaches to the relationship between nature, science, and art created with the use of computers, discussing issues related to the use of visual language in communication about biologically-inspired scientific data, visual literacy in science, and application of practitioner's approach"--Provided by publisher.
   ISBN 978-1-4666-0942-6 (hardcover) -- ISBN 978-1-4666-0943-3 (ebook) -- ISBN 978-1-4666-0944-0 (print & perpetual access) 1. Biologically-inspired computing--Graphic methods. 2. Visual communication--Data processing. 3. Biological illustration. I. Ursyn, Anna, 1955-
   Q222.B56 2012
   006.6--dc23
                              2011049596

British Cataloguing in Publication Data
A Cataloguing in Publication record for this book is available from the British Library.

All work contributed to this book is new, previously-unpublished material. The views expressed in this book are those of the authors, but not necessarily of the publisher.

Table of Contents

Section 1
Visual Data Formation: Biology Inspired Generation and Analysis of Objects and Processes

Section 2
Visualizing the Invisible: Processes for the Visual Data Formation

Section 3
Scientific Communication through Visual Language

Detailed Table of Contents

Section 1
Visual Data Formation: Biology Inspired Generation and Analysis of Objects and Processes

Every day, humans come across billions of data that are beyond their cognitive capacity to perceive and absorb. The data ranges from trivial to highly sophisticated, which can only be understood with proper tools and coding instruments. Moreover, the same data can be received in different ways depending on the background, needs, or tasks of the user. That means there are always possibilities for various interpretations. People strive to make processing flexible, reversible, and editable. For this purpose, man often examines nature to get ideas and solutions.

Chapter 1

Rachel Zuanon, Anhembi Morumbi University, Brazil

The bio-interfaces are widening the notions of complexity, affectiveness, and naturalness to an organismic scale, in which the physiological information about the users acts as the data to configure an interaction that responds to their emotional state in order to match the state of their body at that particular moment. The chapter discusses the role of the bio-interfaces in building an interaction governed by the biology of the users. The author provides applications of bio-interfaces in the areas of design, art, and games, considering their use as wearable devices that provide an organic interaction between man and machine, which could, in turn, lead these systems to a co-evolutionary relationship.

Chapter 2

Mark Stock, Independent Artist, Scientist, and Programmer, USA

While fluid flow is a ubiquitous phenomenon on both Earth's surface and elsewhere in the cosmos, its existence, as a mathematical field quantity without discrete form, color, or shape, defies representation in the visual arts. Both physical biology and computational physics are, at their roots, very large systems of interacting agents. The field of computational fluid dynamics deals with solving the essential formulae of fluid dynamics over large numbers of interacting elements. This chapter presents a novel method for creating fluid-like forms and patterns via interacting elements. Realistic, fluid-like motions are presented on a computer using a particle representation of the rotating portions of the flow. The straightforward method works in two or three dimensions and is amenable to instruction and easy application to a variety of visual media. Examples from digital flatwork and video art illustrate the method's potential to bring space, shape, and form to an otherwise ephemeral medium.

Chapter 3
Mohammad Majid al-Rifaie, Goldsmiths, University of London, UK
Ahmed Aber, The Royal Free Hospital, London, UK
John Mark Bishop, Goldsmiths, University of London, UK

A novel approach of integrating two swarm intelligence algorithms is considered – one algorithm simulates the behaviour of birds flocking (Particle Swarm Optimisation), and the other algorithm (Stochastic Diffusion Search) mimics the recruitment behaviour of one species of ants – Leptothorax acervorum. This hybrid algorithm is assisted by a biological mechanism inspired by the behaviour of cells in blood vessels, where the concept of high and low blood pressure is utilised. The performance of the swarms and the cells in the hybrid algorithm is reflected through a cooperative attempt to make a drawing, which is created by the two nature-inspired algorithms – which lead the swarms – and one biologically inspired mechanism (blood vessel cells and blood flow) that assists the swarms with their performance on the canvas. The scientific value of the marriage between the two swarm intelligence algorithms is currently being investigated thoroughly on many benchmarks and the results reported suggest a promising prospect (al-Rifaie, Bishop, & Blackwell, 2011). The authors of this chapter also discuss whether or not the artworks generated by nature and biologically inspired algorithms can possibly be considered as computationally creative.

Chapter 4
Kuai Shen Auson, Academy of Media Arts Cologne & Cologne Game Lab, Germany

Ants represent a natural superorganism, an autopoietic machine, much like human society. Nevertheless, the ant society stands out due to self-organization. Ants accomplish the generation of bottom-up structures communicating mainly by pheromones, but they also produce modulatory vibrations. This phenomenon represents a fascinating subject of research that needs to be amplified in order to identify the connections between these social organisms and humans; they share the same environment with humans and thus participate in the construction and mutation of posthuman ecology. The human-ant relationship plays an important role in the creation of new ecosystems and the transformations of old ones. Artists can approach and embrace this relationship by means of artistic experiments that explore the bioacoustics involved in the social behavior of ants supported by the combination of cybernetics, autopoiesis, self-organization, and emergence.

Chapter 5
Hironori Yoshida, Carnegie Mellon University, USA

The recent movement from mass production to mass customization enabled by digital fabrication has opened the door for new typologies in architecture and design. The author brought the idea of mass customization to material connection, which normally appears as orthogonal seams that are predominant in man-made objects. This chapter introduces gradient material transitions that seamlessly bridge synthetic and organic matter. Using digital image processing of organic forms, the fabrication process generates 3D tooling paths, culminating in the concept of bio customization, rather than mass customization, a new prospect of digital fabrication.

Section 2
Visualizing the Invisible: Processes for the Visual Data Formation

Quite often new light is cast on existing constructs or current state of knowledge. Many times it is vital to revisit approaches to laws and connections believed to govern the world. Disciplines are so interlocked and at the same time so specialized that the collaborative exchange of knowledge is necessary to deal with many invisible features of nature, those related to physical laws, the micro and macro scale, or the invisible forces (such as energy of wind or strength of underground currents) and dynamic processes that are described differently for each discipline. Thus, knowledge evolves with the developments of tools.

Chapter 6

Humans' complex and dynamic relationship with nature has influenced not only the content but also the physical properties of the moving image since its beginnings. Throughout history, a subset of art and design has used the agency of natural forces on the actual materials as a way to consider the society's connection with the environment. Artists have attempted to harness the physics, biology, and ecology of the natural environment as artistic tools by integrating natural phenomena and by mimicking natural systems in their creative strategies. Today, digital media seems far removed from its organic and natural beginnings. However, as the global conversation shifts towards sustainable development, it is time to revisit artworks that considered the environment as a co-creator in their realization, and to make new works that comment on and even strengthen our relationship with nature. As one of several artists now working in sustainable energy, the author created a series of kinetic public sculptures that use natural power sources to create the moving image. These sculptures are presented here as a case study for a larger perspective on the continuing relationship between the forces of nature and the materials of the moving image.

Chapter 7

To explore enlightened collaborations between art and science, and to probe the ideas, images, and mutual interests connecting art and science professionals and disciplines, the Synapse Group at the University of Akron was formed. This chapter presents selected artworks created by the artists associated with the group. Some of the works were created in collaborations with the scientists in the group, and some were inspired by the science of nature. A major theme of this chapter is visualizing water that is unseen, whether it is invisible underground water or imaginary virtual ocean water. The invisible are made visible by rendering water data with 3D computer graphics or by perceiving interactions between water and other objects. Artworks dealing with digital data in the forms of 2D and 3D imagery are also included. Such digital imagery is processed and interpreted to refocus the attention of the audience and to tell a story. Also explained in the chapter are the inspiration processes by which those artworks were created.

This chapter is an attempt to introduce NanoArt. First, it goes back in time to the first uses of nanomaterials and nanotechnologies to create art and continues with the beginnings of nano art. Then, it follows a status on this new artistic/scientific discipline and the movement that evolved from recent technological developments in the multidisciplinary area known as nanotechnology. The chapter informs about the international juried NanoArt competitions, displays select art works, mostly collected in the NanoArt21 Gallery, and finally presents selected nano artists' thoughts.

It has been generally accepted in history of art that nature ranks as a master and an ideal of the arts. Everybody knows examples of nature-related art works created over centuries in a conventional manner.. Curators of new media art exhibitions are involved in current developments in computing, discussing questions such as whether the computer as a tool be a means to generate new representations of nature-related art. This would demand results different from conventional works of art, as to the conceptual creation processes as well as the output. Some theoretical background and categorizing of such creations are discussed with illustrated by examples from artists participating in a series of "Computerkunst/ Computer Art" exhibitions since 1986. Though it might be too soon to judge computational art works concerning their importance in art history, a closer investigation in the creative processes and social contexts seems helpful and worthwhile.

Section 3
Scientific Communication through Visual Language

Most disciplines rely on visual communication. Visual quality of data presentation gains in importance, because the better it is, the more convincing becomes the message, thought, and even the product. Teams of specialists involve the artists to attain fast, effective, and efficient communication with visual quality.

This chapter explores the use of code, form, and interactivity in translating biological objects into mathematically generated digital environments. The existence of a mathematical language contained in all physical objects that is similar in function to DNA in organisms is proposed as a core component and driving force of this exploration. Code, form, and interactivity makes possible to explore, understand, and teach this hidden biological language by re-writing its algorithms in ways we may readily recognize and absorb. The designer's own works: "Clouds & Ichor," and "Stream" demonstrate and ground the concepts being discussed. "Clouds & Ichor" explores the possibilities of a material that exhibits a mixture of properties of both liquid (ex: water) and fabric (ex: silk or cloth). The resulting material has memory (something liquid does not), and the ability to split and/or combine at will (self healing, something fabric does not do). "Stream" looks into the combination of flocking organisms, curiosity, environmental color response, and human body language that respond interactively to a user's motion and gestures. In both projects, a natural learning experience is at the core of the biological process.

Chapter 11

Anna Ursyn, University of Northern Colorado, USA

This chapter is focused on creating the visual approach to natural processes, concepts, and events, rather than their description for learning. It has been designed as an active, involving, action-based exercise in visual communication. Interactive reading is a visual tool aimed at communication, activation, and expansion of one's visual literacy. It addresses the interests of professionals who would like to further their developments in their domains. The reader is encouraged to read this chapter interactively by developing visual responses to the inspiring issues. This experience will be thus generated cooperatively with the readers who will construct interactively many different, meaningful pictorial interpretations. The chapter comprises two projects about water-related themes; each project invites the reader to create visual presentation of this theme. Selected themes involve: (1) States of matter exemplified by ice, water, and steam, and (2) Water habitats: lake, river, and swamp.

Chapter 12

Anna Ursyn, University of Northern Colorado, USA

"Visual Tweet: Nature Inspired Visual Statements" explores connections between science, computing, and art in a similar way as it is done in a chapter "Looking at Science through Water." This chapter examines concepts and processes that relate to the domains of physics, biology, computing, and other sciences, and at the same time pertain to the planet's life and everyday experience. The reader is encouraged to solve the projects visually, through art, and/or through graphics. Exploration of science-based concepts and nature-related processes will support understanding of the project themes, trigger our imagination, and thus inspire enhancement of an ability to communicate with visual language and create artistic work. Comprehension of what will be noticed, the power of abstract thought, and one's own answer to some evolving issues will result in readers' personal visual projects – drawings, graphics, illustrations, animations, video clips, or web projects. This chapter comprises two projects about science-related themes: (1) Symmetry and pattern in animal world: geometry and art; and (2) Crystals. Each project invites the reader to create visual presentation of the themes.

Chapter 13

Jean Constant, Northern New Mexico College, USA

This chapter describes visualization of the 19th century representations from a Japanese culture – a set of mathematical problems etched on wooden boards. Mathematicians, especially geometers followed the Shinto temples' carving tradition from the Edo period (1603-1867), where worshipers carved the likenesses of horses onto wooden tablets and used those tablets as offerings. The author describes the steps in the creation of artistic statements based on geometrical problems: selecting, scanning, and converting images into digital information followed by vectorization, converting into bitmaps, assigning colors, and then blending the monochrome sketches and colored templates. A QuickTime movie presents (online) the creative process. Discussion refers to the dissemination of the project in art galleries and online, its potential instructional use, and examines the audience responses.

Section 4
Tools for Metaphors: Nature Described with the Use of Mathematics and Computing

While examining and researching processes and events, specific ways to approach a problem are developed. Human needs mandate that the development of particular tools, and in turn, tools stimulate new ideas and solutions found both by scientists and artists.

Small elements in large numbers and densely arranged are a frequently observed phenomena in nature. The chapter uses an arbitrarily chosen stretch of landscape, a dry riverbed, to formulate artistic intentions and design programmed interpretations of them. From the database of recorded findings the author formulates concepts, which he then transforms into programs to generate drawings. This chapter experimentally addresses the formulation of a few concepts inspired by nature, aimed at generating line drawings executed on pen-plotters. Unlike in science and engineering, a piece of code does not produce a solution to a problem for concepts in generative art. Generative drawings are produced through a structured process including a sequence of discrete procedural steps, which are: finding and recording; concept and transformation; programming and testing; and drawing and interpretation.

The relation between the viewer and the artwork has been changed through the development of computer-augmented physical kinetic objects. To explore the specific performance of kinetic interactions, this chapter proposes a biomimetic perspective to demonstrate three kinetic interactive artworks through a modular design approach. MSOrgm is developed as a robot plant to interact with the viewer in a soothing way. Its body is assembled with a hybrid organization, composed of microprocessors, truss structure, and actuators. SSOrgan is designed as an organic skin to interact with the viewer's touch of the top of it. Each sensing cell acts as an individual sensor, which performs the gathering, transmitting, and exchanging the pressure values with neighboring cells in the form of color. LBSkeleton is a robotic instrument that produces pneumatic sound and emits soothing light into space. It consists of dense replicated foldable module, which can make the whole body transformation.

The author discusses her latest digital image series, A New Leaf Series, within the context of early photographic imaging and its connection to science and biology by investigating and connecting to the work of Thomas Wedgewood, William Henry Fox-Talbot, and the early pioneers of photographic technologies. Works of Hippolyte Bayard and Anna Atkins serve as early examples of the scientific fundamentals of photography; the technological advances of the medium still draw on the same subject matter to reveal the basic structure of conceptual and aesthetic investigation. The author discusses how contemporary electronic imaging has returned to its photographic origins through nature-related subject matter.

Section 5
Analytical Discourse: Philosophy and Aesthetics of Nature Inspired Creations

The speed and efficacy of media growth, accessibility, and easiness create a lot of challenges and discourses. Current media and tools cause discovering new solutions that are provoking to ponder how fast the novelty is exchanged with the even newer novelty, how the latest solutions support qualities of the ideas or products, and finally, how novel solutions find their permanent status.

This chapter discusses how both art and science proceed from an appreciation for and application of the natural proportions and forms associated with nature. Descriptions of the Golden Ratio, fractals, and the holographic metaphor are presented with examples from geometry, nature, science, and art. An outline of a personal theory follows, of aesthetics based on emulation of the structure of nature and the work of Thomas Aquinas and James Joyce. A collage series entitled The Elements in Golden Ratio illustrates application of the author's aesthetic theory. The author concludes with personal observations on the commonalities between art and science and how an appreciation of natural form and aesthetics can enhance the practice of both.

The term bio art covers the kind of art that seems to come from the biology lab, with simulations of life forms through generative processes, with data taken from organisms, or even through organisms themselves. This is often at the micro level, invisible to the naked eye, where seeing requires some degree of computer modeling. This chapter discusses works of artists who work alongside biologists to produce visual works of extraordinary quality, in both their decorative and intellectual aspects. Drawing manuals of a hundred years ago advocated the study of plant forms, sometimes as the basis for pattern design. The author describes his own use of scientific sources, arguing there is also a place for art that evokes the wonders of nature without being tied to the visible facts.

In the context of contemporary fine art, the chapter discusses the translation (the finding of equivalences) of a phenomenological experience of water during the activity of swimming into drawing with both traditional drawing media and a tablet computer – an Apple iPad. Firstly, the chapter furthers understanding and gives insights into interaction and relationship with water during this specific activity. Secondly, the author explores and discusses the premise that drawing is phenomenology, considering whether this premise is compromised when drawing with an Apple iPad rather than traditional drawing media. The phenomenological approach to both philosophy (including Merleau-Ponty) and theoretical research (including Rosand) aims at supporting understanding of experiences of water during the activity of swimming and the process of translation of those experiences into drawing.

Art, science, and spirituality comprise a triumvirate of conceptual and process-oriented contexts that are founded on different philosophical tenets. They all help to interpret experience with the universe. This chapter examines how a generalist perspective may counterbalance deconstruction of perceived elemental units, so as to avoid becoming bound by paradigm. Art and science are addressed as related observational methods to explore hypotheses and represent the varied aspects of existence. A practicing artist and a practicing artist/scientist present examples of art works entitled From Zero to Infinity, to illustrate the commonalities that art and science share with respect to pragmatic and creative processes, while not equating art with science as similar cognitive domains.

Foreword

Two decades ago, I was at an international science conference in Japan where a few of the presentations there used the computer's emerging power for visualization. The response from the audience was mixed. "Eye-opening!" was the response of a tiny minority. "Irrelevant!" was the response from the greater majority. Of the latter opinion, what I heard was that, "Pictures don't tell us anything more than the equations can. In fact, they cloud and distract us from how we think."

Fast forward twenty years later, and it's interesting that this body of work on biologically-inspired computing for the arts has been collected, because it represents a kind of reversal in the audience (from scientists to artists), and because the utility of visualization is no longer in question the way it was before. The pragmatic usefulness of visualization is now more evident; and now the aesthetic, emotional satisfaction of visualization is coming into play. We are people, not machines. And we love to see things and experience them. And what better way to understand something than through beauty?

Having spent the last three years at Rhode Island School of Design, having moved here from MIT, I've noticed how artists think differently, and naturally, as a kind of *raison d'être*. Given that discovery is all about working from new perspectives, it is clear that the way artists think differently can have incredible value in the STEM (Science, Technology, Engineering, Mathematics) disciplines today. A STEAM-focused approach – add the A, Art to STEM – can expand the horizons of human discovery with impact to both utility and pleasure. Turning STEM to STEAM is exactly what this body of work represents for computing, arts, and the sciences. The world looks forward to more of it to come.

John Maeda
President, Rhode Island School of Design, USA
September 13, 2011

John Maeda *is a world-renowned artist, graphic designer, computer scientist, and educator whose career reflects his philosophy of humanizing technology. For over a decade, he has worked to integrate technology, education, and the arts into a 21st century synthesis of creativity and innovation. A recipient of the National Design Award and represented in the permanent collection of the Museum of Modern Art, Maeda became president of Rhode Island School of Design in June 2008. He seeks to connect RISD to political, economic, social, and business spheres where artists and designers make a difference, and has prioritized scholarships to ensure the broadest possible access to a RISD education. Maeda taught media arts and sciences at MIT for 12 years and served as associate director of research at MIT Media Lab. His books include The Laws of Simplicity, translated into 14 languages. Redesigning Leadership (2011, with Becky Bermont) expands on his Twitter posts. In 2008 Maeda was named one of the 75 most influential people of the 21st century by Esquire and in 2010 he was called the "Steve Jobs of academia" by Forbes.*

Preface

Art is a short word; however, since it is based on nature, long words cannot be avoided when talking about science and technology. Some words are new and others are forgotten after the school times had ended. The world may be experienced using the senses, but minuscule, invisible fragments of reality, abstract concepts, or even ideas can be visualized. Nature- or science-derived images may serve an artistic purpose, also when transformed into algorithmic structure. The book's contributors keep an eye on nature and its organic forms, from the tiniest nano particles to cosmos (we are all inhabitants of the cosmos, anyway), and then transform this info into art forms with the use of computing. Individual authors refine their study to particular fragments of nature. Some themes appear in more than one chapter, for example, several authors indicate their interest in flow and examine one concept from various perspectives: Mark Stock discusses in Chapter 2 how flow supports the variety and vitality of life on Earth and describes computational fluid dynamics that involves solving the fluid equations of motion, fluid simulations, and related biological computations, while Hans Dehlinger applies in Chapter 14 the generative drawing to offer metaphorical images of the riverbed and ocean; furthermore, chapters 11 and 12 examine water flow from several viewpoints. More themes, such as fractals, nano structures, or swarm computing are interwoven in the book in a similar way, and so are the people who contribute to the developments in the related domains.

This book comprises a collection of individual approaches to the relationship between nature, science, and art created with the use of computers. Themes of the chapters pertain to a wide spectrum of authors' interests; they involve nature and description of nature including mathematics and scientific disciplines. Thus, themes discussed in the book relate to the use of visual language in communication about biologically-inspired scientific data, visual literacy in science, and application of a practitioner's approach: people can understand things better when they can visualize and picture them theirselves. The notion of computing adopted in this book embraces any kind of activities that require the use or benefit from the use of computer hardware and software.

The topic of this book fits in the world today when the chapters explore connections between nature, science, and art, and discuss how art and design support science understanding by visualizing concepts and processes. Art creation benefits from learning about scientific processes and concepts. Processes and products provide inspiration for creation of meaningful art, while art creation helps understand and memorize data framework and structure. The action of designing materials and data helps understand concepts and processes.

Images enhance connections between biology, engineering, and material sciences resulting in growing partnership among academia, laboratories, and industry. Scientists focus on biology-inspired research to understand how biological systems work, and then create systems and materials that would have efficiency and precision of living structures. According to the National Research Council of the National Academies (National Research, 2008), strategies for creation of new materials and systems may be characterized as bio-mimicry, bio-inspiration, and bio-derivation.

Bio-mimicry refers to learning the principles used by a living system to achieve similar function in synthetic material and also create materials that mimic cells in their response to external stimuli. For example, certain cells such as T-lymphocytes can sense particular external stimuli, and then deal with pathogens. The challenge is to design bio-inspired systems and devices for detecting hazardous biological and chemical agents and strengthen national security systems.

Bio-inspiration means developing a system that performs the same function, even with a different scheme. For example, the adhesive gecko foot, the self-cleaning lotus leaf, and the fracture-resistant mollusk shell are examples of inspiring structures. The cutting-edge optical technology solutions can be found in nature: multilayer reflectors, diffraction gratings, optical fibers, liquid crystals, and structures that scatter light are found in animals as well. For instance, Morpho butterfly has iridescence sparkle and blue color visible from hundreds of meters due to periodic photonic structure in scales on wings, without any dye involved.

Bio-derivation is known as using existing biomaterial to create a hybrid with artificial material, such as incorporation of biologically derived protein into polymeric assemblies for targeted drug delivery. The eyes of higher organisms and the photosynthesis mechanism in plants are examples of biological structures and processes that can support harvesting light and also fuels (by converting cellulose polymer to ethanol). Deciphering force and motions in proteins driven by sub-cellular, molecular motors can advance clinical diagnostics, prosthetics, and drug delivery. Molecular motors convert chemical energy (usually in form of ATP - adenosine triphosphate) into mechanical energy. Contrary to Brownian movements, it is not driven solely by thermal effects. Scientists strive to create self-evolving, self-healing, self-cleaning, and self-replicating super-materials that could mimic the ability to evolve and adapt. The challenge is not easy to meet: for example, the gecko's adhesive works in vacuum and underwater, leaves no residue, and is self-cleaning; adhesion is reversible, so geckoes alternatively stick and unstuck themselves 15 times per second as they run up walls. As for now, "all attempts to mimic their design or to synthesize artificial polymers that are analogous to the bioadhesives in structure or function have been largely unsuccessful … and the magic of a gecko's 'dry' glue with its reversible attachments remains unsolved, unmatched, and more challenging than ever" (National Research, 2008, pp. 63-64).

In a process of nature-inspired inquiry about computing for art creation, artists and scientists examine those rules and formulas in science, which define natural processes by abstracting the essentials from specific events or objects, such as elements (e.g., carbon or oxygen) or molecules (e.g., water). One may see organic chemistry as a study of structure, properties, and reactions carbon-based compounds, such as hydrocarbons consisting of hydrogen and carbon, carbohydrates consisting of carbon, hydrogen, and oxygen (for example, with a ratio 2:1 as in water molecule), and other carbon-based compounds. Biological chemistry examines chemical processes in living matter, information transfer, and flow of energy through metabolism, mostly in cellular components such as proteins, carbohydrates, lipids, and nucleic acids, including DNA and RNA. At the atomic level, scientists examine soft condensed materials in states of matter neither liquid nor crystalline solid. Soft matter builds membranes and cytoplasm in human cells, and it is so omnipresent in biological systems that humans may be considered soft matter examples. Scientists apply abstract concepts, for example permeability or electromagnetism, to find rules and patterns that govern these materials. Explorations on structure and functions occurring in living and artificial matter involve intensive use of visualization techniques providing visual representation of information, data, and knowledge through pictures, information graphics, and also artistic display.

All these explorations connect science and art with computing. Art is needed not only in a quest for beauty, but because many times people can apprehend through art the essence of the concepts they attempt to grasp. Art provides the informative qualities of an idea, and thus communicates and explains ideas faster. The process of art creation has its inherent tendency to apply abstract thinking. Artists seek the principles that control the basic elements in art, such as line or color, and then convey the essence of their response to selected slice of reality. People may look at the works of art as if they were not only the aesthetical objects but also as information displays. Scientists and practitioners are showing a growing interest in aesthetics, especially aesthetics of visualization as related to the visual competence in the art, design, and technological solutions in visualization. Analyses of the images, forms, and motions in interactive generative design and art lead to new approaches in defining aesthetic criteria not only in terms of the work beauty. In a growing number of publications, the concept of aesthetics refers to the design effectiveness, efficiency, workability, usability, and easiness to understand (at a low cognitive cost) the visual display, not exclusively the beauty of an image.

In computer based data-, information-, or knowledge-visualization, the use of imaginative thinking leads to discovering new visual metaphors for abstract data, information, or concepts, and consequently to developing several kinds of visualization, for example, tag-cloud visualization of data. In computer science, imaginative approach to natural events and forces resulted in the development of biology-inspired computing, with several branches, such as artificial life, or fractal geometry of nature. Nature serves as a metaphor for developing new computing methods, for example, artificial neuronal networks, evolutionary algorithms, swarm intelligence, and also genetic engineering techniques, and bio-inspired hardware systems. Generative computing resulted in creating art and the developments in biology-inspired design, music, architecture, and other artistic fields.

Attitude towards the environment may influence one's art production, especially in the process of biology-inspired computing for the arts. Many art works obey mathematical order, repeat generative processes already existing in nature, follow randomized processes, rely on information theory, or otherwise support understanding of natural events. People may think about the physical and chemical laws as the essential rules that drive behavior and properties of natural structures and sustain the order in nature. Before examining the new media artists' inspiration with biology or science, people may first explore how the order in nature may apply to art. We may then wonder how physical and chemical laws relate to the elements and principles of art and design. Patterns existing in genetic codes such as the DNA code, or analogies coming from observation of swarm intelligence not only spur the scientists into computing for various technologies, but also inspire the new media artists to create art works built on biological systems. The generative approach makes possible exploring natural phenomena and at the same time allows the creative process. The artists' tools include systems defined by computer algorithms and/or software.

Biologically inspired art graphics may entail applying two-dimensional and three-dimensional graphics. They often present the processed images that show the steady state conditions (systems at equilibrium) or display dynamic conditions in real-time and/or in interactive way. Many times they may involve other techniques and fields of study, e.g., animation and visualization. Artistic rendering often supports creating models that represent empirical objects and allow making assumptions when it is hard to create experimental conditions. Artistic projects, in combination with simulations, aim at implementation of the model and may support testing, analysis, or training.

Generative art, which often uses digital tools such as mathematical or software algorithms, creates a program that displays certain behavior and reshapes our mental plan in computer terms. Such computer-related process may be seen as a task of abstracting essential codes to produce the efficient and evolvable solution. The final product of writing a computer program is often seen dependent on the choice of programming language (Iverson, 1980) in a similar manner as, according to the Sapir-Whorf hypothesis (Marshall, 1998), language shapes our perceptions of reality, so the way of somebody's thinking may depend on one's spoken language. The choice of digital media, a combination of art, science, and technology, often involving computing and programming, may shape the form and content of the new media art. New media art forms that involve or result from computing are widely used to communicate, interact, involve our senses, describe our social patterns, or socially interact. Creators of generative art often focus on the use of bio-inspired techniques, such as evolutionary computing, artificial life, neural networks, or swarm intelligence. Accordingly, notions about art aesthetics, theory, and classification have to follow the evolvements in art production.

The use of visual language supports communication with the readers. Imagination and creativity are needed in every professional or academic discipline and specialization. It has been often asserted that humans live in more and more visual world because of the ongoing changes in the means of communication (social network with videos and pictures), how concepts are defined (concept maps, visual mining), perceiving the meaning of art, learning (using online interactive visuals, videos), and socializing (exchanging visuals, using for example Skype and Facebook). To become habituated and better prepared for the changes in lifestyle and working habits, we need to expand our visual literacy. We need to be able to work with visual quality in mind.

DESCRIPTION OF THE STRUCTURE OF THE BOOK AND CONTRIBUTING CHAPTERS

The content of this book is divided into five sections.

Section 1 - Visual Data Formation: Biology Inspired Generation of Objects and Processes - comprises five chapters. Rachel Zuanon (Brazil) describes in Chapter 1, "Bio-interfaces: Designing Wearable Devices to Organic Interactions," the process of building interaction governed by the biology of the users. The author presents applications of bio-interfaces as wearable devices in the areas of design, art, and games. Mark Stock (USA) describes in Chapter 2, "Flow Simulation with Vortex Elements," a novel method for creating realistic fluid-like forms and patterns via interacting elements presented on a computer using a particle representation of the rotating portions of the flow. The author illustrates the method's potential with examples from digital flatwork and video art and thus makes both fluid simulations and related biological computations deep, interesting, and ready for exploration. In Chapter 3, "Cooperation of Nature and Physiologically Inspired Mechanisms in Visualisation," Mohammad Majid al-Rifaie, Ahmed Aber, and Mark John Bishop (UK) describe a novel way to integrate two swarm intelligence algorithms; one algorithm simulates the behavior of birds flocking (Particle Swarm Optimisation) and the other algorithm (Stochastic Diffusion Search) mimics the recruitment behaviour of one species of ants. This hybrid algorithm is assisted by a biological mechanism inspired by the behavior of cells in blood vessels, where the concept of high and low blood pressure is utilised. Drawings on the canvas reflect the performance of the swarms and the cells in the hybrid swarm intelligence algorithm. The authors discuss whether or not the art works generated by nature and physiology inspired algorithms can possibly be considered as computationally creative. In Chapter 4: "0h!m1gas: a Biomimetic Stridulation Environment" Kuai Shen Auson (Ecuador and Germany) presents an artistic experiment that explores the bioacoustics involved in the social behavior of ants when they communicate by producing modulatory vibrations. The author investigates the connections between these social organisms and humans, as human-ant relationship plays an important role in the creation of new ecosystems and the construction and mutation of posthuman ecology. In Chapter 5, "Bridging Synthetic and Organic Materiality: Graded Transitions in Material Connections," Hironori Yoshida (USA) introduces gradient material transitions that seamlessly bridge synthetic and organic matter, and applies what he learned about nature to architectural and interior design applications using digital fabrication of hybridized materials. Using digital image processing of organic forms, this fabrication process generates 3D tooling paths, culminating in the concept of bio-customization rather than mass customization, a new prospect of digital fabrication.

Section 2: Visualizing the Invisible: Processes for the Visual Data Formation contains four chapters:

Chapter 6, "Sustainable Cinema: the Moving Image and the Forces of Nature," by Scott Hessels (Hong Kong) discusses the continuing relationship between the forces of nature and the materials of the moving image. The author revisits artworks that considered the natural environment as a co-creator in their realization and then presents his own series of kinetic public sculptures that use natural power sources to create the moving image. In Chapter 7, "Seeing the Unseen," Eve Andrée Laramée, Kalyan Chakravarthy Thokala, Donna Webb, Eunsu Kang, Matthew Kolodziej, Peter Niewiarowski, and Yingcai Xiao (USA) present art works created by the artists associated with the Synapse Group at the University of Akron in collaborations with the scientists in the group and/or inspired by the science of nature. The invisible are made visible by rendering water data with 3D computer graphics or by perceiving interactions between water and other objects. In addition, art works dealing with digital data in the forms of 2D and 3D imagery are also included. Chapter 8, "NanoArt: Nanotechnology and Art," by Cristian Orfescu (USA) introduces nano art. First, it goes back in time to the first uses of nanomaterials and nanotechnologies to create art and continues with the beginnings of nano art. Then, it follows the movement that evolved from recent technological developments in the multidisciplinary area known as nanotechnology. The chapter informs about the NanoArt competitions, displays select art works, and finally presents selected nano artists' thoughts. Chapter 9, "Nature Related Computerkunst," by Wolfgang Schneider (Germany) discusses theoretical background, categorizes examples of nature related computer art, and then presents several examples from artists participating in a series of Computerkunst/Computer Art exhibitions during the years 1986-2010.

Section 3: Visual Communication: Scientific Communication through Visual Language comprises four chapters: Chapter 10, "Biological Translation: Virtual Code, Form, and Interactivity," by Collin Hover (USA) explores the use of code, form, and interactivity in translating biological objects into mathematically generated digital environments. The author's own works: "Clouds & Ichor" and "Stream" demonstrate and ground the concepts being discussed. In both projects, a natural learning experience is at the core of the biological process. Chapter 11, "Looking at Science through Water," by Anna Ursyn (USA) is focused on creating the visual approach to natural concepts and events, rather than on their description. It has been designed as an active, involved, action-based exercise in visual communication. The chapter comprises two projects about water-related themes: States of Matter exemplified by ice, water, and steam, and Water Habitats: lake, river, and swamp. Chapter 12, "Visual Tweet: Nature Inspired Visual Statements," by Anna Ursyn (USA), explores connections between science, computing, and art in a similar way as it is done in a previous chapter, examines concepts and processes that relate to particular fields in science, and pertain to Earth's life and personal, everyday experience. Two projects about science-related themes are: Symmetry and pattern in animal world: geometry and art, and Crystals. Chapter 13, "Visualizing Geometric Problems in Wooden Sangaku Tablets," by Jean Constant (Switzerland/USA) describes visualization of the 19th century scientific representations from a Japanese culture - a set of mathematical problems etched on wooden boards. The author describes the steps in the creation of artistic statements based on geometrical problems. Discussion refers to the dissemination of the project in art galleries and online, its potential instructional use, and examines the audience responses.

Section 4: Tools for Metaphors: Nature Described with the use of Mathematics and Computing contains three chapters. Chapter 14, "Drawings from Small Beginnings," by Hans Dehlinger (Germany) experimentally addresses the formulation of a few concepts inspired by nature, aimed at generating line drawings executed on pen-plotters. Generative drawings are produced through a structured process including a sequence of discrete procedural steps. Chapter 15, "On the Designing and Prototyping of Kinetic Objects," by Scottie Chih-Chieh Huang and Shen-Guan Shih (Taiwan) explores kinetic interactions with a biomimetic perspective and demonstrates three kinetic interactive artworks through a modular design approach. "MSOrgm" is developed as a robot plant to interact with the viewer in a soothing way, "SSOrgan" is designed as an organic skin to interact with the viewer's touch of the top of it, and "LBSkeleton" is a robotic instrument that produces pneumatic sound and emits soothing light into space and can make the whole body transformation. In a Chapter 16, "A New Leaf," Liz Lee (USA) discusses her latest digital image series, "A New Leaf Series", within the context of early photographic imaging and its connection to science and biology. The author discusses how contemporary electronic imaging has returned to its photographic origins through nature-related subject matter.

Section 5: Analytical Discourse: Philosophy and Aesthetics of Nature Inspired Creations contains chapters: Chapter 17, "Science with the Art: Aesthetics Based on the Fractal and Holographic Structure of Nature," by Doug Craft (USA) discusses how both art and science proceed from an appreciation for and application of the natural proportions and forms associated with nature: the Golden Ratio, fractals, and the holographic metaphor. An outline of a personal theory of aesthetics and a collage series entitled The Elements in Golden Ratio illustrate application of the author's aesthetic theory. In Chapter 18, "Getting Closer to Nature: Artists in the Lab," James Faure Walker (UK) discusses works of artists who work alongside biologists to produce visual works of extraordinary quality, in both their decorative and intellectual aspects. The author describes his own use of scientific sources, arguing that, there is also a place for art that evokes the wonders of nature without being tied to the visible facts. Chapter 19: "drawing//digital//data: A Phenomenological Approach to the Experience of Water" by Deborah Harty (UK) discusses the translation (the finding of equivalences) of a phenomenological experience of water during the activity of swimming into drawing with both traditional drawing media and a tablet computer - an Apple iPad. The author discusses the premise that drawing is phenomenology, considering whether this premise is compromised when drawing with an Apple iPad rather than traditional drawing media. In Chapter 20, "From Zero to Infinity: A Story of Everything," Clayton S. Spada and Victor Raphael (USA), a practicing artist and a practicing artist/scientist present examples of art works entitled From Zero to Infinity, to illustrate the commonalities that art and science share with respect to pragmatic and creative processes, while not equating art with science as similar cognitive domains. This chapter examines how a generalist perspective may counterbalance deconstruction of perceived elemental units, so as to avoid becoming bound by paradigm. Art and science are addressed as related observational methods to explore hypotheses and represent the varied aspects of existence.

In conclusion, discussion of the role of creativity in artistic process becomes even more complicated with the advent of many new types of art. Working on visual projects based on natural processes is one of possible ways to strengthen one's visual literacy, especially when related to scientific concepts. The resulting artistic projects may be seen as analogy for the way nature works. Many agree the increase in visual literacy and visual imagination supports man's creativity, problem solving, and problem finding abilities. The developments in computing and information science seem to alter the ways of perceiving the notions of creativity, imagination, problem solving, problem finding, and knowledge acquisition and retention. More active approach is observable, and it could happen due to the online interactive learning possibilities and the evolvement of social networks. Changes in the ways of perceiving art may run parallel and be seen comparable to the evolvements in technologies. First of all, art creating is now more often a collaborative process. Many times artists create generative art constructing their works in an algorithmic way, often in multidisciplinary, collaborative manner. The ways of seeking inspiration seem to evolve from non-participative observation of nature and people toward pursuing, researching, and understanding the principles how both the nature and humans work or act. Many artists connect with physical sources of inspiration. Developments in technology achieved in particular domains of knowledge catch an interest and inspire people from other disciplines. Recently developed tools open new possibilities for research, and thus the ascent of computing inspired study of nature through art and data graphics may be observed.

Anna Ursyn
University of Northern Colorado, USA

REFERENCES

Iverson, K. E. (1980). Notation as a tool of thought. *Communications of the ACM, 23*, 444–465. doi:10.1145/358896.358899

Marshall, G. (1998). Sapir-Whorf hypothesis. In A dictionary of sociology. Retrieved February 9, 2011, from http://www.encyclopedia.com/doc/1O88-SapirWhorfhypothesis.html

National Research Council of the National Academies. (2008). *Inspired by biology: From molecules to materials to machines*. Washington, DC: The National Academies Press.

Acknowledgment

The editor of this book wishes to thank many individuals for their input and help with this book:

First, I would like to thank the members of the IGI Global publishing team: Erika Carter and Lindsay Johnston for inviting me to work on the book; Kristin M. Klinger, for setting up the project; Jan Travers, for legal help; Michael Killian and Myla Harty, for all their kind help, and Erika Gallagher, Joel Gamon, Lisandro Gonzalez, Nick Newcomer, Heather Probst, and Sean Woznicki for their cheerful and personal assistance with this project.

I would like to thank John Maeda, the President of the Rhode Island School of Art and Design for writing a Foreword, Marina Mihalakis, Office of the President, RISAD, and all the Co-authors who contributed to this book by writing chapters and providing images illustrating their projects, for their cooperation, in order as they appear in the book: Rachel Zuanon, Mark Stock, Mohammad Majid al-Rifaie, Ahmed Aber, Mark John Bishop, Kuai Shen Auson, Hironori Yoshida, Scott Hessels, Eve Andrée Laramée, Kalyan Chakrawarthy Thokala, Donna Webb, Eunsu Kang, Matthew Kolodziej, Peter H. Niewiarowski, Yingcai Xiao, Cris Orfescu, Wolfgang Schneider, Collin Hover, Jean Constant, Hans Dehlinger, Scottie Huang, Shen-Guan Shih, Doug Craft, Liz Lee, James Faure Walker, Deborah Harty, Clayton Spada, and Victor Raphael. Also, many thanks go to my students who contributed to this book by providing images illustrating their projects.

Many thanks go to the Reviewers who diligently provided supportive suggestions and critiques, and thus helped to make each part of the book better: Mohammad Majid al-Rifaie, Goldsmiths, University of London, UK; John Clinebell, University of Northern Colorado, USA; Jean Constant, Northern New Mexico College, USA; Doug Craft, Doug Craft Fine Art, LLC, CA, USA; Charmaine Cullom, University of Northern Colorado, USA; Hans Dehlinger, Universität Kassel, Germany; Dena Eber, Bowling Green State University, OH, USA; Annie Epperson, University of Northern Colorado, USA; Robert Fathauer, Tessellations Company, Phoenix, AZ, USA; Gary Greenfield, University of Richmond, VA, USA; Joseph Haefeli, University of Northern Colorado, USA; Deborah Harty, Nottingham Trent University, UK; Collin Hover, University of Texas at Arlington, USA; John Antoine Labadie, University of Northern Carolina, USA; Liz Lee, State University of New York at Fredonia, USA; Cristian Orfescu, NanoArt21, USA; Joohyun Pyune, Essex County College, NJ, USA; Philip Sanders, The College of New Jersey and New York University, USA; Wolfgang Schneider, Computerkunst/Computer Art, Cologne/Gladbeck, Germany; Marla Schweppe, Rochester Institute of Technology, NY, USA; Bogdan Soban, Independent Artist, Slovenia; Clayton Spada, Cypress College, Lake Forest, CA, USA; James Faure Walker, University of the Arts, London, UK; Donna Webb, University of Akron, OH, USA; Annette Weintraub, The City College of New York, CUNY, USA; Tom Yingcai Xiao, University of Akron, OH, and Synapse Group,

University of Akron, OH, USA; Hironori Yoshida, Carnegie Mellon University, Pittsburgh, PA, USA; and Rachel Zuanon, Anhembi Morumbi University, Brazil.

I wish also to thank the members of the book's Advisory Board for their help with working on this book: Doug Craft, Doug Craft Fine Art, LLC, Craft Geochemistry Consulting, LLC, USA; Charmayne Cullom, University of Northern Colorado, Computer Information Systems, Monfort College of Business, USA; Hans Dehlinger, University of Kassel, School of Art, Germany; Annie Epperson, University of Northern Colorado, James A. Michener Library, USA; Gary R. Greenfield, Mathematics and Computer Science Department, University of Richmond, USA; Liz Lee, SUNY Fredonia, NY, USA; James Faure Walker, Graduate School, University of the Arts, London, UK; and Wolfgang Schneider, Computerkunst/ Computer Art, Cologne/Gladbeck, Germany.

Warmest thanks to my family, friends, and colleagues.

Anna Ursyn
University of Northern Colorado, USA

Section 1
Visual Data Formation: Biology Inspired Generation and Analysis of Objects and Processes

Chapter 1
Bio-Interfaces:
Designing Wearable Devices to Organic Interactions

Rachel Zuanon
Anhembi Morumbi University, Brazil

ABSTRACT

The bio-interfaces are widening the notions of complexity, affectiveness, and naturalness to an organic scale, in which the physiological information of the users acts as data to configure an interaction that responds to their emotional state in order to match the state of their body at that particular moment. In this context, the chapter discusses the role of the bio-interfaces in building a differentiated condition of interaction governed by the biology of the users. For this, the chapter presents applications of bio-interfaces in the areas of design, art, and games, considering their use as wearable devices that provide an organic interaction between man and machine, which could, in turn, lead these systems to a co-evolutionary relationship.

INTRODUCTION

The research and development of bio-interfaces constitute a transdisciplinary problem involving different fields of knowledge, such as: neurobiology, psychology, design, engineering, mathematics, and computer science. Unquestionably, growth of this research area is driven by the growing knowledge of biological functions, the advent of the computer - as a powerful and low-cost tool, the growing perception of the needs and

potential of individuals with social and / or motor disabilities and, more specifically, the possibility of translating biological functions into numerical data that can be interpreted by computer systems that enable other channels of communication with the external world.

The context of bio-interfaces encompassed by this chapter includes the studies related to functional biometric interfaces as well as brain-computer interfaces, both focused on enabling communication processes between humans and machines and/or humans-machines-humans, based on a co-evolutionary relationship of bio-

DOI: 10.4018/978-1-4666-0942-6.ch001

logical and technological systems. In this sense, aspects that are intrinsic to the application of these bio-interfaces will be addressed from a scientific perspective, considering the contributions by Sutter (1992), Picard (1998), Chapin et al. (1999), Bayliss & Ballard (2000), Wolpaw et al. (2002), among others, as well as within the scope of creation in arts, design and games, focusing on the productions by Gabriel (Wilson, 2002); Gilchrist, Bradley and Joelson (1997); Zuanon and Lima Jr. (2008 and 2010); Pfurtscheller (Friedman et al., 2007). Reflections will be emphasized based on the design of wearable bio-interfaces, specifically the characteristics essential to their design of interaction, taking into account future perspectives for the development of interactive bio-interfaces.

BIO-INTERFACES BACKGROUND

For several years, electrophysiological and electroencephalographic activities, and other measures of brain functions, have been considered means to new non-muscular channels of communication for sending messages and commands to the external world. This possibility becomes reality with the development and application of functional biometric interfaces and brain-computer interfaces (BCI) responsible for actually enabling this communication process between human-machine or human-machine-human, through the acquisition and encryption of the user's biological information. In this section, we will address the main aspects related to this context, to provide an ample understanding of the operation spectrum for both interfaces.

Functional biometric interfaces, based on checking ANS (autonomous nervous system) variability, provide information about the physical state or the behavior of those who use them, continuously gathering physiological data, that is, without interrupting user activity. For such, bio-sensors are used as input channels for a functional biometry system, such as: galvanic skin response

sensor (GSR); blood volume pulse sensor (BVPS); breathing sensor (BS); and electromyogram sensor (EMG).

Galvanic Skin Response Sensor (GSR)

The GSR enables the possibility of measuring the parameters of electrical conductance from skin tissue through the application of two electrodes. This conductance is considered a function of the sweat gland activity, which is a part controlled by the sympathetic nervous system. Thus, when an individual suffers from anxiety or is frightened, a quick increase in skin conductance occurs due to the increase in sweat gland activity. This increase actually reflects the changes that are occurring at the stimulation level of the user's sympathetic nervous system as the result of an internal or external stimulus. The GSR then interprets these alterations and later they may be encrypted as actions in the environment external to the user's body, for example, the light of an environment that turns on after an increase in skin conductivity has been detected as a result of the person's apprehension in entering a dark room. It is important to underscore that an individual's skin conductance baseline is unique and it varies as a result of many parameters, such as: gender, food diet, skin type, social context, among others.

Blood Volume Pulse Sensor (BVPS)

The blood volume pulse sensor (BVPS) uses photoplethysmography to detect existing blood pressure at the extremities of the individual's body. This process consists of applying a light source and then measuring this light when it is reflected on the skin. With each contraction of the heart, the blood is forced through peripheral vessels, which causes their obstruction. In other words, what can be observed at this moment is an alteration in the amount of light that arrives at the photo sensor, thus allowing the reading of the user's blood pressure using BVPS. Also considering that the vasomotor activity is controlled by the sympathetic nervous system, the measurements determined by BVPS may reflect changes in sympathetic stimulation. More specifically, an increase in the pressure range read by BVPS indicates a reduction in sympathetic stimulation and greater blood flow at the tips of fingers. Likewise, with the data related to skin conductance, the reading and interpretation of the individual's blood pressure can also be used to trigger events, whether in the physical or digital environment.

Breathing Sensor (BS) and Electromyogram Sensor (EMG)

When positioned on the sternum, the breathing sensor (BS) enables monitoring the individual's thorax, or, when placed on the diaphragm, it allows monitoring diaphragm activity. This sensor consists of a Velcro belt that extends around the thorax, and a small elastic band that stretches with the expansion of the user's thorax. Thus, the depth as well as the breathing rate of the individual can be recorded based on the change in voltage resulting from the stretching of the elastic belt, working as data to control external actions to the user's body. The electrical activity produced by a muscle at the moment of contraction can be gauged by the electromyographical sensors that capture and amplify the signals. They then send them to the encrypter, where the necessary filtering will be carried out in order to obtain the ideal frequency band, taking into account the applicability of electromyographical activity for interacting with digital devices and/or systems.

All these biosensors also allow the reading of several of the user's physiological protocols, such as: control of anxiety / stress; emotional variability; emotional intensity; muscular variability; respiratory range and frequency; diaphragmatic respiration; sympathetic vascular tonus; cardiac variability; cardiac coherence; sympathetic and parasympathetic activity, among others. And,

therefore, they can be used as input channels for an affective computing system, considering that they effectively contribute towards the detection of patterns in physiological information, which makes possible determining which signals are related to each of the user's emotional states (Picard, 1998). This occurs through the observation of physiological correlates, checked during situations projected to arouse and extract emotional responses. The system thus becomes aware of the user's immediate emotional state and is able to provide useful information about the interactor for applications that can use such data.

Brain-Computer Interface (BCI)

The context of functional biometric interfaces gains even more complex perspectives when brain signals are the substrate of biological information. A brain-computer interface (BCI) transforms the electrophysiological signals of central nervous system activity reflections into the products intended for that activity: messages and commands that act in the world. It transforms a signal, such as an EEG rhythm or a neural trigger rate from a brain function reflection into the final product of this function: an output that, as an output in conventional neuromuscular channels, carries out the person's intention. A BCI replaces nerves and muscles and produces movements with electrophysiological signals associated with the hardware and software that translates them into actions.

At present, BCI research programs are geared towards the exploitation of new technologies for increased control and communication for people with severe muscle disorders, such as lateral amyotrophic sclerosis, cerebral hemorrhage and muscle damage. Thus, the immediate objective of these programs is to provide these users – who may be completely paralyzed – with the capability for basic communication so they can express their desires to those who care for them, or to operate word processing programs and even neuroprosthesis. However, besides providing an option for control and communication for individuals with motor disabilities, BCI systems may also provide individuals with preserved motor abilities and channel for supplementary control or a useful channel for control in special circumstances.

A variety of methods for monitoring brain activity can function like a BCI. That includes, besides the electroencephalograph (EEG) and more invasive electrophysiological methods, magnetoencephalography (MEG), positron emission tomography (PET), functional magnetic resonance imaging (fMRI) and optical imaging. However, MEG, PET, fMRI and optical imaging are still expensive solutions, and from the technical perspective, they still require special care. Furthermore, since PET, fMRI and optical imaging depend on blood circulation, they require longer response time and for that reason they are less appropriate for quick communication. At the moment, only the EEG and related methods, which respond in a relatively short period of time, can function in most environments, because they require considerably simpler and economically more affordable equipment, and thus offer the possibility of a new channel of communication and non-muscular control (Wolpaw & Birbaumer, 2002).

The digital revolution promoted by continuous development and extremely fast computer hardware and software, provides the support for sophisticated online analyses of EEG multi-channels and this leads to the appreciation of the fact that simple communication capability, such as "yes" or "no" and "on" or "off" can be configured in order to serve complex functions – such as word processing and prosthesis control. Many studies (Keirn & Aunon, 1990; Lang et al, 1996; Pfurtscheller 1997; Anderson 1998; Altenmüller & Gerloff, 1999; Mcfarland et al, 2000) have demonstrated correlations between EEG signals and real or imagined movements and between the EEG signals and those from mental tasks.

According to (Wolpaw & Birbaumer, 2002), epidural and subdural electrodes can provide EEGs with high topographic resolution, and the intracortical electrodes can follow the activity of individual neurons (Schmidt, 1980; Ikeda & Shibbasaki, 1992; Heetderks & Schmidt, 1995; (Levine et al., 1999), (Levine, 2000); Wolpaw et al., 2000). Besides that, studies (Georgopoulos et al., 1986; Schwartz, 1993; Chapin et al., 1999; Wessberg et al., 2000) demonstrate that the trigger rates for an appropriate selection of cortical neurons can offer a detailed portrait of simultaneous voluntary movement. However, since these methods are invasive, their use mainly occurs by individuals with extremely severe inabilities since they provide faster and more precise control and communication than the non-invasive EEG.

Current BCIs determine the user's intention based on different electrophysiological signals translated, in real time, into commands that operate a computer screen or some other device: slow cortical potentials, P300 potentials, beta rhythm or mu rhythm – recorded from the scalp – and cortical neural activity – recorded using implanted electrodes. In this sense, satisfactory operations require to encrypt the user commands in these signals since the BCI will derive the commands through these encrypted signals. Thus, the user and the BCI system need to continuously adapt to each other in order to ensure a stable performance (Wolpaw & Birbaumer, 2002).

BCIs are divided into two classes: dependent and independent. A dependent BCI does not use the brain's normal output circuits to send a message, but the activity in these circuits is necessary to generate the brain activity (EEG) that sends it. For example, a dependent BCI presents an individual with a matrix of letters that shine one at a time; then, the user selects a specific letter looking directly at it, so that the visually evoked potential (VEP) recorded from the scalp, just above the visual cortex, is much larger when that letter shines than the VEPs produced when other letters shine (Lauer et al., 2000; Pfurtscheller et al., 2000; Sutter, 1992). In this case, the brain output channel is the EEG, but the generation of the EEG signal depends on the direction of the look, and therefore, on the extra-ocular muscles and the cranial nerves that activate them. A dependent BCI is essentially an alternative method for detecting messages sent to the brain's normal output circuits, such as, the direction of the look.

On the other hand, an independent BCI does not depend in any way on the brain's normal output circuits. The message is not sent by the peripheral nerves and muscles, in other words, the activity of these circuits is not needed to generate brain activity (case of the EEG), which carries the message. For example, an independent BCI presents the user with a matrix of letters that shine one at a time, and the user selects a specific letter by producing a P300 evoked potential when the letter shines (Farwell & Donchin, 1988; Donchin et al., 2000). In this case, the brain output channel is the EEG, and the generation of the EEG signal mainly depends on the user's intention, and not on the precise direction of his / her eyes (Sutton et al., 1965; Donchin, 1981; Fabiani et al., 1987; Polich, 1999). In other words, the normal output circuits present in peripheral nerves and muscles do not play an essential role in the operation of an independent BCI. The fact that they are providing the brain with completely new output circuits makes the independent BCIs of greater theoretical interest than the dependent BCIs. Furthermore, for people with severe neuromuscular inabilities, which may be lacking in all normal output circuits (including extra-ocular muscular control), the independent BCIs are probably more useful.

In addition to the distinction between dependent and independent BCIs, electrophysiological BCIs may be categorized by non-invasive (for example, the EEG) or invasive (case of the intracortical procedure) methodology. They may also be categorized by the use of evoked inputs or spontaneous inputs. Evoked inputs (for example, the EEG produced by shining letters) result from the stereotypical sensory stimulation provided by the BCI. Spontaneous inputs (such as in the case of EEG rhythms on the sensory-motor cortex) do not depend on this stimulation. In this sense,

there is presumably no determining reason that restricts a BCI from combining invasive and no-invasive methods or evoked and spontaneous inputs (Wolpaw & Birbaumer, 2002).

The substantial advances in non-invasive methods are evident for recording brain activity that enables control comparable to that of a computer mouse cursor movement. However, many differences between neural signals recorded with the use of invasive and non-invasive electrodes suggest implantable prostheses have a greater potential over the long term. EEG recordings reflect the average activity of millions of neurons, creating a signal with limited spatial and temporal resolution. In contrast, recordings with hundreds of microelectrodes, each one monitoring the activity of a single or of a small number of neurons, can create highly complex signs of control.

Studies conducted on animals reveal the need of obtaining three or fewer levels of control, since the implantable neuromotor prostheses are developed to foresee the movement the animal makes to reach a spatial target. However, human neural prostheses use a significantly higher number of degrees of control, since the subject's level of involvement for calibrating the device is much greater, and it may be much more complex if the individual is asked, for example, to move of his / her articulations separately (Scott, 2006).

In short, for (Wolpaw & Birbaumer, 2002), progress in the development of invasive and non-invasive brain-computer interfaces depends: on the identification of which signals – the evoked potentials, spontaneous rhythms or neural trigger rates –users are more capable of independently controlling the activity generated in conventional circuits of motor production; on the development of training methods to help users to achieve and to maintain this control; on outlining the best algorithms for translating these signals into commands for devices; on the attention given to the identification and elimination of artifacts; on the adoption of objective and precise procedures for evaluating BCI performance; on the recognition of the need for long and short evaluations of BCI performance; on the identification of the appropriate applications for BCIs; on the attention to factors that affect the acceptance of technologies increased by the user, including user-friendliness and the provision of those capacities for control and communication that are most important for the user.

THE BIO-INTERFACES AT DESIGN, ART, AND GAME AREAS: SOME APPLICATIONS

The adoption of bio-interfaces for the areas of design, art and games turns significantly the forms of participation and audience interaction with these systems. Different from the physicality proposed in the relations with tangible interfaces – of mice and keyboards; of joysticks; of touchscreens – and the ubiquity inherent to intangible interfaces – from position; face; gesture; voice mapping and recognition – the bio-interfaces go beyond both and propose a physicality and ubiquity of another order, of a physiological nature. This condition expands the notion of complexity, of affectivity and of naturalness to a biological scale in which the user's organism begins to provide the information (signals) that will configure the interactive processes between the individual / system in order to correspond to the emotions mapped at that specific moment.

In this section, interactive-media works will be presented and discussed, conducted within the contexts of art, design and games, which use physiological and / or brain activity of participants to propose a coauthor environment of creation. We shall emphasize our approach mainly in aspects involving the use of wearable devices to provide organic interaction between humans-machines that lead them to a relationship of permanent collaboration.

It is important to underscore that within the scope of the proposals considered herein, the applications of brain-computer interfaces occur at non-invasive dimensions.

"Terrain 01" (1993), by Ulrike Gabriel, proposes an interactive space in which robotic beetles are fed by light energy. Interaction with the visitor occurs through its brain waves, captured by a wearable interface comprised of electrodes sensitive to neural activities. The values obtained by this process provide the parameters for controlling the dimming of the facilities lights. In other words, the emotional state of the participant at that moment is responsible for controlling the quantity of energy emitted to the robotic objects. In this sense, the calmer the visitor is, the greater the intensity of light radiated to the beetles and consequently, the greater the speed of locomotion for these beetles when moving through space. The opposite occurs if the visitor presents any signs of stress or tension.[1]

In "Terrain 02: Solar Robot Environment for Two Users" (2001), the artist expands and makes the use of brain waves for the simultaneous control of robotic objects by two people more complex (Wilson, 2002). When placed one in front of the other, the neural signals of the participants, as in Terrain 01, are acquired by a wearable interface. However, in this case, the changes in brain patterns do not only control robot movements, but also affect the fluidity and synchrony of these movements.[2]

In the context of the creation in music, "Thought Conductor #1" (1997), by Bruce Gilchrist, Jonny Bradley, Jo Joelson, consists of a performance that uses software especially developed to translate the composers' brain waves in real time. Connected to a wearable brain interface and a digital biomonitor, the composer directs his / her thoughts to the memory of the largest number possible of details present in the musical structure of the previously created score. During this action, captured brain waves are then translated into musical notes, 'composed' for six interpreters and sent to six computer monitors. Thus, the new score, created through a coauthor process between the composer's organisms and the computer's artificial intelligence, is read and performed live by Nikki Yeoh & Piano Circus. In other words, a creative looping is established in which the composer's physiological information, produced during the practice of his / her creative activity, feed the technological system that returns this information to the composer as musical writing reframed by the collaborative action of both systems.

In "Thought Conductor #2" (2000) and "Thought Conductor #2.1" (2001), the composers Gilchrist and Bradley expand the performance proposal to the collaboration of the public present. In both cases, a previously created database was used with the composers' brain signals, captured when writing the musical notes. After acquired, these signals were associated to the corresponding notations and stored in the referred to database. Several members of the audience were invited to come on stage for the presentations and to contribute with a thought. While connected to a wearable brain interface and to the biomonitor, each was asked to think of a creative act they had already carried out: a jeweler thought of a gold ring he had recently created; a yogi meditated; a painter imagined the production process of his last painting, among others.

Thus, the neural waves of each participant generated original scores – from the association of brain activities acquired during this process to the available notations in the database – which were then sent to laptops to be read and played by a string quartet.[3,4]

In other words, a collaborative process for musical composition is observed mediated by technologies that provide the meeting between the composers' mental states, captured during execution of a creative act, with members of the audience, acquired when they recalled a creative action they had performed. Mental states that when hybridized still dialogue with the interpretation of the quartet musicians and the minds of the public present.

Within the scope of interaction with games, the wearable computers, "BioBodyGame" (2008) and "NeuroBodyGame" (2010), created by artists and designers Rachel Zuanon and Geraldo Lima, allow the user to interact with digital games through their physiological and cerebral signals, respectively.

BioBodyGame (Zuanon & Lima Jr., 2008) constitutes a wearable, wireless interface for functional biometric interaction with onboard games in the system, in which the games as well as the wearable computer react to the user's emotion during interaction. For such, the inter-actor's following physiological parameters are read during playability: emotional variability; anxiety control; emotional response; sympathetic and parasympathetic nervous system; functional oxygen; and cardiac frequency. The mapping of these parameters is done and associated in real time to game functionalities, which begin to react in accordance with the player's physiological state. In other words, playability is facilitated or made difficult based on the user's emotional state as well as how the wearable computer interprets these emotions and reacts to them, altering their color (front / back) and applying vibrations (back).

The NeuroBodyGame (Zuanon & Lima Jr., 2010) consists of a wearable computer that allows

Figure 1. BioBodyGame (© 2008, Rachel Zuanon. Used with permission.)

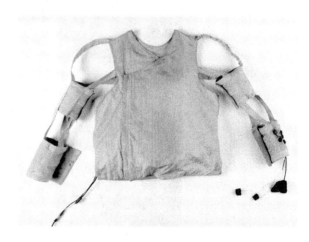

Figure 2. BioBodyGame bio-interface (© 2008, Rachel Zuanon. Used with permission.)

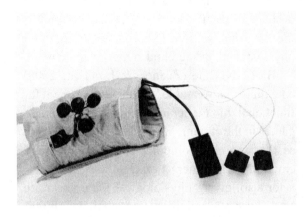

the user to play games with his / her brain signals. It is a wearable wireless interface for the brain to interact with the games bundled in the system. In this sense, games and wearable computers react to the user's brain wave frequencies captured at the moment of playability.

With a BioBodyGame upgrade, the NeuroBodyGame still provides the integration of the brain-computer interface to the functional biometric interaction system, associating user brain activity in real time to his / her physiological parameters related to blood flow; functional oxygen; cardiac frequency; and sympathetic and parasympathetic activities.

The design of both BioBodyGame and NeuroBodyGame is ergonomic and adjustable to different biotypes. That means that the wearable computers can be expanded or contracted in a manner to adjust to the user's body and ensure the interactor's comfort. Any possibility for discomfort can alter the player's physiological and brain signals and, consequently, compromise the organic information.

Other studies (Bayliss & Ballard, 2000; Leeb et al., 2004; Nelson et al., 1997) are carried out to permit applying wearable bio-interfaces as input devices for highly immersive virtual reality environments – such as caves and flight simulators. Pfurtscheller and collaborators (Friedman et al., 2007) propose two navigation experiences: one in which three volunteers rotate a digital room by imagining this movement being carried out by their right and left hands; and the other, in which the same volunteers cover a single dimension inside a digital street by imagining the movement of the feet and hands. In other words, moving physical or digital objects using the force of thought is also a bio-interface achievement.

Figure 3. NeuroBodyGame installation (© 2008, Rachel Zuanon. Used with permission.)

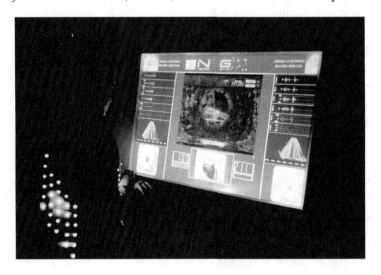

Figure 4. NeuroBodyGame bio-interfaces (© 2008, Rachel Zuanon. Used with permission.)

Figure 5. NeuroBodyGame design (© 2008, Rachel Zuanon. Used with permission.)

Solutions and Recommendations for Design of the Organic Interactions through Bio-Interfaces

From the applications addressed in the above section, it is possible to ascertain that bio-interfaces not only provide a differentiated relationship between the individual and technology, founded on reading, interpreting and associating neuro-physiological data to control commands, but also

a meeting between biological and technological systems for collaborative creation. This tends to become more popular as the use of bio-interfaces, once restricted to research laboratories, expands to artistic, educational and entertainment purposes, among others.

These advances have no doubt been stimulated by a new generation of non-invasive brain-computer interfaces, which come to market for direct use by the final consumer, associated with toys, games and virtual environments; applications geared towards accessibility for controlling physical interfaces (e.g., wheelchair) or computer applications by people with motor disabilities; neurofeedback; applications for marketing research and advertising; so as those developed by NeuroSky Incorporated and Emotiv Systems. While the first provides a wearable interface with only one sensor for detecting user brain waves and monitoring neural activity of controlling objects, the latter, using an Epoc wearable interface, foresees 14 sensors for acquiring interactor brain signals and association at three levels of interpretation: expressive; affective; and cognitive. The expressive level allows identifying the user's facial expressions in real time, providing the direct relationship between the interactor's facial movements and the character of a game. The affective level monitors the user's emotional state, enabling the game to respond to his / her emotions.

And the cognitive level reads and interprets the user's conscious thoughts, enabling the control of virtual objects by the action of thought.

Undoubtedly, the bio-interface design considers all aspects addressed herein to enable communication processes between the user's organism and the computer systems. However, those characteristics intrinsic to interaction design, fundamentally in relation to ergonomics, usability, mobility, as well as the quality of physiological and brain data (proportionally related to the level of existing artifacts in acquired signals) constitute the main concerns while developing bio-interfaces, since they all play a fundamental role in the construction of an effectively discrete and efficient relationship between the user and system.

In relation to ergonomics, anthropometric studies and research geared towards the technology of materials subsidize the elaboration of increasingly more adjustable bio-interfaces to different biotypes and thus promote full adaptation between the wearable device and the user's body. With regard to mobility, in relation to functional biometric interfaces, the wireless communication standard via Bluetooth used until now, although ensuring the user's full displacement without the restriction caused by cables and wires, faces problems related to possible interferences caused by the presence of another device that uses the same communication standard in the same environment. Within the ambit of brain-computer interfaces, studies conducted by researchers at Colorado State University aim to move the EEG analysis to be executed in cloud computing environments. Through this procedure, the current limitations faced by mobile BCIs are believed to be supplanted. For example, the one machine per user ratio is replaced by a set of hundreds of machines serving tens of thousands of users. This action aims at obtaining a significantly larger database for training artificial neural networks. In addition, the diverse small neural networks distributed in this data could act together to produce reports. Besides that, an increase is seen in the temporal aspect of brain signal flow analysis, which currently occurs after an immediate interval, to larger intervals, of around seconds or minutes.

In relation to usability, the implementation of high fidelity prototypes appear as more favorable solutions for obtaining final bio-interfaces, fully adapted to user needs, since, through them, it is possible to map use experiences in advance and thus enable the correction and necessary adjustments, during the wearable device's development process. Also in relation to usability, we see that successive training sessions held during the use of bio-interfaces are fundamental to provide better adaptation by the user to the system.

In relation to the quality of the physiological and brain data, the use of specific algorithms and filters has been presenting itself as one of the most efficient means to annul the possible interferences caused by external stimuli, which introduce artifacts in the biological signals.

INTERACTIVE BIO-INTERFACES

The research geared towards developing increasingly more complex bio-interfaces points to the challenge of these devices to act as output channels while also providing feedback directly to the human organism, in the case of functional biometric interfaces, or the brain, in the case of brain-computer interfaces. In other words, that means considering the possibility of bio-interfaces to also function as information input channels for the human body and thus be interactive.

At present, the operation of a bio-interface depends on the interaction of two adaptive controllers: the user's organism, which produces the signals measured by the bio-interface and the bio-interface itself, which translates these signals into specific commands. An interactive bio-interface shall provide feedback and thus interact in a productive manner with the adaptations that occurred in the user's organism after this feedback.

In this sense, for most neuroscientists, the next step is to introduce a sensory input in the bio-interfaces. Within the scope of brain-computer interfaces, several researchers are already investigating where and how to stimulate the sensory nervous system to reproduce the type of information a member should send to the sensory cortex. Theoretically, this may in the nerves that go from the members to the spinal cord, or in the spinal cord itself. Or it could be in the thalamus, where input sensory signals are integrated and redirected to the appropriate parts of the cortex, or the sensory cortex.

How to stimulate the sensory nervous system refers to the design of the electrical signal to be fed in the cortex. This can imitate the sensory system's natural nervous impulses, based on parameters such as frequency and amplitude. Or it can involve the creation of artificial signals the sensory cortex is apt to distinguish, in the hope that the brain may be trained to associate certain signals to certain parameters (Abbott, 2006).

Andrew Schwartz and Douglas Weber have been working at developing a scientific model for studying sensory inputs. This involves two stimulus procedures for recording neural activity. The first considers the use of electrodes to stimulate the sensory nerves of an anesthetized cat's members, and simultaneously record the neuron activity in the sensory cortex. In the second, the cat's members are moved manually (Schwartz et al., 2006).

After obtaining the data, the researchers compare the standard of neural activity in the cortex in both situations. Weber affirms that, even when encountering disagreements, a more satisfactory context is observed when the central nervous system receives an external stimulus, since stimulation by electrodes at the most central points of the cortex competes with a great convergence of different inputs, and with that obtaining signals without artifacts becomes more difficult.

Lee Miller (London et al., 2008) agrees that Weber may be right, however, stimulation of the body's peripheral nerves, such as in the members, according to Miller, will not function for patients with serious spinal cord injuries. Working with monkeys, the Miller group electrically stimulates the part of the cortex that processes proprioception, and simultaneously records neural activity in the motor cortex. The experiment demonstrated that monkeys recognize and distinguish between low and high frequency stimulations. The researcher expects this to eventually reveal the design of stimulation patterns that can imitate the brain's proprioception processes, the same way Weber plans on imitating the movement processing. These same monkeys are also trained to move a "virtual" arm, created on a computer screen by an algorithm fed by both recordings - from the motor cortex and from the simulated proprioception return.

In his experimental system with monkeys, John Chapin (Chapin et al., 1999) electrically stimulates the thalamus that retransmits signals related to touch and, simultaneously, records the neural activities in the sensory cortex areas that process touch information. Animals, with one of their arms tied, were taught to point with their free arm at an area on their immobilized arm that they felt was being touched. According to Chapin, based on this experience it is possible to produce a sort of natural response in the cortex when stimulating the thalamus. The response proves to be equal to the one normally produced when a specific part of the monkey's arm is touched. With that, he can somehow plan the extension of his research into proprioception studies.

All of the experiments that aim at studying sensory inputs point directly to aspects of adaptability between the user's nervous system and the bio-interface, both involved in this other condition of communication. This suggests a change in paradigm, as the current generation of bio-interfaces, with only one output, constitutes an open circuit systems. In this sense, the notion of co-evolution seems appropriate here, taking into account an instance of correlation between the systems involved, which encompasses non-supervised, that is, non-hierarchical adaptability as a preponderant factor in this communication process.

CONCLUSION

The wearable bio-interfaces presented and discussed in this chapter include the functional biometric interfaces and the brain-computer interfaces. Both consist of solutions that originated in the scientific environment aimed at promoting a differentiated channel of communication for the user with the outside environment, whether through reading and interpreting the variability of the autonomous nervous system or specifically of its brain signals, for controlling digital applications or physical devices.

Within the ambit of art, design, and games, the wearable bio-interfaces play the role of mediators in a collaborative creation process between the user and computer or between the biological and technological systems. However, regardless of the context for wearable bio-interface applications, their design requires attention and special care, considering that this presents itself directly related to the quality of promoted organic interaction. Several parameters guide the design of wearable bio-interfaces. However, ergonomics, usability, mobility, and quality of the acquired biological signals stand out as essential aspects to the interaction design of these devices. In this sense, future perspectives also point to the development of interactive bio-interfaces capable of also providing feedback to the user's organism, from the possibility of bidirectional interactivity, with an output channel (from the user to the external system) and an input channel (from the external system to the user). This condition reconstructs the communication circuit present until this moment since with that, the flows of biological information will not only be used to control the technological systems (hardware and software), but they will also return to the user's organism, thus constructing an effectively co-evolutionary cycle.

When this stage of bio-interface development is reached, certainly other parameters will be considered from a co-evolutionary perspective, in other words, from project definitions that guide the co-evolutionary design of these devices.

REFERENCES

Abbott, A. (2006). In search of the sixth sense. *Nature, 442*(7099), 125–127. doi:10.1038/442125a

Altenmüller, E. O., & Gerloff, C. (1999). Psychophysiology and the EEG . In Niedermeyer, E., & Lopes da Silva, F. H. (Eds.), *Electroencephalography: Basic principles, clinical applications and related fields* (pp. 637–655). Baltimore, MD: Williams and Wilkins.

Anderson, C. W. (1998). Multivariate autoregressive models for classification of spontaneous electroencephalographic signals during mental tasks. *IEEE Transactions on Bio-Medical Engineering, 45*(3), 277–286. doi:10.1109/10.661153

Bayliss, J. D., & Ballard, D. H. (2000). A virtual reality testbed for brain computer interface research. *IEEE Transactions on Rehabilitation Engineering, 8*(2), 188–190. doi:10.1109/86.847811

Chapin, J. K., Moxon, K. A., Markowitz, R. S., & Nicolelis, M. A. (1999). Real-time control of a robot arm using simultaneously recorded neurons in the motor cortex. *Nature Neuroscience, 2*(7), 664–670. doi:10.1038/10223

Donchin, E. (1981). Presidential address, 1980. Surprise!... Surprise? *Psychophysiology, 18*(5), 493–513. doi:10.1111/j.1469-8986.1981.tb01815.x

Donchin, E., Spencer, K. M., & Wijesinghe, R. (2000). The mental prosthesis: Assessing the speed of a P300-based brain-computer interface. *IEEE Transactions on Rehabilitation Engineering, 8*(2), 174–179. doi:10.1109/86.847808

Fabiani, M., Gratton, G., Karis, D., & Donchin, E. (1987). Definition, identification and reliability of the P300 component of the event-related brain potential. In P. K. Ackles, J. R. Jennings, & M. G. H. Coles (Eds.), *Advances in psychophysiology* (pp. 1-78). Greenwich, CT: JAI Press.

Farwell, L. A., & Donchin, E. (1988). Talking off the top of your head: Toward a mental prothesis utilizing event-related brain potentials. *Electroencephalography and Clinical Neurophysiology, 70*(6), 510–523. doi:10.1016/0013-4694(88)90149-6

Friedman, D., Leeb, R., Guger, C., Steed, A., Pfurtscheller, G., & Slater, M. (2007). Navigating virtual reality by thought: What is it like? *Presence (Cambridge, Mass.), 16*(1), 100–110. doi:10.1162/pres.16.1.100

Georgopoulos, A. P., Schwartz, A. B., & Kettner, R. E. (1986). Neuronal population coding of movement direction. *Science, 233*(4771), 1416–1419. doi:10.1126/science.3749885

Gilchrist, B., Bradley, J., & Joelson, J. (1997). *Thought conductor #1*. Retrieved May 23, 2007, from http://www.artemergent.org.uk/tc/tc1.html

Heetderks, W. J., & Schmidt, E. M. (1995). Chronic multiple unit recording of neural activity with micromachined silicon electrodes. In A. Lang (Ed.), *Proceedings of RESNA 95 Annual Conference* (pp. 649-653). Arlington, VA: RESNA Press.

Ikeda, A., & Shibbasaki, H. (1992). Invasive recording of movement-related cortical potentials in humans. *Journal of Clinical Neurophysiology, 9*(4), 409–520. doi:10.1097/00004691-199210000-00005

Keirn, Z. A., & Aunon, J. I. (1990). A new mode of communication between man and his surroundings. *IEEE Transactions on Bio-Medical Engineering, 37*(12), 1209–1214. doi:10.1109/10.64464

Lang, W., Cheyne, D., Hollinger, P., Gerschlager, W., & Lindinger, G. (1996). Electric and magnetic fields of the brain accompanying internal simulation of movement. *Brain Research. Cognitive Brain Research, 3*(2), 125–129. doi:10.1016/0926-6410(95)00037-2

Lauer, R., Peckham, P. H., Kilgore, K. L., & Heetderks, W. J. (2000). Applications of cortical signals to neuroprosthetic control: A critical review. *IEEE Transactions on Rehabilitation Engineering, 8*(2), 205–208. doi:10.1109/86.847817

Leeb, R., Scherer, R., Lee, F., Bischof, H., & Pfurtscheller, G. (2004). Navigation in virtual environments through motor imagery. *Proceedings of the 9th Computer Vision Winter Workshop* (pp. 99-108). Slovenian Pattern Recognition Society.

Levine, S. P. (2000). A direct brain interface based on event-related potentials. *IEEE Transactions on Rehabilitation Engineering, 8*(2), 180–185. doi:10.1109/86.847809

Levine, S. P., & Huggins, J. E., BeMent, S. L., Kushwaha, R. K., Schuh, L. A., Passaro, E. A., … Ross, D. A. (1999). Identification of electrocorticogram patterns as a basis for a direct brain interface. *Journal of Clinical Neurophysiology, 16*(5), 439–447. doi:10.1097/00004691-199909000-00005

London, B. M., Jordan, L. R., Jackson, C. R., & Miller, L. E. (2008). Electrical stimulation of the proprioceptive cortex (area 3a) used to instruct a behaving monkey. *IEEE Transactions on Neural Systems and Rehabilitation Engineering, 16*(1), 32–36. doi:10.1109/TNSRE.2007.907544

Mcfarland, D. J., Miner, L. A., Vaughan, T. M., & Wolpaw, J. R. (2000). Mu and beta rhythm topographies during motor imagery and actual movement. *Brain Topography, 12*(3), 177–186. doi:10.1023/A:1023437823106

Nelson, W. T., Hettinger, L. J., Cunningham, J. A., Roe, M. M., Haas, M. W., & Dennis, L. B. (1997). Navigating through virtual flight environments using brain-body-actuated control. *Proceedings of the IEEE 1997 Virtual Reality Annual International Symposium* (pp. 30-37). Los Alamitos, CA: IEEE Computer Society Press.

Pfurtscheller, G. (1997). EEG-based discrimination between imagination of right and left hand movement. *Electroencephalography and Clinical Neurophysiology, 103*(6), 642–651. doi:10.1016/S0013-4694(97)00080-1

Pfurtscheller, G., Guger, C., Müller, G., Krausz, G., & Neuper, C. (2000). Brain oscillations control hand orthosis in a tetraplegic. *Neuroscience Letters, 292*(3), 211–214. doi:10.1016/S0304-3940(00)01471-3

Picard, R. (1998). *Affective computing.* Cambridge, MA: MIT Press.

Polich, J. (1999). P300 in clinical applications. In E. Niedermeyer, & F. H. Lopes da Silva (Eds.), *Electroencephalography: Basic principles, clinical applications and related fields* (pp. 1073-1091). Baltimore, MD: Williams and Wilkins.

Schmidt, E. M. (1980). Single neuron recording from motor cortex as a possible source of signals for control of external devices. *Annual Review of Biomedical Engineering, 8*, 339–349. doi:10.1007/BF02363437

Schwartz, A. B. (1993). Motor cortical activity during drawing movement: Population representation during sinusoid tracing. *Journal of Neurophysiology, 70*(1), 28–36.

Schwartz, A. B., Cui, X. T., Weber, D. J., & Moran, D. W. (2006). Brain-controlled interfaces: Movement Restoration with neural prosthetics. *Neuron, 52*(1), 205–220. doi:10.1016/j.neuron.2006.09.019

Scott, S. H. (2006). Converting thoughts into action. *Nature, 442*(7099), 141–142. doi:10.1038/442141a

Sutter, E. E. (1992). The brain response interface: Communication through visually induced electrical brain responses. *Journal of Microcomputer Applications, 15*(1), 31–45. doi:10.1016/0745-7138(92)90045-7

Sutton, S., Braren, M., Zubin, J., & John, E. R. (1965). Evoked correlates of stimulus uncertainty. *Science, 150*(3700), 1187–1188. doi:10.1126/science.150.3700.1187

Wessberg, J., Stambaugh, C. R., Kralik, J. D., Beck, P. D., Laubach, M., & Chapin, J. K. (2000). Real-time prediction of hand trajectory by ensemble of cortical neurons in primates. *Nature, 408*(6810), 361–365. doi:10.1038/35042582

Wilson, S. (2002). *Information arts: Intersections of art, science, and technology.* Cambridge, MA: MIT Press.

Wolpaw, J. R., & Birbaumer, N. (2002). Brain-computer interfaces for communication and control. *Clinical Neurophysiology, 113*(6), 767–791. doi:10.1016/S1388-2457(02)00057-3

Wolpaw, J. R., Birbaumer, N., Heetderks, W. J., McFarland, D. J., Peckham, P. H., & Schalk, G. (2000). Brain-computer interface technology: A review of the first international meeting. *IEEE Transactions on Rehabilitation Engineering, 8*(2), 164–173. doi:10.1109/TRE.2000.847807

Zuanon, R., & Lima, G. C., Jr. (2008). *BioBodyGame.* Retrieved March 9, 2011, from http://www.rachelzuanon.com/biobodygame/

Zuanon, R., & Lima, G. C., Jr. (2010). *Neuro-BodyGame*. Retrieved March 9, 2011, from http://www.rachelzuanon.com/neurobodygame/

ADDITIONAL READING

Birbaumer, N., Ghanayim, N., Hinterberger, T., Iversen, I., Kotchoubey, B., & Kübler, A. (1999). A spelling device for the paralysed. *Nature*, *398*(6725), 297–298. doi:10.1038/18581

Guger, C., Schlogl, A., Walterspacher, D., & Pfurtscheller, G. (1999). Design of an EEG-based brain-computer interface (BCI) from standard components running in real-time under windows. *Technik. Biomedical Engineering, 44*(1-2), 12–16.

Jain, A. K., Duin, R. P. W., & Mao, J. (2000). Statistical pattern recognition: A review. *IEEE Transactions on Pattern Analysis and Machine Intelligence, 22*(1), 4–37. doi:10.1109/34.824819

Jones, K. S., Middendorf, M. S., Calhoun, G. L., & McMillan, G. R. (1998). Evaluation of an electroencephalographic-based control device. *Proceedings of the Human Factors and Ergonomics Society 42nd Annual Meeting* (pp. 491-495).

Kalcher, J., Flotzinger, D., Neuper, C., Gölly, S., & Pfurtscheller, G. (1996). Graz brain-computer interface II: Towards communication between humans and computers based on online classification of three different EEG patterns. *Medical & Biological Engineering & Computing, 34*(5), 382–388. doi:10.1007/BF02520010

Kennedy, P. R., & Bakay, R. A. E. (1998). Restoration of neural output from a paralyzed patient by a direct brain connection. *Neuroreport, 9*(8), 1707–1711. doi:10.1097/00001756-199806010-00007

Kennedy, P. R., Bakay, R. A. E., Moore, M. M., Adams, K., & Goldwaithe, J. (2000). Direct control of a computer from the human central nervous system. *IEEE Transactions on Rehabilitation Engineering, 8*(2), 198–202. doi:10.1109/86.847815

Kostov, A., & Polak, M. (2000). Parallel man-machine training in development of EEG based cursor control. *IEEE Transactions on Rehabilitation Engineering, 8*(2), 203–204. doi:10.1109/86.847816

Lopes da Silva, F. (1999). Event-related potentials: Methodology and quantification. In Niedermeyer, E., & Lopez da Silva, F. (Eds.), *Electroencephalogaphy: Basic principles, clinical applications and related fields* (pp. 947–957). Baltimore, MD: Williams and Wilkins.

Lopes Da Silva, F., & Mars, N. J. I. (1987). Parametric methods in EEG analysis. In Gevins, A. S., & Rémond, A. (Eds.), *Methods and analysis of brain electrical and magnetic signals* (pp. 243–260). Amsterdam, The Netherlands: Elsevier.

McFarland, D. J., Lefkowicz, T., & Wolpaw, J. R. (1997). Design and operation of an EEG-based brain-computer interface with digital signal processing technology. *Behavior Research Methods, Instruments, & Computers, 29*(3), 337–345. doi:10.3758/BF03200585

McFarland, D. J., Neat, G. W., Read, R. F., & Wolpaw, J. R. (1993). An EEG-based method for graded cursor control. *Psychobiology, 21*(1), 77–81.

Middendorf, M., McMillan, G., Calhoun, G., & Jones, K. S. (2000). Brain-computer interfaces based on the steady-state visual-evoked response. *IEEE Transactions on Rehabilitation Engineering, 8*(2), 211–214. doi:10.1109/86.847819

Nicolelis, M., & Chapin, J. (2002). Controlling robots with the mind. *Scientific American, 287*(4), 46–53. doi:10.1038/scientificamerican1002-46

Nuñez, P. L. (1995). *Neocortical dynamics and human EEG rhythms*. New York, NY: Oxford University Press.

Parday, J., Roberts, S., & Tarassenko, L. (1996). A review of parametric techniques for EEG analysis. *Medical Engineering & Physics*, *18*(1), 2–11. doi:10.1016/1350-4533(95)00024-0

Penny, W. D., Roberts, S. J., Curran, E. A., & Stokes, M. J. (2000). EEG-based communication: A pattern recognition approach. *IEEE Transactions on Rehabilitation Engineering*, *8*(2), 214–215. doi:10.1109/86.847820

Perelmouter, J., Kotchoubey, B., Kübler, A., & Birbaumer, N. (1999). Language support program for thought-translation devices. *Automedica*, *18*(1), 67–84.

Pfurtscheller, G., & Aranibar, A. (1977). Event-related cortical desynchronization detected by power measurements of scalp EEG. *Electroencephalography and Clinical Neurophysiology*, *42*(6), 817–826. doi:10.1016/0013-4694(77)90235-8

Pfurtscheller, G., Flotzinger, D., & Kalcher, J. (1993). Brain-computer interface – A new communication device for handicapped persons. *Journal of Microcomputer Applications*, *16*(3), 293–299. doi:10.1006/jmca.1993.1030

Pfurtscheller, G., Flotzinger, D., Pregenzer, M., Wolpaw, J. R., & McFarland, D. J. (1996b). EEG-based brain computer interface (BCI). *Medical Progress Through Technology*, *21*(3), 111–121.

Pfurtscheller, G., Kalcher, J., Neuper, C., Flotzinger, D., & Pregenzer, M. (1996a). On-line EEG classification during externally-paced hand movements using a neural network-based classifier. *Electroencephalography and Clinical Neurophysiology*, *99*(5), 416–425. doi:10.1016/S0013-4694(96)95689-8

Pfurtscheller, G., Neuper, C., Guger, C., Harkam, W., Ramoser, H., & Schlögl, A. (2000). Current trends in Graz brain-computer interface (BCI) research. *IEEE Transactions on Rehabilitation Engineering*, *8*(2), 216–219. doi:10.1109/86.847821

Schalk, G., McFarland, D. J., Hinterberger, T., Birbaumer, N., & Wolpaw, J. R. (2004). BCI2000: A general-purpose brain-computer interface (BCI) system. *IEEE Transactions on Bio-Medical Engineering*, *51*(6), 1034–1043. doi:10.1109/TBME.2004.827072

Vaughan, T. M., Wolpaw, J. R., & Donchin, E. (1996). EEG-based communication: Prospects and problems. *IEEE Transactions on Rehabilitation Engineering*, *4*(4), 425–430. doi:10.1109/86.547945

Wolpaw, J. R., McFarland, D. J., Neatb, G. W., & Fornerisa, C. A. (1991). An EEG-based brain-computer interface for cursor control. *Electroencephalography and Clinical Neurophysiology*, *78*(3), 252–259. doi:10.1016/0013-4694(91)90040-B

Wolpaw, J. R., McFarland, D. J., & Vaughan, T. M. (2000b). Brain-computer interface research at the Wadsworth Center. *IEEE Transactions on Rehabilitation Engineering*, *8*(2), 222–225. doi:10.1109/86.847823

KEY TERMS AND DEFINITIONS

Affective Computing: Is a term coined by researcher Rosalind Picard to propose to assign to computers emotional skills and ability to respond intelligently to human emotion.

Artificial Neural Networks: They are based on studies of the structure of the human brain to try to emulate, in a system of programs and computational data structures, its intelligent way to process information. Structurally, the artificial neural network, also known as connectionist model of computing, resembles the biological neural network because of the composition of its neurons and the connection between them.

Beta rhythm or Mu Rhythm: Is a spontaneous rhythm captured by the electroencephalogram (EEG) in the frequency of 8-12 Hz. It is associated to the motor activities and recorded with best potential over the sensorimotor cortex. The alpha rhythm is in the same frequency but it is recorded on the occipital cortex. However, the Biofeedback training can modify the amplitudes of these rhythms.

Brain Computer Interface (BCI): Consists of a communication system that interprets and analyzes brain signals in order to improve human cognitive or sensory-motor functions. In this sense, it allows controlling devices in the external world (prosthetic limb, mouse cursor, wheelchair, etc.) by means of brain signals.

Cardiac coherence: Is related to the variability between the phases of acceleration and decreased heart rate. The balance between these phases is called heart coherence. The absence of this equilibrium characterizes a chaotic heart rhythm.

Co-evolution: In biology, co-evolution is associated with the reciprocal evolutionary change between two species that have dependencies on each other, so that one exerts selective pressure on the other. In evolutionary computation, co-evolutionary algorithms are deployed in order to carry out experiments in artificial life, solve optimization problems, learning games strategies, and other applications.

Functional Biometric Interfaces: They capture, analyze and evaluate neurophysiological user data under different parameters. Such neurophysiological mapping can provide another channel of communication with the external world or, when coupled with knowledge relating to Functional Nutrition and Behavioral Medicine, can be applied to the autonomic rehabilitation through physical and mental training.

Interactive Bio-Interfaces: Consist of biological interfaces that in addition to capture, analyze and evaluate the neurophysiological data of users, enabling their application to control digital systems or devices in the external world; they also promote a return channel to the body of the user. In other words, they provide feedback on actions taken (control systems or devices) in order to set up a co-evolutionary relationship between the systems involved.

Interactor: Individual who establishes an interactive relationship with the interactive digital systems.

P300 Potentials: The P300 consists of a positive potential that arises 300 milliseconds after the stimulus trigger. However, the P300 is related only to stimuli that have some degree of novelty or significance to the individual. The P300 is more evident in the parietal cortex and it is used normally in implementations of BCIs where the individual's expectation is an important factor, as in the case of spellers.

Slow Cortical Potentials: The slow cortical potential denominates the lowest frequencies captured by the EEG, those with periods of oscillation between 0.5 s and 10.0 s. While the negative cortical potentials are related to body movement and other forms of cortical activation, the positive is related to a low cortical activation.

Wearable Computer: Consists of a wearable system, controlled and reconfigurable by the user. Always connected and accessible, a wearable computer allows the user to execute commands while performing other activities.

ENDNOTES

[1]   For more information see: http://www.medienkunstnetz.de/works/terrain/

[2]   For more information see: http://netzspannung.org/cat/servlet/ CatServlet?cmd=netz kollektor&subCommand=showEntry&forward=&entryId=147923&lang=en

[3]   For more information see: http://www.arte-mergent.org.uk/tc/tc2.html

[4]   For more information see: http://www.arte-mergent.org.uk/tc/tc2.1.html

Chapter 2
Flow Simulation with Vortex Elements

Mark Stock
Independent artist, scientist, and programmer, USA

ABSTRACT

While fluid flow is a ubiquitous phenomenon on both Earth's surface and elsewhere in the cosmos, its existence, as a mathematical field quantity without discrete form, color, or shape, defies representation in the visual arts. Both physical biology and computational physics are, at their roots, very large systems of interacting agents. The field of computational fluid dynamics deals with solving the essential formulas of fluid dynamics over large numbers of interacting elements. This chapter presents a novel method for creating fluid-like forms and patterns via interacting elements. Realistic fluid-like motions are presented on a computer using a particle representation of the rotating portions of the flow. The straightforward method works in two or three dimensions and is amenable to instruction and easy application to a variety of visual media. Examples from digital flatwork and video art illustrate the method's potential to bring space, shape, and form to an otherwise ephemeral medium. Though the rules are simple, the resulting behavior frequently exhibits emergent properties not anticipated by the original formulae. This makes both fluid simulations and related biological computations deep, interesting, and ready for exploration.

INTRODUCTION

The state of the Earth and all of the life upon and within it are profoundly affected by flow. The convection in the mantle slowly transfers heat and pushes continents around; the currents and gyres in the ocean regulate and affect climate; the rain, ice melt, and surface runoff erode moun-tains into plains; the wind spreads seeds across vast distances; and tiny vessels inside plants and animals transport life-giving nutrients between organs. Indeed, the shapes of many organisms have evolved to not only accommodate flow, but to thrive in a fluid environment. Birds' wings and fish tails both flap to generate elongated vortex rings to provide thrust, seed pods are dispersed

DOI: 10.4018/978-1-4666-0942-6.ch002

widely because they contain elements that make them to fall very slowly, and the varying strengths of trees' branches allow them to survive high winds by bending to reduce drag. If not an essential quality of life itself, flow clearly seems to support the variety and vitality of life on Earth.

In the context of this chapter, *flow* means the ensemble motion of matter in which the individual elements are allowed to move relative to one another. A *fluid* can be a gas such as air, a liquid such as water, or a collection of solid particles such as sand. Seemingly solid materials can behave as fluids if one observes them over a long period of time; examples of this are ice (glaciers) and rock (mantle convection).

How do we quantify a flow? Flowing matter is composed of disconnected, non-uniformly-spaced molecules, each with its own motion. But it is grossly inefficient to describe flows at human scales with such detail. One solution is to assume that the properties of nearby elements vary smoothly. With this *continuum* assumption, the ensemble motion can be written as a mathematical function. Still, most flows retain more complexity than a single function can easily describe. In these cases, the fluid volume is typically *discretized*: broken up into discrete volumes for which the flow properties in each volume are considered uniform. This turns out to be a useful approximation of the real flow, as it makes it amenable to description and prediction on digital computers.

It is difficult to describe flow using the traditional elements of visual art (texture, form, space, line, color, value, shape). Flow doesn't necessarily have a surface to support a texture, nor does it edges necessary for shape. It defies these categories because it fills space, is constantly moving, and even exists where it is not visible. In many situations, line, form, and texture appear in flow due to visible material being carried by the flow. A collection of clouds, for example, defines negative and positive space, while a thin cloud layer provides texture to the background. Further, the shape and position of foreground subjects can imply their presence in a flow field: hair or branches blown by a breeze, or boats being tossed about on the open ocean.

As an alternative to relying on external elements affected by flow, the properties of flow itself may be used as visual elements. In the methods and artwork presented below, certain properties of the flow, such as volumes of quickly-rotating fluid, or numerical elements used to compute the flow, have been instantiated as solid objects, becoming fluid-like lines or forms within the volume. Flow then allows transformation of spatial entities such as points and lines, and in special cases, those entities themselves recursively define the flow. The non-deterministic nature of this feedback makes fluid simulations powerful and often-surprising tools for visual art.

In the following chapter, we will describe how points, lines, and surfaces can be made into elements which describe a flow, and how their positions and properties can evolve under their self-influence. This capability is described with a simple computer algorithm, but allows spontaneous generation of higher-level dynamics not suggested by the simple elemental rules.

PARTICLE SIMULATIONS

Very simple systems of interacting elements can produce non-deterministic, emergent behavior. Conway created a set of rules governing the life cycle of a square pixel in a grid (a *cellular automaton*): it becomes "alive" if exactly three of its 8 neighbors are alive, survives if two or three are alive, and dies otherwise (Gardner, 1970). Despite the simplicity of these rules, this "Game of Life" generates a remarkable diversity of behaviors—such as the Gosper Glider Gun seen in Figure 1 (Britton, 2011)—and is still the subject of active research forty years after its creation. A limitless number of cellular automata are possible, though most research focuses on emergent behavior of simple rule sets (Wolfram, 2002).

Figure 1. Left: Conway's Game of Life. Right: Mark Stock, Gravtime (© 2005, M. Stock. Used with permission.)

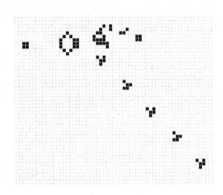

Other sets of rules are used to mimic the behavior of biological systems. For example, the flocking algorithm dictates the motion of independent agents, representing birds or insects, in space (Reynolds, 2001). At every step, each bird will attempt to achieve three goals: move toward the average center of local flock mates, match the flight direction of those neighbors, and steer to reduce crowding. Note that all of these rules require knowledge of the locations of only nearby birds in the flock, though global information is used to determine which birds are nearby. Applying any rule by itself would produce a stable and simple system, but together the algorithm allows much more complex behavior, as if the group were acting as a whole despite having no leader.

A similar system, and one with connections to computational physics, is the gravitational *n-body problem*. Newton's law of universal gravitation states that every mass attracts every other mass in the universe in direct relation to the product of the two masses and to the inverse square of the distance between them. The only other rules governing this system are also Newton's: that an object at rest remains at rest, it maintains its velocity unless acted upon by another object, and it changes its velocity by an amount equal to the

imposed forces divided by its mass. Simulations using rules like are used by astrophysicists to study the formation and collisions of galaxies (Dubinski, 2008), and helped demonstrate how the moon may have been formed by a large impact with the Earth (Ida, Canup, Stewart, 1997). Figure 1 illustrates a small n-body simulation in which the paths taken by particles/bodies as they progress upward are rendered as solid forms. From an even initial distribution, small clusters are born, and those in turn merge to generate larger and larger structures. It is not surprising that emergent phenomena like this exist in the universe, as many physical systems are composed of large numbers of simple elements with straightforward interaction rules.

COMPUTATIONAL FLUID DYNAMICS

The field of computational physics is concerned with recreating the motions of physical phenomena on digital computers. Specifically, *computational fluid dynamics* (CFD) involves solving the fluid equations of motion on a system of discrete elements in order to generate an approximation of a real flow. CFD is used for many scientific and engineering purposes, such as industrial combustion, automobile and truck design, wind power optimization, and obviously aircraft and rocket design and analysis. Scientists, engineers, and now a few artists are using a wide variety of CFD methods, each with advantages and disadvantages relating to accuracy, ease of programming, and aesthetic potential.

To represent field values on a digital computer, the domain of interest must be broken up into small volumes, each with its own unique set of values of the tracked properties. The most common type of CFD method discretizes the domain into adjacent, non-overlapping, non-moving volumes, through which fluid and fluid properties move. In these methods, velocity is a property of the fluid, along with density, pressure, and temperature. The simulation progresses by updating these properties for each cell according to relationships among these cells' neighbors. For example, if a cell sees a higher pressure on its left edge, it will initiate a velocity from the left to the right, and if that cell on the left is warmer, that velocity will carry some of the heat with it. This method appears and acts much like a complex cellular automata simulation.

The rules used to update the cells originate with the Navier-Stokes equations—the primary governing equations of fluid dynamics. These consist of differential equations that relate the change of velocity, pressure, density and temperature in space and time. Terms in these equations represent convection and diffusion of momentum and internal energy, the influence of external forces and heat sources, and the effects of any body forces such as those caused by gravity or rotation. The complete Navier-Stokes equations can only be solved analytically for very specific and simple situations, such as the flow between two infinite flat plates or in a tube. For most applications, especially those for which the flow is turbulent, these equations *cannot* be solved, instead approximate solutions are created on a computer. To do this, the differential equations are discretized in space and time and expressed as difference equations— equations relating the difference between values

in neighboring elements. These equations of fluid motion and their discretization are described in many undergraduate and graduate texts such as those from Hirsch (1988) and Wesseling (2000).

An example of imagery created using this type of method appears in Figure 2. In this work, millions of cells were initialized with horizontal rows of color and a density, but the flow began motionless. The simulation accounted for the density differences by allowing the lower-density (lighter-colored) fluid to rise while the darker/ denser fluid fell. Fluid fills every space always— no voids are created during the evolution of the flow. The consequence of this is that vortices are generated at boundaries between light and heavy fluids, and these vortices jostle with each other and persist for quite a long time.

There are several other popular discretization techniques, each leading to different solution methodologies. In spectral methods, the flow is described by its components in the frequency domain (Karniadakis & Sherwin, 1999). Lattice-Boltzmann methods resolve collisions among macro-particles constrained to move in quantized directions on a grid and use local averages to resolve the fluid properties (Wolf-Gladrow, 2000). Smoothed particle hydrodynamics (SPH) represents the flow as independently-moving spherical parcels of fluid with a location and velocity, and the evolution equations only contain summations over the local neighborhood of elements (Liu & Liu, 2003). This makes SPH methods popular in computer graphics, where fast solutions are more important than accuracy. Finally, particle methods such as SPH are well-suited to visual art, as the motion of their computational elements is easily translated to basic drawing elements.

VORTEX METHODS

A novel way to solve the equations of fluid motion stems from taking a mathematical transformation of the Navier-Stokes equations. For flows that do

Figure 2. Mark Stock, Magma 19. (© 2011, M. Stock. Used with permission.).

not involve shock waves or other compressibility effects, this new formulation—based on a quantity called *vorticity* which represents the rate of rotation at a point in a flow field—is easy to program and solve. A *vortex* is a volume of rotating fluid; normally with decaying circumferential speed and no radial motion. Vorticity and vortices appear frequently in nature and human-made flows, and provide a rich source of dynamical forms for artist and scientist alike (Lugt, 1983). A *vortex method* is a numerical scheme for discretizing and tracking the motion of vorticity. For derivation of the equations of vortex methods in two and three dimensions, and detailed information on the numerical methods for their solution, consult Cottet and Koumoutsakos (2000).

In vortex methods, the fluid volume is broken up into moving particles called vortices or vortons, each with a position and strength. These are not physical particles, but simply spatial markers indicating the rotation of fluid in their vicinity. The

rules governing the evolution of these positions and strengths can be expressed by a few simple equations, though the method will be presented below in the form of an algorithm. For each step of the simulation, the influence of every particle on every other particle must be calculated. This influence depends on the distance and direction between the particles and the strength of the influencing particle, very much like that for universal gravitation.

Note that even though only part of space is ever occupied by vortex elements, their influence covers the entire space—there is a velocity that is computable everywhere. As the particles move relative to each other, these velocity influences will change, further changing both the future motion of the particles and the flow everywhere. Even with just three particles, the resulting motion will be chaotic. With hundreds or thousands, their motion is clearly fluid-like.

A Simple 2D Solver

A vortex simulation can be created relatively easily, even by someone with little programming experience. In fact, the combination of a straightforward algorithm and visually interesting results makes it an ideal exercise for novice programmers. What follows is technically a two-dimensional inviscid (no viscosity) vortex method with a non-singular kernel (Krasny, 1986) and first-order time stepping. Pseudo-code appears in Algorithm 1. It is not from any specific computer language; it is only meant to illustrate the general procedure. Those not familiar with software development should consider using Processing (Fry & Reas, 2001) to create these programs.

The first task of any particle simulator is to define the initial conditions. In the case of a simple vortex method, these are the positions and strengths of the particles, the length of the time step, and in this case, the smoothing radius that stabilizes the simulation. Naturally, particles can be added or removed during the simulation, either arbitrarily or based either on physical rules; such capability can be added at the programmer's dis-

cretion. In the following code fragment, the arrays containing position (x, y), velocity (xvel, yvel) and rotational direction and strength (strength) are defined, and the necessary values set to random numbers.

The remainder of the program must calculate the particle positions as they change over time and call some external routine to display the results. This consists of an outer loop, which never exits containing three major steps, which repeat in order. The first step contains a doubly-nested loop that calculates the new velocities for every particle in the system. The second carries the particles forward a distance equal to their velocity times the time step size dt. Finally, the particles are drawn to the screen. Pseudo-code appears below in Agorithm 1.

Though the first vortex simulations were performed by hand (Rosenhead, 1931), the advent of the digital computer allowed simulations with much larger numbers of particles.

Running the above algorithm and rendering the particle paths as lines generates an image similar to that on the left of Figure 3. On the right is a frame from *Rota 9_8* (2010), a vortex simulation

Algorithm 1.

```
# the simulation will use n particles
integer n = 100
# the following arrays store the properties of each particle
float x[n], y[n], strength[n]
float xvel[n], yvel[n]
# these constants affect speed and smoothness
float dt = 0.01
float rad_squared = 0.01
for each particle i in n
        # random is a function that selects a random real
        #    number between the given bounds
        x[i] = random(-1,1)
        y[i] = random(-1,1)
        strength[i] = random(-1,1)
end loop over i
```

continued on following page

Algorithm 1. Continued

```
while (forever)
        # find the velocities
        for each particle i in n
                # accumulate the velocity influences, start at zero
                xvel[i] = 0
                yvel[i] = 0
                for each particle j in n
                        # first find the vector between the particles
                        dx = x[i] - x[j]
                        dy = y[i] - y[j]
                        # find distance, add the smoothness parameter
                        dist_squared = dx*dx + dy*dy + rad_squared
                        # scale by strength of source particle j
                        factor = strength[j] / dist_squared
                        # add the result to the velocity vector
                        xvel[i] -= dy * factor
                        yvel[i] += dx * factor
                end loop over j
        end loop over i
        # update the position of each particle
        for each particle i in n
                x[i] += dt * xvel[i]
                y[i] += dt * yvel[i]
        end loop over i
        # call a routine to draw the particles
        draw_particles(n,x,y)
end while loop
```

with a slightly different influence formula. In either case, vortices tend to pair up, with those of similar sign spinning around one another, and those of opposite sign marching side-by-side along a curve. Their motion is graceful and seemingly unpredictable. The evolution equations for more than two particles are non-deterministic, so changing any one initial value will generate a completely different flow.

Into Three Dimensions

Things get more complicated in three dimensions. Most importantly, a rotation in three dimensions is described by a three-dimensional vector, where two dimensions requires just a single number. This adds a new set of variables for the strengths (xstr, ystr, zstr) and some new steps to the vortex particle velocity influence code, as seen in Algorithm 2.

An additional complication that will not be addressed in the present method is the treatment of the vortex stretching term. This is a term that results from converting the governing equations

Figure 3. Left: Traces left by 2D vortex flow. (©2011, M. Stock. Used with permission); Right: Frame from Rota 9_8. (© 2010, M. Stock. Used with permission).

Algorithm 2.

```
for each particle i in n
        xvel[i] = 0
        yvel[i] = 0
        zvel[i] = 0
        for each particle j in n
                # find vector between the particles
                dx = x[i] - x[j]
                dy = y[i] - y[j]
                dz = z[i] - z[j]
                # find the distance from that vector
                dist_squared = dx*dx + dy*dy + dz*dz
                # add the smoothness parameter
                dist_squared += rad_squared
                # next two lines find reciprocal of the cube
                #   of the distance
                dist = sqrt(dist_squared)
                factor = 1.0 / (dist * dist_squared)
                # scale the results by that factor
                dx *= factor
                dy *= factor
                dz *= factor
                # compute cross product of strength of source
                #   particle j and scaled distance vector
                xvel[i] += dz*ystr[j] - dy*zstr[j]
                yvel[i] += dx*zstr[j] - dz*ystr[j]
                zvel[i] += dy*xstr[j] - dx*xstr[j]
        end loop over j
end loop over i
```

of fluid motion into those required for vortex motion, and is used to change the particle strengths with respect to the flow. Inclusion of this term is required for accurate simulations, but very flow-like results are possible without it.

A straightforward application of the above algorithm can be seen in Figure 4 in a piece called *Red Streamlines*. In this scene, ten thousand random vortex particles were created inside a cube. Then, one thousand streamlines were created using the above algorithm. For each streamline, an initial point was created, the velocity at that point calculated, and a new point created a short distance downstream. A line was traced between those two points, and the process repeated. Each line was finally converted to three-dimensional geometry, while the background vortices were kept invisible. Even though the simulation does not represent a physically possible flow configuration, the resulting wispy forms and interrelated lines imply dynamic, volumetric flow.

Figure 4. Mark Stock. Red Streamlines. (© 2003, M. Stock. Used with permission.).

Other Vortex Elements

The most common three-dimensional vortex methods use point particles as vortex elements (as above), but alternate vorticity discretization methods use elements that more easily translate to the visual arts. The earliest three-dimensional vortex methods used closed, connected circuits of segments to represent vortex filaments (Leonard, 1975). One nice property of vortex filaments is that their circulation is constant along the entire length of the filament (Saffman, 1992). In the context of the above algorithm, the strength per unit length of the segments is constant, and the direction is always along the axis of the segment. This obviates the need to compute the vortex stretching term, and the resulting method is an accurate viscosity-free three-dimensional vortex method.

Being composed of line segments themselves, vortex filament simulations need to carry no other property, nor affect any external object, to be rendered as artistic elements. Nevertheless, as these vortex filaments are still just numerical representations of flow properties, their instantiation is an attempt to make visible the normally-invisible. Figure 5 shows a simulation of the evolution of a vortex ring—a closed loop composed of one vortex filament. The ring was perturbed slightly, which was just enough to cause the motion to become chaotic. The resulting tangle of tubes represents the hidden details of fluid turbulence, made solid.

If vortex filaments represent lines around which flow rotates, vortex sheets can be considered to be many small, parallel, and adjacent vortex lines. The result is that the vortex sheet separates flows with co-planar, but not parallel, fluid motions. Like the other vortex elements, a vortex sheet moves under its own self-influence, and the evolution of its form can be computed with similar algorithms. See Stock (2006) for a detailed description of the necessary steps to accurate simulation of three-dimensional vortex sheets.

The sheet is normally composed of connected triangles forming a closed surface. The connectiv-

Figure 5. Mark Stock, Turbulence Infinite. (© 2003, M. Stock. Used with permission.).

ity of these elements must be defined and adapted as the simulation progresses, which can require substantial effort. Figure 6 illustrates the contortions and complexity that this triangle mesh can exhibit. That frame is from a larger work called *Smoke Water Fire* that aims to decontextualize fluid flow and leave merely its constituent motions. By rendering only the essential computational elements of a flow, and removing any suggestion of

physical material or appearance, the fluid stands ephemeral – as motion alone.

Vortex sheets can increase in area substantially during the course of a simulation. The repeated stretching, folding, and twisting generates forms in three-dimensional space unlike any other algorithm. Figure 7 shows a very convoluted form that emerged from the simulation of three vortex sheets. They began as separate spherical entities, but in the course of their motion collided with each other, causing rapid swirling and overlapping of their boundaries. The result is a sculptural form, but one that would not support itself if physically constructed. Despite the fluid origins of this and other images using these methods, observers seem quick to draw comparisons to forms with only loose connections to flow, such as octopus heads, or a woman in a flowing dress walking down stairs.

Figure 6. Mark Stock, Frame from Smoke Water Fire. (© 2008, M. Stock. Used with permission.).

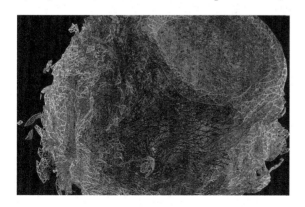

Figure 7. Mark Stock, The Trouble with Algorithmic Art. (© 2009, M. Stock. Used with permission.).

those based on fractals, iterated function systems, or limited-order chaotic systems. When the rules governing the behavior of agents in a large simulation are known (or approximated), the systems can be simulated in a computer. While the rules are often simple, the resulting behavior frequently exhibits emergent properties not anticipated in the original rules. This makes both fluid simulations and other biological computations deep, interesting, and ready for exploration.

REFERENCES

Britton, S. (April 2011). *GtkLife* (Version 5.1) [Software]. Retrieved from http://ironphoenix.org/tril/gtklife/

Cottet, G.-H., & Koumoutsakos, P. (2000). *Vortex methods*. Cambridge, UK: Cambridge University Press. doi:10.1017/CBO9780511526442

Dubinski, J. (2008). *Galaxy dynamics*. Retrieved from http://www.galaxydynamics.org/

Fry, B., & Reas, C. (2001). *Processing* [Software]. Retrieved from http://processing.org/

Gardner, M. (1970, October). Mathematical games: The fantastic combinations of John Conway's new solitaire game "life". *Scientific American, 223*, 120–123. doi:10.1038/scientificamerican1070-120

Hirsch, C. (1988). *Numerical computation of internal and external flows*. New York, NY: John Wiley & Sons.

Ida, S., Canup, R., & Stewart, G. (August 1997). *N-body simulation of moon accretion* [Abstract]. In Interactions between Planets and Small Bodies, 23rd Meeting of the IAU.

Karniadakis, G. E., & Sherwin, S. J. (1999). *Spectral/hp element methods for CFD*. New York, NY: Oxford University Press.

CONCLUSION

Many of the methods presented above for fluid simulation are applicable to other kinds of biologically-inspired computation. This is not surprising, as both physical biology and computational physics are, at their roots, very large systems of interacting agents. Because of the often very large number of highly non-linear equations, artwork formed by these systems is essentially different than other forms of digital algorithmic art such as

Krasny, R. (1986). Desingularization of periodic vortex sheet roll-up. *Journal of Computational Physics, 65*, 292–313. doi:10.1016/0021-9991(86)90210-X

Leonard, A. (1975). Numerical simulation of interacting, three-dimensional vortex filaments. In *Proceedings of the IV International Conference on Numerical Methods of Fluid Dynamics, Lecture Notes in Physics, 35*, (pp. 245-250).

Liu, G. R., & Liu, M. B. (2003). *Smoothed particle hydrodynamics: A meshfree particle method.* Singapore: World Scientific Publishing Co. Pte. Ltd. doi:10.1142/9789812564405

Lugt, H. J. (1983). *Vortex flow in nature and technology.* New York, NY: John Wiley & Sons.

Reynolds, C. (2001). *Boids* (Flocks, herds, and schools: A distributed behavioral model). Retrieved from http://www.red3d.com/cwr/boids/

Rosenhead, L. (1931). The formation of vorticies from a surface of discontinuity. *Proceedings of the Royal Society of London. Series A, Containing Papers of a Mathematical and Physical Character, 134*, 170–192. doi:10.1098/rspa.1931.0189

Saffman, P. G. (1992). *Vortex dynamics.* Cambridge, UK: Cambridge University Press.

Stock, M. J. (2006). *A regularized inviscid vortex sheet method for three dimensional flows with density interfaces.* Doctoral dissertation. Retrieved from http://markjstock.org/research/

Wesseling, P. (2000). *Principles of computational fluid dynamics.* New York, NY: Springer-Verlag.

Wolf-Gladrow, D. (2000). *Lattice-gas cellular automata and lattice Boltzmann models.* New York, NY: Springer-Verlag.

Wolfram, W. (2002). *A new kind of science.* Champaign, IL: Wolfram Media.

ADDITIONAL READING

Cottet, G.-H., & Koumoutsakos, P. (2000). *Vortex METHODS.* Cambridge, UK: Cambridge University Press. doi:10.1017/CBO9780511526442

Flake, G. W. (2000). *The computational beauty of nature.* Cambridge, MA: MIT Press.

Reas, C., & Fry, B. (2007). *Processing: A programming handbook for visual designers and artists.* Cambridge, MA: MIT Press.

Wolfram, W. (2002). *A new kind of science.* Champaign, IL: Wolfram Media.

KEY TERMS AND DEFINITIONS

Automaton: Abstracted machine which executes a sequence of possibly state-modifying instructions in discrete time steps.

Cellular Automata: A regular grid of automatons, each running the same set of instructions.

Computational Fluid Dynamics (CFD): Methods for solving the differential equations that describe fluid dynamics on a digital computer; usually involves discretizing the fluid domain into small, independent elements, and repeatedly solving the discretized form of the Navier-Stokes equations over those elements.

Discretize: To represent a continuous quantity as individual, discrete elements with possibly discontinuous values.

Flow: The ensemble motion of matter in which the individual elements are allowed to move relative to one another.

Fluid: A material that behaves as a flow.

Navier-Stokes Equations: The set of equations most commonly used to describe fluid flow; satisfies conservation of mass, momentum, and energy for a fluid; named after the French mathematician Claude-Louis Navier and the

Irish mathematician-physicist George Stokes, but developed by a number of scientists over the course of several decades in the early 19th Century.

Vector: A quantity that has both magnitude and direction.

Vortex: A finite region around which flow rotates.

Vortex Method: A method for computational fluid dynamics which discretizes and explicitly tracks vorticity.

Vorticity: A field quantity that represents the rotation of a flow; it is calculated by applying the curl operator from vector calculus on the vectorial velocity field.

Chapter 3
Cooperation of Nature and Physiologically Inspired Mechanisms in Visualisation

Mohammad Majid al-Rifaie
Goldsmiths, University of London, UK

Ahmed Aber
The Royal Free Hospital, London, UK

John Mark Bishop
Goldsmiths, University of London, UK

ABSTRACT

A novel approach of integrating two swarm intelligence algorithms is considered, one simulating the behaviour of birds flocking (Particle Swarm Optimisation) and the other one (Stochastic Diffusion Search) mimics the recruitment behaviour of one species of ants – Leptothorax acervorum. This hybrid algorithm is assisted by a biological mechanism inspired by the behaviour of blood flow and cells in blood vessels, where the concept of high and low blood pressure is utilised. The performance of the nature-inspired algorithms and the biologically inspired mechanisms in the hybrid algorithm is reflected through a cooperative attempt to make a drawing on the canvas. The scientific value of the marriage between the two swarm intelligence algorithms is currently being investigated thoroughly on many benchmarks, and the results reported suggest a promising prospect (al-Rifaie, Bishop & Blackwell, 2011). It may also be discussed whether or not the artworks generated by nature and biologically inspired algorithms can possibly be considered as computationally creative.

INTRODUCTION

In recent years, studies of the behaviour of social insects (e.g. ants and bees) and social animals (e.g. birds and fish) have proposed several new metaheuristics for use in collective intelligence.

Natural examples of swarm intelligence (a form of collective intelligence) that exhibit a form of social interaction are fish schooling, birds flocking, ant colonies in nesting and foraging, bacterial growth, animal herding, brood sorting etc.

DOI: 10.4018/978-1-4666-0942-6.ch003

This chapter explores the artistic side of this collective intelligence, which emerges through the interaction of simple agents (representing the social insects/animals) in two nature-inspired algorithms, namely, Particle Swarm Optimisation (PSO) (J. Kennedy & Eberhart, 1995) and Stochastic Diffusion Search (SDS) (Bishop, 1989). Additionally, the mechanisms of blood vessel and blood flow are utilised to add another layer of detail to the drawing.

In the presented work, a user-made sketch is used as an input for the system. Then, the swarms of 'birds' and 'ants' explore the digital canvas they are provided with, going through all the lines made in the sketch and reworking them in their own way. The output of the system would be the swarms' 'interpretation' of the original sketch. As mentioned earlier, at a later stage, the physiologically inspired mechanism of blood flow is also used to add more details to the drawings made by the swarms.

A-Life (Artificial Life), where the boundary between biology and artificial intelligence is blurred (Levy, 1993), inspired many artists and researchers in computer graphics to explore this blurred area. Among the direct responses to A-Life are some works by Karl Sims (e.g. Sims, 1991, 1994). In an earlier work, Harold Cohen, an artist who used techniques of artificial intelligence to produce art, developed a computer program called AARON, which produced drawings as well as paintings (McCorduck, 1991).

Following other works in the field of swarm painting (Moura & Ramos, 2007, Aupetit, Bordeau, Monmarche, Slimane, & Venturini, 2004, Urbano, 2005, 2006) and ant colony paintings (Greenfield, 2005, Monmarche, Aupetit, Bordeau, Slimane, & Venturini, 2003), this work, in addition to exhibiting the cooperation of birds and ants as a new way in making a drawing, benefits from the mechanism used in blood vessels.

There are many works where the input of the nature has been utilised, some of which *are* claimed be to art. As for the presented work, despite the novelty of this hybrid approach, it is not the inten-

tion of the authors to use the results outlined in this work to make neither strong epistemological claims of computational creativity nor strong aesthetic claims of style.

In this chapter, each of the swarm intelligence algorithms used are introduced, and an approach to their possible integration is highlighted. Subsequently, the simplified mechanisms of blood vessel and blood flow are described, followed by an explanation on how the new hybrid algorithm produces a drawing and the role played by blood vessel remodeling. Lastly, the similar individualistic approach of the swarms in making a drawing is highlighted, followed by a brief section on creativity in general as well as a discussion on whether swarms can be computationally creative. The chapter comes to an end with a conclusion and possible future research.

BACKGROUND

After a brief introduction to communication in social systems, this section introduces two swarm intelligence algorithms as well as their integration strategy, followed by the simplified mechanism of blood vessel and blood flow.

Communication in Social Systems

Communication – social interaction or information exchange – observed in social insects and social animals plays a significant role in all swarm intelligence algorithms, including SDS and PSOs. Although in nature not just the syntactical information is exchanged between the individuals but also semantic rules and beliefs about how to process this information (J. F. Kennedy, Eberhart, & Shi, 2001), in typical swarm intelligence algorithms only the syntactical exchange of information is taken into account.

In the study of the interaction of social insects, two important elements are the individuals and the environment, which result in two integration schemes: the first one is the way in which individuals self-interact and the second one is the interaction of the individuals with the environment (Bonabeau, Dorigo, & Theraulaz, 2000). Self-interaction between individuals is carried out through recruitment strategies and it has been demonstrated that, typically, various recruitment strategies are used by ants (Holldobler & Wilson, 1990) and honey bees. These recruitment strategies are used to attract other members of the society to gather around one or more desired areas, either for foraging purposes or for moving to a new nest site.

In general, there are many different forms of recruitment strategies used by social insects; these may take the form of global or local strategies, one-to-one or one-to-many communication, and deploy stochastic or deterministic mechanisms. The nature of information sharing varies in different environments and with different types of social insects. Sometimes, the information exchange is quite complex where, for example it might carry data about the direction, suitability of the target and the distance; sometimes, the information sharing is instead simply a stimulation forcing a certain triggered action. What all these recruitment and information exchange strategies have in common is distributing useful information throughout their community (Meyer, Nasuto, & Bishop, 2006).

In many hive-based (flock-based) agents – like the ones used in this chapter – the benefits of memory and communication seem obvious, but as argued in (Schermerhorn & Scheutz, 2009), these abilities are not beneficial in every environment, depending on the way resources are clustered throughout the environment and on whether the quality of the food sources is sufficiently high.

The algorithms used in this chapter rely both on memory and communication and the communication methods deployed are less greedy than the one presented in (Schermerhorn & Scheutz, 2009), thus allowing the agents to explore various parts of the search space. Nevertheless, the effect communication has on the artistic performance of swarm-based algorithms on this work is under further investigation.

The parable of the *blind men and the elephant* suggests how social interactions can lead to more intelligent behaviour. This famous tale, set in verse by John Godfrey Saxe (Saxe, Lathen, & Chief, 1882) in the 19th century, characterises six blind men approaching an elephant. They end up having six different ideas about the elephant, as each person has experienced only one aspect of the elephant's body: wall (elephant's side), spear (tusk), snake (trunk), tree (knee), fan (ear) and rope (tail). The moral of the story is to show how people build their beliefs by drawing them from incomplete information, derived from incomplete knowledge about the world (J. F. Kennedy et al., 2001). If the blind men had been communicating about what they were experiencing, they would have possibly come up with the conclusion that they were exploring the heterogeneous qualities that make up an elephant.

Birds: Particle Swarm Optimisation

Particle Swarm Optimisation (PSO), first developed in 1995 by Kennedy and Eberhart (J. Kennedy & Eberhart, 1995, Eberhart & Kennedy, 1995), is a population-based, optimization technique which came about as a result of an attempt to graphically simulate the choreography of fish schooling or birds flocking (e.g. pigeons, starlings, and shorebirds) flying in coordinated flocks that show strong synchronisation in turning, initiation of flights and landing. Despite the fact that members of the swarm neither have knowledge about the global behaviour of the swarm nor a global information about the environment, the local interactions of the swarms triggers a complex collective behaviour, such as flocking, herding, schooling, exploration and foraging (Reynolds, 1987, Mataric, 1994, Bayazit, Lien, & Amato, 2002, Janson, 1998).

A high-level description of PSO is presented in form of a social metaphor – The Lost Child in Jungle – demonstrating the procedures through which the information exchange is facilitated between members of the swarm in its simplest possible form. Formal explanation and mathematical equations of standard/basic PSO will be presented in the next section.

The Lost Child in Jungle

A group of villagers realise that a child is lost in the jungle nearby and set off to find him. Each one of the villagers is given a mobile phone equipped with GPS that can be used to communicate with the head of the village. Each villager is also provided with a diary to record some data, as explained below.

The villagers should log the location where they find the best information so far about the child in their diaries (Personal Best position) and inform the head of the village about it. Whenever they find something better that might lead to the location of the child (a location with a better fitness than their current Personal Best position), they should provide the head of the village with the update.

The head of the village is responsible to compare all the Personal Bests he has received so far from all the villagers and pick the best one (Global Best position). The resulting Global Best position is communicated back to the villagers.

Therefore, each villager should log the following three in his diary throughout the search:

- Current position
- Speed in walking
- Personal Best position (which is also called *memory*)
- Global Best position

In the next step, when villagers decide about their next move from their current position, they need to consider their two bests (Personal and Global) and their current speed.

Thus, while each villager does not neglect his personal findings, he has extra knowledge about its neighbourhood through Global Best position (the topology of the metaphor presented here is

global neighbourhood); therefore, preserving a balance between exploration of the search space (e.g. jungle, in this case), and exploitation of potentially good areas around each villager's Personal Best.

In this example, villagers are metaphorically analogous to particles in PSO, where optimisation is based on particles' individual experience (Personal Best) and their social interaction with the particle swarms (via Global Best). Algorithm 1 describes the metaphor chronologically:

At the end of the search, villagers will most likely congregate over the area where the child is likely to be found and hopefully, using this algorithm, the child will be brought back to his family in the village!

Standard PSO

A swarm in PSO algorithm is comprised of a number of particles and each particle represents a point in a multi-dimensional problem space. Particles in the swarm explore the problem space searching for the best (optimal) position, which is defined by a fitness function. The position of each particle, x, relies on the particle's own experience and those of its neighbours. Each particle has a memory, containing the best position found so far during the course of the optimisation, which is called personal best (pbest or p); whereas the best found position so far throughout the population, or the local neighbourhood, is called global best (gbest or) and local best (lbest or) respectively.

The standard PSO algorithm defines the next position of each particle by adding a velocity to the current position. Here is the equation for updating the velocity of each particle:

$$v_{id}^t = wv_{id}^{t-1} + c_1r_1\left(p_{id} - x_{id}^{t-1}\right) + c_2r_2\left(p_{gd} - x_{id}^{t-1}\right)$$

$$(1)$$

$$x_{id}^t = v_{id}^t + x_{id}^{t-1}$$

$$(2)$$

Algorithim 1.

```
Villagers spread in the jungle

While (the child is not found)
   For all villagers
      Evaluate the fitness of the current location
          (how good the current location is
          to lead to the child)
      If (current location is better than personal best)
         Personal Best = current location
      If (Personal Best is better than Global Best)
         Global Best = Personal Best
      Villager decides about his next move
      (using information logged in the diary)
   End For
End While
```

where w is the inertia weight whose optimal value is problem dependent (Shi & Eberhart, 1998) and it is set to 0.5 for the work presented here; is the velocity vector of particle i in dimension d at time step $t-1$; are the learning factors (also referred to as acceleration constants) for personal best and neighbourhood best respectively (they are generally constant and are usually set to 2); are random numbers adding stochasticity to the algorithm and they are drawn from a uniform distribution on the unit interval ; is the personal best position of particle in dimension d (initially set to the value of particle in dimension d); and is global best (or neighbourhood best), initially set to a random particle.

Therefore, PSO optimisation is based on the particles' individual experience and their social interaction with the particle swarms. After updating the velocities of the particles, their new positions are determined.

$$v_{id}^t = \chi(v_{id}^{t-1} + c_1 r_1(p_{id} - x_{id}^{t-1}) + c_2 r_2(p_{gd} - x_{id}^{t-1}))$$
(3)

where χ=0.72984 is reported to be working well in general (Bratton & Kennedy, 2007). The values of other variables are reported earlier (Equation 1).

Algorithm 2 summarises the behaviour of PSO algorithm for a minimisation problem.

Ants: Stochastic Diffusion Search

This section briefly introduces a multi-agent global search and optimisation algorithm called Stochastic Diffusion Search (SDS) (Bishop, 1989), whose behaviour is based on the simple interaction of agents.

Chemical communication through pheromones forms the primary method of recruitment in ants. However in one species of ants, *Leptothorax acervorum*, where a 'tandem calling mechanism' (one-to-one communication) is used, the forager ant that finds the food location recruits a single ant upon its return to the nest, and therefore the location of the food is physically publicised (Moglich, Maschwitz & Holldobler, 1974). In SDS, direct one-to-one communication (which is similar to tandem calling recruitment) is utilised.

Algorithm 2.

```
Initialise particles

While (stopping condition is not met)
   For each particle
      Evaluate fitness of particle
      If (current fitness < pbest)
         pbest = current fitness

      If (pbest < global (or local) best)
         global (or local) best = pbest

      Update particle velocity (Eq 1 or 3)
      Update particle position (Eq 2)
   End For
End While
In this chapter, Clerc-Kennedy PSO (PSO-CK) is used:
```

SDS presents a new probabilistic approach for solving best-fit pattern recognition and matching problems. SDS, as a population-based multi-agent global search and optimisation algorithm, is a distributed mode of computation utilising interaction between simple agents (Meyer, Bishop, & Nasuto, 2003).

Unlike many nature inspired search algorithms, SDS has a strong mathematical framework, which details the behaviour of the algorithm by investigating its resource allocation (Nasuto, 1999), convergence to global optimum (Nasuto & Bishop, 1999), robustness and minimal convergence criteria (Myatt, Bishop, & Nasuto, 2004) and linear time complexity (Nasuto, Bishop, & Lauria, 1998). A social metaphor, *the Mining Game* (al-Rifaie & Bishop, 2010), is used to explain the mechanism through which SDS allocates resources.

The Mining Game

This metaphor provides a simple high-level description of the behaviour of agents in SDS, where mountain range is divided into hills and each hill is divided into regions:

A group of miners learn that there is gold to be found on the hills of a mountain range but have no information regarding its distribution. To maximize their collective wealth, the maximum number of miners should dig at the hill which has the richest seams of gold (this information is not available a-priori). In order to solve this problem, the miners decide to employ a simple Stochastic Diffusion Search.

- At the start of the mining process each miner is randomly allocated a hill to mine (his hill hypothesis, *h*).
- Every day each miner is allocated a randomly selected region of the hill to mine.

At the end of each day, the probability that a miner is happy is proportional to the amount of gold he has found. Every evening, the miners congregate and each miner who is not happy selects another miner at random for communication. If the chosen miner is happy, he shares the location of his hill and thus both now maintain it as their hypothesis, *h*; if not, the unhappy miner selects a new hill hypothesis to mine at random.

As this process is structurally similar to SDS, miners will naturally self-organise to congregate over hill(s) of the mountain with high concentration of gold.

In the context of SDS, agents take the role of miners; active agents being 'happy miners', inactive agents being 'unhappy' miners and the agent's hypothesis being the miner's 'hill-hypothesis'. Algorithm 3 presents the metaphor chronologically:

SDS Architecture

The SDS algorithm commences an optimisation or search by initialising its population, which are the miners, in the mining game metaphor. In any SDS search, each agent maintains a hypothesis, h, defining a possible problem solution. In the mining game analogy, the agent hypothesis identifies a hill. After initialisation, the following two phases are iterated (see Algorithm 3 for these phases in the mining game; for high-level SDS description see Algorithm 4):

Test Phase (e.g. testing gold availability)
Diffusion Phase (e.g. congregation and exchanging of information)

In the test phase, SDS checks whether the agent hypothesis is successful by performing a partial hypothesis evaluation which returns a boolean value. Later in the iteration, contingent on the precise recruitment strategy employed, successful hypotheses diffuse across the population and in this way information on potentially good solutions spreads throughout the entire population of agents.

In the Test phase, each agent performs *partial function evaluation, pFE*, which is some function

Algorithm 3.

```
Initialisation phase
Allocate each miner (agent) to a random
   hill (hypothesis) to pick a region randomly

While (not all/most miners congregate over the highest
   concentration of gold)
   Test phase
      Each miner evaluates the amount of gold
         they have mined (hypotheses evaluation)
      Miners are classified into happy (active)
         and unhappy (inactive) groups

   Diffusion phase
      Unhappy miners consider a new hill by
         either communicating with another miner
         or, if the selected miner is also
         unhappy, there will be no information
         flow between the miners; instead the
         selecting miner must consider another
         hill (new hypothesis) at random
End
```

Algorithm 4.

```
Initialising agents()
While (stopping condition is not met)
    Testing hypotheses()
    Diffusion hypotheses()
End
```

of the agent's hypothesis; $pFE=f(h)$. In the mining game, the partial function evaluation entails mining a random selected region on the hill which is defined by the agent's hypothesis, instead of mining all regions on that hill.

A simple example that SDS's partial function evaluation can be illustrated is text search, where the position of the first letter of each word in the text is a hypothesis (hill). In order to use partial function evaluation, one letter within a word (region within a hill) is compared against the letter in the word which is sought; this way, a full comparison of all the letters is not required. An example of text search using SDS is given in (Bishop, 1989).

In the Diffusion phase, each agent recruits another agent for interaction and potential communication of hypothesis. In the mining game metaphor, diffusion is performed by communicating a hill hypothesis.

Standard SDS and Passive Recruitment

In standard SDS (which is used in this chapter), *passive recruitment mode* is employed. In this mode, if the agent is inactive, a second agent is randomly selected for diffusion; if the second agent is active, its hypothesis is communicated (*diffused*) to the inactive one. Otherwise, there would be no flow of information between agents; instead a completely new hypothesis is generated for the first inactive agent at random (see Algorithm 5).

Cooperation: Birds and Ants

In an ongoing research, an initial set of experiments aimed to investigate whether the information diffusion mechanism deployed in SDS ('ants') on its own improves PSO ('birds') behaviour. Early results show the high potential of this integration. For detailed theoretical work and statistically

Algorithim 5.

```
For ag = 1 to No_of_agents
    If (ag.activity() == false)
        r_ag = pick a random agent()
        If (r_ag.activity() == true)
            ag.setHypothesis(r_ag.getHypothesis())
        Else
            ag.setHypothesis(randomHypothsis())
        End If-Else
    End If
End
```

analysis, refer to (al-Rifaie, Bishop & Blackwell, 2011).

In the hybrid algorithm, each PSO particle (villager, in the Lost Child metaphor) has a current position, a memory (personal best position) and a velocity; each SDS agent (miner, in the Mining Game metaphor), on the other hand, has hypothesis (hill) and status (happy or unhappy).

In the experiment reported here, every particle in PSO is an SDS agent too – together termed *pAgents*. In pAgent, SDS hypotheses are defined by the PSO particle positions, and an additional Boolean variable (status), which determines whether the pAgent is active or inactive (see Figure 1).

The behaviour of the hybrid algorithm in its simplest form is presented in Algorithm 6.

* Each time PSO evaluates the fitness of a particle, evaluation_counter is incremented by 1. The value of n is problem dependent. If n is smaller, SDS is run more often than when the value of n is larger.

In Algorithm 6, when the pAgents are initialised, pbest are initially set to the position of the particles and gbest is set to one of the particles randomly; *evaluation counter* counts the number of function evaluations in PSO and *n* is set to 3000 in this work. Therefore, SDS algorithm is run after every 3000 PSO function evaluations.

Test and Diffusion Phases in the Hybrid Algorithms

In the Test Phase of a stochastic diffusion search, each agent has to partially evaluate its hypothesis. The guiding heuristic is that hypotheses that are promising are maintained and those that appear unpromising are discarded. In the context of the hybrid PSO-SDS algorithm, it is clear that there are many different tests that could be performed in order to determine the activity of each pAgent. A very simple test is illustrated in Algorithm 6. Here, the Test Phase is simply conducted by comparing the fitness of each pAgent's particle's personal best against that of a random pAgent; if the selecting pAgent has a better fitness value, it will become active. Otherwise it is flagged inactive. On average, this mechanism will ensure 50% of pAgents remain active from one iteration to another[1].

In the Diffusion Phase, each inactive pAgent picks another pAgent randomly; if the selected pAgent is active, the selected pAgent communicates its hypothesis to the inactive one; if the selected pAgent is inactive too, the selecting pAgent generates a new hypothesis at random from the search space.

As outlined in the pseudo-code of the hybrid algorithm (see Algorithm 6), after each *n* PSO function evaluations, one SDS cycle[2] is executed. The hybrid algorithm is called *SDSnPSO*, where *n*

Figure 1. pAgent

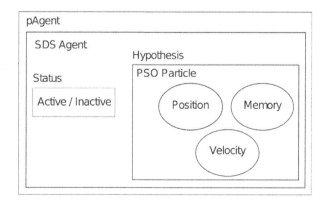

Algorithm 6.

```
Initialise pAgents

While (stopping condition is not met)
    For i = 1 to No-of-pAgent
        Evaluate fitness value of each particle

        If (evaluation_counter MOD n == 0)*
            // START SDS
            // TEST PHASE
            For pAg = 1 to No-of-pAgents
                r_pAg = pick-random-pAgent()
                If (pAg.pbestFitness() <=
                    r_pAg.pbestFitness())
                    pAg.setActivity (true)
                Else
                    pAg.setActivity (false)
                End If-Else
            End For

            // DIFFUSION PHASE
            For ag = 1 to No_of_pAgents
                If (pAg.activity() == false)
                    r_pAg = pick-random-pAgent()
                    If (r_pAg.activity() == true)
                        pAg.setHypo(r_pAg.getHypo())
                    Else
                        pAg.setHypo(randomHypo())
                    End If-Else
                End If
            End For
        End If
        // END SDS

        If (current fitness < pbest)
            pbest = current fitness
        If (pbest < gbest)
            gbest = pbest
        Update particle position (Eq 1 or 3)
    End For
End While
```

refers to the number of PSO function evaluations before an SDS cycle should run.

The next section gives a brief introduction of the mechanism of blood vessels.

The Simplified Mechanism of Blood Vessels

In this part, three different features of blood vessels will be explained in physiological and mechanical terms as they occur in the body. These aspects of the blood vessel mechanism have been imitated to collectively cooperate with the swarms in order to draw. In the presented drawings (see the figures in the next sections), each member of the swarm takes the shape of the blood vessels, as if the vessels are cut in order to see their calibre, thickness, etc. The main focus of attention will be on:

- Vessel calibre, which is affected by the blood flow and its shear stress
- Blood vessel thickness
- Geometrical heterogeneity of endothelial cells lining the vessels

Each of these will be explained independently and details on how these mechanisms influence the drawings of the swarms will be provided at the end of this section.

Blood Flow Shear Stress and Vessel Calibre

Hemodynamic forces of the blood flow have been identified as factors regulating blood vessels (Kamiya & Togawa, 1980, Lowell & O'Donnell, 1986) and influencing development of vascular pathologies such as atherosclerosis (Zarins et al., 1983), and aneurysms (Kerber, Hecht, Knox, Buxton, & Meltzer, 1996). The flow of blood on the luminal vessel wall and endothelial surface creates, by virtue of viscosity, a frictional force per unit area known as hemodynamic shear stress (Fung, 1997, LaBarbera, 1990). Shear stress has been shown to be a critical determinant of vessel calibre (Lowell & O'Donnell, 1986, LaBarbera, 1990, Kamiya, Bukhari, & Togawa, 1984), as well as an important factor in vascular remodeling (Zarins, Zatina, Giddens, Ku, & Glagov, 1987, Gibbons & Dzau, 1994) and pathobiology (Zarins et al., 1983, Kerber et al., 1996).

The luminal surface of the blood vessel and its endothelial surface are constantly exposed to hemodynamic shear stress (Fung, 1997). The magnitude of the shear stress can be estimated in most of the vasculature by Poiseuille's law (Fung, 1997), which states that shear stress is directly proportional to blood flow viscosity, and inversely proportional to the third power of the internal radius (LaBarbera, 1990, Kamiya et al., 1984, Zamir, 1976).

In equation Eq 4, Poiseulle's law states that the flow rate Q is also dependent upon fluid viscosity η, pipe length L and the pressure difference between the ends P by:

$$Q = \frac{\pi r^4 P}{8\eta L} \qquad (4)$$

Measurements using different modalities show that shear stress ranges from 1 to 6 dyne/cm2 in the venous system and between 10 and 70 dyne/cm2 in the arterial vascular network. Studies have shown that shear stress actively influences vessel wall remodeling (Kamiya & Togawa, 1980, Lowell & O'Donnell, 1986, Kraiss, Kirkman, Kohler, Zierler, & Clowes, 1991). Specifically, chronic increases in blood flow, and consequently shear stress, lead to the expansion of the luminal radius such that mean shear stress is returned to its baseline level (Kamiya & Togawa, 1980, Girerd et al., 1996).

This is clearly demonstrated in the radial artery of dialysis patients proximal to their arteriovenous fistula (Girerd et al., 1996) or in feeder arteries supplying cerebral arteriovenous malformations (Rossitti & Svendsen, 1995), both of which lead to the expansion of the blood vessels calibre as a result of increased shear stress in the vessel lumen. Conversely, decreased shear stress resulting from lower flow or blood viscosity induces a decrease in internal vessel radius (Lowell & O'Donnell, 1986). The net effect of these endothelial-mediated compensatory responses is the maintenance of mean arterial hemodynamic shear stress magnitude at approximately 15 to 20 dyne/cm2 (Girerd et al., 1996, LaBarbera, 1990). This shear stress– stabilizing process is dependent on intact endothelial function (Lowell & O'Donnell, 1986).

The effect of this mechanism on the drawing is discussed later in the chapter. In simple terms a proportional correspondence between the speed of drawing on a canvas and the size of the discs' diameter in the drawing (which represents the vessel calibre) is demonstrated.

Remodeling of Vessel Wall Structure and Blood Pressure

Various studies have demonstrated that increased blood pressure is one of the major contributing factors to blood vessel remodeling (Baumbach & Heistad, 1989, Short, 1966). A fundamental tool to understand the varying structure of different blood vessels including their wall thickness is the Laplace law. This law, which can be applied to any tubular element with cylindrical geometry, relates intramural stress (σ), wall thickness (W), lumen radius (r), and transmural pressure (P, or the difference between luminal and extraluminal pressures) according to the following equation:

$$\sigma = \frac{\mathrm{P}r}{W} \qquad (5)$$

which may be rewritten in terms of the W to lumen diameter (D) ratio as:

$$\sigma = 0.5 \frac{P}{(W / D)} \qquad (6)$$

Laplace law dictates vascular structure to maintain σ within a relatively tight domain. Within an individual, there is high plasticity of vascular structure, which continuously adapts to accommodate for the changing conditions.

Blood Pressure and the Concept of Small Vessel Remodeling

Early studies (Baumbach & Heistad, 1989, Short, 1966) have shown that hypertension (or high blood pressure) could be associated with changes in the structure of resistance vessels, such that the vessels had a decreased lumen and increased media:lumen ratio (lumen is the hollow part of the vessel through which the blood passes, and media is the major and the thickest layer of the blood vessel wall), but no change in media cross-sectional area (or volume). (Baumbach & Heistad, 1989) used the term remodeling for the first time to describe these changes.

Vessel Remodeling Classification

It was proposed that the term remodeling should only be used in situations where there is a structurally determined change in lumen diameter. A detailed classification that categorized the remodeling into the six changes is proposed in (Mulvany, Baumbachand, Aalkjær, & al., 1996). It was suggested that remodeling should be termed:

- Inward remodeling: decrease in the vessel lumen
- Outward remodeling: increase in the vessel lumen

Furthermore, since remodeling can result in either increase, no change, or decrease in the amount of vessel wall, there should be a sub-classification into *hypertrophic*, *eutrophic*, and *hypotrophic* remodeling, respectively:

- Hypertrophic remodeling: increase in the amount of blood vessel wall
- Eutrophic remodeling: no change in the amount of blood vessel wall
- Hypotrophic remodeling: decrease in the amount of blood vessel wall

This classification provided a framework for defining various modes of vascular remodeling in order to discuss the mechanisms involved. It is worth mentioning that only certain remodeling categories are used and imitated in this chapter.

Examples of the Different Types of the Remodeling

In this part, the impact of blood flow on the blood vessel remodeling is discussed by giving examples of different types of remodeling:

Primary Hypertension and Inward Eutrophic Remodeling: Histological studies demonstrated increased media:lumen ratios in the small vessels of patient with primary hypertension[3] (Suwa & Takahashi, 1971, Furuyama, 1962, Nordborg, Ivarsson, Johansson, & Stage, 1983). In another study, it was shown that the media:lumen ratio of resistance vessels was increased in hypertensive patients, but that this was not associated with any increase in the cross-sectional area of the media (measured normally to the longitudinal axis) (Short, 1966). Thus, the available evidence indicates that in primary hypertension the resistance vessels have experienced inward eutrophic remodeling. Furthermore, the size of the individual smooth muscle cells within the media is also normal (Korsgaard, Aalkjaer, Heagerty, Izzard, & Mulvany, 1993), while the functional responses of the smooth muscle are slightly affected (Aalkjaer, Heagerty, Petersen, Swales, & Mulvany, 1987).

Secondary Hypertension and Inward Hypertrophic Remodelling: In contrast to the above

inward eutrophic changes in primary hypertension, in human secondary hypertension[4] due to renal causes, the reduction in vessel lumen diameter is accompanied by an increase in media cross-sectional area leading to an inward hypertrophic response (Rizzoni et al., 1996).

Blood Pressure Treatment and Outward Remodeling: Outward remodelling of resistance vessel structure is in general seen during anti-hypertensive treatment and in situations with increased flow. Thus, with a certain class of anti-hypertensive medication called ACE-inhibitor[5], the abnormalities indicated in the previous paragraph (inward eutrophic and inward hypertrophic) are reversed (Thybo et al., 1995, Skov, Fenger-Gron, & Mulvany, 1996) and the remodeling will take the following shape: outward eutrophic and outward hypertrophic remodelling.

The way in which remodeling in blood vessels shapes the drawings are discussed later in the chapter.

Blood Flow and the Heterogenic Geometry of Endothelial Cells

It has been proposed that an important determinant of arterial disease is the local geometry of arteries, which in turn regulates the hemodynamic force distribution that acts on the endothelial cells covering the inner surface of blood vessels (Davies, 1995, 2008). In regions with unstable flow such as curvatures, branches and bifurcations in the arterial circulation, steep temporal and spatial gradients of shear stress are associated with an oscillatory flow that act on the endothelial cells. In these regions of disturbed oscillatory flow, multidirectional forces act on the cells, and as a result, the endothelium, unlike elsewhere in the arterial circulation, lacks preferential cell alignment and often expresses a polygonal morphology (Davies et al., 2010). Disturbed flow regions correlate closely with susceptibility to pathological change such as atherosclerosis in arteries and calcific sclerosis in heart valves.

The action of the oscillatory blood flow that causes a polygonal alignment of the endothelial cells has been imitated in regions of the canvas where the speed of drawing is higher than others; in these regions the discs exhibit a wave-like feature unlike other areas where the lines are unidirectional (see Figure 7).

THE DRAWING MECHANISM

To begin with, this section explains how a sketch is provided to the hybrid swarm algorithm (PSO-SDS) and how the hybrid swarms make a drawing based on the original sketch. Afterwards, the influence of the blood flow and blood vessels mechanisms is explored in this context.

Birds and Ants Set off to Draw

In the experiment setup of this work, a sketch is made on a screen with a mouse. Once the swarm (birds and ants) are presented with this sketch, which is a vector of (x,y) coordinates corresponding to the points constituting the sketch (see Figure 2), they use it as an 'inspiration' and start making a drawing, which is based on the sketch, but utilises the swarms 'style'.

Each one of the points (constituting the sketch and representing the lost child and the richest hill) is traced by the swarms (e.g. of villagers and miners, or birds and ants) as described in Algorithm 6. When the mouse pointer moves on the digital canvas to make a sketch, it is equal to the moving of the child (in the Lost Child metaphor) and to the change of the position of the richest hill (in the Mining Game metaphor). Each member of the swarms has the shape of a disc (with the centre representing the position of the particle) and as they move, their former position is connected to the current one with an arrow. It can be said that 'the trace of the birds' / 'the footprint of the ants' stay on the canvas, creating a drawing inspired by the initial sketch (see Figure 3).

Therefore, the search space of the swarms is the canvas (a two dimensional array corresponding to the width and height of the canvas in pixels), where they are initialised, and the goal of their performance is to trace the constituting points of the sketch. The swarms search on the canvas is terminated when they reach the end of the sketch (in other words, when there are no more points to consider).

In this context, gbest is the closest (fittest) particle to the point (of the sketch) being considered at any time. The hypotheses are the positions of each disc. The method used to determine whether an agent is active or inactive, and whether there should be information exchange, can be found in the test phase and diffusion phase of Algorithm 6 respectively. SDS cycle is carried out after each n PSO function evaluations. Thus, each disc on the canvas represents a pAgent, which is a PSO particle (i.e villager, or bird) and an SDS agent (i.e. miner or ant) at the same time. Twenty pAgents were used in all the drawings of this chapter.

How Blood Flow and Blood Vessels Shape the Drawing

The simplified impact of blood pressure on blood vessels is used in the drawing to reflect the relation between the time spent for drawing each part (e.g. each line) and the form of the discs (e.g. diameter

Figure 2. Sketch - The sketch whose constituting points are used as input to the hybrid swarms (© 2011, al-Rifaie. Used with permission.)

Figure 3. Drawing of the hybrid swarms (PSO + SDS). (© 2011, al-Rifaie. Used with permission.)

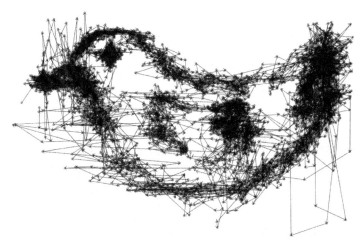

and thickness), which are visible around each member of the swarm.

The size of the discs is affected in either of the following ways (see Figure 4 which shows three types of outward remodeling types, two of which are used for the drawings):

A. Outward Eutrophic Remodeling: Enlarging the lumen (hallow part of the disc) without influencing the media (thickness of its wall)

B. Outward Hypertrophic Remodeling: Enlarging the media while keeping the lumen intact

Here, the concept of speed in drawing a line is analogous to the idea of the blood pressure in the mechanism of blood vessel remodeling. Since blood pressure affects the calibre of the blood vessels (see the earlier sections on blood vessel, blood flow and Eq 4-6), in this context, it implies that the quicker a line is drawn, the bigger the size of the discs around each member of the swarm. In other words, when a line is drawn faster than the other in a drawing, the size of the discs while drawing that line is bigger; but when a line is drawn slower, it will have smaller discs (see Figure 5).

In terms of vessel remodeling, a combination of two concepts are imitated to aid the drawing swarms:

Figure 4. Outward remodeling types. Top: Outward hypertrophic remodeling; middle: outward eutrophic remodeling; bottom: outward hypotrophic remodeling. (© 2011, al-Rifaie. Used with permission.).

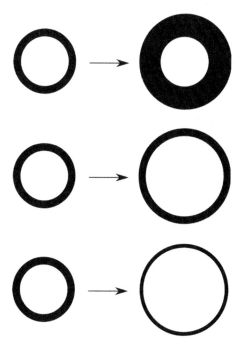

Figure 5. Blood vessels on high and low blood pressure on drawing a line. The speed of drawing the line decreases as it goes towards the right. Top: Demonstrating eutrophic remodeling. Bottom: Demonstrating hypertrophic remodeling. (© 2011, al-Rifaie. Used with permission.).

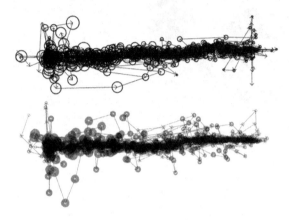

- Outward eutrophic remodeling in small blood vessels that are treated with ACE-inhibitors
- Blood vessel lumen expansion in areas that experience a constant high blood flow

These mechanisms are used simultaneously so that the speed of the drawing 'pen' (mouse) exhibits both the duration of treatment with ACE inhibitor for high blood pressure and the shear stress of the blood flow. For example when the pen speed is high on the canvas (high blood pressure), the disc becomes wider without any change in the disc thickness (see Figure 6-top).

In another approach, in the swarms' drawings, the outward hypertrophic remodeling is imitated by keeping the diameter of the hollow part (lumen) of the discs constant, whereas the thickness of the wall (media) of the discs is in a linear relationship with the speed of the drawing pen on the canvas. For instance, in areas where the speed of the drawing pen is high, the media is thicker than areas where the pressure is low (see Figure 6-bottom).

Earlier in the chapter, oscillatory blood flow has been described. In order to implement the oscillatory flow in the drawing, the equation of the simple sine wave or sinusoid is used:

$$y(t) = A.\sin(\omega t + \alpha) \tag{7}$$

where A is the amplitude, ω is the angular frequency, specifying the number of oscillations in a unit time interval in radians per second and α is the phase which determines where the oscillations begin in its cycle at $t=0$. In this chapter, the main variables are A and ω (α is always set to 0).

Using this equation, when a line is drawn faster than a threshold, the flow of the lines will be oscillatory (e.g. higher angular frequency in Equation Eq 7). Few approaches to implement the oscillations of blood flow in the drawing are listed below:

A. Lines are straight when the drawing speed is below the threshold, and slightly oscillatory when the threshold is crossed (A is a factor of speed and ω is set to 3). See Figure 7-top.

B. Lines are straight when the drawing speed is below the threshold, and highly oscillatory when the threshold is crossed (A is a factor of speed and ω is set to 0.3). See Figure 7-middle.

C. The flow is slightly oscillatory when the drawing speed is below the threshold (A is a factor of speed and ω is set to 3), and highly oscillatory when the threshold is crossed (A is a factor of speed and ω is set to 0.3). See Figure 7-bottom.

The next section presents a brief discussion on creativity, followed by a summary on whether swarms can show creativity in the 'artwork' they produce.

Figure 6. The drawings of the hybrid swarms with blood vessels mechanism. This figure shows the effect of the blood pressure on the disk's lumen and its media respectively (top: Eutrophic bird remodeling; bottom: Hypertrophic bird remodeling). (© 2011, al-Rifaie. Used with permission.).

Discussion on Creativity

The goal of this section is to discuss whether the hybrid swarm algorithms have the potential to exhibit 'computational creativity' in what they draw. In our discussion, we emphasise on the importance of what we later define as 'Swarm Regulated Freedom' (SR freedom) – cf. Gaussian Constrained Freedom (GC freedom) – and the combinatorial creativity of the hybrid swarm system. Then we contrast it with examples of potential non-human assessment of aesthetic judgment and suggestions of creativity in natural distributed systems. Our

modest conclusion would be that SR freedom (vs. GC freedom) – as for example exhibited in the hybrid bird, ant and blood vessel mechanism presented herein – can be useful in generating interesting and intelligible drawing outputs.

On Freedom and Art

For years, it has been discussed that there is a relationship between art, creativity and freedom, among which is the famous German prose, by Ludwig Hevesi at the entrance of the Secession Building in Vienna:

Figure 7. Blood flow oscillation in drawing. This figure shows few implementations of the oscillations of blood flow in the drawings. (© 2011, al Rifaie. Used with permission.).

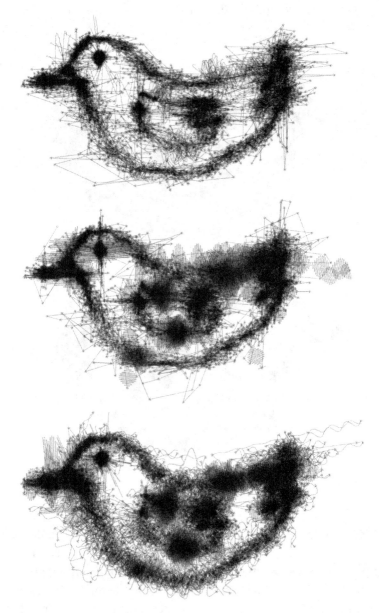

"Der Zeit ihre Kunst

Der Kunst ihre Freiheit"

That is: "To Time its Art; To Art its Freedom".

Or a quote by Aristotle (384-322 BCE) (Etzioni, Ben-Barak, Peron, & Durandy, 2007), which emphasises on the link between creativity and freedom (here, having "a tincture of madness"):

"There was never a genius without a tincture of madness."

Boden, in (Boden, 2010), also argues that creativity has an ambiguous relationship with freedom:

"A style is a (culturally favoured) space of structural possibilities: not a painting, but a way of painting. Or a way of sculpting, or of composing fugues... and so on. It's partly because of these thinking styles that creativity has an ambiguous relationship with freedom."

Among several definitions that have been given to creativity, around sixty of which (as stated by Taylor (Taylor, 1988)) belong to combinational creativity, which is defined as *"the generation of unfamiliar combinations of familiar ideas"* (Boden, 2007), a category that the presented work might fit in. Considering the existence of many influencing factors in evaluating what is creative, might, among other things, raise the argument about how humans evaluate creativity, their aesthetic capacity and that of other animals (e.g. in mate selection). Galanter (Galanter, 2011) suggests that perhaps computational equivalent of a bird or an insect (e.g. in evaluating mate selection) is "all" that is required for computational aesthetic evaluation:

"This provides some hope for those who would follow a psychological path to computational aesthetic evaluation, because creatures with simpler brains than man practice mate selection."

In this context, as stated in (Dorin & Korb, 2011), the tastes of the individual in male bowerbirds is visible when they gather collections of bones, glass, pebbles, shells, fruit, plastic and metal scraps from their environment, and arrange them to attract females (Borgia, 1995):

"They perform a mating dance within a specially prepared display court. The characteristics of an individual's dance or artefact display are specific to the species, but also to the capabilities and, apparently, the tastes of the individual."

The question of whether *'mate selection behaviour in animals implies making a judgment analogous to aesthetic judgment in humans'* is perhaps (pace Nagel's famous discussion in Philosophical review (Nagel, 1974) of 'What it is like to be a bat?') a question whose answer will never be clear.

In contrast, the role of education (or training) in recognising 'good' and 'bad', 'creative' and 'non-creative' has been more experimentally probed. A suggestive study investigating this topic, set by (Watanabe, 2009), gathers a set of children's paintings, and then adult humans are asked to label the "good" from the "bad". Pigeons are then trained through operant conditioning to only peck at good paintings. After the training, when pigeons are exposed to a novel set of already judged children's paintings, they show their ability in the correct classification of the paintings.

This stresses out the role of training and raises the question on whether humans are trained (or "biased") to distinguish good and/or creativity work.

Another tightly related topic to swarm intelligence in this context is the creativity of social systems. Bown in (Bown, 2011) indicates that our creative capabilities are contingent on the objects and infrastructure available to us, which help us achieve individual goals, in two ways:

"One way to look at this is, as Clark does (Clark, 2003), in terms of the mind being extended to a distributed system with an embodied brain at the centre, and surrounded by various other tools, from digits to digital computers. Another way is to step away from the centrality of human brains altogether and consider social complexes as distributed systems involving more or less cognitive elements."

Discussion on creativity and the conditions which make a particular work creative have always been among the heated debates for scientists and philosophers (Rothberg & Hausman (eds), 1976). A dated but excellent source on creativ-

Figure 8. The drawings of the swarms with random behaviour. This figure shows the drawings made with a simple randomized tracing algorithm, using Gaussian random distance and direction from the points of the original sketch. The variance of the figures on top and in the middle is the same. When variance ('freedom') is increased (in the bottom figure), the drawing gradually loses its original 'identity'. (© 2011, al Rifaie. Used with permission.).

ity theory is (Sternberg (ed), 1988), where the authors try to answer questions on the conditions of creativity, systems view of creativity, cognitive approaches, etc.

Although this chapter does not aim to tackle any of these issues or suggest that the presented work fits in the category of creative realm, it attempts to investigate the performance of the swarms in this context.

On the "Creativity" of the Swarms

As stated in the introduction of the chapter, there are several relevant attempts to create creative

Figure 9. Different drawings of the hybrid swarms (and eutrophic remodeling) off a single sketch.

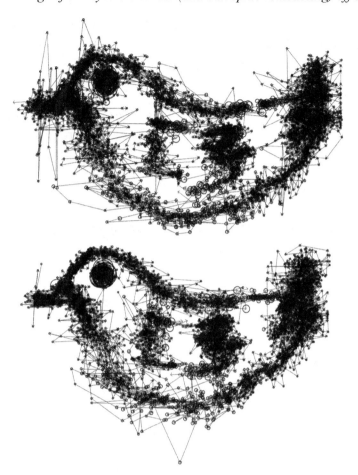

computer generated artwork using Artificial Intelligence, Artificial Life and Swarm Intelligence.

Irrespective of whether the swarms are considered creative or not, their similar individualistic approach is not totally dissimilar to those of the "elephant artists" (Weesatchanam, 2006)):

"After I have handed the loaded paintbrush to [the elephants], they proceed to paint in their own distinctive style, with delicate strokes or broad ones, gently dabbing the bristles on the paper or with a sweeping flourish, vertical lines or arcs and loops, ponderously or rapidly and so on. No two artists have the same style."

Similarly, as it will be discussed next, if the same sketch is given to the swarms several times, the output drawings, made by the swarms, are not the same twice. In other words, even if the hybrid swarm mechanism (of birds, ants and blood vessel) processes the same sketch several times, it will not make two identical drawings; furthermore, the outputs it produces are not merely randomised versions of the input. This can be demonstrated qualitatively by comparing the output of the hybrid swarm system with a simple randomised tracing algorithm, where each point in the sketch is surrounded with discs (similar to the pAgents) at a Gaussian random distance and direction (contrast Figures 8 with Figure 9). The reason why the hybrid swarm drawings are different from using random lines and discs following the points of a sketch, is the underlying algorithms and physiological mechanism [which is used to coordinate the concentrations at any particular point on the canvas] employing proven swarm intelligence techniques; a method which is better (more 'loyal' to the original sketch) than a simple randomisation, but which still has enough 'freedom' to ensure originality in the resulting drawing (i.e. the swarm mechanisms ensure high-level fidelity to the input without making an exact low-level copy of the sketch).

Thus, despite the fact that the swarms are constrained by the rules they follow (rules that were defined earlier in the chapter), the stochastic parts of the algorithms allow them to demonstrate a "regulated difference" rather than a simple "random difference".

Swarm Regulated Freedom versus Gaussian Constrained Freedom

The drawings in Figure 8 (top and middle) show two outputs from the simple randomised algorithm when configured with limited artistic freedom (i.e. there is only small Gaussian random distance and direction from the points of the original sketch – Gaussian Constrained Freedom or *GC freedom*); comparing the two drawings, we note a lack of any significant difference between them. Furthermore, when more 'artistic freedom' is granted to the randomised algorithm (by further increasing the variance in the underlying Gaussian, which allows the technique to explore a wider areas of the canvas), the algorithm begins to deviate excessively from the original sketch. For example excessive randomisation results in a poor - low fidelity - interpretation of the original sketch (Figure 8-bottom). In contrast, although the agents in the hybrid 'birds, ants and blood vessel swarms' are free to access any part of the canvas, they naturally maintain recognisable fidelity to the original input. Thus, it can be seen that simply extending a basic swarm mechanism by giving

it more randomised behaviour (giving it more 'artistic freedom') fails to demonstrate that more creative drawings would be produced.

The Swarm Regulated freedom (SR freedom) or 'controlled freedom' (or the *'tincture of madness'*) exhibited by the hybrid swarm algorithm (induced by the stochastic side of the algorithms) is crucial to the resultant work and is the reason why having the same sketch does not result in the system producing identical drawings. This freedom emerges, among other things, from the stochasticity of SDS algorithm in picking agents for communication, as well as choosing agents to diffuse information (see Algorithm 3); the tincture of madness in PSO algorithm is induced via its strategy of spreading villagers in the jungle as well as the stochastic elements in deciding the next move of each villager (see Algorithm 1). Although the algorithms (PSO and SDS) and the mechanism (blood flow) are nature- and physiologically-inspired, we do not claim that the presented work is an accurate model of natural systems. Furthermore, whilst designing the algorithm there was no explicit 'Hundertwasser-like' attempt – by which we mean the stress on using curves instead of straight lines, as Hundertwasser considered straight lines not nature-like and 'godless' and tried not to use straight lines in his works – to bias the style of the system's drawings.

CONCLUSION AND FUTURE RESEARCH DIRECTIONS

This specific work is the artistic outcome of the marriage between the two swarm intelligence algorithms (PSO and SDS) – whose scientific value is currently being investigated on many benchmarks (al-Rifaie, Bishop & Blackwell, 2011) – and the simplified mechanisms of the blood vessel and blood flow. Nevertheless, the difference between using Gaussian Constrained Freedom (GC freedom) and Swarm Regulated Freedom (SR freedom), which uses known swarm intelligence techniques, is highlighted by emphasising on *regulated difference* versus *random difference*.

This chapter discusses the possible inputs of physiologically-inspired mechanisms in computer-generated artwork. Following this theme, we aim to specifically investigate other physiological mechanisms (e.g. eye lens, bones, HIV virus, etc) and the role they can potentially play herein. We raise the question on whether integrating swarm intelligence algorithms (inspired by social systems in nature) and physiologically inspired mechanisms could possibly lead to a different way of producing 'artworks'. Additionally, the application of the presented nature and physiologically inspired algorithm in producing music is currently being investigated in an ongoing research.

REFERENCES

Aalkjaer, C., Heagerty, A. M., Petersen, K. K., Swales, J. D., & Mulvany, M. J. (1987). Evidence for increased media thickness, increased neuronal amine uptake, and depressed excitation-contraction coupling in isolated resistance vessels from essential hypertensives. *Circulation Research*, *61*(2), 181.

al-Rifaie, M. M., & Bishop, M. (2010). *The mining game: A brief introduction to the stochastic diffusion search metaheuristic*. AISB Quarterly.

al-Rifaie, M. M., Bishop, M., & Blackwell, T. (2011). An investigation into the merger of stochastic diffusion search and particle swarm optimisation. In *Proceedings of the Genetic and Evolutionary Computation Conference GECCO'11* (pp. 37-44). Dublin, Ireland: ACM.

Aupetit, S., Bordeau, V., Monmarche, N., Slimane, M., & Venturini, G. (2004). Interactive evolution of ant paintings. In *The 2003 Congress on Evolutionary Computation, CEC'03,* (Vol. 2, pp. 1376–1383).

Baumbach, G. L., & Heistad, D. D. (1989). Remodeling of cerebral arterioles in chronic hypertension. *Hypertension, 13*(6), 968.

Bayazit, O. B., Lien, J. M., & Amato, N. M. (2002). Roadmap-based flocking for complex environments. In *PG '02: Proceedings of the 10th Pacific Conference on Computer Graphics and Applications* (p. 104). Washington, DC: IEEE Computer Society.

Bishop, J. (1989). Stochastic searching networks. In *Proceedings of the 1st IEE Conference on Artificial Neural Networks* (pp. 329–331). London, UK.

Boden, M. (2007). Creativity in a nutshell. *Think, 5*(15), 83–96. doi:10.1017/S147717560000230X

Boden, M. (2010). *Creativity and art: Three roads to surprise*. Oxford University Press.

Bonabeau, E., Dorigo, M., & Theraulaz, G. (2000). Inspiration for optimization from social insect behaviour. *Nature, 406*, 3942. doi:10.1038/35017500

Borgia, G. (1995). Complex male display and female choice in the spotted bowerbird: Specialized functions for different bower decorations. *Animal Behaviour, 49*, 1291–1301. doi:10.1006/anbe.1995.0161

Bown, O. (2011). Generative and adaptive creativity . In McCormack, J., & d'Inverno, M. (Eds.), *Computers and creativity*. Berlin, Germany: Springer.

Bratton, D., & Kennedy, J. (2007). Defining a standard for particle swarm optimization. In *Proceedings of the Swarm Intelligence Symposium* (p. 120-127). Honolulu, HI: IEEE.

Clark, A. (2003). *Natural-born cyborgs: Minds, technologies, and the future of human intelligence*. Oxford University Press.

Davies, P. F. (1995). Flow-mediated endothelial mechanotransduction. *Physiological Reviews, 75*(3), 519.

Davies, P. F. (2008). Hemodynamic shear stress and the endothelium in cardiovascular pathophysiology. *Nature Clinical Practice. Cardiovascular Medicine, 6*(1), 16–26. doi:10.1038/ncpcardio1397

Davies, P. F., Civelek, M., Fang, Y., Guerraty, M. A., & Passerini, A. G. (2010). Endothelial heterogeneity associated with regional Athero-Susceptibility and adaptation to disturbed blood flow in vivo. *Seminars in Thrombosis and Hemostasis, 36,* 265–275. doi:10.1055/s-0030-1253449

de Meyer, K., Bishop, J. M., & Nasuto, S. J. (2003). Stochastic diffusion: Using recruitment for search. In P. McOwan, K. Dautenhahn & C. L. Nehaniv (Eds.), *Evolvability and interaction: Evolutionary substrates of communication, signalling, and perception in the dynamics of social complexity,* (pp. 60–65). Technical Report.

de Meyer, K., Nasuto, S., & Bishop, J. (2006). Stochastic diffusion optimisation: the application of partial function evaluation and stochastic recruitment in swarm intelligence optimisation . In Abraham, A., Grosam, C., & Ramos, V. (Eds.), *Swarm intelligence and data mining.* Springer Verlag.

Dorin, A., & Korb, K. (2011). Creativity refined . In McCormack, J., & d'Inverno, M. (Eds.), *Computers and creativity.* Berlin, Germany: Springer.

Eberhart, R., & Kennedy, J. (1995). A new optimizer using particle swarm theory. In *Proceedings of the Sixth International Symposium on Micro Machine and Human Science* (Vol. 43).

Etzioni, A., Ben-Barak, A., Peron, S., & Durandy, A. (2007). Ataxia-telangiectasia in twins presenting as autosomal recessive hyper-immunoglobulin m syndrome. *The Israel Medical Association Journal, 9*(5), 406.

Fung, Y. (1997). *Biomechanics: Circulation.* Springer Verlag.

Furuyama, M. (1962). Histometrical investigations of arteries in reference to arterial hypertension. *The Tohoku Journal of Experimental Medicine, 76,* 388–414. doi:10.1620/tjem.76.388

Galanter, P. (2011). Computational aesthetic evaluation: Past and future . In McCormack, J., & d'Inverno, M. (Eds.), *Computers and creativity.* Berlin, Germany: Springer.

Gibbons, G. H., & Dzau, V. J. (1994). The emerging concept of vascular remodeling. *The New England Journal of Medicine, 330*(20), 1431. doi:10.1056/NEJM199405193302008

Girerd, X., London, G., Boutouyrie, P., Mourad, J. J., Safar, M., & Laurent, S. (1996). Remodeling of the radial artery in response to a chronic increase in shear stress. *Hypertension, 27*(3), 799.

Greenfield, G. (2005). Evolutionary methods for ant colony paintings. *Applications of Evolutionary Computing . Proceedings, 3449,* 478–487.

Holldobler, B., & Wilson, E. O. (1990). *The ants.* Springer-Verlag.

Janson, C. H. (1998). Experimental evidence for spatial memory in foraging wild capuchin monkeys, *cebus apella. Animal Behaviour, 55,* 1229–1243. doi:10.1006/anbe.1997.0688

Kamiya, A., Bukhari, R., & Togawa, T. (1984). Adaptive regulation of wall shear stress optimizing vascular tree function. *Bulletin of Mathematical Biology, 46*(1), 127–137.

Kamiya, A., & Togawa, T. (1980). Adaptive regulation of wall shear stress to flow change in the canine carotid artery. *American Journal of Physiology. Heart and Circulatory Physiology, 239*(1), H14.

Kennedy, J., & Eberhart, R. C. (1995). Particle swarm optimization. In *Proceedings of the IEEE International Conference on Neural Networks* (Vol. IV, pp. 1942–1948). Piscataway, NJ: IEEE Service Center.

Kennedy, J. F., Eberhart, R. C., & Shi, Y. (2001). *Swarm intelligence*. San Francisco, CA: Morgan Kaufmann Publishers.

Kerber, C. W., Hecht, S. T., Knox, K., Buxton, R. B., & Meltzer, H. S. (1996). Flow dynamics in a fatal aneurysm of the basilar artery. *AJNR. American Journal of Neuroradiology, 17*(8), 1417.

Korsgaard, N., Aalkjaer, C., Heagerty, A. M., Izzard, A. S., & Mulvany, M. J. (1993). Histology of subcutaneous small arteries from patients with essential hypertension. *Hypertension, 22*(4), 523.

Kraiss, L. W., Kirkman, T. R., Kohler, T. R., Zierler, B., & Clowes, A. W. (1991). Shear stress regulates smooth muscle proliferation and neointimal thickening in porous polytetrafluoroethylene grafts. *Arteriosclerosis, Thrombosis, and Vascular Biology, 11*(6), 1844. doi:10.1161/01.ATV.11.6.1844

LaBarbera, M. (1990). Principles of design of fluid transport systems in zoology. *Science, 249*(4972), 992. doi:10.1126/science.2396104

Levy, S. (1993). *Artificial life: A report from the frontier where computers meet biology*. New York, NY: Random House Inc.

Lowell, B., & O'Donnell, F. (1986). Reductions in arterial diameter produced by chronic decreases in blood flow are endothelium-dependent. *Science, 231*(4736), 405–407. doi:10.1126/science.3941904

Mataric, M. (1994). *Interaction and intelligent behavior*. Unpublished doctoral dissertation, Department of Electrical, Electronics and Computer Engineering, MIT, USA.

McCorduck, P. (1991). *Aaron's code: Meta-art, artificial intelligence, and the work of Harold Cohen*. WH Freeman.

Moglich, M., Maschwitz, U., & Holldobler, B. (1974). Tandem calling: A new kind of signal in ant communication. *Science, 186*(4168), 1046–1047. doi:10.1126/science.186.4168.1046

Moura, L., & Ramos, V. (2007). *Swarm paintings–Nonhuman art*. Retrieved from http://www.leonelmoura.com/aswarm.html

Mulvany, M. J., Baumbachand, G. L., & Aalkjaer, C. (1996). Vascular remodelling. *Hypertension, 28*, 505–506.

Myatt, D. R., Bishop, J. M., & Nasuto, S. J. (2004). Minimum stable convergence criteria for stochastic diffusion search. *Electronics Letters, 40*(2), 112–113. doi:10.1049/el:20040096

Nagel, T. (1974). What is it like to be a bat? *The Philosophical Review, JSTOR, 83*(4), 435–450. doi:10.2307/2183914

Nasuto, S. J. (1999). *Resource allocation analysis of the stochastic diffusion search*. Unpublished doctoral dissertation, PhD Thesis, University of Reading, Reading, UK.

Nasuto, S. J., & Bishop, J. M. (1999). Convergence analysis of stochastic diffusion search. *Parallel Algorithms and Applications, 14*(2).

Nasuto, S. J., Bishop, J. M., & Lauria, S. (1998). Time complexity of stochastic diffusion search. *Neural Computation*, NC98.

Nordborg, C., Ivarsson, H., Johansson, B. B., & Stage, L. (1983). Morphometric study of mesenteric and renal arteries in spontaneously hypertensive rats. *Journal of Hypertension, 1*(4), 333. doi:10.1097/00004872-198312000-00002

Reynolds, C. W. (1987). Flocks, herds, and schools: A distributed behavioral model. *Computer Graphics, 21*(4), 25–34. doi:10.1145/37402.37406

Rizzoni, D., Porteri, E., Castellano, M., Bettoni, G., Muiesan, M. L., & Muiesan, P. (1996). Vascular hypertrophy and remodeling in secondary hypertension. *Hypertension, 28*(5), 785.

Rossitti, S., & Svendsen, P. (1995). Shear stress in cerebral arteries supplying arteriovenous malformations. *Acta Neurochirurgica, 137*(3), 138–145. doi:10.1007/BF02187185

Rothberg, A., & Hausman, C. (1976). *The creativity question*. Durham, NC: Duke University Press Books.

Saxe, J. G., Lathen, D., & Chief, B. (1882). The blind man and the elephant. In *The poems of John Godfrey Saxe*.

Schermerhorn, P., & Scheutz, M. (2009). The impact of communication and memory in hive-based foraging agents. In *IEEE Symposium on Artificial life, ALife'09* (pp. 29-36).

Shi, Y., & Eberhart, R. C. (1998). Parameter selection in particle swarm optimization. *Proceedings of Evolutionary Proramming*, (pp. 591–600).

Short, D. (1966). The vascular fault in chronic hypertension with particular reference to the role of medial hypertrophy. *Lancet, 1*(7450), 1302. doi:10.1016/S0140-6736(66)91206-2

Sims, K. (1991). Artificial evolution for computer graphics. *Computer Graphics, 25*(4), 319–328. doi:10.1145/127719.122752

Sims, K. (1994). Evolving 3D morphology and behavior by competition. [MIT Press.]. *Artificial Life, 1*(4), 353–372. doi:10.1162/artl.1994.1.4.353

Skov, K., Fenger-Gron, J., & Mulvany, M. J. (1996). Effects of an angiotensin-converting enzyme inhibitor, a calcium antagonist, and an endothelin receptor antagonist on renal afferent arteriolar structure. *Hypertension, 28*(3), 464.

Sternberg, R. (Ed.). (1988). *The nature of creativity: Contemporary psychological perspectives*. Cambridge University Press.

Suwa, N., & Takahashi, T. (1971). *Morphological and morphometric analysis of circulation in hypertension and ischaemic kidney*. Munich, Germany: Urban and Schwarzenberg.

Taylor, C. (1988). 4 various approaches to and definitions of creativity . In Stenberg, R. J. (Ed.), *The nature of creativity: Contemporary psychological perspectives* (p. 99).

Thybo, N. K., Stephens, N., Cooper, A., Aalkjaer, C., Heagerty, A. M., & Mulvany, M. J. (1995). Effect of antihypertensive treatment on small arteries of patients with previously untreated essential hypertension. *Hypertension, 25*(4), 474.

Urbano, P. (2005). *Playing in the pheromone playground: Experiences in swarm painting* (pp. 527–532). Applications on Evolutionary Computing.

Urbano, P. (2006). Consensual paintings. *Applications of Evolutionary Computing*, (pp. 622–632).

Watanabe, S. (2009). Pigeons can discriminate âœgoodâ and âœbadâ paintings by children. *Animal Cognition, 13*(1).

Weesatchanam, A. M. (2006). *Are paintings by elephants really art?* The Elephant Art Gallery.

Zamir, M. (1976). The role of shear forces in arterial branching. *The Journal of General Physiology, 67*(2), 213. doi:10.1085/jgp.67.2.213

Zarins, C. K., Giddens, D. P., Bharadvaj, B. K., Sottiurai, V. S., Mabon, R. F., & Glagov, S. (1983). Carotid bifurcation atherosclerosis. quantitative correlation of plaque localization with flow velocity profiles and wall shear stress. *Circulation Research, 53*(4), 502.

Zarins, C. K., Zatina, M. A., Giddens, D. P., Ku, D. N., & Glagov, S. (1987). Shear stress regulation of artery lumen diameter in experimental atherogenesis. *Journal of Vascular Surgery, 5*(3), 413.

ADDITIONAL READING

al-Rifaie, M. M., Bishop, M., & Blackwell, T. (2011). An investigation into the merger of stochastic diffusion search and particle swarm optimisation. In *Proceedings of the Genetic and Evolutionary Computation Conference (GEC-CO-2011)*, Dublin, Ireland.

Bishop, J. (1989). Stochastic searching networks. In *Proceedings of the 1st IEE Conference on Artificial Neural Networks* (pp. 329–331). London, UK.

Boden, M. (2010). *Creativity and art: Three roads to surprise*. Oxford University Press.

Eberhart, R., & Kennedy, J. (1995). A new optimizer using particle swarm theory. In *Proceedings of the Sixth International Symposium on Micro Machine and Human Science* (Vol. 43).

McCormack, J., & d'Inverno, M. (Eds.). (2011). *Computers and creativity*. Berlin, Germany: Springer.

Sternberg, R. (Ed.). (1988). *The nature of creativity: Contemporary psychological perspectives*. Cambridge University Press.

KEY TERMS AND DEFINITIONS

Blood Vessel Remodeling: A process referring to the reshaping of the blood vessel that is caused by blood pressure.

Gaussian Constrained Freedom (GC freedom): A process used to generate new points by applying Gaussian random distance and direction from the already existing points of an original sketch.

Metaheuristics: They are computational methods used to optimise problems by iterative attempts to improve the quality of a candidate solution considering a performance measure.

Optimisation: A simple example of optimisation is when a car is about to be parked; in this case, different parameters should be considered and the best (optimal) choice should be made with regard to the following: the distance of the parking location from the current place, the suitability of the place and probably the duration in which the car be kept parked. In optimisation, these cases are compared against each other and the goal is to balance the trade-off between these parameters. Swarm intelligence algorithms have shown to be of significance in solving optimisation problems.

Particle Swarm Optimisation (PSO): A population based optimisation technique, which came about as a result of an attempt to graphically simulate the choreography of fish schooling or birds flying.

Stochastic Diffusion Search (SDS): A multi-agent global search and optimisation algorithm, which is based on the simple interaction of agents.

Swarm Intelligence (SI): A decentralised, collective approach to solve problems, where intelligence emerges through the simple interactions of the members of the swarm.

Swarm Regulated Freedom (SR freedom): A method used to constrain the freedom of the swarm or their movements by using swarm intelligence algorithms.

Visualisation: A technique deployed in different scientific fields to better understand the behaviour of certain mechanisms by visualising their performance.

ENDNOTES

[1]   NB. In standard SDS such high average activity would not be useful as it entails most agents will continue to exploit their current hypothesis rather than explore the search space, however in the hybrid algorithm the

randomised subsequent behaviour of each pAgent offsets this effect.

2   A full SDS cycle includes:
- one Test Phase which decides about the status of each pAgent, one after another
- one Diffusion Phase which shares information according to the algorithm presented

3   Primary hypertension is the major type of high blood pressure in humans and accounts for almost 95% of the hypertension cases in the human population and it is of unknown cause.

4   Secondary hypertension is the type of hypertension where a cause for the high blood pressure is identifiable, this type accounts for about 5% of high blood pressure in the population.

5   Angiotensin-converting enzyme inhibitor (ACE-inhibitor) is a class of medications used for the treatment of raised blood pressure. ACE inhibitors act by interfering with the action of the enzyme responsible for converting the inactive angiotensin 1 protein into the active Angiotensin 2, this active form causes increased blood pressure. Angiotensin converting enzyme (ACE) is present in the lung, whereas the Angiotensin type 1 is produced in the liver by the action of rennin. (Renin is an enzyme produced by the kidney in response to stress that might be caused by various stimuli). Angiotensin1 is transported in the blood when it passes through the vessels in the lung the ACE convert it into Angiotensin 2. ACE inhibitors interfere with this process and help treat raised blood pressure.

Chapter 4

Oh!m1gas:
A Biomimetic Stridulation Environment

Kuai Shen Auson
Academy of Media Arts Cologne, Germany & Cologne Game Lab, Germany

ABSTRACT

Ants represent a natural superorganism, an autopoietic machine, much like the human society. Nevertheless, the ant society stands out due to self-organization. Ants accomplish the generation of bottom-up structures communicating mainly by pheromones, but they also produce modulatory vibrations. This phenomenon represents a fascinating subject of research that needs to be amplified in order to identify the connections between these social organisms and humans; they share the same environment with humans and participate, thus, in the construction and mutation of posthuman ecology. The human-ant relationship plays an important role in the creation of new ecosystems and the transformations of old ones. Man can approach and embrace this relationship by means of artistic experiments that explore the bioacoustics involved in the social behavior of ants supported by the combination of cybernetics, autopoiesis, self-organization, and emergence.

INTRODUCTION

Media are a contraction of forces of the world into specific resonating milieus: internal milieus with their resonation, external milieus affording their rhythms as part of that resonation. An animal has to find a common tune with its environment, and a technology has to work through rhythmic relations with other force fields such as politics and eco-

nomics. In this context, sensations, percepts, and affects become the primary vectors through which entities are co-created at the same time as their environmental relations. (Parikka, 2010, p. 14)

Oh!m1gas is an artistic research and audiovisual installation that approaches the self-organization in ants as a cybernetic system with emergent manifestations. Oh!m1gas is based on a 'do-it-yourself' approach of bioacoustics, measuring the vibratory

DOI: 10.4018/978-1-4666-0942-6.ch004

sounds and mapping the activity of an ant colony and their relation to the artificial ecosystem where they live. By means of contact microphones and video surveillance interfaced with the computer that feeds this bio-data to two turntables, the life of the ant colony emerges as a soundscape of scratching effects. The source of inspiration for this sound-reactive installation is based on the functional resemblance of the turntable, as an artifact for sound production in human culture, with the stridulatory organ of several highly evolved ants, specifically the Attini leafcutter ants, as an artifact for social organization.

The aim of this artistic research is the exploration of the stridulation phenomena of ants as a modulation mechanism in their self-organization, which can be perceived artistically as well as scientifically like a network of parallel task allocations regulated by local interaction and feedback. My artistic approach is predominantly based on the studies of the first and second wave of cybernetics[1], from Wiener (1948) to Von Foerster (1961), the theory of autopoiesis from Maturana and Varela (1992), which I approached as self-organization in regard to my work, and reflections and abstractions about emergence and its relation to sound creation and propagation in general. Stridulation, is the main bioacoustic focus of my work. In ants, stridulation can be simply put as a stimulus, energy as vibration, which incites decision-making in nestmates. It is a vibratory signal that travels through the soil and the organic material that construct the nest and its surroundings, to stimulate a response. Stridulation is part of the ant's communication repertoire, and along with pheromones and an array of tactile gestures, embodies a social behavior that the human observer and listener can relate to.

The social behavior of ants can be exposed as a complex social soundscape by means of this cybernetic installation based on the observation and audiovisual documentation of their colonial development. This experimental approach has opened new paths for me in understanding the stridulation phenomena and self-organization in the ant society, and has served as a great inspiration for my artistic practice. The impact of ants in the ecosystems, that we think we have taken for ourselves, can be perceived as a communal agency of chemicals and sounds constantly shifting and rearranging the territories occupied by humans. Moreover, to a great extent the relevance of studying ant stridulation and its social implications relates to territoriality. Territoriality in my work is approached as a concrete autonomous system in space defined by the processes of the unity that constitutes it. This is what Maturana and Varela (1992) called autopoietic system. The territories the ants invade can be defined by the communicational nodes and the invisible markings produced by the propagation of pheromones and sounds in their social network. Therefore, and strictly related to the matter of sound production in ants, such ecosystems can be visualized and can be sensed by analyzing those acoustic and vibratory signals that allow these communitarian beings to regulate their communication and survive in human environments.

It is of great importance to mention that my research focuses on two main aspects: the computable analysis of the sounds ants produce when they organize their labor, and the social significance and scope of stridulation with their potential biomimetic application towards a post-human ecology. Furthermore, relations with the human experience as the producer and interpreter of sounds are emphasized taking into account all the cultural implications involved in this investigation. Important to clarify is that in regard to my theoretical framework I decided not to discuss the fundamental inhumanity that technology and media could have. Despite the fact that I feel such discussion can be complemental, and indeed it would need to be integrated in future discourses, I instead decided to concentrate the experience of my research on the relations to human culture. Finally, the key of this research lies in revealing the connection between scratching, as an aesthetic

Figure 1. Left: a photograph of the prototype installation exhibited in Lab 3 at the Academy of Media Arts in Cologne, Germany. Right: a screenshot of the motion tracking program analyzing the movements of leafcutter ants. The crosses depict the pixels that are being tracked. I customized the program in Max/Msp/Jitter. (© 2008, Kuai Shen Auson. Used with permission.).

expression created by human culture, and the stridulation phenomena produced by ants as a modulation mechanism for communication.

BACKGROUND

One of the first pioneer works of the nineteenth century, which showed the fascinating world of insects is the seminal masterpiece An introduction to entomology; or elements of the natural history of insects by Kirby and Spence (1843, 2005). Then, at the beginning of the twentieth century media theoreticians, cultural philosophers, biologists and artists started engaging in the debate of the perception of technology and their relation to natural systems, i.e., comparing, contrasting and intertwining the biologic with the artificial. From Ernst Haeckel's Kunstformen der Natur (1904, 1998) to Jakob von Uexküll's Streifzüge durch die Umwelten von Tieren und Menschen: Ein Bilderbuch unsichtbarer Welten (1934, 2010) and to exemplary media discourses from the beginning of this new century, such as Jussi Parikka's Insect Media: an archeology of animals and technology (2010), artistic practices and scientific researches

have been sharing ideologies and using common tools to perceive, describe, and document the life of those societies of the minuscule living organisms that resemble our social structures. Since then, inspiration by the mechanical, operational, yet sensual world of insect societies have sparked scientists to open to the artistic spheres. Both disciplines intersect knowledge on common ground, signaling the way to a new era of research that is done not only in the lab but in your garden and in your living room. Strongly supported by the technological capacity of our modern media society and the market's predisposition to make advanced instruments accessible and acquirable for any individual, human beings are now more than ever in the privileged position to undergo experiments in their self-created laboratory environments. I am happy to say that my research is one of these examples.

Inspiration by nature has stimulated humans to be creative since the beginning of civilization. In relation to pioneer experiments in the field of bioacoustics, the Slovenian scientist Ivan Regen was the first to study in 1913 the acoustic propagation of the song of male crickets and their influence on female crickets, using a microphone to transmit the signals and a telephone earpiece to receive them (Huber, Moore & Loher, 1989). First the industrial revolution introduced global changes, and then the digital revolution extended and connected the cultural and visual artifacts we have massively produced and distributed, so that science and arts were not isolated endeavors anymore. On one hand, this stimulated an artistic approach for scientists and on the other hand, a scientific approach for artists. Biologists working in the field could take pictures and record sounds, reflecting on the aesthetic aspects of the documentation of living beings and natural processes. The technological apparatus was now accessible for both scientists and artists to engage in an abstract interaction with their study subjects. To this respect, the best visual examples worth mentioning that have influenced my own explorations would be the documentary Microcosmos by Nuridsany and Pérennou (1996), and the photographic documentation of Wild (2008), as well as the related stories and scientific curiosities about ants and other insects he has published online since 2007 on a regular basis at www.myrmecos.net (2011).

Impelled by the scientific discoveries and the possibility to view the microscopic world from a subjective perspective, the human race began to create a diversity of artistic applications, designed ideas and artifacts that derived from a wide range of mapping the natural with the artificial: from swarm intelligence, cellular automata, the culturing of bacteria, the interaction of neurons to the critical mass effect in social networks, everything seemed to be biologically inspired. To this end, the so called 'collective intelligence' of ants has not only been compared to the neurological functionality of the human brain, but it has nowadays established itself as a subject of interest and study for any human endeavor trying to simulate the organization of living organisms in order to replicate its behavior in artificial machines. The debated idea of the superorganism was originally observed only in nature, but nowadays it extends to the artificial realm of posthuman production,

i.e., the networking of cities, brains and bodies with natural environments. For instance, Johnston (2008) discusses several artificial intelligence approaches in his book, such as those of Douglas Hofstadter and Herbert Simon that propose the ant colony as a model of cognition and as a collective information processing system, which can be related to the cognitive processes of the human brain. Furthermore, Johnson (2002) talks about Manchester emerging as the Mecca of the industrialization era in Great Britain mainly because of self-organization and the local interaction of its early inhabitants; the laborers clustered together in their own neighborhoods apart from the riches without a centralized urban planning program forcing them to do so. Academic reflections like these on the relations of ants with manifestations of the superorganism as a multi agent based model mark a celebrated breakthrough in the era of posthuman media culture. Moreover, recognizing the potential relationships of the living with the artificial inspires immense artistic applications profiling political and social purposes, which are not yet fully explored.

During the nineties, projects involving digital media were demonstrating the potential of artificial intelligence and genetic algorithms, thanks to the adaptations and translations achieved by computing programing languages. The highest representatives of these optimizations are the ant colony algorithms. Rendering audiovisual media became a replicating process performed by the computer rather than an analog sequential process of human decision making and design thinking. We suddenly realized the potential of the computer in extending the complexity of nature. The simulation of natural systems was computerized and was mirroring the complex ecosystems surrounding human technology. A need to bring the artificial simulations of the natural out from the lab to interact with the outside world was a consequent and playful thing to do; there was an impetus to observe and test the interaction of the artificial with the biological. A new understanding started to arise. The more artists and scientists engaged in biologically inspired computing experiments, the clearer the parallels were becoming between the biological milieu of insects and the technological achievements of human culture. Fascinating to point out is that we began mimicking natural functions and repurposing the technical achievements of insects in our techno-social experiences a long time ago already: radio telephony, the morphing architecture of the internet, peer-to-peer networking, the colonization of the stratosphere with satellites (which took advantage of progressive rendering and package distribution of images), transfer protocols and data bit rates, all of these encompass problem solving algorithms inspired by insect behaviors. Artists at the dawn of the twenty-first century reflected on the role of the postmodern times and digital media, and started expressing other levels of intensities and experiences that highlighted the organizational achievements and perceptions of insects. Artists like Andy Gracie (Small Work for Robot and Insects, Autoinducer_Ph-1), Garnet Hertz (Cockroach Controlled Mobile Robot), Nigel Helyer (Host), David Bowen (Fly Drawing Device, Fly Blimps), Timo Kahlen (Media Dirt, Swarm) and Theo Jansen (Strandbeest and all his kinetic creations) combined the biomimetics of sound, space, and environment interactions with insect perceptions to create fantastic techno-biological experiences. They made clear that such biologically inspired artistic research is not only possible, but also an intriguing and enlightening enterprise.

There are many sides to the story of being captivated with insect behavior. To be fascinated with ants is probably a matter of feeling akin to that arduous and never ending altruistic labor for the good of the community. My story started around the turn of the new century, 1999, when I sighted for the first time an army ant colony swarming the Amazon rain forests of my home country, Ecuador. Since then I have been researching their behavior for personal interest, specializing on biomimetic stridulation environments based on the stridula-

tion phenomena of ants. I have been concentrating my work on tropical ants and with the aid of audiovisual computing technologies I embarked on a journey to discover the social interactions that characterize an ant system producing a self-organized network. Throughout this time I have been breeding several ants' species in artificial and simulated environments, from leafcutter ants to weaver ants, using my own "do-it-yourself-technology" in sort of a "trial-and-error" fashion. The learning curve has been difficult, as dealing with living beings that do not speak your language can be frustrating. On the one hand, ants cultivated in your own humanly designed private dwelling can become a pest for your neighbors and you can lose control over their territory. On the other hand, keeping tropical ants alive simulating their original environment implies dedication, time and commitment. Out of 6 colonies I had, only 2 of them still live. I failed either in keeping the right temperature, providing the right food, or in keeping their artificial nest sealed enclosed. Nevertheless, the lessons learned from the mistakes I committed have left me with a great deal of knowledge. It has indeed become an obsession that has taken me on fascinating field trips (mentally and physically) to discover the relationships and differences between the myrmecologic microcosmos and the human perception of the world.

STRIDULATION AMPLIFIED

A Cybernetic Instrumentation of Collectivity: The Noise of Self-Organization

Any object, material or organ that produces sounds can potentially become a musical instrument. It depends on its intention, design, adaptation and function. We do not need to define music in order to know what it means. For this purpose we just need to know that music is part of our culture and that music is a form of social communication. Ants can also potentially create music with their stridulatory organ. Ants use stridulation to modulate their main forms of communication (Hölldobler & Wilson, 1990). Every ant species produces distinctive frequencies at different intervals, and even every individual in a colony develops a distinctive stridulatory organ with a unique stridulation pattern. Research by Ferreira, Poteaux, Hubert, Delabie, Fresneau and Rybak (2010) revealed evidence that there is morphological distinctions for every organ of the Pachychondyla workers they studied and there is also a degree of specialization in the stridulatory signals they produced. Hölldobler & Wilson (1990) state that so far stridulation has been identified in numerous species pertaining to the following five subfamilies of ants: Myrmicinae, Pseudomyrmecinae, Ponerinae, Ectatomminae, Nothomyrmecinae (as cited in Markl, 1973). Furthermore, the stridulation behaviors that have been mostly studied belong to the following genera of ants: Atta, Acromyrmex, Pachychondyla, Pogonomyrmex, Messor, Tetraponera, Aphaenogaster, Leptogenys, Ectatomma and Solenopsis

(Hölldobler & Wilson, 1990; Keller, 2009). The stridulatory organ occurs at the point of articulation between the third and fourth segments of the ant's abdomen: the scraper or plectrum lies underneath the posterior region of the third abdominal section, while the pars stridens or ridged file surface is located on the anterior part of the fourth section (Keller, 2009). Stridulation in ants, as a form of social communication, is an amplification process that can be approached as a feedback system, based on cybernetics, that allows the local transmission of vibratory signals from one colony member to another. It is actually a mechanism modulating the transmission of pheromonal messages within the colony's communication network, in order to reinforce tasks or recruit workers depending on the perturbations of the environment.

Communication by pheromone emissions is the primary form of communication in ants. It is a semiochemical form that from time to time needs to be reinforced by another gesture. The secondary, gestural form of communication in ants is tactile communication, which is usually performed

Figure 2. Left: a supersoldier and a minor of the leafcutter ant, Atta Cephalotes. This picture shows the polymorphism in this species. Right: the location of the stridulatory organ of a major of the same species, which was trying to cut my finger. Photographs were taken in the Yasuni rainforest in Ecuador. (© 2011, Kuai Shen Auson. Used with permission.). The inset of the stridulatory organ was hand-drawn, then vectorized. Adapted from "The Ants", Hölldobler B., & Wilson E.O., 1990, Cambridge: The Belknap Press of Harvard University, p. 256. (Copyright 1990 by Bert Hölldobler and Edward O. Wilson. Used with permission.).

in close encounters. Thus, stridulation manifests separately from these two communication forms only when they cannot function properly, like when nestmates are trapped in such a way that the only possible transmission of information is to stridulate for help (Hölldobler & Wilson, 1990). What this points out is that the vibratory signals complement other social expressions, yet stridulation can also appear as a singular gesture if the case requires so; stridulations are complementary and also instinctive, when it is necessary to reinforce a message, or when there is a state of emergency to convey. Take for instance humans, where gestures or caresses accompanied by tender words when we are in love, or screaming and punching when we are attacked or hurt by strangers become examples of modal communication that reinforce the intensities of specific expressions. These expressions derived from either love or stress, evoke social bonding, mainly recognition or rejection, which are not only manifested by humans and other animals with keen aptitude for social bonding, but are also present in the behavior of the individual organisms that make up the ant colony. Ants can express themselves individually and by doing so they amplify a message to the colony.

The ant colony is a cybernetic organization, where each individual is in permanent contact with each other and exchanges information based on proximity and local interaction. Therefore, an ant colony generally responds to stress and perturbations by summing up individual reactions collectively, the colony amplifies its actual parallel operations so that redundancy in actual task performance arises. Redundancy in parallel operations means too many ant workers end up doing the same job after a recruit call or alarming signal was initiated (Hölldobler & Wilson, 1990). In relation to the use of stridulation, this is what happens: when foragers and guards outside the nest perceive something unusual, the pattern of reaction consists of rocking the abdomen up and down so that the scraper, resembling a sharp object

similar in function to the needle of a turntable, rubs against a ridged surface of parallel ribs, producing a chirping sound. This action produces sonic vibrations at different intervals, which every individual decides to perform depending on many factors. It is a complex relationship between the perception of an ant of its surroundings and the changes unfolding in it. This individual manifestation is different for every species, worker and colony, depending on the ecosystem where they live.

When ants decide to stridulate, the sonic effect is a sound wave that expands because it activates a chain reaction amplified by all the members of the colony. All the levels of labor division in the colony get alerted. As a consequence, the speed and effectiveness of workers finding the right job to do increase, thus protecting and defending the queen becomes a priority. The allocation of tasks for the rest of unassigned workers, undecided workers, or workers who were recently recruited to the scene, is then achieved via self-organization. Every single ant perceives and decides on its own which task to choose as the system transits from a warm alerted state to a cool stable one. This auto-regulation can only function if there is an initial signal that amplifies an alert, resulting in a chaotic chain of disordered events that have to settle down and find homeostasis. Redundancy, thus, can be explained by cybernetics. The following observation is based on the analysis of Wiener (1948) to explain heat regulation in a thermostat, and other fluid fluctuations: when there are too many workers performing the same task, which is the case at the beginning of an active alert, then the excess of ants doing one job tends to cancel out over time by moving on to the next available unattended task, so that at the end balance is restored. Consequently, at the beginning of the alert a positive feedback was in progress: the signal was amplified, it was getting stronger until a peak was reached. At this stage, a negative feedback loop regulates the system, lowers the alert, and brings it back to its original state. The key advantage of ants over a compared human equivalent in such redundant problem-solving situations is the quantity of agents involved in an action plus the limitation of decision making determined by their basic brain power. Ants are numerous to the millions but they are simple agents with limited brain power, and their empathy and altruism is unique.

Amplifications have to be de-amplified over time, as is the consequence in any communication system of hyperactive, hot and resonating living beings. The decibels of a high pitched signal cannot be too loud for long periods of time, for we would become deaf. There has to be a regulatory process to turn the volume down. The regulation in the ant system exists because there is a response for every action. They are organisms of a greater social organization. Ants could arguably be seen as trivial machines, but be aware that they do adapt and shape to the conditions of the environment, suggesting there is a level of perception, affects, memory and behavioral actions which challenge the human understanding of the ants' social interaction. That is why it is important to study stridulations in ants to see how far these influence their social behavior, how far these could inspire the design of artifacts that help establish interspecific communication channels, and help in the experimentation of stridulation models for human social interaction. At the beginning it may seem ants are chaotic in their decisions, saturated and overcrowded, but after a while the system achieves knowledge of itself and manages to balance and self-organize. To this extent, according to Hölldobler & Wilson (1990) ants know how to regulate the colony's task allocation by balancing performance and energy invested, in order to do what is best for all. Nevertheless, this greater organization cannot achieve homeostasis, without the amplification of messages originating from initial chaos and disorder. Amplification is a linear process that can become noisy, and in relation to societies and technology, it needs to be modulated so that clear communication channels can be established.

Normally, these positive and negative feedback loops present in the cybernetic ant system, are achieved by means of modal communication: the combination of semiochemical communication (pheromones), tactile rituals and stridulation. Together they reinforce signals that are context specific. This means that communication in ants is multicomponent, almost always occurring as

Figure 3. Graphic representation of the multicomponent communication in ants, imagined as invisible atmospheric fields created by the combination of pheromones and stridulations. (© 2011, Kuai Shen Auson. Used with permission.).

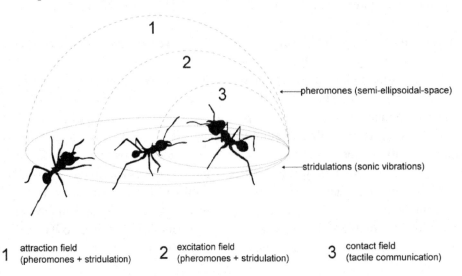

1 attraction field (pheromones + stridulation) 2 excitation field (pheromones + stridulation) 3 contact field (tactile communication)

a combination of the three forms (Hölldobler & Wilson, 1990). This suggests each form appears in the communication act to clarify any of the other forms already present in the exchange of information. Thus, the message is recognized from other situations, because it is rich in chemical, tactile and sonic information describing a specific context. Because the system of communication in ants is still lacking advanced research and field experimentation, it is so important for independent researchers, artists and scientists to undergo experiments with audiovisual media and ants. This can definitely open up new paths for collaboration. We need to pursue a network of knowledge that resonates our cultural perception of the techniques involved in the social communication of ants.

For artists involved in scientific research, this picture of ant's communication system becomes a wonderful open network of possibilities. Ants' network of possibilities should be viewed as networks of relations, a milieu enhanced by pheromones and stridulations. Ants create networks in the complex natural milieu they inhabit connected by a multiplicity of relations. This has served as inspiration for the creation of the ant colony algorithms, which optimize urban transportation systems and provide solutions to the traveling salesman problem. Technology and communication as a medium is in itself a milieu, it can be represented as a computable ecosystem. An ecosystem amplifies its presence in order to differentiate itself from other ecosystems: amplification as delimitation. Deleuze and Guattari (2004) observe the expansion of the rhizome and its roots as an artistic model for reflection because it is a remarkable example of natural unity characterized by connection, heterogeneity, multiplicity, and rupture. Humans take advantage of audiovisual media to deterritorialize themselves, whereas ants do it to define their territories. We are connected by invisible threads in front of the computer without ever leaving home or our workstations. Yet we amplify our messages via online social networking. We resonate. Ants construct

micro-empires, like ancient civilizations did, by succeeding in the operation system and organization of message-carriers: the worker ant transports organic material, which is indeed a container of messages, back to the nest; another worker cuts the leaf and stridulates a recruitment signal, which is transmitted from the closest ant in the foraging area to the closest ant back in the nest. Social behaviors resonate in nature, as well as in the digital worlds constructed by man.

About Resonance: Natural Vibrations versus Acoustic Perceptions Influenced by the Cultural Environment

In his pioneering research on vibrational communication, the German physiologist Hubert Markl discovered that the substrate-borne stridulatory signals of Atta workers can release specific behavioral responses in the recipient nestmates, but the semantic content — that is, the message signaled by the sender and the meaning of the signal for the receiver — varies according to its situational context. (Hölldobler & Wilson, 2009, p. 233)

Visualizing the sound wave spectrum of stridulations is a challenge. For me, an artist working with media, that task becomes less complicated, for media artists in general have a tendency to play and experiment with audio recording devices. As an example, one could record with a directional microphone the area where the ants are stridulating and in post-production (pray to your dearest deity!) filter all the background sounds out with special software. This task is supremely frustrating, if you want to record ants in the field. In most of the cases you end up with a shouting choir of rainforest creatures. It is unavoidable; the rainforest is not a silent ecology. Though interesting for artistic applications involving pre and post-production skills, these results are rendered useless when the goal is to capture the sounds of ants dwelling on the ground. For the purposes of my studies I have found the laboratory environment most beneficial. Usually in a scientific lab one has at his disposal a selection of apparatuses that suit the accurate purpose of measuring vibrations, the best example is the laser Doppler vibrometer. Other secondary gadgets are accelerometers and contact microphones, better known as piezoelectric sensors. These are my favorite choice. Piezoelectric sensors and films are small and light, thus relatively inconspicuous for the colony. They can be amplified and can be applied directly to the surface where the vibration is occurring. Additionally, piezoelectricity is a mechanism that can absorb as well as produce vibrations, providing the right conditions to act as a conversational artifact for the ants.

Where reception of sounds is concerned we want to have a substantial clear recording of the acoustic communication of ants. The attention to undesired sonic effects in the surroundings and its restless overall resonance is of great matter. Like I mentioned before, no ecology is silent. Recording ant sounds in the rainforest, even equipped with the right piezo sensors, is very difficult, for the whole rainforest is made out of organic resonating materials, materials that vibrate and insects that vibrate, too. Therefore, the best environment to record stridulating ants is inside an acoustically isolated chamber, or sound studio for that matter. My experience is based on piezo sensor recordings of leafcutter ant colonies of the species Atta sexdens and Atta cephalotes, which were bred and kept in controlled conditions. Using either one or a combination of all the following sound-proofing materials I tried to dampen the energy of the vibrations: rubber or cork mats, different kinds of polystyrene, and accustomed granular layers of plaster. Interestingly a couple of times I presented the installation with a factor of unpredictability. When the recording surface where your ants stridulate (piezo sensors located in the nest without isolation) is mixed with the sounds produced by the audience, the combination of overlaying sounds initiates a reverberating sonic experience, very similar to the ants themselves, evoking an emergent resonant environment. These experiments in recording can be defined as stridulation environments, because they mimic the use of sound waves in the social communication of ants and are unpredictable in nature.

Studies regarding stridulation research in ants point out that the primary function of the stridulatory organ is the production of information in the form of vibrations, that is energy, and that ants do not possess a specialized hearing organ, rather they perceive those vibrations with their

Figure 4. Photographs of the installation as part of the 6th edition of the Piemonte Share Festival "Smart Mistakes" in Turin, Italy. (© 2010, Kuai Shen Auson. Used with permission.).

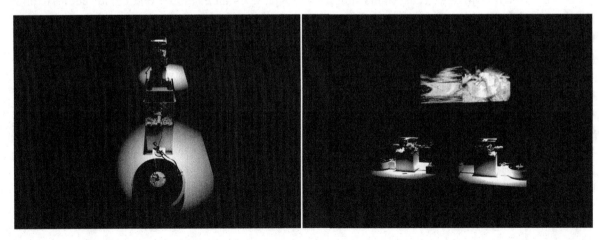

legs (Hölldobler & Wilson, 2009; Ferreira, Poteaux, Hubert, Delabie, Fresneau & Rybak, 2010). Therefore, what ants perceive are vibrations in the form of energy transmitted across the ground. This leads me to believe that the ant body is a resonating body, which is enhanced by the stridulatory organ as an artifact for encoding and decoding energy. The whole exoskeleton of the ant becomes an apparatus for resonance, transmitting energy from one ant to the other, thus being able to produce oscillations with larger amplitudes. From a mechanical point of view, the ant becomes a vibrating agent that produces sound waves that expand and carry information. Additionally, stridulation makes the ant's body resonate acting as a pneumatic mechanism, specifically when it comes to efficiently cutting rough vegetation or excavating hardened terrains (Hölldobler & Wilson, 2009). It is energy that informs and sets materials in motion. The vibrations produced by the stridulatory organ travel along the body making the ant's mandibles vibrate like the cutting blades of a razor machine. At this point one could see a parallel to human invention and the functionality of many tools we have created for different purposes. With respect to artists, this magnificent portrait of ants as social resonating agents for the creation of resonating spaces and biomimetic environments may be of great inspiration.

Ants have six legs, and at the end of their legs they have a tarsus with claws that functions as a foot that can grip to almost any surface. The tarsus is covered with microscopic sensitive hairs that enable ants to sense the material they touch. As a result, this suggests that ants perceive other levels of intensities regarding vibrations transmitted through resonating materials and bodies. How exactly they interpret these vibrations is context-related and deals with every ant's individual perception acting as a member of the colonial organism, and how it reacts to the perturbations in the environment. Wheeler (1912) was the first to see the ant colony as a superorganism that maintains its identity in space, acting and emerging as a whole like a cell or an individual. Moreover, throughout his investigations he was one of the first to recognize the different sensibilities of ant individuals working for the colony. The main distinction to be made here is that ants primarily perceive vibratory sounds, whereas humans primarily perceive airborne sounds. Let's take music for instance. We humans subjectively embrace and appreciate musical compositions, each of us with his or her own hearing capabilities and imagination. Our acoustic perception is strongly shaped by personal experiences and an acquired level of music knowledge. The sounds transform into feelings and recall memories. Augoyard and Torgue (2005) using sociological and psychological analysis refer to this sonic effect as anamnesis. A musical composition carries along memories for the listener, our brains start to connect and reconstruct past experiences so that a temporary meaning emerges in relation to a specific moment in life associated to a musical experience. To this extent, sounds converge in our brain in relation to the knowledge of music that the listener possesses. Nevertheless, how humans give meaning to what we hear, is and still will be a debate. It is not a process we can objectively define, for each human in the world interprets music and sounds in a different way. The human sense of hearing can be educated and it develops according to context, that is, cultural environment. Even among classical musicians with gifted auditive senses, music emerges as past memories, movements, flavors or feelings, to virtualize a re-centered fictional universe and give substance to a composition of sounds, always shifting, always changing depending on experience.

For ants the situation is not much different, at least concerning the development of an organism/organ shaped by the territorial limitations and conditions of a determined ecosystem. In the case of the highly evolved ants, specifically the leafcutter ants whose workers are polymorphic, the stridulatory organ develops naturally according to caste specialization and the pressures of the environment in which the colony lives (e.g., minims or minor ants will develop a smaller stridulatory organ in contrast to majors and soldiers who develop bigger organs). The signaling pattern of stridulation varies according to ant's size, caste and species but also according to the structure of the organ, for not every organism in the colony is born with the same physical features (Hölldobler & Wilson, 2009; Ferreira, Poteaux, Hubert, Delabie, Fresneau & Rybak, 2010). Specialized soldier castes in Atta have the biggest organs because they are strongly developed defense units. The stridulating frequencies of Atta cephalotes specimens oscillate from 2-5 kHz, documented for minors (about 4 mm of body length), to a maximum energy of 38-46 kHz, documented for supersoldiers (about 18 mm of body length). These results are based on indoors' recordings isolating the ants inside custom-made polystyrene casings, and were done in the scientific station of the national park Yasuni, as well as in my atelier, using directional microphones and amplified piezo sensors respectively.

Bergson (1998) reflected on the limitations of humans' cognitive capabilities: the generalization, a tendency to find likeness and similarity in forms of organic and inorganic matter, that which generates and that which is being generated are views of the mind attempting to imitate the operation of nature. Hence, we may be able to recognize, depending on your personal perspective, more than just a few generalized behaviors that seem to be the same in humans as well as in ants regarding the perception of sound arising from the interactions of masses. Human social environments, where activity is high like in a street market, are influenced by the complex interaction of sounds; the closer the radius of interaction is, the more effective the organization develops and the clearer the message becomes. Of course there are many signals in a street market that distract you and influence the intensity of interaction and the desire to interact. The vivid sounds of a street vendor attract and disperse crowds, lure into

personal contact. It becomes a struggle of forces: the perception versus the interest, a negotiation of forces. Hence, your behavior is conditioned by the events unfolding in the market environment and by your determination to find what you desire. The intensity of interaction within this scheme of organization can raise the potential for conflict. We speak, we negotiate in tongues; sound waves carrying messages to convince. It is a fascinating orchestration of sounds, resonating energy catalyzed by individuals interacting with the environment. There has to be a regulation of this conflict, a transformation into settlement. When some play of words and rhetoric resonate better than others, that is when decision making becomes easier and conflict transforms into settlement.

Now take for instance the colonies of leafcutter ants in the rainforests, which can be attacked by other ants, mostly army ants, which prey on their larvae. This is a territorial conflict, a conflict for survival characterized by units of defense and attack resonating their bodies and fighting. Both colonies want the same thing, to breed, expand and reproduce. But they want it only for their own species. Conflict is an everyday issue for ants and reaching settlements with aggressors is not part of their nature. Rather the outcome of the conflict between army ants and leafcutter ants is that either one has to be defeated. It is not always about extermination, but abut recognizing who lost territory and is stronger than the other. It is a measure of forces that not always end up in a massacre. To respond to the imminent presence of predators, these colonies of leafcutter ants produce more soldiers, as a defense mechanism, than controlled colonies bred and studied in laboratory conditions, which normally do not suffer a constant menace. Thus, environment interaction plays a key role in the construction of an ant colony.

If we go back to my reference of Bergson, we can see that the sound waves of a convincing speech in the case of the street market vendor can relate to the waves of army ants attacking the leafcutter colony in the rainforest. Both resonate in the receiver, break the unity of organization, condition its behavior and influence the action to be taken. The environment affects the media of the colony: the army of resonating agents act like sensors reading external perturbations and informing about dangers and casualties, workers start to defend or attack, guard the nest, rebuild the breached architecture. Reaching a settlement in a conflict, as in the case of the street market, mirrors the operation of leafcutter ants reacting to the attack of predators in order to achieve homeostasis.

We all have a general understanding, sometimes vague and abstract, of how sound affects our psyche. Frequently what you hear is what you want to hear and not necessarily what you must hear. As social beings we rely on social learning and this predominantly depends on our cultural background and education. This influences our perception of sounds, because depending on where we are from, our cultural education let us understand certain sound compositions better than others. This is by no means a rule, rather it is a convenience that highlights the importance of the environment interacting with the organs/organisms involved in a conversation. Stridulation is context specific for ants and it is an organic intervention, a rhizomatic dispute, a semantic challenge. The individual notes, which manifest a musical composition, played by any human-made instrument, constitute a combination of patterns, in which each individual chord has a harmonic quality with the interpretation potentially linked to the listener's cultural experience (Augoyard & Torgue, 2005). Furthermore, the contextual sphere in which everything takes place, plays a major role in the process of auditory perception, regardless if we are listening to our own conversations, soundscape creations or listening to ants stridulating. Consequently, the actual interpretation of the resonating events relies on the listener, who then becomes the receiver and author of decoding the acoustic message while interacting with the cultural context. Von Foerster (1961)

repeatedly proclaimed that the listener, not the speaker, determines the meaning of a proposition. When social beings establish an interconnected channel, a conversational milieu, both the listener and the speaker, while interacting with each other instantiate an environment of conditions. A cybernetic ecology arises, where the two become one symbiotic organism, which once conformed tries to negotiate the meaning of its natural existence in a yet-to-be-defined ephemeral string of time and space.

We create our own world out of the input we absorb from the cybernetic chain of events latent in the surrounding environment. Social beings like ants are interested in this resonance of events. Individuals select and filter what they want to hear, or receive. If we compare ants to simple machines that are preprogrammed to compute and can identify only two different frequencies from the environment, as a binary computing resort, what we end up with are merely sensing machines with a specific objective. But if we add a set of social algorithms to these machines and an environment with conflicts, then we can play around with the idea of potentially creating organisms which have the capacity to organize themselves. The principle of the creative resultants postulates the product is not just the sum of the elements involved, but represents a new creation, something genuinely new, which could appear every time we do the same equation (Pask & Von Foerster, 1961). Even though ants can be compared to intelligent machines, and they are approached as such in behavioural models, they are in fact simple essential agents acting sometimes individually and erratically, like us humans, so that sometimes they create things that are not expected. They are constantly changing, resonating, reading the signs from the environment in search for invaders, prey or predators. Ants establish a nonverbal communication with their ecological milieu and the first signal to alert the colony of an unwanted presence is the most simple and instinctive one: to sound the alarm, stridulate. When you get scared, you will instinctively shout, too. Social behaviors have a relationship with the environment. Social behaviors are influenced by the resonating events and the conflicts that emerge from the relationships of the social agents with the environment.

THE TURNTABLE AS A BIOACOUSTIC ARTIFACT FOR STRIDULATION

Scratching and Stridulations: Approximations, Differentiations and Materializations

Music can be considered nonverbal communication and the use, or even abuse, of amplified sounds definitely belongs to the diverse array of bioacoustic strategies we encounter in the world of living organisms. Even organic and artificial materials, which do not strictly fall in the category of animated-mobile-living beings, can influence and contribute to the propagation of sounds. I am referring here to leaves and twigs as organic materials, or plastic and concrete as artificial examples. In order to learn how to interact with the resonating material our world is constructed with, we are compelled to create a relationship with the environment. Ants take advantage of their resonating bodies made out of chitin, an organic polymer of a glucose derivative, to produce and receive vibrations, whereas humans have also created an equivalent medium to store vibrations, a material that in its construction resembles the pars stridens of the stridulatory organ. A music record or vinyl is made out of an organic compound known as polyvinyl chloride, and it is inscribed with grooves and canalizations that contain the phonography of a musical composition. Once played by a turntable, the needle interacts with the vinyl's fractal surface and transmits sound waves to an amplification system. In relation to the stridulatory organ, the mechanism of contact and material interaction are the same. It was then revealed to me that these two materials, namely chitin and vinyl, could be related. After this realization, I delved into turntablism to compare the different scratching sounds with the stridulation frequencies produced by ants, focusing on the expressions rather than the musical content. Scratching is a form of expression that contributes to a sort of swarming in humans, for instance the gathering of crowds in a concert or in a DJ competition. Moreover, scratching reinforces the transmission of lyrical content inciting a reaction in the crowd.

Social beings share information by any means possible, whether it is for summoning soldiers as a preventive response to attacks, or for singing a traditional song to a child. The production of sound waves in ants is just one of many possible mechanisms for the transmission of messages and it has proven to be effective in circumstances where tactile, gestural or other kind of visual communication is not possible. Similarly, scratching is a technique that complements other lyrical expressions and it can also be mastered to manifest by its own means a diverse arrangement of sonic effects, moods and sensations, what is known as turntablism. Thus, through the experimentation with scratching, the turntable has become an artifact for the translation of energy and the transmediality of ideas. Rhythms and beats, clapping, shouting, singing, drumming, stridulating (in ants) and scratching (in humans) represent information that contains messages in need for interpretation, codified and transmitted through air, physical objects or organic material. Ants and humans encode communication and take advantage of tools and instruments to create and share vibratory/acoustical compositions. Additionally, airborne sounds are everywhere and can be misinterpreted, cancelled out, or just regarded as plain noise for living beings who are not interested in listening to certain sound manifestations. This is where the art of amplifying the sounds of ants, with the aid of an instrument of sound production, plays a relevant role in the realm of interspecific

Figure 5. Four seconds of stridulation (top): sample values of one major soldier of Atta cephalotes isolated in a polystyrene box; recorded at 44.1 kHz, 16-bits, using an amplified piezoelectric sensor connected to the computer. Four seconds of scratching (bottom): sample values of baby scratch technique on a 12 inches Hip-Hop vinyl played at 33.3 rpm; recorded at 48 kHz, 24-bits, using a turntable connected directly to the computer. (© 2011, Kuai Shen Auson. Used with permission.).

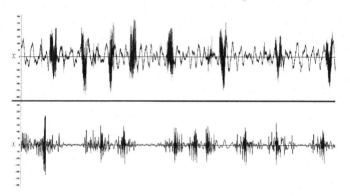

communication: the transformation of stridulation into airborne sounds that humans can listen to, reflect upon and enjoy.

The turntable, as a sound production artifact with its appropriate amplification, can transform the mood of a group of dancers; same is the case for stridulating ants, when resonating social agents incite the mobilization of the colony to a new territory. Colonies of Atta cephalotes produce fantastic concerts composed by a rich variation of high-pitched vibratory sounds, singing and stridulating together like a communal scratching machine (http://kuaishen.tv/stridulations.mp3). Ants, like the carpenter species Camponotus who do not possess a stridulatory organ, but engage in body rapping, rock their exoskeleton and mandibles against the walls of the nest to be able to produce sounds that can alert nestmates (Hölldobler & Wilson, 1990). A fundamental dialect between milieus and living beings has to be created in order for the actors to coevolve with the ecosystem and materialize a relationship.

Taking into account the respective similar functions for sound production in ants and humans, there is a hidden mechanism that relate these two forms. On the one hand, stridulating ants have to be sensed by their nestmates in order for the system to work. On the other hand, the so called turntablism has to be listened to by the people in order for the scratching to be influential in the behavior of the dancers. To this extent, a system materializes if the elements, members, agents, cells, organs of a sensorial apparatus are able to interact with each other and most importantly if they can be interrelated and establish a conversation. Conversations affect and impulse the transitory states of social beings. To these means, a conversation is indeed bioacoustic communication, for it is a natural form for sharing information, both in humans as in ants. Pask (1969) introduced his conversation theory to approach architecture, specially referring to Gaudi's Parque Güell in Barcelona that succeeds establishing a dialogue with its visitor, as an example for informational ecologies and augmented environments, which allow the flow of space and time provoking in the actuating inhabitants a pleasure for exploration, cooperation and self-organization. Everything in this planet is interrelated and contains potential information that just needs to be amplified or accordingly translated in order for the message to be decoded and interpreted. Bioacoustic communication stems from the complex society we belong to; it is an emergent product of active information exchange and feedback mechanisms within the network of living organisms, which can foster new experiences.

Stridulation is nothing more than vibration energy produced by two objects rubbing against each other. Scratching is the production of sounds using a turntable and moving a music record back and forth, so that the needle rubs against its surface. The energy produced from these simple physical mechanisms has a potential to develop into complex forms. Both stridulation and scratching possess emergent properties that can instantiate new stages of social interaction. The emergence of stridulation in ants is a mechanical gesture that can produce sounds similar to the following turntablism techniques: the baby scratch, the chirp scratch, and even the tear scratch. The materials used by both forms of communication are strikingly similar. Chitin is a natural polymer, a derivative of glucose, and it is the material from which the exoskeleton of ants are made, including the stridulatory organ. Vinyls are made of thermoplastic polymers and provide a surface which is easy to be carved in order to encode signals. The profile of the pars stridens approximates the grooves and canalizations of the vinyl. I started to experiment with these two materials and a soundscape driven by movements and stridulations emerged, a soundscape that only existed when the computer communicated with the biological system of the ants. By introducing technology, sensors and artifacts, like the computer and the turntable, I managed to explore a different realm of interspecific communication. 0h!m1gas is a sound reactive installation that depends on the activity of the ant colony, thus becoming an interdependent, interrelated, milieu of resonance with a finite life. The installation works only because the ants work, and according to the labour of the colony, the sounds produced are always different, always evolving.

0h!m1gas is a cybernetic installation that listens to the communication network of ants and is capable of showing visually and acoustically how they self-organize by expressing emergent forms of music: a soundscape that explores the relation of our human-made technological media with insect media, understood as a natural milieu of social organization, cooperation and intensities of relationships. It can be experienced as a cybernetic ecology, where the ants' movements and stridulations are interfaced with a computer that archives the digital data from video cameras and piezo sensors and feeds these to the turntables. It is a cybernetic ecology, because the ants are part of this environment and the artificial presence of surveillance cameras and piezo sensors are adapted and appropriated as part of their territory. But in its essence, it is a biomimetic stridulation environment with the ants performing as scratching DJs, supported by a computer system running an adapted program based on computer vision algorithms that tracks movements and maps frequencies emerging from the ant colony when they sense the vibrations of the turntable[2]. In this regard, the sounds produced by the turntables are amplified as an emergent process that allows tiny bits of information to become bigger bits of information, whose resonance is not predictable. Amplification is a natural action that allows the migration of information far beyond the constraints of a certain social group or species. Amplification strengthens the intensity of messages, increasing its loudness and reinforcing intonation, in order for the audience to perceive, interpret, and participate in the exchange of information. During the ages of our planet social beings have learned to amplify their messages to reach an ample audience, to have a resonance, either developing internal/external organs or using instruments. The best examples are the stridulatory organ in ants and the turntable in humans.

CONCLUSION

Their force is in mutual support and mutual confidence. And if the ant stands at the very top

Figure 6. Diagram of the setup for the installation: the lines show the connection of information and the arrows show the directions of transmission. (© 2011, Kuai Shen Auson. Used with permission.).

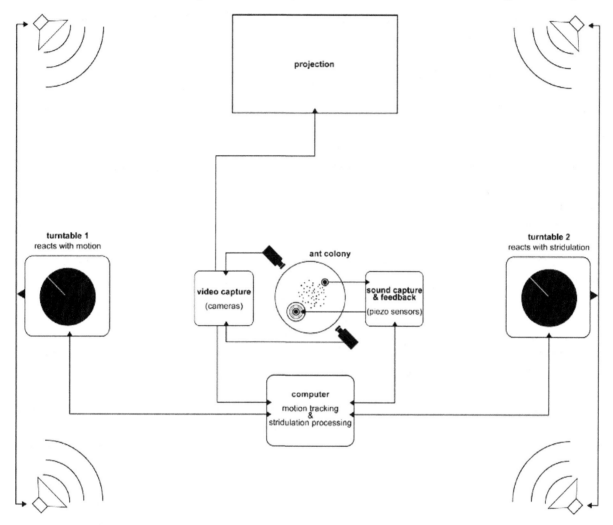

of the whole class of insects for its intellectual capacities; if its courage is only equalled by the most courageous vertebrates; and if its brain — to use Darwin's words — "is one of the most marvelous atoms of matter in the world, perhaps more so than the brain of man," is it not due to the fact that mutual aid has entirely taken the place of mutual struggle in the communities of ants? (Kropotkin, 1987, p. 11)

Interspecific communication with other social beings is still an unknown territory, we need to explore it. We need to experience the perceptions and sensorial apparatuses of complex societies that can inspire our technology, and that can be augmented by it. Ants have a relation with humans, but it started as a troubling, misled, relation since the beginning of the institutionalized studies of entomology. Sleigh (2001) describes briefly the difficulties of the imperialist colonization in Africa because of the conflict and threat posed by the insect world to white man during their invasion, embodied mainly by the numerous and ever present emergence of ants in Congo and Uganda as the most resilient and strangest of all tropical insects opposing to Europe's domination. Our anxiety to alienate them is a result of their non-hierarchical organization challenging our centralized world; a mistake of our illusory superiority. We have to stop addressing concepts of superiority or intelligence when we approach other living beings that are social, too. We should rather see what relations ants can have to the world of humans, and how intense these relations can be in terms of growth, development and transformation.

How can we produce a self-organizing milieu where the artificial and the biological can complement each other? Do we really need to use a self-organized machine or is self-organization a unique social phenomena of the natural kingdom and its organic living beings only? These two questions are explored in my piece, yet the answers are not definite. It is imperative to say that further research needs to be done. We cannot limit ourselves to believe that only several few species of ants possess the communicational instinct for stridulation. Likewise, we cannot just limit our technological capacity to the massive production of artifacts to indulge our human laziness; we have to find new uses for those commercial products that satisfy our needs and repurpose their functionality in order to interact with the ecosystem in novel ways. There are many channels to be explored and connections to be made. Most important, and following Kropotkin's philosophy, mutual aid should be the basis to create collaborative networks of research for non-hierarchical experimentation.

Humans can see potential uses for any natural model. We can approach, embrace and imagine biological principles and behaviors through experiments within the fields of bioacoustics and biomimetics and apply them to human design. To this extent, stridulation is perhaps one of the most underestimated communication mechanisms found in certain social insects with great potential, and it definitely needs to be revived, celebrated and amplified. The cybernetic application of bioacoustics and computing arts has helped me approach the natural phenomena of stridulation in ants to create a complex audiovisual experience that presents an emergent nonhuman social interaction as a resonant acoustic environment. The artistic aim was the creation of a self-organized soundscape based on the integration of surveillant technology inside a colony of ants. In this regard, the project succeeded in capturing and digitizing the social gestures of ants and provided a metaphorical audiovisual representation of their self-organization. Nevertheless, as a scientific research it lacks an objective focus of study of the stridulation phenomena in the Attini species of leafcutter ants. Moreover, it also lacks a methodological scientific framework without being tempted by anthropological associations. Yet, the relations between scratching and stridulation were made clear. It is a hybrid approach, indeed. The artistic research took over the scientific rigor, which is inexistent in my work, and extrapolated the gathered scientific data into the human realm of interpretation.

Biologically inspired art can indeed extend into the social, cultural and political spheres of humanity. Therefore, humans must pursue the investigation of sonic environments that affect our conscience and social behavior. 0h!m1gas has the purpose to communicate the interrelation of sonic effects in the postmodern human-ant ecosystems based on the relatedness of scratching as a cultural expression in humans, and the phenomena of stridulation in ants as a modulatory mechanism in their self-organization. To this extent, I justify that my artistic intentions towards my research opened a new world of possibilities in the readings and the applications of biological driven data. But this artistic research still needs to prove itself valuable as a scientific discipline. Of course, on the one hand bioacoustic communication can impulse creativity and can potentially stimulate channels for interspecific communication between humans and ants. But on the other hand, more experimentation is encouraged based on this actual approach but with more attention to the objective analysis of the biological data.

How objective can we be in the analysis of biological data when our subjects demonstrate more than mere instincts? Drawing conclusions from the study of such a complex subject, can become impartial when your research becomes a passion and obsession, as my case depicts, rather than an objective analysis. I sympathize with ants and this inspires me to dwell on the passionate expression of art, instead of focusing on the impartial documentation of behaviors. Maybe this is not an issue, if your practices are not restrained by science. For this reason, I succeeded in documenting and expressing my results artistically, but lacked the scientific rigor to exercise a universal methodology. My artistic research on the stridulation of ants deals essentially with subjectivity and perceptions. At the end the perception of sound becomes a slave of subjectivity when the human is the observer and controller of the experiments. Therefore, the relevant question is how to unbound oneself from the causality of this vicious circle of being inside your own thought (Bergson, 1998). The way I see it, science and arts can support each other marvelously and work together, but never become one ultimate single discipline. It is in their authentic environments that they succeed, and yet combining them creates an interdisciplinary experience that can yield fantastic insights into the meaning of life and the expressions of nature. It is sort of a sociological, anthropological, ethological condition, which I know many others must also deal with. The reckoning of being a living being who is open to sense the intensities and manifestations in its social environment and the relations between nature and culture is the lesson to be learned and the ultimate issue to be considered in future researches of this kind.

My work with ants is open, it has always been, therefore it cannot be closed. I just began this new relationship, therefore it cannot end. I hope that my research serves for future generations, who want to listen carefully to the environment to design new forms of sonic art without the restriction of approaching social beings, especially ants, as subjects of study, but as collaborators in the creation of new ecosystems.

REFERENCES

Augoyard, J. F., & Torgue, H. (Eds.). (2005). *Sonic experience: A guide to everyday sounds*. Montreal, Canada: McGill-Queen's University Press.

Bergson, H. (1998). *Creative evolution* (New York, N. Y., Trans.). Dover: A. Mitchell. (Original work published 1911)

Cockroach Controlled Mobile Robot. (n.d.). Retrieved July 15, 2011, from www.conceptlab.com/roachbot

Deleuze, G., & Guattari, F. (2004). *A thousand plateaus: Capitalism and schizophrenia* (Massumi, B., Trans.). London, UK: Continuum.

Ferreira, R., Poteaux, C., Hubert, J., Delabie, C., Fresneau, D., & Rybak, F. (2010). Stridulations reveal cryptic speciation in neotropical sympatric ants. *PLoS ONE*, *5*(12). doi:10.1371/journal.pone.0015363

Fly Drawing Device. (n.d.). Retrieved July 15, 2011, from www.dwbowen.com/portfolio.html

Haeckel, E., Breidbach, O., Hartman, R., & Eibl-Eibesfeldt, I. (1998). *Art forms in nature: The prints of Ernst Haeckel (Monographs)*. München, Germany: Prestel Publishing. (Original work published 1904)

Hölldobler, B., & Wilson, E. O. (1990). *The ants*. Cambridge, MA: The Belknap Press of Harvard University.

Hölldobler, B., & Wilson, E. O. (2009). *The superorganism: The beauty, elegance, and strangeness of insect societies*. New York, NY: W. W. Norton & Company.

Host. (n.d.). Retrieved July 15, 2011, from http://www.sonicobjects.com/index.php/projects/more/host

Huber, F., Moore, T. E., & Loher, W. (1989). *Cricket behavior and neurobiology*. Cornell, NY: Cornell University Press.

Johnson, S. (2002). *Emergence: The connected lives of ants, brains, cities, and software*. New York, NY: Simon & Schuster.

Johnston, J. (2008). *The allure of machinic life: Cybernetics, artificial life, and the new AI*. Cambridge, MA: MIT Press.

Keller, R. (2009). Ant reconstruction one homology at a time. Homology Weekly: Stridulatory Organ. Retrieved March 26, 2011, from http://roberto.kellerperez.com/2009/02/homology-weekly-stridulatory-organ

Kirby, W., & Spence, W. (2005). *An introduction to entomology; or elements of the natural history of insects*. London, UK: Elibron. (Original work published 1843)

Kropotkin, P. (1987). *Mutual aid: A factor of evolution*. London, UK: Freedom Press. (Original work published 1902)

Markl, H. (1973). The evolution of stridulatory communication in ants. In *Proceedings IUSSI 7th International Congress* (pp. 258–265). Southampton, UK: University of Southampton.

Maturana, H., & Varela, F. (1992). *The tree of knowledge*. Boston, MA: Shambhala.

Media Dirt. (n.d.). Retrieved July 15, 2011, from www.timo-kahlen.de/soundsc.htm

Myrmecos. (n.d.). Retrieved July 14, 2011, from www.myrmecos.net

Nuridsany, C., & Pérennou, M. (Directors), Barratier, C., Mallet, Y., & Perrin, J. (Producers). (1996). Microcosmos: Le peuple de l'herbe. USA: Miramax.

Parikka, J. (2010). *Insect media: An archeology of animals and technology*. Minneapolis, MN: University of Minnesota Press.

Pask, G. (1969). The architectural relevance of cybernetics. In Spiller, N. (Ed.), *Cyber reader: Critical writings for the digital era* (p. 78). London, UK: Phaidon Press.

Pask, G., & Von Foerster, H. (1961). A predictive model for self-organizing systems, Part 2. *Cybernetica*, *4*(1), 20–55.

Sleigh, C. (2001). Empire of the ants: H.G. Wells and tropical entomology. *Science as Culture*, *10*(1), 33–71. doi:10.1080/09505430020025492

Small Work for Robots and Insects. (n.d.). Retrieved July 15, 2011, from hostprods.net/projects/small-work-for-robot-and-insects/

Strandbeest. (n.d.). Retrieved July 15, 2011, from www.strandbeest.com

Von Uexküll, J. (2010). *A foray into the world of animals and humans*. Minneapolis, MN: University of Minnesota Press. (Original work published 1934)

Wheeler, W. M. (1912). The ant colony as an organism. *Journal of Morphology*, *22*, 307–325. doi:10.1002/jmor.1050220206

Wiener, N. (1948). *Cybernetics*. Cambridge, MA: MIT Press.

Wild, A. (2008). Breaking news: The atta phylogeny. Retrieved March 12, 2001, from http://myrmecos.net/2008/11/13/breaking-news-the-atta-phylogeny

ADDITIONAL READING

Ball, P. (2001). *The self-made tapestry: Pattern formation in nature*. Oxford, UK: Oxford University Press.

Bassett, P., Salisbury, M., Appleby, B., & Dunleavy, S. (Directors), Salisbury, M. (Producer) (2005). Life in the undergrowth, Episode 5: Supersocieties. United Kingdom: BBC Natural History Unit & Animal Planet.

Bennett, J. (2009). *Vibrant matter: A political ecology of things*. Durham, NC: Duke University Press Books.

Berthoz, A. (2000). *The brain's sense of movement*. Cambridge, MA: Harvard University Press.

Buchanan, B. (2008). *Onto-ethologies: The animal environments of Uexküll, Heidegger, Merleau-Ponty, and Deleuze*. New York, NY: State University of New York Press.

Corbett, J. (2006). *Communicating nature: How we create and understand environmental messages*. Washington, DC: Island Press.

Delanda, M. (2011). *Philosophy & simulation: The emergence of synthetic reason*. New York, NY: Continuum.

Encyclopedia Britannica. (2011). *Evidence of hearing and communication in insects*. Retrieved April 1, 2011, from http://www.britannica.com/EBchecked/topic/555378/sound-reception/64794/Evidence-of-hearing-and-communication-in-insects

Hellström, B. (2003). *Noise design: Architectural modeling and the aesthetics of urban acoustic space*. Göteborg, Sweden: Bo Ejeby Förlag.

Hölldobler, B., & Roces, F. (2001). The behavioral ecology of stridulatory communication in leafcutting ants. In Dugatkin, L. A. (Ed.), *Model systems in behavioral ecology - Integrating conceptual, theoretical, and empirical approaches* (pp. 92–109). Princeton, NJ: Princeton University Press.

Hölldobler, B., & Wilson, E. O. (2010). *The leafcutter ants: Civilization by instinct*. New York, NY: W. W. Norton & Company.

Kelly, K. (1995). *Out of control*. Cambridge, MA: Perseus Books.

Krause, B. (2002). *Wild soundscapes: Discovering the voice of the natural world*. Birmingham, AB: Wilderness Press.

Morgan, C. L. (1927). *Emergent evolution*. London, UK: Williams and Norgate.

Riedelsheimer, T. (Director). (2004). Touch the sound: A sound journey with Evelyn Glennie [DVD]. Germany & UK: Filmquadrat & Skyline Productions.

Serres, M. (2007). *The parasite*. Minneapolis, MN: University of Minnesota Press.

Thaler, W. (Director). (2006). Ameisen: Die heimliche Weltmacht [DVD]. Germany: WVG Medien GmbH.

Väliaho, P. (2005). Simulation, automata, cinema: A critique of gestures. Theory and Event, *8*(2).

Von Foerster, H. (1960). On self-organizing systems and their environments . In Yovits, M., & Cameron, S. (Eds.), *Self-organizing systems* (pp. 31–50). London, UK: Pergamon Press.

Werber, B. (1997). *Les Fourmis*. Paris, France: Livre de Poche.

Wilson, E. O. (1984). *Biophilia*. Cambridge, MA: Harvard University Press.

Wilson, E. O., & Gómez, J. (2010). *Kingdom of ants: José Celestino Mutis and the dawn of natural history in the new world*. Baltimore, MD: The Johns Hopkins University Press.

Zielinski, S. (2008). *Deep time of media: Toward an archeology of hearing and seeing by technical means* (Custance, G., Trans.). Cambridge, MA: MIT Press.

KEY TERMS AND DEFINITIONS

Attini: The singular denomination for the tribe comprising 13 genera of leafcutter ants, including the highly evolved Atta and Acromyrmex (e.g., Attini is a tribe > Atta is a genus > Atta sexdens is a species).

Autopoiesis: This is the fundamental term introduced by Humberto Maturana and Francisco Varela to originally describe the nature of living systems. It derives from the Greek auto, meaning self, and poiesis, meaning creation or production.

Bioacoustics: The combination of biology and acoustics to study the production of sounds in living beings.

Biomimetics: The observation and analysis of nature, its processes, models and systems for the application of its biological principles and behaviors to human design.

Cybernetics: An interdisciplinary field that studies regulatory systems. In relation to my research, it refers to the definition by Norbert Wiener: control and communication in the animal and the machine.

Emergence: The arising of complex systems and patterns out of simple interactive relationships. Emergence is the formation of a higher organization with a bottom-up structure, whose outcome cannot be deduced from the sum of its parts.

Homeostasis: The state achieved by an organism by regulating its internal conditions using feedback to stabilize its health and functioning.

Myrmecology: It is the scientific study of ants and it is a branch of entomology (the study of insects).

Polymorphism: The occurrence of different forms among the members of the same colony.

Scratching: The production of distinctive sounds by moving a vinyl record back and forth on a turntable, usually by means of manual gestures. Scratching originated from the hip hop culture during the late 70's.

Semiochemical: Any chemical substance that carries messages or information, which can only affect individuals of the same species involved in the exchange of information.

Stridulation: The action of rubbing together certain body parts. This mechanism can produce vibrations and resonance, depending on the structural form of the objects involved in the contact. This behavior is typically associated with many species of insects, including cicadas, spiders, crickets, beetles and ants.

Turntablism: The creation of music using turntables in a distinctive manner, not just playing records.

ENDNOTES

[1] Briefly put, the first wave of cybernetics initiated the study of regulatory systems and how the transmission of information, and feedback with the environment play a role in the evolution of these. The second wave of cybernetics delved into the self-organization of the systems and how these identify, reflex and auto-produce themselves.

[2] I designed the motion tracking program with Max/Msp/Jitter 5.0, using pixel tracking differentiation based on the computer vision algorithms of Jean Marc Pelletier (http://jmpelletier.com/cvjit/).

Chapter 5
Bridging Synthetic and Organic Materiality:
Gradient Transitions in Material Connections

Hironori Yoshida
Carnegie Mellon University, USA

ABSTRACT

The recent movement from mass production to mass customization enabled by digital fabrication has opened the door for new typologies in architecture and design. The author brought the idea of mass customization to material connection, which normally appears as orthogonal seams that are predominant in man-made objects. This chapter introduces gradient material transitions that seamlessly bridge synthetic and organic matter. Using digital image processing of organic forms, the fabrication process generates 3D tooling paths, culminating in the concept of 'bio customization' rather than mass customization, a new prospect of digital fabrication.

INTRODUCTION

If mass produced parts and components are the atoms of modern design, jointing techniques are the bonds between these atoms, the nucleus of today's built world. "The art and technology to build is based on the skill to combine, to connect and to join similar, various or different parts, materials or components in order to construct a new whole" (Emmitt, Olie & Schmid, 2004). Seams between standardized parts and components are everywhere in our physical environment from products to buildings. These lines reveal how built objects are assemblies of standardized parts and components. There is a well-established tradition of assembling structures according to this method in human history. Building with adobe bricks has over 9,000 years of history and the Egyptian pyramids are made of millions of standardized stones. It is no exaggeration to say that throughout history, people have continuously flattened and standardized the diverse natural materials into regular, uniform, repeatable, measurable forms. Our living environment today consists mainly mass produced artifacts, which is typically considered to be the consequence of Industrialization

DOI: 10.4018/978-1-4666-0942-6.ch005

and subsequent mass production. The nature of mass production is such that it creates uniformity, which became a dominant aesthetic trend: Functionalism. Adolf Loos (1908/1998) claimed in his essay 'Ornament and Crime' (1908) "the evolution of culture is synonymous with the removal of ornamentation from objects of everyday use," and expressed his "passion for smooth and precious surface" (Rykwert, 1973). In part, due to new materials and tectonics, Functionalism could create a dialogue that questioned standard perceptions of the built environment. Although the means of standardization have evolved, there has been continuous criticism to this process by organizations such as the Ludites in early 19th century and the Arts and Crafts Movement. This criticism of anti-machine trends is today continued in the form of organic fluid shapes enabled by recent digital tools, resulting in 'blobby' reforms. "The biomorphic structures and organic designs referred as "blobitecture" have their roots in the postmodernist rebellion against the perceived mechanistic dryness of modernism, with its well-known emphasis on function, scientific analysis, and order" (Walters, 2003). CAD/CAM technologies realize efficient construction process of such structures: mass customization rather than mass production. "Mass customization of buildings means that all produced building components have a unique identity, are individuals that can be addressed independently. Each building component is different, and fits only in one place" (Oosterhuis and Biloria, 2008).

MATERIAL CONNECTIONS

Before humans, nature discovered jointing techniques long ago. Organisms developed biological forms and jointing techniques such as suture joint on skulls and the connection of a tooth to the jawbone. Joining techniques such as mechanical fasteners are simplified techniques to hold man-made structures together. In the design process, designers and engineers subdivide a required

function into parts and components ultimately built with mono-materials. They specify materials to fulfill assigned requirements taking advantage of material properties; for example a window component with a transparent sheet glass and a well insulated frame. As long as man-made structures are fabricated as complex assemblies of parts and components, whether mass-produced or digitally mass customized or one-off hand crafted, connections between components are inevitable. "From a philosophical and practical stance we can see that where materials or building components meet each other - at the points, at the lines or at the planes or surfaces – there is nothing" (Emmitt et al., 2004). Thus, assembled objects typically have pronounced seams between parts and components. Designers and architects do not have many choices to deal with these seams: to accentuate the contrast between components by using parting lines as graphical elements, disguise them from the eye using complex tooling, surface finishing or processing methods. The technological limitation of standardized parts and components is represented by their seams and appears as orthogonal seams that are predominant in man-made objects.

Konrad Wachsmann, a forerunner in architectural details, "emphasized the need in any age to understand technical possibilities – in terms of machine-made standardized elements" (Creighton, 1969). Consequently his focus on architectural details such as joints and mechanical fasteners contributed to detail qualities of modern architecture. Mies van der Rohe (1959) stated that God is in the details. The details do influence how people perceive the quality of a built structure or fabricated product. We simply appreciate the quality of details and connections such as well-fitted stone works from Inca civilization or Japanese wood joinery. The number of books and magazines focusing on details illustrates how much people pay attention to detail. "Details – connections, joints and knots – have an extraordinarily crucial place and meaning, both technologically and culturally" (Emmitt et al., 2004).

GRADIENT MATERIAL TRANSITION

What if materials are gradually connected to one another instead of pronounced seams between them? Is it possible to construct contiguous product forms with gradual material transitions between types of materials or components? Gradient effects are frequently used in architecture and design, but historically served only as graphical visual transitions. "Gradation is found everywhere in our environment. Frequently found in nature, gradation is, however, little used in architecture. More regular rhythms are preferred for obvious reasons of economy of building methods" (Van Meiss, 1990). Patterning of floor tiles and wall panels is a popular design technique to personalize spaces; however these are mechanically assembled using adhesives or fasteners. This is different than transitioning a weave pattern in a rug. Moreover, our perception of three-point perspective and diminishing views creates a gradation effect. A repetition of columns gradually scales down towards the vanishing point and as the columns recede from the viewer, the eye perceives them to move closer to each other. Recent advances in 3D printing technology can construct mono-structures with multi-material transitions. "Complete electromechanical devices can be made entirely by printing with a single fabrication system" (Alonso, Malone, Moon, & Lipson, 2009). Taking a look at organic structure like the human body, tendons connect bones and muscles with gradient transitions from mineral (bone) to organic collagen (muscle). This transition aids in its functionality and thereby affects its form. Functionally Graded Material (FGM) is an emerging research area in material science and nano science. The concept is to make composite materials by varying the microstructure from one material to another with a specific gradient pattern or structure.

DEVELOPMENT OF GRADIENT MATERIAL TRANSITIONS

The author launched a project aiming to construct a recognizable gradient material transition in place of standardized connections. Comparing the visually apparent transition of parting lines and assemblies versus a multi-material mono-structure without apparent seams provided the basis for experimentation. The transition in micro scale like FGM is not relevant, because the transition is not obvious for human eyes. On the other hand, at human scale, visually recognizable gradient effects could be achieved by tiling components, however, there is a risk of ending up with just an exploration of gradient patterns. For those reasons, this project envisions to fabricate a mono-structural piece composed of different materials with gradient transitions. Moreover, creating the correct amount of gradient transitions where different materials are equally hybridized. The project fabricates two-dimensional surfaces projecting interior applications e.g. table surfaces and wall panels. The development of gradient material transitions was an iterative process of fabrication and reflection.

Prototype 1: Selecting Different Materialities

To observe how gradient material transitions mediate contradicted materialities, plywood (organic, opaque, subtractive) and castable polyester resin (synthetic, transparent, additive) are selected. Figure 1 illustrates the first prototype of gradient transition between plywood and polyester resin. Transition patterns cited from material texture was used for visually apparent transitions.

For a smooth transition of different materialities, the straight incisions referred to the layers of the plywood (Figure 2). The result demonstrates a smooth transition from plywood to polyester resin without any gaps due to the castable nature of polyester resin.

Figure 1. Prototype of gradient material transition between plywood and polyester resin (© 2010, Hironori Yoshida. Used with permission).

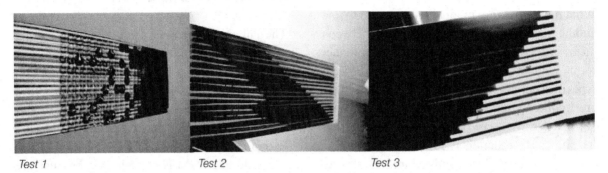

Test 1 Test 2 Test 3

Figure 2. A transition pattern cited from material texture integrates different materialities (© 2010, Hironori Yoshida. Used with permission).

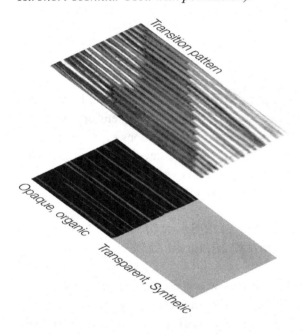

Prototype 2: Various Transition Patterns

Prototype 2 explores generating various transition patterns aiming to fabricate mass customized connections. The bowed veneer strips refer to the elasticity of the material and helped to create a gradient transition (Figure 3).

At Figure 4, prototype 2 successfully fabricated several transition patterns by controlling the amount of compression or pinching of the veneer strips.

Prototype 3: Mass Customization of Gradient Material Transitions

Aiming for mass customized connection, prototype 3 automates the process of generating transition patterns. For mediating different ma-

Figure 3. Process of bowing veneer strips (© 2010, Jeremy Ficca, Hironori Yoshida. Used with permission.).

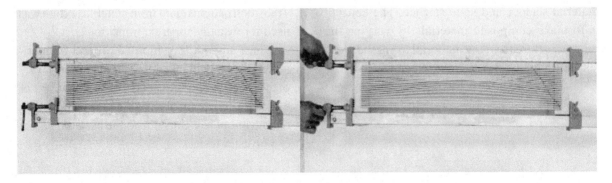

Figure 4. Uniformed veneer strips and castable resin by a pattern of bowed shape (© 2010, Jeremy Ficca, Hironori Yoshida. Used with permission.).

terialities, a plywood panel and polyester resin were selected and the wood grain pattern was used for the transition pattern. The grain pattern was first scanned (Figure 5) and then analyzed by a developed algorithm that converts the 2D image into 3D tooling paths.

The algorithm simplifies the scanned image by pixelating and thresholding color values (Figure 6).

The algorithm transforms the 2D image to 3D model by converting the color values to depths of each pixel and connecting them with vector lines. Figure 7 illustrates the generated tooling path and Figure 8 shows the CNC (computer numerical control) tooling process.

Result and Reflection

Figure 9 shows a 24" x 48" fabricated board with a gradient material transition. The developed algorithm automatically converts a 2D image to 3D tooling paths by image processing. Since wood grain is a biologically developed structure unique to wood, the generated tooling paths from the grain pattern identifies the original wood panel thus

Figure 5. Original grain image (© 2010, Hironori Yoshida. Used with permission.)

Figure 6. Processed original grain image by the algorithm (© 2010, Hironori Yoshida.).

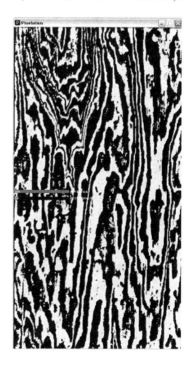

Figure 7. Generated tooling path by the algorithm (© 2010, Hironori Yoshida. Used with permission.).

Figure 8. A CNC router tooling a plywood panel (© 2010, Hironori Yoshida. Used with permission.).

Figure 9. A board with gradient material transition (© 2010, Hironori Yoshida. Used with permission.).

can only be used for that particular wood panel. This automation process of tool path generation and the usage of organic materials realized mass customization of gradient material transitions.

In terms of the quality of gradient material transition, a visually apparent transition effect was achieved by leveraging the inherent material quality of the wood and its organic grain pattern. At the same time, the transparency of the polyester resin emphasizes the contrast of materialities of wood and polyester. Since the fabricated piece presents a uniformed surface between wood and resin, the piece has a continuous mono-structure made of different materials, which is an essential element of gradient material transition, declared in the beginning of this section.

CONCLUSION

We began by reflecting on the history of standardization and the dominance of material connections with joints and mechanical fasteners in man-made structures. This observation formed the concept of 'gradient material transition' and the fabricated board. In the fabrication process of gradient material transition, computation was used to extract the biologically developed structure of wood grain. Now the digital fabrication process interacts with organic structures, and materials automatically defining the tooling process. As a consequence, they form as if they already knew how they were supposed to be composed. This fabrication process could be described as bio customization rather than mass customization.

The built piece raises a question: What is the boundary between organic and inorganic? Since the degree of hybridization of organic/inorganic materialities varies, the boundaries will blur. Apparently a tree in the forest is natural, but once cut down, is it artificial just because the human hand is involved? Further, is a 90%-10% wood-resin piece artificial? We label many artifacts in our living environment as strictly 'organic' or 'natural'. These artifacts may have organic shapes built with natural materials through natural fabrication processes or may be synthetic man-made forms with very "inorganic" materials. Although artifacts are temporally distinguished from natural objects through the different methods with which materials are connected, our notion of nature will need to be transformed since the boundary between natural and artificial will blur. We need to invent a new category for the new nature; objects formed or fabricated through biologically inspired processes.

REFERENCES

Alonso, M. P., Malone, E., Moon, F. C., & Lipson, H. (2009, August). *Reprinting the telegraph: Replicating the Vail register using multi-materials 3D printing*. Paper presented at Solid Freeform Fabrication Symposium (SFF'09). Austin, TX.

Creighton, T. (1969). *Building for modern man*. Manchester, NH: Ayer Publishing.

Emmitt, S., Olie, J., & Schmid, P. (2004). *Principles of architectural detailing*. Oxford, UK: Wiley-Blackwell.

Loos, A. (1908/1998). *Ornament and crime. Selected essays*. (M. Mitchell, Trans.). Riverside, CA: Ariadne Press. (Original work written in 1908).

Oosterhuis, K., & Biloria, B. N. (2008). Interactions with proactive architectural spaces: The muscle projects. *Communications of the ACM, 51*(6). doi:10.1145/1349026.1349041

Rykwert, J. (1973). Adolf Loos: The new vision. *Studio International, 186*, 957.

van der Rohe, M. (1959, 28 June). A quotation, "God is in the details." Speaking about restraint in design. *New York Herald Tribune*. Retrieved September 26, 2011, from http://architecture.about.com/od/20thcenturytrends/a/Mies-Van-Der-Rohe-Quotes.htm

Van Meiss, P. (1990). *Elements of architecture*. London, UK: Taylor & Francis.

Walters, J. (2003). *Blobitecture: Waveform architecture and digital design*. Boston, MA: Rockport Publishers, Inc.

ADDITIONAL READING

Gramazio, F. Kohler, M. (2008). *Digital materiality in architecture.* Lars Müller Publishers.

Pye, D. (1995). *The nature and art of workmanship.* Fox Chapel Publishing.

Wake, W. (2000). *Design paradigms: A sourcebook for creative visualization.* Hoboken, NJ: John Wiley and Sons.

Weiser, M. (1996). *The coming age of calm technology.* Palo Alto, CA: Xerox PARC.

Willis, K., Xu, C., Wu, K. J., Levin, G., & Gross, M. (2011). Interactive fabrication: New interfaces for digital fabrication. *TEI'11, Proceedings of the Fifth International Conference on Tangible, Embedded, and Embodied Interaction,* Funchal, Portugal.

KEY TERMS AND DEFINITIONS

Customized Connections: Joining techniques to connect raw materials together. Typically fabricators customize such joining to connect such non-standardized raw materials by manual analysis of material conditions.

FGM (Functionally Graded Material): Composite materials by varying the microstructure from one material to another with a specific gradient pattern or structure to improve functionality of materials.

Joining Techniques: Such as joinery, mechanical fasteners, adhesives, glues and so forth to connect machine-made standardized parts and components to construct a new whole.

Mass Customization: Producing goods and services to meet individual customer's needs with near mass production efficiency.

Mass Customized Connections: Joining techniques customizing their typologies by automated analysis of material conditions.

Material Connections: Where materials, parts and components are connected to hold structures together.

Materiality: Materiality is defined with the most dominant properties among sensual properties (sight, touch, smell, taste, and hearing), technical properties (e.g. strength and elasticity) and expressive characteristics (organic, artificial). The most dominant properties of a material among sensual properties (sight, touch, smell, taste, and hearing), technical properties (e.g. strength and elasticity) and expressive characteristics (organic, artificial).

Parts and Components: Standardized construction units typically mass-produced by a machine.

Standardization: Transforming diverse natural materials into regular, uniform, repeatable, measurable forms for rational construction and quality of artifacts.

Standardized Connections: Simplified joining techniques to connect mass produced standardized parts and components. Typically these connections are already embedded in parts and components for economical and productive construction.

Section 2
Visualizing the Invisible: Processes for the Visual Data Formation

Chapter 6
Sustainable Cinema:
The Moving Image and the Forces of Nature

Scott Hessels
City University, Hong Kong

ABSTRACT

While nature has often inspired art, a subset of artists has given the natural world an even more influential role in the outcome of their work. These artists have harnessed the physics, biology, and ecology of the natural environment as artistic tools and have used natural phenomena as a co-creator in the realization of their work. This use of natural force impacting the actual form of an artwork has also been explored in the kinetic and moving image arts. As one of several artists now working in sustainable energy, the author of this chapter has created a series of kinetic public sculptures that use natural power sources to create the moving image. These sculptures will be presented here as a case study for a larger perspective on the continuing relationship between the forces of nature and the materials of the moving image.

INTRODUCTION

The organic origins in art forms like painting and sculpture are easily recognized when one considers the ancient mixing of colored pigments found in nature, and the wood and stone chiseled by early sculptors. Musical forms, drawing and theatre share this foundation as many of their first materials came from plants and animals. The moving image, including the mediated versions of cinema and computer forms, also has traceable

roots in the natural environment yet in a less obvious and inimitable way. Through tools and materials alone, nature has directly affected the outcome of nearly all creative expression.

Kinetic sculpture is a time-based, often narrative art form and its 'moving image' is its changing shape, dimension, light, materiality, site, *etc.* As art forms that can be watched over time, cinema and kinetic sculpture share a unique perceptual connection. In addition, while all art forms reflect the society of their times, both the picture and the sculptural versions of the moving image are often used to directly comment on their context

DOI: 10.4018/978-1-4666-0942-6.ch006

Figure 1. Scott Hessels, "The Image Mill" at night, Gerald R. Ford Presidential Museum, Grand Rapids, Michigan. (© 2010 Scott Hessels. Used with permission.).

and physical presence. More than many other types of artistic expression, it seems cinema and moving three-dimensional art are by design highly self-aware of their contexts. Because of this, when one considers society's changing views on nature over the past two hundred years, a thread of artworks becomes evident that shares and envisions those views.

This chapter presents a series of my sculptures that use natural power to generate the moving image. As background to these artworks, I will look at society's changing relationship with forces in nature and how other artists have mirrored those relationships. These artists embraced the natural and organic beginnings of their mediums and allowed natural energy to write upon their works as a co-author. When placed parallel with the evolving global perspectives on the natural environment, a relationship emerges that creates a deeper context for the artworks and a clearer understanding of cultural views on nature.

BACKGROUND

Physics, biology, ecology and now sustainable design have all played into the moving image evolution. The optical illusions and electricity that led to the birth of the mediated moving image were seen as natural phenomena harnessed or recreated by man. Shadows plays, one of the earliest media presentation systems, were made from biological skins and fibers, and early moving images were often spoken of as being infused with a living force. The first screens were silk, celluloid itself was made from plants and animals. In the last mid-century, sculpture began to reflect and use the concepts of ecology that were emerging in society at the time by using natural systems integrally in their time-based, environmentally-conscious artworks.

Over the past two centuries, we have greatly advanced our comprehension of physics, biology and ecosystems. Now we hope use the forces found nature in ways that do not diminish them yet still benefit us. Once again the moving image will likely reflect society's views on the environment, but this time with an emphasis on sustainability. The winds that blew Calder's mobiles and changed their sculptural form are once again being considered as both a power source and a creative strategy. However, artists now are not limited to the direct elements of wind, water, light, and fire. Emerging sensing technologies are providing data that is being used to visualize hidden natural forces – and poetry – that we never knew was in the landscape around us.

Natural Phenomena: The Moving Image and Physics

For centuries, civilizations have looked at the stars and ascribed characters, connections and stories to them. These myths and narratives were not groundless flights of imagination, but a complex merging of science, art, and culture. Nearly every civilization has considered nature as a proactive character integrated into a complex pattern of belief. More than just giving human characteristics to natural phenomena, it is the recognition of both force and intent in the environment.

Early moving image media had their origins in scientific experimentation in physics. Early optics was viewed as occurring outside of the body, images were 'projected' onto our eyes by invisible natural phenomena. Optics follows a heritage spanning Aristotle, Bacon and Da Vinci that involved research in light, lenses, shadow and reflection. Combining these elements into the principles of mediated projection appeared as early as *Ars Magna Lucis et Umbrae* written by Athanasius Kircher in 1645 (Gorman, 2001). The scholar explored the creation of images by sunlight, mirrors and lenticular lenses and his catotrophic lamp made advances in the emerging technology of magic lanterns.

In her book on 19th century electric communications, Caroline Marvin (1998, p. 120) explains that electricity was first thought of as "the production of lightning," a creation of an anti-nature that caused consternation in a divided society. Nature was viewed as in battle with man-made nature and would proactively respond. "Recurring in all these expressions of popular concern was the fear that man was throwing nature wildly out of balance in his manufacture of electricity, and that nature would sooner or later redress that balance" (Marvin, p. 121).

When wireless technologies were first introduced, nature was considered a conduit. The popular idea in 19th century physics was that a natural 'luminiferous aether' served as a ubiquitous but invisible transmitter of electricity and communication waves through space. The metaphors that helped society understand the emerging technologies were often tied to a proactive, engaged nature. "Not only did the metaphor of the 'etheric ocean' encourage the idea that one could become 'lost at sea,' but it also implied that, as with oceans of the earth, unknown creatures might stalk this electronic sea's invisible depths" (Sconce, 2000, p. 69).

Several artists explored physics as a force to affect the moving image. In 1976, Mary Lucier (1975/1993) allowed for direct environmental impact when she created "Dawn Burn" by aiming a camera at the morning sun as it rose. Slowly, the direct sunlight damaged the camera's tube, leaving a dark, arcing scar on the video image. Her video's confrontational face-off with natural force and its eventual pounding into submission is still one of the most poignant examples of the moving image being directly modified by nature at the behest of the artist. As part of an installation that included video, Doug Hall's (2009) "The Terrible Uncertainty of the Thing Described" makes a direct association between nature and technology by using a Tesla coil to transmit huge electrical bursts between two steel chairs. "Inspired by ideas related to the sublime, the video shows scenes of intense weather…which it compares to extreme technological and industrial situations that replicate, or are modeled after, natural phenomena" (Hall, 2009).

Natural Processes: The Moving Image and Biology

As mentioned earlier, biological materials and early moving image systems have been intertwined through design for centuries. In a sense, Plato's cave was an organic system – the wood fire, the silhouettes. Dried translucent animal skins and local woods were used in the shadow puppet plays of Asia (Groenendael, 1987). In the early days of the cinema industry, the name 'silver screen' came from the embedding of silver into woven silk. As mobile media evolves today, media archeologists are also considering 18th century formal garden designs, framed panoramas explored by strolling, as part of moving image history.

The biological ancestry of moving image materials did not end as distantly as one would expect. Celluloid resulted from the mix of natural and organic materials. *The Book of Film Care* (Gordon, 1983), a publication by Kodak, boasted that their film was 'animal, vegetable, and mineral' – bragging how all the materials used to make the celluloid of the movie industry came from the natural world. It is easy to forget that the first century of cinema was completely founded on a stock made from wood pulp and a coating of boiled cattle bones and cartilage.

Several artists and filmmakers have acknowledged the forces of biology in their work through direct application of natural materials onto the film stock. Both the Structuralists and the Expanded Cinema movement explored this relationship. In 1966, George Landow embraced the dirt that appeared on the material in his "Film in Which there Appear Sprocket Holes, Edge Lettering, Dirt Particles, Etc." and Nam June Paik's "Zen for Film" (1962-1964) was one hour of dust particles on unprocessed celluloid. However, the most direct application of nature onto the materials of the medium is likely Stan Brakhage's (1963) experimental silent film "Mothlight." A film with no camera, he pressed moth wings, flower petals and blades of grass between two sheets of mylar.

Both a lyrical and literal imprinting of nature onto the moving image, Brakhage successfully invented a new film process that used "real world elements" (Elder, 1998, p. 389).

One of the most striking uses of biology directly influencing the materials of cinema is Australia's Bio-Kino project that produced a collection of screen/organism hybrids. "The Living Screen" 2005, is a series of screens grown or scavenged from living organisms including skin tissue and blood, sperm, or cornea cells. As the specially made 'nano-movies' (only 25 microns in size and shown through a modified microscope) are projected onto the living screens, the surfaces change, respond, and die. The artists explain that "in overlaying digital pixels over biological pixels we intend to explore the tension between the inanimate and the animate and the digital versus the biological" (BioKino, 2011).

Natural Systems: The Moving Image and Ecology

Although not considered moving image artworks *per se*, the Land Art sculptures of the 1960's and 1970's were often both programmatic and time-based. As temporal forms that changed 'image' as part of their design, they can be included in discussions here. Robert Smithson's (1995-2011) "Spiral Jetty," 1970 has ominously, grandly resurfaced in the Great Salt Lake, once again changing color, form, aesthetic, and meaning. "Spiral Jetty" is becoming one of the century's great artistic narratives. In a broad sense, Earthworks (and later Environmental Art) were moving images in that each work had its own lifespan and presented itself to a viewer in stages. Sculptor Robert Morris explained, "What art now has in its hands is mutable stuff which need not arrive at a point of being finalized with respect to time or space. The notion that work is an irreversible process ending in a static icon-object no longer has much relevance" (Morris, 1969/1998, p. 231).

The emphasis on time and process was directly tied to dynamics in the environment for these artists. The sculptures were interactive through contextuality—the artist interacted with the landscape, the user interacted with the artwork as a space, the environment interacted with the work by actively changing its form. It was "a programmatic approach to the work and advocates sculpture which experiences, reacts to its environment, changes, is non-stable… art is gradually entering into a more significant relationship with the viewer and the component parts of his environment" (Sharp, 1970/1998, p. 200). Nature was chisel, paintbrush, pen.

"During the period, many artists worked with natural materials, often fascinated by their evolution and their organic decomposition. To better observe this process, the artist became almost a laboratory assistant, engaging in artistic experiences" (Tiberghien, 1993/1996, p. 14). Robert Smithson wrote, *"by excluding technological processes from the making of art, we began to discover other processes of a more fundamental order"* (Smithson, 1968/1998, p. 213).

A curator familiar with kinetic art, Guy Brett explains that art began to open up in the 1960's and allow for a greater direct impact of nature on the form and narrative of an artwork. "We begin to see that 'natural phenomenon' and 'aesthetic decision' were at this time in a shifting and reciprocal relationship to one another. The working-out of natural processes was allowed to change the conception of the beautiful; artists ceded their 'will to form' to certain degrees and in certain ways, and allowed natural events to prevail, which was seen as an emancipatory process, and to offer deeper insight into reality" (Brett, 2000, p. 31).

Many examples of artworks partially controlled by eco-systems surfaced in this period—each containing a very direct environmental agency with the sculpture. Some were created to specifically react to natural systems, for example Hans Haacke's "Fog, Flooding, Erosion" (1969) and Robert Smithson's "Asphalt Rundown" (1969). Others mimicked natural systems. Haacke's "Rhine Water Purification Plant" (1972) paired an artificial ecosystem with an endangered one, Agnes Denes harvested wheat in lower Manhattan ("Wheatfield: A Confrontation," 1982), Helen and Newton Harrison researched land use and ecosystems ("The Lagoon Cycle," 1972-1982), and Mel Chin used plants as remediation tools ("Revival Field," 1990-present). As Don Krug explained, "the artists are doing cultural work, through art, in relation to the systemic characteristics of human, plant, and animal interactions within particular geographic locations" (Krug, 2011). Artist and nature had joined forces to create temporal, changing image sculptures.

Natural Forces: The Moving Image and Sustainable Energy

If ecology was the recognition of the relational systems in nature and their fragility, sustainability is partially how those systems can healthily survive and endure without diminishing over time, in a sense, empowering natural systems. The Earthworks emphasis on complex organic and natural relations has shifted towards an emphasis how an environment can keep those relations running through its own natural forces and our respectful interaction. Sustainable design often includes a direct agency with environmental forces—wind power, water currents, sunlight, etc.

These sustainable forces of nature being used as a formal property in art making has some precedence in art history. If nature is perceived as an energy force, artists have used it to power kinesis in their work. Alexander Calder's mobiles alluded to the movements of nature—leaves rustling, insects and birds fluttering—but also used those forces to change their form. When describing his early mobiles, Calder wrote, "I have made a number of things for the open air: all of them react to the wind, and are like a sailing vessel in that they react best to one kind of breeze" (Calder, 1937). His simple description of his mobiles conceals their revolutionary break from sculptural traditions. "He introduced an intricate dynamic of dispersed and reciprocal forces that took the notion of sculptural mass beyond the uni-directional force of gravity, and he opened it up to outside influences" (Brett, 2000, p. 15). This direct impact of wind on sculpture continues today with the kinetic works of Theo Jansen (Frazier, 2011), whose wind-powered skeletal 'strandbeests' lope across the Dutch beaches.

The mutating form of kinetic art and sculpture ties directly to energy. In the *Artforum* review of "Force Fields: Phases of the Kinetic," an exhibition of kinetic art in Barcelona, Yve-Alain Bois (2000) emphasized curator Guy Brett's interest in the natural power sources inherent in the works:

It should be noted here that what's at stake for Brett is less "movement" per se than "energy"--the specific desire of a tremendous number of artists in the twentieth century to materialize energy, to give form to something that is eminently nonvisual. Movement, in this account, is only one of several formal possibilities in this quest, but a particularly efficient solution; no matter how concrete, movement can always be expressed as an equation, like energy itself. The qualities that define movement (slow/fast; continuous/discontinuous; regular/irregular; accelerating/decelerating; etc.) are shared by every object or being that produces and expends energy. This very universality, which is an abstract quality, makes of movement an ideal metaphoric switchboard: Every work exhibited in "Force Fields" alludes to either the organic, the mechanic, or the cosmic--in all cases concepts of energy that we, as human beings, have learned to apply in our daily life without a second thought (Bois, 2000).

A year earlier, a 1999 exhibition at the Hudson River Museum called *Drip, Blow, Burn: Forces of Nature in Contemporary Art* presented artworks that used wind, water, and fire as integral components to shape the materials of the artworks.

The artists employed these elements as power to animate, alter, or destroy their creations. The curator, Thomas Weaver (1999) observed how using natural process as a material in art allows for a unique dual transformation:

It manipulates structures of mediation and representation, and shifts the viewer's awareness of nature, space, time, and movement. This dual process is reciprocal, with modes of signification affecting referents and referents affecting modes of representation...The natural here is not just a subject, and certainly not just a material...moving natural elements are primal elements that, by rupturing the boundaries that govern the significations of visual art, embody the power of art to wrestle with the world (Weaver, 1999, p. 24).

SUSTAINABLE CINEMA: CREATING THE MOVING IMAGE WITH NATURAL POWER

I am working with natural energy in my own artworks. Sustainable Cinema is a series of kinetic public sculptures I am fabricating that harness natural forces in the environment to power a perceptual illusion of a moving image. Large-scale and made from steel or wood, the artworks reference early optical illusion toys that were part of the history of cinema as well as early energy sources that are now experiencing a revival. By examining the concurrent histories of film and industrialization, they are meant to trigger consideration of environmentally sustainable media. In many respects, sustainable energy is a re-imagining of the oldest energy forms like wind and water and these sculptures do the same with the moving image.

Mediated Earthworks

Natural energies are often invisible, often indiscernible. To be able to read and design artworks that utilize the environment's invisible dynamics, computational sensing technologies come into play. Sensing allows for a new form of interplay with nature. As changes in motion, light, sound, and temperature can now be measured with great computational detail, our modern surveillance technologies are no longer dedicated to watching people—they are now reading the environment as well and offering unique information about the shifts and patterns in our world. Hewlett-Packard's "Central Nervous System for the Earth" is a corporate initiative to deploy a trillion sensors into the natural and built environments (Sutter, 2011). A global swarm of miniature wireless devices would observe ecological systems, seismic vibration, natural energy activity, *etc.* Computers are about to take over the role as explorer and revealer of essential truths in our world.

I've experimented with this type of sensor-driven environmental agency in two cinema projects. "Brakelights" (2004) is a real-time computer system that uses changing color information in the environment by reading the RGB levels of every pixel in every frame coming into a camera. The program analyzes the color levels and then selects elements from a visual database, in this case two hundred pre-shot scenes between and man and woman delineated into five distinct emotions. When the camera was placed on a Los Angeles traffic jam at night, the red brakelights controlled the narrative. When traffic jammed, the red became brighter, the system pulled shots from the 'anger' database, the couple fought; when traffic flowed, fewer red brakelights, they spoke of their love. Designed as a live cinema-making machine, the artwork makes a film that is directed by the environment. The ebb and flow of my daily traffic jam, something I did not even realize had existed, became a powerful narrative generator. While I used a completely non-natural phenomenon in this piece, automobile brakelights, the system was originally designed to read color changes in nature like clouds in the sky or the wind on leaves.

2005's "Mulholland Drive" was a mediated earthwork I created with programming by Michael Chu and sound design by Martin Bonadeo. Together, we drove the length of Los Angeles' famous Mulholland Drive with five types of sensors—computationally measuring the tilt, direction, altitude, speed and engine sound of the car. The precise captured data was then used to create an exact 3-D path in a computer, duplicating every curve and pothole of the journey. That computer path was then used to control two robotic lights in a dark room filled with fog. Two beams of light and the processed sound of the engine recreated the journey of driving the road. The road's topography creates a new form of visual experience and sculpture. In a sense, the artwork is cinema without an image.

Media Archeology

While this paper focuses on natural environmental agency, my sculptures cannot be separated from their debt to media archaeology and the popular 19th century optical toys. I am one of several artists who are currently exploring this history in their new media art practice. In a forthcoming paper, media archeologist and scholar Erkki Huhtamo considers the trend:

There seems to be a parallel between the emergence of the archeological art and some changes taking place in the cultural and intellectual ambience. The general framework seems to be the gradual displacement of the 1980's postmodernist discourse in favour of an approach which once again seeks foothold in "real" space and time....I see the activity of this gaze as an attempt to go beyond postmodernism, to initiate a dialogue with the past with the aim of countering the constant blurring of boundaries and definitions which is characteristic of the "postmodern condition" and largely a product of the spreading of audiovisuality (Huhtamo, in press).

In many ways postmodernism has muddied the waters. By mixing everything and anything, we may have created some unnecessary complication and possibly lost touch with the purity of the individual elements. The simplicity of these sculptures in creating a moving image offers a glimpse into the mystery of cinema; they are simple illusions made with simple energy. By doing this, I hope to initiate a conversation about our distancing from the sources of power, both literal and sociological, in our world. They are meant to be a *primal* media experience; in the age of rapid technological development, this is no longer an oxymoron. This theme of demystifying invisible power has surfaced in several of my works, notably the dome visualizations I created of the increasingly dense aerial technologies above us in my planetarium artwork "Celestial Mechanics" (2005).

Referencing the early optical toys served another purpose. Their inherent interactivity, a dialogue between man and illusion machine, were part of a historical trajectory of recognizing that systems could be art. Duchamp made it official, but the distancing from a static art object had begun. In media, we watch machines to watch the moving images. The Sustainable Cinema sculptures are meant to simultaneously create and break the illusion by revealing the machinery of cinema. The tools of the mediated moving image are inherent in the sculptures' materiality, and because of this, the images shown in them serve a dual purpose of proscenium art and abstraction of the machines' own narrative.

Using natural energy to power these cinema-generating machines adds an additional layer of meaning to the sculptures. These hulking steel artworks are not powered conventionally. We have come to equate media with electricity and by changing the source of power in creating the moving image, the sculptures very clearly capture the energy of the earth. The animations seem to be part of a life force continuum. They are animated in the mediated sense, but also animated in a way associated with living nature. We see a

Figure 2. Scott Hessels, "The Image Mill" during ArtPrize, Gerald R. Ford Presidential Museum, Grand Rapids, Michigan. (© 2009, Scott Hessels. Used with permission).

natural energy captured by a machine, injected into a representation, and come alive.

Sustainable Cinema No. 1: The Image Mill

The first completed sculpture was installed at The Gerald R. Ford Presidential Museum in Grand Rapids, Michigan in 2009. "The Image Mill" is a rotating steel machine that uses the force and beauty of falling water as the energy to create a moving picture. As water falls over the 4-meter-tall wheel, a transmission assembly causes two disks to spin in opposite directions. On the interior wheel are a series of animation frames painted onto plexiglass; on the black outside wheel, rotating in the opposite direction, are cut slits. As the two wheels spin, the slits act as a shutter and the animation becomes visible; a movie plays in the falling water.

The site of the work in the heart of America's 'rust belt' determined the content for the sculpture. One of the first movies created was a galloping horse and this sculpture also uses it as a metaphor for the struggling Michigan automobile industry; the animation is part Muybridge, part Ford Mustang. As the waterwheel spins, the pony stumbles, but continues on. This 32-frame narrative suggests that the 'horsepower' that drove the state's industrial age is at a transition to a new age of alternative energy. This theme was also revealed in the fabrication. Made by Michigan metal workers, the artwork was meant to be an optimistic hope that the skills of industrial-era tradesmen could be tapped as a valuable resource now that the region is considering new sustainable directions.

Figure 3. Scott Hessels, Design rendering of "Rickshaw Cinema" (© 2010, Scott Hessels. Used with permission).

Sustainable Cinema No. 2: Rickshaw Cinema

Although not an energy source created by the natural environment, pedal power is often considered in sustainable design. The recycling and redesign of bicycles to build simple systems to help facilitate the work of small-scale, self-sustaining projects is receiving global attention. This sculpture explores regional bicycle traditions as a starting point for a greener future.

The crudely chopped bikes seen throughout Southeast Asia combine found metals, recycled wood, concrete and other cheap materials to create a hybrid 'hack' that assists a struggling family to better their lives. Inspired by this heritage, this sculpture is a mechanically re-engineered regional bicycle. In the artwork, the pedals both generate the electricity and advance the celluloid film to project a film on a coarsely made screen that folds up in front of the handlebars. The sculpture references the vernacular of Asian mobile small-scale businesses to celebrate the folk beauty, ingenuity and compelling history of these machines.

Sustainable Cinema No. 3: The Praxinoscope Windmill

The third sculpture uses mirrors similar to the design of another early animation device called a Praxinoscope. A windmill at the top turns a gear system that powers the spinning of a beveled, diamond-shaped mirror at the base that reflects two disks of animation frames rotating directly above and below it. Using wind as the energy and

Figure 4. Scott Hessels, Model of "Praxinoscope Windmill." (© 2010, Scott Hessels. Used with permission).

Figure 5. Scott Hessels, "Shadow Play Windmill." (cc 2010. Scott Hessels. Used with permission).

a tower structure that references futuristic 19th century innovation and design (the Praxinoscope and the Eiffel Tower occurred at nearly the same time in history), the simple animation is completely controlled by the speed and direction of the wind.

Sustainable Cinema No. 4: Shadow Play Windmill

In this wind-powered shadow puppet show, the silhouettes are also achieved by light penetrating a translucent screen. The rotation of the windmill powers the backlight for the shadows as well as turns a series of gears and plates that animate the puppets and move a background diorama. Unlike the other sculptures which function as 'players' for animation content that can be easily changed, "Shadow Play" required the content to be created in tandem with the overall design. Instead of a machine that plays an animation, this sculpture is an animation that determines the structural design of the machine.

Sustainable Cinema No. 5: The Phenakistoscope Windmill

Figure 6. Scott Hessels, Model of "Phenakistoscope Windmill." (© 2010, Scott Hessels. Used with permission).

As with the "Image Mill", the phenakistoscope was the foundation for the fifth sculpture. This windmill uses a dual-blade system where one fan acts as a shutter by overlapping another fan that contains the animation frames. In this artwork, the front windmill fan is black, the rear contains fifteen frames of animation. As the wind spins the two blades, the moving image is visible in the intersection of the two fans.

CONCLUSION

The history of the moving image has rode astride culture's views of nature. Society's perceptions of physics, biology, ecology and sustainability have all surfaced in artworks and media theory over the past two centuries. We've journeyed from phenomena to organism to system to force. In each case, the direct integration of the natural environment into an artwork has generated a reconsideration of both nature and culture. With the Sustainable Cinema series of sculptures, natural and sustainable energy is used in a visible, understandable and startling way, to generate the moving image. As with other artists who have worked with natural forces, I hope these works will lead to enduring conversations about the environment.

REFERENCES

Audesirk, T., Audesirk, G., & Byers, B. E. (2001). Biology: Life on earth. *Benjamin Cummings.*, *ISBN-10*, 0321598466.

BioKino Collective. (2011). *The living screen: About*. Retrieved April 2, 2011, from http://www.biokino.net/about.html

Boettger, S. (2002). *Earthworks: Art and the landscape of the sixties* (pp. 23–27). Berkeley, CA: University of California Press.

Bois, Y. (2000). Review of force fields: Phases of the kinetic. *Artforum*. New York. Retrieved on April 4, 2011, from http://findarticles.com/p/articles/mi_m0268/is_3_39/ai_67935450/

Brett, G. (2000). The century of kinesthesia. In S. Cotter & C. Douglas (Ed.), *Force fields: Phases of the kinetic* (pp. 9-68). Barcelona, Spain: Museu d'Art Contemporani de Barcelona and Actar. ASIN: B003U3Y7Z8.

Calder, A. (1937). Mobiles. In M. Evans & G. Howe (Ed.), *The painter's object*. Retrieved from http://calder.org/historicaltexts/text/9.html

Elder, R. B. (1998). *The films of Stan Brakhage in the American tradition of Ezra Pound, Gertrude Stein, and Charles Olson*. Waterloo, Canada: Wilfrid Laurier University Press.

Encyclopædia Britannica. (2011). *Phenakistoscope*. Retrieved July 24, 2011, from http://www.britannica.com/EBchecked/topic/455469/phenakistoscope

Frazier, I. (2011, September 5). The March of the Strandbeests: Theo Jansen's wind-powered sculpture. *New Yorker (New York, N.Y.)*, 54–61.

Freeman, M. H. (2003). *Optics* (11th ed.). London, UK: Butterworths-Heinemann.

Gordon, P. L. (1983). *The book of film care*. Rochester, NY: Eastman Kodak Company.

Gorman, M. J. (2001). Between the demonic and the miraculous: Athanasius Kircher and the baroque culture of machines. In D. Stolzenberg, (Ed.), *The great art of knowing: The baroque encyclopedia of Athanasius Kirche* (pp. 59-70). Stanford, CA: Stanford University Libraries. Retrieved August 10, 2011, from http://hotgates.stanford.edu/Eyes/machines/index.htm

Greenslade, T. B., Jr. (2011). *Instruments for natural philosophy*. Retrieved on 26 July, 2011, from http://physics.kenyon.edu/EarlyApparatus/Optical_Recreations/Praxinoscopes/Praxinoscopes.html

Groenendael, V. M. C. (1987). *Wayang Theatre in Indonesia*. Dordrecht, The Netherlands: Foris Publications.

Hall, D. (2011). *Media installations: 1987-The terrible uncertainty of the thing described*. Retrieved from http://doughallstudio.com/1987-the-terrible-uncertainty/the-terrible-uncertainty-of-the-thing-described/3305605

Hecht, E. (2001). *Optics* (4nd ed.). Reading, M A: Addison-Wesley Publishing. ISBN-10: 0805385665

Huhtamo, E. (2010). Media archaeology and media art . In Sommerer, C., & Jain, L. (Eds.), *The art and science of interface and interaction design* (*Vol. II*). New York, NY: Springer Verlag.

Kastner, J. (1998). Preface . In *Land and environmental art*. London, UK: Phaidon.

Krug, D. (2011). *Introduction*. Retrieved March 10, 2011, from http://www.greenmuseum.org/c/aen/Issues/intro.php

Marvin, C. (1988). *When old technologies were new: Thinking about electric communication in the late nineteenth century*. New York, NY: Oxford University Press.

Morris, R. (1998). Notes on sculpture part 4: Beyond objects . In Kastner, J. (Ed.), *Land and environmental art* (pp. 230–231). London, UK: Phaidon. (Original work published 1969)

Popper, F. (1968). *Origins and development of kinetic art*. (S. Bann, Trans., p. 121). London, UK: Studio Vista. *SBN, 28979592*, 3.

Ratner, B. D. (2004). Sustainability as a dialogue of values: Challenges to the sociology of development. *Sociological Inquiry, 74*, 59–69. doi:10.1111/j.1475-682X.2004.00079.x

Robert, K. H., Daly, H., Hawken, P., & Holmberg, J. (1996). A compass for sustainable development. *International Journal of Sustainable Development And World Ecology, 4*, 79-92. ISSN: 13504509

Sconce, J. (2000). *Haunted media: Electronic presence from telegraphy to television*. Durham, NC: Duke University Press.

Sharp, W. (1998). Notes towards an understanding of earth art . In Kastner, J. (Ed.), *Land and environmental art* (pp. 199–200). London, UK: Phaidon. (Original work published 1970)

Smithson, R. (1998). A sedimentat ion of the mind: Earth projects . In Kastner, J. (Ed.), *Land and environmental art* (pp. 199–200). London, UK: Phaidon. (Original work published 1968)

Sutter, J. D. (2011). Smart dust aims to monitor everything. Retrieved April 4, 2011, from http://edition.cnn.com/2010/TECH/05/03/smart.dust.sensors/index.html

Tiberghien, G. A. (1996). *Land art* (Green, C., Trans.). New York, NY: Princeton Architectural Press. (Original work published 1993)

Tilakasiri, J. (1968). *The puppet theatre of Asia.* Ceylon, MA: The Department of Cultural Affairs, Department of Government Printing.

Tufnell, B. (2006). *Land art* (pp. 15–17). London, UK: Tate Publishing.

Warren, J. F. (2003). *Rickshaw coolie: A people's history of Singapore 1880-1940.* Singapore: Singapore University Press.

Weaver, T. (1999). *Drip, blow, burn: Forces of nature in contemporary art.* Yonkers, NY . *The Hudson River Museum.*, ISBN-10, 094365128X.

Wilson, J. (1977). *Physics: Concepts and applications.* Lexington, MA: D. C Heath and Co.

ADDITIONAL READING

Andrews, M. (Ed.). (2006). *Land, art: A cultural ecology handbook.* London, UK: Cornerhouse.

Beardsley, J. (1984). *Earthworks and beyond.* New York, NY: Cross River Press.

Cartwright, L. (1995). *Screening the body: Tracing medicine's visual culture.* Minneapolis, MN: University of Minnesota Press.

Dempsey, A. (2010). *Destination art.* Berkeley, CA: University of California Press.

Eisaesser, T. (Ed.). (1997). *Early cinema: Space, frame, narrative.* British Film Institute.

Goldberg, K. (Ed.). (2001). *The robot in the garden: Telerobotics and telepistemology in the age of the internet.* Cambridge, MA: MIT Press.

Judson, W. (Ed.). (1988). *American landscape video: The electronic grove.* Pittsburgh, PA: The Carnegie Museum of Art.

Kagan, S. (2011). *Art and sustainability: Connecting patterns for a culture of complexity.* Bielefeld, Germany . *Transcript Verlag.*, ISBN-10, 383761803X.

Manovich, L. (2001). *The language of new media.* Cambridge, MA: MIT Press.

Novak, B. (1980). *Nature and culture: American landscape painting 1825-1875.* Oxford, UK: Oxford University Press.

Petro, P. (Ed.). (1994). *Fugitive images: From photography to video.* Indiana University Press.

Prather, M. (1998). *Alexander Calder 1898-1976.* New Haven: Yale University Press.

Reboratti, E. E. (1999). Territory, scale and sustainable development . In Becker, E., & Jahn, T. (Eds.), *Sustainability and the social sciences: A cross-disciplinary approach to integrating environmental considerations into theoretical re-orientation* (pp. 207–222). London, UK: Zed Books.

Reiser, M., & Zapp, A. (Eds.). (2002). *New screen media: Cinema/art/narrative.* British Film Institute.

Rossell, D. (1998). *Living pictures: The origins of the movies.* Albany, NY: State University of New York Press.

Stiney, P. A. (1979). *Visionary film: The American avant-garde.* Oxford, UK: Oxford University Press. ISBN-10: 9780195148862

Vesna, V. (Ed.). (2007). *Database aesthetics*. Minneapolis, MN: University of Minnesota Press.

Youngblood, G. (1970). *Expanded cinema.* Toronto, Canada. *Clarke, Irwin & Company Limited.*, *ISBN-10*, 0525472630.

KEY TERMS AND DEFINITIONS

Biology: Broadly, the branch of natural sciences that includes living organisms, used here interchangeably with 'organic' (Audesirk, Audesirk, & Byers, 2010).

Earthworks: Although usually used interchangeably with Land Art and Environmental Art, the phrase coined by Robert Smithson is usually applied to artworks that involved a sculptural gesture that involved direct manipulation of the soil and terrain (Boettger, 2002).

Environmental Art: Also used interchangeably with Land Art and Earthworks, this term appeared later and includes work that is usually more direct in its support of eco-friendly practices. Many of the Land Art works were systems that mimicked natural processes and Environmental Art became the term that encompassed a type of 'stewardship' towards the earth that many of these artists supported (Kastner, 1998).

Kinetic Art: Artworks, usually three-dimensional sculptures, that use real movement. Often powered by motors, environmental forces (e.g. wind) or human interactivity (Popper, 1968).

Land Art: Also used interchangeably with Earthworks and Environmental Art, it often includes a broader range of sculptures beyond the soil-specific pieces associated with Earthworks. Here, the sites, materials and gestures are more diverse yet still include physical (and ususally non-respresentational) interactions with the natural environment (Tufnell, 2006).

Luminiferous Aether: One of several 'ethers' that were falsely considered as mediums for a wide range of movement in space; a way to explain the invisible including conduits for magnetics, planetary movement, and electricity (Hecht, 1987).

Optics: A branch of physics that studies the properties of light and vision, as well as other radiations that cannot be seen by man (Freeman, 1990).

Phenakistoscope: A 19th century optical illusion toy that simulated movement through the use of two disks—one with slits, the other with frames of animation. When spun in different directions, the illusion of movement appears, usually presented in a rotating mirror ("Phenakistoscope", 2011).

Physics: The study of natural phenomena and the patterns and principles found there; the search for fundamental properties in physical phenemomena (Wilson, 1977).

Praxinoscope: Another 19th century animation device where a strip of animation cells is reflected off a rotating ring of beveled mirrors creating the illusion of movement (Greenslade, 2011).

Rickshaw: Invented in Japan in 1869, the man-powered carriage quickly spread throughout Asia in a variety of forms well into the 20th century. Today, they exist as transportation novelties but have influenced a mobile culture where bicycles are converted into shops, entertainment, and a host of other functions (Warren, 2003).

Shadow Play: One of the oldest art forms and possibly the first moving image system, several ancient cultures developed variations of presenting cut, usually flat characters made from woods or skins against a cloth or hide screen, backlit by fire, oil or kerosene lamps to create the shadows. The players usually performed dual roles, moving the puppets and vocalizing the dialogue and effects (Tilakasiri, 1968).

Sustainability: Sustainability is the ability to endure and has been applied to a wide range of fields. It is used here more specifically as the potential of a biological system or ecosystem to subsist and remain productive over time (Riboratti 1999).

Sustainable Design: Although first used in connection with architecture (notable 'green' buildings), the definition can now include several other design fields that involve fabrication. The approach attempts to use resources fairly and efficiently so that substances from the earth do not increase in the ecosphere (*e.g.* oil, coal), substances made by man do not increase in the ecosphere, and the productivity and diversity of nature is not be systematically diminished (Robert, K.H., Daly, H., Hawken, P., Holmberg, J., 1996).

Sustainable Development: Although the term is also applied to a wide range of beliefs and approaches, it is used here in a multidimensional point of view, beginning with ecosystem integrity. From there it recognizes that human society and economics are closely tied and cannot grow faster than the consumption of the resources (Ratner, 2004).

Chapter 7
Seeing the Unseen

Eve Andrée Laramée
Maryland Institute College of Art, USA

Eunsu Kang
University of Akron, USA

Kalyan Chakravarthy Thokala
University of Akron, USA

Matthew Kolodziej
University of Akron, USA

Donna Webb
University of Akron, USA

Peter Niewiarowski
University of Akron, USA

Yingcai Xiao
University of Akron, USA

ABSTRACT

The Synapse Group at the University of Akron was formed to explore enlightened collaborations between art and science, and to probe the ideas, images, and mutual interests connecting art and science professionals and disciplines. This chapter presents selected artworks created by members of the group. A major theme of this chapter is visualizing water that is unseen, such as invisible underground water or imaginary virtual water. Also explained in the chapter are the inspiration processes by which those artworks were created.

INTRODUCTION

In her book, Art & Science (Ede, 2005), Sian Ede, the Arts Director of the Calouste Gulbenkian Foundation, UK, (2011) raised the question "Is science the new art?" In the same book she showed us that in today's world "'art' is as vital to our existence as 'science'" and "There is much in contemporary science that can stimulate art's flexible, intuitive and visceral response to the world." New York Times columnist Amy Wallace (Wallace 2011a) recently wrote an article in her monthly Prototype column titled "Science to Art, and Vice Versa" (Wallace 2011b), in which she profiled sculptor Nathalie Biebach and scientist Matthew McCrory. Biebach uses scientific measurements to create three-dimensional objects and Matthew McCrory uses art to benefit science. "Both promote understanding by finding new ways of seeing the world" and "both are invested in the idea that better visualization leads to better thinking."

Visualizing with data, noticing the effects of change, using direct observation, and examining the gaps in information are motivations for the

DOI: 10.4018/978-1-4666-0942-6.ch007

interaction between scientists and artists. These processes are essential to both disciplines and take the work into a range of possible ways of making the invisible visible and making the visible more meaningful. Artistic explorations reflect upon either an appreciation of this world or a desire to make sense of it. Whether from a systemic view or from the point of view of a detail, the scientist and artist use data gathering, physical interaction with the environment, observation, and consideration of dynamic forces working in conjunction with the focus of study. Through the eyes of installation, new media interactive performance, ceramics, and painting, the possibilities of using scientific processes and pursuits are reconsidered and energized. These collaborations invite innovative views of both fixed and time-based descriptions of space and material.

The Synapse Group (Synapse, 2005) was formed at the University of Akron to encourage conversations between arts and science professionals. Through initial discussions within this group it was clear that mapping, material properties, and environmental restoration were central concerns for both disciplines. A process of making and consultation resulted in the group's interactions between computer science, geology, biology, and the arts, and it demonstrated the possibilities of these collaborations. Forming an investigation of both the process of science and art, as well as what can be made as a result of this intersection, is demonstrated through the examination of a specific issue or design problem. These interactions flow from either a vision that is about systemic relationships or from a fascination with the details adding up. At the Synapse Group, the participants in this process used water as a metaphor, subject, and material involved with biological structures and systems. The subject of water is a global issue. Water makes life possible and sustainable. Water affects all facets of cultural, political, and organic systems. How this material functions, is used, is owned, and is preserved touches life on this earth from the micro to the macro levels.

Biology is the study of life. Modern biology, at least as recognized by most biologists today, has been a formal discipline for about 200 years, but biological study of various sorts formed the basis of an older recognized area of inquiry known as 'natural philosophy.' Whatever its exact origins, Biology has become a central and possibly a definitive scientific discipline of our time, with, for example, scientists across many fields declaring the 21st century as the 'Age of Biology.' Biology, in this view, can be placed at either the core or interface of nearly every interesting question we might wish to ask in our modern society. Consider the prominence of just two different sources of news continually bombarding us through newspapers, blogs, radio, television and other mediums: healthcare issues (e.g., policy, costs, technologies, etc.) and environmental catastrophes (e.g., the BP oil spill, Japanese nuclear reactor meltdowns, greenhouse gases and global warming).

Presumably, it is rather obvious that biology has much to offer in computing and computer science (and vice versa) as they relate to many problems and endeavors, including applications where artists use computers and related technologies as a way to create, interpret or otherwise inform their art. It is likely the rare biologist who doesn't comprehend the interesting dualities of explicitly biology-computer interfaces: computational biology and bioinformatics. In either of these areas, a biologist might emphasize how the technology of the computer has transformed biological exploration and discovery (gene sequencing and the human genome project are just two examples), while the computer scientist might be more captivated by how genetic algorithms and neural nets lead to novel computational models and even the creation of capabilities such as 'artificial intelligence.' It does not require a big extension to bring art into this mix and see the possibilities. In our modern age, computing is used to code and define the graphic and statistical information in both science and art. But as with any interactive relationship, science and art explorations are increasingly having an effect on what digital designers consider possible and relevant. Perhaps biology and computers are just tools to help shape or communicate artistic expression? There is probably a deeper relationship that is more fundamental and more interesting. For example, if biology, computers and art are ways of knowing and communicating about the world around us, do novel, new forms emerge by bringing their methods, language and cultures together? What are the barriers to such an interaction? What are the likely benefits? We are intrigued in how these collaborations around the central issue of water manifest an array of experimental and expressive impulses.

In the rest of this chapter, the artists in the Synapse Group share their experiences in exploring the synergy between art and science. As they prepare for an exhibit on the subject of water at the Cleveland Sculpture Center (2011), they use the main theme of water to connect the projects in this chapter together and to demonstrate how something that is colorless and shapeless can be represented using an array of diverse media. In the session of "Seeing the Unseen: Invisible Fire, Detail of Installation," Eve Andrée Laramée and Kalyan Chakravarthy Thokala visualize underground water contaminated with radioactive isotopes by interpreting water quality data with 3D computer models. In "Out of Sight / Out of Mind: Observing What Lies beneath the Surface," Donna Webb establishes a connection in the viewer between the ground water and the image on her ceramic artwork so that the invisible water becomes assessable through the image. In "Body, Voice, and Ocean: Biological Processes Visualized Through Interactive Technologies," Eunsu Kang creates water-like multi-media interactive spaces in which the participants enjoy conversations with the spaces through their bodily movements as if they were swimming in the water. Finally, in "The Gaps Between: Biological Structures Reconsidered through Entropy and Digital Translation," Matthew Kolodziej discusses and demonstrates the impact of water on paintings.

Seeing the Unseen: Invisible Fire

Interdisciplinary artist and researcher Eve Andrée Laramée creates artwork at the confluence of art and science (Laramée et al., 1999, Heon et al., 2000, Lippard et al., 2007, Reynolds, 1999, Shanken, 2009, Strelow, 1999, Weintraub, 2003). Her research focuses on the environmental and health impacts of Cold War atomic legacy sites (Laramée, 2009). In collaboration with computer scientist Kalyan Chakravarthy Thokala, this artist-scientist team visualized underground water resources contaminated with radioactive isotopes. The former Department of Energy Fernald Uranium Feed Material Production Plant, a nuclear weapons complex in southwestern Ohio, contaminated groundwater in a buried valley resulting in a plume 1.5 miles long by 1.8 miles wide that extends beyond the facility boundary. Fernald was the largest producer of uranium metal for nuclear weapons production and also received radioactive wastes from the WWII Manhattan Project, which created the bombs dropped on Hiroshima and Nagasaki. The 1,050-acre site is located eighteen miles northwest of Cincinnati. During its 37 years of operation, 620,000,000 gallons of contaminated water were produced, and over 2/3 of its campus was contaminated with radioactive materials (Center for Disease Control, 2000, Makhijani et al., 2000, Rainey, 2008, Rhodes, 1986, Wasserman & Solomon, 1982).

The invisible was rendered visible (Figure 1) by interpreting water quality data with 3D computer modeling using OpenGL software (OpenGL, 2011) and GoogleEarth (Google, 2011). The Department of Energy Office of Legacy Management Geospatial Environmental Mapping System (GEMS) was the source of water sample data from 474 wells (Office of Legacy Management, 2011). Imagery was created visualizing points where plutonium, uranium, radium, technitium, and thorium were present in water samples. Based on the depths of the monitoring wells, the plume is shown to be below the water

Figure 1. Eve Andrée Laramée and Kalyan Chakravarthy Thokala, Invisible Fire, computer graphics, detail of installation. (© 2011, E. A. Laramée and K. C. Thokala. Used with permission.)

table of the Great Miami Aquifer. Laramée and Thokala hope to continue their collaboration to create animations that visualize the movement of the plume in the aquifer, and how that plume may change over time due to climate change and other environmental factors.

Biologically-inspired computing played a central role in Laramée's 2009 installation, Halfway to Invisible, questioning the environmental legacy and biological impact of uranium mining in the Four Corners region of the American Southwest (Cochran, 2009). Between 1949 and 1989, uranium mines in the Western United States produced more than 225,000,000 tons of uranium ore (Brugge et al., 2006 and Mogren, 2002). This activity affected a large number of Native American nations, including the Laguna, Navajo, Zuni, Southern Ute, Ute Mountain, Hopi, Acoma and other Pueblo cultures (Eichstaedt, 1994). Many of these peoples worked in the 4,000 mines, mills and processing plants in New Mexico, Arizona,

Utah and Colorado (Hevly & Findlay, 1988). These workers were not only poorly paid, they were seldom informed of the dangers of working with uranium and were not given appropriate protective gear (Masco, 2006). The government, mining companies, and scientific and health communities were all well aware of the hazards of working with radioactive materials at this time (Johnston, 2007).

Due to the Cold War demand for increasingly destructive and powerful nuclear weapons, these laborers were both exposed to and brought home (in the form of dust on their clothing and skin) large amounts of radiation. Epidemiologic studies of the families of these workers have shown increased incidents of radiation-induced cancers, miscarriages, cleft palates and other birth defects.

Halfway to Invisible (Figure 2), questions how "Atomic Age" events may have influenced evolutionary processes and produced genetic casualties in these communities: Is our atomic

Figure 2. Eve Andrée Laramée, Halfway to Invisible, installation (© 2010, E. A. Laramée. Used with permission.)

legacy producing genotoxic effects in indigenous human populations? If so, what is the extent of DNA damage, and how might this affect these populations in the future?

The artist engaged biologically-inspired computing in the sixty light-boxes that were distributed throughout the room. These contained photographic transparencies of radial gene maps and cancer cells with superimposed text, microphotographs of extremophile organisms, such as *Deinococcus radiodurans*, currently under study as bioremediation agents. This extremophile grows in pools of water in which spent fuel rods from nuclear reactors are stored, as well as in the hot springs and geysers of Yellowstone National Park. A video sculpture in the installation depicted an intuitive interpretation of genetic mutation, and a video projection showed genetic material breaking off from a cell immersed in a solution of uranyl acetate.

Laramée's research-driven art practice[1] addresses global environmental and health impacts of atomic weapons production and the post-Cold War nuclear power industry (Admundson, 2002 and Dalton, 1999). Groundwater, surface water,

and deep aquifer resources are polluted in areas where these activities took place (Kuletz, 1998). Water systems fundamentally affect food production bio-dynamics. By targeting the sources of radiotoxic ingestion within animal and vegetable food contamination, the work addresses issues of systemic pollution.

Out of Sight / Out of Mind: Observing What Lies beneath the Surface

Donna Webb's art brings together the history and geology of the landscape, current research about water, and ceramic processes. She establishes connections between the structural features of hidden water and the medium of clay and glaze to make the invisible visible.

One of the conclusions reached through discussion with other members of the Synapse Group was that much of what is compelling about water is invisible most of the time or all of the time. The group concluded that finding ways to make information about water visible to the viewer could be transformative for both the artist and the viewer. For artists, observation of the world is a necessary prerequisite to translating it to traditional materials such as paint and clay or new materials like polymers and digital sensors. Those who share this attention and intention to observation find it a necessary component to the process of discovery.

Webb's medium is ceramics. The impulse to use ceramic materials to express ideas about the natural world, such as water, earth, and rock, is recorded in the long history of nature-oriented ceramics, perhaps best exemplified by medieval Japanese pottery. Rather than telling stories like those on Greek pots or displaying patterns like the Islamic potters, Japanese potters celebrated forms of nature from mountain streams to snowy bushes. Describing a first rate set of Japanese tea bowls, ceramic historian, Robert Yellin wrote (Hayes 2010), "They have no fancy glazes or deftly painted iron under glaze design; they just 'are.' Full like the moon they quietly invite you to pick them up. The balance is perfect, the touch sensual, and the feeling of holding earth, water, fire and air combined is very grounding."

Scientific research on the nature of silica, the glassy part of ceramic glazes, and water bring the ceramic-water relationship up to date. According to H. Eugene Stanley of Boston University, Center for Polymer Studies, "This 'silicon work' is a real breakthrough. People have always thought of silicon as a perfectly straightforward element. They're now finding that liquid silicon is anything but straightforward … It's like water." "The apparent similarities of liquid water, silica, and silicon are more than just coincidences. The common properties of these very different substances may reflect patterns of structure and function that had previously eluded the scientific community" (Weiss 2004). It seems the capacity of ceramic materials to express earth, rock and water can be attributed not only to the obviously earthy quality of the clay, but to the water-like quality of the glaze as well.

Webb's home town of Akron, Ohio owes its existence to the hundreds of laborers who dug the Ohio Canal by hand. The Canal connected water from the Ohio River north to Lake Erie. Water in the Cuyahoga River was diverted to a race that drove woolen and grist mills. The water in the river and the canal are the visible part of a vast invisible water system. Visualizing the connection between these two, the seen and the unseen, is a critical aesthetic component as well as the driving environmental probe of Webb's work.

Like the citizens of Akron, human beings throughout history have been interested in the mostly visible: fast moving water in lakes, streams and rivers. Humans were distrustful of slow moving water in swamps and wetlands. Now we know that water, moving slowly through the ground and collecting in unseen reservoirs is perhaps the most important water of all. This is water we may have never seen. Out of sight is out of mind; our lack of understanding and awareness of these waters makes us behave in unthinking ways. For some time, media coverage about the invisible water system has been increasing in scientific literature as well as the popular press. The New York Times series, "Toxic Waters" was a six-part exposé of ways in which problems within the invisible water system have begun to manifest themselves in the form of illness and death (New York Times, August 2009-March 2010).

On March 17, 2011 a devastating magnitude 9.0 earthquake that struck off the east coast of Japan temporarily impacted groundwater supplies as far away as America. At the Edwards Aquifer in Texas, which supplies water to about 1.7 million people, water levels fluctuated wildly for about two hours after the earthquake, rising by one foot and continuing to oscillate afterwards. Instruments gathered information about the hidden water at Edwards Aquifer (Vance 2011). This data makes us aware of the interconnectedness of water resources on earth. However the search for data that would generate images of ground porosity and water storage capacity was frustrating. It seemed beyond the capability of a nonscientist. Difficulty in obtaining data led Webb

Figure 3. Donna Webb, Porites, drawing for ceramic tile mural (© 2011, D. Webb. Used with permission.)

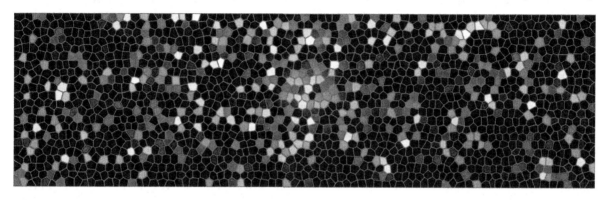

to a discussion with geologist, Ira Sasowsky, who said that he looks directly at rocks, and that his labs are full of rock samples. Looking at the rock samples allows Webb to use direct observation to gather information. Webb recognizes these rocks as being like still lifes or landscapes depending on the application of scale. Her goal is to create visualizations of otherwise invisible underground water supplies. She examines samples of porous rock, such as sandstone, which often holds water underground. Using imaging software she distills the topography and skin of these 'landscapes' into a pixilated network of color and shape (Figure 3).

She combines images of porous rock with images of ceramic tile maps she has made of the Cuyahoga River Valley and the Ohio Canal System that run through Akron. Using a computer imaging system to simplify the information helps provide an abstract grasp of the structural features. The simplification and abstraction serves a practical application in her work by providing a structure realized in ceramic tiles (Figure 4).

Webb is following in the footsteps of artists who, since the 1960's, have developed various strategies to engage the viewer with the natural world. Sometimes these were bleak, barren or

Figure 4. Donna Webb, Cross Sections of Geologic Strata, computer image (© 2011, D. Webb. Used with permission.)

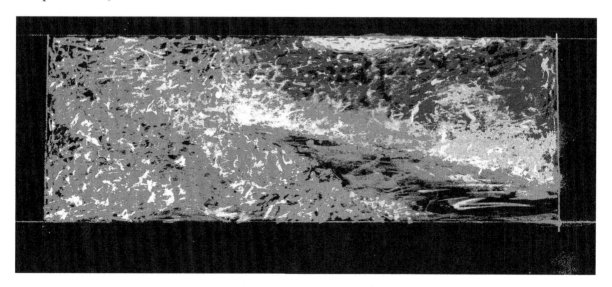

remote sites such as Robert Smithson's *Spiral Jetty*, Patricia Johanson's "wet lands and brooks paved over, fenced off, channelized and used as a dumping ground" (Kelley, 2006), or Roni Horn's frozen waters of Iceland in the *Library of Water*. These artists provide their audience with a view of these otherwise inaccessible waters.

Webb's goal can also be extended to include, as in the words of Lucy Lippard about the achievement of eco-artist, Patricia Johanson, "Most importantly, the interconnection she establishes between the ground and the image are visual reflections of ecological principles" (Kelly, 2006). Webb wants to establish a connection in the viewer between the ground (water) and the image so that the invisible water becomes assessable through the image. This can be the beginning of a learning process. "There is no getting around the fact that an abstractive grasp of structural features is the very basis of perception and the beginning of all cognition" (Arnheim, 1997).

According to Beacon Journal Art and Architecture Critic, Dorothy Shinn, "Among the aspects of Akron's history is the one-time existence of a match factory and Akron's geographical location at a continental divide, where water runs south to the Mississippi basin on one side and north to the Great Lakes basin on the other. Webb's work,

Fire and Water expounds on the subject in both *content and medium*" (Shinn 2011).

Body, Voice, and Ocean: Biological Processes Visualized through Interactive Technologies

Media artist Eunsu Kang creates water-like spaces that interact with the participants, who formerly were in the audience passively observing artworks, but now become active members of the creative process. The participants are immersed in the interactive space and enjoy a conversation with the space through their bodily movements as if they were swimming in the water (Figure 5). Such fluidity is achieved by several digital technologies including computational sound generation, spatial sound movement, interactive audiovisual projection, and computationally generated visuals using fluid algorithms and particle systems. Kang's frequent use of water sound and video input enhances the illusion of fluid space.

Fluidity is the key in Kang's works to create an experience that is not invasive or oppressive but open and intuitive. That space where anyone can dive in and interact is a language for which Kang has searched throughout her artworks. It began with her ongoing interest in the creation of

Figure 5. Eunsu Kang, Membranes (Invisible Walls), interactive audiovisual space (© 2011, E. Kang. http://vimeo.com/26902851. Used with permission.)

Figure 6. Eunsu Kang, Struldbrugg, single channel video (© 2002, E. Kang. http://vimeo.com/26906691. Used with permission.)

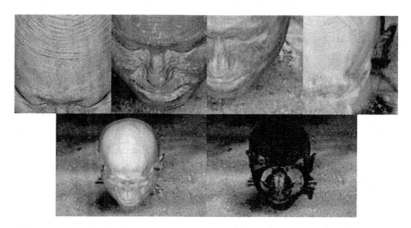

a new language for the "aliens" who are shunned from their society and do not have audible "voices" or sometimes visible "faces" allowing them to express and transmit their existence to the others. How do the "aliens" speak? What kind of language can be created for them to erase the invisible, but strong boundaries? These inquires have been explored in various ways, including in her videos created with medical data.

One such example, Kang's (2002) project *Struldbrugg* (Figure 6), is a single channel video that was inspired by the character from Gulliver's Travels. *Struldbrugg* is an interpretation of an immortal human kind that becomes old and frail as time goes on, yet does not die (Swift, 1927). Through the generations their population becomes scarce and they lose their connection with their "normal" family and friends, as well as their language and culture. Their cultural isolation and deteriorating bodies cause them to transform into "invisible" citizens. This project presents one such *Struldbrugg* as a symbolic creature without a body but with a head that slowly becomes transparent as it straddles the line between two worlds. The gradual transformation happens almost below the conscious threshold, appearing frozen until an imperceptible wind blows the sand on the ground. To create this effect, Kang used a 3D volumetric visualization (Schroeder, 2006) of medical data through Computer Tomography (CT). The head was created from medical data that allowed her to visualize the gradual decay of layers of skin, muscle and bone structures of one head. It was modeled and manipulated with medical 3D volumetric modeling software, Vworks (CyberMed, 2002).

In a subsequent work, Kang (2004) used a Magnetic Resonance Image (MRI) of her own

Figure 7. Eunsu Kang, Siren III, single channel video (© 2005, E. Kang. http://vimeo.com/26905620. Used with permission.)

head and a digital recording of her voice to create the Siren III project (Figure 7). Sirens, the sea nymphs of Greek mythology, are known to have beautiful voices that lure sailors to their doom. Kang interpreted this story from a new point of view: what if the Sirens were not singing with malice in their hearts, but due to language differences, their intent was misunderstood? Taken further, what if they had no voice, but only a body with which to communicate? To illustrate this, Kang created a 3D volumetric model of her head using Vworks and then imported the image to the Maya 3D imaging software (Autodesk, 2004). Each node of the polygon model corresponds to the waveform of her pre-recorded voice. As a result, her head distorts as if it is liquefying and expresses her "voice" with no sound.

Later Kang creates audiovisual spaces that intuitively interact with the participant's body. With the advent of new media technologies and its osmosis through our lives and society, our body transforms into a cyborg; "a cybernetic organism, a hybrid of machine and organism, a creature of social reality as well as a creature of fiction" (Haraway, 1991). Like how the cyborg wades through the realms of both the cyber and organic worlds, the participant connects himself or herself to the interactive space in Kang's recent project *Shin'm* (Kang, 2009, Figure 8). Spatial movement of water sound and video projections create a perceptive experience of swimming in an "ocean." This "ocean" and the body interact and reshape each other.

As the participant dives into this space, bubble images as well as the water sound in the space

Figure 8. Eunsu Kang, Shin'm, interactive audiovisual space (© 2009, E. Kang. http://kangeunsu.com/ shinm. Used with permission.)

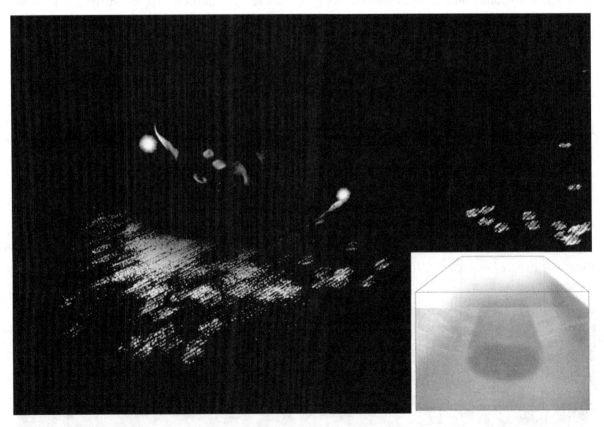

follow their movements. Their movements may provoke the bubbles and change them into a swirling body. The participant's body, sound, and lights dance, draw, and transform themselves together. Bubble images, which were originally an image of a nebula, vortex form of body in the video projection, and water sound that spatially follows the participant collaboratively enhance the participants' illusion of them swimming in the *Shin'm* space as if they are splashing invisible water.

The Gaps between: Biological Structures Reconsidered through Entropy and Digital Translation

In painting, how structure is formed and perceived has become as important as what we observe. The material that we choose to build with, the lens through which we observe, or the application is the content of modern painting. Ever since Cézanne began to pixelate the topography of Mont Sainte Victoire (Cezanne, 1885-87), the content of the image was not the observed object, but rather the very tenuous and fluctuating nature of observation itself. Cézanne's interest was not in the details, but rather in the phenomena of color, light and form. The image is broken down into consistent dashes of color laid next to each other in a loose grid format. The image is held together in a fragile composition by each mark. His goal was not to depict the mountain, but to capture in the image the fact that fixation was unattainable. For Cezanne, change was the constant.

The biologist, computer scientist, and artist are linked together by the proposition that if you change the means for observation you will have a greater understanding or appreciation of the world. For a painter the difference is that there is a value given to the elusive quality of this observation. The difficulty and gap in understanding structure provides a strong metaphor for describing emotional and psychological spaces. As Maurice Merleau-Ponty (1964) wrote, "Cézanne introduced doubt in the act of observation as the subject for art."

The means that artists visualize this relationship between material, nature, and human perception ranges from careful construction to the use of chance operations and processes beyond the control of the hand.

In this century, computer generated images provide us with factual accounts predicated on a system of logic. We tend to believe in these images without question. For a painter, the computer is a tool that facilitates limitless possibilities for definition. The digital information of the computer offers a means for examining greater complexity of both the microscopic and macroscopic worlds. But it does not erase the vital quality of painting which is to examine those moments where gaps in understanding exist between those observed or those experienced.

The substance of water offers a means to challenge this digitally defined structure and provides a strong metaphor for change and adaptation. Water is a medium that erodes an image or landscape as much as it facilitates its definition. What was once farmland can suddenly become a navigable lake. A picture can be wiped away, appear atmospheric or solid depending on how water is manipulated. Water will subscribe to the boundaries defined by design or nature, but it will just as easily flood or redefine those constraints and uses. Erosion and entropy are forces through which water redefines the landscape or the perceived image.

Matthew Kolodziej's paintings use references to architectural structures to project a sense of dislocation, which is a central theme in his work. These acrylic paintings are a fusion of forms generated by digitally constructed architectural fragments and the processes formed by water. Making the work and looking at the work are processes of negotiating logical and geological descriptions.

Kolodziej's process begins with documenting construction and demolition sites with photographs. Using the computer, he collages multiple conflicting points of view. The states of transition, dilapidation and rejuvenation, evident in

Figure 9. Matthew Kolodziej, Good Neighbors, acrylic and ink on canvas, 108" x 144" (© 2009, M. Kolodziej. Used with permission.)

the texture, physical structure, color, and light of this architecture provide a composite image that is the foundation for his painting.

In the example shown here, the process of making the painting Good Neighbors, 2009 (Figure 9) uses a filter in the program "Illustrator" to translate the collage of photographic fragments into a technical line drawing (Figure 10). This is, in practice, a map of the site. By changing the variables on the computer, he is able to find multiple readymade descriptions of the same image. This describes a map that is simultaneously a record of disintegration and formation. These drawings are projected onto canvas and traced. The successive layers of maps are offset or shifted in scale to develop a labyrinth of line. The projected images of temporary molds, scaffolding, and debris form a network of intertwined structures. The recon-

structed images of the site present a space that alternates between a tenuous and fragile façade and a believable illusion of stability. Much like a biological system of circulation or digestion, the paintings depict a maze of complexity, but one that has an inherent formal logic in how each part relates to the next.

Kolodziej's project engages how this factual information appears and is redefined when it is undermined by processes beyond human control. Water provides the catalyst for this doubt in the image. In recent work like *Good Neighbors*, Kolodziej traces over the projected drawings with thick gel medium to develop a raised surface. The drawing is essentially made into a topographical relief map. Kolodziej then lays the painting on the ground and pours liquid paint between the lines. Water moves the paint through the canals

Figure 10. Matthew Kolodziej, Illustrator file for Good Neighbors. (© 2009, M. Kolodziej. Used with permission.)

and corridors of the heightened surface. Small concentrations of paint make the image transparent, while increased pigment alters the viscosity and opacity.

Gravity is a force affecting both the geological and biological systems. Using the fluid paint to define the original collected information forces a deterioration of the foundation image. The image becomes a record of both the digital composite and the fusion of paint rippling through and bubbling over a network of lines. Cracks mimic lines. Paint yields to or overflows from the banks of the raised drawing. There is a constant dialogue between the fixed structure chosen from the photographs and the editing and decomposing of that structure in the medium of paint. Kolodziej sees the structure of architecture affected by time and entropy as being analogous to the process of evolution and the transfer of genetic material. The final effect is a solid cast, or enduring fossil, of the original structures, but defined paradoxically with artificial color and material. Plastic paint replaces the organic line. The viewer tries to decipher what is the original image and that which is distorted by the liquid.

In the 1960's and 1970's artists such as Robert Smithson worked with the earth and environment to explore the relationships between culturally and naturally constructed structures. In the sculpture, *Spiral Jetty* (1970), water took a central role in defining structure. The sculpture located on the shore of the Great Salt Lake in Utah is a 1500' long spiral composed of mud, salt crystals, basalt rocks, earth, and water. Over time, the rising and falling waters of the lake reveal and conceal the piece.

In an interview with Pa Norvell (Smithson & Jack, 1969) Smithson said: "There is no escape from matter. There is no escape from the physical nor is there any escape from the mind. The two are in a constant collision course. One might say that my work is like an artistic disaster. It is a quiet catastrophe of mind and matter." In the same vein as Smithson, Kolodziej's paintings blur interpretations of what is designed and what is a function of entropy. Meaning in this context comes not from accuracy and completeness of information, but rather from the gaps in data and in the ambiguity of interpretation.

We experience paintings both visually and with senses of touch. The digital contribution to painting is both in the complexity it so easily affords and in the ability to take this information and distill it quickly. A painting slows this process of understanding by forcing the viewer to look at the paint drying and the layers of touch and time implicated on the surface. The residues of both evaporation and fragmentary information are fused forming a space to consider how structure is constantly in flux.

In the process of observation and experimentation, a vital aspect of discovery is the moments when what is observed is disrupted, morphed, or reconstituted. In Kolodziej's paintings (Kolodziej, 2011), these transitions are depictions of several states of being, either juxtaposed or superimposed upon one another. Relationships of scale, amount of information, and the quality of information shift over the surface of the image. This means of visualization at the intersection of the natural world of water and the artificial construct of digital information provide a place to examine perception itself.

CONCLUSION

Software designers are increasingly aware of the need to develop a new paradigm for design. How do intuition and trial-and-error inform design?

Simply designing a program to perform a certain function is different from a program that allows for failure and response to be an integral part of the software platform. Information is central to biological, digital, and painterly systems. Organisms transfer DNA, digital means provide a way of developing infinitely complex networks, and art uses the five senses to translate material into expression. Research and understanding depends on examining not only patterns, but also the gaps in information and the nature of transformation processes. The work reported here introduces examples of how such explorations are informed by the intersection of digital, biological, and artistic languages.

Consider how an artist and a computer scientist collaborated to produce a visualization of the distribution of radioactive contaminants that have infiltrated the groundwater beneath a site formally dedicated to the production of nuclear materials for weapons (Fernald). Seeking new methods for visualizing the unseen so that people can be more aware of important phenomena, the landscape scale of the graphics and juxtaposition of a menacing glow beneath aerial images of the Fernald site also beg questions that bring biology back into the mix. For example, radionuclides can persist in the environment for very long times, even thousands of years. How does one represent the potential biologic effects on such time scales from snapshots of data that map distributions over just tens of years? Laramée has proposed a way to visualize this contamination in an expanded format that explores biological consequences and ramifications, and that is not just a distribution of concentrations, but rather is a "deep map" of change over time, taking into consideration climate change. Presumably, solutions to these kinds of questions might lead to a heightened awareness of the true environmental and health costs of activities (nuclear weapons production) that we know little about, even though they have profound implications on our lives and last over many generations. This sort of interdisciplinary collaboration helps us create and understand those new visualizations.

There is a long history of art inspired by science, beginning with Leonardo, if not before. Private, government and corporate sponsorship of art-science collaborations are known to result in innovation, as proven by the Bell Labs sponsored residencies, Experiments in Art and Technology (E.A.T.) in the 1960's, Xerox Parc in the 1990's, and for decades at the San Francisco Exploratorium. However, artists' access to technological tools, software, and personnel with specialized skill sets, as well as to revenue streams that fund the sciences is an ongoing challenge. Can innovative think-tank initiatives involving art-science collaborations that directly involve communities impacted over time emerge in the future to support art research over a period of years, similar to the research model found in the sciences? Such limitations mean that these opportunities are too few and far between, as most sponsors, including academia, expect to know the concrete results of collaboration for accountability and outcomes assessment purposes before the creative experimentation fully gestates and comes to fruition. Great ideas get put on hold indefinitely as most institutions fail to create interdisciplinary structures to support and nurture necessary periods of time for collaborative teams to work side-by-side in studio and laboratory situations.

Biology can also frame the way artists use new media technologies to explore reaction to and communication about the natural world. In this case, collaboration gives us access to art that helps viewers understand and interact with biological themes like species interactions, dependencies, and system properties. Whether the computer scientist and artist create a simulated 'ecosystem' with species that live, grow, and die based on random encounters that are a source of nutrition, or build an interactive interface that blends light and sound inputs into dance and movement that invite participation of viewers, the results motivate questions about human sensory modalities and perception.

Traditional arts such as ceramics and painting afford an understanding of biological systems simply from their affinity as a material. Both are often compared to flesh and skin. Both are dependent on structure, gravity, and chemistry to work conceptually and visually. The importance of the computer in this context is how the digital can afford a way of either distilling or developing complexity in visualization. How can the perception of the artist meld with that of scientific exploration through the technology of the computer. How can the computer be used as a tool to not simply show the accuracy of information, but to allow for a visualization that shows the gaps and the fallibility of systems as a motivator and strength of innovative learning and thinking? In the big picture, the sustainment of life is in adaptability and anomalies, as well as in function and clarity of design.

The most important resource for sustaining life is water. The main effort of this chapter is to explore ways to visualize water. Water's colorless and shapeless character enables artists to render it in any color and any shape, and lures artists to put their creativity and imagination to full use. In "Invisible Fire," Laramée and Thokala presented underground water with an unlikely candidate: "fire." The "fire" was artistically depicted based on scientific measurement data. It reveals the severity of underground water pollution and makes us feel the urgency of protecting our most precious resource from pollution. Water not only sustains life, but its shapelessness allows it to move in ways that enable it to overcome invisible boundaries as shown in Kang's interactive spaces where participants can "reshape" the imaginary water-filled space. Water is powerful and it can find paths in anything, including rocks. By observing rocks (some of them porous), Webb drew inspiration on how to create images in ceramics to help viewers to perceive water that is out of sight. Water can be destructive too. As Kolodziej pointed out, water can erode landscapes as well as paintings. But if properly guided, water can help us to irrigate and to create entropy-driven art, as demonstrated by Kolodziej. Water, a resource of ultimate importance to us, needs to be protected and properly used.

ACKNOWLEDGMENT

The authors would like to thank the reviewers for their valuable suggestions on improving the quality of this chapter and Jason Xiao for serving as an independent proofreader of the manuscript.

The current and past members of the Synapse Group at the University of Akron: Matthew Kolodziej, Peter Niewiarowski, Joseph Schubauer, William Lyons, John Roloff, Eve Andrée Laramée, Donna Webb, Eunsu Kang, Judit Puskas, Jessica Hopkins, Jean Marie Hartmann, Yingcai Xiao, Kalyan Chakravarthy Thokala, Elisa Gargarella, Francisco (Paco) Moore.

REFERENCES

Arnheim, R. (1997). *Visual thinking*. Berkeley, CA: University of California Press.

Autodesk. (2004). *Maya*. Retrieved April 17, 2011, from http://usa.autodesk.com/maya/

Brugge, D., Benally, T., & Yazzie-Lewis, E. (Eds.). (2006). *The Navajo people and uranium mining*. Albuquerque, NM: University of New Mexico Press.

Calouste Gulbenkian Foundation. (2011). Retrieved July 18, 2011, from http://www.gulbenkian.org.uk/

Center for Disease Control. (2000). *Fernald risk assessment project*. Atlanta, GA: National Center for Environmental Health. Retrieved August 28, 2011, from http://www.cdc.gov/nceh/radiation/fernald/default.htm

Cézanne, P. (1885-87). *Mont Sainte Victoire*. Oil on canvas. Courtauld Institute of Art, London, England. Retrieved August 28, 2011, from http://www.ibiblio.org/wm/paint/auth/cezanne/st-victoire/1885/

Cleveland Sculpture Center. (2011). Retrieved July 18, 2011 from http://www.sculpturecenter.org/

Cochran, R. D. (2009). Eve Andrée Laramée. *Sculpture Magazine, 28*(9).

CyberMed. (2002). *Medical software: Vworks*. Retrieved August 28, 2011, from http://www.cybermed.co.kr/e_pro_dental_vworks.html

Dalton, R. J. (1999). *Critical masses: Citizens, nuclear weapons production, and environmental destruction in the United States and Russia*. Cambridge, MA: MIT Press.

Ede, S. (2005). *Art & Science*. London, UK: I. B. Tauris. Retrieved August 5, 2011, from http://books.google.com/books?id=iiE3RsvK248C

Eichstaedt, P. (1994). *If you poison us: Uranium and native Americans*. Santa Fe, NM: Red Crane Books.

Google. (2011). *Google Earth*. Retrieved April 15, 2011, from http://www.google.com/earth/index.html

Graf, W. (1994). *Plutonium and the Rio Grande: Environmental change and contamination in the nuclear age*. New York, NY: Oxford University Press.

Haraway, D. J. (1991). *Simians, cyborgs, and women: The reinvention of nature*. New York, NY: Routledge. Retrieved August 5, 2011, from http://books.google.com/books?id=ejHWRgAACAAJ

Hayes, J. (2010). *Japanese pottery and lacquerware*. Retrieved August 5, 2011, from http://factsanddetails.com/japan.php?itemid=693&catid=20&subcatid=129jtt

Heon, L. S., Ackerman, J., & Massachusetts Museum of Contemporary Art. (2000). *Unnatural science: An exhibition, spring 2000 - spring 2001, MASS MoCA.* New York, NY: Te Neues Publishing Company. Retrieved August 5, 2011, from http://books.google.com/books?id=H7PpAAAAMAAJ

Hevly, B. W., & Findlay, J. M. (1998). *The atomic west.* University of Washington Press. Retrieved August 5, 2011, from http://books.google.com/books?id=ugdHhzX3Fl8C

Johnston, B. R., & School for Advanced Research. (2007). *Half-lives and half-truths: Confronting the radioactive legacies of the cold war.* School for Advanced Research Press. Retrieved August 5, 2011, from http://books.google.com/books?id=ReAeAQAAIAAJ

Kang, E. (2002). *Struldbrugg.* Retrieved August 28, 2011, from http://vimeo.com/26906691

Kang, E. (2004). *Siren III.* Retrieved April 15, 2011, from http://kangeunsu.com/siren3/

Kang, E. (2009). *Shin'm.* Retrieved April 15, 2011, from http://kangeunsu.com/shinm/index.htm

Kang, E. (2011). *Membranes.* Retrieved August 28, 2011, http://vimeo.com/26902851.

Kelley, C. (2006). *Art and survival: Patricia Johanson's environmental projects.* BC, Canada: Islands Institute.

Kelley, C., & Johanson, P. (2006). *Art and survival: Patricia Johanson's environmental projects.* Islands Institute. Retrieved August 5, 2011, from http://books.google.com/books?id=ghDqAAAAMAAJ

Kolodziej, M. (2011). *Matthew Kolodziej - Home.* Retrieved August 5, 2011, from http://www.mattpaint.com

Kuletz, V. (1998). *The tainted desert: Environmental ruin in the American west.* New York, NY: Routledge.

Laramée, E. A. (2009). *Halfway to invisible.* New York, NY: Emory University. Retrieved August 28, 2011, from http://evelaramee.com/

Laramée, E. A. & MIT List Visual Arts Center. (1999). *A permutational unfolding: Eve Andrée Laramée: MIT List Visual Arts Center, Cambridge (Mass.), 23.4.-27.6.1999.* MIT List Visual Arts Center. Retrieved August 5, 2011, from http://books.google.com/books?id=6AHVSAAACAAJ

Lippard, L. R., Smith, S., & Revkin, A. Boulder Museum of Contemporary Art, & EcoArts. (2007). *Weather report: Art and climate change.* Boulder Museum of Contemporary Arts. Retrieved August 5, 2011, from http://books.google.com/books?id=p6JOGgAACAAJ

Makhijani, A., Hu, H., & Yih, K. (2000). *Nuclear wastelands: A global guide to nuclear weapons production and its health and environmental effects.* MIT Press. Retrieved August 5, 2011, from http://books.google.com/books?id=0oa1vikB3KwC

Mann, R. (2003). Yellowcake towns: Uranium mining communities in the American west. *The Journal of American History, 90*(3), 1082-1083. Boulder, CO: University Press of Colorado. doi:10.2307/3661002

Masco, J. (2006). *The nuclear borderlands: The Manhattan project in post-cold war New Mexico.* Princeton, NJ: Princeton University Press.

Merleau-Ponty, M. (1964). *Sense and non-sense* (Dreyfus, H. L., & Dreyfus, P. A., Trans.). Northwestern University Press.

Mogren, E. W. (2002). *Warm sands: Uranium mill tailings policy in the atomic west.* University of New Mexico Press. Retrieved August 5, 2011, from http://books.google.com/books?id=S3LbAAAAMAAJ

Office of Legacy Management. (n.d.). *Department of energy geospatial environmental mapping system.* Retrieved April 1, 2011, from http://gems.lm.doe.gov/imf/ext/gems/jsp/launch.jsp?verify=true

OpenGL. (2011). Retrieved April 15, 2011, from http://www.opengl.org

Rainey, C. (2008). *One hundred miles from home: Nuclear contamination in the communities of the Ohio river valley: Mound, Paducah, Piketon, Fernald, Maxey Flats, and Jefferson proving ground.* Cincinnati, OH: Little Miami Press.

Reynolds, A. (1999). *Histories of science, histories of art.* Austin, TX: Austin Museum of Art.

Rhodes, R. (1986). *The making of the atomic bomb.* Simon & Schuster. Retrieved August 5, 2011, from http://books.google.com/books?id=aSgFMMNQ6G4C

Schroeder, W. (2006). *The visualization toolkit: An object-oriented approach to 3D graphics.* Clifton Park, NY: Kitware.

Shanken, E. A. (2009). *Art and electronic media.* Phaidon Press. Retrieved August 5, 2011, from http://books.google.com/books?id=qXpTAAAACAAJ

Shinn, D. (2011, June 19). Summit ArtSpace showcases books as art. *Akron Beacon Journal,* p.1.

Shuey, C. (1992). *Contaminant loading on the Puerco river: A historical overview.* Albuquerque, NM: Southwest Research and Information Center.

Smithson, R. (1979). *Fragments of an Interview with Robert Smithson by P.A. Norvell, collected writings* (p. 194). New York, NY: New York University Press.

Smithson, R., & Jack, D. F. (1996). *Robert Smithson, the collected writings.* Berkeley, CA: University of California Press.

Swift, J. (1726). *Gulliver's travels.* Retrieved April 17, 2011, from http://publicliterature.org/books/gullivers_travels/1

Synapse. (2005). Retrieved April 15, 2011, from http://www2.uakron.edu/phn/synapse.html

Times, N. Y. (2009, August). Toxic waters. *New York Times.*

Vance, C. (2011). Japan earthquake a reminder about importance of groundwater. *News Hawk Review, News Update.* Retrieved July 13, 2011, from http://newshawksreview.com/japan-earthquake-a-reminder-about-importance-of-groundwater-protection/42305/

Wallace, A. (2011a). *Home page.* Retrieved July 18, 2011, from http://www.amy-wallace.com/

Wallace, A. (2011b, July 9). Science to art, and vice versa. *New York Times.* Retrieved July 18, 2011, from http://www.nytimes.com/2011/07/10/business/science-to-art-and-vice-versa-prototype.html

Ware, C. (2004). *Information visualization: Perception for design.* Morgan Kaufman. Retrieved August 5, 2011, from http://books.google.com/books?id=ZmG_FiqqyqgC

Wasserman, H., & Solomon, N. (1982). *Killing our own: The disaster of America's experience with atomic radiation.* Delacorte Press. Retrieved August 5, 2011, from http://books.google.com/books?id=Km0gAQAAIAAJ

Weintraub, L. (2003). *In the making: Creative options for contemporary art.* D.A.P./Distributed Art Publishers. Retrieved August 5, 2011, from http://books.google.com/books?id=h6NPAAAAMAAJ

Weiss, P. (2004). *Wet 'n' wild: Explaining water's weirdness.* Boston University, Center for Polymer Studies. Retrieved July 13, 2011, from http://www.phschool.com/science/science_news/articles/wet_n_wild.html

Wilson, S. (2002). *Information arts: Intersections of art, science, and technology.* MIT Press. Retrieved July 13, 2011 from http://books.google.com/books?id=sHuXQtYrNPYC

ADDITIONAL READING

Cunningham, K. J., Sukop, M. C., Huang, H., Alvarez, P. F., Curran, H. A., Renken, R. A., & Dixon, J. F. (2009). Prominence of ichnologically influenced macroporosity in the karst biscayne aquifer: Stratiform "super-K" zones. *Geological Society of America Bulletin, 121,* 164–180.

Harmon, K. A. (2004). *You are here: Personal geographies and other maps of the imagination.* Princeton Architectural Press. Retrieved from http://books.google.com/books?id=Hohb0VFSl-QC

Harmon, K. A., & Clemans, G. (2009). *The map as art: Contemporary artists explore cartography.* Princeton Architectural Press. Retrieved from http://books.google.com/books?id=iJpT_EuL-7gAC

Jones, C. A., Galison, P., & Slaton, A. E. (1998). *Picturing science, producing art.* Routledge. Retrieved from http://books.google.com/books?id=j26nlIKmypkC

Kerren, A. (2008). *Information visualization: Human-centered issues and perspectives.* Springer. Retrieved from http://books.google.com/books?id=O6_fnpty330C

Moura, L., & Pereira, H. G. (2004). *Man + robots: Symbiotic art.* Institut d'Art Contemporain. Retrieved from http://books.google.com/books?id=CGT2OwAACAAJ

Salter, C., & Sellars, P. (2010). *Entangled: Technology and the transformation of performance.* MIT Press. Retrieved from http://books.google.com/books?id=ZBJbIP0fMr0C

Sandford, R. W. (2009). *Restoring the flow: Confronting the world's water woes.* Vancouver, Canada: RMB.

Schwabsky, B. (2002). *Vitamin P: New perspectives in painting.* London, UK: Phaidon.

Spence, R. (2007). *Information visualization: Design for interaction.* Pearson/Prentice Hall. Retrieved from http://books.google.com/books?id=bKQeAQAAIAAJ

Walker, J. F. (2006). *Painting the digital river: How an artist learned to love the computer.* Prentice Hall. Retrieved from http://books.google.com/books?id=oX4auslgVHEC

Wands, B. (2006). *Art of the digital age.* Thames & Hudson. Retrieved from http://books.google.com/books?id=HguVQgAACAAJ

KEY TERMS AND DEFINITIONS

Bioremediation Agent: An agent which significantly increase the rate of biodegradation to mitigate the effects of discharge.

Eco artist: One who makes art that revitalizes natural ecosystems and introduces them to urban dwellers.

Entropy: The degree of order and disorder in a system. Entropy increases as the system gradually declines into disorder.

Extremophile: an organism that thrives in physically extreme conditions.

Genotoxicity: An action capable of altering DNA, thereby causing cancer or mutation.

Grains, Textures, Porosity: Soil properties that affect groundwater.

Ground Water: Water that is out of sight, underground in the soil or in pores and crevices in rock.

Ichnology: the scientific study of fossil footprints.

New Media Art: A field encompassing art works and creative projects using and/or concerning the new media technologies and following cultural/social paradigm changes.

Radionuclide: An unstable element that radioactively decays, resulting in radiation.

Synapse: A specialized junction through which neurons send signals to each other and to non-neuronal cells.

Visceral: The suggestion through materials of a particular emotion or condition. Visually recognizing or anticipating that a surface or material will feel a certain way when touched.

Visualization: Seeing the unseen. The unseen objects or concepts are usually made visible through computer graphics.

ENDNOTE

[1] Laramée first became interested in the radioactive pollution of water resources in the American Southwest after hearing about the Church Rock Uranium Mine tailings-pond spill into the Rio Puerco River in the Four Corners region in 1979 (Shuey, 1992). In subsequent years she made numerous sculptures, installations, photographs, and works on paper dealing with the pollution of water with radioactive isotopes from uranium mining and milling, plutonium production for nuclear weapons research and development, and the production of fuel rods and storage of waste from the nuclear power industry (Graf, 1994).

Chapter 8

NanoArt:
Nanotechnology and Art

Cris Orfescu
NanoArt21, USA

ABSTRACT

This chapter is an attempt to introduce NanoArt. It goes back in time to the first uses of nanomaterials and nanotechnologies to create art and continues with the beginnings of NanoArt. Then, it follows a status on this new artistic-scientific discipline and the movement that evolved from recent technological developments in the multidisciplinary area known as nanotechnology. The chapter informs about the international juried NanoArt competitions, displays select artworks collected in the NanoArt21 gallery, and finally presents thoughts of select nanoartists and art people.

INTRODUCTION

Nature, including people, is built from nanostructures (Jones, 2008). Nanotechnology is part of the human evolution and enables people to visualize and manipulate objects that were invisible in the past. During previous centuries people applied nanotechnologies without realizing that fact. Most people are still not aware of nanotechnology although they are using nanotech products.

Over the past two decades, the ability to measure and manipulate matter at atomic and molecular scales has led to the discovery of novel materials and phenomena. These advances underlie the multidisciplinary areas known today as nanotechnology. The responsible development and application of nanotechnology could lead to create jobs and economic growth, to enhance national security, and to improve the quality of life. Some of the benefits would be cleaner manufacturing processes, stronger and lighter building materials, smaller and faster computers, and more powerful ways to detect and treat disease (The Nanotechnology Initiative Strategic Plan, 2004).

Due to the quality of images obtained by studying the nanostructures, most people perceive them as artistic objects. One of the aims of creating NanoArt is to familiarize people with the omnipresence of the nano world and raise the public awareness of the impact of nanotechnology on our lives. There are legitimate concerns about nano products from health and environmental

DOI: 10.4018/978-1-4666-0942-6.ch008

point of views, and nanotech companies should develop their products responsibly. NanoArt can be considered one of the best vehicles to promote a responsible scientific and technological development to the general public.

NanoArt is a complex artistic-scientific process that comprises three major components:

1. Creation of the nanosculpture (sculpture at atomic and molecular levels, by manipulating atoms and molecules using chemical reactions and physical processes) or discovery of the nanolandscape (natural nanostructures, including biological)

2. Visualization of the nanostructure (which is facilitated by the use of advanced microscopes) and image capture

3. Artistic interpretation of the scientific images using different artistic techniques in order to convert these images in pieces of artwork to be showcased for large audiences and to educate the public with creative images that are appealing and acceptable (Orfescu, 2011). Figure 1 shows a nanosculpture created by embedding graphite nanoparticles in a polymer cast on glass. The structure was coated with gold and visualized with a scanning electron microscope. The image was captured in a computer and printed on luster ultra premium photo paper with archival ink.

ART AND NANOMATERIALS IN PAST CENTURIES

Altamira, Spain, 13000 B.C. The man grabbed a piece of charcoal from the cave floor, put his hand on the wall, and drew its contour without knowing that he was using a nanomaterial to create a piece of artwork. He just wanted to draw his hand. He also deposited layers of graphene (which is a nanomaterial) on the cave's wall without any

Figure 1. Cris Orfescu, "NanoMaiastra – Brancusi, In Memoriam." (© 2008, C. Orfescu. Used with permission).

knowledge about nanotechnology (Museo de Altamira, 2011).

Altamira cave in Spain is famous for its Upper Paleolithic cave paintings featuring drawings and polychrome rock paintings of wild mammals and human hands (Cave of Altamira and Paleolithic Cave Art of Northern Spain, 2011). Archaeological excavations in the cave floor found rich deposits of Upper Solutrean (c. 18,500 years ago) and Lower Magdalenean (between c. 16,500 and 14,000 years ago) artifacts. These artifacts are part of the Paleolithic Age, or Old Stone Age (Grey, 2008). The artists used charcoal and ochre or hematite to create the images, often scratching or diluting pigments to produce variances in intensity and creating strong contrast between light and dark.

Scientists are continuously evaluating the age of the cave artwork. In 2008, scientists utilizing uranium-thorium dating estimate that parts of the artwork are between 25,000 to 35,000 years old (Owen, 2009). Further discoveries suggest that some of the paintings were completed over the thousands of years by successive artists, so they were not created just by individual artists in their own lifetime. Hundreds of caves with elaborate prehistoric paintings and carvings on their walls have been discovered across Europe. It is thought, the designs which often depict scenes of animals, like bison, and grazing or hunting expeditions, were created up to 40,000 years ago – sometime after humans began moving from southern Europe into northern Europe during the last ice age.

Nanotechnologies from the Past Centuries

"The History of Nano Timeline" (2011), a website published by the Northwestern University dates the beginning of the art-nanotechnology intersections to over 2000 years ago. The above findings and numerous other discoveries suggest that art-nanotechnology interactions are much older than that. Nanomaterials have been used about 2000 years ago to create art objects like the famous Lycurgus cup that resides in the British Museum in London (Freestone, Meeks, & Higgitt, 2007). The cup's glass contains gold and silver nanoparticles, which make the cup change colors from green to red when light is shone through it.

All cave artworks have something in common, namely, the drawing and painting materials (charcoal and pigments). According to Guineau Delamare and Ber Francois (2000), pigments are pure colors in powder form, which must be suspended in a medium in which they are insoluble in order to make paint. Pigments are micro and nanopowders of the size ranging from less than 0.01 to 1 micron. When converted in colloidal or in clay form by mixing with water, they are used for tinting with permanent colors. A pigment changes the color of reflected or transmitted light as the result of wavelength-selective absorption. Many materials selectively absorb certain wavelengths of light. Materials that humans have chosen and developed for use as pigments usually have special properties that make them ideal for coloring other materials. A pigment must have a high tinting strength relative to the materials it colors and must be stable in solid form at ambient temperatures (Grey, 2008). Clay-sized hematite crystals (ranging within micrometer and nanometer scales) can also occur as a secondary mineral formed by weathering processes in soil, and along with other iron oxides or oxyhydroxides such as goethite; it is responsible for the red color of many tropical, ancient, or otherwise highly weathered soils. The name hematite is derived from the Greek word for blood aima because hematite can be red, as in rouge, a powdered form of hematite (Hematite Mineral Data, 2011).

Ochre is clay that is colored by different amounts of hematite, ranging within 20% to 70% in content. Ochre, derived from naturally tinted clay containing mineral oxides, is among the earliest pigments used by mankind. Chemically, it is hydrated iron (III) oxide. Modern artists' pigments continue to use the terms "yellow ochre" and "red ochre" for specific hues. The two pieces of ochre engraved with abstract designs found in Blombos Cave in South Africa are often considered to be the world's first known art (Blake, 2008), along with shells pierced for use as jewelry and a complex toolkit including finely crafted bone tools dated to around 75,000 years ago (Edgar, 2008). Early historical records suggest the use of ochre as a pigment by numerous cultures for painting on walls or as body paint (Minerals Zone, 2011).

Figure 2 shows a nanosculpture created by drying a drop of colloidal graphite (graphite nanoparticles in a liquid suspension) in liquid nitrogen at 196 degrees Celsius bellow zero. The structure was visualized with a scanning electron microscope.

Figure 2. Cris Orfescu, "Nanographite Psychedelic Mushrooms." Print on luster ultra premium photo paper with archival ink. (© 2010, C. Orfescu. Used with permission.).

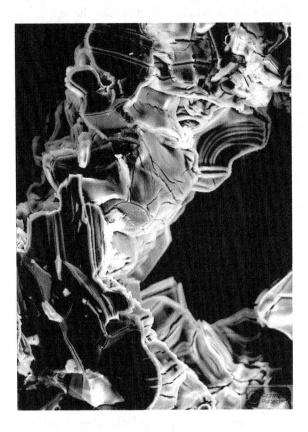

In the 10th and 11th centuries the stained glass began to flourish as an art. Glass was usually colored by adding nanoparticles of metallic oxides and metals to the glass while in a molten state. Copper oxides were added to produce green, cobalt for blue, silver for yellow, and gold for red glass. After coloring, small pieces of glass were arranged to form pictures, held together (traditionally) by strips of lead and supported by a rigid frame.

In the 15th and 16th centuries, ceramists in Deruta (in Umbria region, Italy) created metallic glazes using nanoparticles of copper and silver metal (Deruta Ceramics, 2011). Earlier Deruta ceramics do not have the lustre. The luster majolica of Gubbio owes its celebrity almost entirely to the work of Maestro Giorgio Andreoli who most probably learned the technique from a Moslem potter and developed it to perfection. Finished painted pieces were sent from other factories to receive the addition of lustre at Gubbio.

Known since ancient times, the colloidal gold was originally used as a method of staining glass. A so-called 'elixir of life', a potion made from gold was discussed, if not actually manufactured, in ancient times. In the 16th century, the alchemist Paracelsus claimed to have created a potion called 'aurum potabile' (Latin: potable gold). In the 17th century Andreus Cassius and Johann Kunchel refined the glass-coloring process. In 1842, John Herschel invented a photographic process called chrysotype (from the Greek word for gold) that used colloidal gold to record images on paper. Herschel's system involved coating paper with ferric citrate, exposing it to the sun in contact with an etching used as mask, then developing the print with a chloroaurate solution. This did not provide continuous-tone photographs. The modern chemist, photographer, and photography historian Mike Ware (2011, 1994) has experimented on re-inventing of the process giving more subtle tones.

The scientific evaluation of colloidal gold did not begin until Michael Faraday's work in the 1850s. Faraday prepared the first metallic colloids in 1856. The Royal Institution of Great Britain (2011) houses now the entire set (over 600) of specimens. Colloidal gold, also known as "nanogold" is a suspension (or colloid) of sub-micrometer-sized particles of gold in a fluid, usually water. The liquid has usually either an intense red color (for particles less than 100 nanometers) or a dirty yellowish color (for larger particles). The nanoparticles themselves can come in a variety of shapes. Spheres, rods, and cubes are some of the more frequently observed ones. Due to the unique optical, electronic, and molecular recognition of properties of the gold nanoparticles, they are the subject of substantial research, with applications in a wide variety of areas, including medicine, electronics, nanotechnology, and the synthesis of novel materials with unique properties.

Photography, another example of using nanotechnology to create art, is defined as the process, activity, and art of creating still or moving pictures by recording radiation on a sensitive medium, such as a photographic film, or an electronic sensor (Spencer, 1973). Light patterns reflected or emitted from objects activate a sensitive chemical or electronic sensor during a timed exposure, usually through a photographic lens in a device known as a camera that also stores the resulting information chemically or electronically. The photographic film is a transparent cellulose acetate base coated with a thin layer of gelatin containing silver halides. The light decomposes the silver halides, producing nanoparticles of silver, which are the pixels of the photographic image (History of Nano Timeline, 2011, Discover Nano).

NANO ART: THE BEGINNINGS

There are numerous sources that mention the art–nanotechnology intersections from early times of the human history. When did nano art come into the picture? In my opinion, once the electron microscope became commercially available we could talk about the first nano art works. Even though the scientists who were imaging those small structures apparently didn't have any artistic intention, they created images that could be considered artworks.

One of the first nano artists in the history, probably without his intention to create art was George Emil Palade (1912 – 2008), a Romanian cell biologist. Described as "the most influential cell biologist ever" (Hopkins, 2008), he was awarded in 1974 the Nobel Prize in Physiology and Medicine (2011), together with Albert Claude and Christian de Duve, for innovations in electron microscopy and discoveries concerning the structural and functional organization of the cell that laid the foundations of modern molecular

cell biology; the most notable discovery being the ribosomes of the endoplasmic reticulum – which Palade first described in 1955. The George E. Palade Electron Microscopy Slide Collection (2011) of electron microscopy images at Harvey Cushing/John Hay Whitney Medical Library, Yale University, derived from high-resolution images scanned by James D. Jamieson is freely available to students and scientists worldwide.

The collection of images includes some of the earliest electron micrographs taken by the collaborators of George Palade both at the Rockefeller University (1945-1973) and at Yale (1973-1990), such as micrographs taken by Marilyn Farquhar (the glomerular basement membrane in renal filtration), Maya and Nicolae Simeonescu (capillary endothelium), James Jamieson (secretory pathway in the exocrine pancreas; atrial granules), Lucien Caro (electron microscopic autoradiography), Philip Siekevitz, John Bergeron and Japoco Meldolesi (microsomes, Golgi fractions), and Sanford Palay (synapses) among others. All these scientists, consciously or not, created valuable scientific imagery, and in the same time they pioneered in a new discipline, nano art.

MODERN NANO ART

Modern nano art is created intentionally by individual scientists who deliver artworks, artists with interest in science, and teams of scientists and artists. The micro and nano worlds bring forth aesthetically sound imagery. A multitude of scientists manipulate the scientific imagery they capture and create artworks. In the words of Liz Else (2011) from the New Scientist, "while science is about understanding the complexity of the structure of the material world, art indicates the deeper implications of scientific advancement and helps shape new paradigms. In this sense, art is not only close to science but it is complementary, and even necessary. Thus the scientific eye is able to penetrate the smallest sub-atomic particle,

Figure 3. Jan Schmoranzer, "Starved Fibroblasts 1. (© 2008, J. Schmoranzer. Used with permission.).

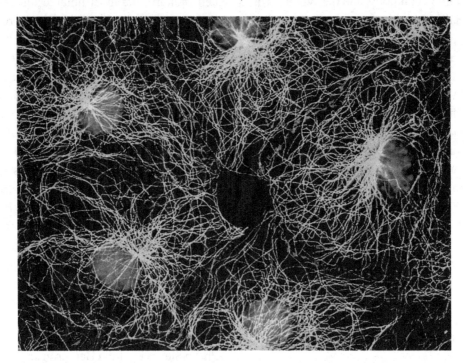

which moves perpetually creating energy waves and makes one realize that the structure of matter consists of emptiness. The artistic eye can see in that void, in that fluid "emptiness," a seed for a new vision of the world." Figure 3 shows digital multi-color immuno-fluorescence microscopy of fibroblast cells in culture stained with various antibodies: green – microtubuli, red – cell-cell contacts, and blue – DNA.

The depth and three dimensions achieved in nano art sets this process of electron imaging apart from photography where images are created by photons (particles of light) rather than by electrons (electrically charged particles) as in nano art. The electrons penetrate deeper inside the structures, generating images with more depth, more natural 3D-look than the photographic images. Therefore, in my opinion, nano art could become for the 21st Century what photography was for the 20th Century.

NanoArt21: New Venues to Display Nano Art

Showcasing the nano art works is one of the challenges that nano artists have to deal with. The author is the founder of the NanoArt21 Online Gallery and the annual NanoArt International Online Competitions and Exhibitions that are dedicated to NanoArt as an artistic expression of nanotechnology (NanoArt21, 2011). The competitions are juried by both scientists and artists, and best entries are hosted by nanoart21.org (2011). The mission is to promote worldwide the NanoArt as a reflection of the technological movement and to raise the public awareness of nanotechnology through art. It would be very difficult and non-productive to show the nanosculptures directly on the electron microscope to a large number of people in the same time, so artists have to find ways to show their nano art works. Some artists alter the scientific images using traditional painting or sculpture, animation, digital painting and manipulation, digital drawing, fractals, digital collage, colorized electron micrographs, and paper collage. Other artists are using video, installations, and multimedia to bring the NanoArt works to the public at large. Web exhibitions of NanoArt included pioneers such as Donald Eigler, Anastasios John Hart, Jack Mason, Tim Fonseca, Robert A. Freitas Jr., Joe Lertola, to name only a few who started producing works in the early 1990s and some of them even earlier.

The author creates NanoArt works from early 1980s and participates in numerous group and personal exhibitions all over the world. He prefers to use digital painting, manipulation, and multimedia to display artworks. Figure 4 presents a nanosculpture created by embedding graphite microparticles in a polymer matrix. The structure was visualized with a scanning electron micro-

Figure 4. Cris Orfescu, "Quantum Tunneling." Print on canvas with archival ink. (© 2010, C. Orfescu. Used with permission).

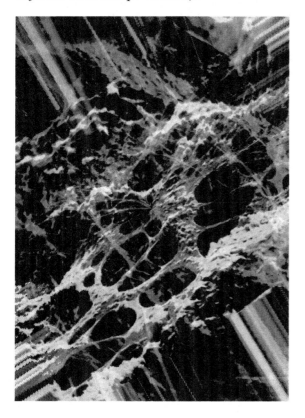

scope and captured in a computer where the image was digital painted and manipulated.

NanoArt has been exhibited in many venues all over the world. In the last few years there was an abundance of online competitions hosted by universities and organizations, such as the "NANO" 2003 show at Los Angeles County Museum of Art followed by a publication by Victoria Vesna and James Gimzewski (2011), and "Nanomandala," the 2004 and 2005 installations in New York and Rome by Victoria Vesna and James Gimzewski. The brick-and-mortar gallery shows produced worldwide by the NanoArt21 organization include the 1st International Festival of NanoArt in Finland, 2007, and the 2nd International NanoArt Festival (2008) in Stuttgart, Germany, as well as NanoArt21 exhibitions like the one hosted by the 2009 EuroNanoForum in Prague, Czech Republic or the one in San Sebastian, Spain hosted by the Passion for Knowledge Festival in 2010.

Selected Statements about the NanoArt

Below is a series of thoughts by artists and art people that show the level of interest in nano art as a new discipline and the extent of the NanoArt movement.

Chris Robinson (2011), Art Professor at the University of South Carolina, senior and co-principal investigator on NSF funded research, says, "We have the privilege of watching this fascinating science develop and can assist in providing information about its meaning, assets, and liabilities. But we should be careful to make sure that we provide accurate information and inform rather than confuse and deter public understanding."

Jeanne Brasile, curator of the Eye Tricks Show at Walsh Gallery at Seton Hall University, New Jersey, USA (Orfescu, 2007) says, "I've always been interested in producing interdisciplinary exhibitions that question the role of art, as well

Figure 5. Cris Robinson, "NeurFor+" Digital drawing - 3D neural network model. (© 2011, C. Robison. Used with permission)

as break down barriers between what I deem to be artificial separations between design, craft, high-art, low-art, etc… I think that art, science and technology are quite symbiotic. Think back to ancient Greece or the Renaissance – there wasn't this artificial separation of art and science. Artists use art as the vehicle to enact scientific principles, while others incorporate technology into the creation of their work… I don't believe that NanoArt should be relegated to only shows of NanoArt. There is validity to this work aesthetically, artistically and conceptually and one would hope NanoArt begins to gain acceptance in more galleries. I think it is very important that NanoArt is being displayed alongside art of all media… I believe that as nanotechnology becomes more of a household word, people will become aware of NanoArt as well. The public is very interested in the imagery displayed…they become fascinated by the concept…It functions on aesthetic and conceptual levels."

Jack Mason (Orfescu, 2008c), a NanoArt pioneer, introduces his "pixels as atoms" concept.

His work is based on the quantum wells of electrons spinning in an array of quantum dots: "The Nanographs I produce are developed with layers of images and structures from nanoscience and nanotechnology. Just as nanotechnology is about finer control over the order or structure at the scale of atoms and molecules, my 'pixels as atoms' approach seeks to both create new visual materials out of the building blocks of pixels … and the quantum surprise of using digital tools. I would like to see artists working in different media including video, sculpture, and 3D and collaborate with us to extend the dimension of NanoArt in new directions. For my own work, which I call Nanotechno, the definition I've gravitated toward is 'envisioning the invisible.' The realm of atoms and molecules is so tiny that it really is invisible in the optical or photographic sense … As a genre or subject matter, art about or inspired by nanotechnology will likely produce the deep, dramatic breakthroughs in energy, medicine, and materials that have been touted. By definition, any way of imaging things at the nanoscale is

Figure 6. Frances Geesin, "Cell Group." A sculpture inspired by nanostructures that can exhibit complex electronic properties. (© 2010, Frances Geesin. Used with permission).

inherently not photographic ... things at the scale of atoms and molecules are smaller than the wavelength of light, so they are too small to be seen via traditional optical means, even with the most powerful magnification. In this sense, the source materials for NanoArt are inherently digital, the results of measuring things like the atomic force of atoms and molecules, or their magnetic fields ... I certainly hope that art might be a way to interest young people in the creative aspect of scientific careers."

Paolo Manzelli (Orfescu, 2008b), Director of LRE/EGO-CreaNet, Firenze, Italy, says, "We know that with the nanotechnology, science understanding picked up new interest in the epistemology of forms. On the other hand, contemporary computer art allows new graphic representation and visual aids in terms of original making structures as a pre-vision in a non-observable dimension… Referring to the phenomenon in which the quantum states of two or more objects have to be described with reference to each other, even though the individual objects may be spatially separated,

Manzelli states: "the entanglement between science and art, working in a trans-disciplinary profile of nanotechnology manufacturing will furnish new areas of complementary research and an innovative professionalism in science and art that can be able to recover the ancient creative tradition of Florentine Renaissance, historically mediated by a unitary cooperation between Art, Science, and Technology."

Tereza Majerus (2011), Luxembourg, winner of the 1st place at the NanoArt 2007 International Online Competition, is describing her winning artwork: "Rather than use the nanoflower seed image provided by NanoArt21 as a basis for the further electronic manipulation, I decided to use it as inspiration for an acrylic painting on canvas. The painted canvas shows a view of the nanoworld from the particle perspective. We can clearly recognize the eye of the scientist looking via microscope onto the complex structure. The model of the atom plays here the role of an engine."

Hugh McGrory (Orfescu, 2008a) says, "I'm interested in the nanoworld because I'm human

Figure 7. Tereza Majerus, "Eye of Science," acrylic painting inspired by "Nanoflower" nanosculpture by Cris Orfescu. (© 2010, Tereza Majerus. Used with permission).

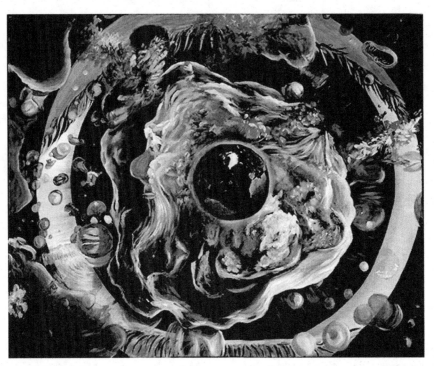

and curious. The scientists I have worked with could see the science in what I did and I could see the art in their processes. At Yale, for instance, the scientists described the process of finding 'The Happy Cell' – the cell chosen specifically from hundreds or thousands to be used for imaging. This is a key decision since an 'unhappy' cell will not necessarily 'perform' under the microscope and can lead to wasted hours in the lab. It's similar to a nano beauty contest, the cell is defined as happy from how it looks, how it moves, what kind of shape it has, etc. The scientist uses an artistic eye for this. It is about feeling, gut, and instinct … What needs to be stressed is that NanoArt is examining an area that will define the 21st Century, an area that will grow exponentially and change the way we think about the world. The images created in science labs (taken at the nanoscale) are NanoArt if they are presented as art … My artistic process involves working with technology to create images. I use the same basic tools as an imaging scientist … The process is as interesting as the work, probably more interesting in fact, since I meet people who are passionate and inspiring, people who are awake to the possibilities that emerging technologies can offer, and tools, which require a steep technical learning curve for their operation."

CONCLUSION

NanoArt is the expression of the new technological revolution and reflects the transition from science to art using technology. A new artistic movement was born at the beginning of the 21st Century where sciences, technologies, and arts interact generating a multidisciplinary form of art. We can talk now about an artistic–scientific creative process instead of two separate processes, scientific and artistic. More and more artists are moving towards new technologies which offer them added flexibility and power to express their thoughts and feelings in a timely manner. These technologies are real time savers and offer unlimited opportunities for creativity. In the same time, scientists are becoming more interested in art. Let's not forget that both, science and art have a big common ground, both are creative processes.

REFERENCES

Blake, E. (2008). Letter from South Africa: Home of the modern mind. *Archeology, 61*(2). Retrieved August 8, 2011, from http://www.archaeology.org/0803/abstracts/letter.html

Cave of Altamira and Paleolithic Cave Art of Northern Spain. (2011). Retrieved August 8, 2011, from http://whc.unesco.org/en/list/310

Delamare, G., & Francois, B. (2000). *Colors: The story of dyes and pigments*. Harry N. Abrams.

Deruta Ceramics. (2011). *That's Arte.com: Fine Italian ceramics*. Retrieved August 8, 2011, from http://www.thatsarte.com/region/Deruta

Else, L. (2011, 15 March). What art can do for science (and vice versa). *New Scientist*. Retrieved March 11, 2011, from http://www.newscientist.com/blogs/culturelab/2011/03/where-science-and-art-collide.html

Freestone, I., Meeks, N., Sax, M., & Higgitt, C. (2007). The Lycurgus Cup – A Roman nanotechnology. *Gold Bulletin, 40*(4), 270-277. Retrieved August 8, 2011, from http://www.goldbulletin.org/assets/file/goldbulletin/downloads/Lycurgus_4_40.pdf

George, E. Palade EM Slide Collection. (2011). *Harvey Cushing/John Hay Whitney Medical Library*. Retrieved March 9, 2011, from http://cushing.med.yale.edu/gsdl/cgi-bin/library?p=about&c=palade

Grey, R. (2008, 5 October). Prehistoric cave paintings took up to 20,000 years to complete. *The Telegraph*. Retrieved August 8, 2011, from http://www.telegraph.co.uk/earth/3352850/Prehistoric-cave-paintings-took-up-to-20000-years-to-complete.html

Hematite Mineral Data. (2011). *Mineralogy database*. Retrieved August 8, 2011, from http://webmineral.com/data/Hematite.shtml

History of Nano Timeline. (2011). *Discover nano*. Northwestern University. Retrieved August 8, 2011, from http://www.discovernano.northwestern.edu/whatis/History/#

Hopkins, C. (2008, 22 October). Prof George Palade: Nobel prize-winner whose work laid foundations for modern molecular cell biology. *The Independent: Obituaries*. Retrieved August 8, 2011, from http://www.independent.co.uk/news/obituaries/prof-george-palade-nobel-prizewinner-whose-work-laid-the-foundations-for-modern-molecular-cell-biology-968560.html

Jones, R. (2008). *Nano nature*. New York, NY: Metro Books.

Majerus, T. (2011). *Eye of science*. Retrieved August 9, 2011, from http://nanoart21.org/nanoart-exhibitions/index.php.

Minerals Zone. (2011). *Industrial minerals, ochre*. Retrieved August 8, 2011, from http://www.mineralszone.com/minerals/ochre.html

Museo de Altamira. (2011). Retrieved July 3, 2011, from http://museodealtamira.mcu.es/ingles/index.html

NanoArt21. (2011). *Art/science/technology*. Retrieved August 8, 2011, from http://www.nanoart21.org/

NanoArt Festival, Stuttgart, Germany. (2008). Retrieved August 8, 2011, from http://nanoart-festival-stuttgart.blogspot.com/

Orfescu, C. (2007, November 27). NanoArt at the eye tricks show at Walsh Gallery – Interview with Jeanne Brasile. *Nanotechnology Now*. Retrieved August 9, 2011, from http://www.nanotech-now.com/columns/?article=138

Orfescu, C. (2008a, November 27). NanoArt pioneers - Interview with Hugh McGrory. *Nanotechnology Now*. Retrieved August 7, 2011, from http://www.nanotech-now.com/columns/?article=222

Orfescu, C. (2008b, February 8). NanoArt and nanotechnology - New frontiers. Nanotechnology Now. Retrieved August 9, 2011, from http://www.nanotech-now.com/columns/?article=169

Orfescu, C. (2008c, January 7). NanoArt pioneers - Interview with Jack Mason. *Nanotechnology Now*. Retrieved August 9, 2011, from http://www.nanotech-now.com/columns/?article=153. Also, http://www.nanotechno.biz

Orfescu, C. (2011). *NanoArt: Art/science/technology*. Retrieved August 8, 2011, from http://nanoart21.org/html/nanoart.html

Owen, E. (2009, March 14). After Altamira, all is decadence. *The Times*. Retrieved July 3, 2011, from http://www.timesonline.co.uk/tol/travel/specials/artistic_spain/article5904206.ece

Robinson, C. (2011). *NanoArt21 exhibitions*. Retrieved July 31, 2011, from http://nanoart21.org/nanoart-exhibitions/index.php

Royal Institution of Great Britain. (2011). Retrieved August 8, 2011, from http://www.rigb.org/registrationControl?action=home

Spencer, D. A. (1973). *The Focal dictionary of photographic technologies*. Focal Press.

The Nanoscale Science, Engineering, and Technology Subcommittee. (2004). *National nanotechnology initiative strategic plan*. Retrieved September 28, 2011, from http://www.nsf.gov/crssprgm/nano/reports/sp_report_nset_final.pdf

The Nobel Prize in Physiology or Medicine. (1974). Retrieved September 28, 2011, from http://www.nobelprize.org/nobel_prizes/medicine/laureates/1974/

Vesna, V., & Gimzewski, J. (2011). *At the intersection of art and science: NANO*. Los Angeles County Museum of Art. Retrieved August 8, 2011, from http://nano.arts.ucla.edu/files/nano_lacma_book.pdf

Ware, M. (1994). Photographic printing in colloidal gold. *The Journal of Photographic Science*, *42*(5), 157–161.

Ware. M. (2011). *Alternative photography*. Retrieved August 8, 2011, from http://www.alternativephotography.com/artists/mike_ware.html

KEY TERMS AND DEFINITIONS

Atom: A basic unit of matter that consists of a dense, central nucleus surrounded by a cloud of negatively charged electrons and other subatomic particles

Colloids: Nanoparticles suspended in a liquid

Electron: A subatomic particle with a negative elementary electric charge. It has no known components or substructure; in other words, it is generally thought to be an elementary particle.

Electron microscope: A type of microscope that uses a particle beam of electrons to illuminate the specimen and produce a magnified image. Electron microscopes (EM) have a greater resolving power than a light-powered optical microscope, because electrons have wavelengths about 100,000 times shorter than visible light (carried by photons), and can achieve better than 50 picometers resolution and magnifications of up to about 10,000,000x, whereas ordinary, non-confocal light microscopes are limited by diffraction to about 200 nanometers resolution and useful magnifications below 2000x.

Graphene: One-atom-thick planar sheets of carbon atoms that are densely packed in a honeycomb crystal lattice

Micrometer: One millionths of a meter

Molecule: An electrically neutral group of at least two atoms held together by covalent chemical bonds.

NanoArt: New art discipline at the art-science-technology intersection. It features nanolandscapes (molecular and atomic landscapes, which are natural structures of matter at molecular and atomic scales) and nanosculptures (structures created by scientists and artists by manipulating matter at molecular and atomic scales using chemical and physical processes). These structures are visualized with research tools like scanning electron microscopes and atomic force microscopes and their scientific images are captured and further processed by using different artistic techniques to convert them into artworks showcased for large audiences.

Nanomaterials: Materials composed of nanostructures

Nanometer: One billionths of a meter (approximately 80,000 times smaller than human hair diameter)

Nanolandscapes: Atomic and molecular landscapes that occur naturally (without being modified by people)

Nanoparticles: Particles with size bellow 100 nanometers

Nanosculptures: Sculptures at atomic and molecular levels, by manipulating atoms and molecules using chemical reactions and physical processes

Nanostructures: Structures composed of particles with size bellow 100 nanometers

Nanotechnology: A combination of technologies facilitating the manipulation of matter at atomic and molecular scales

Photon: An elementary particle, the quantum of the electromagnetic interaction and the basic unit of light and all other forms of electromagnetic radiation.

Scanning Electron Microscope: (SEM): A type of electron microscope that images a sample by scanning it with a high-energy beam of electrons in a raster scan pattern. The electrons interact with the atoms that make up the sample producing signals that contain information about the sample's surface topography, composition, and other properties.

Chapter 9
Nature Related Computerkunst

Wolfgang Schneider
Computerkunst/Computer Art, Germany

ABSTRACT

It has been generally accepted in art history that nature ranks as master and ideal of the arts. Everybody knows examples of nature-related artworks created over centuries and decades in a conventional manner. Most of the contemporary readers witnessed the invention of the computer as a tool used in natural sciences, and later, in the arts as well. As a natural scientist and curator of art exhibitions, the author of this chapter was continually involved in this contemporary development which raised a fundamental question: Would the computer as a tool be a means to generate new representations of nature related art? This would demand results that ought to be different from conventional works of art as to the conceptional creation processes as well as the output. Some theoretical backgrounds and categorizing of such creations are discussed in this chapter and then illustrated by several examples from artists participating in a series of 'Computerkunst/Computer Art' exhibitions during the quarter of the last centuries (1986-2010). Though it might be too soon to judge computational art works concerning their importance in Art History, a closer investigation in the creational processes and social contexts seems helpful and worthwhile.

INTRODUCTION

'Natura est via in naturam'

- Thomas Aquinas

Nature related art will doubtlessly be estimated as old as art itself. In history there are countless examples of this understanding starting from the cave images of early mankind, witnessing Leonardo da Vinci`s scientific and artistic works, and art works still spreading in a broad diversity of representations in modern times. In overviewing this development, we have to state that all of those examples were 'handmade' products in form of sketches, drawings, paintings, models, sculptures, etc. All of them were made of real world materials, as paper, wood, metal and others. The invention of the computer in the last century as a result of the developments in science and technology, especially mathematics and applied physics turned out to cause a radical change. No longer graphic or pictorial creations had a life in the so called real

DOI: 10.4018/978-1-4666-0942-6.ch009

world alone but could also exist parallel or even solely in a virtual state. Additionally this means that the replacement of accustomed production tools of art by computer, monitor, keyboard, and mouse must lead to a change of the mechanisms in the creative processes as such and its public and individual reception.

Any creation of artistic works demands ideas, experience, and means, though each of these aspects may weigh differently to carry them out. Concerning those fundamentals there can not be any difference between conventional and electronic art generation. So it was of growing interest and importance for me to observe the different approaches of scientists and artists towards the kind of electronic art works they presented to the public in a row of Computer Art exhibitions I curated over the years in Germany since 1986.

Use of the Computer for the Arts and the Author's Classification

Digital or computer art has grown multifaceted. Which basic tools and materials did scientists and artists use for the purpose of creating artistic works? Generally we can discern different 'inputs' and 'outputs' concerning computational art. With the evolution of software and growth of computational capacity it became easier and steadily more affordable for each user to handle commercial machines and peripheral gears. So I propose to define one category of computer art as creations achieved by using commercial painting and picture processing programs; in such cases there are no pre-existing samples, the artist only uses the given possibilities of 'free hand' drawing or painting, with different means of output. A subcategory can be recognized in works that use transformation and processing of existing samples, e.g. in form of digitized photographs, graphics or paintings as input. These procedures are based on the timely developed algorithms, the available software, and the peripheral gears concerning input and output

as well. In the following text I will refer to some examples presented on exhibitons.

A second and different category of computational art we can identify in the algorithmic procedures that scientists and artists develop themselves following their own intentions and purposes. A main partition of this category encompasses the group of the 'Algorists' who almost exclusively have been using plotters as graphical output gears. Another algorithm-based mathematical method is the performance of cellular automata for artistic and/or scientific generation of works.

We can discern the third category of electronic art works, clearly distinguishable from the above mentioned, which is generated as nature-related art. Applications emerge with growing intensity from the convergence of digital and scientifical, especially biological investigations, and fuel the possible impetus for artistic concideration and examination.

Many art works can be attributed to one of the sketched categories, others will be perceived as mixtures of these and sometimes additional techniques. Because of the enormous span of these fields I have to confine myself and leave out here other branches of computer based art like video (and video-installation), AI, game art, net art and others.

ELECTRONIC ART: APPROACHING AND EXTENDING NATURE

There are many different ways to generate art that in a broad sense is based or related to nature and natural sciences. Since it is the spirit that unifies art and science, which originates in human being, and which communicates to human being (Alcopley, 1994), the representations of the human and all relations of his/her physical or spiritual background have been permanent constituents of art. So it is only consistent that a great deal of computer generated art works, beside biologic connexions in general, encounters with the human body and human environment.

Some years ago the Gesellschaft für Elektronische Kunst (Electronic Art Society) presented an exhibition of electronic art based on biologic backgrounds to a broad public in Dortmund, Germany (Digit@l körper, 2002). For this I surveyed and selected artworks that had been on show up to then in the biennial series of 'Computerkunst/ Computer Art' organized over the years since 1986 by this society and the Gladbeck authorities. Main motivation was to encounter with the changes in conceptions and expressions of artworks they have undergone from the traditional to the evolving electronic manner of creation.

What happened to the conventional art topic of portrait when turning electronic? A portrait of Konrad Zuse, inventor of the computer may serve as an example of art that use transformation and processing of existing samples. This print is the result of a transfer of a photographic or painted picture by scanning and further processing by means of a commercial paint program. The portrait no longer tries to give a real picture of the person Zuse but instead only a resemblance of the face translucently changed and set onto a blue mysterious mathematical background by computational methods, indirectly made possible by the inventor himself.

A very important question that arose with the development of computer technologies was and still is the maintenance of individuality of the human being. In a world of numbers and barcodes some people felt more and more uneasy about the future state of possibly just being a countable thing instead of a human of flesh, blood and soul. Artists as the sensors in our society very soon saw this sensible challenge and found adequate expressions by means of electronically produced pictures. Elga Morgenstern-Hübner from Essen, Germany presented a graphic example at the "Computerkunst in Deutschland 1987" exposition in Cologne and Langenhagen (Blobel, 1987). The print was titled "Erkennbarer Prozess" – another

example of category one. In six steps it shows a continuous appearance of a barcode and fading of the artists individual face - a challenge of individuality.

A further example of the first category aims at the perception of man's individual appearance through the computer. What happens if my counterfeit or that of other person are cascading the pixelled pathway through scan, hard disc, programs in the PC, and the printer/plotter? In search of this question Gerd Struwe (1988) investigated positions in works like 'Ich am/im Rechner' (Me at/in the computer) he presented to the Computerkunst '88 exhibition in Gladbeck and seven further venues in Germany. "By detaching the human body shapes from narrative or spacial contexts" in a first step "I want to question conventional imaginations of visual realities as to body, space and time connections", he states (Struwe, 1988, p. 102, translation by the author). His new approach aims at a more complex, multiperspective and simultaneous sight of the human. Once caught in the lattice of pixelled existence, the individual may be outlined then in many possible ways and changed in its expressions, even to total disappearence. Corinne Whitaker (2000) caring for the latter illustrated and commented the loss of human existence in her work "The Vanishing Human."

The jury of 'Computerkunst '90' awarded an outstanding work of art consisting of a series of 34 graphics and an animation (video) with the same title 'Auflösung' (Dissolution). The author and prize winner of the Gladbeck Golden Plotter Award in 1990 was Iran born Shahin Charmi who lived and worked in Kiel, Germany (Charmi, 1990). Starting from a scan of one of his own painted self-portraits he zooms gradually into his face focusing almost on the eye's lightspot. Final point is a nearly empty square holding only parts of recognizable rectangles of no further detectible meaning (Figure 1).

In this procedure, to zoom is equal to changing position and standpoint making aware that the difference between realistic and abstract art is just

Figure 1. Shahin Charmi: Auflösung, series of 34 B&W Prints (excerpt). (© 1988, Collection of Museum der Stadt Gladbeck. Used with permission.).

a question of perspective. In a very dense and precise art work Charmi herewith shows parallels to the development of modern art from the renaissance to the twentieth century. The individual is bound to disappear the nearer you try to get to it. But this is only one aspect of this important work. Charmi followed his socially inspired path by making obvious how easily people and events can be manipulated by media for political or social motivations. His body of works contains many other examples of this kind.

NATURE AND HUMANS IN ALGORITHMIC PROGRAMMING

The following examples of nature based art illustrate the algorithmic procedures of creation. Conceptions of this include the generation of shapes or faces, a task demanding programming skills but opening new (in)sights or ways of interpretation.

In Hans Dehlinger's plotted human shapes, general starting point is the definition of dot and line by means of algorithmic programming. The generative drawings of human shapes in his works evolve out of filling and/or omitting spacial regions on the given surface where the borders of the shapes may be defined 'from outside or within' mutually (Figure 2). An interesting experience is introduced by this experimental programming method of 'clipping' (Dehlinger, 1981). This leads us to phenomenological aspects of a double existence of the body. The borders of the human shape in the pictures remind us that we are external beings as well as internal ones. Simultaneously our body is an external being that can be experienced from outside and an internal being that experiences the outside world (Becker, 2000).

Software developed by the artist became his pool of countless shape variations, the 'genotype' as Roman Verostko (1988/2003) used to call it in his paper on 'Epigenetic Painting.' Verostko's

Figure 2. Hans Dehlinger: Figures 3. Silksprint from pen-plotter-drawing, 50 x 70 cm. (© 1990, H. Dehlinger. Used with permission)

Figure 3. Michael Badura, Nadel 12, Needle print on endless paper, about 350 cm high. (©1984, Michael Badura. Used with permisssion.).

'Cyber Flowers' are examples of bio-related plotted art works. Dehlinger (2004) and Verostko belong to the group of 'Algorists' mentioned above. Using the biological terms 'genotype' and 'phenotypes' for this kind of mathematically defined art they make clear that their way of creation may serve as a representation of a natural process, the 'genotype' standing for the 'invisible,' a hidden universe of possible creations, and different 'phenotypes' for it's visible outputs.

In later years, Gerd Struwe developed 'Automatic Drawers' – self developed programs that continuously draw scenes and persons appearing and fading, communicating and departing - parallel or time shifted - an ongoing computerized reflexion of daily life. The output of mathematical art generation in this case is animated graphics to be watched on the monitor screen or as beamed projection.

GENETICS AND PROGRAMMING

Over the last years the growth of knowledge and possibilities in natural sciences and arts have made it possible for scientists and artists to generate genetic interactions on the real and computational level. Will there evolve a conversion of mathematical and genetic data programming in the future? A state of art that Stephen Wilson (1989) illustrated in his provocative vision 'Carbon and Silicon playing a game of skill.' In establishing a 'genetic code' the artists have learned to produce more or less well defined cells, faces and bodies following their mutual imagination and their mutual purposes. Not in a real manner like Eduardo Kac's luminescent bunny but still only existing on monitors and graphic paper, they use the electronic media to add to the discussion in this growing field of contemporary challenges.

Gerd Struwe (2011) ran the Institute of Biogenic Art, the aim of which was to deal with the development of postevolutionary biogenetic aesthetics. The power to generate and manipulate figurative, especially human forms of expression is an important step in Struwe's artistic career. The new defined aesthetics can only be reached by first abandoning the determination of imaginations we know of form and beauty given by evolution. Struwe's institute wants to transfer purposeless aesthetics into the biologic sphere. In a second step it demands models and concepts of behavior free of restrictions in life existence, which the institute investigates by means of new biological entities, determined genetically. Defined are three levels of algortihmic developments: 'Monopersonal Entity' (mpe), 'Microsocial Entity' (mse), and 'Postevolutionary Portrait Design' (pep). While the first level, with the design of his organs, skeletons, and sensors is still comparable to the evolutionary human, the second emerges out of at least two monopersonal gene pools and may be designed mono- or multi-sexual. Further, they may be equipped with two or even more brains configuring a novel organic complex. In the most advanced development, the institute offers at a third level the postevolutionary design of the body and especially the head because the latter is estimated the most important aesthetical aspect and operational center (details in: Struwe, 2011 and Catalog 2000, pp.15 ff.).

One of precursors of environmental art in Germany is Michael Badura who created and exhibited in conventional manner pictures, drawings, and installations emphasizing the challenges and threats to natural resources including men. Then he experimented with and discovered the possibilities of a computer and printer. In spite of the restricted capabilities of the early affordable machines like C 64 or Amiga, the artist found a way to convey messages concerning the attitude of men towards nature and living creatures. In 1984/6, after some experimental work in programming and printing pixelled creations of nature and men, he presented a series of prints he called 'wood of needle leaves' (Nadelwald) carried out in shapes of towers, leaves and blades by a needle printer on endless paper about three and a half meter high (Badura, 2011). Probably for the first time an artwork results from the direct analysis of the possibilities of the computer and needle printer, more convincing than other attempts resulting in conventionally looking paintings or graphics. Medium and message coincide here consistently. Badura took up this topic again in 2005 in a second generation of generative plants and beings, calling it a 'digital herbarium'. Going on with pixelled animations of 'cloned fighters' the artist tried to get down to the scientific developments of cell cloning in animal reproduction.

The next step to create human clones by means of algorithmic programs was only consequential during the eighties and later on, when we were confronted with 'Adam and Eve' (1984/5), 'men made to measure' (1990/2) or 'homo genes' (1991). The latter may be traced back from the above mentioned shapes of needle leaves to new forms that were taking over the tops or whole shapes of human beings in endless variations. The artist seemed to play with his once discovered mathematical possibilities of sound, strange, or even curious figurations approaching, or better questioning the scientists' positions of taking over a role of god somehow. Badura (2002) was awarded the Golden Plotter Prize with Computerkunst/ Computer Art 2.002 in recognition of his merits in his early and continual search for computational expressions of urging contemporary problems. In his works 'Klon PAP 1-3' (Clone PAP 1-3 – Figure 4) we are confronted with heads of humans open mouthed and staring into space. The scull being an excavated hole and the skin a freckled surface in red and yellow. In the subtitle 'In Erwartung des Feuers' (In expectation of the fire, 2002) we may find some hints at further interpretation of these algorithmically developed clones of men. The next step into the third dimension of mathematically created representations of natural beings or artificial creatures done by Michael Badura is the algorithmic programming of his modules that has been expanded into the 3D output by means of rapid prototyping technique.

Figure 4. Michael Badura, Klon PAP 1 (In Erwartung des Feuers), Color Print. (© 2001. Collection of Museum der Stadt Gladbeck. Used with permission.).

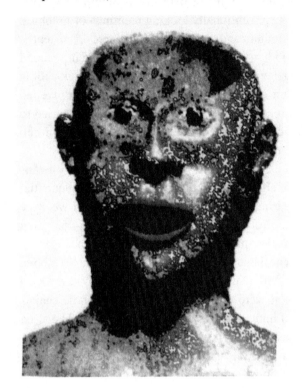

ART USING SCIENTIFIC DATA

An example of this kind of artistic transformation or the aesthetical interpretation of scientific data can be discovered in the works of Thorbjorn Lausten from Denmark. The artist used geomag-

netic measurements, meteorologic or solar wind data in colaboration with scientific stations in Norway, the geostationary satellite Meteosat, and the so called 'Soho' (Solar and Heliospheric Observatory). The visualizations in projects and exhibitions like 'Magnet' or 'Datablik' (Lausten, 2008) were intended to open eyes for a meaning of such data beyond mere illustration of science. The artist points out that the data do exist freely and universally and must not be considered to only have an inevitable or unequivocal meaning. Collected by scientists they are supposed to serve one special purpose, but since they are not independent of a medium they also may be used to produce other forms of information or interpretation, performed through artistic processes.

For several years Ingrid Hermentin has been creating art works that consider the topic of individuality and human identity. In her project of the years 2006 to 2008 called 'Transcriptions_decoded' (Hermentin, 2010) she aimed at assigning the identity of a human being by means of a restricted genetic investigation. She combined individual genetic fingerprints transformed into sound parameters, physiognomic projections on acrylic glass (5 pieces, 84 x 84 cm each) and transcription of the DNA information superimposed on the pictures (Figure 5).

In a first step the artist used the determination of genetic structure of individuals by their unique DNA profiles (genetic fingerprints) and con-

Figure 5. Ingrid Hermentin: Transkriptionen_dechiffriert, 2007. Inkjet prints on acrylic glass and mp3-players (exhibition sight). (© 2007, Ingrid Hermentin. Used with permission.).

 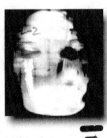 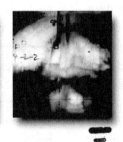 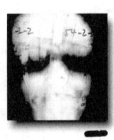 

verted these genetic informaton into musical parameters such as frequency, tone height, and tone length. She made transcriptions of the dinucleotide sequence of the DNA and translations of the trinucleotide (codon) sequence of the DNA into a 13 accord music to achieve this. The profiles of these DNA investigations were collected from five volunteering female individuals by cooperating with genome scientists and firms. Secondly she created two-dimensional black and white portraits of the individuals as physiognomic projections of the candidates including herself. The pictures were carried out on foils between acrylic glass. In a third step further small sets of individual DNA informations were superimposed on the mutual shapes as short literal notes. The artist's aim of the project was to combine the genetic identity - defined via the genetic fingerprint and the musical domain - defined via acoustics, and thus to create a novel measure of human

personality and identity that is perceivable in a form of common human reception and understanding.

Another field of artists` interest is the search for understanding how the human brain and its cells function. Ray Kurzweil (1999) predicted that with the growth of computational power and miniaturization of chips the scanned brain will show its complex connections of information units. We would just need to upload these data onto a computer and then would be able to prolong our lives by programming them. Following his earlier commitments in cellular automata simulations, as in 'Screen Heads' (1993) and `Match-id (#1- #9, 1993), where he unrolled the history of human life and races, Georg Mühleck, Germany/Canada (1999) creates now prints and 'live' pictures of the congruent growth and decay of cells in our brain (Figure 6). They are products of an intensive and ongoing cooperation between the artist and the

Figure 6. Georg Mühleck: sTEAmulus_pond_subculture4. Color Print. (© 2010, Georg Mühleck. Used with permission.).

microbiology scientist Sylvia Niebrügge (2010) using embryonic stem cells of mice enriched with simulations of cellular automata. Their project 'Cell-Cell' is an experimental cooperation in cell culture and artificial life technology. The authors investigate possibilities of combining two (still) separate systems, one derived from real life consisting of organic cultures and the other one generated in the computer as cell simulations. Will there be realisations of such metasystems in the future? Would we as responsible contemporary humans even want to have the power to do so?

CONCLUSION

In this overview I could examine only a few examples of nature related art works presented at the Computerkunst/Computer Art exhibitions that united artists from Germany, Europe, and Overseas. Many of these participated as well in comparable events like NY Digital Salon, Prix Ars Electronica, etc. None of these venues may claim they represent the topic in a holistic sense. I am convinced that art works exhibited at Computerkunst/Computer Art may stand for a broad variety of methods used in electronic art generation and thus may be considered a substantial part of the general developments in respective times.

Keeping this in mind we may return to the introductory question of artists' approaches to creating electronically works inspired by nature or natural sciences. We can ascertain that in comparison to conventional understanding computers evoked other and new conceptions of topics such as nature, human and society. Examples of a traditional theme such as a portrait reveal the changes where multilayering and time shifting may be realised in one representation, accompanying signs and metaphors creating an intrinsic entity. In the run of time we could witness the development from a single print to outputs in serial pictures and moving pictures (animation), meeting the habits of modern onlookers. When

contemporary philosophical thinkers derive a necessity of new mental orientation in a global and telematic world, we cannot avoid reconsidering our understanding of body and personality. Art works like „Auflösung" (Dissolution) by Shahin Charmi and other ones introduced here opened a door in this very direction.

There are art works that reveal the creative capability of the computer as a tool and which could not have been represented by conventional means (Dehlinger, Verostko, Badura). The computer behind these works helped to explore and visually experiment with forms that were hidden before. Dehlinger (2004) calls such forms the examples of a second universe beside the conventional one, the universe of machine generated drawings, a universe in its own right. Epigenetic painting and creations of artificial environments by L-systems have comparable backgrounds in the developments of algorithmic computing. The early works of generative art turn out to be roots and predecessors of the developments that in recent time are still expanding in terms of artificial life, agent algorithms, self organization, and artifial societies.

While natural sciences aim at adequate representations of objective reality on the one hand and the methods and tools they use were getting more sophisticated and scholarly but less understandable in a common sense on the other hand, the demand for a perception by means of an artistic approach is steadily growing. Following the intention to enlighten what is going on in our societies when scientific research in genetics and algorithmic optimization methods open a field of hardly predictible results in e.g. reproduction, medicine, or artificial limb design, we need indicators and – even more important – imaginations of processes happening and possible outcomes thereof. Who else but artists may help to better 'see' developments and future states while conditions of environments have been rapidly changing over the last years? This is what we partially are confronted with when looking at the representations of nature related Computer Art, not only revealing a superficial beauty but also giving hints to messages behind the aesthetics.

Biologically based art works, which I tried to introduce with a few examples, clearly show a means of 'translation' of natural processes and of investigation results in the natural sciences.

The conceptions and processes of their creation may range as art works of their own, widening our perception of the world and making visible the hidden rules of nature. Experimental and investigational approaches, as well as new forms of output spread and communicated via modern media surely may help to address and reach a broader audience directly or indirectly.

Electronic art uses true outcrops of natural sciences and nature-related laws in the form of mathematical algorithms to create analogous nature-related art, a procedure that may enlighten the self-reflective saying of Thomas Aquinas above. In this sense art opens a sight on nature as a steadily renewing entity out of it's own potential, the rules of which we try to understand.

REFERENCES

Alcopley, L. (1994). Art, science and human being. *Leonardo, 27*(3), 183. doi:10.2307/1576049

Badura, M. (2002). *Computerkunst/Computer Art 2.002 catalog,* (pp. 22–25). ISBN 3–923815–40–9

Badura, M. (2011). *Badura Museum.* Retrieved July 1, 2011, from http://www.baduramuseum.de/

Becker, B. (2000). Cyborgs, agents, and transhumanists. *Leonardo, 33*(5), 363.

Blobel, W. (Ed.). (1987). *Computerkunst in Deutschland.* Munich, Germany: Barke-Verlag.

Charmi, S. (1990). *Computerkunst '90 catalog.* Gladbeck.

Dehlinger, H. E. (1981). Bildnerische Experimente mit der geplotteten Linie . In Bauer, H., Dehlinger, H. E., & Mathias, G. (Eds.), *Design Kunst Computer –Computer in den künstlerischen Bereichen* (pp. 81, 84, 85–87). Kassel, Germany: Jenior & Pressler.

Dehlinger. (2004). *SIGGRAPH'04 catalog.* Digit@lkörper. (2002). Exhibition with Hobbytronic, Dortmund. In *Computer Art Faszination,* (p. 316).

Hermentin, I. (2010). *Transcriptions decoded. Computerkunst/Computer Art 2.010 catalog.* Gladbeck.

Kurzweil, R. (1999). *The age of spiritual machines: When computers exceed human intelligence.* New York, NY: Viking Adult.

Lausten, T. (2008). Datablik. *Computerkunst/ Computer Art 2.008 Catalog.* ISBN 3-923815-44-1.

Niebrügge, S. (2010). *Computerkunst/Computer art 2.010 catalog.* Gladbeck.

Struwe, G. (1988). *Computerkunst '88 catalog.* Gladbeck.

Struwe, G. (2011). *Bio gen art.* Retrieved July 1, 2011, from http://www.biogenart.de

Verostko, R. (1988). Epigenetic painting - Software as genotype. *Leonardo, 23*(1), 17–23. Retrieved July 1, 2011 doi:10.2307/1578459

Whitaker, C. (2000). The vanishing human. *Leonardo, 33*(5), 438–438. doi:10.1162/leon.2000.33.5.438b

Wilson, S. (1989). Carbon and silicon playing a game of skill. *Leonardo, 22,* 1.

Section 3
Scientific Communication through Visual Language

Chapter 10
Biological Translation:
Virtual Code, Form, and Interactivity

Collin Hover
University of Texas at Arlington, USA

ABSTRACT

This chapter explores the use of code, form, and interactivity in translating biological objects into mathematically generated digital environments. The existence of a mathematical language contained in all physical objects that is similar in function to DNA in organisms is proposed as a core component and driving force of this exploration. Relative to current education tactics, using code, form, and interactivity as a set of common lexicons creates an increasingly universal method, to explore, understand, and teach this hidden biological language by re-writing its algorithms in ways we may readily recognize and absorb. Two case studies of the designer's own work, (a) Clouds & Ichor, and (b) Stream, will be used to demonstrate and ground the concepts being discussed. In both projects, a natural learning experience is at the core of the biological process.

INTRODUCTION

Strange Behavior

If I told you that I had a material, one made expressly for the purpose of play and, dare I say it, magic, and that had a mind of its own and could not be hurt, you might think me odd. Perhaps it will bring to mind the fictional liquid metal T-1000 character from Terminator 2, or an imagined combination of the material with the metal. If I then gave you this material within the bounds of

a room, your first action would likely be to touch it, and your second to physically set up a forceful meeting between the material and the walls of that space. I would not think this strange at all, and in fact this is the point. Not, specifically, to slam this material into walls (though it would be fun), but rather to play with a digital material informed by properties of amoebic organisms and liquid, that exists in an environment created to promote agency. Agency, as explained so well by Beeker Northam, executive strategy director for creative communications agency Denstu London, may be "the ability to control and affect your own and your shared environment in the face of com-

DOI: 10.4018/978-1-4666-0942-6.ch010

Figure 1. Clouds & Ichor, located at http://www. collinhover.com/lab/ichor/. (© 2010, C. Hover. Used with permission).

munications. Magic, play, and information is a choice, never an infliction" (Northam, 2010). The latter part of this definition will be revisited later in this chapter (Figure 2).

Now if, after becoming familiar with the above project, I explained that I had several thousand creatures composed entirely of a drive to learn more about human body language and environment, as if curiosity might be considered a physical material, you may not find this so strange. I would also not think it out of place for you to make the most wild and outlandish movements with your limbs and body should you (and perhaps others) find yourself face to face with a group of these creatures. It seems difficult, when presented with a physical or digital system that exhibits sentience, for us humans, to resist exploring and interacting with it. This is the concept of

Figure 2. Stream and user interacting, located at http://www.collinhover.com/lab/stream/. (© 2010, C. Hover. Used with permission.).

polite information, wherein something earns curious attention instead of needing to interrupt for attention (Northam, 2010).

What we might encounter here is a swarm or flock of relatively diminutive creatures, just as curious about our actions as we of theirs, and in communication with the environment they "see" through colored bioluminescence. The behavior of this group of creatures is based on the "scale-free flocking" (Hayes, 2011) methods used by flocks of starlings, as discovered and explained by STARFLAG researchers: "Scale-free correlations imply that the group is, in a strict sense, different from and more than the sum of its parts. The effective perception range of each individual is as large as the entire group and it becomes possible to transfer undamped information to all animals, no matter their distance, making the group respond as one" (Cavagna et al., 2010). Though it is neither initially obvious nor intentional, observers – through their interaction with these creatures – become performers in a live generated play of social experiences and ambient information. Utilizing only consumer level technology (and only the cheapest of it), this project comes together physically by watching the environment through a web camera, translating this visual data into the language of the creatures, allowing each of the creatures to interpret and react to the data through group decisions, and finally translating these decisions back into visual data which the "performers" see on screen as the creatures follow and swarm around their bodies. I have observed quite a few people's performances with these swarming creatures, and this simple matching of designer's purpose with live interaction never ceases to bring laughter to both the "performers" and me.

I have titled these two projects "Clouds & Ichor," found at http://www.collinhover.com/lab/ichor/ and "Stream," found at http://www.collinhover.com/lab/stream/.

I used these experiments as a step into the shallow end of a mathematical structure that defines our reality. The idea here is that for each object or system in our universe, from the unthinkably small atom to the infinitely large planet, there may be a set of rules, equations, or patterns that it follows. Some of these patterns are seemingly specific, such as the rule of the binary tree, where each branch can either split into two new branches or continue as a single branch. Other patterns are multipurpose, such as the atomic hypothesis: "all things are made of atoms – little particles that move around in perpetual motion, attracting each other when they are a little distance apart, but repelling upon being squeezed into one another" (Feynman, 1989). Both of these patterns seem to define the behavior, appearance, and functionality of part(s) of our universe.

Here I will propose a universal human set of languages and argue that we can use these languages for exploratory travel between the natural systems of our universe and each of their individual underlying rule sets or patterns. I hope to demonstrate, using these projects and other examples, reasons for increased crossover between design, science, and art through a biologically inspired, creative computing process I refer to as "Biological Translation."

A Determined Query

Before going further, it may help to note that throughout this paper, there will be some terminology used interchangeably. For the purposes of this paper, 'logic', 'rules', 'patterns', 'instructions', and 'reason' might all be thought of as mathematical implementations of ideas or information, while 'biological constructs', 'natural systems', 'physical manifestations', and 'expression' all correspond to any object existing in an external physical reality independent of human-kind.

There could be concern as to whether a pattern defines an object or system, or if the reverse is true. With respect to this concern, my argument will make the same assumption that the Max Tegmark's (2008) Mathematical Universe

Hypothesis makes: that reality is external and independent from human-kind, as described by the External Reality Hypothesis (ERH). As Tegmark writes, "assuming an external reality exists, physics theories aim to describe how it works" (2007, p. 1). It's notable that concerns similar to this one engendered attempts to find a clear set of rules that define the way everything works, and my own query should not be confused with this search for the theory of everything (TOE). Additionally, although I use 'Biological Translation' to name the process I am arguing for here, it does not directly utilize biological material to create or build and has little or no connection to the practice of BioArt.

The two creations we defined above, "Clouds & Ichor" and "Stream," are the results of the process of Biological Translation; the exact process from which they sprung is unclear. Before a concrete process can be determined, I believe we must address the question that generated this process, as well as the ways in which it may change perceptions of our environment. To clarify this question, we might ask, "Is it possible that each natural system contains and is defined by an individual set of instructions?" We will explore this question by beginning with an example of two universes.

BACKGROUND

Instruction and Expression

In one universe, language and logic exist as tools to communicate experience of biological beauty, "i.e. that which makes something interesting" (Flake, 2000). The universe itself and its biological constructs are self-evident, existing as the origin, rather than the result, of logic.

In the other universe, a similar collection of biological objects/systems are as beautiful as any other and with as necessary a balance between regularity and irregularity to generate Flake's "beauty." Within this universe, biological constructs are sensory expressions of equations, where "Geometrical ideas correspond to more or less exact objects in nature, and these last are undoubtedly the exclusive cause of the genesis of those ideas" (Einstein, 1916). It is probable that each individual object contains the instructions necessary for its own continued physical existence (this will be explained later). Here, the relationship between logic and biological constructs is a cyclical one in which logic creates existence and existence suggests logic.

The latter universe described above is the model that this paper will use. I will build an exploratory definition, consulting a collection of theories, including Chaos Theory, String Theory, Albert Einstein's theories of relativity, and Max Tegmark's Mathematical Universe Hypothesis. It is not my intention to discuss these theories at length, but it is important to note that the justification for a logic or equation based origin and process in nature is derived from the testing of these theories (rather than strictly from the theories and equations themselves), and these tests have had much success in mathematically describing natural systems and biological constructs. One case of note is that of Benoît Mandelbrot, a mathematician and advocate of fractal geometry, who suggested that within nature most shapes are fractals, showing that "clouds are not spheres, mountains are not cones, coastlines are not circles, and bark is not smooth, nor does lightning travel in a straight line" (Mandelbrot, 1982, p. 1). Fractals are a great example of a simple set of instructions generating extremely complex natural constructs. With these thoughts in mind, the following statements, applied to the scope of our "rather incomplete experience" (Einstein, 1916), seem reasonable:

i.   If a system exists, it may be mathematically described.
ii. If there is a mathematical description of a system, it may exist.

Evidence of (i) has already been discussed, i.e. the many theories and equations describing our universe, and (ii) is supported by Tegmark's (2008) Mathematical Universe Hypothesis (MUH), which postulates that "our external physical reality is a mathematical structure" (p. 1), and "that only computable and decidable (in Gödel's sense) structures exist" (p. 1). Therefore, our universe may display a stimulating relationship between logic and existence, where logic is originator and existence the expression. To further expand this relationship, one might say that (a) nothing can be without logical backing, and (b) nothing can be propagated (i.e. continued existence over time) without continued logical evaluation of natural behavior. One cannot say, however, that logic does not hold without physical manifestation (i.e. the inverse of (a)), as logic is not constrained to the realm of natural expression and can easily be used to describe other logic.

Additionally, systems, as defined above in points (i) and (ii), may become observable (i.e. come into existence) to humans at different points along humankind's timeline, so human observability should not preclude existence. String theory provides support for this claim through an example explained by physicist Brian Greene: "The full name of string theory is superstring theory. The "super" refers to something known as supersymmetry, a kind of mathematical pattern which implies there should be a whole class of particles, called supersymmetric particles, that we have not yet seen" (Greene, 2011). Further, one is left with two extremes (logic and existence) and a lot of 'grey area', or distance, between the two. This area will be addressed in the following section.

Language

Language is this 'grey area', and in this sense, is an infinite space of information formats with each individual language acting as bridges along a continuum of logic and expression. Each indi-

vidual language instance is separated from any other language instance only by encoding (i.e. the mapping of two information formats). As described by notable computer scientist and artist Jonathan Harris, "Language is basically a system for expressing ideas" (Harris, 2008). The following definition, for the purposes of this paper, seeks to expand Harris' general description:

a. Language is a translation in any direction along the above continuum.
b. Language is anything that does not qualify as logic or a natural expression of logic.
c. Any language is functionally equivalent to any other language, but each may differ in its audience.

Using language in this manner allows fluid movement between instructions and their natural manifestation. This also suggests that to be expressed over time, as opposed to existing only for a single moment, any biological construct must have instructions for its own behavior readily available. It would not be efficient to have each biological construct constantly requesting these instructions from some sort of central control, but rather to have them contained within the object to allow for autonomous existence. We might equate this setup to DNA in organisms.

These instructions must somehow be communicated, or translated, into their intended physical expression. Conversely, physical expression must be translated back into input for these instructions, or rules, to evaluate. By definition, this information cycle needs a proper method or container for transport, which leads us directly back to language.

Fortunately, the language in use by natural systems, and by extension the logic contained within these systems, is not directly observable by humans. One might question the use of "fortunate" in relation to the content of the previous sentence by posing the following: "The ability of see, read, and understand the underlying equations of our universe would solve every problem known to man. How does one justify this as unfortunate?" This is neither a question easily answered nor a problem easily settled, as one might counter this concern with another of seemingly equal weight: "If we knew the answers to everything, what would remain to explore?"

Science, as phrased so well by Flake, is "doomed to uncertainty – but this is a good thing... regardless of how much 'data' one collects, it's not always possible to build a perfect theory" (Flake, 2000). And, while humans are able to observe the physical expression of this logic (i.e. we see nature), the exact equations driving this expression are elusive and uncertain. This inability stems directly from the process of observation, which is itself at best an interpretation of an interpretation of the generative logic.

We have seen that Einstein's (1916) observations and calculations led to a theory (and set of equations) that have thus far closely approximated some cosmological rules of nature using language a human can understand. In fact, these theories have been translated into many different languages without loss or change of content. Additionally, as the expected expression described by these equations is consistent with the physical expression found in nature, they are strong evidence for a natural system wherein identical results may be obtained from any number of different sets of logic. In any given set of observationally identical objects in this system, not only may the logic of expression be variable between them, but the language in which the logic is written may be variable as well.

Accessibility

At this point we still face two problems among the above proposed relationship of logic and existence: language choice and uncertainty. First, we cannot choose any single human language to reliably and universally translate between logic and nature. All languages are a far cry from universally understood and spoken by humankind in practice. A clear example can be made by choosing the languages of science, art, and technology, of which the mastery and understanding of any one would be reasonable for an individual. We might also think it close to impossible to find a single individual that exhibits a clear mastery of all three languages, as languages are not instinctual and must be learned. Hence, the low probability of finding such a person is a result of the breadth of the languages chosen for the example and, by extension, the time required to master them. However, should languages with very narrow ranges of application be chosen, one could easily counter their usage with the argument that we cannot expect highly specialized languages to be capable of universal translation between logic and nature. Therefore, while it seems necessary to use a single broad and flexible language, we also cannot choose a single language and expect it to be universally understood.

Our second problem may be described as the inability to access the exact generative logic of nature. Because there is not a single universal human language able to cover all aspects of a translation between logic and nature, our only choice is to use the biological expressions of that logic as the qualifier for our own logic, theories, and processes. In other words, any approximate logic created by humans that expresses a natural system/process may be considered a reasonable approximation of the exact logic of nature if the natural system it expresses is consistent with that in nature. This leads us back to the need for a universal language to translate between these human approximations and nature. However, before we explore the possibilities of a universal human language and clearly define its parent process of Biological Translation, it would be best to begin with an answer to the question of why we would want to find such a thing.

MAIN FOCUS OF THE CHAPTER

Complementary Function

Through Biological Translation, we seek to build knowledge and discover rational approximations of the underlying instructions of the universe. One may compare these goals to those of the sciences. It would be fair to say that many societies hold science with the highest esteem. Given that the goals of a process often determine the worth of the process to its performers, and that the goals of Biological Translation coincide in some ways with the goals of science, exploring Biological Translation may be described as of interest to the sciences.

Further, in the dissemination of knowledge (generally speaking, this includes all academic fields) there has historically been more emphasis on knowledge conveyed using only the underlying logic, or very small and specific ideas. This is opposed to knowledge conveyed through the natural expression of that logic: the larger ideas whose responsibility it is to show the incredible beauty of the underlying logic. Focus on the former creates an exclusionary situation in which only audiences that absorb knowledge through the former method are able to learn. Greene emphasizes this imbalance, explaining that

"In the broader public, there is significant resistance to engaging with science. This is largely due to the way that many have encountered science in the classroom, where there's a tendency to focus on details without an equal focus on the big, wondrous scientific ideas—the very ideas that can inspire passionate interest in learning those details. We need to embark on a radical cultural shift in which science takes its rightful place alongside music, art, theater and literature as an absolutely indispensable part of a full life. We need to make clear that science is not something that you can willfully ignore. All of the major decisions going forward, from stem cells to nuclear proliferation

to nanotechnology to genetically modified food to alternative energy sources to climate change, have a scientific component. How can you be part of a democracy if you can't participate in the discussion about these ideas?" (Greene, 2011).

Biological Translation attempts to place equal emphasis on logic and its expression, by using languages relatively native to both as well as to the transition between both. As noted earlier, the concept of agency, or the idea that "Magic, play, and information is a choice, never an infliction" (Northam, 2010) is stressed heavily in this process for the simple reason that the absorption of information must always be a choice. Communication to any given audience is then done with much more clarity by conveying information through familiar absorption pathways for each individual of that group. This allows Biological Translation, as a process of exploration, generation, and learning to include rather than exclude, while also being flexible in its implementation so as to complement any other method with similar goals, rather than replace it. This and the previous reason will serve as justification for further exploration.

Biological Translation (A Universal Human Codex)

If reduced to a less complex definition, Biological Translation is a process composed of a loosely defined and flexible pattern of deconstruction and reconstruction, allowing fluid movement of information between the continuum of logic and biological expression, with the ability to communicate that information to as wide an audience as possible. We may further simplify this definition through correlation to the previously suggested non-standard definition of language, as follows: Biological Translation is a universal human language for a crossing of the space between logic and natural systems.

However, as we begin the search for a language to deconstruct, encode, transfer, decode, and reconstruct information, we must remind ourselves that finding a single universal human language will prove close to impossible. An answer to what to use does not come from a single language, but instead from a pool of languages. These languages are related in non-trivial ways, they are complementary in the function of translation, and as a whole the language pool's accuracy is greater than the sum of its parts. More concretely: one may use a relatively small and discrete (i.e., not every possible) set of languages to approximate the functionality of a single universal human language in the quest for fluid Biological Translation. These languages are as follows: a primary pair composed of code and interactivity, complemented by a secondary tetrad containing form, sound, haptics, and flavour.

Code and interactivity coexist in digital media, and are the languages that generate and sustain systems. Code is used here to denote any language that uses some type of information in programmatic and algorithmic manner to generate some type of representation. Generally speaking, the end goal of using code within Biological Translation is to create interactive or biologically based communication by converting logical information into one or many of the process' four secondary languages, thereby becoming understandable by a receiver. For example, we may observe a school of tiny creatures that seem to be swimming through the air, moving to and from randomly chosen points, splitting and grouping at random times, and glowing in random patterns of color. If we do not interact and only observe, we may initially believe that these creature's choices are random. This helps to demonstrate deviation of knowledge gained from information obtained without interaction and experimentation. When we interact with these creatures by using body language and gestures, we may understand how the application of 'random' to these creature's choices is wrong. They see our movements, try to learn the biologically based language of our gestures, and respond through their own movement and color change. More importantly, the code that generates these creatures is incomplete without our interaction.

The code gives us information in a representation we can understand, and we react in a language to which the code can respond to in kind.

The languages of the secondary set are chosen for their interchangeability and universality. The first property of the set, interchangeability is used loosely to indicate the many intuitive ways in which humans may use different senses, captured by the languages of form, sound, haptics, and flavour, to arrive at the same or similar information. These languages are not primary because they are not often able to create systems or patterns by themselves, but their power lies in universal understanding. Of all the languages known to humankind, the senses are instinctual. And while we have created higher-level languages, such as writing, that allow us to understand and express complex sets of rules, we still need the senses to mediate. Even more powerful is the cultural shift away from these higher-level languages and back into the languages of the senses as a primary form of communication, as noted by designer David Crow (2006). In fact, physicist Freeman Dyson wrote of Richard Feynman's greatest contribution to science as the way in which he visualized the patterns of our physical reality:

"Feynman visualized the world with pictures rather than with equations... Skipping the equations was his greatest contribution to science. By skipping the equations, he created the language that a majority of modern physicists speak. Incidentally, he created a language that ordinary people without mathematical training can understand." (Dyson, 2011, p. 40).

These secondary languages allow both quantitative understanding, for those with training, and qualitative understanding, for those without. Because similar information is often gained from these languages, each language functions flexibly within Biological Translation, and any successful implementation may utilize one or many of the secondary languages.

In referring to this set of languages as an approximate universal human codex, we've begun to concretely fill out Biological Translation by establishing a medium for information travel between any desired start (problem) and end (solution) points. Such a medium is initially infinite in expanse and direction to allow for flexibility in application, but this also makes it unusable, as we cannot settle on a single solution point from an infinite set of possibilities without a meaningful focusing of the process relative to the problem.

Hybridization

A focusing of Biological Translation is informed and shaped by a hybrid of disciplinary concerns stemming from science, art, and design. Though these considerations are numerous, it would be doing the reader a disservice not to cover each at least briefly. At a very general level, this shaping begins with science and art, often seen as separate and even opposite disciplines, and is completed by the joining of these two using design.

Science informs Biological Translation first by suggesting that knowledge may be translated into algorithmic systems, by which we are able to make biological systems modular, general, and reusable. The knowledge that leads to these functional systems is initially gathered through the use of the scientific method, which (for our purposes) we may reduce to observation and experimentation. For example, in "Clouds & Ichor" the digital material's behavior and properties are heavily influenced by mathematical knowledge we have obtained through observation of and experiments on both amoeboid organisms and liquid. We should not forget the visual nature of our universe and what we have so far referred to as the expression of knowledge as algorithmic system: knowledge as aesthetic system. Art is not seen as a mirror or derivative of nature but, much like language, is instead a tool for articulation of natural / physical experiences (McCormack, 2003). This is where art inserts its influence on

the process, and though I only list it as a single consideration, it is as significant as any other set.

The teachings of design play a significant role through several principles, the first of which is an analysis of a system's function and form. With any object that is designed to accomplish specific goals within a specific environment, we must be mindful (as designers) of the balance between the functionality, or ability to accomplish said goals, and the form, i.e. sensitivity to its environment and human context. This principle is illustrated in the emphasis of human motion tracking versus the reactive color swarming of the creatures in "Stream." Following this is the belief that there are always multiple ways to solve a problem. Next, audience and accessibility are fundamental to design as ways in which we craft, target, and make available our communication. Lastly, play, a concern too often ignored in design, is used to enable agency and to create something honest in its intent to contribute culturally (Northam, 2010). Following the previous example, "Stream" may be used as a demonstration of design that seeks to include the understandings of play at a very high level, by allowing the user to play as the creatures in a social dance of bioluminescence.

Though the points at which science, art, and design intersect may be as numerous as the considerations from each, there is one major point of note. Science is, as mentioned, quite good at the discovery of knowledge and the transfer of objective knowledge into algorithmic systems. Art, on the other hand, is well versed in the manipulation of what we see and the creation of aesthetic systems from which we derive subjective information. The third discipline, Design, is the agent that ensures the algorithmic systems are utilized to generate aesthetic systems from which the subjective information perceived has little deviation from the intended objective knowledge. It is at this point that Biological Translation becomes notably focused through a hybrid lens constructed by the perceptions of science, art, and design as they apply to a given problem.

CONCLUSION

Application

With a focused method to give us both reason and means for exploring, we return to our most basic question of the ideas and logic that define the biological constructs of our universe. It is not necessary to use these means to find an absolute or comprehensive answer for application to everything, especially with a lens tailored to excel in the exploration of a flexible range of individual cases. We start, as we did similarly at the beginning of this paper, with several questions or problems to which we wish to find an answer, this time more specific and personal.

I began "Clouds & Ichor" with the intent to translate my physical self into a digital organism as a way to understand what I do creatively and explain it to others. It may seem strange to some that a person would not fully understand what he/she does, but I must stress here that, relatively speaking, it is easy to define oneself should you be clearly working within the boundaries of a single discipline, as you may simply name the discipline and others will supply their own understanding to fill in the gaps. However, if an individual begins to work at the intersection point of a number of disciplines, a definition becomes exponentially more difficult to find. This is where I find myself mixing a background in design with science and art, and face a problem of coherently removing the fog from the ways in which I synthesize these disciplines.

With a problem identified and a clear intent to change it in hand, we will need a method for solving the problem. A method both to find a meaningful solution and a ways to implement the chosen solution, which may be a long process in itself, as we must explore and evaluate as many solutions as necessary to justify a single remaining design. To solve this problem, I decided on an environment that generates a cloud of material of which each piece of the cloud represented a modular element of

my ideology. The material's expression is derived from the properties of amoeboid organisms and liquid, so that each piece appears alive through its irregular cellular shape and pseudopodium driven movement, while also malleable due to its fluid dynamics (i.e. compressibility, viscosity, turbulence, etc). The user is then given a simple cellular construction, as a representation of the mind, within which a chemical reaction between any combination of these pieces may be initiated.

The fact that this solution involves the use of information gathered from natural systems and biological constructs illustrates that this solution seeks to be scientific in nature. In the intended configuration, the use of the languages of code and interactivity is, for me, a reasonable choice for this solution, but this may not be the case for everyone. Code allows the algorithmic systems provided by the scientifically gathered information to be quickly used in a logical manner to generate an array of desired representations. Interactivity is added upon that to allow the user to indirectly but tangibly interface with the code through language that is familiar to the user. For example, consider when the user takes hold of several pieces (or ideas) of the cloud and tears them away to be recombined as an entirely new miniature cloud. The resulting solution is a sustained cycle of user-generated ideas and is therefore self-taught, which expands both the explanation and absorption of information.

The artistic and aesthetically driven framework of this solution demonstrates that with the use of one or more of the secondary languages in conjunction with our primary languages, there is communication. Any information transmitted would be left uncommunicated without the ability to be seen, heard, felt, smelled, or tasted. While the thought of smelling and tasting digital organisms is exciting, and here I joke, but only a little, the technology is not available. Additionally, though the possibility for physical feedback (i.e. feeling) from a digital world is increasing, it is still primarily in its infancy and may not yet be feasible. However, the other two are certainly applicable, though with different responsibilities. Sound in this solution could not correctly convey the intended information and interactivity, and so serves a reduced role of rounding out the illusion of life and environment by providing subconscious stimulus. Form, on the other hand, is used as the conscious language bridge between code and user by translating mathematical system into visually tangible meaning.

As the design takes shape, there are a number of less obvious decisions that have significant effect on both the underlying system as well as its surface. Throughout this process, I have to be constantly aware of how well "Clouds & Ichor" works to recreate the properties of the biological constructs that inform it, while also being mindful of how this functionality comes across aesthetically and whether it obscures or promotes the primary message about the synthesis of disciplines. I wonder often for whom this is intended, but often answer my own question by realizing my interest in speaking to as wide an audience as possible, even if I can only work from my own experiences. Interestingly, I have been taught that consciously designing with one's own experiences makes for more powerful and universal results. Because play and agency are such important personal concerns, to bring play in was natural, and was done by presenting an intuitively malleable, yet unknown, material and setting no explicit goals, thereby leaving the user free to manipulate as he/she wishes.

By engaging Biological Translation we pass the knowledge we've gained in our exploration back through the same lens we used to generate the solution, and we've completed the process as it is intended to work. We use Biological Translation to ask questions about our universe, and to explore possibilities not only for ourselves but for as many others as possible.

REFERENCES

Cavagna, A., Cimarelli, A., Giardina, I., Parisi, G., Santagati, R., Stefanini, F., & Viale, M. (2010). Scale-free correlations in starling flocks. *Proceedings of the National Academy of Sciences of the U.S.A.*

Crow, D. (2006). *Left to right: The cultural shift from words to pictures.* Switzerland: AVA Publishing.

Dyson, F. (2011). The dramatic picture of Richard Feynman. *The New York Review of Books, LVIII*(12), 39–40.

Einstein, A. (1916). *Relativity: The special and general theory.* Methuen & Co Ltd. Retrieved February 20, 2011, from http://www.gutenberg.org/ebooks/5001

Feynman, R. (1989). *The Feynman lectures on physics: Commemorative issue (Vol. 1).* Massachusetts: Addison-Wesley Publishing Co., Inc.

Flake, G. W. (2000). *The computational beauty of nature: Computer explorations of fractals, chaos, complex systems, and adaptation.* Cambridge, MA: MIT Press. Retrieved January 14, 2011, from http://mitpress.mit.edu/books/FLAOH/cbnhtml/home.html

Greene, B. (2011). *An elegant multiverse? Professor Brian Greene considers the possibilities.* Retrieved March 22, 2011, from http://news.columbia.edu/briangreene

Harris, J. (2008). *Beyond Flash.* Retrieved August 8, 2010, from http://www.number27.org/beyondflash.html

Hayes, B. (2010). Flights of fancy. *American Scientist.* Retrieved January 20, 2011, from http://www.americanscientist.org/issues/pub/2011/1/flights-of-fancy/1

Mandelbrot, B. (1982). *The fractal geometry of nature.* W. H. Freeman.

McCormack, J. (2003). Art and the mirror of nature. *Digital Creativity, 14*(1), 3. doi:10.1076/digc.14.1.3.8807

Northam, B. (2010). *Making future magic: Media surfaces*. Dentsu London. Retrieved November 11, 2010, from http://www.dentsulondon.com/blog/2010/11/03/mediasurfaces/

Tegmark, M. (2007). *Shut up and calculate*. Retrieved March 3, 2011, from http://arxiv.org/PS_cache/arxiv/pdf/0709/0709.4024v1.pdf

Tegmark, M. (2008). The mathematical universe. *Foundations of Physics, 38*(2), 101–150. Retrieved March 3, 2011, from http://arxiv.org/PS_cache/arxiv/pdf/0704/0704.0646v2.pdf

ADDITIONAL READING

Bache, P. (2010). Digital world: Art in the computer age. *Aesthetica, 32*, 34–37.

Barberio, N. (2011). *Video feature: 'Flock Logic' collaboration unites science and dance*. Princeton University. Retrieved February 2, 2011, from http://www.princeton.edu/main/news/archive/S29/62/46S65/index.xml

Barcucci, S., & Niessen, B. (2011). The machine that makes art. *Digimag, 60*. Retrieved February 10, 2011, from http://www.digicult.it/digimag/article.asp?id=1963

Edmonds, E. (2003). Logics for construction generative art systems. *Digital Creativity, 14*(1), 3. doi:10.1076/digc.14.1.23.8808

Gips, T. T. (1990). Computers and art: Issues of content. *Art Journal, 49*(3), 228. doi:10.2307/777112

Golan, L. (2006). Computer vision for artists and designers: Pedagogic tools and techniques for novice programmers. *AI & Society, 20*, 462–482. doi:10.1007/s00146-006-0049-2

Goodman, C. C. (1990). The digital revolution: Art in the computer age. *Art Journal, 49*(3), 248. doi:10.2307/777115

Harris, J. (2008). *Cold + bold*. Retrieved August 8, 2010, from http://www.number27.org/today.php?d=20100319

Hayes, B. (2010). Flights of fancy. *American Scientist*. Retrieved January 20, 2011, from http://www.americanscientist.org/issues/pub/2011/1/flights-of-fancy/1

Hertz, P. (2009). Art, code, and the engine of change. *Art Journal, 68*(1), 72.

McLuhan, M., & Fiore, Q. (1967). *The medium is the massage*. United Kingdom: Penguin Books.

Reas, C., & McWilliams, C. (2010). *Form + code*. New York, NY: Princeton Architectural Press.

Russell, S., & Norvig, P. (2002). *Artificial intelligence: A modern approach*. New Jersey: Prentice Hall.

Verostko, R. (2010). Form, grace and stark logic: 30 years of algorithmic drawing. *Leonardo, 43*(3). doi:10.1162/leon.2010.43.3.230

KEY TERMS AND DEFINITIONS

Art & Logic: Logically constructed form with a purpose, sometimes known as graphic design

Art & Science: An undefined interdisciplinary relationship between disciplines of form and logic

Code & Form & Interactivity: A method of deconstructing natural systems and reconstructing them as digital environments.

Computer Art: Form created through the use of a computational methods and computer tools

Generative Art: Form generated by algorithms and computational methods

Interactive Art: Form that creates the illusion that it may be tangible and changes as it is used

Chapter 11
Looking at Science through Water

Anna Ursyn
University of Northern Colorado, USA

ABSTRACT

This chapter is focused on creating the visual approach to natural processes, concepts, and events, rather than their description for learning. It has been designed as an active, involving, action-based exercise in visual communication. Interactive reading is a visual tool aimed at communication, activation, and expansion of one's visual literacy. It addresses the interests of professionals who would like to further their developments in their domains. The reader is encouraged to read this chapter interactively by developing visual responses to the inspiring issues. This experience will be thus generated cooperatively with the readers who will construct interactively many different, meaningful pictorial interpretations. "How to produce texts by reading them," asks a philosopher, semiotician, and writer Umberto Eco, (1984, 2). The chapter comprises two projects about water-related themes; each project invites the reader to create visual presentation of this theme. Selected themes involve: (1) States of matter exemplified by ice, water, and steam, and (2) Water habitats: lake, river, and swamp.

INTRODUCTION

The Overall Structure of this Chapter

Projects in this chapter open with an introduction telling about the theme and the objectives that describe the essence of the suggested task. Annotated examples of related art works illustrate and inform the readers about the artistic approaches and styles. Project description and hints for solv-

ing the task guide the reader in the process of working out the project. Then come suggestions for further reading, along with description of the key terms and definitions.

Interactive Response

Since communications media are storing and delivering information visually, pictures happen to be ubiquitous. Everything pivots on images, which are available as dynamic, multi dimensional, interactive, or real-time displays. What's

DOI: 10.4018/978-1-4666-0942-6.ch011

even more, they are continually updated and improved every day. For all these reasons we all need to reinforce connections between visual and verbal thinking. The reader is invited to read about a selected theme and then organize the data by creating visual presentation. While reading a small part of the text in this chapter, researching the web, or reading texts written by scientists, you are encouraged to visualize mentally what you are reading, and then use the acquired knowledge as an inspiration for creating a picture.

Creating Imagery that Interacts with Text

Projects about biologically inspired computing for the art creation aim at enhancing visual communication skills of the readers. For this purpose, background information related to the science-inspired topics prepares the reader for particular projects by supporting visual literacy and cognitive imaging. Color boxes with background information and a web space support the inquiry, planning, and creating phases of project production. The reader will find the visual ways of gathering and delivery of information and will be asked to respond in the form of their own projects. A companion website helps to amplify visual learning and instruction with the use of art enhanced by computer graphics and digital media technologies.

Before creating visualization, it is good to organize one's thoughts about a theme and a project. One may want to make a structural sketch or a graph that explains one's goals, their hierarchical order, relative importance, cause-and-effect features, their parent-child-siblings relationship (in terms of computer science), and a sequence of actions. It may be useful to use arrows to represent vectors (with position, orientation, and magnitude). It may be helpful to write a storyline with a storyboard. One may also want to think about the available pictorial tools: one may prefer to apply color coding and/or pattern coding, using shapes, a change of size, placement, or the amount of shading to signal perspective; maybe include some tables, pie charts, vectors, arrows, pointers, links and nodes, or other graphic ways of picturing, and maybe also add sound, animation, and/or video.

Background Information Boxes

To meet the needs of the readers that are advanced in their own specific fields but probably not in all areas, projects contain the background information boxes. A distinct style of coding the boxes indicates the content of each box. The coded boxes focus on the themes: natural events and processes, art concepts and principles, and computing or technology.

a. Background Information Type A comprise supporting materials about a natural events, processes, and science concept to be solved and discussed as a theme of a project. That will serve as an inspiration for the visual solution. These boxes provide research into the theme and tell about the methods of investigating and disseminating information visualization that links art, nature, and science.

b. Background Information Type B present information about art concepts and principles, and traditional versus generative art that refer to the project. They provide background information related to visual literacy, basic facts, elements and principles in visual arts, essential art and art criticism concepts, suggestions about browsing for visuals and web-based supplemental materials, issues related to semiotics (imaging with signs, symbols, icons, and metaphors), as well as the cognitive processes and cognitive learning related to imaging with the use of the media.

c. Background Information Type C tell about computing or technology-related issues, instruction, or examples that may be useful in applying computing, information technology, computer graphics, animation, digital storytelling, and digital photography.

Integrative Approach to Art, Science, and Technology

"Looking at sciences through the water" explores connections between science, computing, and art. As it was said, we measure physical laws but mathematics gives us answers. Evidence coming from measurements and observations is confirmed by the mathematical theories and equations describing our universe. Mathematics is an exquisite example of the connectivity between abstract theories of numbers, groups, graphs, or order and the visual practice of showing and explaining the space, shapes, and patterns. The Italian painter, mathematician, and geometer of the Early Renaissance Piero della Francesca (1415-1492) was familiar with this subject when he combined his theoretical study of geometric forms with the humanist attitude toward contemplative portrait painting (one way to see his art works is to type in Google search 'Piero della Francesca' and select 'images').

After reading about basic facts and principles in visual arts, and then concepts and data in science, readers are guided in creating technologically based projects. Hopefully, the themes discussed would inspire them to respond interactively by putting theoretical knowledge into practice, making visuals, and creating artwork. Water-related themes, such as micro–macro structures in water, water life, and water in human life are the dominant issues here. Project descriptions provide integrative, concise information about water, seen both from the scientific and artistic point of view. Projects focus on presenting concepts and data and creating practical applications for technologically based creativity. They serve as a means to understand and interpret nature-related themes and then combine metaphorical visualization with

the artistic principles. One may use a metaphor as a form of thought and then present knowledge with the use of electronic media. This distinctive approach involves turning data into pictures, and thus comparing difficult to understand notions to the well-known, common objects. Examples of computer graphics and discussion of works done by scientists, computer science professionals, and artists, illustrate the presentation of views and concepts.

These projects will provide a good occasion to exercise the readers' cognitive processes related to imaging. It may serve well to enhance their level of confidence about both passive and active familiarity with art, when one acts both as the perceiver and the creator. By solving projects we may enhance our visual literacy, as we query and use information about art, graphics, and visual ways to communicate our response to the project. For those having little self-confidence in their background in art or design, projects will help to become art and design savvy and assured about their ability to present technical and scientific material in an interesting visual way. In this respect, completing the projects may assist programmers, scientists, engineers, as well as computer science or science-oriented students and teachers in creating and then effectively communicating their work using science-related knowledge and data as their main resources.

We will examine biologically inspired computing in relation to the aesthetics of the data displayed through art. It may be a challenging and rewarding activity to collect information taken from certain disciplines in order to make visual presentation of selected topics, support our study of concepts, and show underlying processes, products, relationships, and forces. That means we create a thought provoking and comprehensible graphical display of facts and processes.

Media, Materials, and Tools Needed

The reader is invited to read this book interactively: first, visit the interactive companion site and suggested websites to complement this text with visual content, and then react actively and create one's own pictorial response. Materials and tools needed would depend on one's choice of an artistic medium. They may comprise computer hardware and software with a web connection and a scanner, a digital camera or, if one prefers hand drawing, sketching, and then posting one's scanned images, it's good to prepare a stack of white, color, or Manila paper, pencils, crayons, charcoal, paints, and a compass. If someone would choose to make finger drawings in wet sand, or make sand constructions on the beach, and then to photograph them for further thoughts, it would work as well. Many readers may prefer to draw on a smart phone such as iPhone or a tablet computer such as an Apple iPad, a computer with a drawing tablet or a mouse; they may utilize any imaging software for drawing, and/or any image-manipulation software package. Projects can be also solved as computer-generated art produced by employing programming skills of the reader, or generating an image from a mathematical model created by the reader. The project may as well become an animated story. Whatever way you choose, make your projects exploratory, derived from your previous observations, showing your understanding of concepts just discussed, and focused on problem solving.

PROJECT 1: THE STATES OF MATTER

Introduction to the Project "The States of Matter"

When we encounter, even as a written account, the essential powers that rule everything in our world, we can draw inspiration out of knowledge, which we can gain or recount, and then create our visual response. Such inspiration may result in a burst of creativity in our artistic endeavor. The following text about the states of matter (solid, liquid, gas, and plasma) will involve creating artistic graphics. First, in a box (A) we will focus on three states of water: steam (which is water vapor in a gaseous phase), liquid, and ice. The theme of water is truly inspirational: first, the intrinsic nature of water is very special, and then the theme, because of the indispensable quality of water, refers to the very essence of life.

The emerging technological advancements will support further examination of the biology-inspired computing applied for artistic tasks and computing-based approaches to art creation, which are presented in the background information boxes of the kind [B]. Discussion about visual communication techniques and the ways to convey one's statement, presented in the boxes of the kind [C], maybe seen as exploration of the tools for a visual solution of the project about the states of matter.

The objective of this material is to provide an insight about the states of matter and encourage the reader to present in a visual way the very essence of the concepts examined, connotations, ideas, and feelings one have derived from the perusal of the text: for example, the hardness of solids, the fluidity of liquids, and the heat or cold feeling of steam. Figure 1a and 1b show art works about water done with two different approaches. "Water" presents the enchanted underwater world, while "Phases of Water" tells about transitions between the states of matter, with the use of both images and symbols.

Phase Characteristics and Transitions

In further text we will first recount basic properties and processes that determine different phase characteristics and transitions, then we will focus on water, water inspiration in art, as well as in-

Figure 1. a) Anthony Bianchi, "Water" (© 2010, A. Bianchi. Used with permission); b) Steve Smart, "Phases of Water" (© 2010, S. Smart. Used with permission).

 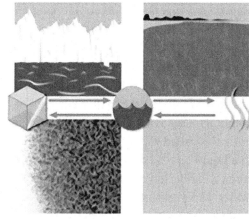

spiration with elemental forces in nature, which will be also discussed in semiotic terms.

Background Information Type A: Natural Events And Processes

Background Information Related to the Four States of Matter

Matter takes on multiple phases that can coexist in a stable equilibrium (which in fact in living matter is never stable). These forms are called the states of matter. Solid, liquid, gas, and plasma go through the phase transitions depending on the surrounding temperature and pressure conditions. A solid can melt into a liquid, and then a liquid vaporizes and becomes a gas, while a gas can be ionized into a plasma state. With the decreasing energy of an entire system, plasma can undergo deionization to a gaseous state; gas condensates to a liquid state, and a liquid can freeze and become a solid. In some cases there is a direct phase transition between a gas and a solid: a solid sublimates into a gaseous state, and a gas can be deposited as a solid. This way we can experience a snow falling from the sky and then disappearing without melting into

water. It's a common knowledge that physicists relate to four states of matter:

- A solid-state substance is resistant to changes of volume and shape. Crystals have atoms tightly bound in a geometric lattice (as in diamonds, metals, or ice), while amorphous solids have irregular position of atoms (for example, in glass). Solids are to some extent resistant to deformation caused by the applied stress or external impact. They also display some viscosity, for example, ice responds with compression and shear to the applied stress and its rate (Morland & Staroszczyk, 2009, Zaretskii & Fish, 1996).
- A liquid has a fixed volume, but it flows to take on the shape of a container. Steam is water in the vapor state. It is formed when heat of vaporization is supplied to water at boiling point (it varies with the pressure of formation). Fluids yield to some degree to external pressure; deformation of fluid's surface depends of its viscosity. For example, water is more 'thin' and has greater fluidity than the volcano's magma,

which is 'thick'. Viscosity increases with temperature but is independent of pressure (if it is not enormous). *At the companion website one can find a link to a looped file and watch a demonstration of viscosity (Viscosity, 2011).*

- A gaseous matter expands to fill any space available. Atoms, molecules, or ions of a gas move freely, so the matter expands indefinitely. Gas at a temperature lower than critical is called vapor; it can be condensed to a liquid or a solid by increasing its pressure without lowering the temperature. Water vapor absorbs heat from the Sun. Molecules of water escape from the water surface when the Sun energy breaks the bonds between molecules, and float into air as vapor. Water vapor then changes into rain or snow.

- If any substance is heated high enough it enters plasma state. Plasma is described in physics and chemistry as a very high-temperature ionized gas: electrons leave their parent atoms or are added to atoms, and thus atoms become ions that have free electric charges. Free electric charges of ions or electrons make plasma electrically conductive; plasma responds also to electromagnetic fields. However, plasma has no electric charge, with the number of positive and negative ions being equal. In nature, plasma is the most common phase of matter, up to 99% of the entire visible universe, where it fills the interplanetary and interstellar space. (However, the outer envelope of cool stars is cool, so the gas isn't ionized, because decreasing energy (measured as temperature) stops all molecular motion. The temperature at which molecular motion stops is called absolute zero and has been calculated as -273.15 degrees Celsius. Plasma is also present in the ionosphere, appears in lighting, as luminous plasma in St. Elmo fires, and in polar auroras. Plasma is artificially made by application of electric and/or magnetic fields. Figure 2a and 2b show student works.

In a chapter 2 of this book, Mark Stock describes flow as "the ensemble motion of matter in which the individual elements are allowed to move relative to one another. A fluid can be a gas such as air, a liquid such as water, or a collection of solid particles such as sand. Seemingly solid materials can behave as fluids if one observes them over a long period of time; examples of this are ice (glaciers) and rock (mantle convection)" (Stock, 2012).

In Figure 2a "Solid Me" a dynamic silhouette of a surfer serves as a metaphor of forces that rule water movement and transitions. Figure 2b "Snow and water" provides a painterly approach to the theme.

Background Information Type A: Natural Events and Processes

Background Information about Water Characteristics

Water has an ability to exist at ordinary temperature and pressure in all three stages in dynamic equilibrium – as a liquid, solid, and vapor. The large proportion (about 71%) of the Earth's surface is covered with water in all three stages, and 97% of this water is in the oceans. Water combines with many salts as water of crystallization, and many substances dissolve in water as a universal solvent.

It is a common knowledge that water is a hydrogen oxide H_2O, so its molecule consists of three atoms: two of hydrogen and one of oxygen. A molecule of water is about 0.29 nm (nanometer is 10^{-9} m). As a comparison, the size of a human cell is between 4 μm (4×10^{-6} m) and 135 μm. The ostrich egg is the largest known cell and weights over 3 pounds (over 1,360 grams).

Figure 2. a) Brennan Nelsen, "Solid Me" (© 2010, B. Nelsen. Used with permission); b) Aki Tawa, "Snow and Water" (© 2010, A. Tawa. Used with permission)

Water molecules have molecular polarity, with negative and positive charges on opposite sides. Hydrogen atoms provide a water molecule with a positive charge, while on the oxygen side it has a negative charge. This electrochemical feature causes attraction between water molecules, thus building strong molecular bonds. These bonds, which depend on temperature and pressure, determine the arrangement patterns of water molecules (ordered, semi-ordered, or random) and hence the physical state of water, whether it is gas (vapor), liquid, or ice. Molecules stick to one another: show cohesive attraction because of their hydrogen bonds to other polar molecules. Water has a low melting and boiling point. Except mercury, water has the highest surface tension of any liquid. Because of the high surface tension of water some insects such as water striders or even small reptiles such as a basilisks, can run on a water surface. Apart from this, the water resistance of spiders' legs comes from their physical structure. A great number of tiny, oriented hairs with fine nano-grooves cover their legs. Moreover, chemical properties add to the effect because their legs are wax-coated (Gao & Jiang, 2004).

Water has its maximum density of 1000 kg m^{-3} at a temperature of 4° C (39.2 F) that means its molecules are densely packed. The freezing of water in ponds and lakes depends on its density. In winter, the water at 4° C sinks to the bottom of ponds and lakes. Ice at 0° C forms on the surface; it has a crystalline hexagonal arrangement of molecules with empty spaces in-between, that supports flotation.

Clouds, fog, and mist are visible, as they are liquid water droplets. Clouds cover usually more than half of Earth. Fog begins to form when vapor condenses into the minute water droplets suspended in the atmosphere. It is a kind of a cloud that reduces visibility, even more than mist. Droplets of fog have radii about 1 to 10 μm (micrometer, 10^{-6} m). Water can absorb and hold heat; it has one of the highest heat capacity. Strong ocean currents, such as the Gulf Stream transport heated water over the long distance, and thus play an important role in Earth's climate.

Figure 3. a) Brodie Chinatti, "Ice–Water–Gas" (© 2010, B. Chinatti. Used with permission); b) Ben Mooney, "Water–Ice–Steam" (© 2010, B. Mooney. Used with permission).

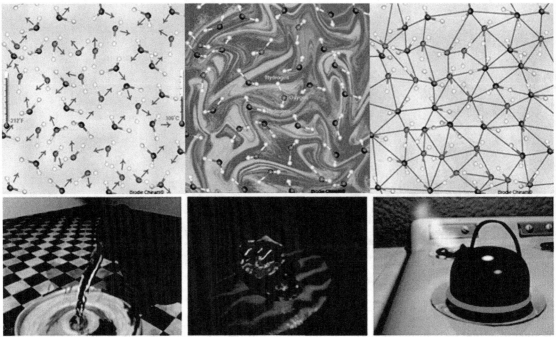

Figure 3a and 3b present artistic presentations of the three states of water. "Ice–Water–Gas" is informal visualization of the relations among water molecules in three states, with the use of symbols for molecules and bindings. The second work, "Water–Ice–Steam" shows the phase transitions of water symbolized by everyday iconic objects serving as metaphors.

Images of Water

When we type on Google a word 'water' and select 'images,' first of all we can see many works picturing a drop bouncing away from a surface of water. Some people used to connect this image with Feng Shui, as the five Feng Shui elements are earth, metal, wood, fire, and water. Some are inspired with the shape of droplets frozen in mid-splash. For example, a physicist and artist Martin Waugh (2011) creates a series called "Liquid Sculpture"–using high-speed flash photography, and a photographer Corrie White (2011) creates

"Liquids in Motion." Kenneth G. Libbrecht (2011) is an expert in snowflakes, an author of several books, a designer of images for the commemorative U.S. Postal Service stamps, and a creator of Snow Crystal Photo Galleries. A droplet in the air proves to be impressive and serves as an almost iconic image. It often illustrates all kinds of published water-related texts. In many cases a droplet of water announces research, information, data, or software related to works on water quality, or is placed to share experiences and ideas on various other themes.

Background Information Type B: Art Concepts and Principles

Background Information about Examples of Water-Inspired Art

In art, manifestation of powerful elemental forces in water takes form of pictures that show stormy clouds, tempests on the sea, or the beauty of calm water habitats or even the swimming pools, such as in case of David Hockney (2011) considered by many the most influential contemporary British artist. Hockney devoted many of his works to the theme of water: for example visit the sites http://www.hockneypictures.com/works_paintings_60_10.php, or http://www.hockneypictures.com/works_paintings_70_17.php. Currently, the artist draws every day on his iPad with the edge of his thumb and then sends his works digitally to 15 or more of his friends.

An Armenian seascape painter Ivan Konstantinovich Aivazovsky (1817-1900) has been considered by many the best marine painter in the figurative style of the Romanticism period. You may want to look at the artist's rendition of the light, waves, and wind when you type on Google the name Aivazovsky and then go to the 'Images.'

A British painter J. M. W. Turner (1775-1851) was called at the National Gallery site "the painter of light" (London National Gallery, 2010) because of his atmospheric seascapes, and not truly realistic, sometimes barely recognizable depictions of natural phenomena, such as sunlight, storm, wind, and tempest on the sea, created in his oils, watercolors, and engravings.

On the web one can find traditional, realistic paintings on water; however, art works created in contemporary media are scarce. Some artists focus on the theme of a solid state of matter, except for some examples of the earth art and the ice art. Michael Hansmeyer (2011) creates "Platonic Solids" using recombined algorithms to create generative 2D and 3D art. Probably the world's largest ice art can be found on the Lake Baikal in Siberia, where Jim Denevan (2011) created enormous ice circles. The theme of the gaseous state of matter evokes connotations with neon art, as well as art about gas masks and death. An art historian Chris Witcombe (2011) conducted a study on water in art, often stylized or shown in the form of a symbol. He examined, with examples from the traditional art forms, some water symbols, water related processes including change, destruction, and motion, as well as several social and cultural connections related to water.

Figure 4a and 4b are designed as visual/verbal presentations of the three states of water. "Water Trifold" shows the painterly image with added textual information, while a folding brochure "Water" combines text and image in the same place.

Elemental Forces as Inspiration

In the wide world perception, as well as in many philosophies, classical elements were accepted as the essential parts of the world and fundamental powers that rule everything that happens there. We may say watching the phases of matter inspired ancient beliefs. For Babylonians classical elements comprised sky, sea, wind, and earth, while Greeks, who introduced concepts of air, water, fire, and earth, added a quintessential ("quint" meaning "fifth") element of aether – immutable, heavenly substance setting up the stars. One may think, wasn't it a premonition of the contemporary concept of plasma – the fourth state of matter? Hinduism and Buddhism have also seen the four states of matter describing earthly material and a fifth element that is beyond the material world. Water as an elemental force is also present in ancient India, China, Tibet, and Japan.

Human imagination responds strongly, especially in a visual way, to the ideas and forces people perceive or believe to exist and influence our life. People create both the archetypical images and a visual record showing the manifestations of the powerful elemental forces. Archetypes, original models and prototypes that form our further imaging of an idea, refer to water as a mystery force of creation, purification, resurrection, fertility, and growth.

Figure 4. A) Jael Esquibel, "Water Trifold" (© 2010, J. Esquibel. Used with permission); b) Pat Mapes, "Water" (© 2010, P. Mapes. Used with permission).

Background Information Type C: Computing or Technology

Background Information about Biology Inspired Computing

Current interest in natural forces and events comes from researchers and engineers who develop natural computing and its branch, biology inspired computing that deals with advances in artificial life, fractal geometry, and computing with natural means, among other areas. Evolutionary computation, artificial life, artificial neural networks, or swarm intelligence are often used as examples of bio-inspired techniques. Genetic engineering techniques serve for designing new computers based on molecules, such as membranes, or for designing controllers for robots. Nature is considered a metaphor for developing such natural means computing methods as molecular, membrane, and quantum computing. For example, dynamical transport network in a single-cell organism is considered as a virtual computing material that allows approaching spatially represented geometry problems (Jones, 2010), and developing a Physarum machine – a biological computing device that computes by propagating diffusive or excitation wave fronts (Adamatzky, 2010). Bio-inspired algorithms enable solving complex problems, modeling, and designing simulations. For example, scientists and engineers examine swarm intelligence, collective intelligence of groups (such as birds, ants, or schools of fish) where each agent is a peer that acts and is interacting independently, and there is no central controller that directs the activities of other members of the swarm. Systems that depend on a central controller are often robust to disasters, such as a damage of the controller (Bonabeau, Corne, & Poli, 2010).

The Semiotic Content of Visual Design

In terms of semiotics, we can say people have developed systems of signs, symbols, and icons, to convey meaning. They also devised the ways to visualize and communicate their knowledge about natural processes and events using metaphors, analogies, and a variety of the biology data visualization tools. In the arts pictorial signs may be arbitrary, for example, showing resemblance of a stimulus to its symbol, or conventional, which are often unrelated. The existing trend in applying biology-inspired research and computing has been conducive to the advancement in biosemiotics, which examines communication and signification in living systems in terms of the production, action, and interpretation of signs, and approaches biology as a sign system study.

Humans use signs to communicate or to express something. The semiotician Roland Posner (1992, 1993) called string codes those sign systems that have all complex signs reducible to a string; he considered natural languages, writing systems, musical notations, vestment codes, culinary codes, and traffic signs the examples of sign systems. A collection of signs that can be combined in a system makes a code, simple or a double articulated one. Communication among people is possible due to different types of articulation of signs used. In a double articulated code, an infinite number of possible combinations may be done from a finite number of signs. This is possible because communication takes place under the rules acting on two structural levels. It is so in a case of speech, where a great potential for making sentences results from a double articulation on a syntactic level. Meaning in any language arises through the interplay of two types of elements. Morphemes, the smallest elements: words or parts of words that convey meaning are developed through combining of phonemes, single speech sounds without meaning. A finite number of morphemes, along with the rules of syntax, may combine into a sentence. An infinite number of correct sentences may be constructed this way.

Possibly, double articulation is not unique for verbal or artistic messages, so one may look for some analogy of double articulation of speech in other systems, for example, in organization of the Japanese calendar or in formation of protein molecules and the genetic code. Maybe, the organization of some parts of the Japanese calendar could be discussed as an example of the double articulation of symbols. The names for days of the seven-day week correspond in some cultures to the names that come from the five visible planets (with names of planets given according to the Chinese elements – wood, fire, earth, metal, and water), and from the moon and sun (yin and yang).

Double articulation may possibly be also seen as a characteristic of the formation of protein molecules. Proteins are developed from amino acids, according to the four-sign code. Nucleic acids contain four kinds of basic amino acids joined in triplets, and just code for specific amino acids making a molecule of a protein. Four bases assembled this way in groups of three in each triplet make possible 64 different codings. However, only 20 existing amino acids are coded this way. Such a wide margin of coding possibilities makes the code open and ambiguous, so more than one coding is possible for the most of amino acids. The traditional way of presenting a double helix of amino acids is one of the most popular educational applications of scientific visualization.

Working on a Project

The project about the states of matter requires some research about the state transitions, especially on the molecular level. Visual, artistic representation of the abstract concepts related to the phase transitions may become easier when we focus on water as a unique element of our life. To recapitulate, the special properties of water include the fact that it exists in all three states at typical temperature and pressure, has polarity - with the hydrogen bonds, a low melting and boiling point, expands (floats) when it freezes, has one of the highest surface tension, heat capacity, heat of vaporization, and is a nearly universal solvent, so it contains most organic components of the biosphere that are necessary for life. One may want to adopt a micro–macro approach in examining the theme and examine various levels of magnification, from nano structures including atoms or particles to some big expanses of water such as oceans, or water-related facilities for example, a water mill, a power station, and plants recovering oil from the sea bottom through pumping ammonia. Figure 5 "Ice–Liquid–Gas" shows an artistic impression about phases of water.

After completing your research on the Internet or in books and maybe drawing some sketches, create a triptych about the three states of water – a project divided into three sections. You may want to focus on the essence of each particular

Figure 5. Liz Hergert, "Ice–Liquid–Gas" (© 2010, L. Hergert. Used with permission).

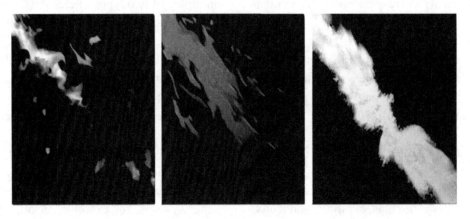

condition and the connotations you can bring about from your study of the theme. You may accomplish your project in representational or abstract way of imaging, but the three parts should be consistent in style to make a whole artwork.

Background Information Type B: Art Concepts and Principles

Background Information about Symbols – Concrete and Abstract

When we think about the arts in terms of semiotics, we talk about visual communication between the artist who is the sender of the message, and the viewer who is its receiver. Many concur with the opinion that images become messages when a distinction is made between a signal and its referent. When thinking about our imagery, we can see relations of signals, symbols, and signs to their referents.

To convey an own visual interpretation of the state transitions and elemental forces that cause them, the reader may choose a symbolic presentation of the theme and utilize some abstract thinking. Symbolic drawings may convey messages about universal forces of which we are not always conscious, such as a ying-yang – contrasting, complementary symbol that endangers and sustain the universe. Artists often apply symbolism to convey meaning. Colors are often used as symbols, for example, they signal the cold-warm water on faucets. Abstract art does not concern literal description; for example, idea sketching is abstract. We use abstract symbols when we order parts for the electrical installation. When we have a map of an island, we can picture what visiting the island would be like or even write a fiction about events on that island without being there. Writing programs requires using abstract thinking about described concepts. Visual communication occurs through visual symbols, as opposed to verbal symbols or words. This way

of thinking is related to the methods of simulation and visualization because it brings forth an ability to perceive complex systems. Current approaches to product design apply images for visual thinking and use imagery as a medium for thought. We need to recognize a difference between concrete and abstract images or concepts because this way we can organize our knowledge and use only what we need. Semiotics is useful in knowing how it is all connected and make a distinction between a signal and its referent. We use symbols and link-node diagrams for abstract concepts in graphic languages. Symbolic shortcuts in human perception make a meaning of what we see or hear. And signals of that kind are grounded deeply in neural system. Signs, symbols and their meanings are the focus of art education. While cognitive scientists are usually focused on looking for the sources of human communication that are grounded in precise thinking, artists often use purposefully transformed simple signs to direct thoughts of the viewers.

Caveat (a Warning or Caution)

Some symbols become a cliché and evoke an enormous amount of various connotations, hints, and associations, for example, the "heart" symbol. Therefore, one has to be careful where and how to apply symbols.

Symbols are not the same in different parts of the world. For example, a sign "WC" is used in some parts of Europe for a restroom. It happened not once that someone asked in the US, "Where is WC?" and the answer was, "WC? I do not know him."

A song "Tell me something I don't know" is a cliché about a concept of cliché.

Symbols may change their meaning. For example, an image of smoke going out of factory chimneys was considered a sign of progress in the times of industrial revolution and was even pictured on currency bills. Nowadays, it means smog and pollution, so it gives a negative connotation.

Some usages of symbols result in misunderstandings. For example, children can often see a bulb drawn over Einstein's head as a symbol of his genius. They sometimes think, Einstein + the light bulb = a bright idea, so he was the one who invented a bulb.

Background Information Type C: Computing or Technology

Background Information about Semantics and Semantic Networks

Semantics (from the Greek semantikos, "significant,") defines the nature of meaning in language and its role in a sentence. The interconnection of topics to search for information goes through the associations (relations between topics) and roles linking the topics. Semantics make this network meaningful through making definitions of types for the different object, defined by the topics and used by these roles, topics, associations, and occurrences. Visual semantics is used in design and in presentation of three-dimensional objects, for example, in experimenting with the design products: how to apply in practice semiotics of utility products when describing purpose, function, and qualities of this product. In the '80s the process of developing the product semantics changed the concepts about the optimization, marketing, and aesthetics of commercial design.

Semantic networks are large structures comprising knowledge about interconnected categories, for example, taxonomies of knowledge about animals and plants. An extensive research is conducted in semiotic terms in relation to communication with the use of multimedia. Topic maps are being designed, which bridge knowledge representation and information management by building a structured semantic network above information resources. Topic maps help navigate

on the web. According to Sir Tim Berners-Lee who started the World Wide Web and its evolving extension – the semantic web, information can be expressed in a format that is readable and usable not only for humans but also for the software applications. The Data Web and the Web 3.0 are aimed to grow as a universal database, a medium for data, information, and knowledge exchange. A Web3D Consortium is working on transforming the Web into a series of 3D spaces, realized also by the Second Life – a free 3D virtual world where users can socialize, connect and create using free voice and text chat (http://secondlife.com/).

A Folding Brochure about States of Water

This could be a good time for drawing and describing the states of matter in a way that seems to be rich in the semantic meaning: the general data about the states of matter (solid, liquid, gas, and plasma), with special attention to the states of water. The result from this action may be now changed into a two-sided printout and then designed as a folding three-page brochure. The presentation may include general data about the states of matter and the results of the research about water, its solid state – ice, and turning water from liquid into vapor, steam, fog or mist.

The use of signs and symbols in a given design is often called signage. Signage may include billboards, posters, placards, etc. It may refer to a number of signs thought of as a group. Symbols, iconic and canonical objects are used in commercials. They often cause that we take a suggestive commercial message for granted, without thinking. Also, body language may encompass some iconic features. A big problem may arise when we travel to another country and the same signs mean something different from what we intended to convey, and we do not even know that we are conveying strong messages. To help the travelers, a pocket book "Point it" (2009) contains photographs of

Figure 6. Anna Ursyn, "Change of Matter" (© 1999, A. Ursyn. Used with permission).

typical objects and situations; travelers can point to in order to address their questions.

Figure 6 "Change of Matter" tells about how changing seasons result in phase transitions in water: each year comes a new cycle, which brings changes on the ground, sky, and water. As we change various types of communities, we change our perspective and routines, while surviving snow and rain, ice and sunshine, liquid and solid phases.

PROJECT 2: LAKES, RIVERS, AND SWAMPS

Introduction to Project 2

This subchapter examines some of the factors that make people conduct water-inspired investigations. It would be rewarding experience to inquire into the living conditions in water, the aesthetic qualities of water environments, and then, with intuitive feeling, create a synthetic, contemplative, and informative triptych about water environments. We will explore three kinds

of water resources – lakes, rivers, and swamps. It is the variety of intensive activities taken by water creatures that makes such search so enjoyable. Lakes, rivers, and swamps are interesting not only because they constitute rich habitats, they inspire scientists and artists to examine these complicated, interactive systems, with many variables, because of the ensuing vital issues for debate and applications of ensuing knowledge for art and technology. Examining biology and ecology provides a potent paradigm for performance-oriented design that correlates environment with architecture. Studies into the morphology, physiology, and evolution of biological systems and their ecological relation supply insights and methods for architectural design and sustainability of the built environment. For example, Johann-Gerhard Helmcke and Ulrich Kull (2004) investigated the specific shell construction of diatoms – the unicellular algae that live in fresh water and as the plankton of the oceans.

The objective of this text is to take macro-micro approaches to the three water environments, search for analogies with current technological solutions, and aim for possible inspiration to create artistic projects. First we will examine lakes as big water systems that act on the surrounding environments. A need for providing clean water to all people resulted in the developments in technologies, research, and implementations that reduce the enormous costs of water purification. Some of research and technology progress results from the studies of biological structures, often in a nano scale, and applies biology inspired solutions, for example, in the form of carbon nanotubes. Skimming through the issues referring to the water cycle and management of water resources may provide a good reason to create a project about water cycle in the form of a manhole cover design. Next, we will glance through the ways in which water has become an inspiration for people to create myths and art works, and then inspect the current technologies that support computing for arts and creating biology-inspired art. Lakes may mean reflection of objects on a water surface, seen upside down. Static, cold water is often seen as majestic. We expect lots of animal traffic and more static plant life down below.

We will then take a look at rivers as a natural home for big and small living creatures. We will examine some of the approaches to computing that are inspired by animal behavior, such as evolutionary computation, swarm computing, genetic programming, or swarm intelligence. We will then examine closer some issues related to nanoscale objects and technologies – soft matter, liquid crystals, DNA crystals, carbon nanotubes, nanoshells, and again water purification, this time in micro and nano scale.

Perusal of these issues may provide a good reason to write a limerick (or another form of a short verse) about water and water creatures. Some fish, such as trout, hatch after going upstream. If the river would ever stop, so would the fish.

Finally we will inspect swamps with a magnifying glass to survey small microorganisms and inquire into the building blocks that decide about their biochemistry and metabolism, and then we will look into visualization of biological data. It may provide a background explaining the biology-inspired trends in computing and biotechnology. The green color of the swamp makes one think about its living, ever changing content. There is not much light let insight: too dense environment. A short text about creating an iconic image will connect the theme to the next task – creating "The Traffic on the Sky, the Horizon, and a Hidden Treasure in Water" project.

A triptych entitled "Habitats: Lakes, Rivers, and Swamps" will result as a synthesis of intellectual activity and the emotional response of the reader to all these themes. Figure 7 "Just do something" shows an artistic impression about water habitat.

Water: Threats and Answers to Threats

Water brings life, but it also often poses a threat to health, and this happens for many reasons. Humans cannot live without water, or any other living creatures; yet, many times we suffer because of water-induced maladies. The fascinating fact that we can die from something we need the most evokes a wide range of intense activities. We explore a possibility of life on any other planet or even a star system, and make quests for alternative, water-independent forms of existence, both in biological and ontological meaning. A single cell may contain billions of water molecules. Scientists conduct explorations about previous and possibly present existence of water on Mars, and investigate potential life forms.

However, people survive regardless of so many hazards and the life-threatening perils. The crucial task is preserving water purity and providing efficient supply of clean water for people. Aside from the long established, expensive technologies for filtering water, this involves making use of the developments in nanoscale technologies and the availability of nanoscale objects – soft matter, liquid crystals, carbon nanotubes, nanoshells, and

Figure 7. Jerod Wilson, "Just do something" (© 2010, J. Wilson. Used with permission).

molecular-scale technologies involving carbon nanotubes. These technologies make a background for progress in water purification in micro and nano scale. We will examine what kinds of threats are hidden under the water surface and what kinds of methods have been developed to secure pure water for people, animals, and plants.

Water inhabitants – big and minuscule – are being as much as humans submitted to harmful components of the contaminated and polluted environment. There is no need to read more than we see in the daily news to become scared about the future and encouraged to preserve whatever we can preserve. People conduct research in many domains of science and develop technologies to control threats coming from the water content and harmful contamination or pollution. Some pollutants come from the soil, while mercury (Hg) present in fish, lobsters, and shrimps has a tendency to concentrate it in their bodies.

Many both simple and advanced methods serve to purify water and thus make water safe for human needs. The United Nations international committee has adopted "The Millennium Development Goals" and put forward a target: "Halve, by 2015, the proportion of the population without sustainable access to safe drinking water and basic sanitation" (MDG, 2008).

1. Lake

Lakes present big masses of water that have an effect on their surroundings: air, land, and living beings. Fresh water (called also sweet water) takes part in an overall motion of water on the Earth's surface. Water comes from the groundwater resources, upland lakes and reservoirs, rivers canals, and low land reservoirs (where water is not always clean), from collecting rainwater and fog, desalinating seawater, and extracting water from humid air by cooling and thus condensing the water vapor.

In many regions where water is scarce, fog catching is a method that uses fog nets to provide easy-to-collect drinking water. A 40 square meter net can collect up to 200 liters of water per day (DW-World, 2010). Fishermen and miners from the Atacama Desert in northern Chile, one of the driest coastal deserts of the world (Wild World, 2010) catch water on fabric stretched between two poles, and thus avoid buying expensive water delivered in trucks. Thus, they are even able to replant the endemic tamarugo trees (that are threatened with extinction) on the site of the cut high-altitude forest, and water saplings by installing fog-catching nets (Vis, 2010).

Figure 8a "A frog habitat" shows an art graphics, while Figure 8b "Water our resource" shows a visual/verbal brochure about water resources.

Background Information Type A: Natural Events and Processes

Background Information about the Water Cycle

The water cycle relates to the endless movement of water on Earth and the processes that cause this movement. Water molecule has an atomic structure as simple as H_2O, and yet water dominates our environment, covering over 70% of the Earth surface and being life's essential component. Water is present in all living organisms and is indispensable for living. Human body contains 55% to 78% of water. Water existing on, below, and above the Earth surface changes its phases among liquid, vapor, and ice in constant movement of water molecules. As we all know, water goes from streams to rivers, then to oceans; water from lakes, rivers, swamps, and oceans goes to the atmosphere. Plants contribute to the amount of evaporated water. Air humidity, heat from the sun, and wind decide on the dynamics of the water cycle. Earthquakes and volcanic eruptions let water trapped deep below the rocks escape in the form of steam. At the Google images we can find tens of approaches to visualizing the water cycle.

Physical processes of evaporation, condensation, precipitation, infiltration, runoff, and subsurface flow determine the water movement, still maintaining the balance of water on Earth. Changes in heat energy cause variations in temperature; for example, evaporation of water from lakes, rivers, swamps, and oceans has a cooling effect on the surroundings, while condensation warms the environment. Fog condensation is important for the growth of trees, such as coast redwoods on the US west coast. Precipitation

Figure 8. a) A. Gaggini, "A frog habitat"; b) Candace Haywood, "Water our resource" (© 2010, A. Gaggini, C. Haywood. Used with permission).

caused by water condensation unloads fresh water both on the dry land and onto the oceans. Sublimation, the transition of a substance from the solid phase directly to the vapor phase without passing through an intermediate liquid phase (NSIDC, 2010) – adds to the dynamics of water cycle. Scientists use mathematical models to examine infiltration, runoff, and channel flow; they also make measurements with a variety of devices such as permeameters or infiltrometers (Oram, 2010) to predict and improve river flow rates and water quality.

Water cycle has an influence on the amount of fresh water and its purity, climate (through heat exchange when it heats oceans and seas), geology dynamics (through transport of minerals, erosion, and sedimentation), and life of the ecosystems on Earth (when plant foliage hold up water from precipitation and roots convey water from the soil). According to Pidwirny & Jones (2010), average time a water molecule spends in atmosphere is 8 days, while it stays in Antarctica for 20,000 years.

There is a feedback between cryosphere and climate: cryosphere has an impact on the climate and its change, because it influences moisture of the ground and air, energy exchange, precipitation, and hydrology. Snow and ice reflect solar energy and transfer heat, both as ice and during the change of state, and thus they have an important role in climate change. Albedo is the ratio of reflected to incident solar radiation that comes as microwave energy, with shortwave electromagnetic spectrum of ~0.3 to 3.5 nm. It changes with the physical properties of ice and snow cover. Melting of the glaciers, mostly from the Antarctic, results in a rise of the sea level; about 1 mm per year while total observed rise is about 2 mm per year.

Snow and ice reduce the flux of heat, they insulate the surface from energy loss in winter and delay the spring warming. They influence the hydrological cycle because moisture cannot escape from water or ground covered by even a small amount of snow. Snow covered area may be as large as 47 million km^2. Seasonal snow packs – layers of accumulated snow in mountain ranges – are major sources of the runoff water and groundwater recharge, as snowmelt runoff fills the rivers and aquifers – underground water-bearing rocky containers – and also act on summer rainfall in distant places (Gutzler & Preston, 1997).

The "Water Cycle" manhole cover project

When you type 'manhole cover art' on Google and then go to 'Images,' you will see several pages full of artistic manhole covers from all over the world. The theme of a manhole as an art form fascinates many artists (e.g., Dan Heller, 2004) who share their experiences on the web (e.g., Damncoolpics, 2006). Several actions resulted in the art-in-public-spaces programs, for example, in Minneapolis in 1983.

If you like manholes created as an art form, you may want to make your own artistic design for a manhole cover. Thus, the next stage of the project – with water taken as an example – consists in creating an artistic design for a manhole cover that shows the water cycle. The "Water Cycle" manhole cover should have a radial symmetry, with imagery showing the three constituting components (evaporation, condensation, precipitation) placed around its center, so, when installed on a street, it can be approached from every direction. Figure 9 presents four computer graphics with various approaches to showing manhole covers about the water cycle.

Background Information Type B: Art Concepts and Principles

Background Information about Myths and Art Works about Water

Because it is essential to humans and all living creatures, water has always stirred human imagination. We are made of water, partially at least. We

Figure 9. a) Betony Coons; b) Halina Kadiszewski; c) Mike Huscroft; d) Nathan White – Four Manhole Covers about the Water Cycle. (© 2010. Used with permission.)

have it strongly imprinted in our minds that water means purity – mythical, spiritual, and physical. Early and advanced human civilizations, which grew mostly around rivers, developed systems of symbols, myths, beliefs, rituals, prayers, and celebrations derived both from philosophical and religious reasons. People worshiped numerous gods they associated with water. They created pictorial representations of deities in the form of painted images, reliefs and sculptures, written or spoken epics, lyrics and poems, musical lamentations, hymns, and songs, as well as ritual dances or solemn ceremonies.

In Sumerian and Akkadian myths, supernatural entities were imagined as primordial waters, first told and then written in cuneiforms. Babylonian epic, telling on clay and stone tablets about the beginning of heaven and earth, introduces the god Enlil. Ancient myths of the Near East link the creation of humans with a mother goddess and Enki, the god of freshwater and practical inventions (Mythology, 2008). In the Babylonian myth, the masculine underground freshwater (Euphrates River) combined with the feminine saltwater – a gigantic monster). The god Atum of the early Egypt created himself from Nun, the primordial waters. Belisama was the Celtic goddess of fire, bodies of water, and metallurgy, along with other Celtic deities linked to various rivers and wells. Poseidon, brother of Zeus, was the god of the seas and rivers. He sent a sea monster against Troy (which was killed by Heracles), and then other sea monsters Scylla and Charybdis (his daughter) against Odysseus. The Maya peoples believed that life emerged from the lifeless, dark universe filled with water. The Aztec deity Tlaloc was called the Rain Sun because he was the god of rainwater. He reportedly carried four magic jugs. Water from the first jug caused crops to grow, water from the second jug was killing crops, the third jug contained water that frosted plants, and the fourth jug destroyed everything. Tlaloc's wife, the jade-skirted Chalchiuhtlicue was a goddess of lakes and streams. Priests tortured and killed children to sacrifice them in honor of Tlaloc (Mythology, 2008).

The Deluge

The flood stories exist in Sumerian, Babylonian, and Hebrew myths. George Smith (1875) translated a Chaldean account of the Great Flood from a cuneiform tablet found in Nineveh. The great Flood as the divine retribution was described in the Bible, in the Hindu story of Manu, in the Greek mythology, and in many other myths.

The theme of the Deluge – the great flood inspired artists from many times and origins. Examples of a deluge as a theme in art can be found on the Internet, for example:

- The Michelangelo Buonarroti's (1475-1564) fresco "The Deluge" (1508-1512), was created as the eighth scene from the Old Testament for the ceiling of the Capella Sistina, Vatican. The fresco (Michelangelo Buonarroti, Deluge, 2011) visualizes the Great Flood from a human point of view, showing passion and torment caused by this event (Michelangelo Buonarroti, Sistine Chapel, 2011).
- The Lithuanian artist Mikalojus Ciurlionis (1875-1911) created in 1904 a series of five paintings entitled "Deluge" (Ciurlionis, Deluge, 2011).
- The French painter, engraver, illustrator, and sculptor Gustave Doré (1832-1883) created the engraving "The Deluge" as a

frontispiece of the illustrated edition of the Bible (Doré, 2011).
- The French painter and lithographer Theodore Gericault (1791-1824), one of the pioneers of the Romantic Movement, created oil on canvas painting entitled "Scene of the Deluge" (Gericault, 2011).
- The English Romantic landscapist, aquarelle (watercolor) painter, and print-maker Joseph Mallord William Turner (1775-1851) painted around 1843 "The Morning after the Deluge" (Turner, 2011).

Figure 10 presents personal approach to water environment. The light emanates from water. Reflections coming from the sky enlighten the sight and one may feel almost united with nature, feeling like being a tiny part of it. Many like to go fish in order to breath the light.

Background Information Type C: Computing or Technology

Background Information about Technologies that Inspire Computing for the Arts

An acronym GRIN has been coined for genetics, robotics, information technology, and nanotechnology as the four most fundamental venues in technology development. Geneticists develop model organisms for genetics research studies on gene regulation and the role of genes in organisms' development or falling ill with diseases such as cancer. Model organism serve for educational purpose as well (Model Organisms, 2008). Models based on molecular genetics are applied to create images and structures processed with the use of artistic techniques. Organisms, modified genetically by insertion or deletion of genes, have been serving for creating various types of genetic art projects and also genetically modified pets. Artists

Figure 10. Anna Ursyn, "Lake, River, Swamp" (© 2011, A. Ursyn. Used with permission.)

transform living organisms by their structure and processes manipulation. They model, simulate, and engineer selected ecosystems and habitats and apply artificially designed visual effects and soundscapes to create generative art. Evolutionary computation and genetic algorithms serve for creating evolutionary and generative art projects that operate with some autonomy, leading later to producing synthetic animals that can evolve collective behavior or interact with the viewers. Evolutionary techniques are applied to develop controllers for animated motion of real or virtual creatures, and to create artificial evolution of shape. Participatory, web-based art projects also use evolutionary computation to create online interactive evolution of biomorphs. Art installations feature real-time interaction between people and evolutionary creatures. Interactive genetic algorithms create and learn to create music (Reynolds, 2002). In some cases generative artists draw inspiration and technical solutions from the genetics and evolution related concepts to introduce automated behavior, artificial intelligence, and swarm intelligence features to their products. This approach may lead to creating artificial DNA. For example, Celestino Soddu (2011) generated the artificial DNA of medieval towns that can produce 3D architectural models in a selected style.

Robotics relates to electronics, mechanics, and software. This technology deals with actuators that convert stored energy (taken from various kinds of power sources) to movement, sensing, computer vision, effectors manipulating objects with grippers, locomotion, and other elements. Application of neural networks to robotics includes directing a manipulator, the steering, and path planning. Some robots act autonomously in a dynamic environment, other can interact with humans, being equipped with speech recognition, gestures, facial expression, artificial emotions, and even personality (Biever, 2006). With the developments in AI, artificial intelligence that uses machine learning, sophisticated sensors, and algorithms aimed at discrete tasks, robot constructors no longer try to mimic human mind with its logic-based reasoning. Robotic systems derive meaning from massive data sets using probability-based, genetic algorithms that produce evolving, continuously improving codes. Therefore, robots designed to perform specific tasks (for example, iRobot or Roomba) do not resemble humans (Levy, 2011).

Information and communication technologies (ICT) deal with processing data, information, and knowledge using hardware, software, and programming languages, to create applications of different kinds, design computer networks and information databases. According to the Global Information Technology Report (2009) network readiness correlates with the GDP per capita and depends on the market environment, political and regulatory environment, and infrastructure environment. Mobile telephony occupies a special place among information and communication technologies in terms of both its diffusion and impact on economic growth and poverty reduction.

Background Information Type B: Art Concepts and Principles

Background Information about Biology Inspired Art

We may notice many collaborative and hybrid artistic projects where biology-inspired research results are combined with the use of genetic algorithms, adaptive formal and structural design, architectural approaches, and new fabrication techniques. Works of the EvoNet, the European Network of Excellence in Evolutionary Computing exemplify trends in bio art that uses biotechnology as its medium, and applies evolutionary computing. EvoMUSART events on Evolutionary and Biologically Inspired Music, Sound, Art and Design make a forum for introducing advancements in the use of bio-inspired techniques, such as evolutionary computation, artificial life, artificial neural networks, and swarm intelligence, in the scope of the generation, analysis and interpretation of art, music, design, architecture and other artistic fields. Biologically inspired design and art-making systems create drawings, images, animations, sculptures, poetry, text, objects, designs, websites, buildings, etc. Biologically inspired sound-generators and music-systems create music, aggregate sound, or simulate instruments, voices, and effects. Evolutionary art includes also robotic-based evolutionary art and music, and other related generative techniques (EvoMUSART 2010). Computers serve as design optimization tools employing options provided by the natural selection principles. Transformed or invented living structures are used for developing engineered ecosystems and simulations of biotic habitats (Dorin and Korb, 2007). Interactive projects are also made with a therapeutic perspective. For example, Corwin Bell, my former master's degree student, produces interactive computer video games with biofeedback sensors that measure heart rate and skin conductance; players not only learn to control their breathing, build mental serenity, and reduce stress; they also can access their innate power of visualization and see how their thoughts and emotions may impact their ability to play the game (Bell, 2010).

An interactive painting created by Christa Sommerer and Laurent Mignonneau (2010), professors at the University of Art and Design in Linz Austria, entitled "The Value of Art (Unruhige See)" deals with the economy of attention (as measured with sensors and thermal printers) and value of art in the art world. At the Mediations Art Biennale in Poznan, Poland (2010), the painting starts counting the number of visitors and the amount of time they spend looking at the painting. A digital media artist, computer graphics research scientist, and software entrepreneur Karl Sims (2009) is known for his interactive works, computer animations, and the GenArts, Inc., visual effects software he founded.

Eduardo Kac (2011) develops transgenic art with genetic material artificially modified. For example, in his "Cypher" (2009), Kac introduced synthetic DNA where genetic sequence was encoded according to the artist's poem. His "Natural History of Enigma," awarded the 2009 Golden Nica, comprises a genetically engineered flower that is a hybrid of Kac's DNA and petunia. The gene selected by the artist is responsible for the identification of foreign bodies.

Figure 11 (a and b) shows a computer art graphics inspired by biotechnology.

2. River

We may think of a river as a watercourse with a sufficient flow to serve as a navigable waterway deep and wide enough to travel by water. Rivers carry lumber and goods in barges, self-propelled, towed by tugboats, or pushed by towboats. We will also inquire into the environmental flow of a river that is able to maintain ecosystems. Thus, we might want to seek who lives in a river and why, taking into account possible changes of address, for example, of salmon or trout jumping against

Figure 11. a) Kati Stanford, "Nano"; b) Ryan Napier, "The cell," were inspired by a lecture about nanotechnology. (© 2010, K. Stanford and © 2010, R. Napier. Used with permission.)

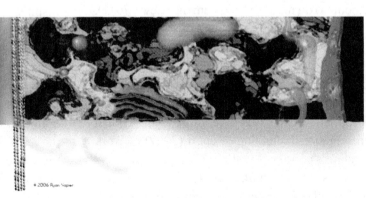

the cascades and even boatlifts, to swim far away upstream and hatch in clear, cold water. We may want to make the acquaintance with animals that can be found in a river, and avoid contacts with other not so gentle creatures. We will examine not only living conditions in a river but also its aesthetic qualities, so vividly shown in art.

Background Information Type A: Natural Events and Processes

Background Information about Management of Water Resources

A growing number of international networks comprising organizations, cooperation agencies, associations, research centers, banks, and other institutions develop coordinated programs aimed at development and management of water, land, and related resources. For example, since 1996 the Global Water Partnership (2010) fosters integrated water resource management. An Intergovernmental Panel on Climate Change (IPCC, 2010), honored with the 2007 Nobel Prize, works on the assessment of information related to water cycle: precipitation; temperature; water vapor; extremes; runoff, river flow, and discharge into the oceans; water storage, soil moisture, lakes, ground water; drought, evaporation; sea level; cryosphere changes; and air pollution. Observations made by the Panel will be used to evaluate models and simulations.

Water Purified

Water can be called the 'drinking water' when it is free from any microorganisms that can cause an acute disease, a well as of any chemical compounds that may cause a chronic disease. Effects of pathogens are immediate, while effects of chemicals are distant in time. Substances that are added to water in order to kill microorganisms often cause chronic diseases. However, if not added, consumption of water may cause diarrhea.

Balancing act means a trade-off between these two factors: killing pathogenic organisms with substances and suffering the side effects of these substances. There are nutrients in water: potassium, carbon, phosphorus, and organic residues, e.g., from leaves. For example, proportion of nutrients can be about: carbon - 100, nitrogen – 10, and phosphorus - 1. Decomposition of organic matter provides too small amount of phosphorus. Engineered bio-filtration can provide phosphorus acid. Introducing bacterial mutations is a controversial issue because people create problems about introducing analytic methods.

Water should not be totally clean; for example, lactobacillus is common and usually benign. Many types of water biota – natural aquatic systems comprise coexisting, often symbiotic organisms. Daphnia – tiny (0.2–5 mm long) freshwater crustaceans are everywhere, the same way as algae are. In a similar way as snails in water reservoirs and canaries in the coalmines, daphnia are used as security agents because they dramatically increase their activity in the presence of any upsetting agent and start to swim in big zigzags. For example, after a drop of gasoline is added to a compartment, sensors register on a computer the increased activity of daphnia.

It's a common knowledge that over 97% of water in the world is saltwater and less than 3% of water that is fresh. 70% of water is frozen at the poles, so humans and animals (except the marine life) have to survive on less than 1% of the planet's accessible water (Global Change, 2010). The process of water purification, aimed at removing harmful chemicals and physical or biological materials, produces usable water for human consumption and industrial applications. When we need safe water for drinking, medical, pharmacological, chemical, or industrial purposes, we have to purify water to rid of dissolved or suspended contaminants and unwanted living organisms. Pollutants can be naturally occurring or introduced; dissolved substances, particles of different kind, viruses, bacteria, algae, fungi, and other living microorganisms, many of them parasitic, as well as toxins, pathogens, poisons, and radioactive contamination create a threat to our life or health. Giardia and Cryptosporidium are ubiquitous pathogens and common protozoan parasites existing in surface water. Giardia, also called a Beaver fever, lives inside human and animal intestines after it is swallowed with contaminated food, water, or soil. Cysts are opening inside human intestines and cause a disease. Cryptosporidium is smaller than Giardia; it is transmitted by domestic animal – person contact, and the results are similar. During an outbreak that occurred in 1993 in southern Wisconsin about 400,000 people became ill and estimated 69 people died, according to Corso, Kramer, Blair, Addiss, Davis, & Haddix, 2003). Scientists continuously perform research projects and environmental assessment, for example, whether bacterium Escherischia coli (*E. Coli*) may be considered an appropriate surrogate for Cryptosporidium occurrence in water (Nieminski, Durrant, Hoyt, Owens, Peterson, Peterson, Tanner, Rosen, & Clancy, 2010).

Multiple barriers protect water. The multiple barrier concept can be realized in many ways:

1. Watershed protection provides a secure water source. Water in a watershed should be protected from swimming, urinating, throwing objects, or adding pesticides.
2. Water treatment; for example, sometimes bad taste, odor, or arsenic must be removed.
3. Distribution system: for example, there may be a pitcher of clean water in a restaurant but glasses may be dirty. Or good water may run in old rusty pipes at 100 degree, in dirty hoses that siphon water.

The challenge of improving an access to clean water involves developing a multitude of methods that reduce concentration of particulate inorganic and organic matter. Water is pre-treated and its pH-adjusted. Further methods for water purification involve technologies such as coagulation, flocculation, sedimentation, and filtration. Typically processes include:

- Desalination of seawater that makes sea- or ocean water potable. Saltwater can only be transformed into drinking water by an expensive desalination process.
  - Physical processes, for example filtration through sand and membranes, and ultrafiltration (where oversize particles cannot pass through the lattice structure of the filter) and *sedimentation* (where the contaminants settle down in response to the forces acting on them).
  - Biological processes, such as slow sand filters or *activated sludge* (involving adding air or oxygen combined with organisms to a sewage or wastewater),
  - Chemical processes, for example, flocculation (using coagulants – chemicals that cause colloids and other suspended particles in liquids to aggregate), chlorination (adding chlorine to water), and other methods for killing bacteria or other pathogens that could pass through filters. Such treatment can be done with chlorine dioxide, chloramine, and hydrogen peroxide.
  - The use of electromagnetic radiation, such as ultraviolet light, ozone, and solar energy.
  - Further treatment involves water fluoridation (or excess fluoride removal), conditioning to reduce water hardness, and removal of lead, radium, and arsenic. Also, boiling, distilling, and passing through activated carbon can improve water purity. Many treatment plants take raw water from rivers and lakes. It is also possible to

obtain clean water from sewage. The first station of sewage treatment to obtain drinking water on industrial scale was in Denver, CO. Scientists presented their 12-step technology (including the use of activated carbon and ozone treatment), and installed a drinking fountain at the end; but at that time people did not want to drink this water.

Oil is one of pollutants that are extremely difficult to remove from water. It deprives water of air and thus kills living organisms. Methods applied to purify water in polluted lakes and rivers include physical and chemical separation of solid matter, and then biological purification through breaking down the organic elements. Some ancient methods for removing oil or salt from water make use of lagoons – shallow, separated bodies of water – where sun, wind, and specific species of plants absorb pollutants. In many places wastewater is still effectively processed with the lagooning method. We can see an impressive image of a water purification center on the online gallery posted by Yann Arthus-Bertrand (2011). This center, located in Marne, France, is one of 15,000 centers that are able to process about half of wastewater in France. Oil is there turned into foam by forcing air through the liquid, and then removed or destroyed by burning.

Developments in Nanoscale Technologies

We have figured out now that we all are built from the nanoscale building blocks and we deal with nanoparticles often without realizing it. Long before the emergence of nanotechnology, while ancient or medieval people did not know about the nanoscale domain and could not see it, they did make use of its potential. We may find several instances from the past of applying specific courses of action without knowing why this action is effec-

tive. For example, Romans used 2,000 years ago the gold and silver nanoparticles in their artwork not knowing they are so minuscule. Medieval artists created stained glass adding nanoparticles of gold that produced colors from yellow-orange to ruby red to purple; so did the Renaissance Italian pottery makers, Irish stain glass designers, and the Damascene masters of sword making (PennState modules, 2009, Goodsell, 2006). People applied molds on wounds without knowledge about the antibiotic properties of penicillin, and used cultured molds to produce cheese, bread, or soy sauce. Developments in nanotechnology allow understanding both the benign and toxic effects of molds (such as toxic molds that produce sometimes deadly mycotoxins). We have realized now what there is in the nanoscale and how can we use nanoparticles and nanotechnology. The Institute for Complex Adaptive Matter, established in 1999, became in 2004 the International Institute for Complex Adaptive Matter, ICAM-I2CAM. It has grown rapidly to a constellation of branches: 31 in the US, 15 in Europe, 5 in Asia, 1 in Australia, 1 in the Middle East, 1 in South America and one European affiliate (ICAM-I2CAM, 2010). Knowledge about the nanoscale biology, which is still in the developmental stage, inspires technology-oriented people to develop and design biologically inspired models, materials, applications, tools, and devices. For example, since 1999 the nature-inspired biomolecular motor 'Myosin V' (Yildiz, Forkey, McKinney, Ha, Goldman, & Selvin, 2003) walks by transducing chemical energy of the ATP hydrolysis to mechanical work. Google images about myosin V display several pages of various solutions.

Nanoscale Objects: Soft Matter

Nano world is an entity that inspires scientists and practitioners to explore complex soft matter and to understand general principles that drive behavior and properties of structures. Developments in technology, especially advances in microscopy opened for us the whole new world. They resulted in discoveries in a nano scale and evolving new epistemologies allowing us to see the world in a new way.

A macro-scale comprises visible objects with sizes of a millimeter or more (1 mm = 1/1,000 meter – 1×10^{-3} m).

A micro-scale relates to objects with sizes about a micrometer (1 μm = 1/1,000,000, one millionth of a meter – 1×10^{-6} m) to about 1/10 of a millimeter.

A nano-scale encompasses a range of subjects with sizes from about a nanometer (1 nm = 1/1,000,000,000, one billionth of meter – 1×10^{-9} m) to about 1/10 of micrometer.

A pico-scale is a size range of single atoms, both found in nature (and represented in the periodic table) and atoms man-made in accelerators for nuclear technology. 1 ångström or angstrom (symbol Å) = 1×10^{-10} meters.

To visualize something that is one nanometer large and to compare it to one inch, we may think about comparing a dice to the Earth. Many familiar objects are millions of nanometers big: a human nail on a little finger is about ten million nanometers across, and a human hair is about 80,000 nanometers wide. A dollar bill is 100,000 nanometers thick. A small reptile gecko can cling upside down to the pane of glass because it has millions of microhairs on its toes; each hair is split into hundreds of tips 200 nanometers wide, which form nanohairs on its microhairs). The van der Waals force causes intermolecular attraction and pulls glass and tips together. Scientists in several institutions fabricate gecko-inspired lamellar and nanofibrillar structures to make surfaces adhere (Lee, Bush, Maboudian, & Fearing, 2009; Sitti, & Fearing, 2003).

When we think about nano scale we mean a great variety of so-called soft condensed matter that is in a state neither liquid nor crystalline: liquid crystals, biological tissues, cells and a cytoplasm, biological membranes, microfilaments and filamentous networks, e.g., a cytoskeleton present in all cells, molecular mono-layers, polymers and biopolymers (such as DNA or filaments in neuronal or muscle fibers), gels, and also food, soap, ink, paint, cosmetics, and putty. In colloids at least a part of a system has a dimension of one micrometer or less. Colloidal systems may form a suspension of a solid in liquid – as in an Indian ink, an emulsion of liquid in liquid – as in mayonnaise, a foam of gas in liquid – as in beer or a soap foam, or a sponge containing gas in solid – in a bath sponge or ice cream (Smalyukh, 2010).

Some properties of nano-scale objects are unique, such as a small size comparable to biological structures and macromolecules, large surface to volume ratio, quantum mechanical effects, and wave properties (caused by the size of nanostructures that is smaller than the wavelength of visible light, so light interacts with nanostructures (scatters and diffracts) differently (Penn State modules, 2009). Familiar materials develop odd properties when they're nanosize because their atomic structure is determined at this level. For example, aluminum foil will behave like aluminum when it is cut in strips, until the strips become 20 to 30 nanometers, when they can explode.

Soft materials have chemical and mechanical characteristics that are useful in technology, such as quantum size effects, responsiveness to small electrical fields and to chemical or thermal actions, and flexibility, so they are used in a fast growing number of applications (for example, in flat panel LCD TVs). However, nanotoxicology, the study of toxicity of nanomaterials is intended to determine a threat to the environment and humans. Research papers and conference proceedings, for example, Nanotoxicology Conference (2010) in Edinburg comprise approaches that promote interaction between different disciplines and discuss exposure and risk assessment, human toxicology, and ecotoxicology.

Liquid Crystals

Liquid crystals have usually a structure of rods with dipole characteristics and general orientation along a common axis. They are not so ordered as in crystalline matter, and not fully isotropic (without orientation) as liquids. Liquid crystal materials have different types of states depending on the amount of order. Molecules of lyotropic liquid crystals have the hydrophilic (water loving) and hydrophobic (water-hating) parts. Thermotropic liquid crystals, which are in a phase of matter intermediate between solids and liquids, are further classified into smectic, nematic, and cholesteric (also known as chiral nematic), among other types. The nematic phase, with no positional order but aligned in the same direction, smectic phases, also with general orientation but in addition aligned in layers or planes, chiral (not identical to its mirror image) nematic phases, and columnar phases, with stacked columns of disks. As dipoles, liquid crystals respond to electric and magnetic fields.

Soap bubbles are made of liquid crystals. Bubbles change colors when light is reflected through the bubble walls. First, the bubble wall is thicker and reflects all the full spectrum of colors in a rainbow. Part of light is reflected from the outer surface of a bubble, and part is reflected from the inner surface that is a few nanometers further. When the two waves interfere, we see color, which is more intense when the waves reinforce each other. When the bubble wall gets thinner, with a smaller distance between surfaces, the reflected waves of light start to coincide, cancel each other out, and the bubble loses its color (Bubbles, 2011).

Self-assembled 3D DNA Crystals

The best description of the structure of matter is at the atomic and molecular scale, which is observable in two dimensions. By producing precisely designed 3D macroscopic objects it is possible to bridge the macroscopic and molecular worlds, which is required to understand the relationships with atomic precision. Zheng and others (2009) formed the crystal structure at 4Å resolution of a designed, self-assembled, 3D DNA crystal. The helically repeating nature of DNA facilitates the construction of a periodic array. The authors formed a crystalline arrangement of a DNA crystal that fulfilled criteria necessary to produce a 3D periodic system: a robust 3D structure and affinity interactions between parts of the DNA with predictable structures when it self-associates by its sticky ends. They demonstrated that it is possible to design and self-assemble a well-ordered macromolecular 3D crystalline lattice with precise control.

Carbon Nanotubes

Biologically inspired nanoscience includes nano materials such as fullerenes and nanotubes (carbon, inorganic, DNA, and membrane nanotubes), and nanotechnologies, for example molecular electronics, nanolithography, or nanorobotics. Carbon as a chemical element has eight allotropes (coexisting different structural forms), three of them being common: diamond with a tetrahedral lattice of carbon atoms, graphite with a hexagonal lattice, and fullerenes with atoms in a carbon molecule bonded in a form of an empty sphere, ellipsoid or tube. A nanotech pioneer, the 1996 Nobel Prize-winning chemist Richard Smalley (Smalley-resources, 2011) discovered a strong molecule made of 60 carbon atoms. He called this spherical molecule a buckminsterfullerene or a buckyball, because it resembled geodesic domes created by Richard Buckminster Fuller. Richard Smalley envisioned a power grid laced with nanotubes that would distribute electricity from solar farms. He was confident that nanoscale missiles would target cancer cells in human body. He spoke this on June 1999 but he died of non-Hodgkin lymphoma on October 2005. The IBM Research – Zurich scientists Gross, Mohn, Moll, Liljeroth, & Meyer (2009) succeeded in imaging of single molecules and their chemical structure with unprecedented atomic resolution by probing the short-range chemical forces with use of noncontact atomic force microscopy. They are able to imagine not only the physical shape of a single carbon nanotube but to show up the chemical bonds.

Thus, carbon nanotubes are cylindrical fullerenes, usually a few nanometers wide, tens of thousands times smaller than the diameter of human hair. In August 2009 scientists provided images of single carbon nanotubes, where even the bonds to the hydrogen atoms could be seen (Palmer, 2009). Carbon nanotubes may be micrometers up to centimeters long. Thin nanotube sheets are 250 times stronger than steel and 10 times lighter. Their mechanical tensile strength, high electrical and heat conductivity, and chemical inactivity makes them useful in nanotechnology, electronics, optics, material and architectural science domains, and many other applications, such as for strengthening materials, gluing, coating transparent conductive display films, building artificial muscles (Aliev, Oh, Kozlov, Kuznetsov, Fang, Fonseca, Ovalle, Lima, Haque, Gartstein, Zhang, Zakhidov, & Baughman, 2009), space elevators, a body armor (in the MIT's Institute for Soldier Nanotechnologies: ISN, 2010), waterproof and tear-resistant textiles (Dalton, Collins, Muñoz, Razal, Von Ebron, Ferraris, Coleman, Kim, & Baughman, 2003), non-cracking concrete, and a lot of other implementations. While nanoparticles have been considered extremely toxic, Chan (2007) concludes that the evidence, which was gathered since the discovery of fullerenes, overwhelmingly points to C_{60} being non-toxic.

Nanoshells

A nanoshell consists of a dielectric core covered by a thin metallic (usually gold) shell. Light interacts with nanoparticles; hence nanoshells possess optical and chemical properties involving quantum plasma oscillation where the electrons simultaneously oscillate with respect to all the ions (plasmon hybridization). They are often used for biomedical imaging, fluorescence enhancement of weak molecular emitters, some kinds of surface enhanced spectroscopy, and therapeutic applications. For example, gold nanoshells act as a Trojan horse when they enter a tumor cell in a macrophage and cause a photo-induced tumor cell death (Choi, Stanton-Maxey, Stanley, Levin, Bardhan, Akin, Badve, Sturgis, Robinson, Bashir, Halas, & Clare, 2007). Nanoparticles can be made "top down" by chopping a bulk material into nanosize bits or "bottom up" by growing molecules like crystals in controlled conditions.

Water Purification in Micro and Nano Scale

Scientists are focusing on novel ways to produce clean drinking water from contaminated or salty water. They focus on efficient flow of water through a novel class of filter materials: carbon nanotubes, stacked in arrays so that water must pass through the length of the tubes. Along with the developments in a micro scale, several nanoscale processes, nano science and technology (a nano unit is a thousand times smaller then a micron) serve for water purification. Some methods apply the nanoscale adhesion process, in which nanofibers coated with a thin metallic film attract electrostatically charged particles; other methods include nanoceramic, nonmetallic materials synthesized from inorganic powders, and less than 100 nanometer nanofibers. The ultrafiltration method uses 10^{-7} m to 10^{-8} m membrane filters to remove particles from water under very high pressure; the nanofiltration method applies the 10^{-8} m to 10^{-10} m nanoceramic filters, and the *reverse osmosis* pushes the solvent through a 10^{-9} m to 10^{-11} m membrane by applying pressure on the higher concentration side.

World Community Grid (2010) is a network of more than 400 partners to create the world's largest public computing grid. It joints many individual computers, creating a large system with massive computational power, to tackle projects that benefit humanity. One of these is the Computing for Clean Water project (2010) aimed at understanding the molecular-scale processes that could produce more efficient water filters for clean water and desalination. Current extensive research is focused on efficient water filtering with the use of carbon nanotubes stacked in arrays. For example, the Computing for Clean Water Project group (CNMM, 2010) is developing nature-inspired molecular simulations using computer programs and researching processes that facilitate water flow in nanotubes. Researchers from this group developed simulations that show motion of individual water molecules through the nanotubes that are only a few water molecules in diameter.

Background Information Type C: Computing or Technology

Background Information about Drawing Inspiration from Nature for Evolutionary Computing

Self-organization is a typical characteristic of biological systems, from the sub-cellular structures to ecosystems. The origin of life from the self-organizing chemical matter, the swarm behavior of social insects (such as bees or ants), mammals living in groups, and the flocking performance of birds and schools of fish – are considered self-organizing phenomena. Collective action performed by self-organized (without a central authority), biological or artificial systems is called swarm intelligence. People also display swarm behavior in some circumstances.

The inspiration for applying swarm intelligence concept in computing came in great part from the self-organized natural systems. Mathematical models describe swarm behavior as the collective motion of self-propelled units following simple rules that do not result from any central coordina-tion. For example, individuals in a swarm, whether comprising animals or agents in a model, move in one direction without collisions, one close to another. Drawing their inspiration from nature, scientists develop evolutionary computing that uses evolutionary systems to build problem-solving techniques based on general ideas of biological evolution, like natural selection and genetic inheritance. They achieve it by building evolutionary models and techniques for computation, such as genetic algorithms, artificial evolution strategies, classifier systems, evolutionary programming, genetic programming, swarm intelligence (e.g., ant colony optimization and particle swarm optimization), and other techniques. Computer scientists build decentralized systems such as networks that are aimed at information processing, even at the global level, with the use of self-evolving cellular arrays or evolutionary computation.

With ambient intelligence, processing of information is interactively embedded in our ordinary activities and objects, often without our awareness. This model, which relates to pervasive computing and ubiquitous computing, is considered a future paradigm, and an advanced stage in comparison with the desktop paradigm, because of its capability to record and oversee our surroundings and support our interactions with other people or objects.

A Limerick about Water

Water and all just discussed things about water may inspire the reader to write and illustrate a limerick. This project comprises writing and drawing. The task involves exploration of the meaning carried by the notion of water and then showing your verbal and visual power of conveying your response. It starts from writing a limerick, a comic, frequently nonsensical verse that consists of five lines, rhyming aabba. The verse and the picture will tell about a water encounter (so the theme requires some research). Try to express the very

Figure 12. David Frisk, Melissa Nakamura, and Crystal Schuller, Limericks. (© 2010, D. Frisk, M. Nakamura, C. Schuller. Used with permission).

essence of the encounter with water environment or the enjoyment of it. To fulfill this task, create a picture illustrating the limerick. Figure 12 shows three students' limericks about water illustrated on a computer.

David Frisk:

There once was a boy on a boat,

Who set sail across a great moat;

To rescue a maid, from a fierce tirade,

And thus a legend was wrote.

Melissa Nakamura:

I don't know how to write a limerick

Something about water? What a trick!

You can swim, you can jump

You can swim, you can pump

Hey! I guess I can write a limerick.

Crystal Schuller:

My brand new watch was pricey

It kept the time quite nicely.

I thought it would be cool

To take it with me into the pool,

By now my watch does not work so precisely.

3. Swamp

Swamps, wetlands and freshwater marshes (such as Florida Everglades) are swarming with animals that live deep in water, near the surface, or above the water surface. When we think about swamps, the spectacular variety of animals may be a first thing that comes to mind. Deep in dark, low-oxygen water live many kinds of fish, crayfish (small freshwater lobsters), shrimp, crabs, tadpoles, and insect larvae (e.g., mosquito larvae), among many other species At the surface of water live meat-eating alligators, caimans (that live in Amazon basin waters of the rain forest habitat), Chinese and American alligators, plant-eating nutrias, and capybaras (the biggest rodents in the world living in Central and South America) that would eat everything of both animal and plant origin. Some animals live above water, such as birds (such as black-and-white Downy woodpeckers, flamingoes, great blue herons, great egrets, or cranes), insects (e.g., dragonflies) while other, such as scorpions, spiders, frogs, toads, turtles, beavers live at the surface of water, as well as raccoons, opossums, muskrats, snails, or white tail deer, which used to live around the swamps (Enchanted Learning, 2011).

However, we will focus on examining swamps in a micro scale, by looking at the plankton, which can be seen under a microscope, the macro–micro relations, and the nanobiology of the water ecosystem that is full of tiny or even single-celled plants and animals. Plankton consists of microscopic organisms floating in water. Phytoplankton is composed of plants and zooplankton of animals. Phytoplankton organisms are autotrophic: they use their chlorophyll to convert sunlight into energy, and also produce carbohydrates from inorganic chemicals and dissolved carbon dioxide. Figure 13 (a and b) presents works about water ecosystem.

Background Information Type A: Natural Events and Processes

Background Information

Creatures Down under

In the project, one may want to picture an underwater world full of bizarre creatures. There is no necessity to imagine such pictures from your fantasy because nature has already developed a multitude of creatures with strange, weird, sometimes grotesque shapes (which can be easily found in water samples using a microscope or while making an online search). Two examples of amazing water inhabitants are described below. The Dutch painter Hieronymus Bosch (~1450-1516) did not have an access to the Internet, nor to a microscope, when he created fantastic, often astonishing creatures in his "Earthly Delights" or a "Garden of Eden" (which could be easily seen at Google images after typing "Hieronymus Bosch").

Square Creatures

One may wonder, are there any square-shaped organisms in nature and why this shape, if existing, is so unusual. It seems there is one genus, called Haloquadratum walsbyi that has this unique shape. However, it is still unknown why haloquadra take this unusual form. Haloquadra are about 0.15 μm thick (1 μm = 10^{-6} m). Their square cells join with others to build sheets up to 40 μm long. They move forward rotating their flagella clockwise, or backward when rotate them counterclockwise. Haloquadra, discovered in 1980, were considered impossible to cultivate in a lab up to 2004. Now the mapping of the organism's 3.1 Mb large genome is underway (Haloquadra, 2010). Haloquadra be-

Figure 13. a) Jessica Oxton, "Mangrove swamp"; b) Anna Melkumian, "Lake, River, Swamp" (© 2010, J. Oxton, A. Melkumiann. Used with permission).

long to archaea (single-celled organisms without cell nuclei or other membrane-bound organelles, different in many aspects from other organisms, such as bacteria or eukaryote). Like other archaea, haloquadra are common in different waters, but they also can live in extreme harsh environments such as volcanic hot springs or salt lakes (in concentration of salt up to 18%); they can also survive organic solvents. They can draw energy from numerous sources, using as nutrients organic compounds, ammonia, metal ions, and hydrogen.

The 0.1 mm Long Water Bear

Tardigrades live in waters of the entire world, from above twenty thousand feet (6,000 m) in Himalayas to about thirteen thousand feet (4,000 m) below the sea level. In 1777 they were called Tardigrada (which means 'slow walkers'), and are also known as water bears because they walk like bears (Water Bear, 2011). Tardigrades are 0.1 mm to 1.5 mm long, and their larvae may be smaller than 0.05 mm; they can be seen with a microscope or on a multitude of pictures online. It's easy to find them in moss growing on a roof, so they are also called 'moss pigs'. One can find as much as 25,000 tardigrades in one liter of water, in lichens and mosses, freshwater sediments, dunes, or beaches. According to researchers from the Center for Tardigrade Research (CTR, 2010), moss cushions or lichens are microhabitats that may be considered as nanoecosystems inhabited by a community dominated by nematodes, rotifers and tardigrades. They are almost indestructible: they survive extremely hard conditions, such as living a decade without water, temperatures close to absolute zero or about 300^0 F, and 1,000 times more radiation than other animals or humans. According to Jönsson, Rabbow, Schill, Harms-Ringdahl, & Rettberg, 2008), tardigrades were taken into low Earth orbit mission and for 10 days were exposed to the vacuum of space. After they were returned to Earth, it was discovered that many of them survived and laid eggs that

hatched normally (Flemming, Verolet, Goldstein, Hobgood, & Raines, 2008).

Visualization of Biological Data: DNA

Researchers utilize visualization tools to understand better the massive amount of complex biological data and provide new biological insights. Designing visualization tools that support research results usually from collaboration between biology and computing science specialists. Maybe the most popular biological visualization on the molecular, nanoscale level is a colorful, often rotating, animated picture of a DNA (deoxyribonucleic acid) structure.

The DNA molecules store the long-term information and instructions needed to build components of cells, such as proteins, molecules of ribonucleic acid RNA. They influence organism characteristics through information stored within regions of DNA called genes. Development and survival of a living organism depends on the precise regulation of the expression of genetic information (Watson & Crick, 1953). Following the solution of DNA structure and the deciphering of the genetic code instructing the translation of RNA transcripts, Francis Crick (2010) introduced the term 'Central Dogma', which depicted the flow of genetic information between macromolecules as proceeding from DNA to RNA to protein. Beginning in 1990 scientists worked on international Human Genome Project resulting in multiple publications on the project's progress on sequencing approximately 20,500 genes present in human beings. Following this research, Venter et al (2001) published in Science magazine "The Sequence of the Human Genome." And then on November 5, 2009, Radoje Drmanac (2009) and 64 coauthors published online in *Science* magazine a report about a DNA sequence completion of the sequencing of the human genome. They examined each base from patterned nanoarrays of self-assembling DNA nanoballs and identified 3.2 to 4.5 million sequence variants per genome.

The authors opened their article with a statement, "genome sequencing of large numbers of individuals promises to advance the understanding, treatment, and prevention of human diseases, among other applications." Currently genetic information is used in many technologies, such as genetic engineering, forensics, bioinformatics, DNA nanotechnology, history, anthropology, and many other branches of knowledge.

"The Traffic on the Sky, the Horizon, and a Hidden Treasure in Water" Project

This artistic theme would be focused on including action into a composition. This picture can be envisaged as consisting from three parts arranged vertically, with the top, middle and bottom parts representing action in the sky, on a horizon, and the underwater area.

Actions and events on the skies may consist from clouds carried by the wind, storms with thunder and lightning, heavy rain or hail, but also flocks of birds, planes, gliders, balloons with gondolas, and kites. A horizon surface where water meets the sky may be populated with ships, sailboats, and surfers. A hidden treasure region includes fish, reefs, or sunken galleons.

The challenging part of this project is in furnishing the picture with an overall feel of dynamics and action rather than representing separate objects. Also, composition of the three parts will be decisive for its integrity and overall aesthetics. Figure 14 (a, b, and c) presents three projects about traffic in water.

Background Information Type C: Computing or Technology

Creating an Icon

While responding to this project, one may want to design one's own icon. In visualizations, we often use icons, images of iconic objects that are familiar to all viewers, such as an old-style electric bulb, a

Figure 14. a (left) Jael Esquibel, b (middle) Sean Norman, and c (right) Jessica Wilson. (© 2010, J. Esquibel, s. Norman, J. Wilson. Used with permission).

DNA double helix, or a telephone handset. In an everyday practice we use icons to easily allude to concepts or issues that may be far from our specialty. Most often, we use icons referring to concrete objects; however, many icons stand for abstract ideas. For example, an old-style electric bulb shining above a head is often meant to stand for a bright idea. However, one may wonder why so many objects and ideas, for example, intelligence (not to mention artificial intelligence) do not yet have their visual counterparts in the form of iconic images. Many icons have a long life, sometimes longer than the shapes of the objects they stand for; we already seldom use the old-style phones with handsets but we can see the icon when we want to use such a phone and look for a phone booth. In the same way, in spite of the developments in robotics, a picture of an anthropomorphic, humanoid robot still serves as an icon for a great many industrial, servicing robots, those designed for specific tasks, or bots (virtual software agents), all of them not resembling humans. By the way, the word "robot" was coined in 1920, in the course of conversation between the Czech writer Karel Čapek (1890-1938) and his brother, the cubist painter and writer Josef Čapek (Zunt, 2005); it was given to an artificial man that could be mistaken for humans. The U.S. writer of Russian origin Isaac Asimov (1920-1992) introduced to the readers in 1941 the term 'robotics' building on Karel Čapek's concept of the robot.

After many encounters with the water related creatures, issues, and images, you may want to create water-inspired icon, which would signal some specific function, situation, or event. You may create a series of icons signifying, for example, your typical daily activities.

Working on a Project

The "Habitats: Lakes, Rivers, and Swamps" Triptych

This project can be done as a synthetic, contemplative, and informative triptych (a work consisting of three panels that are hinged together) about water environments. It may be proving quite a challenge to create a triptych "Habitats: Lakes, Rivers, and Swamps" containing drawings (made on a computer or hand drawings) showing a mental picture of water life – a synthetic, contemplative or cheerful image. It requires inquiring both into the living conditions and the aesthetic qualities of this environment.

The "Habitats: Lakes, Rivers, and Swamps" project might contain a title placed on top, a triptych made from color printouts of this artwork placed in the center, and three (optional) pieces of writing describing three states of water. The light qualities and the colors around water may come into question for further consideration. In a shallow lake, pebbles at the bottom throw the light back; deep water reflects and thus repeats the line of horizon and shows an inverted image of a landscape. In a river, light changes incessantly because of fast-moving currents. Swamps may be mysteriously static, opaque, textured, and without reflections.

The answer to the "Habitats: Lakes, Rivers, and Swamps" theme may also take a form of an open work (Eco, 1989), where the viewers construct interactively many different, meaningful interpretations. An Italian philosopher, semiotician, and writer Umberto Eco (born 1932) wrote, "The problem is not to challenge the old idea that the world is a text which can be interpreted, but rather to decide whether it has a fixed meaning, many possible meanings, or none at all." (Eco, 1994, 23). Decoding of a message is possible when a message is decoded on a basis of a code shared by both the artist and the viewer. However the codes of the addressee are often different from

Figure 15. a (top) Sam Dailey; b (bottom) Jael Esquibel. (© 2010, S. Dailey, J. Esquibel. Used with permission).

those of the sender. For example, it would be such a case, were the American allegorical painter Albert Pinkham Ryder (1847-1917, an artist known for this poetic art) evaluated as a seascapist only, and the Swiss symbolist painter Arnold Böcklin (1827-1901, an artist who influenced numerous music composers and also Surrealist and Art Nouveau artists) as an illustrator of mythology. There are also deliberately open messages, using periphrases, symbols, or synaesthetic signs that could be freely interpreted.

Figure 15 shows two works entitled "Lake, River, Swamp Triptych," one depicting the physical appearance, and another done as an abstract artwork.

A Title as a Part of the Work

A title may provide a connection between visual and verbal communication. Perception of the artwork often depends on knowledge of the title. In electronic art, a distance between the artist's eye and the computer screen is rather small, unless the artwork is meant to be displayed on a big screen or through a projection system. The Polish painter Stanislaw Fijalkowski titled his work "Walk back seven steps". Due to the artist's imperative, the viewers are drawn into the space laid out between them and the surface of the artwork, so its reception is improved due to their involuntary reaction.

In many computer art graphics, the title and/or the artistic statement becomes an integral part of the artwork and is often decisive for its understanding. When a non-figural artwork is provided with a title, viewer's attitude to the work may be changed or guided by the title. For example, the American painter Jackson Pollock (1912-1956) entitled his non-figurative painting "Night Mist" (1944), whereas the characteristics of the American painter Mark Rothko's (1903-1970) painting have been enhanced by its descriptive title "Light Red over Black" (1957). That way, one may successfully apply a title that would guide the reception of an artwork.

CONCLUSION

"Looking at sciences through the water" explores connections between science, computing, and art. This chapter consists of two projects about water-related themes: (1) States of matter exemplified by ice, water, and steam, and (2) Water habitats: lake, river, and swamp. You have been invited to create visual presentation of each theme. The reason behind this interactive enterprise is an attempt to create an interactive process that would result in generation, visualization, constructive criticism, analysis, productive reactions to criticism, and the resulting changes toward refinement. In the artistic, conceptual, cognitive, critical, and visualizing terms, this endeavor offers support in one's work on a project, lowers the cognitive load inferred by such work, provides valuable, often multicultural connections with others, along with an exposure to great sources for inspiration. Working on each

project makes a favorable occasion to exercise our skills in using communication media for gathering interesting facts and ideas and actively responding to them in a pictorial way.

REFERENCES

Adamatzky, A. (2010). Physarum machines: Encapsulating reaction-diffusion to compute spanning tree. *Naturwissenschaften, 94*(12), 975–980. doi:10.1007/s00114-007-0276-5

Aliev, A. E., Oh, J., Kozlov, M. E., Kuznetsov, A. A., Fang, S., & Fonseca, A. F. (1575-1578). … Baughman, R. H. (2009). Giant-Stroke, superelastic carbon nanotube aerogel muscles. *Science, 323*(5921). doi:doi:10.1126/science.1168312

Arthus-Bertrand, Y. (2011). *The image of a deoiling basin at a water purification centre*. France: Marne.

Bell, C. (2010). *Wild divine*. Retrieved January 4, 2011, from http://www.wilddivine.com/company_bios.html

Biever, C. (2006). A good robot has personality but not looks. *New Scientist, 2561*. Retrieved January 9, 2011, from http://www.newscientist.com/article/mg19125616.400-a-good-robot-has-personality-but-not-looks.html

Bonabeau, E., Corne, D., & Poli, R. (2010). Swarm intelligence: The state of the art special issue of natural computing. [Springer.]. *Natural Computing, 9*, 655–657. doi:10.1007/s11047-009-9172-6

Bubbles. (2011). Retrieved February 1, 2011, from http://bubbles.org/html/questions/color.htm

Buonarroti, M. (2011). *Deluge*. Retrieved January 27, 2011, from http://www.wga.hu/frames-e.html?/html/m/michelan/3sistina/1genesis/2flood/02_3ce2.html

Buonarroti, M. (2011). *Sistine Chapel*. Retrieved January 27, 2011, from http://www.wga.hu/frames-e.html?/html/m/michelan/3sistina/1genesis/2flood/02_3ce2.html%20and%20http://www.wga.hu/tours/sistina/index3.html

Chan, W. C. (2007). Toxicity studies of fullerenes and derivatives. In *Bio-applications of nanoparticles*. New York, NY: Springer Science+Business Media. ISBN 0-387-76712-6

Change, G. (2010). *Human appropriation of the world's fresh water supply*. Retrieved December 11, 2010, from http://www.globalchange.umich.edu/globalchange2/current/lectures/freshwater_supply/freshwater.html

Choi, M., Stanton-Maxey, K., Stanley, J., Levin, C., Bardhan, R., & Akin, D. (2007). A cellular Trojan Horse for delivery of therapeutic nanoparticles into tumors. *Nano Letters, 7*(12), 3759–3765. doi:10.1021/nl072209h

Ciurlionis, M. (2011). *Deluge*.

CNMM. (2010). *Computing for clean water project*. Center for Nano and Micro Mechanics. Retrieved December 11, 2010, from http://cnmm.tsinghua.edu.cn/channels/495.html

Corso, P., Kramer, M., Blair, K., Addiss, D., Davis, J., & Haddix, A. (2003). Cost of illness in the 1993 waterborne Cryptosporidium outbreak, Milwaukee, Wisconsin. *Emerging Infectious Diseases, 9*(4), 426–431.

Crick, F. H. C. (1958). On protein synthesis. [from http://profiles.nlm.nih.gov/SC/B/B/Z/Y/_/scbbzy.pdf]. *Symposia of the Society for Experimental Biology, 12*, 138–163. Retrieved April 13, 2011

CTR. (2010). *Center for Tardigrade Research*. Retrieved December 19, 2010, from http://www.tardires.ch/

Dalton, A. B., Collins, S., Muñoz, E., Razal, J. M., Von Ebron, H., & Ferraris, J. P. (2003). Super-tough carbon-nanotube fibres. *Nature, 423*, 703. doi:10.1038/423703a

Damncoolpics. (2006). *Japanese manhole cover art*. Retrieved December 3, 2010, from http://damncoolpics.blogspot.com/2006/12/japanese-manhole-cover-art.html

Denevan, J. (2011). *The art of Jim Denevan*. Personal website. Retrieved April 11, 2011, from http://www.jimdenevan.com/

Doré, G. (2011). *The deluge*. Retrieved January 27, 2011, from http://en.wikipedia.org/wiki/File:Gustave_Doré_-_The_Holy_Bible_-_Plate_I,_The_Deluge.jpg

Dorin, A., & Korb, K. (2007). Building artificial ecosystems from artificial chemistry. *9th European Conference on Artificial Life* (pp. 103-112). Springer-Verlag.

Drmanac, R., Sparks, A. B., Callow, M. J., Halpern, A. L., et al. (5 November 2009). Human genome sequencing using unchained base reads on self-assembling DNA nanoarrays. *Science, 327*(5961), 78-81. Retrieved December 19, 2010, from http://www.sciencemag.org/content/327/5961/78.abstract

DW-World.DE Deutsche Welle. (17.08.2010). Retrieved December 15, 2010 from http://www.dw-world.de/dw/article/0,5918010,00.html

Eco, U. (1984). *The role of the reader: Explorations in the semiotics of texts*. Bloomington, IN: Indiana University Press.

Eco, U. (1989). *1979). The open work*. Cambridge, MA: Harvard University Press.

Eco, U. (1994). *The limits of interpretation (advances in semiotics)*. Bloomington, IN: Indiana University Press.

Enchanted learning. (2011). Retrieved January 23, 2011, from http://www.enchantedlearning.com/biomes

EvoMUSART. (2010). *Eighth European Event on Evolutionary and Bio-inspired Music, Sound, Art, and Design.* Retrieved January 9, 2011, from http://eden.dei.uc.pt/~machado/evomusart2010.pdf

Flemming, A., Verolet, M., Goldstein, B., Hobgood, N., & Raines, G. (2008). *The most important microbe you've never heard of* [Video]. Retrieved October 10, 2011, from http://www.npr.org/templates/story/story.php?storyId=99800021

Gao, X., & Jiang, L. (2004). Biophysics: Water-repellent legs of water striders. *Nature, 432*(7013), 36. doi:10.1038/432036a

Gericault, T. (2011). *Scene of the deluge.* Retrieved January 27, 2011, from http://www.wikigallery.org/wiki/painting_218864/Theodore-Gericault/Scene-of-the-Deluge

Global Information Technology Report 2008-2009. (2009). *Mobility in a networked world.* Retrieved January 9, 2011, from https://members.weforum.org/pdf/gitr/2009/gitr09fullreport.pdf

Global Water Partnership. (2010). Retrieved January 4, 2011 from www.gwp.org

Goodsell, D. S. (2006). Fact and fantasy in nanotech imagery. *Leonardo Journal, the International Society for the Arts . Sciences and Technology, 42*(1), 52–57.

Gross, L., Mohn, F., Moll, N., Liljeroth, P., & Meyer, G. (2009). The chemical structure of a molecule resolved by atomic force microscopy. *Science, 329*(5944), 1110–1114. doi:10.1126/science.1176210

Gutzler, D. S., & Preston, J. W. (1997). Evidence for a relationship between spring snow cover in North America and summer rainfall in New Mexico. *Geophysical Research Letters, 24,* 2207–2210. doi:10.1029/97GL02099

Haloquadra. (2010). Retrieved January 27, 2011, from microbewiki.kenyon.edu/index.php/Haloquadra

Hansmeyer, M. (2011). *Computational architecture.* Personal website. Retrieved April 11, 2011, from http://www.michael-hansmeyer.com/html/

Hartman, N. W., & Bertoline, G. R. (2005). Spatial abilities and virtual technologies: Examining the computer graphics learning environment. *Proceedings of the Ninth International Conference on Information Visualisation,* (pp. 992-99). Washington, DC: IEEE Computer Society.

Heller, D. (2004). *Manhole covers of the world.* Retrieved April 11, 2011, from http://www.danheller.com/manholes.html

Heller, E. (2011). *Personal website.* Retrieved April 11, 2011, from http://www.ericjhellergallery.com/index.pl?page=image;iid=68)

Helmcke, J. G., & Kull, U. (2004). *IL38 Diatoms II: Shells in nature and technics III.* Universität Stuttgart, Germany: Institut für Leichte Flächentragwerke.

Hockney, D. (2011). *Personal website.* Retrieved April 11, 2011, from http://www.hockneypictures.com

ICAM-I2CAM. (2010). *The International Institute for Complex Adaptive Matter.* Retrieved December 11, 2010 from http://icam-i2cam.org/index.php/about/

IPCC. (2010). *Intergovernmental Panel on Climate Change.* Retrieved December 4, 2010, from http://www.ipcc.ch/index.htm

ISN. (2010). *Massachusetts Institute of Technology, Institute for Soldier Nanotechnologies.* Retrieved December 11, 2010, from http://web.mit.edu/isn/

It, P. (2009). *Traveller's language kit* (16th ed.).

Jones, J. (2010). Influences in the formation and evolution of *Physarum polycephalum* inspired emergent transport networks. *Natural Computing, 4,* 793–1006. doi:doi:10.1007/s11047-010-9223-z

Jönsson, K. I., Rabbow, E., Schill, R. O., Harms-Ringdahl, M., & Rettberg, P. (2008). Tardigrades survive exposure to space in low Earth orbit. *Current Biology, 18* (17), R729-R731. Retrieved December 19, 2010, from http://www.cell.com/current-biology/abstract/S0960-9822(08)00805-1

Kac, E. (2011). *Website of Eduardo Kac.* Retrieved January 26, 2011, from http://ekac.org/

Lee, J., Bush, B., Maboudian, B., & Fearing, R. S. (2009). Gecko-inspired combined lamellar and nanofibrillar array for adhesion on nonplanar surface. *Langmuir, 25*(21), 12449–12453. doi:10.1021/la9029672

Levy, S. (2011, January). The AI revolution. *Wired.* Retrieved from http://www.wired.com/magazine/2010/12/ff_ai_essay_airevolution/

Libbrecht, K. G. (2011). *Snow crystals.* Retrieved April 11, 2011, from http://www.its.caltech.edu/~atomic/snowcrystals/

London National Gallery. (2010). Retrieved November 20, 2010, from http://www.nationalgallery.org.uk/server.php?show=ConConstituent.539

Mateo, J., & Sauter, F. (Eds.). (2007). *Natural metaphor: Architectural papers III, Zurich: The Millennium Development Goals Report.* United Nations. Retrieved December 11, 2010, from http://mdgs.un.org/unsd/mdg/Resources/Static/Products/Progress2008/MDG_Report_2008_En.pdf#page=44

Morland, L. W., & Staroszczyk, R. (2009). Ice viscosity enhancement in simple shear and uniaxial compression due to crystal rotation. *International Journal of Engineering Science, 47*(11-12), 1297–1304. doi:10.1016/j.ijengsci.2008.09.011

Mythology, (2008). *National Geographic essential visual history of world mythology.* Berlin, Germany: Peter Delius Verlag GmbH & Co KG. ISBN 978-1-4262-0373-2

Nanotoxicology Conference. (2010). Retrieved April 13, 2011, from http://www.certh.gr/A806416C.el.aspx

Nieminski, E., Durrant, G. C., Hoyt, M. B., Owens, M. E., Peterson, L., & Peterson, S. (2010). Is *E. Coli* an appropriate surrogate for *Cryptosporidium* occurrence in water? *Journal - American Water Works Association, 102*(3), 65–78.

NSIDC. (2010). *National Snow and Ice Data Center.* Retrieved December 4, 2010, from http://nsidc.org/arcticmet/glossary/sublimation.html

Oram, B. (2010). *Soils, infiltration, and on-site testing.* Wilkes University. Retrieved December 4, 2010, from www.water-research.net/powerpoint/soilinfiltration.ppt

Organisms, M. (2008). *The use of model organisms in instruction.* University of Wisconsin: Wisconsin Outreach Research Modules. Retrieved January 9, 2011, from http://wormclassroom.org/teaching-model-organisms

Palmer, J. (2009). *Single molecule's stunning image.* Retrieved August 20, 2011, from http://news.bbc.co.uk/2/hi/science/nature/8225491.stm

PennState modules. (2009). *NACK educational resources.* The Pennsylvania State University. Retrieved December 11, 2010, from http://nano4me.live.subhub.com/categories/modules

Pidwirny, M., & Jones, S. (2010). *Fundamentals of physical geography.* Retrieved December 4, 2010, from http://www.physicalgeography.net/fundamentals/chapter8.html

Posner, M. I. (1993). *Foundations of cognitive science.* Cambridge, MA: The MIT Press.

Posner, R. (1992). Origins and development of contemporary syntactics. *Languages of Design, 1*(1), 37–504.

Reynolds, C. (2002). *Evolutionary computation and its application to art and design.* Retrieved January 9, 2011, from http://www.red3d.com/cwr/evolve.html

Sims, K. (2009). *Karl Sims website.* Retrieved January 9, 2011, from http://www.karlsims.com/

Sitti, M., & Fearing, R. S. (2003). Synthetic gecko foot-hair micro/nano-structures as dry adhesives. *Journal of Adhesion Science and Technology, 18*(7), 1055–1074. doi:10.1163/156856103322113788

Smalley, R. (2011). *Resources.* Retrieved April 13, 2011, from http://4snk.info/links/richard-e-smalley.html

Smalyukh, I. I. (2010). *Intro to soft condensed matter physics.* Retrieved December 10, 2010, from http://www.colorado.edu/physics/SmalyukhLab/SoftMatter/

Smith, G. (1875). *Assyrian discoveries: An account of explorations and discoveries on the site of Nineveh, during 1873 and 1874.* Retrieved December 30, 2010, from http://books.google.com/books? vid=01cHWlP8ACrFcxC4bHx3bKB&id=1RudUM1WeQEC

Soddu, C. (2011). *Website of Celestino Soddu.* Retrieved January 26, 2011, from http://www.celestinosoddu.com/

Sommerer, C., & Mignonneau, L. (2010). *The value of art (Unruhige See).* Retrieved January 9, 2011, from http://www.interface.ufg.ac.at/christa-laurent/WORKS/FRAMES/FrameSet.html

Stock, M. (2012 in press). Flow simulation with vortex elements. In Ursyn, A. (Ed.), *Biologically-inspired computing for the arts: Scientific data through graphics.* Hershey, PA: IGI Global.

Tomasula, S. (1998). Bytes and zeitgeist. Digitizing the cultural landscape. Sixth Annual New York Digital Salon. *Leonardo, 31*(5), 338.

Turner, W. (2011). *The morning after the deluge.* Retrieved January 27, 2011, from http://www.william-turner.org/The-Morning-after-the-Deluge-c.-1843.html

Venter, J. C., Adams, M. D., Myers, E. W., Li, P. W., Mural, R. J., & Sutton, G. G. (2001). The sequence of the human genome. *Science, 291*(5507), 1304–1351. doi:10.1126/science.1058040

Vis, K.-M. (2010). *Chile – Protection of the Tamarugal Forest in the Atacama Desert.* Retrieved November 15, 2010, from http://www.suite101.com/content/chile--protection-of-the-tamarugal-forest-in-the-atacama-desert-a223618#ixzz15NUQxz2W

Water Bear. (2011). Retrieved October 10, 2011, from http://www.fcps.edu/islandcreekes/ecology/water_bear.htm

Watson, J. D., & Crick, F. H. (1953). Molecular structure of nucleic acids: A structure for deoxyribose nucleic acid. *Nature, 171*(4356), 737–738. doi:10.1038/171737a0

Waugh, M. (2011). *Liquid sculpture – Water drop art.* Retrieved April 11, 2011, from http://www.liquidsculpture.com/index.htm

White, C. (2011). *Liquids in motion.* Retrieved April 11, 2011, from http://www.liquiddropart.com/myliquiddropart/index.html

Witcombe, C. (2011). *Water in art.* Retrieved April 11, 2011, from http://witcombe.sbc.edu/water/art.html

World, W. (2010). *Atacama desert NT 1303.* WWF Full Report. Retrieved November 15, 2010, from http://www.worldwildlife.org/wildworld/profiles/terrestrial/nt/nt1303_full.html

World Community Grid. (2010). Retrieved December 17, 2010, from http://www.worldcommunitygrid.org/about_us/viewAboutUs.do

Yildiz, A., Forkey, J. N., McKinney, S. A., Ha, T., Goldman, Y. A., & Selvin, P. R. (2003). Myosin V walks hand-over-hand: Single fluorophore imaging with 1.5-nm localization. *Science, 300*(5628), 2061–2065. doi:10.1126/science.1084398

Zaretskii, Y. K., & Fish, A. M. (1996). Effect of temperature on the strength and viscosity of ice. *Soil Mechanics and Foundation Engineering, 33*(2), 46–52. doi:10.1007/BF02354293

Zheng, J., Birktoft, J. J., Chen, Y., Wang, T., Sha, R., & Constantinou, P. E. (2009). From molecular to macroscopic via the rational design of a self-assembled 3D DNA crystal. *Nature, 461*, 74–77. doi:10.1038/nature08274

ADDITIONAL READING

Blossfeldt, K., Bataille, G., & Mattenklott, G. (2004). *Art forms in nature*. Schirmer/Mosel (Complete edition). ISBN 3888146275

Gardner, H. (1983a). Artistic intelligences. *Art Education, 36*(2), 47–49. doi:10.2307/3192663

Gardner, H. (1983b). *Frames of mind: The theory of multiple intelligences*. New York, NY: Basic Books.

Jones, O. (2001). *The grammar of ornament*. New York, NY: A Dorling Kindersley Book. ISBN: 0-7894-7646-0

Phaidon Press. (1999). *The 20th century art book*. London, UK: Author.

Phaidon Press. (2001). *The American art book*. San Francisco, CA: Author.

Phaidon Press. (2008). *1994) The art book*. San Francisco, CA: Author.

Phillips, R., Kondev, J., & Theriot, J. (2008). *Physical biology of the cell*. Taylor & Francis Group.

Tufte, E. R. (1983). *The visual display of quantitative information*. Cheshire, CT: Graphics Press.

Tufte, E. R. (1990). *Envisioning information*. Cheshire, CT: Graphics Press.

Tufte, E. R. (1997). *Visual explanations: Images and quantities, evidence and narrative*.

Tufte, E. R. (1997). *Visual and statistical thinking: Displays of evidence for making decisions*. Cheshire, CT: Graphics Press.

KEY TERMS AND DEFINITIONS

Activated Sludge: Treatment process serves for the wastewater treatment, with flocs created in sedimentation tanks by biological processes

Akkadian: The ancient and extinct languages, which include Sumerian and Babylonian-Assyrian, the earliest Semitic languages spoken in ancient Mesopotamia in the Bronze Age. Along with the Hittite, the extinct Indo-European language, Akkadian utilized cuneiform scripts in the form of logograms representing words or morphemes (the smallest meaningful units of language).

Canonical Objects: Objects that have an easy to recognize shape. Some items should always look in an obvious way and be easy to recognize, for example, a fire extinguisher should not look fancy, and it should be easy to find. Scissors should fit to a hand and a hammer should be easy to use. In spite of the new line in a design of cellular phones, we still draw an old-style telephone with a round dial to signal where we can find the much more modern touch-tone ones in the phone booths.

Cohesion: Water forms hydrogen bonds with other water molecules. Example – surface tension

Condensation: A change of physical phase from gaseous into a liquid one, conversely to evaporation, which turns liquid into gas. It occurs when vapor is cooled or compressed. Water vapor (for example, in humid air) condenses as droplets on a cold surface. Condensing molecules of water transfer their kinetic energy to an absorbing contact surface.

Contamination: Water contamination means addition of poisonous or polluting substance to water environment, which causes harm to humans, other organisms, and the indispensable for life environment.

Critical Temperature: The highest at which this substance can exist as a liquid.

Cryosphere: The frozen surface of the Earth: ice on the seas, freshwater ice on lakes and rivers, glaciers and ice sheets (ice masses flowing on the ground), frozen ground, including permafrost (permanently frozen ground that covers about 54 million km^2 on the Northern Hemisphere alone), and the snow covering the land and frozen water. Ice sheets provide about 77% of the global freshwater. Average time water spends in these subsystems varies from seasonal existence to hundreds of thousands years.

Density: The mass of a substance divided by its volume

Evaporation: A kind of phase transition that converts liquid into gas (water molecules change into vapor); it is the reverse of condensation that converts gas into liquid. Water molecules need heat kinetic energy to escape from the surface. It may be solar energy that causes evaporation of water from the surface of oceans, lakes, and rivers, electric or other type of heat we provide to boil water in a pot, or metabolic energy necessary for transpiration of water through a plant stoma – the minute pore in a plant leaf or stem epidermis. Wind supports evaporation by increasing the airflow rate.

Evolutionary Computing: Transforms computers into automatic optimization and design tools, utilizing the power of the natural selection mechanisms: reproduction, mutation, the Darwinian principle of survival of the fittest through inheritance, selection, and crossover. Various approaches to evolutionary computing include

genetic algorithms (that mimic natural evolution to solve optimization and search problems), evolutionary programming (strategies using mutation as main variation operator, where a parent generates an offspring according to survivor selection principle), evolution strategies (using mutation and selection as search operators aimed at optimization techniques), and genetic programming (finding programs that would perform a user-defined task). Evolutionary computing resulted in a progress in quantum computing, search algorithms development, sorting, electronic design, evolvable hardware (containing hardware, artificial intelligence and autonomous systems that change their architecture and behavior in response to its environment), and advances in computer programming.

Filtration: Separates solid matter from fluids (in a liquid or gaseous form). Filtration for water treatment may involve biological films that absorb unwanted matter.

Flocculation: Groups colloids and other suspended particles together into flocs, is used for the purification of drinking water and the wastewater treatment, e.g., sewage treatment.

Fluids: Deform when submitted to shear stress. Liquids, gases, plasmas, and even some solids have properties of fluids.

Fluidity: The ease of movement of a substance in a liquid state. However, some solid-state materials are characterized by some fluidity.

Gene: A region of the nucleic acid DNA (deoxyribonucleic acid) that influences particular characteristics in an organism. The hereditary information carried by DNA is encoded in the sequence of pieces of DNA called genes. DNA is condensed in multicellular organisms in a genome and the complete set of this information in an organism is called its genotype (in many types of viruses information is stored in the ribonucleic acid RNA). The set of chromosomes in a cell makes up its genome; the human genome has approximately 3 billion base pairs of DNA arranged into 46 chromosomes (Venter, Adams, Myers, Li, Mural, Sutton, Smith, Yandell, et al., 2001).

Heat capacity: Amount of energy that is required to change body's temperature by given amount, for example, to raise 1 gram of water 1^0C

Icon, Iconic Object or Image: An icon represents a thing or refers to something by resembling or imitating it; thus a picture, a photograph, a mathematical expression, or an old-style telephone may be regarded as an iconic object. Thus, an iconic object has some qualities common with things it represents, by looking, sounding, feeling, tasting, or smelling alike.

Infiltration: Process that moves water through soil from the ground surface down.

Ionosphere: The part of the upper atmosphere that is ionized by solar radiation,

Microscopy: In nano scale comprises the electron beam-based techniques, such as transmission electron microscopy (TEM), and scanning electron microscopy (SEM); scanning probe microscopy (SPM), such as atomic force microscopy (AFM), scanning tunneling microscopy (STM, with a spot size of 1 to 10 Å), and near-field optical microscopy (NSOM); polarizing optical microscopy (PM – 2D imaging); and fluorescent confocal microscopy (FCPM, 3D imaging), including confocal laser scanning microscopes, spinning disk confocal microscopes, and programmable array microscopes (PAM).

Nanoscience and Nanotechnology: Very small objects, roughly 1 to 100 nanometers in size.

Ontology: A philosophical study about being and existence, and their categories and relations.

Osmosis: Allows the passage of water through a semi-permeable membrane from a region of low solute concentration to a region of high solute concentration. The flow of solvent that equalizes solute concentrations generates osmotic pressure.

Plasmon: A quantum of plasma oscillation, a quasiparticle associated with a local collective oscillation of charge density (All reference sources: New Oxford American Dictionary,

Oxford American Writer's Thesaurus, Apple Dictionary, Wikipedia).

Pollution: The presence of naturally occurring contaminants or introduction of harmful energy, substances or objects into the environment, physical body, a workplace, or material. Water pollution results from releasing waste products and contaminants into surface water. Water can collect soil contaminants, petroleum, pesticides, or fertilizers, and then run into rivers, drain into groundwater. Liquid waste – domestic, commercial, industrial, or agricultural – if not properly disposed, adds to water pollution.

Precipitation: A product of condensation that results in rain, snow, sleet, hail, and small snow pellets, which usually fall under gravity. It happens when air becomes saturated with water as result of cooling or adding moisture by the weather fronts.

Referent: In semiotics, a word or a phrase stands for or denotes something (usually an object) that is called a referent.

Reverse Osmosis: Removes from water large molecules and ions by applying external mechanical pressure on the higher concentration side to counter the osmotic pressure that occurs across semi-permeable membranes. The solute remains on the side under pressure and the solvent passes to the other side. In the reverse osmosis method external pressure reverses the natural flow of solvent.

Runoff (or surface runoff): The flow of water over land resulting from rain, snow melting, and other sources. Water runoff occurs because of the imbalance between evaporation and precipitation over the Earth's land and ocean surfaces (Physical Geography, 2010). The soil becomes saturated and absorbs no more water, or precipitation rate is higher than infiltration rate.

Sedimentation: Separates and removes suspended solid particles (of various sizes, but above 10 μm). In potable water treatment, they are settled out due to the action of gravity, usually after chemical coagulation and flocculation.

Semiotics: The study about the meaningful use of signs, symbols, codes, and conventions that allow communication. The name 'semiotics' is derived from the Greek word 'semeion' which means "sign". "Meaning" is always the result of social conventions, even when we think that something is natural or characteristic, and we use signs for those meanings. Therefore, culture and art is a series of sign systems. Semioticians analyze such sign systems in various cultures; linguists study language as a system of signs, and some even examine film as a system of signs. The semiotic content of visual design is important for non-verbal communication applied to practice, especially for visualizing knowledge.

Sign: Tells about a fact, an idea, or information; it is a distinct thing that signifies another thing. Natural signs signify events caused by nature, while conventional signs may signal art, social interactions, fashion, food, interaction with technology, machines, and practically everything else.

Signs, Symbols, and Icons: Collectively called signage. Signs take conventional shapes or forms to tell about facts, ideas, or information. Icons and symbols help compress information in a visual way. An icon represents a thing or refers to something by resembling or imitating it; thus a picture, a photograph, a mathematical expression, or an old-style telephone may be regarded as an iconic object. Thus, an iconic object has some qualities common with things it represents, by looking, sounding, feeling, tasting, or smelling alike. Designers choose signs, symbols, and icons that are powerful and effective; for example, a designer may look for an icon showing the scissorness, the essence of the meaning related to scissors: some common features characteristic for this product. Effective design of a complicated product may help memorize and learn how to use this product (for example, 'Where is the switch?' or 'How to open this thing?').

Solute: Is a substance that is dissolved in another substance in a homogeneous mixture. Salt in the salt water may serve as an example.

Solvent: Is a substance in which a solute is dissolved. Water in the salt water may serve as an example.

Subsurface Flow of Water: Another part of the water cycle: water travels underground through infiltration and recharges aquifers.

Surface Tension: The tension of the surface film caused by attraction of the particles on the surface: which allows a liquid to resist an external force. Surface tension is measured in units of force per unit length or as energy per unit area.

Symbol: Does not resemble things it represents but refers to something by convention; for example, the word "red" represents red. We must learn the relationship between symbols and what they represent, such as letters, numbers, words, codes, traffic lights, and national flags. A symbol represents an abstract concept, not just a thing, and is comparable to an abstract word. Highly abstracted drawings that show no realistic graphic representation become symbols. Symbols are omnipresent in our life, for example: An electric diagram that uses abstract symbols for a light bulb, wire, connector, resistor, and switch; An apple for a teacher, or a bitten apple for a Macintosh computer; A map – typical abstract graphic device; A 'slippery when wet' sign.

Viscosity: A measure of resistance of a fluid deformed by stress applied in a perpendicular, parallel or tangential direction to the fluid's surface.

Chapter 12
Visual Tweet:
Nature Inspired Visual Statements

Anna Ursyn
University of Northern Colorado, USA

ABSTRACT

"Visual Tweet: nature inspired visual statements" explores connections between science, computing, and art in a similar way as it is done in the previous chapter, "Looking at sciences through the water." This chapter examines concepts and processes that relate to some fields in physics, biology, computing, and other sciences, and at the same time pertain to the planet's life and humanity's everyday experience. This chapter solves the projects visually, through art and/or graphics. Exploration of science-based concepts and nature-related processes support the understanding of the project themes, triggers imagination, and thus inspires enhancements to the ability to communicate with visual language and create artistic work. Comprehension of what is observed, the power of abstract thought, and an answer to evolving issues will result in personal visual projects – drawings, graphics, illustrations, animations, video clips, or web projects. This chapter comprises two projects about science-related themes: (1) Symmetry and pattern in animal world: geometry and art, and (2) Crystals and crystal caves. Each project invites the reader to create visual presentation of this theme.

PROJECT 1: SYMMETRY AND PATTERN IN ANIMAL WORLD: GEOMETRY AND ART

Introduction to Project "Symmetry and Pattern in Animal World"

When we plan to create biologically inspired art, the theme of symmetry can certainly be considered inspirational for many of us. It may be so because symmetrical forms and shapes possess an aesthetic

beauty and an order reflected by their geometry. Also, it is so because there are so many kinds of symmetry existing not only in geometry but also in natural world and human works. For example, water, when in liquid state, has bilateral symmetry, with the symmetric stretch of the two O-H bonds and some molecular vibrations (Kettle, 2007); when frozen, water becomes symmetrical in various ways (however, not always) usually developing the hexagonal crystals. Ice, snowflakes, feather ice on the twigs, hail, sleet, icicles, glaciers, and polar caps, all have their own order of symmetry

DOI: 10.4018/978-1-4666-0942-6.ch012

and develop various arrangements of symmetry axes. We discuss some topics related to symmetry in a project 2 about crystals and snowflakes.

Mathematicians, anthropologists, artists, architects and designers who conduct computer analysis of the facades, friezes, and some architectural details, as well as researchers in many fields of natural sciences, biology, geology, or chemistry see a purpose in symmetry investigations. Many artists have created masterpieces this way; we will examine some of their works later. By finding mathematical order in natural forms and re-creating it in our own artwork we can appreciate these forms and also understand the importance of adaptations that animals develop as an answer to the conditions of life.

"Symmetry and pattern in animal world" integrates several art concepts, such as symmetry, pattern, tessellation (natural or human-made filling a surface with figures with no overlaps or gaps), and general composition of the artwork, with issues related to:

- Geometry (symmetry, tessellation),
- Biology (animal shapes and forms, their symmetry and patterns, adaptation),

- Art and art history (patterns in artistic or decorative design, animals in art, and general composition of the artwork), and
- Computer graphic skills.

The objective of this project is to look over living forms in nature and in art, and examine how the nature-related concepts of symmetry (bilateral, radial, or helical), asymmetry, and patterns pertain to the general design of animal bodies, the animals' look, and behavior. We will examine symmetry (or lack of symmetry) in animal surface patterns, for example in fish scales or bird feather. Working on symmetry for artistic projects promotes application of our spatial visualization skills. Then, after some study about the use of symmetry and pattern in the art works, some readers may want to combine this knowledge with art and computer graphic skills and create an artistic representation of the animal world using symmetry and patterns. One may also want to apply tessellation in order to design a background for the artwork. Figure 1 (a and b) shows impressions about animal symmetry and pattern.

Figure 1a. Anna Melkumian, "Symmetry." (© 2010, A. Melkumian. Used with permission.); b) Betony Coons, "Symmetry." (© 2010, B. Coons. Used with permission.)

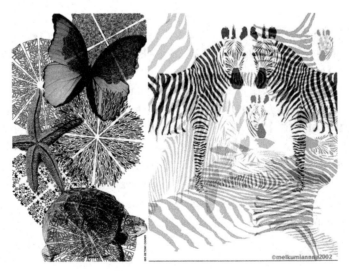

Background Information Type A: Natural Events And Processes

Background Information About the Concept of Symmetry as Related to Geometry

Geometry studies properties of space: shapes, sizes, positions of figures, and distance concepts. As a starting point from which we can develop further statements we accept some axioms, universally established propositions, truths that are accepted without proof. For example, a symmetry axiom tells that for all points A and B, AB = BA. Axioms seem to be self-evident for human reasoning; however, many of the inventive and significant discoveries, such as the *Heisenberg's uncertainty principle* in quantum mechanics, resulted from the questioning of axioms and mixing a subject and an object of investigation. As Julian Voss-Andreae wrote, "Quantum theory remains philosophically problematic because 'objective realism' turns out to be incompatible with quantum theory (Einstein, Podolsky, & Rosen, 1935). There is no accurate space-time representation of, say, an electron: It is neither a particle nor a wave or any other "thing" (Voss-Andreae, 2011, p.14).

Symmetry is present when similar parts of an object are arranged on the opposite sides of a point, line (axis), or plane. There are several types of geometrical symmetry, for example, bilateral (reflection or mirror), rotational (when an object looks the same after rotation), cylindrical, spherical, and helical symmetry (like in a drill bit), not to mention some kinds not so obviously seen in everyday objects, such as translational (where a particular translation - moving in a specified direction does not change the object), glide reflection (in a line or plane combined with a translation), or rotoreflection symmetry, which presents rotation about an axis, combined with reflection in a plane perpendicular to that axis.

A figure that has bilateral symmetry has two mirror-like halves, which correspond exactly if folded along its line of symmetry. The halves are congruent, they are the same size, shape, and coincide exactly when superimposed. In nature, optical *isomers* are symmetrical around a plane. Molecules of some sugar isomers are deflecting the rays of light in right or left direction. Symmetrical objects show several elements of symmetry, for example, a crystal may show rotation axes, a center of symmetry, or mirror planes - the imaginary planes that separate an object into halves.

An object has a rotational (radial) symmetry when it can be rotated around an imaginary line called the rotation axis and retain the same appearance as before rotating, repeating itself several times during a complete rotation. For example, with a six-fold rotation axis the crystal repeats itself each 60°. A center of symmetry is equally distant from any point on the surface of a symmetrical object.

Objects with helical symmetry combine symmetry such as that of a circle with the translation of this object along a long axis. For example, springs, screws, drill bits, or slinky toys have helical symmetry. An infinite helical symmetry appears when a cross section of a helix doesn't change after every small rotation. The N-fold helical symmetry exists when a cross section repeats itself regularly. Double helix is the case when it repeats after every full rotation, when it returns to its initial position. A molecule of DNA, a deoxyribonucleic acid, has a non-repeating helical symmetry.

Fractals represent form of scale symmetry that appears when the objects magnified or reduced in size have the same properties. Mathematicians name some objects symmetrical with respect to a given mathematical operation applied to this object, when this operation preserves some property of the object. Such operations form a symmetry group of the object.

Symmetry in Living Organisms

Humans and animals evolve and adapt to a continuously changing environment. In the course of indefinitely long periods of time the wonderful ways of animal adaptation resulted in a variety of extraordinary shapes and forms. The general design of animal bodies, their symmetry, and patterns has also been changing in time. Symmetry and its changes are used in biology to introduce the concept of classification.

Many of the earliest organisms lacked symmetry. Then, animals sitting mostly in one place at the bottom of the ocean, as well as some floating animals developed radial symmetry. Having the rotational symmetry, such creatures did not change their appearance after rotating a certain number of degrees around the center of their body. Radial arrangement of body parts strengthens an animal's skeleton. Also, animals with rotational symmetry can sense the danger from all directions. Most of these animals, often in relation to the times past, have a three-rayed symmetry, but other, for example, jellyfish, retain a pentagonal symmetry of their skeleton, major organ systems, and rays radiating from the mouth in five tube feet. There are also seven-armed starfish, while sea lilies develop 10 to 200 arms resembling fern fronds. Ernst von Haeckel (1834-1919, Haeckel, Breidbach, Hartman, & Eibl-Eibesfeldt, 1998), German naturalist, philosopher, physician, and artist described thousands of new species and life development processes through evolution, stressing their aesthetic value. His work from 1904 "Kunstformen der Natur" (Art Forms in Nature) contains images of marine animals, often displaying symmetry of various kinds (Figure 2).

Cylindrical symmetry around the vertical axis (such as in balloon-shaped creatures swimming in the oceans, and also in pollens) facilitates forward motion. In any body with the spherical symmetry, for example in spherical pollen, everything is the same on all sides.

Figure 2. Marine animals: Pheodaria, Circogoniaicosahedra, (Ernst von Haeckel, 1904. Image in the public domain, available at Wikimedia Commons.)

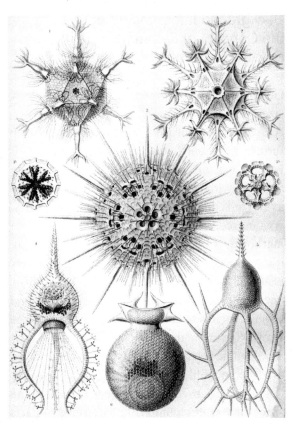

Bilateral symmetry occurs in all living groups and is especially marked in the larval stages. During evolution, muscle contraction replaced the beating of cilia, so streamlined bodies with bilateral symmetry (similar to line symmetry) became dominant. This type of symmetry occurs when the animal has the front and the rear parts developed differently and it displays the forward motion. In bilaterally symmetrical animals, for example in butterflies, the halves of their bodies, when seen along the horizontal or the vertical axis (x or y axis) form each other's mirror images.

Patterns in Animals

We may see many patterns in our surroundings on everyday basis; they are of natural or accidental origin. Patterns we can see in plants and animals have consistent forms, traits, or features characteristic of an individual or a group. Animal patterns, such as the designs on scales of fish, or on feathers of birds, enable animals to recognize individuals of their own species. Humans can describe and classify these species on the basis of these characteristics (Neville, 1977).

Asymmetry in Living Organisms

Patterns on animal exteriors are not always symmetrical. For example, some species of salamanders, frogs, vipers, fly larvae, and fish have asymmetrical patterns. Asymmetry of a pattern may be useful in terms of the camouflage possibilities: they aid to conceal their bodies from enemies by making them appear to be part of the natural surroundings. An asymmetrical pattern can help an animal with bilateral symmetry to change its appearance, to hide and become invisible against the background. In later stages of evolutionary development, body forms became not so simple. Most animal bodies, including people, cannot be divided exactly into two halves, even when they look symmetrical from external appearance. Other forms, for example marine animals holothurians (2011) also called sea cucumbers (echinoderms), show bilateral symmetry outside and radial symmetry of hemal sinuses inside.

We can find many examples of asymmetry in animals. It can be expressed as a zigzag pattern down the back of a viper, or as a position of a liver or a heart. Not only internal organs, but the skull and the brain are also asymmetrical in humans, as well as in some animals and birds. Organisms develop not only a structural but also a behavioral asymmetry. Two halves of the human brain display different abilities, ways of learning, and thinking. Human and animal handedness is an asymmetry in skill development. For example, Fiddler crabs have one claw much bigger than another. Earthworms, when put in a maze, display a behavioral asymmetry when they can recognize the difference between right and left. Some insects use their jaws like left-handed or right-handed scissors, depending on the species they belong to.

Some technologies are applied in zoology to explain existing symmetry or asymmetry. For example nuclear transplantation or application of a mutagen drug may induce biased symmetry. The notion of asymmetry pertains also to several other disciplines. For example, in organic chemistry chirality refers most often to molecules: chiral molecules display lack of an internal plane of symmetry, usually because of the presence of an asymmetric carbon atom. Chirality means, in simple terms, the existence of left/right opposition (IUPAC, 2010; Leffingwell, 2003). Chirality is also present in biological structures; it often determines bioactivity (for example, odor perception) and is an important factor in drug efficacy. As was stated at the 2011 Congress of the European Society for Evolutionary Biology, "asymmetric shapes in animals and plants can come in two mirror-image forms. However, such chiral dimorphism is found in some structures but not in others. This makes chirality one of the very few developmental traits that can be studied consistently across all multicellular organisms, offering a goldmine of research questions in evo-devo, evolutionary ecology, and macro-evolution" (Schilthuizen & Gravendeel, 2011).

Asymmetry as Seen by Humans

The art theorist and perceptual psychologist Rudolf Arnheim (1988) stated that gravity makes the space asymmetrical, not in a geometrical but in dynamical sense, because an upward movement requires energy, whereas downward movement can be done by removing any support that keeps an object from falling. We perceive this asymmetry by two senses, with kinesthesia (awareness of the tension in the muscles and joints of the body) and vision.

Michael Leyton (2006) discussed his asymmetry principle. He proposed in his "The Foundations of Aesthetics" that the two principles, maximization of transfer and maximization of recoverability are the basic principles both of geometry and aesthetics. They are fundamental to aesthetic judgment in the arts (painting, music, and poetry), the sciences (general relativity and quantum mechanics), and computer programming (object-oriented programming). Recoverability of the backward history is possible due to the asymmetry principle: to ensure recoverability of the past, any asymmetry in the present must go back to symmetry in the past. According to the author, in mathematics and physics "asymmetry" really means distinguishability, and "symmetry" means indistinguishability. Thus, the asymmetry principle really says that, to ensure recoverability, any distinguishability in the present must go back to indistinguishability in the past.

Humans, often in a similar way as animals, apply asymmetrical patterns as a camouflage, a way of blending with the environment; they use hunting camouflage clothing in colors (for example, bright orange) that are perceived as dull by the game animals, and battledresses or camouflage netting for military purposes. Artists and designers contribute with their projects. For example, for warplane and ship camouflage, in order to confuse the periscope view of the submarine gunners during World War I, Norman Wilkinson, Everett L. Warner, and other artists painted the high-contrast, asymmetric shapes on ship surfaces, thus confusing the periscope view of the German submarines (Berens, 1999). Other, non-military applications include art. Artists, for example, Liu Bolin (2009) or Bev Doolittle (2011) create camouflage art, while architects and designers construct unusual camouflage restaurants (2011) of different kinds.

Background Information Type B: Art Concepts and Principles

Background Information about Aesthetic Values of Symmetry and Asymmetry

In a book entitled "Aesthetic Measure" American mathematician George David Birkhoff (1884-1944) proposed a mathematical theory of aesthetics: in an equation $M=O/C$, Aesthetic Measure (M) is a function of Order (O) divided by Complexity (C.) The Gestalt psychology theory of mind postulated that brain has self-organizing tendencies and recognizes the whole of a figure rather than its individual parts (Birkhoff, 2003).

Aesthetics has been investigated as part of cognitive science, since Semir Zeki (1993, 1999), professor of neuroaesthetics at London University College associated perception of the great works of art with working principles of the brain. Artists, acting like instinctive neuroscientists, capture in their art works the essence of things in a similar way as the brain acts when it captures the essential information about the world from a stream of sensory input. Neuroesthetics explores the visual brain using anatomical, electro-physiological, psychological methods and imaging techniques.

Symmetry plays a remarkable role in most human visual endeavors. Natural objects displaying symmetry evoke wonder and surprise because their intricacy. For example in architecture, such architectural details as stain-glass windows, mosaics, and friezes, visual arts, pottery and ceramics, quilts, textiles, and carpets many times make a varied use of symmetry as an important principle in their design. Maybe for that reason symmetry is so often seen not only beautiful but also conducive to visual communication.

One may discuss the aesthetics of visualization as related to the visual competence in the art, design, and technological solutions in visualization.

In a growing number of publications the aesthetics concept refers to design effectiveness, efficiency, and easiness to understand (a low cognitive cost) of visual presentation, not exclusively the beauty of an image. Researchers who deal with advancements in visualization associate aesthetics with readability, and readability with understanding. Intensive research on the optimal layout aesthetics has been conducted in the field of graph drawing and the aesthetics of graph drawing *algorithms* (for example, Purchase; 2010, Lau & Vande Moere, 2007). Spatial relationships between nodes and edges and the overall layout, including graph's symmetry, area, flow, and aspect ratio, determine the aesthetics of a graph (Bennett, Ryall, Spalteholz, & Gooch, 2007). Methods of measuring the aesthetics of a layout and the results obtained suggested reducing the number of edge crossings and making the best use of symmetry, e.g., by maximizing symmetry of subgraphs.

A mathematician, an anthropologist, and an architect conducted together a computer analysis of friezes covering the facades of hundreds of buildings in the village of Pirgi, a small town on the Greek island of Chios in the eastern Aegean Sea (James, A. V., James, D. A., & L. N. Kalisperis 2004). Gray and white friezes contain squares, triangles and rhomboids, different on each house. Mathematic analysis of friezes' symmetry revealed five basic actions of moving a frieze (translation, vertical and horizontal mirror, half-turn and glide reflection). The aesthetic value of asymmetry has been appreciated in Chinese art and art criticism. In Chinese calligraphy, the "dynamic asymmetry' proportion of a Chinese character, with a subtle discrimination, is prized by Chinese artists and art theorists (Huang & Balsys, 2009).

Patterns in Art

In art and design domains, pattern is an artistic or decorative design made of lines. Patterns make a basis of ornaments, which are specific for different cultures. Pattern is based on the repetition of

units coming from the natural or artificial origin. Patterns that are used in decorative arts and architecture have distinctive styles, which are specific for each culture or ethnic group. A great part of ornaments display motifs as elements of patterns. Owen Jones made a huge collection of ornaments typical for different countries. In 1856 he wrote a monographic book entitled "The Grammar of Ornament" (Jones, 2001). Works of art created according to various art movements or artistic groups display patterns characteristic of this group, for example, decorative patterns typical of the Art Nouveau or Secession styles. In cultural anthropology, a study of decorative patterns, ornaments, and their characteristics support the detailed analysis of an individual culture. Some common leading ideas on which patterns of ornaments are based are in accordance with the arrangement typical of the distribution of form in nature.

Animals in Art

We may easily find wonderful pictures of animals when we look at the cave walls (regardless of a debate as to whether the cave paintings were created for artistic intent), ancient or antique paintings, as well as the paintings from the Renaissance or modern times. Real and fantastic animals served in the medieval paintings (from most of the Gothic period of the 12th through the 15th century) as a part of decorative vocabulary and vehicles for religious allegory and moral instruction (Animals in Medieval Art, 2011). One can also find fantastic animals and beasts in classical paintings of ancient Egypt, Greece, and Rome, and in the dreamlike or nightmarish pictures from the times of the Surrealism movement (originated in France in the 1920s). Such bizarre, fictional beasts were derived both from mythology and pure fantasy.

In order to examine paintings containing representations of animals, and make the animal theme in art more familiar, we can easily find them in Google Images, and on web art galleries and collections, for example, http://palimpsest.

stanford.edu/icom/vlmp/usa.html for American art, and http://palimpsest.stanford.edu/icom/vlmp/world.html for the rest of the world; The Parthenet: http://witcombe.sbc.edu/ARTHLinks.html, specifically, http://witcombe.sbc.edu/ARTH20thcentury.html#general20century for the contemporary art; or World Art Treasures: http://sgwww.epfl.ch/BERGER/. We may surely find artwork in books. Many of the titles of art works collected below come from the Art Book (1994), The 20th Century Artbook (1996), and The American Art Book (1999).

While looking at the artwork, it may be interesting to fix one's eyes on the painting and give serious thought to a real cause or a motive the artist might have in mind to create it. It may not necessarily be an accurate and detailed representation of a scene with the animals but a message to convey or an artistic statement that provides a reason for bringing this work into being. You are requested to figure out the content of the artwork, and then, in the same way, to make an effort to include some meaning into your animal representations. Below, some approaches to the animal theme are shown in works from various periods of time.

- Jacopo Bassano, c1590, "The Animals Entering the Ark," "Sacrificio di Noe"
- Jan Breugel, c1620, "The Garden of Eden," "Paradise"
- Frans Snyder, 1620s, "A Game Stall," "Still Life of Dead Game"
- Aelbert Cuyp, c1650, "Cattle with Horseman and Peasants," "Cows in Water"
- Carel Fabritius, 1654, "The Goldfinch"
- Edward Hicks, 1833/4, "The Peaceable Kingdom"
- John James Audubon, 1835-8, "Roseate Spoonbill"
- George Catlin, c.1857, "Ambush for Flamingoes"
- Sir Stanley Spencer, 1935, "Saint Francis and the Birds"
- Henri Rousseau, 1906, "The Monkeys"

- Giacomo Balla, 1913, "Flight of Swallows"
- Raoul Dufy, c1926, "The Paddock"
- Marcel Broodthaers, 1964-5, "Casserole and Closed Mussels"
- Arthur Boyd, 1987, "The Australian Skapegoat.

Background Information Type C: Computing or Technology

Background Information about Visual Appeal of Mathematics for Mathematicians and Artists

The visual world of mathematics-derived art forms may be of interest for art majors and computer graphics majors as inspiration for learning, thinking, and creating. We can realize how much the mathematical way of thinking is a visual process and how often the beauty of forms derived from mathematical formulas becomes an inspiration and a source for creating an artwork. Visual mathematics may be examined as the language of space design and is often used for the composition of an artwork. This idea may provide a common language for mathematicians, visual artists, architects, musicians, crystallographers, cartographers, and many other professionals. In his work *On Growth and Form*, Scottish embryologist D'Arcy Wentworth Thompson (1860-1948) looks for explanation of evolutionary changes in mathematical and physical laws of 'economy and transformation' (Thompson, 1992).

Intuition, along with knowledge and calculations, has been stressed for many years as a leading force in problem solving. Arthur Loeb (1993), in his book entitled, "Concepts & Images – Visual Mathematics," claimed that intuition is a form of non-verbalized knowledge. Some scientists and artists use their knowledge and intuition in such a way that their abstract reasoning takes form of images, rather than words or formulas. Rudolph Arnheim (1969) stressed the role of the visual thinking, which allows gifted minds with intuitive wisdom to avoid troubles with formalistic thought operations due to their brilliant cross-circuits.

Several topics of research in visual mathematics provide inspiration for artists. For example, geometry provides unlimited possibilities for creating patterns and ornaments that are present in the variety of design styles characteristic of all of cultures of the world. Artists from different periods, such as the Italian Renaissance painter Piero della Francesca (1410/20-1492) or the Italian Surrealist artist Giorgio de Chirico (1888-1978) explore symmetry and perspective, some of them making exciting tricks, such as Hans Holbein, who applied *anamorphosis* in "The Ambassadors" (1533), or the Dutch graphic artist Maurits Cornelis Escher (1902-1972) in his impossible sceneries. Some shapes and forms that contain mathematical regularities and can be described by equations seem to be especially inspirational and aesthetically appealing. For example, complex

polygons, tessellations of strings and lattices, the geometry displayed by soap bubble films, tiles, Oriental mosaics, Roman mosaics, or mazes motivated mathematicians and artists to create art- and design-related works.

Study of geometric two-dimensional shapes and three-dimensional forms resulted in works of art done in various media, both traditional and digital, including painting, sculpture, printmaking, and architecture. Computer programs and computer graphics produced with the use of software packages give a boost to such studies. They make a separate category of digital art and, at the same time, serve as a tool for creating works in other media. Teams working on visualization or simulation projects usually include a mathematician, and the direct results of their work look many times like artistic productions.

Figure 3 (a and b) shows the student's abstract, and then the painterly way of exploring the theme of symmetry and asymmetry.

Figure 3. a) Sam Dailey, "Symmetry." (© 2010, S. Dailey. Used with permission.); b) Bolor Vandan, "Lovely Winter." (© 2010, B. Vandan. Used with permission.)

Background Information Type B: Art Concepts and Principles

Background Information about Aesthetical Concerns: From Nature, through Math, to Art

One may ask, does the beauty of an object presented (its aesthetic value) make its representation an artwork? Helaman Ferguson (1994), mathematician and sculptor, claims that mathematics is an invisible art form. As he states, "computer graphics make mathematics visible." What are the distinguishing characteristics of natural forms, their mathematical descriptions, and mathematics-derived artwork? The shell of a mollusk contains a logarithmic spiral. It is a natural phenomenon, not the result of some mathematical program in the nautilus. A drawing of a logarithmic spiral is a biology-inspired, mathematics-derived form. Spiral forms have been explored, discovered and modified by people, but they are hardly an artwork. In the same way, when we visualize the laws of nature and develop their representations, can we consider those representations an artwork? Which criteria concerning the artistic quality of mathematically developed art may be accepted by art criticism?

A need for embellishing things seems to be universal among people who are not necessarily educated in mathematics. Intricate designs of old embroideries and patterns for laces seem to be derived from mathematical principles in an intuitive way. In the same way, we knowingly employ mathematics in developing complex polygons and fractal images to create an artwork. Artistic expressions based on natural and calculated patterns or on a tessellation principle had been applied both by old Islamic artists and by the twentieth-century Dutch artist M. C. Escher. Other concerns about determining artistic quality of mathematically developed art may also relate to its precision.

While designing an artwork, a mathematician is careful to avoid ambiguity. Everybody can see the exact and precisely defined formula representation. On the contrary, visual communication in fine arts is often based on metaphors. Everyone may receive different, unique, and individual messages from the same artwork. It may well be that a representation of mathematical formulas cannot inevitably become an art form, but it is their intentional transformation that may become an artwork.

Art Criticism and Mathematically Developed Art: Beauty of Nature, or of Mathematics?

Laces of complex ornamentation, geometric representations of polygons, and interlaced patterns, all evoke in us the sense of beauty. Some paintings and photographs explore the beauty of natural objects that have been magnified or reduced. However, Rudolph Arnheim (1990) wrote that photographs might affect our observation by singling out accidentals as readily as essentials, and thus making everything equally important. In a similar way, the exquisite perfection of soap bubble geometries, as well as fractal shapes rose to the form of art because of their natural beauty. A question arises, does the art critics' evaluation of the mathematics-derived artwork depends on:

- The aesthetic quality of patterns,
- The beauty of underlying mathematical formulas which give those ornamental arrangements, or
- Has some human intervention occurred between these two points of interest?

Graphic elegance, which can be found in the simplicity of the image demands, "every bit of ink on a graphic requires a reason" (Tufte, 1983). Where is the secret of perfect design – in its simplicity or its elaborate intricateness?

Figure 4. Anna Ursyn, "Fish" (© 1986, A. Ursyn. Used with permission.)

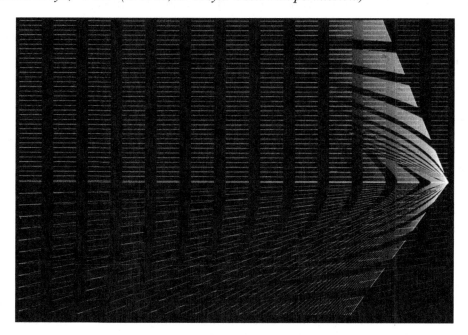

Figure 4 represents argonautic marine engineering properties merged with corresponding design in the form of patterns and colors.

Background Information Type C: Computing or Technology

Background Information about Concepts and Processes Related to Fractals

Fractals can be found virtually everywhere in the natural world. Fractal geometry departs from traditional Euclidean geometry. In 1975, Benoit Mandelbrot, a Polish-born French mathematician (who moved to the United States in 1958), developed the mathematical theory of fractals. The concept of self-similarity is forming the groundwork for fractals because fractal geometry describes objects that are self-similar. Fractal objects have the same structure, whatever their scale. They can be subdivided into parts, each of which is a smaller copy of the whole. The smaller parts are like the larger ones. When fractal objects are magnified, their parts are similar to the whole, the likeness continuing with the parts of the parts and so on, forever. That means, the part, whatever its size, has the same topology as the whole. Self-similarity can be seen in many plants, including the fern leaves. Each leaf branching off the fern is a smaller version of the entire plant.

Some Ways to Calculate a Graphic or Acoustic Fractal

Fractals are produced by algorithms. Final results may vary depending on odd or even, left or right values and situations chosen. Fractals can be used to create visual art or visual music, where the results of calculations can be presented graphically or acoustically. Fractals, especially fractal music, result from iteration (repeated application of an equation) in the recursive operations, where the items are repeated in a self-similar way during the process. By using fractal-generating applets we may bring into being images of plants, snowflakes, landscapes, and many other forms, including fractal art, music, and fractal music generators.

The Cantor Set, the simplest fractal, may be constructed using the following algorithm: we may build a simple fractal by dividing a line in 3 parts and removing the middle part. When we repeat this series of steps, first on the 2 remaining parts, then on the 4 parts produced by that operation, and so on, the fractal will have an immeasurably great number of infinitely small parts.

Fractals in Science and Technology

The basic ideas in fractal geometry are concepts of self-similarity and of kinetic growth, in which particles that are added to a structure neither come off nor rearrange themselves. Using a fractal theory, physicists can describe the chaotic course of events occurring in dynamical systems and build visually models of what we see in nature. Fractals are used to model soil erosion and to analyze seismic patterns. In biology, polymer chains building proteins have the fractal shape, as well as patterns of atoms on the protein surface. In geology, coastlines, surfaces of mountains, and the interior brittle crust, such as California's San Andreas Fault (Okubo & Aki, 1987), have a fractal nature and can be modeled with fractal geometry. Small earthquakes are fractal in time as well as space. Fractals are able to describe complex figures, such as coastlines, clouds, or trees. They are used in a variety of applications ranging from special film and TV effects to economy and physics. Fractal nature of many materials could be put into service of technology. Scientists investigate the fractal character of objects and events in biology, geology, meteorology, along with their implications for physics, electrical conductivity, and the atomic structure of glasses, gels, and other amorphous materials. Biology inspired computing draws to a great extent from the developments in fractal geometry.

Fractals in Nature and Art

Fractals are exceedingly common in nature, and fractal art can imitate nature. As they often elicit an aesthetic response in us, fractals are often given the status of a work of art. On the interface of science and art, computer-graphics artists and specialists have produced fractal images of great statistical complexity.

Fractal art, which came about as a consequence of the developments in fractal geometry, has been presented in tens of handsomely printed books and displayed at art exhibitions. Computer-graphics artists create fractal images of great statistical complexity. For example, fractal landscapes serve as backgrounds in motion pictures, while trees and other branching structures can be seen in animations. Decorative arts are often produced with fractals.

The appearance of fractal designs may resemble various styles in art, depending on the method of calculation. With all their decorative merits, fractals have often evoked discussions about their aesthetic values in terms of fine art. In one of his books Claude Lévi-Strauss, French philosopher and anthropologist associated with the development of structuralism, characterized the essence of fractals in art. As he noticed, in 1854 the French Romantic artist Eugène Delacroix (1798 - 1863) observed in nature the distinctive property that objects have the same invariant structure whatever their scale. Lévi-Strauss recalled the opinion of a German philosopher Immanuel Kant (1724-1804) about an aesthetic judgment. In an aesthetic theory developed by Kant, judgments about beauty rest on feeling but they should be validated in harmony with mental structure, so they are not merely statements of taste or opinion. According to Kant, there are judgments of taste that are subjective and judgments of reason that are universally valid. Aesthetic judgment falls somewhere between these two kinds. Lévi-Strauss (1997) stated that, in this intermediary space, fractals are given the status of a work of art, because they are appealing and at the same time, objectively governed by reason. Innumerable individual art works reside on the Internet, for example when we go to Google Images, such as Helaman Ferguson's Umbilic or Clifford Pickover's Lensflare VTT.

Figure 5 "Clean Water Act" presents a water scene containing some symmetry. We may reflect our still actual concerns whether now, more than twenty years after the Clean Water Act had set up water quality standards, we can find many rivers, lakes, and bays safe enough for swimming.

WORKING ON THE PROJECT IN SEVERAL STEPS

A Composition with Symmetry

Now you may want to make an abstract composition made of concrete geometric representations using simple geometric forms. Draw on the computer screen some forms showing several types of symmetry: the bilateral, the radial, cylindrical, or spherical symmetry, copy them and arrange on the screen. It may be useful in further work on your composition. Explain a relation between the type of symmetry and the animal moving capacity, drawing two- and three-dimensional models and applying visualization made with the use of color and pattern coding. You may also want to construct models out of paper to explore principles of symmetry.

To create an body with a bilateral symmetry, draw a left or right side of a shape you plan to design, then perform a "Save as ..." operation, and create it's another side using the "Brush mirror" option. It can be a geometric form, for example, an acute triangle (having angles less than 90°), and the right-angle triangle or, if you prefer so, it may also be a butterfly or a flower. Organize

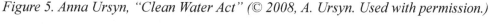

Figure 5. Anna Ursyn, "Clean Water Act" (© 2008, A. Ursyn. Used with permission.)

several such shapes; for example, create a steel bridge applying copying, flipping, and mirroring triangles.

To show an object with radial symmetry, for example, an open umbrella or a flower, draw a segment of your object: an isosceles triangle (having two sides and two angles the same) or a petal of a flower, then rotate it three, four, five or six times around an imaginary line called the rotation axis, so your segment will repeat itself each 120°, 90°, 72°, or 60°. Now you may find a center of symmetry equally distant from any point on the exterior surface of your object. You can also see that your shape will retain the same appearance after rotation.

Make a sketch of an object with a cylindrical symmetry, for example, a glass, a top hat or a tube.

To show a spherical symmetry, design a spherical object, for example, a space ship that fulfills the space explorers' needs and demands. How will you divide the sphere interior? Draw a plan of the interior. Name your file and perform a "Save as ..." operation.

Background Information Type C: Computing or Technology

Background Information about Tessellation

Applying tessellation may now create another abstract art piece. Starting with a geometric form, begin working on a tessellated composition – a Virtual Garden. You may want to apply tessellation in order to design a background for your artwork. Look at the examples of art created with the use of tessellation, for example, at the works of Maurits Cornelis Escher (1898-1972), and then, create your own tessellation. To create tessellation, choose a rectangle or a geometric shape you have already sketched. Take away a fragment from this rectangle by cutting out a shape of your choice from its left side. Slide this fragment so that it becomes closely attached with its straight-line edge to the bottom line of your rectangle. It would be sensible to save your work often. Now, repeat this procedure, now on the other side of the rectangle: select and subtract a fragment on the right side, and attach its straight-line side to the upper border of the rectangle. Copy and paste the new shape you have just created, making several copies. Select one color for a half of these shapes, choose another color for the rest of them, and color them all using the paint bucket tool. Arrange all fragments as a two-colored whole. In some graphic programs, (for example, Adobe Photoshop), the stages of your work are being organized in layers, so you may color shapes from each layer separately, then flatten the image and arrange the shapes into a tessellation pattern.

Figure 6 "Frog Issues" is about our relationship with water environment. A whole landscape can change when the frog leaps. We visit pristine swamps and lakes to contemplate the static and dynamic life and build our memories according to the frog issues. We list endangered species, not necessarily recognizing them. We do extensive research by cataloging, sketching, making X-rays, and learn about their habits, fears, and food chains. We protest against mining, changing water systems, cutting trees, and installing pipelines. However, when the animal is no longer on the endangered species list, we eat it.

Virtual Garden: Art Production

Continue creating an imaginative drawing of the virtual garden built out of previously created images of animals and plants. Using your tessellation as a background, create a virtual garden. Create a landscape with animals, emphasizing symmetry and patterns in nature. Looking at small, plastic toy animals make several images of animals on the screen. You have many options in doing this. You may create hand drawings in pencil and then scan them, or draw with a mouse or graphic tablet

Figure 6. "Frog Issues" (© 2006, A. Ursyn. Used with permission.)

straight on the screen. You may scan pictures or your photos of animals and paste the images into your work. Also, you may import animal pictures from the web (being careful to obey copyright rules!) or from clip-art, but the artwork would be more genuine, original, and authentic with your hand-drawn animals. Remember that no two animals look alike, even when they belong to the same population, so avoid copying and pasting the images of animals several times.

Add some plants: trees, flowers, and grass, carefully composing them together with your tessellation background. Create a sense of perspective by placing bigger objects in the foreground,

Figure 7. a) Andrea Carvalho, "Natural Symmetry." (© 2010, A. Carvalho. Used with permission.); b) Jasmine R. Wilson, "Natural Symmetry." (© 2010, J. R. Wilson. Used with permission.)

partially covering farther objects by the nearer ones, and applying lighter shades in front than in the back of the space of your virtual garden. Try to imagine the impact of the environment you depict on each of the animals, resulting from changes and events you invented. How is your virtual garden experienced and felt by all of the creatures living there?

In your work, use patterns to convey the sense of variety. Assign a specific pattern to each of the specimens. Select one pattern that indicates that this individual belongs to its class. Arrange patterns (that means, animals with patterns) in order to bring harmony in your composition. Make your landscape purposeful, and organize it into a whole, not resembling a piece of fabric that had been cut at random from a bale to make a tablecloth.

Remember one general principle, which is usually expressed sententiously as "form follows function." Each animal shape you draw should indirectly convey the characteristic of movement, which is specific to the animal you choose to portray, while each symmetrical or asymmetrical pattern may tell about animal's locomotion or its possible ways of disguising its true appearance.

Figure 7a shows yet another study on symmetry, while Figure 7b shows an imaginary creature striking a symmetrical pose.

Working on Composition

When you are ready with the general design of your picture, examine it in a detailed and complete manner: does the artwork convey the message you intended to express by art, or is it just an accurate depiction of the object of your attention you have been working on? After saving your image under a new name, select the best and most meaningful part of your work and crop it, so you can endeavor now toward completing a new, blown-up segment. Work on it, having in mind both the meaning you want to convey and the aesthetic matters of artistic beauty and taste. Your new work may be less descriptive than your initial composition, but you may find it more engaging and intent. After you feel you have completed your work, compare it critically with the first rendering in terms of your initial goals and your actual answer to the issues you were working on.

PROJECT 2: CRYSTALS AND CRYSTAL CAVES

Abstract

We will examine crystals and then make a geometric composition with lines and patterns. Then we will discuss rock art and its preservation problems, and examine modern and contemporary art. This project also relates someway to mathematics (by examining crystals' angles and symmetry or making fractal design), chemistry (studying how crystals take on a precise crystalline form), and geology (learning about crystal caves). We examine a concept of crystallization, combined it with art and graphic skills, and created a composition of crystalline forms. Then we will create a three-dimensional representation of the interior of a cave using symmetry, repetition, and pattern.

Introduction to Project "Crystals and Crystal Caves"

Project about crystals relates to several areas of interest: physics, geometry, chemistry, visual arts, and computer graphic skills. This interactive project involves also an application of spatial visualization skills of the reader. We will examine *crystals* and then will make connections with all these fields of interest, to discuss this project in terms of:

- Mathematics, by examining crystals' angles and their symmetry, or making fractal design,
- Chemistry, by studying how crystals take on precise crystalline forms; we will give special attention to water in a solid state: ice and snowflakes.
- Geology, by learning about crystal caves,
- Design principles, for example, when making a geometric composition with lines and patterns, and apply tessellation,

- Art and art history, by contemplating rock art, cave art, preservation problems, and at the same time looking at modern and contemporary art.

The objective of this project is to use our knowledge derived from all these inquiries to create beautiful projects about minerals: gems and other more mundane earth baubles. In this project, we will examine a concept of crystallization, combine it with art and graphic skills, and then create a composition of crystalline forms. Finally, we will draw a crystal and then, through copying and pasting to selection, and then create a three-dimensional representation of the interior of a cave using symmetry, repetition, and pattern.

Some Physical Concepts and Processes Related to Crystals

Before working on the project it may be useful to examine the properties of crystals, such as their chemical composition and structure. We will first examine a crystal in terms of its physical properties, such as size, shape, texture, flexibility, and color. Figure 8 shows a computer art graphics created by a student.

Background Information Type A: Natural Events And Processes

Background Information about Science Connections: The Structure of Crystals

Some substances don't have any order in the array of atoms; we call them amorphous. Many other materials have a crystalline structure, where atoms are set in a three-dimensional pattern. Crystals display such repeating pattern of atoms, *ions*, or molecules, with constant distances between these parts. A set of atoms makes a unit cell of such a pattern and is repeated in a regular way. Some crystals, such as table salt or copper are built of

Figure 8. Liz Hergert, "Crystal Cave." (© 2010, L. Hergert. Used with permission.)

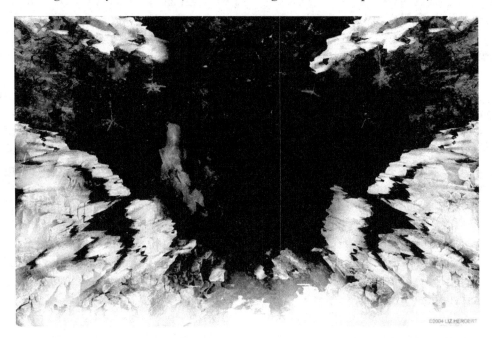

few kinds of atoms and have a simple structure. Some proteins, such as those building teeth, have complex crystalline structure and many kinds of molecules. Physical tests made with the use of light, electricity, pressure, ultrasound, and other factors show the internal symmetry of crystals.

Most of the minerals that form the Earth's crust have a crystalline structure. Thus, most rocks, metals, and ice are made of crystals. The most widely known materials have crystalline structure, for example, sand and clay that are used for pottery and ceramic tiles, gypsum (used for finishing wall surfaces), as well as many edible substances, such as sugar. Human-made forms, sculptures, and architectural designs often reveal crystalline structure.

Grown Crystals

More diamonds are grown rather than produced by mining. People produce crystals for industrial applications and for the purpose of scientific research. Geologists grow crystals in their laboratories and learn about processes involved in building up the mountains. Rubies, sapphires and many synthetic gems are grown for jewelry and industry. Industrially grown diamonds, the crystalline forms of carbon (C), are the hardest of solids. Crystals are very useful in electronics, semiconductor industry, optics, the production of television screens and tapes for videocassettes.

The computer industry uses crystals showing superconductivity. Silicon (Si) crystals are grown in layers to produce integrated circuits. Grown quartz SiO_2 crystals show piezoelectricity: when their shape is changed by rapid stress, they produce the electric current that is used in piezoelectric circuits. A seeded growth method serves for the fabrication of high-permeance membranes. Grown quartz crystals change shape when a voltage is applied, so they are used for radio oscillators. In watches, quartz crystals modulate the time-keeping circuits. Many kinds of interactions can produce changes in a system, although the total quantities of matter and energy remain unchanged. When we learn about the structure of a crystal, we recognize that solids, unlike liquids and gases, tend to retain memory of the events that changed them, because they preserve their shapes, while liquids and gases keep the shape of the container as long as they are inside.

Crystalline material has been separated from the tobacco-mosaic virus protein in 1933 (Stanley, 1937). We cannot ascribe the crystalline structure to inanimate forms only, after a closer look into organic forms on the nano level revealed that some viruses have an ability to organize themselves into liquid crystals.

Thus, for several reasons, "current knowledge about nanostructures makes difficult defining the distinction between organic and inorganic, living and inanimate, natural and artificial, or human and machine" (Cheetham, 2010).

Crystal Caves

On the web and in books we may find pictures of caves built out of crystalline minerals such as calcite, a form of calcium carbonate $CaCO_3$. Examples of such caves come from different parts of the world. Caves are the roofed cavities in the rocks produced by underground water or by the waves of the sea. The biggest caves in North America are the Carlsbad Caverns in New Mexico (2011), more than 117 limestone caverns located on 46,766.45 acres, that is, 189.26 km^2, and the Mammoth Cave in Kentucky, which is 25 feet high and 4 miles long. The Big Room in the Carlsbad Caverns National Park is the third largest chamber in North America and the seventh largest in the world. The largest in the world is the Sarawak Chamber in Malaysia. Chambers formed when sulfuric acid dissolved the surrounding limestone. Calcite from limestone dissolved and later deposited by water forms beautiful, white, pink or yellow structures called stalactites (which grow downward from the wet roof, like big icicles) and stalagmites (growing upward, like trunks of trees or stacks of saucers). Sometimes they meet, making columns. In many places paintings dating from prehistoric times cover the cave walls and ceilings.

Background Information Type B: Art Concepts and Principles

Background Information about the Stone Age

The Stone Age is a prehistoric period of human culture before the use of metals, and before the use of writing. It is divided into the Old, or Paleolithic age, which lasted from about 3.5 million to 10,000 years ago, the Middle or Mesolithic age, which means "middle stone," and the New, or Neolithic age. The Paleolithic was the stage of hunting and gathering, and the only domesticated animals were dogs. Realistic and symbolic cave paintings created by early humans from before 20,000 years were found in many places: for example, in Altamira (Spain), Lascaux (France), Africa, India, and Australia. Mesolithic started about 8300 BC. Farming and herding practices characterized Neolithic Period, and also the use of small, chipped stone tools. Isolated Stone Age cultures survived on many continents until the 19th and 20th centuries. Estimation of the age of the findings involves many up-to-date technologies, such as radiometric age dating used to measure the amount of radioactive decay of isotopes present in the rocks and in organic tissues. Isotopes are pairs of atoms that have the same number of protons (atomic numbers) but a different number of neutrons. In radioactive decay, one atom is converted into another one with emission of radiation. The amount of changed isotopes in a rock gives a measure of its age.

Art in the Caves

Prehistoric paintings and engravings produced on rock surfaces of caves by their early non-literate inhabitants have been discovered mostly in the 19th and 20th centuries. Thousands of sites in America, Europe, Asia, Africa, and Oceania contain ancient art, with thousands, and even millions of figures carved, engraved, or painted on the walls of rock shelters and caves. Drawings of bison, horses, deer, and cattle are in the caves of Altamira in northern Spain, Lascaux in France, and in New Mexico in the USA. The authenticity of the Paleolithic, Mesolithic, or Neolithic paintings is accepted many years after the discovery of a cave, after examination with the use of many methods; for example, with X-ray analyses. The earliest cave art was created some 32,000 years ago by the nomadic tribes. North American Indians and the tribes who traveled on the plains and in the woods of Europe were hunting animals, eating their meat, employing the skins for clothing and building shelters, and using bones and antlers as tools, weapons, and domestic utensils. Maybe they created their beautiful artwork to communicate with other people or the gods.

Pictographs – pictorial symbols for phrases and objects were used in prehistoric times, for example, for creating drawings and paintings on rock walls. Ancient people created beautiful images on the cave walls and ceilings, providing an artistic expression and an account of everyday human life. However, the basic subject is the animal. Some images were engraved with stone tools or bones on the rock surfaces. Decorated bones, dear-antlers and stone tools were found nearby in the caves. Ancient artists made their drawings with charcoal, and created paintings often using water solution of iron oxides and the golden-yellow earth pigment called ochre, so the rocks absorbed the paints. When the treasures of ancient art were discovered after tens of thousands years, they were well preserved in the stable humidity and temperature of the caves. When caves were opened to the public, many problems of conservation arose due to the physical, chemical, and microbiological reason. Rocks began to fall, fade and peel of the paint due to the cave lighting, and sometimes acts of vandalism happened as well. For this reason, cave art specialists built in many locations the replicas of the caves and reproductions of the cave paintings, while the original caves have been closed to the public or they are open for a very limited number of people interested in scientific research and education. In his film "Roma," Fellini shows a moment of discovery of Roman frescoes, which fade in front of the viewers' eyes the moment the flashlight affects them.

Figure 9 (a and b) presents student semi-abstract art works about the crystalline structure.

Figure 9. a) Adrian Nunenkamp, "The World Matrix." (© 2010, A. Nunenkamp. Used with permission.); b) Patrick Boulac. (© 2010, P. Boulac. Used with permission.)

Background Information Type C: Computing or Technology

Background Information about Fractals

We can model crystalline structures using geometric concepts and describing crystals by means of the horizontal and vertical coordinates. In two and three dimensions, we can draw the geometric relationships in crystals and allocate their points and edges along x, y, and z-axes. Transformations of drawings, such as reflections, translations, and rotations may help extend our knowledge about geometric relationships.

The concept of fractal design is helpful in understanding a structure of the natural phenomena, such as crystals. It allows a pictorial representation of objects that involve patterns of self-similar shapes. It could be helpful to examine the web-based tutorials about how to create fractals with the use of a computer and learn about various kinds of software for creating fractals.

Some types of fractals that are in use today include:

- Iterated Function System (random and deterministic), where the process is repeated and results in a self-similarity independent of a scale, with all the frames being simply iterations of the original frame. The Sierpinski Gasket, one of the most basic types of fractals built from equilateral (or other) triangles can be formed as an iterated function system.
- *Mandelbrot sets*, the nonlinear fractals where the relationship between their parts is subject to change. They become the source of stunning color computer graphics images. They are also important in the dynamical system theory.
- *Julia sets*, with objects generated through an iterative process called after a French mathematician, Gaston Julia. By counting the number of times each point goes through the function before it gets a certain distance away, we can determine what color to make that point. Therefore all points that are equally far away will be the same color.
- The L-System is a parallel rewriting system used to generate self-similar fractals. The Hungarian biologist and botanist Aristid Lindenmayer designed this technique in 1968 for the study of biological models for plant growth.

Fractals and the Structure of Matter

Fractal geometry describes objects in a different way than the traditional Euclidian geometry. It takes for granted that objects are self-similar so, when magnified, their parts are similar to the whole, and the likeness continues when the parts are magnified more and more.

We can find fractals everywhere in the natural world – in the eroded landscapes of mountain surfaces, crystalline caves in the crust, in the patterns of frost on a cold window, as well as on the surface of a virus. Specialists in a great number of domains analyze the fractal character of objects in biology, geology, and meteorology and put fractals in service of technology, so one could change physical features, electrical conductivity, and the atomic structure of glasses, gels, and other amorphous materials. Fractal models serve in chemistry, physics, and materials science to describe a passage from one state in which matter can exist (solid, liquid, gas, or plasma) to another, which depends on temperature and pressure. Researchers control the growth of polymers and colloids in liquid and gaseous phases. Fractals are useful in explaining the atomic structure of materials, and heat- and electrical conductivity. Physicists can describe with the use of fractal theory the chaotic changes in dynamical systems.

Fractal geometry is a branch of bio-inspired computing, and involves *cellular automata*, L-systems, iterated function systems, particle systems, Brownian motion, and fractal proteins for landscape design, growth processes, and modeling. Inspiration for designing cellular automata comes from complex natural systems, such as colonies of insects or the nervous system, and pertains decentralized systems, such as sensory networks and networks showing the intrinsic connectivity and conductance (Packard, 2001). With evolutionary approach, scientists can solve a variety of problems, for example, the Rubik's cube (El-Sourani, Hauke, & Borschbach, 2010).

Artists have often applied fractal design in their work. When we look (for example, at the Google Images) at the photographs taken by the American photographer and environmentalist Anselm Adams (1902-1984), such as his "Moon and Mount McKinley, Denali National Park" or the "Oak Tree, Sunset City," we can see a striking resemblance between the fractal and photographic rendering of natural scenery. Artists saw such resemblance and drew analogies with their own fractal art. For example, an algorithmic artist Kerry Mitchell (2011) wrote, "I varied the thickness of the curve in accordance with the grayscale level of the target photograph, Ansel Adams' *Oak Tree, Sunset City, California.* I contrasted the straight, precise lines of the curve with the natural branching of the tree and tried to pay homage to Adams' image of a fractal with one of my own." A photography artist Julia Jones (2005) wrote, "Great photographs are like living things, subject to the laws of life. They are made up of cells or parts, each as significant as the whole. There are photos within photos: fractals. Fractals work and exist in nature and in Adams' photographs; these fractals play out to recreate what Adams saw in the scene, making it alive again to the viewer. Adams saw and captured pictures within pictures; masterpieces within the one masterpiece. Adams once argued, no note is beautiful on its own: it is the repetition, variation, and the note's place in the whole that allows one to hear its beauty." Using a recursive splitting technique, artists produce fractal images of great statistical complexity. Landscapes with trees and other branching structures made with the use of fractal geometry have been used as backgrounds in many motion pictures, still life works, and animations.

Background Information Type B: Art Concepts and Principles

Background Information about Modern and Contemporary Art Connections

Visual communication in fine arts is often based on a metaphor, where one thing developed in the mind represents another thing, so each viewer may receive the unique and individual message from the same artwork. For example, abstract sculptures created by the American artist Joel Shapiro (born 1941, accessible at the Google Images) in the Minimalist style from regular blocks, arranged in larger-than-life, human-like forms may evoke a feeling of movement.

On the web or using books on art we may examine reproductions of works of artists inspired by the beauty of the natural order. For example, natural forms served the American artist Aaron Siskind (1903-1992), as a theme for almost abstract photography, such as "Martha's Vineyard." We can see how often geometric shapes inspired artists as a source for creating art.

Fascination with patterns and regular arrangements inspired a great many artists in the 20th century. For example, Frantisek Kupka (1871-1957) composed his imaginative "Cathedral" of geometrical shapes filled with colors. American artist Lyonel Feininger (871-1956) composed his "Sailing Boats" from overlapping triangles of color.

In the Constructivism style, Ljubov Popova (1889-1924) set up the "Space-Force Construction" and Naum Gabo (1890-1977), created a delicate constructivist sculpture "Linear Construction in Space No.2" from a complex 3-dimensional arrangement of nylon strings.

William Latham is a creator of the Organic Art that can be seen on his website at http://doc.gold.ac.uk/~mas01whl/media/images.htm. Latham and Todd created in the early 1990s the FormGrow system, which translated DNA data to 3D computer art forms. They continue their work (Latham, Shaw, Todd, Leymarie, Jefferys, & Kelley, 2008) by developing biological software that performs analysis of the biochemical properties of the proteins encoded by genes in DNA, and then controls the parameters of a fixed FormGrow structure.

Background Information Type A: Natural Events And Processes

Background Information about Crystallization

Snowflakes Have a Crystalline Design

Crystals take diverse kinds of forms, many times evoking our wonder because of their beauty. *Crystallography* is a study of crystals: their form, growth, structure, chemistry, bonding, and physical properties. The nature of *binding among atoms*, compounds, and molecules determines the way they form crystals. When crystals grow, they develop various arrangements of symmetry axes. For example, snowflakes grow with great variety of designs, with their shape depending on the internal pattern. In most cases, the outer surface of a crystalline matter (for example, of an ice cube) does not reveal the arrangement of crystals. Only certain angles of rotational symmetry are possible for crystals: 60 degrees, 90 degrees, 120 degrees, 180 degrees, and 360 degrees. Due to the possible combinations, there are 32 crystal classes, which are grouped into the 7 crystal systems.

Sometimes water in the atmosphere changes directly from gas to solid, omitting the liquid phase; we can see the result as the snow. Snowflakes, looking like the six-armed stars or feathery jewels, are actually ice crystals, sometimes as large as six inches (15 centimeters) from one side to the other. Snowflakes develop when the supercooled cloud droplets, which can remain liquid even at 0^0 F, start to freeze around an ice lattice arranged around a few molecules of different kinds acting as a nucleus (Glossary of Meteorology, 2010). When examining a snowflake, we may think about the elements and principles of design, such as shape, or symmetry, and see the uniqueness of their structures. We can see rotational (mostly six-fold) symmetry. This kind of symmetry occurs in nature in flowers, fruits, starfish, jellyfish, and other sea animals. Leonardo da Vinci conducted studies on rotational symmetry. It occurs universally in decorative arts, prehistoric and contemporary.

Years ago, in the times when photography was black-and-white only, Wilson A. Bentley (1865-1931) created more than 5000 photographs of snow crystals, not finding any two alike. Bentley had done his pioneering work on photomicrography by connecting a folding (bellow) camera to a microscope. Many versions of his book entitled "Snow Crystals" (Bentley, 1995) are still available in bookstores and on the web. Images of crystals, never repeating their awesome shapes, can be seen at the Google Images after typing 'Bentley snowflake.'

Most of us accept that regular patterns are perceived as beauty in nature: it may be a natural meander of a river; it may also be a fractal design of a mollusk shell, a snowflake, a pinecone, a sunflower, or a foliage arrangement on a tree, many of them displaying properties of cellular automata. Common, primary, simple elements of our environment, such as raindrops, snowflakes, and simplified animal shapes might serve as a carrier of a notion. The use of natural metaphors might yield art works that are massively structured in cognitive terms. We may find an extensive use of metaphors in literature, visual arts, and music. In a visual mode of communication, images that have iconic properties or serve as generally accepted symbols. They are considered crucial to visualization of the hard to explain objects and notions.

Simple subjects, like snowflakes, are often being pictured in art works, serving as metaphorical statements about the theme itself and the artist's thoughts on the theme. It might be interesting to understand rules that control movements of a single snowflake, then compare and contrast them with dynamics of a composition created for the ballet dancers, and examine to what degree nature might inspire visual and performing artists.

Natural phenomena such as the snowflakes, involve patterns. Fractals, which are usually generated by computers, represent such patterns. Fractal-generating applets may be useful in bringing into being images of snowflakes or snowy landscapes. You may then examine your final product made up by grouping of the single structures. The pattern of snow falling on the city street transforms the way we see an order of windows and the whole town. By lowering the brightness and contrast, snowflakes intensify each other to the point of dizziness of the viewer. To picture this effect, you may want to experiment with the shades of white and to show depth in your composition. In other respect, you may want to develop an interior scene with a pattern made with snowflakes, with light passing through a window.

Now it's a good time to create images of snowflakes, on paper or on the computer. Use cutouts of snowflakes: choose an image as a background and then paste multiplied and resized images of snowflakes as a new layer onto the background image. Figure 10 (a and b) shows an artistic presentation of a snowflake, and then a postcard, both created by students.

Creating a Cave Project in Several Stages

Making Hand Drawings and Models

On the web or in illustrated books examine pictures of various kinds of crystals. Some of them are famous jewels; some, for example quartz crystals,

Figure 10. a) Watsatree Diteeyont, "Snowflake." (© 2010, W. Diteeyont. Used with permission.); b) Amber Johnson, "A Postcard." (© 2010, A. Johnson. Used with permission.)

may be found easily both in the countryside and in stores. Create a drawing in your sketchbook of a crystal using traditional tools, such as pencil or chalk. Then, make a simple three-dimensional model out of wooden sticks or matches in order to explain the crystalline structure of matter. Explain properties and composition of crystals through two- and three-dimensional models and visualizations made with the use of color and pattern coding.

Geometric Composition Derived from an Image of a Crystal

While working on the project, apply your spatial visualization skills – spatial reasoning skills, so you can draw upon your understanding of the three-dimensional world. Build a three- dimensional representation of a cave out of two-dimensional pictures. Figure 11 shows stages of work in progress, first by drawing a single crystal, and then copying an image and repeating it over the surface of the drawing.

Looking at a sample of a crystal, draw an angle of your choice. While working on the proj-

Figure 11. a) Tory Wagoner, Mike Wyckoff. (© 2010, T. Wagoner and M. Wyckoff. Used with permission.); b) Loren Music, Peter Vrazsity. (© 2010, L. Music and P. Vrazsity. Used with permission.)

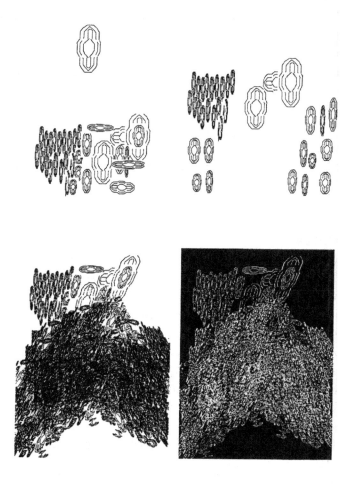

ect, apply geometric concepts and examine shapes of crystals and their symmetry, thus recognizing geometry in nature. Draw a single crystal, then copy and repeat the image over the surface of your drawing. Look, the angle in a crystal does not change! An angle between any pair of crystal faces remains constant; it is the same for all minerals. The crystal may change the size but not an angle, because in a crystal, the angle between any pair of crystal faces is constant, the same for all pieces of a mineral, regardless of its overall shape or size. Measure the angles on the drawings and check the crystals to see whether they keep the same angle. This structure cannot be seen in amorphous minerals: that is, in minerals displaying no pattern to the arrangement of atoms.

You may also generate this project in another way, with any graphic software or by writing a program. Create an image of a crystal with the use of any graphic software, or, if you have some experience in programming, you may write a program for developing a structure of a crystal. When you write a program, remember that a small change in a program makes a big difference in a crystal design. This is the way the connoisseurs appreciate the works of art. Geometric composition derived from an image of a crystal may also serve as a starting point for creating an animation about growing crystals.

Abstract Composition Showing Symmetry and Pattern

While working on the project, recognize and use your art as a form of communication, so by applying visual art materials, tools, techniques, and processes, you will make connection between visual arts and other disciplines. Explore the concepts of symmetry (as a repetition of units) and pattern while drawing direct representations of crystals and crystalline materials. Use and modify patterns, change proportions, and repeat selected details, changing their scale and slant, distorting or rotating them, and applying perspective.

Manipulate the image by using color selections, adding lines, applying textures, and enhancing the depth of the picture.

Combine these skills with concepts related to crystals to create artwork that visually conveys your understanding of the crystallography-related concepts, and communicate your experiences gained in this assignment. Using samples of crystals and drawings of crystal lattices as the stimulus for creating art, work on your composition of crystals applying symmetry and pattern. Transform the image of the crystal the same way as nature does.

Crystal Cave

Make an imaginative drawing of a crystal cave built out of previously created crystal rocks. Contrary to the Paleolithic tradition, create an interior of a cave in the spirit of contemporary art. Explore the concept of symmetry. Copy a small part of your abstract composition and use symmetry and pattern to create a composition that would embellish the cave and reflect its crystalline structure. Everybody can create their own solution to this art production and create a different image of the cave interior, because everybody began with selecting different angle and building different crystals. You may experiment with a few different angles and compare the results. Show the effect of the movement of the tectonic plates. How does it look when rocks are heated, bent, twisted, squeezed, stretched, and the crusted fragments collide? Try to imagine what kind of light might be found in a cave, and how it may affect your image. Figure 12 presents student works about a crystal cave.

A Fractal Design Composition

While working on this project, it would be helpful to examine some information about the developments in electronic media for art and learn about utilizing fractals as an artistic tool in art. To create a cave interior, build a composition out of the

Figure 12. a) Gregory Effinger, "Crystal Cave." (© 2010, G. Effinger. Used with permission.); b) Dina Waddell, "Crystal Cave." (© 2010, D. Waddell. Used with permission.)

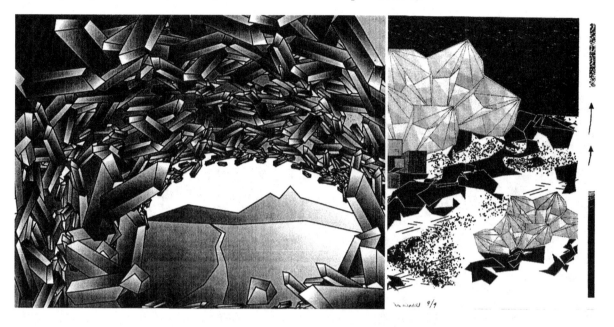

small elements. For this project, you may use a concept of fractal design. We may build a simple fractal by dividing a line in 3 parts and removing the middle part. When we repeat this series of steps, first on the 2 remaining parts, then on the 4 parts produced by that operation, and so on, the object has a great number of parts, each of which is very small. On the web, there are many sites about fractals, helpful fractal tutorials, and beautiful examples of fractal art.

Artwork resulting from writing a program is often as pleasing and impressive as nature itself, despite any possible remarks and disagreements about the essence of art and about conditions that identify what it is. You may also prefer to design a fractal image, with geometric shapes that are self-similar and have fractional dimensions. Figure 13 presents other examples of student works about a crystal cave.

A Story about Crystal Growth

Now you may want to write a story in your journal, on your listserv, or elsewhere on the web about your imaginative trip to a cave, and then you may incorporate this story into your picture using the story itself as a pattern for the background. Now, you may want to create an animated story about growing crystals in a crystal cave. You can also apply a design with the flipbook approach, where, in order to put things in motion, each next image has added lines. Again, you may use a concept of fractal design. You may also want to participate in a web discussion that you may initiate, about different uses of pattern (as a repetition of units) in the design created in this project, as well as about the use of symmetry.

CONCLUSION

In a similar way as in previous chapter, "Visual Tweet: nature inspired visual statements" discusses

Figure 13. a) Steve McDonald. (© 2010, S. McDonald. Used with permission.); b) Peter Musset. (© 2010, P. Musset. Used with permission.)

possible visual explorations about connections between science, computing, and art. This chapter consists of two projects about science-related themes: (1) Symmetry and pattern in animal world – geometry and art, and (2) Crystals and crystal caves. The readers have been invited to engage in interactive reading that would result in creating visual presentation of each theme. The projects are aimed at enhancing the reader's skills in using visual communication media, gathering interesting facts and ideas, and actively responding to them in a pictorial way.

REFERENCES

Animals in Medieval Art. (2011). *Heilbrun timeline of art history*. Department of Medieval Art and The Cloisters, The Metropolitan Museum of Art. Retrieved July 27, 2011, from http://www.metmuseum.org/toah/hd/best/hd_best.htm

Arnheim, R. (1969). *Visual thinking*. Berkeley, CA: University of California Press.

Arnheim, R. (1988). *The power of the center: A study of composition in the visual arts*. Berkeley, CA: University of California Press.

Arnheim, R. (1990). Language and the early cinema. *Leonardo, Digital Image Digital Cinema, Supplemental Issue*, 3-4.

Bennett, C., Ryall, J., Spalteholz, L., & Gooch, A. (2007). *The aesthetics of graph visualization. computational aesthetics in graphics, visualization, and imaging* (pp. 57–64). Eurographics Association.

Bentley, W. A. (1995). *1931). Snowflakes in photographs*. Mineola, NY: Dover Publications.

Berens, R. R. (1999). The role of artists in ship camouflage during World War I. *Leonardo, 32*(1), 53–59. doi:10.1162/002409499553000

Birkhoff, G. D. (2003, 1933). *Aesthetic measure*. Kessinger Publishing. ISBN 0766130940.

Bohr, N. (1935). Can quantum-mechanical description of physical reality be considered complete? *Physical Review, 48*, 696–702. doi:10.1103/PhysRev.48.696

Bolin, L. (2009). *Camouflage art*. Retrieved July 27, 2011, from http://www.toxel.com/inspiration/2009/10/04/camouflage-art-by-liu-bolin/

Camouflage restaurants. (n.d.). Retrieved July 27, 2011, from http://www.toxel.com/inspiration/2009/06/20/10-unusual-and-creative-restaurants/

Cheetham, M. A. (2010). The crystal interface in contemporary art: Metaphors of the organic and inorganic. *Leonardo, 43*(3), 251–255. doi:10.1162/leon.2010.43.3.250

Doolittle, B. (2011). *Camouflage art*. Retrieved July 27, 2011, http://www.bnr-art.com/doolitt/

Einstein, A., Podolsky, B., & Rosen, N. (1935). Can quantum-mechanical description of physical reality be considered complete? *Physical Review, 47*, 777–780. doi:10.1103/PhysRev.47.777

El-Sourani, N., Hauke, S., & Borschbach, M. (2010). An evolutionary approach for solving the Rubik's cube incorporating exact methods . In Di Chio, C. (Eds.), *Applications of evolutionary computing, LNCS 6024 EvoApplications 2010 Proceedings* (pp. 80–89). Berlin, Germany: Springer. doi:10.1007/978-3-642-12239-2_9

Encyclopædia Britannica. (2011). *Holothurian*. Retrieved July 27, 2011, from http://www.britannica.com/EBchecked/topic/269645/holothurian

Ferguson, C., & Ferguson, H. (1994). *Mathematics in stone and bronze*. Erie, PA: Meridian Creative Group.

Glossary of Meteorology. (2010). Retrieved November 19, 2010, from http://amsglossary.allenpress.com/glossary/search?p=1&query=cloud+seeding&submit=Search

Haeckel, E., Breidbach, O., Hartman, R., & Eibl-Eibesfeldt, I. (1998). *Art forms in nature: The prints of Ernst Haeckel (monographs)*. München, Germany: Prestel Publishing.

Huang, Q., & Balsys, R. J. (2009). Applying fractal and chaos theory to animation in the Chinese literati tradition. *CGIV, Sixth International Conference on Computer Graphics, Imaging and Visualization* (pp.112-122). Los Alamitos, CA: IEEE Computer Society.

IUPAC. (2010). *Compendium of chemical terminology*, 2nd ed. Oxford, UK: Blackwell Scientific Publications. Retrieved October 2, 2011, from http://goldbook.iupac.org/C01058.html

James, A. V., James, D. A., & Kalisperis, L. N. (2004). A unique art form: The friezes of Pirgi. *Leonardo, 37*(3), 234–242. doi:10.1162/0024094041139409

Jones, J. (2005). *Fractals & frequencies*. Retrieved July 28, 2011, from http://fractalsandfrequencies.blogspot.com/

Jones, O. (2001, 1856). *The grammar of ornament: Illustrated by examples from various styles of ornament*. London, UK A Dorling Kindersley Book, The Ivy Press, Limited. ISBN 0-7894-7646-0

Kettle, S. F. A. (2007). *Symmetry and structure: Readable group theory for chemists*, 3rd ed. Wile-Blackwell. ISBN-10: 0470060409

Latham, W., Shaw, M., Todd, S., Leymarie, F. F., Jefferys, B., & Kelley, L. (2008). Using DNA to generate 3D organic art forms . In Giacobini, M. (Eds.), *Applications of Evolutionary Computing, LNCS 4974 2008 EvoWorkshops Proceedings* (pp. 433–442). Berlin, Germany: Springer. doi:10.1145/1276958.1277049

Lau, A., & Vande Moere, A. (2007). Towards a model of information aesthetics in information visualization. In *Proceedings of 11th International Conference on Information Visualisation* (pp. 87-92). Los Alamitos, CA: IEEE Computer Society.

Leffingwell, J. C. (2003). Chirality and bioactivity I: Pharmacology. *Leffingwell Reports, 3*(1). Retrieved April 13, 2011, from http://www.leffingwell.com/download/chirality-phamacology.pdf

Lévi-Strauss, C. (1997). *Look, listen, learn* (B.C.J. Singer, Trans., pp. 83-87). Basic Books, a division of Harper-Collins Publishers. ISBN 0-465-06880-4

Leyton, M. (2006). The foundations of aesthetics . In Fishwick, P. A. (Ed.), *Aesthetic computing* (pp. 289–314).

Loeb, A. L. (1993). *Concepts & images: Visual mathematics*. Boston, MA: Birkhäuser.

Mitchell, K. (2011). *A celebration of beauty*. Digital Art Guild; Art through Technology. Retrieved July 28, 2011, from http://www.digitalartguild.com/content/view/56/26/

Neville, A. C. (1977). Symmetry and asymmetry problems in animals . In Duncan, R., & Weston-Smith, M. (Eds.), *The encyclopedia of ignorance: Everything you ever wanted to know about the unknown* (pp. 331–338). Oxford, UK: Paragon Press.

Okubo, P. G., & Aki, K. (1987). Fractal geometry in the San Andreas Fault system. *Journal of Geophysical Research, 92*(B1), 345–355. doi:10.1029/JB092iB01p00345

Packard, A. (2001). A neural net that can be seen with the naked eye . In Backhaus, W. (Ed.), *Neuronal coding of perceptual systems* (pp. 397–402). Singapore: World Scientific.

Phaidon Books. (1996). *The 20th century art book*. San Francisco, CA: Author. ISBN: 0-71483542 0

Phaidon Press. (1994). *(The) art book*. London, UK: Author. ISBN # 07148 2984 6

Phaidon Press. (1999). *American art book*. London, UK: Author.

Purchase, H. (2010). Graph drawing aesthetics in user-sketched graph layouts. In *AUIC '10 Proceedings of the Eleventh Australasian Conference on User Interface*, Vol. 106. ISBN: 978-1-920682-87-3

Schilthuizen, M., & Gravendeel, B. (2011). *Evolution of chirality symposium*. The 13th Congress of the European Society for Evolutionary Biology, Tuebingen 20-25 August 2011. Retrieved August 26, 2011, from http://www.eseb2011.de/

Stanley, W. M. (1937). Crystalline tobacco-mosaic virus protein. *American Journal of Botany, 24*(2), 59–68. doi:10.2307/2436720

Thompson D'Arcy, W. (1917, 1992). *On growth and form*, rev. ed. Dover Publications. ISBN-10: 048667135

Tufte, E. R. (1983). *The visual display of quantitative information*. Cheshire, CT: Graphics Press.

Zeki, S. (1993). Vision of the brain. *Wiley-Blackwell., ISBN-10*, 0632030542.

Zeki, S. (1999). Art and the brain. *Journal of Conscious Studies: Controversies in Science and the Humanities*, 6(6/7), 76–96.

ADDITIONAL READING

Arnheim, R. (1974). *Art and visual perception.* Berkeley, CA: University of California Press.

Briggs, J. (1992). *Fractals, the patterns of chaos. A new aesthetic of art, science, and nature.* Touchstone Books.

Falconer, K. (2003). *Fractal geometry: Mathematical foundations and applications.* John Wiley & Sons, Ltd. doi:10.1002/0470013850

Gleick, J. (2000). *Faster: The acceleration of just about everything.* Vintage Books, ISBN# 067977548X

Harrison, A. (1996). *Fractals in chemistry.* Oxford University Press.

Henisch, H. K. (1996). *Crystal growth in gels.* Dover Publications.

Holden, A. (1991). *Shapes, space, and symmetry.* ISBN-13: 978-0486268514

Holden, A., & Morrison, P. S. (Photographer), (1982). Crystals and crystal growing. ISBN-13: 978-0262580502

Novak, M. M. (Ed.). (2004). *Thinking in patterns: Fractals and related phenomena in nature.* ISBN-13: 978-9812388223

Sands, D. E. (1994). *Introduction to crystallography.* Dover Publications.

Schroeder, M. (1992). *Fractals, chaos, power laws. minutes from an infinite paradise.* W H Freeman & Co.

Stevens, R. (2005). *Creating fractals.* Graphics Series.

Wynn, C. M., & Wiggins, A. M. (1996). *The five biggest ideas in science.* Wiley.

KEY TERMS AND DEFINITIONS

Algorithms: Are mathematical recipes telling how to carry out a process. They are actually mathematical equations used to create repetition. An algorithm is a procedure for solving a complicated problem by carrying out a fixed sequence of simpler, unambiguous steps. A recursive process means that an algorithm is applied multiple times to perform operations on its previous products. Such procedures are used in computer programs and in programmed learning.

Anamorphosis: Is a way of distorting perspective in such a way that an image seems to be meaningless until viewed from a particular angle. Anamorphic drawings have appeared in the Renaissance art. Leonardo da Vinci experimented with such optical illusions. Hans Holbein the Younger placed an anamorphic picture of a skull in his painting "The Ambassadors" (1533). It is visible only when viewed from close up and to one side of the painting.

Cellular automaton: Is a discrete model consisting of a grid of cells, each in a finite number of states (such as 'on' or 'off'), in sets called neighborhoods. The fixed rules, such as mathematical functions, determine the creation of new generations of sets with the new states of cells. Plant leaves, seashells, and even neural networks are examples of naturally occurring cellular automata.

Crystal Binding: There are many types of crystal binding: covalent (sharing electrons in pairs), ionic (with a charge transfer from cations to anions), metallic (with cationic atoms weakly bound to the ion cores), and molecular (with van der Waals interactions between molecules). In most crystals, the binding is a mixture of ionic, covalent and metallic binding, with a three-dimensional array of unit cells.

Crystallography: The study of the crystal's form, growth, physical properties resulting from its structure, the nature of the bonding among its atoms, and its chemical composition. Molecular biologists and organic chemists are often crystallographers. They make use of crystallographic data to examine the structure of organic molecules and ways to concentrate and crystallize the molecules in plants and animals. For example, Rosalind Franklin and others examined DNA crystals using X-ray diffraction. In 1952, James D. Watson and Francis Crick proposed the double helix structure of the DNA molecule determined with the use of crystallographic data.

Evo-Devo: An informal term that means evolutionary developmental biology. This is a study of evolution and generation of form and pattern, through research on comparative gene function/expression, embryogenesis, genomics, phylogenetics, and paleontology, among other venues. Materials on this topic can be found in the EvoDevo Journal, http://www.evodevojournal.com/

Ions: Cations and Anions: An atom or a molecule that has an electric charge is called an ion. An electric charge results from the presence of single, double, triple, or even higher negative electrons unequal to the number of positive protons in the nucleus of an atom. The removal or addition of one or more electrons changes a neutral atom into an ion. Cation is an ion or group of ions that have a positive charge. Anion is a negatively charged ion. Polyelectrolytes are large molecules with many charged groups. During electrolysis (produced in an electrolyte solution by applying an electric current) cations move toward the cathode (negative electrode) and anions migrate to an anode.

Isomers: Chemical compounds that have the same molecular formula and mass but different structural formulas. Isomerism may be structural (when atoms are bonded together in different orders) or spatial (when atoms are placed in different positions in space). They may some different physical or chemical properties caused by different arrangement of atoms in their molecules. For example, ethyl alcohol (CH_3CH_2OH) and methyl ether (CH_3OCH_3) contain the same atoms bonded in different ways (Retrieved November 18, 2010 from http://www.britannica.com/EBchecked/topic/378561/methyl-ether).

Julia Sets: The function for Julia sets is $f(z)=zA2-i$. Each point in the Julia set must be passed through a function many times to determine whether the point will eventually go to infinity. Julia set uses one equation that does not change, while in the Mandelbrot set equation changes with the point that is being plotted.

Mandelbrot Set: The function for the Mandelbrot set is $z(n+1)+z(2/n)+c$ (c is a constant). Fractal shapes are distorted from one length to another and retain some degree of self-similarity. In these nonlinear fractals, the more the set is magnified the more its unpredictability increases.

Pattern: Is an artistic or decorative design made of recurring lines or any repeated elements. We can see patterns everywhere in nature, mathematics, art, architecture, and design. A pattern makes a basis of ornaments, which are specific for different cultures. Owen Jones (1856) made a huge collection of ornaments typical for different countries. He wrote an amazing monographic book entitled "The Grammar of Ornament."

Permeance: The degree to which a material allows a flow of magnetic energy. In electromagnetic circuits permeance is usually larger for cross-sections.

Symmetry: The correspondence in size, form, and arrangement of parts on opposite sides of a plane, line, or point. A crystal shows symmetry when it has s a center of symmetry, rotation axes, or mirror planes (imaginary planes that divide it into halves). There are several types of symmetry: for example, line or mirror symmetry, radial, cylindrical, or spherical symmetry. A figure that has line symmetry has two identical halves when folded along its line of symmetry, and these halves are congruent, meaning they are the same size and shape. An object has a radial symmetry when it can be rotated around the rotation axis. For example, with a fourfold rotation axis the crystal repeats itself each 90°. Angles of rotational symmetry possible for crystals are: 60 degrees, 90 degrees, 120 degrees, 180 degrees, and 360 degrees. The halves of the bilaterally symmetrical animals, for example, butterflies, when seen along the axis, form each other's mirror images. Most animals and people cannot be divided into two identical halves, even when they look symmetrical from external appearance. Two halves of the human brain display different abilities and ways of learning and thinking.

The Heisenberg's Uncertainty Principle: A part of quantum mechanics. This principle states that we cannot know precisely about certain pairs of physical properties, such as a particle's position and momentum (the product of the mass of a particle and its velocity) at the same time, because the measuring process involves interaction, which disturbs the particle. For example, a photon of light used in a measurement is bouncing off the particle. Thus, one cannot, even theoretically, predict the moment-to-moment behavior of a system consisting of the subject and the object of examination (somebody who makes an observation and an object observed). There is a theoretical limit for simultaneous measuring at an atomic scale because the more precisely is figured one amount, the more uncertain is the other one.

Chapter 13

Digital Approaches to Visualization of Geometric Problems in Wooden *Sangaku* Tablets

Jean Constant
Northern New Mexico College, USA

ABSTRACT

This chapter describes the digitalization process of 19ᵗʰ century scientific representations from the Japanese culture – a set of mathematical problems etched on wooden boards. The object of the demonstration is to apply computing techniques to the creation of artistic statements based on geometrical problems, highlight the dynamics of interaction between art and science, and examine how much both fields enrich the larger discourse and appreciation of Art. The following text describes the steps adopted in a visualization project. First, the data collection included selecting specific geometry problems from various Sangaku wooden tablets and converting them into digital information as a single black and white outline to define shapes, volumes, and textures. The vectorization of the underlying shapes transferred the exact mathematical information onto the virtual canvas. In the next step, the vector outlines were converted into bitmaps. Each individual plate was assigned a specific color scheme to enhance object size, positioning, and dynamic of the composition. At the last stage, vector-based sketches, colorizations, and the monochrome sketches were blended together to complete full color visualization. Finally, the step-by-step development of the creative process was recorded as a QuickTime movie, including an original soundtrack. Discussion refers to the dissemination of the project in art galleries and online, its potential instructional use, and it examines the audience responses.

DOI: 10.4018/978-1-4666-0942-6.ch013

INTRODUCTION

The abstract beauty of *Sangaku* – Japanese temple geometry problems (2011) and the unusual medium on which they are presented provide a fertile ground to explore alternative means of effective scientific communication. The aesthetic quality of the *Sangaku* design as well as the exactitude of the scientific demonstration they convey provide an intriguing challenge from which to start an evaluation how objective science affects aesthetics and creativity.

Sangaku or San Gaku (算額), lit. mathematical tablets are geometric problems engraved on wooden tablets. They were very popular in Japan during the Edo period (1603-1867) where worshipers carved the likenesses of horses onto wooden tablets and used those tablets as offerings. They etched mathematical problems on wooden boards and dedicated them to a shrine or a temple. Japanese mathematicians and geometers followed the Shinto temples' carving tradition. Their geometric puzzles, or *Sangaku* were originally conceived as topological pursuits. Mathematicians, especially geometers followed this tradition. As Z.M. Ruttkay (2008) points out, most of such problems were of a geometric nature and the figures were often exquisite in style and color. From a larger perspective, *Sangaku* tablets can be seen as representations of the problems driven from biology because objects driven from nature are used as part of explanatory process.

Sangaku problems are problems in Euclidean geometry concerning area and volume, the number of units that cover a closed figure, and a set of points in space. Mathematicians and *Sangaku* experts Fukagawa Hidetoshi and Tony Rothman collaborated on the mapping and cataloguing this form of visualization and published a book titled "Japanese Temples Geometry" (Hidetoshi & Rothman, 2008), which includes over two hundred *Sangaku* mathematical problems. Insight, reasoning, and accurate information are essential elements of effective practices in all scientific fields and in the creative process as well. Science inspired computing techniques collect data to create models of natural systems that help artists create visual statements. The aim of this article is to engage readers to broaden their appreciation of abstract concepts, increase their awareness of multidisciplinary interaction, and encourage artists to apply an approach that blends technology and art, and use scientific knowledge and methodology as a source of inspiration and creativity.

Art provides a context in which artists express their individual perception of nature and may become an individual and subjective quest to represent and communicate emotion to others. It is also a tool of communication that conveys information. Artwork based on the understanding of how we are affected by shape, color, sound, and all the components that constitute a visual statement help artists create a more effective narrative and enrich the spectator's experience. Explorations that blend technology and art such as the electron microscope nano-landscapes of Cris Orfescu (NanoArt 21, 2011), the experiments performed in the Digital Art and Science Program at NUS (2011), as well as the works of many artists in the fractal environment (e.g., Fractal Foundation, 2011) stand as examples of this cross-interaction.

The following experiment incorporates elements of computing to create meaningful visualization. The project initially draws from the particular sequence of lines and shapes of well-known mathematical principles and integrates the visual components of geometrical figures into aesthetic statement. The specific framework of this demonstration is based on a series of artistic representations built around the data collected from the geometry problems carved on the *Sangaku* tablets. The reader is invited to follow the step-by-step progression of the art process from extracting an outline to create a multimedia product including sound. The resulting images were deployed to encourage the development of visually attractive propositions inspired by a rigorous objective discipline and add to the effectiveness of the larger exchange of information of a scientific nature in the aesthetic environment.

PROCEDURE

The quality of the source material and the sophistication of tools being used bring to light the larger scope of methodology and invite further investigation. Understanding and mapping out the patterns by which emotions are created benefits both the maker and the viewer of art. In the Nobel Prize winning physicist Richard Feynman's own words: "The nature of a rose fragrance and beauty may be privileged information, but knowledge and skill at communicating the complexity of its design greatly enhances the experience" (Feynman, Leighton, & Dyson, 2005). Figure 1 illustrates how the mathematical tablets showing geometric problems were composed as visual propositions.

Data Collection

Twenty tablets showing examples of the geometry problems were identified and selected from the collection of the International Society for Mathematical Sciences (2011) and the Mathematics Museum (2011) that have both an extensive catalog of *Sangaku* wooden tablets pictorials. The source material for this project was selected according to the simplicity-complexity of the problem, the line dynamic of the example, and the visual narrative potential.

Japanese *Sangaku* tablets represent powerful but simple graphic representations of well-known universal mathematical theories, such as:

- The Pappus Chain (presented in Figure 2) identified by Pappus of Alexandria in the 3rd century AD is found on numerous wooden Japanese *Sangaku* tablets. This is a well-know problem in topology. The dynamics of the circle eversion process is

Figure 1. Portion of a wooden Sangaku tablet hung in the Fukushima prefecture, 1885. (© Public Commons. Courtesy of Princeton University Press/Asahi Shinbun. Used with permission.)

a model that inspired many scientific and artistic computer aided visualizations.

- The Casey theorem describes the relation between four circles that are tangent to a fifth circle or to a straight line. It makes for a visually intriguing challenge.
- The Egyptian Triangle is a direct application of the Pythagorean theorem applied to triangles. This principle of geometry can be found in the architecture of the Egyptian pyramids and the application the golden section that many artists used from Leonardo da Vinci to Salvador Dali.

The 3–4–5 triangles progression and other examples of later recursive computer programming are distinctly identifiable in several original woodcarvings.

Extraction of the Data: Vectorization

Vector graphics use geometric primitives and shapes resulting from mathematical equations to represent images in 2D computer graphics. They are used in laser light shows, mirroring experiments, in physics, and developmental biology. Vector graphics are made of paths defined by a start and end point, along with other points, curves, and angles. Paths in this particular environment are used to create two-dimensional objects, from simple drawings to complex diagrams. The lines, colors, curves, and all other geometric attributes are stored in the form of mathematical formulae. Reas and Fry (2007) sum up the flexibility of the formula in a programming handbook for visual designers and artists, "Every time an image is constructed, those equations create an image scalable to any size and detail, regardless of the screen dimension and resolution with no noticeable degradation of quality even if the image is made a thousand-time larger or smaller."

To transform the exact mathematical information into a virtual canvas, the *Sangaku* images were first scanned and thus converted into digital information. Image scanners allow graphic artists and designers to transfer information from one format into another. Scanners used by graphic professionals do not have the same level of resolution as medical and scientific scanners, but they operate according to the same principle: an optical signal is converted into a set of points or bit maps that can be displayed on a computer screen and manipulated by computer driven software. After the scanning was completed, pre-defined templates were created in Adobe Illustrator to extract a vector outline from the underlying shapes. Many types of vector graphic programs are available in graphic environment, such as CorelDraw,

Open-Office Draw, and several other kinds of open-source and proprietary software. Designers and artists can create and manipulate documents using various elements such as panels, bars, and windows to recreate a studio work environment on a computer screen and save the outcome in many different formats.

Twenty new files were created to host the scanned images. The document size was set to 8,5x11 inches to accommodate the various formats in which the final product would be displayed. The color mode display was calibrated to red, green, and blue (RGB). The visual computer environment originates directly in the extensive research and scientific observation made on the physiology of the eye and the visual process. The color space in which computer art is being created evolved from the Young–Helmholtz theory of tri-chromatic color vision. Davson & Perkins (2009) explain the specifics of the RGB calibration as created by mixing three colors: when the highest intensity of each color is mixed together, white light is created, when each hue is set to zero intensity, the result is black.

The image conversion of the original files was completed in two steps to insure the accuracy of the lines and positioning of the extraction. In Illustrator, the user can draw lines with tools or enter specific numeric information in contextual menus. While the tools fit more an intuitive and art oriented approach, the numeric boxes on the menu bar allow maximum accuracy and control of the form created. An exact calculation of shapes and positioning was done in an Excel spreadsheet - a software that uses a set of grid of cells arranged in numbered rows and letter-named columns to organize data and allow arithmetic calculation. The spreadsheet results were transferred to the Illustrator documents and the data entered in the 'transform' and 'dimension' contextual boxes of the menu bar. This approach, while slower at the beginning, made the vectorization of the image easier and more consistent. The computer's ability to transfer numeric information of a geometrical

Figure 2. Extraction: from original to outline. The example of the Pappus chain from a Sangaku tablet dated 1788 and found in the Tokyo Prefecture. (© 2007-2011 Jean Constant. Used with permission.).

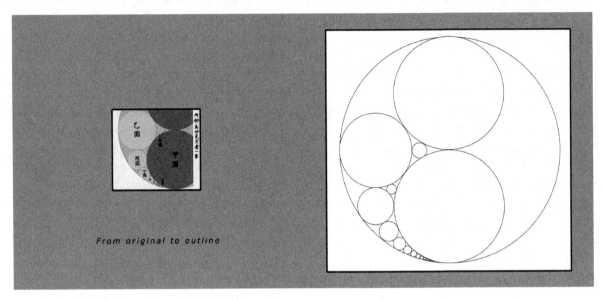

nature onto a canvas eliminated approximation and effort at creating geometric forms and positioning elements, as draughtsmen, architects, and artists used to do in the past. Figure 2 shows how the vectorization process allows for a definition of the outline, size, and positioning of the circles and an exact conversion of the mathematical progression.

Pixelation

The *Sangaku* vector outlines were converted back into a bitmap environment to explore the drawings in terms of shapes and forms. Bit-mapped graphics, also referred to as raster graphics, are the choice format to create a visualization that looks like a photograph of an existing object or a photo-realistic composition. A bitmap image is part of the computerized framework in which rows and columns of dots create a picture. The value of each dot is stored in one or more bits of data and the density of the dots determines the sharpness of the image. Bitmaps are translated into pixels to project images on a screen. The bitmap process allows the designer to add elements of

contour, volume, and perspective to a flat surface or simulate a three dimensional experience. New templates were created to import the vector-based documents in a bitmap environment and set at a resolution of 350 dots per inch to ensure quality printing. The virtual canvases were adjusted to a dimension of 720 pixels wide x 480 pixels long, the standard video frame size engineers commonly use when the product is going to be deployed outside of a controlled environment.

The program selected for converting vectors into bitmaps was Adobe Photoshop™, one of the industry standard image-editing software for bitmap graphics that allows for complex image building. Similar programs, such as the open source Gimp and Paint, or the proprietary Corel Paintshop have near identical capacities, yet are more restricted in terms of flexibility and performance. Like Illustrator this programs is meant to recreate a virtual artist studio. It is made of five main components that facilitate the designer's workflow including an application bar, a tools panel, an options bar, a document window, and a panel dock. The application bar contains the menu bar where most of the necessary commands are located. The menu bar allows to quickly access controls for managing and editing files. The tools panel displays a collection of tools used for creating, selecting, and manipulating images. Panels help manage and edit images, allowing for quick and easy access to the most common controls for a particular task. Drafting and graphic techniques have been merged with the scientific calibration relating to light and visual representation to produce spectacular imagery in engineering and medical visualization programs, such as Osirix software and widely used in computer games design as well (Rosset, Spadola, & Ratib, 2004).

The computer performs the task the user asks it to do but is not a creating entity per se. A fundamental element of good design is to approach a composition first in terms of space, lines, and shape and add color at the last stage because, in the words of Marvin Bartel (2010), "Color provides its own excitement and sensory motivation." Color would have been an unneeded and distracting element at this stage of the project development. Shapes are self-contained areas of geometric forms. Lines give the eye explicit directions about where to look and how to interpret what it sees. They group related

objects together and divide unrelated objects. The lines are also the edge where two shapes meet. Well known to scientific, technical, and professional image-makers, directional lights on still life objects that are painted white make shadows and shading easier to see.

This stage of development of the project was aimed to explore form, shape, and composition alternatives appearing from the *Sangaku*'s outlined sketch. The task was completed with a tool called paint bucket, in this instance set in a scale of grey. After the form of the composition was defined, each element was given a distinct shape by applying effects with the program's filters gallery, the image adjustment tools, and various optional layer styles. The mechanical process was done freely and spontaneously to recreate a studio like situation in which the artist' decision is guided by how the light reflects on each element or the combination of emerging shapes. Although the graphics at this stage were built without concern for an exact representation of the mathematical problem, the underlying geometry present in the design established a sense of stability and harmony to the entire composition. Figure 3 shows the steps adopted in the pixelation process: Step

Figure 3. Pixelation: from outline to shape (© 2007-2011 Jean Constant. Used with permission.)

From outline to shape

1 - Different gradation of grey is applied to each individual element of the outline. Step 2 - Shapes and textures are added to extract singular forms and create an original composition.

Color Scheme

In the next step of the project, colors were added to the black and white sketch to highlight the mathematical demonstration key points and make the image aesthetically more pleasant. Color represents emotion and allows objects to stand out from the background. A designer's choice of color combinations can greatly influence the character of a display. In science, in particular in genetics, biochemistry, and molecular biology, color is an important tool used in the mapping and cataloguing of elements. The entire field of radiological imaging is based on a strict color-coding mapping of the information. Color-coding is a very specific and exact language people working in a collaborative environment can quickly understand and relate to.

The human retina through which visual information is sent to the brain is composed of rods and cones that are light-sensitive receptors. Color is a signal made of light wavelength and frequency. It is interpreted by cones that are extremely sensitive to the light spectrum and is processed by the visual system (Kimball, 1983). Albert H. Munsell at the beginning of the 20th century developed a color system based on three-color dimensions: hue, value, and chroma (Cleland, 1921). He created a five-color wheel with no triad that became the base from which most color combinations have been developed and refined since. Color wheels are extremely useful when putting together a color scheme – a series of colors that will compliment each other: analogous colors, colors that are adjacent to each other, complementary colors that are opposite to each other, triadic color that are a combination of three colors of equidistant distribution on the color wheel, and tetradic color that are any four colors with a logical relationship on the color wheel.

Adobe Kuler software (2007) was used to determine each image color theme. Kuler is a web-hosted application that generates color themes according to any chosen input. Color themes are created around a base color to determine a variety of color combination such as analogous, monochromatic, triad, complementary, compound, and shades based on a mathematical algorithm. Themes can be applied to various image formats such as RGB, CMYK, and LAB, and are easily integrated into Internet coding protocols.

The palettes created in the Kuler application were imported in Photoshop and loaded in the swatch panel. Each closed area of the vector outline sketches were colored with the paint bucket to highlight the key points of the mathematical demonstration and to obtain a coherent statement that would be both effective and visually pleasing. As noted by Itten (1970), the juxtaposition of colors changes the perception of volume; therefore many tests had to be effected before the final composition came together in a satisfying manner. Figure 4 presents how the vector-based sketch is colorized with the Kuler theme palette. Notice the central square (orange) from which each complementary color is calibrated according to the light and reflection of the color scheme. The actual colors register only in terms of light intensity because of the black & white printing constrains.

Merging

In the next step, the black and white sketches and color compositions were merged as separate layers in a new Photoshop file. In graphic computer programs, layering replaces the traditional oil painting technique of adding coats of pigment to build the final composition. A document is composed of a series of images or layers, stacked on top of each other. Individual layers can be manipulated, drawn on, and moved around independently of any other

Figure 4. Color theme: from outline to color (© 2007-2011 Jean Constant. Used with permission.)

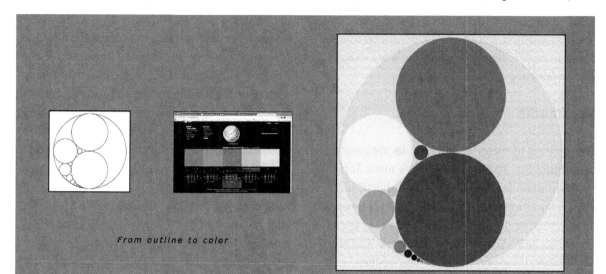

layer. In addition, the program's palette includes several tools such as blending and opacity controls that adjust each layer transparency. Figure 5 shows the layering process that takes a classic painting technique to a new level of practical possibilities. The colors in this example register only in terms of light and intensity. The full color plate can be checked on the publication's website.

Each document was printed several times to insure that the effect seen on the screen would also register in print. Fine details showing in a backlit environment do not always register in a front-lit situation. The object being defined by different light sources, in one case from the back of the object, in the other case in the front, it is not uncommon to find differences both in the

Figure 5. Merging black and white and color documents (© 2007-2011 Jean Constant. Used with permission.)

definition of the shapes and the accuracy of the color. Those issues were addressed and reworked in the Photoshop workspace with various image filters to insure the print would replicate exactly what would appear on the screen.

Multimedia

The amount of material gathered in the process of creating the 20 *Sangaku* images made for an interesting challenge to illustrate in a short Quick-Time animation the step-by-step development of the creative process. Communication experts often use MS PowerPoint and iWork Keynote to illustrate their presentation. The material can later be saved in a multimedia portable format viewable on various platforms. Those programs consist of a number of individual pages or 'slides' arranged in a given order that can be displayed on a screen, exported for a projection, or posted on the Internet. While very similar in nature to PowerPoint, Keynote is favored by designers because of the quality of its rendering, the film-like character of its transition and blending, and its many dynamic graphic options. It supports coding standards that allow for quick and stable display on today's mobile devices such as iPhone, iPad, and most other. Technical research in the industry and many academic programs such as the Center for Research in Computing and the Art in Singapore (NUS, 2011) or the Museum of Moving Image in New York (2011) that provides curriculum-based educational experiences to approximately 60,000 students each year underscore the extend of this mode of communication that brings together researchers, engineers, programmers, media experts, and the visual artists.

The process of building moving images consists of putting together a succession of single frame images and assembling them into one unified composition readable by the user. Hochberg and Brooks (1996), who studied the physiological aspect of this occurrence in cognitive film theory state, "These displacements are small, and within the range of the low-level sensory receptors of the visual system ... Pictures 'arrest' the figure imaged, presenting a single moment from all possible moments of the subject in motion."

Each individual stage of the creative process was attributed an identification number and inserted in the Keynote document. Slide transition, effect build in, build out, and actions were added to animate and highlight the mathematical discourse and the step-by-step development of the reasoning behind the visualization. The slide show was timed and reviewed several times by third parties and re-adjusted for cohesion and consistency. Contrary to art making which is mostly a singular process, filmmaking is a collaborative effort. To be consistent, it necessitates input and perspective from many different sources.

A soundtrack was added to sustain and complement the rhythm of the presentation. An original digital loop was selected from an Internet sound library. The soundtrack and the slide show were imported in a digital audio editor used for professional presentations. Audio editors allow create sound effects, blend soundtracks, and slow or accelerate the pitch according to the specific needs of the production. The sound was scored to match the slide transition and individual effects within each sequence. The final product was saved in the QuickTime movie format to meet multimedia, cross-platform display requirements, and Internet deployment protocols. Figure 6 shows selected movie frames. Each slide has been timed to last 5 seconds. Different image effects and a fade-in fade-out transition have been added for an even progression.

DISCUSSION

Dissemination and Assessment of the Project

The twenty final plates were printed in fine art archival quality paper. Selected plates were

Figure 6. Movie frames selected to overview the process: 1) Title, 2) Original Sangaku, 3) Vectorization and mathematical problem, 4) Transformation progress, 5) End of animation. (© 2007-2011 Jean Constant. Used with permission.)

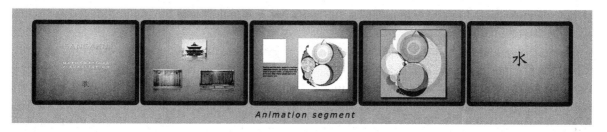

displayed in galleries as part of several Mathematics and Art exhibitions. The multimedia file was deployed on an institutional website and a multimedia aggregator for a larger outreach with the Internet community (Constant, 2011).

The public reaction in the gallery environment was a combination of curiosity and interest in both the cultural and scientific aspect of the representation. One unexpected but very prevalent aspect of the audience's response was that, even in the particular context of a gallery environment, the artistic component of the image was quickly set aside and the attention focused on the mathematical significance of the demonstration. Most of the exchange had to do with the impact of colors and the dynamics of the shapes in reinforcing or distracting from finding the solution to the geometry problem. However, it is often difficult to be party to a work and objective analyst of an audience reaction. One can only encourage similar experiments in a controlled environment to assess objectively the effect of the work, the implication of the audience reaction, and possible direction for future experiments.

Internet traffic analysis tool keeps good record of the numbers of queries, time spent on any given page, and origin of the queries. The site was composed of three parts: gallery, animation, and problem solving pages. It has had consistently over one hundred visitors a month since it was first posted, with most visitors spending significantly more time in the problem solving pages.

Most of the graphics from the site have been collected by various search engines like Google and Bing and can be seen on their image pages when searching for *Sangaku*. Individuals contacted the author to offer new *Sangaku* examples or alternative solutions to existing mathematical problems. Several sites, particularly in Japan, extended invitations to feature the artwork, and an academic institution in the Reunion Island has adapted the methodology to teach geometry classes. Indeed those data do not qualify for a proper assessment of an experiment of a scientific nature. The context in which this experiment was conducted was started on the personal interest of the author to explore the nature of scientific and artistic interaction in terms of visual representation. The information collected from those few sources is nonetheless significant and can only encourage further studies of similar reach in a more controlled environment to build valuable data and further the understanding of the arts and human expression.

CONCLUSION

The initial objective of this project was to examine and transform the biology inspired technical schemes through geometry into the creative process. The outcome of this project invited the viewer to reassess the linear and exclusive approach of traditional teaching methodologies and validate collaborative effort in which a more global, all-inclusive approach helps shape a significant statement.

Forms, color, and sound studied in the context of biological experiments are also inspiring to the art community. Their objective understanding helps create more meaningful aesthetic statements. It made accessible to all information that greatly benefit individual projects both in science and in art. Using knowledge-based elements of neuroscience, optical physiology and computer-aided techniques, many biology inspired scientists create representations that are both aesthetically satisfying and significant in terms of understanding better the nature of perception. Larger scientific experiments continue to enrich further the reach and extend of such multidisciplinary approach to knowledge. Already, institutes such as the DFG Research Center MATHEON (2011) involved in modeling, simulation, and optimization of real world processes, or the Blue Brain Project (2011) are providing artists with invaluable data affecting the decision making in creative process and influence the outcome, as can be noticed in recent visual trends in design, art, and architecture.

This limited and intuitive experiment based on universally accepted concepts depicted in representations from the 19th century Japanese culture adds another narrative to a larger trend that encourages the use of scientific data as a source of all-inclusive inspiration in the creative process. The detailed description of this process was intended to inspire and encourage artists to narrow the distance between science and art in the digital and computer-aided environment. The informal but sustained interest of the audience about this project is a positive signal that can only encourage further collaborative interdisciplinary effort in that direction.

ACKNOWLEDGMENT

I would like to acknowledge Dr. T. Rothman & Mr. F. Hidetoshi for having introduced me to the world of

Sangaku and supported my effort in this project; Mr. Alexander Bogomolny, without whom I could not

have completed the mathematical part of it, Mr. Urabe who hosted me in his Mathematics Museum, Dr.

Richard Palais and Professor Claude Bruter for their support and advice, Dr. Anna Ursyn for her thoughtfulness and focus, Ms. C. Besa and all who were an inspiration and a guiding force through the writing of this text.

REFERENCES

Bartel, M. (2010). *Composition and design. Elements, principles, and visual effects.* Goshen College Art Department. Retrieved July 15, 2011 from http://www.goshen.edu/art

Blue Brain Project. (2011). *Ecole Polytechnique Fédérale de Lausanne.* Lausanne, Switzerland. Retrieved July 16, 2011, from http://bluebrain. epfl.ch/

Cleland, T. M. (1921). *A practical description of the Munsell color system, with suggestions for its use.* London, UK: British Library Collection.

Constant, J. (2011). *Wasan geometry.* Retrieved July 16, 2011, from http://www.hermay.org/ jconstant/wasan/, http://hermay.org/jconstant/ animation/animSangaku.html

Davson, H., & Perkins, E. S. (2009). *Eye anatomy.* Retrieved July 10, 2011, from http://www.britannica.com/EBchecked/topic/1688997/human-eye

DFG Research Center Matheon. (2011). *Mathematics for key technologies*. Berlin, Germany. Retrieved July 16, 2011, from http://www.matheon.de

Feynman, R. P., Leighton, R., & Dyson, F. (2005). *All the adventures of a curious character. Collection of essays and lecture series*. W. W. Norton Publisher.

Fractal Foundation. (2011). *Interconnections of natural systems and their essential nonlinearity*. Albuquerque, NM. Retrieved July 16, 2011, from http://fractalfoundation.org/

Hidetoshi, F., & Rothman, T. (2008). *Sacred mathematics: Japanese temple geometry*. Princeton, NJ: Princeton University Press.

Hochberg, J., & Brooks, V. (1996). *Movies in the mind's eye*. University of Wisconsin Press International Society for Mathematical Sciences. (2011). *Osaka, Japan*. Retrieved July 10, 2011, from http://www.jams.or.jp/

Itten, J. (1970). *The elements of color: A treatise on the color system of Johannes Itten, based on his book The Art of Color by Johannes Itten*. Van Nostrand Reinhold Co.

Japanese Temple Geometry Problem. (n.d.). *Sangaku*. Retrieved July 10, 2011, from http://www.wasan.jp/english/

Kimball, J. W. (1983). *Biology*. Addison Wesley Publishing Company.

Kuler. (2007). *Internet application*. http://kuler.adobe.com/

Mathematics Museum. (2011). *Mathematical visualizations*. Tokyo, Japan. Retrieved July 10, 2011, from http://mathinfo.sci.ibaraki.ac.jp/open/mathmuse/

Museum of the Moving Image. (2010). *Advances the public understanding and appreciation of the art, history, technique, and technology of film, television, and digital media*. New York. http://www.movingimage.us/education/teachers

NanoArt 21. (2011). *Art/science/technology*. Retrieved July 10, 2011, from http://www.nanoart21.org/

NUS. (2011). *The National University of Singapore, Center for Research in Computing and the Arts*. Retrieved July 16, 2011, from http://amas.cz3.nus.edu.sg/art

Palais, R. S. (1999). The visualization of mathematics: Towards a mathematical exploratorium. *Notices of the American Mathematical Society, 46*(6), 647-658. Retrieved July 16, 2011, from http://3d-xplormath.org/DocumentationPages/VisOfMath.pdf

Reas, C., & Fry, B. (2007). *Processing: A programming handbook for visual designers and artists*. Cambridge, MA: The MIT Press. Retrieved July 16, 2011, from http://processing.org/img/learning/Processing-Contents-070603.pdf

Rosset, A., Spadola, L., & Ratib, O. (2004). OsiriX: An open-source software for navigating in multidimensional dicom images. *Journal of Digital Imaging, 17*(3), 205–216. doi:10.1007/s10278-004-1014-6

Ruttkay, Z. M. (2008). A *Sangaku* revived. *Bridges Mathematics, Music, Art, Architecture, & Culture Conference Proceedings*. EEMCS University of Twenet, Leeuwarden, the Netherlands.

ADDITIONAL READING

Bogomolny, A. (2007). *Sangaku: Reflections on the phenomenon*. Retrieved April 20, 2011, from http://www.cut-the-knot.org/pythagoras/Sangaku.shtml

Emmer, M. (Ed.). (2005). *Mathematics and culture II: Visual perfection: Mathematics and creativity (Pt. 2)*. Springer.

Fukagawa, H. (1989). *Japanese temple geometry problems San Gaku*. Winnipeg, Canada: Charles Babbage Research Ctr.

Fukagawa, H., Rothman, T., & Freeman, D. (2008). *Sacred mathematics: Japanese temple geometry*. Princeton University Press.

Peterson, I. (2001). *Temple circles*. Mathematical Association of America. Retrieved April 20, 2011, from http://www.maa.org/mathland/math-trek_4_23_01.html

Sangaku Problems. (2009). *A project conceived & directed by Jean Constant. Completed by the students of the NNMC-Visual Communication program, Spring 2009*. Retrieved July 16, 2011, from http://hermay.org/jconstant/wasan/nnmc.html

The Virtual Math Museum. (n.d.). *Department of Mathematics - University of California, Irvine, CA*. Retrieved April 20, 2011, from http://virtualmathmuseum.org/gallery4.html

KEY TERMS AND DEFINITIONS

Animation: Animations are made up of a series of individual images called frames. When these images are shown rapidly in succession, a viewer has the illusion that motion is occurring. The viewer cannot see the flickering between frames due to an effect known as persistence of vision, whereby the eye retains a visual image for a fraction of a second after the source has been removed. (http://wordnetweb.princeton.edu/. Princeton University).

Bitmap: Digital representation composed of dots arranged in rows and columns, each represented by a single bit of data that determines the value of a pixel in a monochrome image on a computer screen. In a gray scale or color image, each dot is composed of a set of bits that determine the individual values of a group of pixels that in combination create the visual impression of a specific shade or hue. The greater the number of bits per dot, the wider the range of possible shades or hues. The number of dots per square inch (density) determines the resolution of a bitmapped image. (Merriam-Webster, online dictionary).

Computer Visualization: "Conveying information using graphical techniques." (Barbara Tversky, Psychology department, Stanford U. CA) Computer visualization include but are not limited to data and image models, perception and cognition, space, color, conveying shape with lines, conveying shape with shading and texturing, conveying interior structure with volumetric techniques, conveying process and narrative with animation. - Pat Hanrahan. (2005). (*Teaching Visualization*. Journals of the ACM/SIGGRAPH, issue 39).

Digital Art: Digital art is art that allows us, through an interface with technology, to immerse ourselves in the image and interact with it. New media art humanizes technology through its emphasis on interactivity, its philosophical investigation of the real and the virtual, and its multisensory nature. What distinguishes the artists who practice virtual art from traditional artists is their combined commitment to aesthetics and technology. Their "extra-artistic" goals—linked to their aesthetic intentions—concern not only science and society but also basic human needs and drives. Digital or (Virtual) art, offers a new model for thinking about humanist values in a technological age. (Frank Popper. (2007). *From Technological to Virtual Art.* MIT Press).

Multimedia: Text, graphics, video, animation, and sound presented in an integrated way. Multimedia on the web includes sound, music, videos, and animations. Media literacy education implemented in the US sine the early 20th century promotes students' critical thinking and communication skills. (http://cinema.usc.edu/ Institute for Multimedia Literacy - USC School of Cinematic Arts).

Sangaku: Sangaku problems, often written "san gaku," are geometric problems of the type found on devotional mathematical wooden tablets ("*Sangaku*") which were hung under the roofs of shrines or temples in Japan (http://mathworld. wolfram.com/*Sangaku*Problem.html) 1683 Earliest reported *Sangaku* tablet, in Tochigi Prefecture.

Vector: Vector images are a collection of individual objects. A vector image can be composed of points connected by lines, or nodes connected by Bezier curves. Each individual object contained in a vector image is defined by a mathematical equation. Vector images are not resolution dependent. Thus, each vector object is scalable and can generally be resized without any loss of image quality. (Tech-Faq (2011) www. tech - faq com).

Section 4
Tools for Metaphors: Nature Described with the Use of Mathematics and Computing

Chapter 14
Drawings from Small Beginnings

Hans Dehlinger
Universität Kassel, Germany

ABSTRACT

Small, densely arranged elements in large numbers are frequently observed phenomena in nature. The author uses an arbitrarily chosen stretch of landscape, a dry riverbed, to formulate artistic intentions and design programmed interpretations of them. From the database of recorded findings the author formulates concepts, which then transform into programs to generate drawings. Many different programs can satisfactorily assist in this task. The conceptual formulation is a crucial step in the procedural chain for attempts in generative art. This chapter experimentally addresses the formulation of a few concepts inspired by nature, aimed at generating line drawings executed on pen-plotters. Unlike in science and engineering, a piece of code does not produce a solution to a problem for concepts in generative art. Generative drawings are produced through a structured process including a sequence of discrete procedural steps, which are: finding and recording; concept and transformation; programming and testing; and drawing and interpretation.

INTRODUCTION: THE RIVERBED OF RAMBLA DE CERVERA

Imagine that we are walking down a dry riverbed, in which we observe and digitally record impressions drawn from nature. Nature-induced generative shaping resulting in visual formations on large and small scales is particularly visible in this type of environment. We choose the *Rambla de Cervera*, a large seasonal riverbed, most of the year dry and barren, which is cutting through the southern Cervera Mountains in the Comarca of Bajo Maestrazgo in the east of Spain. The river dried up a long time ago. The riverbed is the *locus* of a great number and a great variety of soft and forceful past events, which have generated its present visual state. We use it as a starting point for our reflections on nature-inspired, computer-generated drawings.

With the help of a collection of digital photographs, the purpose is to extract generative concepts from the visual impressions of this particular

DOI: 10.4018/978-1-4666-0942-6.ch014

landscape. We want to invent generative schemes, which transform our findings into generative, line-based aesthetic events. We can, for example, decide to focus on elements, repetitions, and arrangements of similar things. There are plenty of them around us: shaped by the forces of gravity, geotectonic pressure, wind, temperature changes, or flash floods, and formed in time slots ranging from a fraction of a second to millions of years.

We see dried parts of plants, petrified remains of animals, flowers and leaves, trunks and branches in aggradations, and dry and live trees. We hike over solid rocks, large and small stones, pebbles, sand, cracked branches, torn-up roots, rusty parts of metal, and flattened tin cans. Rain, flood, tumbling stones, seasonal changes and other impacts have shaped everything we see.

The embankment on one side of the riverbed towers over it with layers of sediments cut through geological time, while the other side is rolling out into soft hills with olive trees, many of them a thousand years old. Small and large elements and repetitions are everywhere, each one with an individual shape. They are unique and precious, and yet each is just one among trillions. On the way down the riverbed the visible elements are complemented by the elements of sound as a repetitious sequence: slowly-dripping water, a bird with a simple tune, and the croak of a frog.

What do we expect; what do we want to find? A small element is an instance, a singularity, and a tiny spot in the universe. Drawn up in large numbers it turns into a grayscale, a background noise, and a shadow of something else. A multitude of similar elements turns into something different. This and similar ideas are the themes we want to explore experimentally. Our intention differs only marginally from many other attempts to use nature as a template for drawings that may be found in art collections all over the world.

TRANSFORMING PHENOMENA IN NATURE INTO PROGRAMS FOR GENERATIVE DRAWINGS

Constraints Imposed

Our approach for constructing drawings is purposefully constrained on the grounds of artistic reasoning and from a self-restriction stemming from the generative approach we follow: the resulting drawings are realized on pen-plotters. We convert a computer-generated image into a line drawing with a physical pen, which is guided by a program controlled and driven algorithmically by a mechanical device rather than by the skilled hand and imagination of an artist. Refraining from all enhancements is a deliberate decision, which opens up a specific line-oriented window of expression where subtle differences significantly contribute to the quality of an image. These decisions, which seem to be limiting at the first impression, have certain desirable effects. For example, pencil-drawn lines cross differently than printed lines, and a pen, which partially fails to perform under high speed[i] and acceleration when guided by a mechanical device, can add something like a context-sensitive fingerprint to each generated line. A range of such effects imprints special characteristics and distinctly recognizable features on the generative drawings. And they are, of course, artistically wanted properties.

Procedural Steps

We have chosen to use the metaphor of a hike as a starting point. The realization of generative drawing of the imagined hike will be structured by a sequence of discrete procedural steps which are: finding and recording; concept and transformation; programming and testing; and drawing and interpretation.

Finding and Recording

To become more specific, we turn to the dry riverbed of the *Rambla de Cervera* again. The collection of photographic images in Figure 1 provides illustrations of the impressions we receive from the surroundings there. Behind each of the images we can clearly identify nature-induced generative processes by which the pebble, rocks, roots, plants, and all we see have been shaped into their present existence. We see (and our findings are) unexpected events that are suddenly appearing and resistant to planning. Equipped with a digital camera, we record arrangements, particular for-

Figure 1. Images from the dry riverbed of Rambla de Cervera, Comarca Bajo Maestrazgo, Spain. (©2005, Hans Dehlinger. Used with permission).

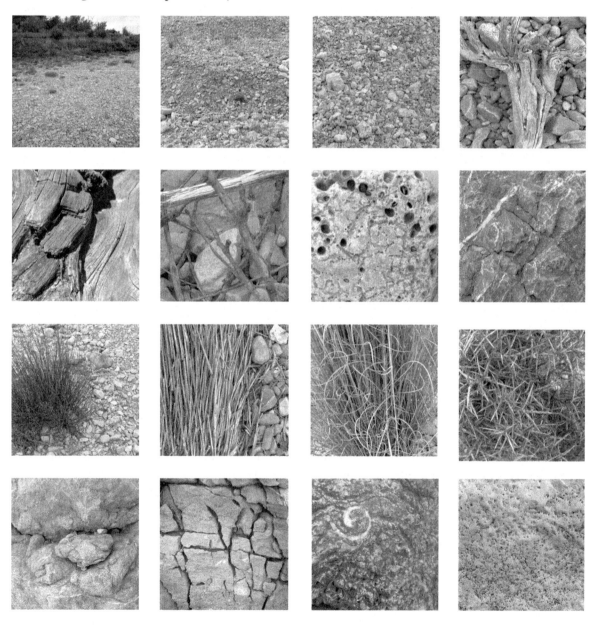

mations, elements and structures, the small and the large, the old and the young, the organic and inorganic. We observe surfaces and solids, rough and smoothly washed or even polished. We see details, tiny things, and focus on the very small. We observe, reflect, touch, pick things up and drop them again, and we move on. We look at arrangements, shapes of rocks, and collections of seemingly incompatible things, piled up and clinched into each other. We have long views taking in the entire riverbed as a visual panorama, and we scan and zoom in, literally and digitally. All the way along we take hundreds of pictures with the digital camera.

Concept and Transformation

For the purpose of discussion we restrict the number of designs for conceptual schemes to a few distinctly different examples. It is not nearly possible to be exhaustive in this attempt, as an infinite number of such schemes are conceivable.

Looking back to the beginnings of computer-generated art, we find beautiful examples of drawings by the pioneers of computer art. Casting a concept into a code to generate art was only possible in these early attempts within a strictly constrained environment. What we admire today are the astonishing results of these intellectual experiments. Artists such as Georg Nees (2006), Frieder Nake (1989, 2007), Michael Noll (1964), Charles Csuri (2011), Harold Cohen (2001), and many others have, right in the beginning of computing, tried to transform conceptual ideas into algorithms for the purpose of generating art. Only recently have we seen some major efforts to present the history of this early computer art. For example, at the University of Bremen, Germany, Nake initiated "CompArt" in 2007, an ambitious project of a "structured space for computer art." Herzogenrath and Nierhoff-Wielk (2007) from the *Kunsthalle Bremen* have published a Catalog at the occasion of the 80th birthday of Herbert W. Franke, a German pioneer in the field. The *Kunsthalle* also holds a substantial collection of works from the beginnings of computer art. The early period of British computer artists from 1960-1980 has been thoroughly researched and is now documented by Brown, Gere, Lambert, & Mason (2009). In addition, in the CACHe Archives (2011), pioneering British computer art has found a home. The necessity to transform a concept into an algorithm is a constant from the early beginnings. We can also get a glimpse of the diversity in the design of such schemes and artistic approaches to drawings by the study of famous historic collections of drawings; for example, the Uffenbach-Collection in Göttingen (Unverfehrt, 2000).

Conceiving an *idea* or a *concept* for a work of art is a fundamental process, and it is the most important aspect in conceptual art. First we try to find a verbal description of the concept, and then extend it into a set of rules from which the work can be generated at any time in any location. Turning back to the river again and taking a view down the riverbed (Figure 1, row one), we see a sort of a plain stretching to the embankment. Thousands and thousands of pebbles can be seen, in all sizes, formed over thousands of years. We formulate from this impression a *conceptual scheme number 1* and name it: *small elements in very large arrays*. Elements and their shapes will become parameters in our program, as well as their specific locations in particular arrangements. The generative engine, following the proper settings, will draw them algorithmically in great numbers. But beforehand we have to define precisely how the program will interpret and process an *element*. Such an element can be a simple straight line, a small shape, a short fat stroke, a dot, an assembly of other even smaller elements, or anything else that will serve to transform them within the conceptual scheme into something the program can manipulate and place into a generative drawing.

The idea of nearly similar elements arranged in large numbers can be formulated in many ways. As a further example, we formulate a *conceptual scheme number 2: long, equally directed poly-lines stretching across a canvas.* Looking at Figure 1 again, we can imagine many other *concepts* abstracted from nature. The view towards the embankment is suggesting trying a *conceptual scheme 3: metaphoric landscapes.* The remains of a trunk (Figure 1, row one, right image) suggest the shape of a tree and can be formulated as a *conceptual scheme 4: metaphoric trees.* The arrangements of branches and stones, washed out holes in stones, and surface structures on a rock (Figure 1, row two) suggest even other schemes. Linear elements formed by plants (Figure 1, row three) will be used to formulate a *conceptual scheme number 5: fine interwoven poly-lines.* Structures on rocks, a spiral petrifaction, and fungi on a rock (Figure 1, row four) are other images recorded on the hike, and they too are potential sources for conceptual schemes that can be transformed into actual drawings. In the following section we will demonstrate further steps towards their generation.

Coding, Programming, and Testing

We have to recognize that, contrary to a common perception of how art is done, we follow a rather different direction. Instead of working on a piece of art directly and with constant, immediate feedback during all stages of its production, we focus on the design of a process that can generate not one but a potentially endless sequences of pieces, all related to each other by the conceptual idea behind the generating program. The act of creation here is not focused on a particular image; it is focused on the generative process and the rules necessary to set this process into motion. The idea of a *sequence* as the result of a generative design, or the idea of a generative variety, is fundamental to this approach.

For the nature-inspired generative drawings, we try to write programs on the basis of a formulated conceptual scheme. In conceptual scheme number 1 we have mentioned *small elements in very large arrays,* and were thinking about the uncountable pebbles in the riverbed. What is a small element supposed to look like? To arrive at an answer, we need a few more steps in defining the essence of the concept and transform it into a programmable entity. As an experimental transformation for *a small element* we use a circle, a simple geometrical shape that we can easily manipulate and arrange in any desired order. In Figure 2a we see a cutout of a drawing that consists of a sample arrangement of circular elements. As we can see, they are all line-based, of equal size, and in slight disorderly arrangement. Obviously, size and type of arrangement are program-controlled parameters. In the programs for generative drawings we typically use such parameters. The other three examples of elements are also line-based.

Figure 2. Transformations of impressions from the riverbed- a: Small circular elements in an array; b: Poly-lines from equally spaced point sets; c: Upward arrangement of lines from random point set; d: Outlined random lines; (©2005, Hans Dehlinger. Used with permission.).

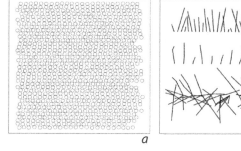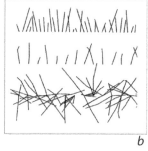

a   *b*   *c*   *d*

In Figure 2b a set of programmed poly-lines of various lengths originates from equally distributed linear sets of starting points. In Figure 2c we have a program-controlled random arrangement of upward directed lines. In a second image in Figure 1, row three, some thick, dry, linear plant remains are visible. We have chosen to transform this finding into the shape of outlined linear elements as shown in Figure 2d and will use such lines in a drawing discussed below.

Since we use a pen-plotter for the execution of drawings, we have to recall that this output device relies on a code, which mechanically moves a pen. Three important commands in the operation mode of a pen-plotter are *pen-up*, *move*, and *pen-down*. Moving with *pen-up* will position the pen, moving with *pen-down* will draw. One of the early standards in machine supported codes for drawing is the HPGL-language (HP, 1983). It was widely used for plotting, but with the replacement of pen-plotters by digital printers it has lost its importance for the output of drawings. Today it is instead used in mechanical engineering for the cutting of sheet metal with laser-cutters. The transition into this area is rather plausible, because the only essential adaptations necessary are a simple replacement of the commands *pen-up* and *pen-down* for plotting into the commands *laser-off* and *laser-on* for cutting. For the drawings we discuss here, the HPGL-code is fundamental, and all of the drawings here have been coded this way. But it must also be remembered that this code is remarkably simple and effective in describing a line drawing. Despite the fading popularity of pen-plotters, there is still very useful software around, running smoothly on today's advanced operating systems. An example is the 2D CAD-software CADintosh[i1], which, among others formats, accepts this code and displays the respective drawings on the screen.

As an example of the HPGL-code we again inspect the *small circular elements*, which have been used to realize one version of the *conceptual scheme number 1*. To draw a simple circle through the origin with a diameter of 5 units, all

we need is the character-string PD;AA0,5,360; in which we first set the pen down with PD, then code an absolute arch through zero with AA0, give it the diameter of 5 units, and mention the 360 degrees of the full circle. This string of code submitted to the CADintosh package will draw a proper circle. Likewise, for a poly-line consisting of five segments and starting at the origin, we will have to formulate the code: PD;PA63,64; PA123,102;PA174,140;PA228,175;PA250,197;. Again we start with a PD, the pen-down command, followed by a chain of identical PA (*pen-absolute commands*), each accompanied by the coordinate pair it is supposed to go next to. As we can see we have five PA commands, hence the five segments mentioned. Any programming language that can handle alphanumeric strings can generate HPGL-code for drawings. It is even possible to write such a "program" by subjecting a table of coordinate pairs to a sequence of character-replacement operations in a standard word-processing system. While the old HPGL-code has the advantage of directly supporting the pen-plotting hardware, this is not the case for many of the contemporary image generating software systems. Images created with them need to be converted into vector formats and in many cases this is not at all possible. Nevertheless, in spite of the fact that such systems offer a range of other advantages and much more comfort in programming, the old code seems to be doomed to fade away into history. We can use *Processing*[2i] as an example of a contemporary software tool to generate some different instances for the *elements*, which we also may regard as a useful and potential candidate for realizing the *conceptual scheme number 1*. You, Dehlinger, & Wang (2010) show examples of images generated with the Processing environment. The idea is to confine elements into a square and use grid-like arrangements of such squares for density in large numbers. In a project carried out at Sun Yat-Sen University in Guangzhou (You, Dehlinger, & Wang, 2010), we have explored to some extend the theme of *Lines and Squares*.

Figure 3. Small circular elements in a very large array. Interpretation: View onto the ocean. Computer generated drawing, pencil on paper, A0+. (©2005, Hans Dehlinger. Used with permission.).

Executing and Drawing

The concept of a circular element to generate a drawing is an abstraction. Contrary to what we see in the riverbed, all small *circular elements* in this image series make use of equally sized[3] elements. The program parameters were set to draw them slightly disarranged in a random fashion, and their number for a drawing can be indeed *large*. Figure 3 displays an image resulting from the series following *conceptual scheme_1*. It is entirely composed of small circular elements of the same size[4] and they are arranged in long rows.

The plotting equipment and the pen for which this image was generated have definitely not been designed with the idea in mind to realize such tremendous numbers of repetitive movements. In forcing the plotter to execute the code, we very likely push pen and equipment beyond a reliable, predictable, and precise operation. Inspecting Figure 3 again, we can identify slight variations in line thickness and precision. They are distortions, due to a partially failing pen. It would not be tolerable in a technical context, but in the context in question here, it is a wanted, provocative effect, and a deliberately produced element

Figure 4. Long equally directed poly-lines stretching from left to right. (©2005, Hans Dehlinger. Used with permission.).

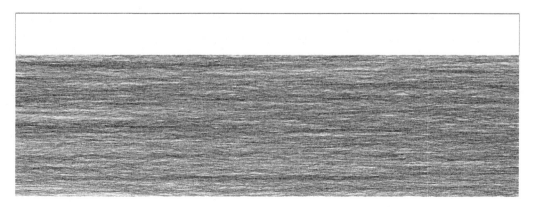

of the final result. To operate beyond the limits is an adventure and an artistic challenge. In the drawing in question, numerous ups and downs of the pen have to be performed, which is mechanically demanding on the equipment. Jean-Pierre Hébert (2011) constructed plotter-drawings by executing only one pen-up and one pen-down command, and the resulting drawing – a tremendously long singular line producing an incredibly dense, large-scale drawing, is also pushing the capabilities of pen and equipment beyond its intended states of operation. In terms of mechanical challenge, it is another extreme position to the execution of Figure 3. Further examples of deliberately designed artistic abuse of plotting equipment are the pen-plotter driven ink-brush-plots of Roman Verostko (2011) generated by mounting brushes to the machine, or the poetic sand-pieces by Hébert, where the plotter is driving a metal ball through a sand-bed, generating a sophisticated relief of grooves in sand instead of a line drawing.

Our attempts here are restricted to the simple line, while trying to explore its rich possible expressions. The *conceptual scheme number 2* addresses the idea of *conceptual scheme number 1* with a very different notion. It uses a poly-line, stretching with slight variations from one side of the canvas to the opposite side over and over again. The resulting drawings have some resemblance to the ones from scheme number 1, but they are based on an entirely different definition for the parametric construction of an element. Also, in *conceptual scheme number 3* and *conceptual scheme number 4* we use different approaches in the application of lines.

Both metaphoric landscapes in Figure 5 are based on the same set of data: on the left side we use simple lines and on the right side we use outlines of lines with the inside area left blank. In the metaphoric trees on Figure 6, simple lines on the left side are used and horizontally hatched patches are used on the right side.

As with line drawings performed by the hand of an artist, we can imagine an equally rich universe of line drawings performed by machines or mechanical devices. There seems no limit to the creative mind in inventing modes of operation for

Figure 5. Metaphoric landscapes. Two different schemes applied to the same data set. The left image uses simple lines, the right image outlined lines. (©2005, Hans Dehlinger. Used with permission.).

Figure 6. Metaphoric trees. The left image is based on a scheme using poly-lines from randomly distributed point sets. The right image is based on a scheme using filled shapes. (©2005, Hans Dehlinger. Used with permission.).

a dynamic relationship between a marking device (pen, laser, etc.) and a receiving surface (paper, sheet metal, wood, etc.). We have experimented with a number of them (Dehlinger, 2004).

Evaluation and Interpretation

The drawings presented in this chapter are algorithmically generated, and a program is driving the pen and controlling the movement of the paper.[5] On closer inspection we can sort them into two classes: one-pass drawings; for example, Figure 3, and collage-type drawings; for example, Figure 5. The distinction makes only sense by including the conceptual scheme behind a drawing.

The generated images have no meaning assigned to them whatsoever. For identification they usually have a date and a code. They are abstractions based on concepts, which are cast into rules, and then executed mechanically, driven by algorithms. The rules have been designed to bring *aesthetic events* into existence. It is a legitimate position in art to completely deny sense or meaning in a work and shift the issue to the primary

side of an aesthetic reception by the viewer: The assumption of a sense, implied or constructed by the viewer during the process of an aesthetic experience, does not provide motivation for the artist. If we desire so, an interpretation of Figure 3 may read: On a quiet day we look out over the ocean. The position of the viewer is away from the beach and fairly elevated above the shoreline and overlooks a section of a flat beach. The horizon merges at some point with the sky. The overall impression is calmness, width and openness. We see only water, no distractions by other elements or any activity but the waves rolling in, coming to rest on the sand.

CONCLUSION

Usually, any drawing executed on a plotter will come to existence in an uninterrupted one-pass mode, because a conceptual scheme of a drawing is represented by a piece of code which will produce a result. Imposing purist or minimalist constraints on the design may require formulating the code as a minimalist set of commands. To satisfy such constraints is usually a challenge however; the resulting drawings may mirror the effort by (partially) disclosing the generative principles behind the conceptual scheme. With geometric entities (Dehlinger, 2002) and with small elements (Dehlinger, 2005), such schemes may be easily realized as a collage that can be viewed as multiple-pass process where each step is based on feedback from the previous step. Fragment by fragment is conceived and coded and may be added to the drawing with the possibility of feedback and under the evaluative control of the artist.

REFERENCES

Brown, P., Gere, C., Lambert, N., & Mason, C. (Eds.). (2009). *White heat cold logic, British computer art 1960-1980*. Cambridge, MA: MIT Press.

CACHe. (n.d.). *Archive of pioneering British computer art*. Retrieved July 14, 2011 from http://www.e-x-p.org/cache/index.HTM

Cohen, H. (2001). *Biography of Aaron Cohen, creator of Aaron*. Retrieved September 29, 2011, from http://www.kurzweilcyberart.com/aaron/hi_cohenbio.html

Csuri, C. (2011). *Charles Csuri: Art & ideas*. Personal website. Retrieved September 29, 2011, from http://www.csuri.com/

Dehlinger, H. (2002). *Instance and system: A figure and its 2^{18} variations*. Paper presented at the International Conference Generative Art 2002, Politecnico di Milano: Italy.

Dehlinger, H. (2004). *Zeichnungen*. Kassel, Germany: Kassel University Press.

Dehlinger, H. (2005). *Programming generative drawings with small elements*. Paper presented at the International Conference Art+Math=X, Boulder, Colorado.

Hébert, J.-P. (2011). *Website of the Artist*. Retrieved April 1, 2011, from http://jeanpierrehebert.com/

Herzogenrath, W., & Nierhoff-Wielk, B. (2007). *Ex machina - Frühe Computergrafik*. Berlin, Germany: Deutscher Kunstverlag.

Hewlett-Packard Company. (1983). *HP7475A graphics plotter: Interfacing and programming manual*. San Diego, CA: Author.

Nake, F. (1989). Art in the time of the artificial [Editorial]. *Leonardo, 31*(3), 163–164.

Nake, F. (2007). Retrieved July 12, 2011, from http://viola.informatik.uni-bremen.de/typo/

Nees, G. (2006). *Generative Computergraphik*. Berlin, Germany: Vice Versa.

Noll, A. M. (1964). *Vertical- horizontal: Example of early computer art*. Retrieved 14 July, 2011 from http://www.citi.columbia.edu/amnoll/CompArtExamples.html

Unverfehrt, G. (Ed.). (2000). *Zeichnungen von Meisterhand: Die Sammlung Uffenbach aus der Kunstsammlung der Universität Göttingen*. Göttingen, Germany: Vandenhoeck & Rupprecht.

Verostko, R. (2011). *Website of the artist*. Retrieved April 2011, from http://www.verostko.com

You, F., Dehlinger, H., & Wang, J.-M. (2010). *Generative art: Aesthetic events from experiments with lines and squares*. Guangzhou, China: Lingnan Art Publishing House.

ADDITIONAL READING

Baume, N. (2001). *Sol Lewitt: Incomplete open cubes*. Cambridge, MA: MIT Press.

Beddard, H. (2009). Computer art at the V&A. *V&A Online Journal, 2*. Retrieved July 14, 2011, from http://www.vam.ac.uk/content/journals/research-journal/issue-02/computer-art-at-the-v-and-a/

Boden, M. A. (1990). *The creative mind: Myths and mechanisms*. London, UK: Weidenfeld and Nicholson.

Boden, M. A. (2003). *The creative mind. Myths and mechanisms*. London, UK: Routledge.

Boden, M. A., & Edmonds, E. A. (2009). What is generative art? *Digital Creativity, 20*(1-2), 21–46. doi:10.1080/14626260902867915

Candy, L., & Edmonds, E. (2002). *Explorations in art and technology*. London, UK: Springer-Verlag. doi:10.1007/978-1-4471-0197-0

Faure Walker, J. (2006). *Painting the digital river: How an artist learned to love the computer*. New Jersey: Prentice Hall.

Foley, J. D., van Dam, A., Feiner, S. F., & Hughes, J. F. (1990). *Computer graphics, principles and practice* (2nd ed.). Reading, MA: Addison-Wesley.

Galanter, P. (2003). What is generative art? Complexity theory as a context for art theory. In C. Soddu (Ed.), *Proceedings of the 6th International Conference on Generative Art* (216–235). Milan, Italy: Generative Design Lab of Politecnico di Milano. Retrieved 14 July, 2011, from http://www.philipgalanter.com/downloads/ga2003_paper.pdf

Krawczyk, R. (2001). *Curving spirolaterals*. Conference Mathematics & Design 2001, Geelong, Australia. Retrieved July 14, 2011, from http://mypages.iit.edu/~krawczyk/brdg01.pdf

Lieser, W. (2010). *Digital art. Neue Wege in der Kunst*. Potsdam, Germany: H. F. Ullmann.

McCorduck, P. (1991). *Aaron's code*. New York, NY: W. H. Freeman.

Nake, F. (2008). *Behind the canvas: An algorithmic space*. Reflections on Digital Art, CHArt 24th Annual Conference, Birbeck, London. Retrieved August 9, 2011, from http://www.chart.ac.uk/chart2008/papers/nake-koster.pdf

Nake, F., & Stoller, D. (Eds.). (1993). *Algorithmus und Kunst - Die präzisen Vergnügen: Texte und Bilder zu einer Ausstellung und Werkstattgespräch*. Hamburg, Germany: Sautter & Lackmann.

Programming language and programming artists. (n.d.). *Website*. Retrieved 14, July 2011 from http://processing.org/

Reichardt, J. (Ed.). (1968). *Cybernetic serendipity: Studio international 168*. London, UK: Institute of Contemporary Art.

Rosen, M. (2011). *Little-known story about a movement, a magazine, and the computer's arrival in art: New tendencies and Bit International*. Cambridge, MA: MIT Press.

Spalter, A. M. (1999). *The computer in the visual arts*. Reading, MA: Addison Wesley.

Stiles, K., & Selz, P. (1996). *Theories and documents of contemporary art*. Los Angeles, CA: University of California Press.

Struwe, G. (1996). *Temporary tenderness. Dynamische Bilder und Automatischer Zeichner*. Retrieved July 14, 2011 from http://www.youtube.com/watch?v=A3scAWv6_gA

The V&A's computer art collections. (n.d.). Retrieved July 14, 2011, from http://www.vam.ac.uk/content/articles/t/v-and-a-computer-art-collections/

Verostko, R. (1988). *Epigenetic painting. Software as genotype, a new dimension of art*. Presented at the first International Symposium on Electronic Art (FISEA'88). Retrieved 14, July 2011 from http://www.verostko.com/epigenet.html

Wilson, S. (2001). *Information arts. Intersection of art, science, and technology*. Cambridge, MA: MIT Press.

KEY TERMS AND DEFINITIONS

Algorithm: An algorithm is a procedure that terminates after a final number of steps. A procedure is a step-by-step instruction, where at each step it is clear what the next step will be.

Constraint: Restrictions introduced deliberately and by design, or accepted (in an act of resignation), which fence in the breathtaking epistemological freedom of an artist. In programmed art, constraints often take the form of an upper and/or lower limit of the value ranges of variables, e.g. in the use of controlled random processes.

Generative art: An art practice where the artist follows a self-designed formal system of rules. It is not necessary that a computer is part of the process. However, generative art on computers is a widespread and growing area of interest for many contemporary artists worldwide. In the context of art history, new challenges arise here in the struggle with the particular problems of this kind of art practice.

HPGL (HP-GL): Acronym, derived from Hewlett-Packard Graphics Language. An early and important set of commands for controlling the interface of a computer to a pen-plotter. HPGL, originally designed as a language to generate 2D graphics on the Hewlett-Packard range of plotters, it became a standard language for almost all plotters. It is efficient, easy to write and read. Most of the commands are composed of two upper case letters, followed by arguments, e.g. SP,3 (select pen number 3 from stocker). The early pen-plotters have basically been line drawing output devices, and consequently, the commands that were most commonly used were concerned with drawing lines: PU (pen up), PD (pen down), PA (plot absolute), PR (plot relative).

Metaphor: A metaphor is usually thought of as a construction in speech. Some tangible entity is pointed at or referenced (e.g. grains of sand, pebble), and from this reference a less tangible entity is constructed for a situational use (e.g. as countless as the grains of sand in the riverbed). A visual metaphor moves conceptually away from the image it originated from but remotely preserves some of the features of the triggering image. The transformational process is characterized by information-loss on the one side and information-gain on the other side. The metaphoric image stands in its own *space of meaning* and allows for other associations.

Pen-plotter drawing: An image, normally on paper, drawn with a physical pen such as a pencil, rollerball-pen, or any other suitable pen, which is fitted to a mechanical device instructed and controlled by a computer.

ENDNOTES

[i] Around 1000 mm/second

[ii] Retrieved July 8, 2011, from http://www.lemkesoft.com/content/189/cadintosh.html

[iii] Processing. Retrieved April 1, 2011, from http://processing.org/

[iv] The radius of one circular element in the real drawing is about 1 mm

[v] The image displayed in Figure 3 is plotted on a sheet of paper of size A0+

[v] A pen-plotter in action can be seen at: http://www.generativeart.de/ Retrieved April 2011

Chapter 15
On the Designing and Prototyping of Kinetic Objects

Scottie Chih-Chieh Huang
Chung Hua University, Taiwan

Shen-Guan Shih
National Taiwan University of Science and Technology, Taiwan

ABSTRACT

MSOrgm (Huang, 2009), SSOrgan, and LBSkeleton (Huang, 2011) were created to contain computation, aesthetic, and structural characteristics to employ physical kinetic motion to embody and communicate to people. MSOrgm raises its branches when it senses someone who is looking at it. MSOrgm was developed as a robot plant to interact with the viewer in a soothing way; it uses transformable module to build interconnected fabric and produce unexpected behavior. SSOrgan provides a novel tangible interaction, which generates color in response to touch. SSOrgan is an artificial skin system composed by dense individual sensing module; it creates the responsive behavior executed by its external contact and its internal computing mechanism. LBSkeleton explores a mutual interaction that happens between "the piper and the snake" — through the change of the sound performance that should triggered by body movement reflectivity. LBSkeleton shows a kinetic structural system, which is engaged with the sensor networked framework and the origami tessellation module to perform a kind of growling behavior with sound. These works bring the specific type of modeling, controlling, and interacting on the designing of the kinetic creatures. The artworks are bringing novel user experiences with the biomimetic mechanism in a space.

INTRODUCTION

The development of computer-augmented physical kinetic objects has changed the relation between the viewer and the artwork. To discover the feature of kinetic object, this chapter used biomimetic aspect to develop modular design method in the three digital artworks. Physical computing (Sullivan & Igoe, 2004) is bringing new opportunities to develop diverse and multiple design forms in the field of new media art. It integrates traditional fine arts and modern art forms with computational features and creates a closed relationship between the viewer and the

DOI: 10.4018/978-1-4666-0942-6.ch015

artwork. In approximately 1820, modern materials of electric and machine technology came to be used into kinetic artworks. Since then, numerous artists, designers, and architects have created kinetic objects involving the representation of illusion and natural movement. From 1960, during the introduction of the computer graphics and interactive techniques, several research directions have been attempted to take computational resources from the cyber space into the physical world, such as Augmented Reality (AR) and robotics technology. These novel technologies, which are used as design media, bring new possibilities for designing computer-augmented physical objects in the space (Liu & Lim, 2009).

This chapter used a biomimetic aspect to develop a modular design method in three digital art works. MSOrgm (Huang, 2009), SSOrgan, and LBSkeleton (Huang, 2011) contain computation, aesthetic, and structural characteristics to employ physical kinetic motion to embody and communicate to people. We treat them as pioneers to investigate the ongoing relation between the viewer and the artwork – the digital artworks' body and behavior may change dynamically and lively as if to reflect echoes of environment and human communications.

Computer-Augmented Physical Kinetic Objects

The developments in research on kinesthesia are playing an indispensable role in contemporary spatial design projects. Bubbles (Fox & Kemp, 2009) demonstrated that interactive installation could be aware of a visitor coming and react with a spatially pneumatic form at an urban scale. Deforming and performing dynamical behavior is generated by real time calculations. The rolling bridge (Ahlquist & Fleischmann, 2009) presents a transformable design, which opens smoothly, curling from a conventional, straight bridge, into a circular sculpture. The structure uses a series of hydraulic rams integrated into its eight segments,

causing its rolling character. The expanding video screen (Hoberman, 2010) demonstrates a giant screen that can change its size and shape, morph into a 7-story high cone-shaped structure, enveloping the band as it extends in the U2's concert. And the actuated tensegrity structure (Sterk, 2003) demonstrated a vision of building adaptability, which could change the shape of building's envelope in response to outside/inside sensors in the structure.

The field of kinetic art offers a rich motion vocabulary both in the functional and perceptual areas. Hylozoic Soil (Beesley, 2010) is an immersive, interactive environment made of tens of thousands of lightweight digitally-fabricated components fitted with meshed microprocessors and sensors. It contains infrared proximity sensors, micro-controllers, strands of titanium nickel memory wire, and custom circuit boards to perform mutual interactions between viewers and the kinetic object. The robotic dog Aibo (Otsuki, 1999) attempted to simulate animal or human forms and movements coexisting into our living space. Outerspace (Andre Stubbe and Markus Lerner, 2007) appears as a playful, curious creature exploring the surrounding space, looking for light, motion, and contact. To create a kinetic sculpture Ferrofluid (Kodama, 2008), the shape-changing material that appears as a black fluid was prepared by dissolving nanoscale ferromagnetic particles in a solvent such as water or oil; it remains strongly magnetic even in a fluid condition.

Computation embedded interactive objects give the electronics hardware and software a manipulable and perceptible form. The computational construction objects can self-describe the spatial organization and form a decentralized computing framework while they are assembled (Gorbet, Orth, & Ishii, 1998; Aish, Frankel, Frazer, & Patera, 2001; LeClerc, Parkes, & Ishii, 2007; Schweikardt & Gross, 2010; Weller, Gross, & Goldstein, 2010). It can combine organization with topology to form and conduct further computational behavior. In systems created by

Lifton et al. (2002, 2003), each individual sensing object provides distributed and decentralized hardware/software architecture for practicing with algorithms in cellular computing and test emergent behavior with light, sound, and vibration applications.

Modular Design Approach

We attempt to represent the kinetic characters from the natural life into artificial object. To make the organic and diverse growing patterns and the adaptability from the environmental situation changed into dynamic posture or behavior responding into real object, we purpose three modular design attitudes: (1) the Recursive Algorithmic for Shape Modeling (RASM); (2) the Adaptive Properties for Emergent Behavior Control (APEBC); and (3) the developments of Computational Constructive Design Toolkits (CCDTs).

Recursive Algorithmic for Shape Modeling (RASM)

In order to represent the organic and diverse growing patterns as nature-like, we are using the recursive algorithm to establish the probably natural growing process. The replication and reorganization mechanism is utilized as a set of modeling rules with the recursive data structure to generate diverse nature-like forms. As can be seen in Figure 1, through the use of coding to restriction the basic principle (boundary) of predefined modular object and its interconnected relationship in Processing (2011) language and its environment. It is able to generate organic-like form efficiently, and also may changing the generation result through its internal parameter adjustments.

Figure 1. Through the parameter changed the diverse shape is generated simultaneously (© 2011, Scottie Chih-Chieh Huang. Used with permission.).

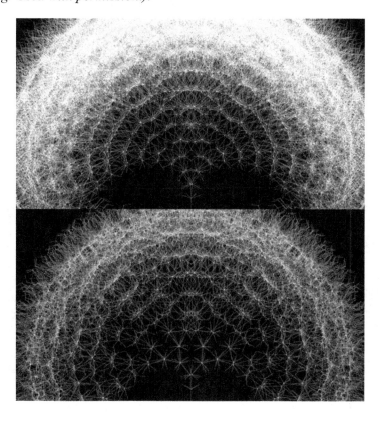

Adaptive Properties for Emergent Behavior Control (APEBC)

Adaptive behavior is a property that natural life used to present their current postures according to their internal condition and the external condition changes. We attempt to explore a kind of dynamic behaviors as presented on Mimosa - each motor cells may be stimulus by perceives touch and then disseminating electrical signals to turn on the neighboring motor cells to display emerged rolling behavior. On the designing of this emerged adaptive behavior, Processing (2011) software is used to develop decentralized framework toward to make unexpected behavior control for the string objects. As see in Figure 2, the leave is consisted by twelve module objects interconnected together, which could see as a one-dimensional Cellular Automata (CA) framework. In which, each module objects has two possible states of live and dead, and the next state of the module depend on the internal conditions of the state of the self-module, neighboring modules, and the external state that sensed from perceives contact through a simple rule we defined. While the state of the module object is live, the joint of the object will make shrinking behavior; if the opposite, it will make stretching behavior. Therefore, as one module objects lives, it will produce disseminate phenomenon from local objects to global behaviors.

Computational Constructive Design Toolkits (CCDTs)

In order to make the computational mechanism from the virtual module (as above-mentioned in RASM and APEBC) into real object, we invent CCDTs, which contained of the flexible joints and the tubing materials, and attached shape-changing materials as of pneumatic cylinder and shape-memory alloy within it. And also, we develop the specific Constructive Printed Circuit Boards (C-PCBs, shows in Figure 3), used Atmega 328 microprocessor programmed by Arduino (2011) programming language and its development environment to contain the computational capabilities of (1) the sensibility of the environmental condition changing, perceives touch, and the proximity sensing, (2) the controllability of the pneumatic sounds, shadow and full-color light, and the kinetic movement, and (3) the computability of the external communication with other C-PCBs and the internal data processing, to make physical artifacts embed with the robotic capability as living objects.

Figure 2. Rolling behavior is occurred in one-dimensional CA framework. (© 2011, Scottie Chih-Chieh Huang. Used with permission.).

Figure 3. C-PCBs engaging with the flexible joints and the tubing materials to produce kinetic objects. (© 2011, Scottie Chih-Chieh Huang. Used with permission.).

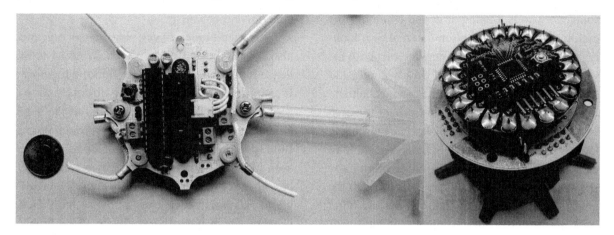

DEMONSTRATION

MSOrgm

In order to realize kinetic expressions of creature-like movements and shape changing, we build MSOrgm (Motivational Sensitive Organism) as a technical application to demonstrate and the performance of its transformable movement. In the development, the controllability of actuating the shape-memory alloy on CCDTs is used to develop the specific transformable module for MSOrgm, called trans-module. Through the use of code to define the trans- module in computer graphics, the RASM is able to applied for generate its interconnected fabric. And then, we used APEBC to study CA rules loading and loading the rules into each CCDTs to make emergent behavior.

MSOrgm is a plant-like structure that presents itself as a biological form not only in terms of shapes but with the way it interacts with people who pay attention to it. The concept comes from plants that are capable of rapid motion in reacting to external stimulation, such as mimosa.

Figure 4. MSOrgm — Motivational Sensitive Organism, MOCA Taipei, Taiwan, 2008. (© 2008, Scottie Chih-Chieh Huang. Used with permission.)

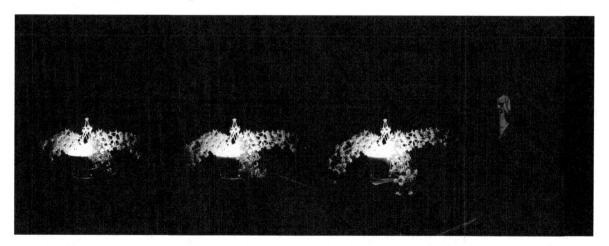

Equipped with cameras and a face recognizing program, MSOrgm raises its branches when senses someone who is looking at it, and continues the dialog with a kind of motion that makes it looking like a living creature. It may interact with the viewer in a quiet and graceful way, in contrast to the unnatural movements of most mechanism. Shape-memory alloy is used as mussel for each of the kinetic motor cell to shorten the cell in length. In another mode, MSOrgm is capable of displaying various motions and configurations by stimulating some of the motor cells through the proximity contact, which in turn stimulate other cells that are connected to them. Although it is one single object when seen as a whole, MSOrgm can be regarded as an organization consisting of autonomous cells, which are capable of reacting to other cells, and altogether, display cooperated and sometimes unexpected behaviors.

SSOrgan

SSOrgan (Stimulus Skin Organ) is aim to build a sensor networked framework for demonstration and performance of the emergent behavior toward biomimetic exploration. In the development, we used APEBC for defining CA rules in each CCDTs to explore the unexpected behavior emerged by 2-dimentional grid organization. Through the controllability of lighting and the sensibility of perceives touch on CCDTs, makes the responsive

processes of the autonoetic consciousness are able to execute by physical contact and the digital generative mechanism.

Skin membrane is a very sensitive organ, and also a complicated organization. It consists of dense individual sensing cells working together. It can sense touch from outside objects, and react by developing specific features on the skin (such as gooseflesh and bruises). Through blood fluid specific conditions affecting the skin can be seen visually. SSOrgan inspired by organic skin, attempts to build an artificial system. We create an artificial skin composed of dense individual sensors which have the ability to sense touch, has activities for processing information input and output within its organization, and displays touch in the form of color. Full-color LED is used to express the stimulated information on each piece through whole organization processing in a direct way. SSOrgan provides a novel tangible interaction, which generates color in response to touch. A viewer may use hands to stroke or press the SSOrgan to create an interactive lighting pattern. The emerging processing appears on the skin surface. It is also wants to make people imagine a dense interconnected organization that works like the organic skin system. We make this working system through sharing and exchanging haptic information to reveal touch sense, and make people feel a new contact experience between human and artifact.

Figure 5. SSOrgan – Stimulus Skin Organ, NTUST, Taiwan, 2009. (© 2009, Scottie Chih-Chieh Huang. Used with permission.).

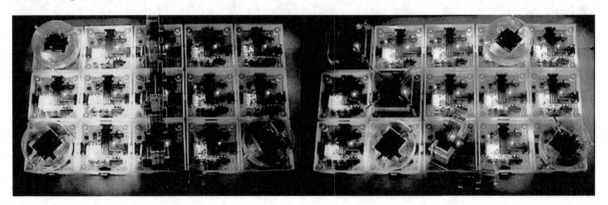

LBSkeleton

LBSkeleton (Listening Bio-Skeleton) is aim to build a kinetic structural system to perfect engaged with APEBC by the sensor network framework and the origami tessellation module to generate and perform growling behavior. It applied CCDTs to develop the replicated foldable space frame units, and grouping it into grid organization to form the 3-dimentional cylinder. And through the controllability of actuate the pneumatic cylinder and the sensibility of the proximity sensing on CCDTs, it is able to make the circular cylinder perform crawling movement and behavior, and create the kinetic interaction with the viewers' motion.

LBSkeleton is a robotic musical instrument, creating an alternative ambient display from a blend of pneumatic sound and magnificent shadows, and showing an emotional communication between audience and the kinetic sculpture in a soothing way. The sculpture is made of dense replicated foldable space truss studying the con- figuration of origami magic balls and mechanical techniques, to design a transformable body. LBSkeleton explores a mutual interaction that happens between "the piper and the snake" — through the change of the sound performance that should triggered of body movement reflectivity. LBSkeleton detects the presence of one or more persons in the space and reacts through a change of shape, sound, light, and gracefully enables the audience to immerse and control a harmonious and augmented musical environment through the body movement.

FUTURE RESEARCH DIRECTIONS

Creation of artificial-life is bringing new aspect to use computer graphics technique as a design method of modeling and behavioral animation. Through the use of program for defining the expect rule, and then utilize the algorithm to produce unexpected result of both the gener-

Figure 6. LBSkeleton – Listening Bio-Skeleton, Digital Art Center Taipei, Taiwan, 2010. (© 2010, Scottie Chih-Chieh Huang. Used with permission.)

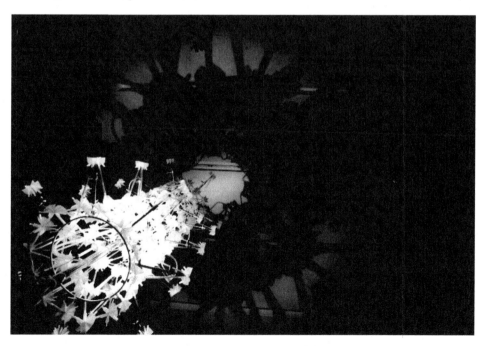

ated modeling and emerged behavior, it is able to attach the biomimetic features in this design process. Physical computing technique is enable designer to express and produce any types of physical interactive system they wish. Through the custom of their own software and hardware, designer is able to develop specific mechanism and the materials of electronic, structure, and computation as their toolkits for instructing novel interactive opportunities in the physical world. These computer techniques bring new directions in the development the unexpected in a predictable feature in the future of design.

CONCLUSION

These digital artworks are used as application to demonstrate modular design approach in this chapter. It brings rule-based design method to execute forms and its contained behaviors in the design. Recursive Algorithmic for Shape Modeling (RASM) is useful to generate nature-like growing patterns in the modeling process. And the Adaptive Properties for Emergent Behavior Control (APEBC) is useful to design the nature-liked behavior in kinetic object controls, through the networked computing property. In the prototyping, we aim to make Computational Constructive Design Toolkits (CCDTs) to make virtual simulation and ideas into meaningful object in the context of real world. These artworks are bringing novel user experiences with the biomimetic mechanism in a space.

REFERENCES

Ahlquist, S., & Fleischmann, M. (2009). Computational spring systems: Open design processes for complex structural systems. *Architectural Design*, *79*(2), 130–133. doi:10.1002/ad.870

Aish, R., Frankel, J. L., Frazer, J. H., & Patera, A. T. (2001). Computational construction kits for geometric modeling and design. In *Proceedings of the ACM Symposium on Interactive 3D Graphics, I3D 2001*, North Carolina, March 19-21, 2001. New York, NY: ACM Press.

Arduino. (2011). Retrieved August 14, 2011, from http://www.arduino.cc/, http://arduino.cc/en/Main/ArduinoBoardLilyPad

Beesley, P. (2010). *Hylozoic ground*. Ontario, Canada: Riverside Architectural Press. Also, retrieved August 14, 2011, from http://www.philipbeesleyarchitect.com/sculptures/0635hylozoic_soil/hylozoic.html and http://www.hylozoicground.com/

Fox, M., & Kemp, M. (2009). *Interactive architecture*. New York, NY: Princeton Architectural Press.

Gorbet, M. G., Orth, M., & Ishii, H. (1998). Triangles: Tangible interface for manipulation and exploration of digital information topography. In *Proceedings of the 4th International Conference on Human Factors in Computing Systems, ACM SIGCHI 1998*, Los Angeles, California, April 18-23, 1998. New York, NY: ACM Press.

Hoberman, C. (2010). Expanding video screen for U2 360° tour. *Architecture and Urbanism*, *2010*(2), 119-121.

Huang, S. C. C. (2009). MSOrgm (Motivational Sensitive Organism). *Leonardo/ISAST*, *42*(4), 374-375.

Huang, S. C. C. (2011). *LBSkeleton (Listening Bio-Skeleton). Analogue is the new digital*. Retrieved Auguest 10, 2011, from http://sonotonialand.org/siggraph2011/

Kodama, S. (2008). Dynamic ferrofluid sculpture: Organic shape-changing art forms. *Communications of the ACM*, *51*(6), 79–81. doi:10.1145/1349026.1349042

LeClerc, V., Parkes, A., & Ishii, H. (2007). Senspectra: A computationally augmented physical modeling toolkit for sensing and visualization of structural strain. In *Proceedings of the 13th International Conference on Human Factors in Computing Systems, ACM SIGCHI 2007*, San Jose, California, April 28–May 3, 2007. New York, NY: ACM Press.

Lifton, J., Broxton, M., & Paradiso, J. A. (2003). Distributed sensor networks as sensate skin. In *Proceedings of the 2th IEEE International Conference on Sensors, IEEE SENSORS 2007*, Atlanta, Georgia, October 22-24, 2003. Los Alamitos, CA: IEEE Computer Society.

Lifton, J., Seetharam, D., Broxton, M., & Paradiso, J. (2002). Pushpin computing system overview: A platform for distributed, embedded, ubiquitous sensor networks. In F. Mattern & M. Naghshineh (Ed.), *Pervasive Computing, First International Conference, Pervasive 2002* (pp. 139-151). Berlin, Germany: Springer

Liu, Y. T., & Lim, C. K. (2009). *New tectonics: Towards a new theory of digital architecture: 7th FEIDAD award*. Basel, Switzerland: Birkhauser.

Otsuki, T. (1999). *AIBO* (ERS-110). Japan Media Arts Plaza. Retrieved January 7, 2011, from http://plaza.bunka.go.jp/english/festival/1999/degital/000330/

Processing. (2011). Retrieved August 14, 2011, from http://processing.org/

Schweikardt, E., & Gross, M. D. (2010). Experiments in design synthesis when behavior is determined by shape. *Personal and Ubiquitous Computing, 15*(2), 123–132. doi:10.1007/s00779-010-0310-z

Sterk, T. D. (2003). Using actuated tensegrity structures to produce a responsive architecture. In *Proceedings of the 23th International Conference of the Association for Computer Aided Design in Architecture, ACADIA 2003*, Indianapolis, Indiana, October 24-27, 2003. Retrieved August 25, 2011, from Cumulative Index on CAD (CUMINCAD).

Stubbe, A., & Lerner, M. (2007). *Outerspace: Reactive robotic creature*. Retrieved August 14, 2011, from http://www.andrestubbe.com/outerspace/

Sullivan, D. O., & Igoe, T. (2004). *Physical computing: Sensing and controlling the physical world with computers*. Boston, MA: Thomson Course Technology.

Weller, M. P., Gross, M. D., & Goldstein, S. C. (2010). Hyperform specification: Designing and interacting with self-reconfiguring materials. *Personal and Ubiquitous Computing, 15*(2), 133–149. doi:10.1007/s00779-010-0315-7

ADDITIONAL READING

Beesley, P. (2005). Orgone reef. *Architectural Design, 75*(4), 46–53. doi:10.1002/ad.102

Berzowska, J., & Coelho, M. (2005). Kukkia and vilkas: Kinetic electronic garments. In *Proceedings of the 9th IEEE International Symposium on Wearable Computers, ISWC 2005*, (pp. 82-85). Osaka, Japan, October 18-21, 2005. Los Alamitos, CA: IEEE Computer Society.

Breazeal, C., Brooks, A., Gray, J., Hancher, M., McBean, J., Stiehl, W. D., & Strickon, J. (2003). Interactive robot theatre. *Communications of the ACM, 46*(7), 76–85. doi:10.1145/792704.792733

Cadet, F. (2008). *Hunting trophies*. Retrieved August 14, 2011, from http://cyberdoll.free.fr/cyberdoll/index_a.html

Coelho, M., & Zigelbaum, J. (2010). Shape-changing interfaces . *Personal and Ubiquitous Computing, 15*(2), 161–173. doi:10.1007/s00779-010-0311-y

Delbruck, T., Whatley, A. M., Douglas, R., Eng, K., Hepp, K., & Verschure, P. F. M. J. V. (2007). A tactile luminous floor for an interactive autonomous space. *Robotics and Autonomous Systems, 55*(6), 433–443. doi:10.1016/j.robot.2007.01.006

Glynn, R. (2008). *Performative ecologies*. Retrieved August 14, 2011, from http://www.interactivearchitecture.org/portfolio/performativeecologies.html

Goulthorpe, M., Burry, M., & Dunlop, G. (2001). Aegis Hyposurface©: The bordering of university and practice. In *Proceedings of the 11th International Conference of the Association for Computer Aided Design in Architecture, ACADIA 2001*, Buffalo, New York, October 11-14, 2001, (pp. 344-349).

Jansen, T. (2008). Strandbeests. *Architectural Design, 78*(4), 22–27. doi:10.1002/ad.701

Kerstin, E. (2010). *Whiskers in space*. Retrieved August 14, 2011, from http://www.nodegree.de/

Kusahara, M. (2001). The art of creating subjective reality: An analysis of Japanese digital pets. *Leonardo/ISAST, 34*(4), 299–302.

McNerney, T. S. (2004). From turtles to tangible programming bricks: Explorations in physical language design. *Personal and Ubiquitous Computing, 8*(5), 326–337. doi:10.1007/s00779-004-0295-6

Negroponte, N. (1975). *Soft architecture machines*. Cambridge, MA: MIT Press.

Oosterhuis, K., & Biloria, N. (2008). Interactions with proactive architectural spaces: The muscle projects. *Communications of the ACM, 51*(6), 70–78. doi:10.1145/1349026.1349041

Oxman, N. (2010). Structuring materiality: Design fabrication of heterogeneous materials. *Architectural Design, 80*(4), 78–85. doi:10.1002/ad.1110

Paradiso, J. A., Lifton, J., & Broxton, M. (2004). Sensate media-multimodal electronic skins as dense sensor networks. *BT Technology Journal, 22*(4), 32–44. doi:10.1023/B:BTTJ.0000047581.37994.c2

Parkes, A., Poupyrev, I., & Ishii, H. (2008). Designing kinetic interactions for organic user interfaces. *Communications of the ACM, 51*(6), 58–65. doi:10.1145/1349026.1349039

Romero, M., Pousman, Z., & Mateas, M. (2008). Alien presence in the home: The design of tableau machine. *Personal and Ubiquitous Computing, 12*(5), 373–382. doi:10.1007/s00779-007-0190-z

Roosegaarde, D. (2010). Lotus 7.0. *Leonardo/ISAST, 43*(4), 408-409.

Rowe, A., & Birtles, L. (2010). Glowing pathfinder bugs: A natural haptic 3D interface for interacting intuitively with virtual environments. *Leonardo/ISAST, 43*(4), 350-358.

Stedman, N., & Segal, K. (2010). ADB. *Leonardo/ISAST, 43*(4), 414–415.

Tenhaaf, N. (2008). Art embodies A-life: The VIDA competition. *Leonardo/ISAST, 41*(1), 6-15.

Terzidis, K. (2009). *Algorithms for visual design: Using the processing language*. Indianapolis, IN: John Wiley & Sons.

Zykov, V., Mytilinaios, E., Adams, B., & Lipson, H. (2005). Self-reproducing machines. *Nature, 435*(7038), 163–164. doi:10.1038/435163a

KEY TERMS AND DEFINITIONS

Actuator: An actuator is a device for controlling a mechanism or system, and converts that energy into some kind of motion.

Autonoetic Consciousness: Autonoetic consciousness is the human ability to mentally place ourselves in the past, in the future, or in counterfactual situations, and to analyze our own thoughts

Biomimetic: Biomimetic refers to human-made processes, substances, devices, or systems that imitate nature.

Cellular Automata (CA): CA is a discrete model studied in computability theory, It consists of a regular grid of cells, each in one of a finite number of states according to some fixed rule (generally, a mathematical function) that determines the new state of each cell in terms of the current state of the cell and the states of the cells in its neighborhood.

Haptic: Haptic is the senses of touch, is extremely important for humans; as well as providing information about surfaces and textures it is a component of nonverbal communication in interpersonal relationships, and vital in conveying physical intimacy.

Tensegrity Structure: Tensegrity is a structural principle based on the use of isolated components in compression inside a net of continuous tension, in such a way that the compressed members do not touch each other and the prestressed tensioned members delineate the system spatially.

Chapter 16
A New Leaf

Liz Lee
State University of New York at Fredonia, USA

ABSTRACT

The author and artist, Liz Lee discusses her latest digital image series, "A New Leaf Series", within the context of early photographic imaging and its connection to science and biology by investigating and connecting to the work of Thomas Wedgewood, William Henry Fox-Talbot, and the early pioneers of photographic technologies. Hippolyte Bayard's "Arrangement of Specimens" and Anna Atkins' "Photographs of British Algae: Cyanotype Impressions" serve as early examples of the scientific fundamentals of photography; the technological advances of the medium still draw on the same subject matter to reveal the basic structure of conceptual and aesthetic investigation. The author discusses how contemporary electronic imaging has returned to its photographic origins through nature-related subject matter.

INTRODUCTION

The first photographic image, a Heliograph on pewter, *View from the Window at Le Gras,* was taken by Joseph Nicéphore Niépce in 1826. This documented fact has been, and still is, taught in every History of Photography course at every leading educational institution in the world. But now a modifier must be placed in front of that declarative statement: *Allegedly* the first photographic image, a Heliograph on pewter, *View from the Window at Le Gras,* was taken by Joseph Nicéphore Niépce in 1826. A deceptively simple,

delicate, silver nitrate-coated piece of paper that displays a perfectly intact negative image of the "Quillan Leaf" (Figure 1) named after the Quillan Company Collection, in which the image is housed along with a small group of anonymous photogenic drawings as part of an album assembled by Henry Bright) could now claim this distinction. Previously attributed to Henry Fox-Talbot, the leaf image was believed to have been created in 1839, a period still considered the dawn of photography. However a recently discovered small inscription of a handwritten "W" in bottom corner of the leaf image questions the image creator; reassigning it from Fox-Talbot to, it is believed, Thomas Wedgewood, descendant in the long line of the

DOI: 10.4018/978-1-4666-0942-6.ch016

Figure 1. Leaf, attributed to Thomas Wedgewood. Photogenic drawing, n.d. (© n.d., The Quillan Collection, Used with permission).

Wedgewood pottery manufacturers, who died in 1805 (Sotheby's 2008). The date of Wedgewood's death would place the creation of this photogenic drawing as early as 1802, some speculate even as far back as 1790 (Associated Press 2008). This revelation could reshape the history of photography. The first surviving mechanical means of reproduction, the art of capturing a shadow, is not an image of another manmade creation, a building in the view from a window, but a contact print of nature. A delicate, seemingly insignificant image of a poplar leaf that was never fixed to protect it from continual exposure so must forever be kept in the dark, now casts new light and transforms the history of image making. If the "Quillan Leaf" is attributed to Wedgewood it may cause Niepce's image to fade away into obscurity like so many unfixed photogenic drawings.

William J. Mitchell begins his well known text, *The Reconfigured Eye: Visual Truth in the Post-Photographic Era* (1997), with a brief history lesson: that the origin of painting is uncertain, some Greeks claim it was discovered in Sicyon, while others in Corinth, but there is universal agreement that it began by outlining a man's shadow. A mythic tale told by Piney the Elder explains that a Corinthian maiden traced the shadow of her departing lover; his image forever captured by the work of her hand and painting is born. Mitchell continues:

William Henry Fox Talbot traces a scene at Lake Como with the help of a camera obscura. He begins to wonder 'if it were possible to cause these natural images to imprint themselves durably.' By 1839 he has perfected the art of chemically fixing a shadow. He announces to the Royal Society his invention of a way to record images permanently on specially treated paper 'by the agency of light alone, without the aid whatever from the artist's pencil.' Simultaneously, Daguerreotypes make their public appearance in France. The history painter Paul Delarouche exclaims, 'From this day on, painting is dead' (Mitchell 1997, p. 3).

I too have introduced my lecture on the History of Computer Art in my Digital Imaging classes at SUNY Fredonia with this same passage for the last ten years. In my introductory remarks I make sure to emphasize the developments of capturing and recording a life-like image to man's continual quest to reproduce his likeness. People are spellbound by the "mirror with a memory". (Marien 2002). It was man's ego and his continual search for fame and recognition that was the driving force behind most technological achievements. From Hershel and Fox-Talbot's competition with Daguerre and Niepce to win the patent for the first photographic process to Paul Delarouche's and Pablo Picasso's flamboyant declarations that the invention of photography was the death of painting ("I have discovered photography. Now

I can kill myself. I have nothing else to learn."), photography's history appeared to be marked by masculinity, competition and triumph. But now, a quite, little leaf poplar leaf; a muted brown salt-print, its veins exposed, reveals unexpected details about the discovery and use of photography and imaging technologies.

BACKGROUND

One of the most remarkable aspects of photography, and what has been attributed to its status as the first imaging technology, is it ability to take a picture directly of the visible world; the mechanical act of light on film. The relationship between camera image and the scene it portrays has been termed "indexical" by American philosopher Charles Sanders Pierce. The photograph's one-to-one relationship to the scene is similar to smoke as a signal to fire, the photograph is a signal of light reflected off the object and recorded on film. This concept led Roland Barthes to declare "the referent adheres" to the photograph, or in other words that the photograph can never distinguish itself from that which it represents. The evolution, however, of film-based to digital photography has created a separation between photography and reality. The revered position photography once held is gone. The photograph is no longer indexical, no longer faithful to the physical world but determined by a set of data. Unlike light, digital data has no referent in the outside world.

The camera was not designed to unleash a new way of seeing; "what" is being represented remains unchanged, but this does not diminish the camera's importance in defining an image. On a functional level, the photograph is dependent on its context. The "fixed" image offers its subject a continuous state of transformation and metamorphosis. The French Romantic painter Eugene Delacroix wrote the photograph is "the dictionary of nature," not so much a "mirror" up to nature but a veritable catalogue of the world (Clark, 1997).

American photographer Edward Weston speaks of photography's capacity "for looking deeply into the nature of things", and cultural critic Siegfried Kracauer states "the power of the medium" lays in its ability "to open up new, hitherto unsuspected dimensions of reality" thus, "photographs do not just copy nature but metamorphose it". But against this sense of the actual and the literal has always existed a powerful vocabulary, most associated with "art photography," which insists on the medium's capacity to express something beyond the surface of things (Clark, 1997).

The use of a flatbed scanner as camera certainly is not new. The scanner in fact could be compared to the earliest photographic techniques. Before fixing the image was discovered; artists used a lens that projected light onto ground glass producing an image that could then be traced. Cameras have used this fundamental structure – a point projecting a circle of definition onto a flat plan. The scanner uses this same basic method for gathering visual data.

As photography is defined as "light writing" it is essentially just image capture and display. Enumerated by John Szarkowski (1966) with elements "peculiar to photography:" "The Thing Itself," "The Detail," "The Frame," "Time," and "Vantage Point," digital technology has not radically transformed any of these. Using a scanner as camera encompasses all of the traditional devices associated with medium: exposure, contrast, depth of field and motion. The scanner in essence is a camera with an incredibly slow film speed and, just like the traditional film support, the pay off is amazingly sharp detail with little grain (noise), but even the slightest movement will create a dynamic pattern of displaced pixels (equivalent to an analogue motion blur). The desktop flatbed scanner uses a series of sensors strung along a linear bar, which passes along the object placed on the glass surface in a direction of right angles to its array of sensors. The scanner records strings of data taken from an area and literally builds a picture. Desktop scanners could be compared to a multi-lens camera, making pictures with incredible detail over an extended period of time, but the photographs they take are not taken from a single point as the scanning bar moves and sees its subject from more than one location on the glass surface. The comparisons to early photography become even more pronounced as optical character recognition technology improves. As one of Talbot's earliest photogenic drawings was little more than a trace of a simple object on paper which he spoke of having "the utmost truth and fidelity" and was part of the "natural magic" and "natural chemistry" with the potential for both science and art, the scanner allows digital photographers to use technology to step back into history and allow nature to be built within the scanner like "auto-graphy", nature's automatic writing (Marien 2002). Unlike capturing the thing in a negative or digital file where it is transformed by the photographer's eye, what is placed on top of scanner, as it was centuries ago placed on paper, is the thing: a contact print of biology.

STAGES OF "LEAF" DEVELOPMENT

Photography was born as the golden age of botanical illustration drew to a close. "Nature's gems", as Victorians loved to call flowers, were among the first subjects to be pictured in photographs (Ewing 1991). Hippolyte Bayard's *Arrangement of Specimens* (Figure 2) serves as an early example of scientific fundamentals of photography - the light sensitive nature of certain chemical compounds. Without the use of a camera or lens, Bayard carefully arranged a delicate selection of laces and flora on a sheet of paper that was made sensitive to light with a combination of iron salts that produced a blue-toned cyanotype when developed. The sheet of sensitized paper with the objects placed upon was exposed with sunlight in order to make a camera-less direct-positive print. The opacity of the object blocked the light in relation to its density, thus creating a

Figure 2. Hippolyte Bayard, direct positive print, about 1842, 10 15/16 x 8 1/2 in

silhouette of the object on the paper. Although the exposure times were long the cyanotype process was relatively uncomplicated, provided a quick method of recording easily recognizable shapes and patterns. Bayard filled entire sheets of paper, creating a catalog of specimens that reveals the basic structure of each object.

A photograph in a textbook was rare in 1892. Not until the turn of the 20th century did extensive plant surveys come into their own (Ewing 1991). In 1843 Anna Atkins (the world's first female photographer) self-published *Photographs of British Algae: Cyanotype Impressions*, the first book with photographic illustrations (Figure 3). Atkins collected the specimens herself and made direct contact cyanotypes to illustrate William Harvey's Manual of British Algae (1841) utilizing her own nomenclature. Although artistic expression was not her primary goal, she was extremely sensitive to the visual appeal of the algae and

Figure 3. Anna Atkins, photogram of algae (as part of her 1843 book, Photographs of British Algae: Cyanotype Impressions, the first book composed entirely of photographic images.) Cyanotype, 1843-53

arranged her specimens in imaginative and elegant compositions, thus uniting the rational sciences with aesthetic sensibility.

From the beginning photographers have been driven to look deeper, more discernibly, at nature than their artist and scientific forebears were able to. It was quickly realized that the camera extended human vision. Attaching cameras to microscopes and tooling lenses for even greater precision reveals a complex and ordered universe beyond our imagination. Using imaging technology to observe things not ordinarily seen with the naked eye, the scanner reveals unexpected details. Divorced from their natural environments such images astound us with the range of color and

minute detail revealed by high resolution scans; reexamining through imagery what might otherwise seem pedestrian or everyday.

Leaf Morphology

My series, *A New Leaf* series (Figure 4), focuses on the visual depiction of various human emotions, ever-changing emotionally, culturally and intellectually subjective states of mind. The images of disintegrating and decaying leaves are paired with text from a variety of scientific, philosophical and anecdotal self-help resources interpreting interconnection, transformation, symbols and patterns. Each leaf in the series reveals, and simultaneously obscures, the surrounding interpretive language, giving each leaf its own distinct character, a series of related explorations that enact a different way of relating to language and social practice through imagery. The insect devoured leaf of the Pin Oak

Figure 4. Liz Lee, A New Leaf Series – Guilt. Digital image – archival ink-jet print on photo rag. 12.694" x 16.156". (© 2009, Liz Lee. Used with permission.).

Figure 5. Liz Lee, A New Leaf Series - Depression. Digital image – archival ink-jet print on photo rag, 12.694" x 16.156". (© 2008, Liz Lee. Used with permission.).

(Figure 5) may be a strikingly beautiful object in and of itself, but when entitled "Depression" and matched with the passage "If you suffered from manic depression in recent years…" the fragility of the strong, majestic oak revered for its longevity and brilliant fall foliage is exposed.

The physical decay of the structurally intact leaf visually describes the human affliction. Reading the text in-between the veins of the diseased structure reveals the significance of image title and leaf's "affliction" as the passage describes future changes in medical diagnosis and treatment through biochemical networking of the human cell and genetic mapping. The series takes its cues from Niels Bohr's statement, "Isolated material particles are abstractions, their properties being definable and observable only through their interaction with other systems" and asks the viewer to consider the importance of subjective perspective. Just as a quantum object can be registered as either a particle or a wave, it is our psyche, through conscious discrimination, that determines if an event reveals a deeper order of significance. The need to turn over *A New Leaf* can be triggered by a specific incident or simply as part of the quotidian flux; spontaneous, simultaneous or synchronous, the need to understand what is beyond the individual is universal, connecting human beings to a larger order. It is the deeper interconnection between representation and reality that gives the image its meaning and its shape, as Virginia Woolf declared in *A Room of One's Own*, emotion "is not made by the relation of stone to stone, but by the relation of human being to human being." The beauty and elegance found in the death of the organic substance is juxtaposed against the speculative ideology of various thinkers.

To create the series actual leaves were collected throughout New York and Vermont and scanned into Photoshop™ then paired with the corresponding text that suggests the image title. Each leaf shadow and page blur was enhanced within the electronic environment to force an illusion of "shallow" space to create a completely fabricated "hyper" reality. The series dramatize the print's dual identity as illusion and substance, as a document of reality and artistic creation. Referencing the post-modern declaration that we are a culture not just of the image, but one in which the image has replaced that which it is supposed to represent (that all representations only refer to other representations), *A New Leaf* series plays with the content and context of the subject – leaf as noun: foliage, paper, folio and as verb: to grow, to develop, to turn over, to scan. It is the deeper interconnection between representation and reality that gives the image its meaning and its shape - a language of depth replaces that of the surface.

In my work I use the scanner and software applications to link media and to draw connections and parallels to photography and new media as well as painting, printmaking, illustration and the written word. When I first began working with digital processing and spoke of my work in the relatively new medium of digital imaging, I compared its use to language structures. I likened the computer to a grammatical counterpart, the conjunction. Abiding to the School House Rocks lyrics I grew up with as a child, "Conjunction Junction what's your function, linking up words and phrases and clauses", I regarded the computer as a foundation media, like paper or paint, with a distinct difference, its successful promise to be used in conjunction with other media. To reinforce this linguistic comparison I recently read another comparison in Christopher James' (2009) *The Book of Alternative Photographic Processes*, in which he states, "Sophisticated software programs, as you well know, are quite content to sit on your monitor screen forever, mocking your ignorance, until you provide the correct "noun" to go with the correct "verb" to complete the digital action." Continuing to support my theory is the *Digital Mosaics: The Aesthetics of Cyberspace*; the author Steven Holtzman (1998) claims that the computer really is "the supreme vehicle of postmodern expression." He supports this claim on the computer's ability to make copies, combinations, juxtapositions and contrasts. So in my view, the successful digital photograph harkens back to its photographic roots and uses the medium to trespass its normal conventions by simply expanding its grammar.

Issues, Controversies, Problems

As photography's primary role has been writing an image at a particular point in time and space, digital imaging breaks the rules by allowing the image-maker to manipulate not only the time and place, but space and time. Digital photography in fact becomes not based on actual events but the inner workings of the creator's imagination. The primary issue should be what is being said, not how it is made.

In Robert Hirsch's influential text *Seizing the Light: A Social History of Photography* he claims "[w]estern society's compact with the photograph as empirical catalog of the real is being appropriated" (Hirsch 2000, p. 473). "A key element of postmodern discourse can be understood in terms of photography's relinquishing its role as society's authoritative chronicler, in favor of a position that acknowledges that reality is constantly evolving in our culture" (Hirsch 2000, p. 477). As the Postmodern thinker believes reality does not exist until it is analyzed by the viewer, when contemplated from this post-modern perspective is the "Quillan Leaf" even real, or merely a Baudrillard simulacrum? It cannot be seen, only imagined, as it cannot be taken out into the light of day. Hirsch argues that "if electronic imagery is going to radically affect our consciousness and perception of reality, artists and scientists need to go beyond using computers as convenient means for mimicking visions of the past and discover their native diction" (Hirsch 2000, pp. 479-480). But what if digital simulation is used in fact to revisit the past? Not to "re-write" it or "improve" it as some fear (deleting people and events who fall out of favor), but to reinvestigate and reinterpret the collection of images interwoven into our daily existence. Photographs are not neutral containers of reality, or mirrors, because, as mentioned earlier, the photograph, digital or analog, is always dependent on its context, even if it is contained within a darkened box.

Solutions and Recommendations

Digital technology has reawakened the natural history of photography. Whether it's the contemporary Anthotypes of Carol Golemboski (2007) created by sandwiching the concentrated blueberry juice-coated positive ink-jet prints with glass for week long outdoor exposures, or the chlorophyll process of Binh Danh's Photosyhthesis Art, digitally rendered photographs printed on the surface of leaves through the natural process of photosynthesis, the addition of "digital" mechanisms to aid the photographic "process" changes very little of the medium except time (physically and metaphorically). Stephen Kurtz' (of the Critical Art Ensemble) definition of "digital" as anything that is recombinant, in which the starting elements and end results have different meanings, is not new. The same transformation, in a slightly different *language*, has been applied to the photographic arts for centuries.

FUTURE RESEARCH DIRECTIONS

A quick Google search using a term such as "digital cyanotypes" and the first results explain the process with declarative pronouncements such as, "the digicam is the best thing that's happened to photography" (Reed, 2010). As Christopher James (2009) describes in the "Digital Options" chapter of *The Book of Alternative Photographic Processes*, "It is significant that the first edition (published 2001) detailed a 26-step sequence for making CMYK ink jet separations for gum bichromate contact negatives. In this new edition I can tell you how to do the same thing in a few simple steps…changing the mode to CMYK and clicking >Channels." The ease and flexibility of digital processing allows artists like Yvette Drury Dubinsky (2006) to create *Macro-Array*, an enormous 5 by 12 feet collage of an imagined micro array where gray light intensities representing gene activity are artificially converted to color from scanned cyanotype and Van Dyke photograms. Artist John Neff (2008) writes in his artist statement, "the rich and unpredictable materiality of the cyanotype printing process gives substance to digital images, typically imagined to be disembodied and perfectly replicable." While post-modern bad boy Douglas Prince (2005) embraces digital technology in his statement "Evolution of a Creative Vision in a Digital Environment", "Whether I'm working with the camera, in the darkroom, or on the computer, I'm looking for juxtapositions, relationships and

transformations that create new perceptions, fostering an insight into the elementary nature of things…An important breakthrough for me has been the freedom to pursue new ideas outside pre-determined constructs. An early, important motivation has been a quest for a unified vision. Like the physicist searching for a unified theory, I was looking for the ability to transform everything I saw into a significant image." The formation of websites and blogs such as the Plate to Pixels Gallery (2007) whose mission is "to promote the evolution of photography from the archaic wet-plate process to the new digital format of pixels and includes everything in between" continues to support the popularity of my thesis – a rebirth of photographic history through a digital evolution.

CONCLUSION

As there are those who will cry that digital photography remains largely in the simulacrum stage of mimicry that has barely scratched the surface of its unique possibility (Lynch 2010), I believe the mistake being made here is the expectation that digital imagery must in fact be something *different*. Just as painting did not die with the advent of photography, it simply evolved to embrace abstraction and conceptualism and adhered to the formalities of the medium (referencing critic Clement Greenberg's (1971) influential suggestion in his critical essays on *Art and Culture,* that Modern Art painting was an unfolding tradition), photographers should not feel compromised or challenged by the Digital Revolution but embrace its evolution.

Photography has been described as an inherently analytic discipline that unlike the painter that builds a picture from a blank canvas, the photographer starts with the chaos of the world and simplifies the mess by giving it structure (Shore, 2007). The photographer chooses a vantage point and perspective and selects the photograph. The contact print of nature, however, by placing the thing on the paper or glass, breaks the transformative rules of photography. The four ways in which the world in front of the camera is transformed into the photograph: flatness, frame, time, and focus (Shore, 2007), are not contained within the first photographic image, the Quillan Leaf; it is missing time. Without a lens, it has been said, there is no photograph, but could it be in some cases that the biological structure, such as a leaf, becomes an everlasting lens?

Photography's pioneers Henry Fox Talbot, Louis Daguerre, and Nicéphore Niépce, each insisted that photography originated in nature and was disclosed by nature. Talbot (1844) wrote that photography depicts its images "by optical and chemical means alone ... the image is impressed by Nature's hand." Daguerre put it this way: "the Daguerreotype is not an instrument which serves to draw nature; but a chemical and physical process which gives her the power to reproduce herself." Niépce defined his accomplishment as "spontaneous reproduction through the action of light." The initial legal agreement, drawn by Niépce and Daguerre, spoke of Niépce's attempts "to fix the images which nature offers, without the assistance of a draughtsman". Each was keenly aware of the medium's relationship to nature. As the investigation of Thomas Wedgewood's signature, the single "W" continues, it may just prove that the first photographic record and the history of the medium simply evolved from a single new leaf.

REFERENCES

Associated Press. (2008). *Early "leaf" photo could fetch fortune*. Retrieved January 31, 2011, from www.cbsnews.com/stories/2008/03/28/tech/main3977071.shtml

Clark, G. (1997). *The photograph*. Oxford, UK: Oxford University Press.

Danh, B. (2006). *Chlorophyll prints*. Posted by David Pescovitz. Retrieved August 13, 2011, from http://boingboing.net/2006/10/23/binh-danhs-chlorophy.html

Danh, B. (2010). Retrieved April 25, 2011, from http://www.binhdanh.com

Dubinsky, Y. D. (2006). *YDD Studio*. Retrieved April 25, 2011, from http://www.yddstudio.com

Ewing, W. A. (1991). *Flora photographica: Masterpieces of flower photography*. London, UK: Thames & Hudson, Ltd.

Golemboski, C. (2007). *Portfolio*. Retrieved April 25, 2011, from http://www.kevinlongino.com/portfolio.cfm?a=39&p=131&t=collector

Greenberg, C. (1971). *Art and culture: Critical essays*. Boston, MA: Beacon Press.

Hirsch, R. (2000). *Seizing the light: A history of photography*. Boston, MA: McGraw-Hill Companies, Inc.

Holtzman, S. (1998). *Digital mosaics: The aesthetics of cyberspace*. Touchstone.

James, C. (2009). *The book of alternative photographic processes* (2nd ed.). Clifton Park, NY: Delmar, Cengage Learning.

Lipkin, J. (2005). *Photography reborn: Image making in the digital era*. New York, NY: Abrams.

Lynch, M. (2010). *In her own lens: A look at Aida Laleian*. Retrieved April 1, 2011, from http://www.stockyardmagazine.com/galerie/in-her-own-lens-a-look-at-aida-laleian/

Marien, M. W. (2002). *Photography: A cultural history*. Upper Saddle River, NJ: Prentice-Hall, Inc.

Mitchell, W. J. (1997). *The reconfigured eye: Visual truth in the post-photographic era*. Cambridge, MA: The MIT Press.

Neff, J. (2008). *Artist's statement*. Retrieved April 25, 2011, from http://artistregistry.artadia.org/registry/view_artist.php?aid=34

Plates to Pictures Gallery. (2007). Retrieved August 13, 2011, from (http://platestopixels.com/)

Prince, D. (2005). *Evolution of a creative vision in a digital environment*. Retrieved April 25, 2011, from http://www.douglasprince.com and http://www.douglasprince.com/statement-04-19-05.pdf

Read, J. (2010). *The digital camera, the cyanotype and grain*. Retrieved April 1, 2011, from http://www.alternativephotography.com/wp/cameras-film/the-digital-camera-the/cyanotype-and-grain

Shore, S. (2007). *The nature of photographs* (2nd ed.). London, UK: Phaidon Press Limited.

Sotheby's. (2008, April 7). *The Quillan collection of nineteenth and twentieth century photographs*. Auction catalog. New York, NY: Author.

Szarkowski, J. (1966). *The photographer's eye*. New York, NY: The Museum of Modern Art.

ADDITIONAL READING

Bajac, Q. (2002). *The invention of photography*. New York, NY: Harry N. Abrams, Inc.

Benson, R. (2008). *The printed picture*. New York, NY: The Museum of Modern Art.

Peres, M. R. (2007). *The focal encyclopedia of photography* (4th ed.). Kidlington, UK: Elsevier Focal Press.

Schaaf, L. J. (1992). *Out of the shadows: Hershel, Talbot & the invention of photography*. New Haven, CT: Yale University Press.

Talbot, W. H. F. (1844). *The pencil of nature*. London, UK: Longman, Brown, Green and Longmans.

The History of photography (an Archive Farms collection). (2011). Retrieved July 25, 2001 from http://www.photohistorytimeline.com/?page_id=52

Woolf, V. (1987). *A room of one's own*. London, UK: Grafton Books.

KEY TERMS AND DEFINITIONS

Anthotype: An image created using photosensitive material from plants invented by Sir John Herschel in 1842. An emulsion is made from any other light-sensitive plant, fruit or vegetable. A coated sheet of paper is then dried, exposed to direct full sunlight until the image is bleached out.

Anna Atkins: (1799 - 1871) An English botanist. She learned directly about the invention of photography through her correspondence with William Henry Fox Talbot and the cyanotype printing method through the astronomer and scientist Sir John Herschel.

Roland Barthes: (1915 - 1980) A French literary theorist, philosopher, critic, and semiotician. His ideas explored a diverse range of fields and he influenced the development of schools of theory including structuralism, semiotics, existentialism, social theory, Marxism, anthropology and post-structuralism.

Hippolyte Bayard: (1807 - 1887) A French photographer a pioneer in the history of photography. He invented his own process known as direct positive printing. His invention of photography actually preceded that of Daguerre, for on 24 June 1839 he presented the world's first public exhibition of photographs but postponed the publishing of his work and thus goes into the record books as being the first person to hold a photographic exhibition but not the inventor of photography.

Niels Henrik David Bohr: (1885 - 1962) A Danish physicist who made fundamental contributions to understanding atomic structure and quantum mechanics, for which he received the Nobel Prize in Physics in 1922.

Louis Jacques Mande Dauguerre: (1789 - 1851) A French Photographic pioneer, the inventor of the daguerreotype, a photograph produced on a silver-coated copper plate treated with iodine vapor. Around 1826 he, in conjunction with Nicephore Niepce, perfected the photographic process named after him. Until Niepce's death in 1833 they worked together on the photographic process. Daguerre completed the invention of the daguerreotype alone, and in 1839 it was made public and ceded to the Academy of Sciences.

Paul Delaroche: (1797 - 1856) Born Hippolyte Delaroche, was a French painter whose painstakingly realistic historical subjects made him one of the most successful academic artists of mid-19th-century France.

Gum bichromate: A 19th century photographic printing process based on the light sensitivity of dichromates. In 1839, Mungo Ponton discovered that dichromates are light sensitive. William Henry Fox Talbot later found that colloids such as gelatin and gum arabic became insoluble in water after exposure to light. Alphonse Poitevin added carbon pigment to the colloids in 1855, creating the first carbon print. In 1858, John Pouncy used colored pigment with gum arabic to create the first color images.

Heliograph: This process uses bitumen (a black, sticky carbon liquid), as a coating on glass or metal, which hardens in relation to exposure to light. When the plate is washed with oil of lavender, only the hardened image area remained.

Sir John Frederick William Herschel: (1792 - 1871) An English mathematician, astronomer, chemist, and experimental photographer/inventor. Herschel published details of his chemical and photography experiments in 1819, which, 20 years later, would prove of fundamental importance in the development of photography.

Joseph Nicéphore Niépce: (1765 - 1833) A French inventor, most noted as one of the inventors of photography and a pioneer in the field. In 1822 Niépce produced the world's first permanent photograph (known as a Heliograph). He partnered with Daguerre three years later, beginning a four-year cooperation but suddenly died in 1833 before their "partnership" was complete.

Pablo Picasso: (1881 - 1973) A Spanish expatriate painter who lived most of his life in France was a sculptor, printmaker, ceramicist, and stage designer, one of the greatest and considered one of the most influential artists of the 20th century and the creator (with Georges Braque) of Cubism.

Salt Print: The first type of paper print used in photography, and remained the most popular paper print until the introduction of the albumen in the 1850's. The salted paper technique was created by British photographer William Henry Fox Talbot. He called his process calotype printing, but today the method is more commonly known as salt prints or salted paper prints.

Gaius Plinius Secundus: (23 AD - 79 AD) Better known as *Pliny the Elder*, was a Roman philosopher and naturalist who wrote an encyclopedic work of the knowledge of his time, *Naturalis Historia*, which has become a model for all such written works.

William Henry Fox Talbot: (1800 – 1877) A British inventor and a pioneer of photography. He was the inventor of calotype process, the precursor to most photographic processes of the 19th and 20th centuries. He was also a noted photographer who made major contributions to the development of photography as an artistic medium.

Van Dyke Process: a direct-contact, iron-silver photographic printing process. The process was so named due to the similarity of the print color to that of a brown oil paint named for Flemish painter Sir Anthony Van Dyck.

Adeline Virginia Woolf: (1882 - 1941) An English author, essayist, publisher, and writer of short stories, regarded as one of the foremost modernist literary figures of the twentieth century.

Section 5
Analytical Discourse: Philosophy and Aesthetics of Nature Inspired Creations

Chapter 17

Science within the Art:
Aesthetics Based on the Fractal and Holographic Structure of Nature

Doug Craft
Doug Craft Fine Art, LLC, USA

ABSTRACT

This chapter discusses how both art and science proceed from an appreciation for and application of the natural proportions and forms associated with nature. Brief descriptions of the Golden Ratio, fractals, and the holographic metaphor are presented with illustrative examples from geometry, nature, science, and art. This material is followed by an outline of a personal theory of aesthetics based on emulation of natural form, and concepts from Thomas Aquinas and James Joyce. Application of the aesthetics are illustrated with art from a series of collage entitled, The Elements in Golden Ratio. A discussion of the four classical elements (earth, air, fire, and water) and application of the Golden Ratio forms used in the art underscores how the emulation of form in nature is central to the author's artistic process. The author, an artist and scientist, concludes with personal observations on the commonalities between art and science.

INTRODUCTION

Science and art are creative vocations, and form and structure are important aspects of both. Form will be defined here as the organizing structure, geometry, and causality we observe in nature. The scientist may use mathematical equations to describe the behavior or structure of a system where mathematics is used to emulate or model the form observed in nature, and the success of a scientific theory is judged according to the elegance and simplicity of its mathematical equations, the falsifiability or refutability of the hypothesis, and how closely the theory actually emulates nature. Form to an artist refers to the geometric arrangement of elements (color, line, shape) in a work of art that defines composition, and I would suggest that the composition of a successful work of art should emulate the forms and structures that appear in nature (Boles & Newman, 1987; Ghyka, 1946).

DOI: 10.4018/978-1-4666-0942-6.ch017

Science and mathematics have revealed that nature is sublimely organized from the subatomic to the cosmic scale (Mandelbrot, 1977; Ball, 1999; Gazalé, 1999). Many of the structural forms in nature embody the Golden Ratio, a universal constant that has been known and used by artisans, architects, and artists since antiquity (Livio, 2002; Herz-Fischler, 1987; Cook, 1979). The development of fractal mathematics and computer graphics has revealed that nature also creates forms that have a fractal structure (Mandelbrot, 1977). If we observe nature at different size scales, we often see similar fractal structural forms repeated: windblown clouds, wood grain, and sand may all exhibit herringbone patterns, and protein molecules on cellular membranes show structural branching similar to trees (Bak, 1996; Doczi, 1981). Wilbur (1982, 1992) and others have also observed that subtle structures in nature might be organized in a holographic manner, where the structural form of the part suggests the structural form of the whole. For example, the model of the atom (electrons orbiting a nucleus) is repeated at the solar system as well as the galactic scale. Metabolic and excretory functions within the cell are repeated at the organismic and societal levels.

This chapter will discuss how both art and science may benefit from an appreciation for and application of the natural proportions and forms associated with the structure of nature. Brief descriptions of the Golden Ratio, fractals, and the holographic metaphor will be presented along with examples of each from nature, science, and art. I will then outline my theory of aesthetics based on the structure of nature and illustrate the application of the theory using images from my collage series, *The Elements in Golden Ratio* (Craft, 2010a). A discussion of the Golden Ratio forms used in my art work and the classical elements (earth, air, fire, and water) will underscore how the emulation of form in nature is central to my art process. As an artist who is also a scientist, I will conclude with some personal observations of the commonalities

between art and science and how an appreciation of natural form can enhance the practice of both.

THE STRUCTURE AND FORMS OF NATURE

Some of the important structures and forms of nature that both artists and scientists see, hear, feel, and touch may be summarized by reference to the Golden Ratio, fractals, and the holographic metaphor. Form in nature is a profound and humbling subject that has been studied by many great minds since antiquity. As a student of the subject, I recommend Theodore Andrea Cook's 1914 book, *The Curves of Life* (Cook, 1979) and D'Arcy Wentworth Thompson's 1917 book, *On Growth and Form* (Thompson, 1961), as excellent introductory sources and reference material. I hope reading this chapter might encourage the reader to begin or expand upon their personal study of nature's forms by considering the work by scholars, scientists, and artists who made the observation and elucidation of nature's forms their life's work.

The Golden Ratio

Many forms in nature feature a very special mathematical constant: the Golden Ratio, or Golden Section (section referring to a cut or division). The Golden Ratio is an irrational number equal to 0.618034... (where the dots indicate that the decimals continue infinitely with no repeated number patterns), and is usually represented by the Greek letter *phi*, φ, after the sculptor Phidias, one of the architects of the Parthenon. I will begin by showing the algebraic derivation of φ, discuss some unusual mathematical properties of φ, describe Fibonacci and Lucas numbers, discuss examples of φ in simple polygons studied by the classical Greeks, and then provide examples how φ appears in nature and art.

The Extreme and Mean Ratio

Geometry has two great treasures: one is the theorem of Pythagoras; the other, the division of a line into extreme and mean ratio. The first we may compare to a measure of gold; the second we may name a precious jewel. – Johannes Kepler (1571 – 1630) (Huntley, 1970, p. 23)

The Golden Section was defined by Euclid as the division of a line segment into "extreme and mean ratio" in Book VI of his *Elements* (Herz-Fischler, 1987). To understand what this means, and to help set up an algebraic equation to solve for φ, a diagram may be constructed as seen in Figure 1.

Another way to state the extreme and mean ratio problem is, how do you section a line segment so that the ratio of the smaller to the larger sub segment is the same as the ratio of the larger sub segment to the whole segment? By assigning 1 as the length of the whole segment, φ as the length of the larger sub segment, and $(1 - \varphi)$ as the length of the smaller sub segment (Figure 1), we can set up the following ratios that must be true if φ is the Golden Section:

$$\frac{1-\varphi}{\varphi} = \frac{\varphi}{1}$$

If you recall high school algebra, we can simplify this expression of the ratios by multiplying the extremes (the upper left term, $(1 - \varphi)$, and the lower right term, 1), and the 'in between' means (the lower left term, φ, and the upper right term, φ) to get:

$$\varphi^2 = 1 - \varphi$$

This expression may be rearranged to obtain the 2nd degree polynomial equation we can use to solve for φ:

Figure 1. Diagram of a line segment of length = 1 (middle gray and black line segment) illustrating how the Golden Section may be calculated by setting up ratios that correspond to the extreme and mean ratios as defined by Euclid. (© 2010, Doug Craft. Used with permission.).

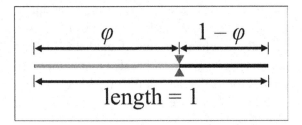

$$\varphi^2 + \varphi - 1 = 0$$

Solving this polynomial using the quadratic formula gives us two solutions, notable for the appearance of the irrational number square root of 5 ($\sqrt{5}$):

$$(-1 - \sqrt{5})\,/\,2 \text{ and } (-1 + \sqrt{5})\,/\,2$$

The first solution is −1.6180339..., which we ignore because it is a negative number with an absolute value greater than the length of our line segment. The other solution is the irrational number 0.6180339... I prefer this value for φ following Runion (1990), because I like to think of the Golden Ratio as a fractional portion of the whole associated with the number 1. It should be noted that some authors define φ as 1.618..., with its reciprocal = 0.618... (Walser, 2001; Huntley, 1970). Here I will refer to the Golden Ratio as φ (the lesser) and its reciprocal, $1/\varphi$ as the capital letter *Phi*, Φ (the greater).

Odd Mathematical Properties of φ and Φ

There are some peculiar mathematical properties associated with φ and Φ, and I will only present a few of the examples that have been described. It is one of the few numbers whose reciprocal can be calculated by adding or subtracting 1 to or from itself:

$$1 / \varphi = \varphi + 1 \text{ and } 1 / \Phi = \Phi - 1$$

Other interesting properties are associated with the integer exponent powers of φ. Table 1 shows that successive powers of Φ (denoted by the exponent *n*) are calculated by *adding* the previous 2 powers, and that powers of φ are calculated by *subtracting* the previous two powers as the following formulas suggest:

$$\Phi^n = \Phi^{(n-2)} + \Phi^{(n-1)}$$

$$\varphi^n = \varphi^{(n-2)} + \varphi^{(n-1)}.$$

Fibonacci and Lucas Numbers

The Golden Ratio may also be derived using Fibonacci and Lucas numbers. Leonardo Pisano (Leonardo of Pisa, called Fibonacci, c. 1170 – 1250), wrote the *Liber Abaci* in 1202, a revolutionary book that introduced the Hindu-Arabic decimal number system and several other mathematical topics to European culture (Hoggett, Jr., 1969; Livio, 2002). *Liber Abaci* included topics on geometry, algebra, and a discussion of a special additive number series we now call the Fibonacci series. This series was illustrated by Leonardo's observation of the way numbers of rabbits increased from a single mating pair. From this example he defined the generalized series where starting with 1 and 1 (or 0 and 1 as used in the Table 1 formulas), successive numbers are determined by adding the previous two numbers, *Fn = F(n-2) + F(n-1)*, to produce the series:

Table 1. Properties associated with powers of Φ (upper portion of table), and φ (lower portion of table). Powers of Φ and φ may be calculated based on addition or subtraction of lower powers, or by use of Fibonacci number formulas.

$\Phi = 1.61803398...$					
Exponent	*Calculated Value*	*Additive Exponent Formula*	*Additive Exponent Value*	*Fibonacci Formula* $\Phi^n = F_{n-1} + (F_n \times \Phi)$	*Fibonacci Formula Value*
Φ^0	1	$\Phi^{-2} + \Phi^{-1}$	1		
Φ^1	1.61803...	$\Phi^{-1} + \Phi^0$	1.61803...	$0 + 1\Phi$	1.61803...
Φ^2	2.61803...	$\Phi^0 + \Phi^1$	2.61803...	$1 + 1\Phi$	2.61803...
Φ^3	4.23606...	$\Phi^1 + \Phi^2$	4.23606...	$1 + 2\Phi$	4.23606...
Φ^4	6.85410...	$\Phi^2 + \Phi^3$	6.85410...	$2 + 3\Phi$	6.85410...
Φ^5	11.0901...	$\Phi^3 + \Phi^4$	11.0901...	$3 + 5\Phi$	11.0901...
$\varphi = 0.61803398...$					
Exponent	*Calculated Value*	*Subtractive Exponent Formula*	*Subtractive Exponent Value*	*Fibonacci Formula* $\varphi n = 1 \div (F_n + (F_{n+1} \times \varphi^{-1}))$	*Fibonacci Formula Value*
φ^0	1	$\varphi^{-2} - \varphi^{-1}$	1		
φ^1	0.618033...	$\varphi^{-1} - \varphi^0$	0.618033...	$1/(0 + 1\varphi^{-1})$	0.618033...
φ^2	0.381966...	$\varphi^0 - \varphi^1$	0.381966...	$1/(1 + 1\varphi^{-1})$	0.381966...
φ^3	0.236067...	$\varphi^1 - \varphi^2$	0.236067...	$1/(1 + 2\varphi^{-1})$	0.236067...
φ^4	0.145898...	$\varphi^2 - \varphi^3$	0.145898...	$1/(2 + 3\varphi^{-1})$	0.145898...
φ^5	0.0901699...	$\varphi^3 - \varphi^4$	0.0901699...	$1/(3 + 5\varphi^{-1})$	0.0901699...

0, 1, 1, 2, 3, 5, 8, 13, 21, 34, 55, 89, 144, 233, 377, 610, 987, ...

Dividing adjacent numbers in the Fibonacci series can calculate an approximation of the Golden Ratio. With greater Fibonacci numbers, the ratios of adjacent numbers (for example 21 ÷ 34 = 0.6176... and 89 ÷ 144 = 0.6180...) begin to converge on the irrational value of φ. After the 17th Fibonacci number, φ is approximated to 6 decimal places (1,597 ÷ 2,584 = 0.618034). Higher Fibonacci number ratios yield changes in estimates of φ only in the 7th decimal place and beyond. Curiously, each successive paired ratio alternates between values that are slightly greater than φ and slightly less than φ, for example: 5 ÷ 8 = 0.625 (> φ), 8 ÷ 13 = 0.6153...(< φ), and 13 ÷ 21 = 0.6190... (> φ).

Table 1 shows that the powers of Φ and φ can also be expressed using formulas based on the Fibonacci series. The general formulas for calculating powers greater than 1 of Φ and φ are as follows: where Fn represents the Fibonacci number with sequence number, n, and I define $F_1 = 0$ in the Fibonacci series,

$$\Phi^n = F_{n-1} + (F_n \times \Phi)$$

$$\varphi^n = 1 \div (F_n + (F_{n+1} \times \varphi^{-1}))$$

Another additive number series that is observed in nature, but less frequently, is the *Lucas Series*. This series also calculates successive numbers in the series by adding the previous 2 numbers, but begins with 2 and 1:

2, 1, 3, 4, 7, 11, 18, 29, 47, 76, 123, 199, 322, 521, 843, ...

The ratios of adjacent Lucas numbers also converge on φ, but not as quickly as the Fibonacci series. In fact, ratios of adjacent numbers in *all* similar additive number sequences exhibit the property of convergence to φ (Livio, 2002; Olsen, 2006).

Fibonacci numbers appear frequently in living and growing things and are the way that nature embodies and approximates φ. This occurs because as things grow, they usually grow on top of a previous structure, so that the new growth is "added to" the existing structure (e.g., new chambers in mollusk shells or new offspring added to the existing population). Doczi (1981) documents many examples of how Fibonacci and Lucas numbers appear in vegetative life.

Many plants exhibit Fibonacci numbers in phyllotaxis (from the Greek *phullon*, leaf + *taxis*, arrangement). In the early 19th Century Karl Friedric Schimper observed Fibonacci numbers and common divergence angles in phyllotaxis, and the Bravais brothers noted an optimum divergence angle for some plant species of 137.5°. Curiously, this angle is equal to 360°/Φ2 (Livio, 2002). Adjacent bones in your fingers and the positions of many features on the human body are also approximately scaled according to φ as Fibonacci number ratios. Fibonacci numbers are also observed in plant and crystal branching, and in spiral structures like the arrangement of rows of bracts on pinecones, petals on an artichoke, and scales on a pineapple (Doczi, 1981; Ghyka, 1946; Thompson, 1961; Cook, 1979).

The Golden Rectangle

The Golden Rectangle (GR) is a rectangle whose height = 1 and length = 1 + φ (aspect ratio = 1: 1.618...) and is one of the basic Golden polygons. It is featured in the composition of many art works and is often used by architects and designers of industrial goods (Elam, 2001; Droste, 1998). It is also a polygon commonly associated with animal and plant life forms (Doczi, 1981).

An interesting property of the Golden Rectangle (GR) may be seen in Figure 2 where a GR is subdivided into smaller φ-proportional squares and GRs. The square was called a *gnomon* by

Figure 2. A GR subdivided by φ-proportioned squares suggests a logarithmic spiral that converges on the Eye of God. The Eye of God is also defined by the intersection of the diagonal of the initial GR_0 and the diagonal of the first subordinate GR_1 (diagonals are light gray). (© 2010, Doug Craft. Used with permission.).

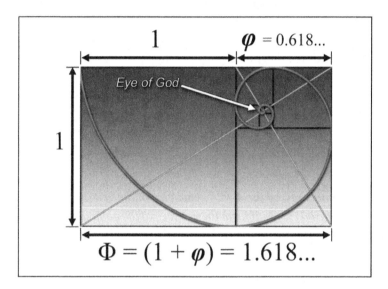

Thompson (1961), defined as a polygon that sections a larger polygon to produce another smaller proportional polygon. The square gnomon on the left sections the long side at 1 and leaves a φ-proportioned smaller vertical GR_1 that is also rotated 90°, sometimes called the reciprocal of the original GR_0. The GR is the only rectangle with the square as its gnomon (Ghyka, 1946; Runion, 1990; Hambidge, 1967).

This proportional sectioning by the square gnomons can be continued producing smaller and smaller squares and GRs that converge on a point mathematician Clifford A. Pickover called the *Eye of God* (Livio, 2002). The Eye of God is explicitly defined by the intersection of the diagonal of GR_0 and the diagonal of the reciprocal GR_1 created by sectioning with the 1 x 1 square. The intersection of these diagonals also forms a right (90°) angle. Figure 2 suggests that the 'coiling' square gnomons implied by the proportional subdivision of the GR approximates a logarithmic spiral that converges on the Eye of God. Thus the GR implies a nonlinear curved spiral often associated with living growth (Gazalé, 1999; Hambidge, 1967; Dozci, 1981; Cook, 1979).

Symmetry of the Golden Rectangle and the √5

There are further curious properties of GRs that may be observed by investigating the polygons implied within a GR by the diagonals arising from the proportional sectioning seen in Figure 2. This use of proportional subdivisions with squares and GR diagonals was called harmonic analysis by Ghyka (1946). We should not be surprised that the √5 that appeared in the quadratic formula solutions for φ would also appear in the internal geometry implied by the diagonals in a GR.

The division of the GR using proportional squares can proceed in 4 different directions (left up, left down, and right up, right down) and thus shows a 4-fold symmetry that implies 4 possible Eyes of God within the GR. Figure 3 shows how the harmonic analysis of a GR proceeds using diagonals and squares revealing the geometric presence of the √5. The smaller 5 stepwise GRs (Figures *3a–3e,* top) show intersecting diagonals for GR_0 (*3a*), the division of GR_0 into 2 smaller reciprocal GRs with overlapping squares (*3b*), and the addition of diagonals for the 2 reciprocal GR_s (*3c*). The 4 Eyes of God can be seen in Figure *3d* at the intersections of the diagonals of GR_0 and the diagonals of the 2 subordinate GRs. Horizontal and vertical lines that intersect the 4 Eyes of God are seen in Figure *3e*, and these lines produce some interesting rectangles within GR_0 seen in the larger GR Figures *3f* and *3g*.

The upper larger GR in Figure *3f* shows a shaded central inner $GR_{\sqrt{5}}$ with vertices at the Eyes of God, and both horizontal and vertical sides in √5 ratio (1: 2.236...) to the *sides* of the original GR_0. To either side of the central $GR_{\sqrt{5}}$ are two lighter gray vertical rectangles with aspect ratio of 1: √5. These are called √5 rectangles and two additional larger √5 rectangles implied by horizontal lines intersecting the Eyes of God may be seen in Figure *3g* (only the lower √5 rectangle is shaded gray). The √5 rectangle can be thought of as overlapping GRs that share a central square.

Figure 3. Intersecting diagonals reveal the 4-fold symmetry of the GR (smaller GRs a through e, at top) and the presence of 4 Eyes of God (☼) that form the vertices of the central $GR_{\sqrt{5}}$ (darker gray rectangle in f.). The central $GR_{\sqrt{5}}$ (in f.) sections GR_0 to form 2 vertical lighter gray rectangles with aspect ratio of 1: √5. A larger √5 rectangle is also seen in the lower GR (g.). (© 2010, Doug Craft. Used with permission).

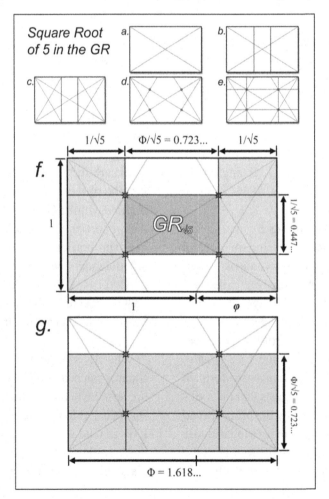

The Regular Pentagon and the Golden Triangle

Another important Golden polygon considered sacred by the Pythagoreans is the regular, or equilateral pentagon, and the regular pentangle that is formed by the intersection of the diagonals within the pentagon. These polygons are simply full of the Golden Ratio (Lawlor, 1982; Olsen, 2006). The Pythagoreans noted the Golden Section in the regular pentagram but did not mathematically explore the irrational mysteries of φ because it could not be expressed as a simple ratio of sacred whole numbers (Lawlor, 1982).

Harmonic analysis of this polygon gives us another Golden Polygon, the acute Golden Triangle (GT) and its gnomon the obtuse GT. Note that a multiplicity of acute GTs (a larger one is shaded in Figure 4), an isosceles triangle with base:side length ratio of 1: Φ, base angles of 72°, and an acute angle of 36°, are created by the diagonals within the regular pentagon. The pentagon diagonals create 5 large acute GTs with base = Φ and sides = Φ^2, 10 acute GTs with base = 1 and sides = Φ that overlap the base sides of the larger GTs, and 5 acute GTs associated with the points of the pentagram with base = φ and sides = 1.

The acute GT can also be proportionally divided like the GR, and this gnomonic division may also be seen within the intersecting diagonals of Figure 4. The gnomon here is the obtuse GT, an isosceles triangle with base:side length ratio of Φ: 1, base angles = 36° and obtuse angle = 108°. This division of the acute GT also produces a rotation of the smaller acute GTs and can be used to approximate the logarithmic spiral.

Both Φ and φ can be used to express the segment lengths *and* the trigonometric functions associated

Figure 4. Diagram of the regular pentagon and its diagonals show the Golden Triangle (shaded). This polygon contains many φ-based ratios and was a favorite of the Pythagoreans. (© 2010, Doug Craft. Used with permission.).

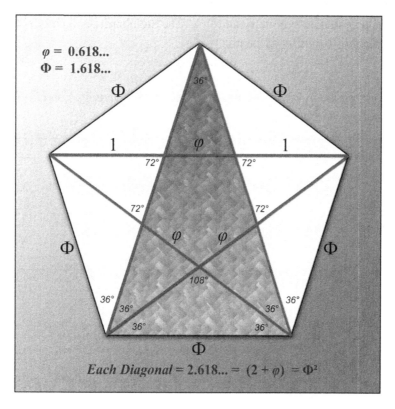

with the angles that appear in the regular pentagon and the diagonal pentagram seen in Figure 4. Table 2 summarizes trigonometric functions for some of the Golden Pentagon angles θ (Olsen, 2006) expressed as functions of φ and Φ.

The Golden Ratio in Nature

Besides appearing often in animals and plants, φ and its Fibonacci number approximations also appear in many unexpected places elsewhere in nature. Martineau (2001) provides many examples of Fibonacci and Φ relationships between the orbits and timing of planetary conjunctions and the synodic cycles of the planets with the sun in our solar system. Interestingly, the motions of Venus (orbital period = 224.7 earth days) as seen in the sky from earth, trace out a perfect pentagon around the sun over an 8-year synodic cycle. During this same synodic cycle, Venus has made 13 orbits (8 and 13 are Fibonacci numbers). Similar Φ and Fibonacci ratios may be observed between the synodic patterns between the Earth, Jupiter, and Saturn.

Topologists have long studied symmetry and plane filling with polygons (tiling), and Islamic artists are well known for their complex tiling using Golden geometric forms (Critchlow, 1999). The regular pentagon cannot be tiled to perfectly fill the space on a plane, so it was assumed for many years that this was a property of all polygons with 5-fold symmetry. However, in 1974, astrophysicist Roger Penrose discovered a plane-filling tiling of polygons that was based on the acute and obtuse GTs and thus contained many Φ traits. These polygons, called *kites* and *darts*, have 5-fold symmetry and can be combined to fill a plane using *non-periodic* tiling. This is a more complex plane filling, called long-range order, compared to the regular repeatability of periodic tiling with squares or hexagons (Gardner, 1989).

Material scientists working with aluminum alloys in the 1980s unexpectedly found that the alloy crystals showed long-range order and 5-fold symmetry, which they called quasi-crystals. During the 1990s, Steinhardt and Jeong applied a physical model of quasi-crystals that used a form of Penrose tiling with decagons embodying Φ and found that this mode of crystal packing provided greater stability (lower energy and higher density). The Steinhardt-Jeong model was later confirmed

Table 2. Trigonometric functions for angles present in the regular pentagon and its diagonals expressed as a function of Φ and φ (after Olsen, 2006).

Angle θ	$\sin\theta$	$\cos\theta$
18°	$\dfrac{\sqrt{1-\phi}}{2}$	$\dfrac{\sqrt{2+\Phi}}{2}$
36°	$\dfrac{\sqrt{2-\phi}}{2}$	$\dfrac{\sqrt{1+\Phi}}{2}$
54°	$\dfrac{\sqrt{1+\Phi}}{2}$	$\dfrac{\sqrt{2-\phi}}{2}$
72°	$\dfrac{\sqrt{2+\Phi}}{2}$	$\dfrac{\sqrt{1-\phi}}{2}$

for some alloys using X-ray and electron diffraction (Livio, 2002).

At the small extreme of the size scale, El Naschie (1994) suggested that the subatomic particles arising out of the quantum vacuum field could be modeled using a geometry based on a fractal Cantor set with Φ scaling. While this theory has not been embraced by most physicists, the ubiquity of Φ in nature suggests that Φ may be lurking somewhere in the geometry and organization of the ultra-small quantum universe, as well as other natural processes not yet investigated by science.

The Golden Ratio in Art

Because of its observed universality in nature, the Golden Ratio has been long recognized by shamans, priests, and philosophers, and used as a formal element by architects, artists and designers at least since Egyptian civilization and perhaps earlier (Livio, 2002; Gazalé, 1999; Boles & Newman, 1987). Lawlor (1982) noted pentagonal symmetries based on Φ, the $\sqrt{2}$, and $\sqrt{5}$ in the Egyptian *Osirion* temple, and the Great Pyramid's sides are composed of a diagonally bisected GR rearranged to form a isosceles triangle. Classical Greek architecture, visual art, and household goods commonly used Golden Ratio forms like the GR (aspect ratio 1: 1.618...) and the $\sqrt{5}$ rectangle (aspect ratio 1: 2.236...) (Ghyka, 1946; Doczi, 1981; Elam, 2001). The layout of Beijing's Forbidden City uses three adjacent GRs and each of these spaces were further divided into squares and other GRs (Olsen, 2006).

During the Renaissance, the influence of the Golden Ratio on artists began in earnest after the monk Luca Pacioli published his influential book in 1509 about the Golden Ratio, *Divina Proportione*. This book was illustrated by Leonardo Da Vinci, and led to the widespread study of proportions by artists and architects based on Pythagorean musical harmonies and the Golden

Ratio. The Golden Rectangle and other proportional rectangles were widely utilized as formal elements by artists during the Renaissance and more recently by Seurat (Smith, 1997), Le Corbusier, and others (Ghyka, 1946; Elam, 2001). The underlying aesthetic implied by these artists is that beauty in art depends on emulation and congruence with natural laws of form as suggested by the Golden Ratio.

Fractals

The term fractal was coined by Benoit Mandelbrot and refers to a geometric figure that is composed of repeating identical or quasi-identical geometric units that look the same (that is, they are self similar) no matter how much the figure is enlarged or reduced. A mathematical fractal is created when an equation or geometric transformation undergoes iteration to smaller scales – a form of mathematical feedback called recursion (Barnsley & Rising, 1993).

Self Similarity

Self similarity is a basic property of fractals that may be visualized in Figure 5. At the top of Figure 5 are the first three recursive geometric iterations of a simple fractal, the Koch Snowflake, that is constructed from an equilateral triangle (the self similar unit). Each iteration involves adding a new equilateral triangle in the middle third of each side and removing the base of the new triangle. Each iteration increases the complexity and length of the perimeter of the Koch Snowflake. In the middle of Figure 5 (a and b) are two views of the mathematically generated Mandelbrot set fractal, which features quasi-self similarity. I generated these images using the Ultra Fractal program, version 5 (Slijkerman, 2010). At the bottom of Figure 5 are two microphotos of rock thin sections I shot using a polarizing microscope (c and d) that show examples of natural fractal

Figure 5. Examples of fractals. At the top are the first 4 iterations of the Koch Snowflake, a simple fractal created using recursion of a simple geometric rule. Below are two views of the quasi-self similar Mandelbrot set fractal (a and b) showing the entire set (a) and a zoomed image (b). At the bottom are microphotos of rock thin sections by the author (c and d). (© 2010, Doug Craft. Used with permission).

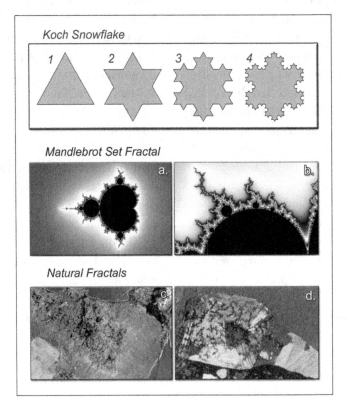

structures. Interestingly, the image in Figure 5c is reminiscent of images of the earth taken from orbiting satellites.

Fractal Dimension

An additional characteristic of fractals is a property called fractal dimension (Lauwerier, 1991; Mandelbrot, 1977), denoted as D. While Euclid tells us that a point has zero dimension, a line has one dimension, a plane has two dimensions, and that we live in a three-dimensional world, dimension for fractals is not a simple concept. From a topological perspective, '2-dimensional' fractals (that can rendered on a sheet of paper)

occupy an intermediate dimension between a line (one dimension) and a plane (two dimensions), and hence have a non integer or fractional dimension, D, between 1 and 2. In Figure 5, the Koch Snowflake has $D = 1.26$ (Mandelbrot, 1977) and the Mandelbrot set fractal (images a and b) has $D = 1.64$ (Elenbogen & Kaeding, 1989). Coastlines and river networks show a fractal dimension $D = 1.2$ which is similar to the Koch Snowflake (Mandelbrot, 1977). Three-dimensional fractals, such as broccoli florets or a cauliflower, have a fractal dimension between 2 and 3. This in-between dimensionality is one of the characteristics that differentiate fractal geometry from traditional plane and solid geometry.

Fractal Noise

Another more subtle way that fractal structures appear in nature is through random processes such as noise in signals, and what we commonly call noise. Audible noise is a complex sound composed of many frequencies that is not perceived as a discrete pitch or note as in music. For example, white noise is sound that contains a random distribution or spectrum of all audible frequencies and amplitudes. No single pitch (frequency) or loudness level (amplitude) appears more often than any other. Natural noises, on the other hand, feature a frequency distribution (or spectrum) with a bias that favors certain pitches and loudness levels (Bak et. al., 1987).

The bias observed in natural noise is called $1/f$ or fractal noise, and sometimes also called pink noise. The reason why natural noise and noise in signals measured over time from complex natural and man-made systems show $1/f$ spectra remains a mystery of physics (Bak, 1996). Yet $1/f$ noise is observed in all electronics devices and circuits (from ceramic capacitors and vacuum tubes to large scale integrated circuits), the movements of automobiles in traffic, and changes in the annual Nile River flood stages (Voss, 1988; Mandelbrot, 1998). Voss and Clark (1975) observed $1/f$ noise in music and speech, noting that most people do not hear tones generated randomly as 'musical.' Widely different types of traditional and classical music from many cultures and historical eras show a similar $1/f$ fractal noise structure.

Fractals in Nature

Almost everywhere the scientist or artist looks in nature, fractal forms dominate. Mandelbrot was interested in the self similarity of fractals because this iterative geometry seemed to emulate the complex forms he observed in nature, and the mathematics of fractal recursion is the basis of many computerized special effects that mimic natural landscapes now used in cinema (Voss,

1988). Many of the simple and complex structural features in nature are fractal, or approximately fractal: crystals, glycoproteins on cell surfaces, artichokes, wetting and drying cracks in soil and rock, rock formations, coastlines, clouds, landscapes, and the melodic and time domain structure of music and language (Peitgen & Saupe, 1988; Briggs, 1992).

Nature is complex and random processes are often adjacent to and influencing other processes, introducing a blurring or approximation of the fractal forms that is called statistical self similarity (Mandelbrot, 1977). An example of a random process common in nature is the dissipative influence of entropy which constantly wears and erodes emergent natural structures at all size scales in the universe. This may be seen in the complex abstract shapes of coastlines and rocks, and in the Figure 5 microphotos (bottom images 5c and 5d). Note the dark fractal crack features on the surface of the rock crystal in Figure 5d. These cracks approximate the Julia set dendrite fractal, a fractal closely related to the Mandelbrot set.

Abstract Art and Fractals

Figurative and representational art depict objects and living things, and therefore naturally embody the fractal elements of landscapes and living things. However, the subtle fractal structure in nature also gives us an insight into abstract art and the widely held idea that abstraction is somehow *not* related to nature or representation.

Before the industrial revolution, art served as the medium for accurately rendering representational images of reality such as portraits, great events, landscapes, and still lifes. The development of photography through the 19th Century, however, provided a new technological means to render and document life, and this trend gradually allowed painters and sculptors to explore the creation of non-representational or abstract art. With photography providing liberation from the task of representation, many Modernist artists sought to create a 'pure art' free of visual representation that suggested a rejection of the imitation of nature (Klee, 1966). A progression of decreasing figurative content and increasing abstraction in art can be seen from early 20th Century Post Impressionism to Cubism, to Dada and Surrealism, culminating in the mid 20th Century 'pure' abstract images of Jackson Pollock, Franz Kline, Helen Frankenthaler, Robert Motherwell, and Mark Rothko.

The discovery and study of fractals, however, have cast a new light on abstraction in art. Jackson Pollock's famous drip paintings, which have been variously described as chaotic, random, and not art, were analyzed by Taylor and others for fractal properties (Taylor et al., 1999; Taylor, 2002). Taylor mathematically analyzed several of Pollock's drip paintings and found that these art works embodied fractal dimension and had an inherent structure associated with nature. Apparently, despite a non-intentional or random drip painting technique, the patterns created though Pollock's improvisational method embodied a fractal structure. It should not be surprising that humans, being creatures of nature with brains evolved to recognize natural fractal patterns, would also possess an innate ability to create fractal patterns.

I have noted while taking microphotographs that many microscopic images of rock thin sections and chemical crystals have a notable abstract quality, and the same kind of abstract/fractal quality can be seen in satellite images from space, and also at the macro- and landscape-size scales. Note again how the microphoto of a rock thin section in figure 5c resembles Landsat photos from space of coastlines and mountain ranges. The implication is that what is thought of as being "abstract" may really be representational of the deeper and subtle fractal structure of nature, and that perhaps the distinction between representation of nature and abstraction is sometimes a false dichotomy.

The Holographic Metaphor

The holographic metaphor suggests that nature is organized similarly to the way a laser hologram behaves, where the full dimensional structure and form of an object is encoded throughout the hologram's complex interference pattern at the very small scale: that the whole is embodied in the part. By analogy, we could surmise that nature is structured holographically such that small forms and systems in the universe emulate the structural form of the whole. This is similar to the concept of self similarity in fractals, but is not applied with the same kind of mathematical rigor.

The idea that the part embodies the whole and the whole is present within the part is not new. It has been associated with many different philosophical and mystical religious traditions (Suzuki, 1973; Campbell, 1991a). Carl Jung's concept of the collective unconscious is a psychoanalytic version of the idea.

The Laser Hologram

The term "holographic" refers to the photographic laser hologram. To create a hologram, a laser beam, a focused and coherent light of a single wavelength, is split using a partially transparent mirror. The reflected beam is directed to illuminate an object and the laser light that bounces off the object is recombined with the original non-reflected beam. This recombination creates a complex *interference pattern* that is then captured on a photographic plate. When the photographic plate is developed, the original object is not visible and we instead see the interference pattern: a complex matrix of finely detailed whorls and apparent smudges that were created when laser light waves bouncing off the object at many different angles (and with varying reflectances) interacted with the non-reflected laser light waves (Kock, 1981).

An analogy for the way the holographic interference pattern appears could be the collection of waves generated on a pond when different sized raindrops hit the surface during a shower. As the circular water waves propagate outward from each drop's impact, the waves collide with each other, sometimes in a constructive (additive) way creating larger waves, and sometimes in a destructive (subtractive) way creating smaller waves or even flat surfaces. The rippled surface of a pond during rain represents a complex interference pattern, and a photograph of such a pond from above approximates the way a hologram plate might look.

The strangeness of holography begins when the laser light is beamed back through the interference pattern on the photographic plate. Diffraction of the laser light by the interference pattern re-creates a projected image of the original object that appears some distance beyond the plate, not as a flat 2-dimensional object like a photograph, but as a complete 3-dimensional representation. You can walk around the projected hologram and the details of the object are visible much like the original object would have been seen. So, the interference pattern on the flat photographic plate contains *all* the information (shape as viewed from different angles, reflectance properties, dimensionality) associated with the object originally under laser illumination.

From Optical Phenomenon to Metaphor

The hologram becomes the basis for a metaphor of universal structure because of a unique property of the hologram interference pattern. If the photographic plate is cut into four equal sections and the laser is again beamed though any one of the plate quarters, the original object once again appears, complete, in the projected hologram. The sectioning process could be repeated into 16th- or 64th-sized sections of the plate and the result would be the same. In actual practice, the resolution of the projected hologram will become fuzzier as the sections become smaller and smaller,

but even the smaller sections of the hologram still contain most of the information (shape, texture, etc.) needed to recognize the object.

This suggests that the dimensional and reflectance information about the complete object is imbedded throughout the interference pattern *practically down to the atomic scale*! Each minute part contains the information about the whole. This is the basis for the analogy with the structure of the universe, wherein, for example the structure of the galaxy is implied in the atom.

Metaphor vs. Theory

The idea of the universe as a giant hologram (or holographic system) is a powerful integrative concept that helps us understand nature and form. It remains a metaphor because it is not yet a fully falsifiable or predictive hypothesis in the scientific sense. However, since the development of holography in 1947 by physicist Dennis Gabor (who later won the 1971 Nobel Prize for the discovery) there has been notable scientific interest in the subject (Talbot, 1991; Wilbur, 1982). Three scientists who have proposed holographic models are the neuroscientist Karl Pribram (b. 1919), physicist David Bohm (1917 – 1992), and biologist Rupert Sheldrake (b. 1942).

Karl Pribram observed hologram-like behavior during his studies of memory and cognition. Pribram observed that memories were not localized in specific small regions of the brain, then called *engrams*, but were instead distributed over the 3-dimensional peripheral structure of the brain. He suggested that information was being encoded throughout the brain in a quantum-scale hologram. Pribram called this model *holonomic brain theory*, and speculated that our sensory organs and their associated brain structures were actually manifesting what we see, feel, and hear as reality by creating a three-dimensional representation from an external universal hologram (Pribram, 1991).

Observing that many subatomic particles have very short life spans, manifesting measureable properties and then disappearing back into the quantum vacuum field, David Bohm suggested that this field, which he called the *implicate order*, was a dynamic hologram he called the *holomovement* (Bohm, 1995; Wilbur, 1982). All matter and phenomena we observe in our 3-dimensional reality, which he called the *explicate order*, arise from the fluctuating energy field of the universal and nonlocal implicate order holomovement. Bohm suggested that the holomovement is the fundamental ground of matter and causality, rather than the collection of subatomic particles, atoms, and molecules that are proposed to make up what we perceive as solid matter and dimensionality. He also noted that the idea is philosophical, but is certainly a reasonable deduction based on the nonlocal behavior of nature observed at the quantum level (Wilbur, 1985).

Biologist Rupert Sheldrake has also proposed the holographic metaphor in a tangential manner. Sheldrake posits nonlocal organizing fields that govern forms and behaviors in nature called *morphic fields*. Nonlocality suggests that the fields communicate instantaneously across distances and likely operate at the quantum scale. These hierarchically nested fields are an underlying causal structure associated with organisms, postulated to coordinate the shape and behavior of the individual, the group, and the species (Sheldrake, 1981). For example, there is a morphic field associated with an individual bird, a related field associated with the local flock, and another field for the entire species. Information between these nested fields is exchanged and communicated by what Sheldrake calls *morphic resonance*, thus implying a wave structure to the fields.

Sheldrake suggested that morphic fields are formed and reinforced by repetition that he calls habits of nature (Sheldrake, 1988). According to his theory, the difficulty in crystallizing newly synthesized organic compounds arises because of the variety of possible stable crystal forms with similar stable (degenerate) energy states. Sheldrake notes that after initial crystallization, other chemists find that the compound crystallizes much more quickly and adopts a single stable form. Plant hybrids also go though an exploratory phase where different leaf shapes and phyllotaxis initially appear, but within several generations, the hybrid adopts a leaf pattern that becomes dominant (Sheldrake, 1988). To date, the hypothesis of morphic fields has been tested experimentally with ambiguous results.

Nested Structures

The holographic metaphor suggests that structural organizing forms and processes of the universe repeat themselves in a nested hierarchical pattern. Structures at higher (or more complex) levels contain structural elements and patterns associated with simpler systems. These more complex structures are themselves part of larger scale structures. Ken Wilbur calls these nested and similar organizational structures *holons* (Wilbur, 1982, 1992) after Sheldrake (1981). Examples of nested holons are:

cell → organism → family → tribe → society

quantum particles → atom → matter → solar system → galaxy → meta galaxy

The solar system shows structural similarities to the atom, which is also suggested in the galactic organizing structure. An organism repeats the functions of individual cells (metabolism, catabolism, reproduction), which are also repeated at the social level of organization.

Cohan and Cole (2002) suggested that hurricane Hugo in 1989 caused increased marriages, divorces, and childbirths in disaster areas in South Carolina compared to areas not affected by the hurricane. While these decisions may be a collective result of people individually reassessing their life plans in light of a tragedy, perhaps there is also a morphic field that is also causing the country or region to respond to disaster much like an organism responding to an injury or a cell to an invading virus. Similarly, one might think of empires re-enacting feeding by "devouring" and "absorbing" other nations and cultures. The intermarriage following conquest might be considered a form of genetic assimilation, or "digestion." These examples are suggestive of the nested holons associated with the holographic metaphor.

Other Holographic Correspondences

I think that the holographic metaphor can also be observed when similar mathematical equations or organizing principals can be applied to different phenomena at different size scales. I call this a holographic correspondence. For example, diffusion equations may be applied to model chemical transport processes that occur at cell membranes, the mixing and dilution of pollutants in a body of water, or the dissemination of ideas in a population (Banks, 2010). The quantum field equations of high energy physics (the Standard Model) can also be applied to condensed matter physics (solids and liquids) (Marder, 2010). Periodic behavior observed with the atomic elements (as seen in the Periodic Table of the Elements) can also be seen among subatomic particles like quarks, leptons, and bosons (Gell-Mann & Ne'eman, 2000). Logistic equations (growth curves) can be used to describe the growth of individuals, populations of individuals, and processes such as the expansion of technology and resource depletion (Modis, 1992).

Consider the vibration of strings and musical intervals, which were studied by the Pythagoreans, and the correspondence with electrons in an atom. A vibrating string will have a fundamental pitch associated with the entire string moving back and forth in one motion. But the string will also vibrate in a more complex manner, with waves and nodes associated with integer fraction divisions of the string length (one-half, one-third, one-fourth, etc.). These integer division vibrational modes create higher harmonic frequencies that are not as loud as the fundamental pitch, but contribute to how

the string sounds – the timbre. The electrons in an atom also have a "harmonic" structure with discrete levels associated with the energies of the electrons in orbitals surrounding the nucleus, usually electromagnetic energies in the visible and ultraviolet frequencies that determine the physical and chemical properties of the atom. Erwin Schrödinger used the analogy of a vibrating string to help develop the wave equation for describing the electron in the hydrogen atom. This is the basis for the theory of quantum mechanics, that the electron behaves in some ways like a vibrating string on a guitar.

Theory as Metaphor

The holographic theories advanced by Pribram, Bohm, and Sheldrake are not yet widely accepted by neuroscientists, physicists, or biologists as the current scientific paradigm. After all, many physicists note that quantum mechanics and general relativity do a good job of predicting the results of experiments and observed data. Yet, the active search for a unified field theory able to join these separate views of reality suggests that scientists are also seeking a new level of causation and its underlying mathematics that will imply universality and wholeness. Perhaps unification in physics will be found in the mathematics of a model that refers to the holographic metaphor. My fantasy is that the new unified field theory will include the Golden Ratio and some kind of fractal scaling.

AESTHETICS BASED ON THE STRUCTURE OF NATURE

Aesthetics may be defined as the philosophy of art creation and art appreciation. To an artist, aesthetics is usually a set of principles that defines what art is (or should be), the purpose of art, the definition of and attributes associated with form, beauty, creativity and inspiration, and the role the of the artist in society. Theories of art are not subject to validation or falsification in the manner associated with scientific theories, yet philosophy applies its own criteria of logic, elegance, and internal consistency. A theory of aesthetics is important because it establishes standards and goals for artists, guidelines for assessing art work by the viewing public, and provides for a deeper appreciation of the mystery associated with human creativity. Edward Tufte also suggests that scientists could benefit from aesthetics through the application of form, composition, and elegance when they create data visualizations (Tufte, 1983, 1990, 1997).

Personal Aesthetics

My personal aesthetic theory, which I have developed using the ideas of many others, includes the following elements and goals:

1. The higher purpose of art is spiritual and belongs to the domain of consciousness and the universal mystery of life. With proper intention, the creation of art can function as a spiritual practice.
2. The higher calling of the artist is to create *proper art*, as defined by James Joyce in *A Portrait of the Artist as a Young Man* (Joyce, 2010). By creating proper art, an artist serves culture by revealing beauty and harmony through his or her art.
3. Form and composition are the fundamental elements of a work of art, and form in art should emulate the forms, proportions, and structures we observe in nature. Because of resonance or harmony, a work of art with properly executed form is able to embody and transmit aesthetic ideas to the viewer.
4. The creation of proper art is enhanced if the skilled and experienced artist works in a non-personal or meditative state of mind and allows for improvisation.

The Spiritual in Art

Science may account for many examples of causality (the 'how') and deepen our appreciation of nature's forms, but only human consciousness can contemplate the meaning (the 'why') of the universe we experience. I define as spiritual those issues associated with consciousness, meaning, mystery, and creativity. I also refer to spiritual as being contemplative rather than religious, and this is what I mean by the term "the spiritual in art."

An artist or scientist who has experienced the sensation of inspiration – the 'eureka moment' – during his or her work likely suspects that creativity is often inexplicable and not a product of intellectual reason or planning. In fact, creative insight often happens in spite of the intellect and at times when the mind is unoccupied with the problem at hand. The origin of creativity is unknown, hence mysterious, and thus I would consider it a part of the spiritual domain.

There is another context where a creative vocation may be associated with the spiritual, and that is when a person intentionally uses the activity as a personal *spiritual practice*. A spiritual practice can be defined as a set of activities a person follows regularly to develop wisdom or relationship with the divine, such as a yoga discipline. The Hindus developed a variety of yoga practices to account for the different spiritual inclinations of people. Bakhti Yoga is a devotional approach that relies on chanting the name of an avatar (an incarnation of God) such as Krishna. Raja Yoga is a practice based on meditation and experiencing *samadhi*, the enlightenment experience associated with the union of the personal soul (*Atman*) and the universal soul (*Brahman*). Karma Yoga is the intentional use of work or the unselfish performance of duty as a spiritual practice (Vivekananda, 1953).

The idea that art could be considered a spiritual activity was discussed by Wassily Kandinsky (1866 – 1944) and other Bauhaus artists such as Johannes Itten (1888 –1967) and Paul Klee (1879 – 1940) who were influenced by theosophy and Buddhism (Droste, 1998). In his 1911 essay, *Concerning the Spiritual in Art*, Kandinsky suggested that the artist must allow *inner necessity* to define the visual content and form of works of art (Kandinsky, 1977). I interpret inner necessity similarly to Zeno of Citium's (c. 333 BC – 264 BC) concept of the logos (λόγος), as an active animating force of reason or divine consciousness in the universe (Pearsons, 2010).

The model of creation espoused by these artists is not a personal act grounded in the ego or intellect, but rather an intuitive, nonpersonal, and even mystical process whereby a universal consciousness is allowed to animate the work of art. Itten further suggested that a calm and meditative state of mind was needed before inner necessity could manifest a suitable form through art, and he had his classes at the Bauhaus perform meditation exercises before working on art projects (Itten, 1975, 1997; Droste, 1998).

This nonpersonal model of art creation bears some similarity to the traditional practice of shamanism, though to a much lesser degree. The shaman receives knowledge and insight during trance states entered via prolonged privation, chanting, dancing, or ingesting psychoactive plants. While the artist does not need to enter the profound trance state of the shaman, both the artist and shaman are revealing new knowledge to their culture, and are thus performing similar duties (Campbell, 1991a).

The Creation of Proper Art

James Joyce formulated an aesthetic theory via his protagonist Stephen Dedalus in *A Portrait of the Artist as a Young Man*, that I have incorporated into my philosophy of art. For his aesthetics, Joyce drew upon Aristotle (384 – 322 BC) from his *Poetics* and *Rhetoric* (Rhys Roberts & Bywater, 1984), and Thomas Aquinas' (1225 – 1274) *Com-*

mentary on the Divine Names (Campbell. 1991a; Eco & Bredin, 1988).

Joyce builds on Aristotle and Aquinas when he defines *improper art* and *proper art*, suggesting that the goal of true artists should be to create proper art. Improper art is either *pornographic*, an image causing desire in the viewer for a tangible object in the image, or it is *didactic*, causing fear and loathing in the viewer. Accordingly, all advertising imagery would be termed pornographic, and advocacy art, political art, and propaganda would be considered didactic. Improper art provokes in the viewer either a movement desiring or being repelled by the image and is thus termed *kinetic* by Joyce.

Proper art, on the other hand is *static* and should produce what Joyce called "esthetic arrest," an impassive capture or rapture of the viewer's attention. To paraphrase Aquinas, proper art embodies a sublime beauty, "something the mere apprehension of which gives pleasure." (Eco & Bredin, 1988, p. 36). Proper art has no application or purpose other than to act as a transmitter of the aesthetic idea or inner necessity, and thus is associated with the spiritual or transcendent. Because proper art functions as a object of contemplation, rather than a means to excite or create fear, its content is better suited to the domain of mythology, universal and human archetypes, and trancendent truths and beauty.

Joyce further defined proper art by referring to three characteristics of beauty suggested by Aquinas: *integritas* (wholeness), *consonantia* (harmony), and *claritas* (radiance) (Eco & Bredin, 1988; Joyce, 2010). Art having integritas suggests that that the work is complete in and of itself and represents a distinct wholeness. The artist selects the boundaries of the art work and thus frames the work to create a visual field that denotes its separateness and wholeness. Consonantia, which Joyce calls the "rhythm of beauty," refers to the harmonious placement of objects, colors, lines, and space within the art work – a statement of the importance of form and composition in art. Successful inclusion of consonantia in the art work suggests that the art can create radiance and aesthetic arrest in the viewer, and thus function as proper art (Joyce, 2010; Campbell, 1986, 1991a).

Form in Art and Nature

Following Joyce and Aquinas, I would suggest that form and composition are *fundamental* to artistic beauty, and I define this sublime beauty as harmony or resonance with the forms, geometry, and structures of nature. This is not beauty as a cultural or personal idea of attractiveness, but rather a correspondence with or emulation of nature. Paul Cezanne (1839 – 1906) noted that, "Art is a harmony parallel to nature," (Campbell, 1991a, p. 250). The Golden Ratio and the natural proportions in nature were significant inspirations to the classical Greeks, the artists of the Renaissance, and Bauhaus artists also made the connection between natural forms, the Golden Ratio, and design aesthetics (Droste, 1998; Elam, 2001). In 1950, Le Corbusier published *Le Modulor*, his theory of design in architecture based on his analysis of the Golden Ratio and proportion in the human body (Le Corbusier, 1996).

Resonance and Form

Another reason I assign importance to form in art is related by analogy to one of the ways energy and information are transmitted and exchanged in nature: through the process of *resonance*. The physical universe we can sense and all energy are vibratory and have the wave properties of wavelength and frequency. Einstein showed us that matter and energy are equivalent, so both have wave properties. Light is vibratory electromagnetic energy – sound is vibratory mechanical pressure energy. Solid objects have wave properties because they are composed of atoms that contain particles having wave properties. I would

suggest that consciousness and thought are also vibratory and have wave properties.

We do not yet know the nature of thought waves or how they might propagate. Insight, reason, memory, perception, and other conscious mental functions likely have an electromagnetic component associated with neurochemistry and the electrical activity of the neural networks in the brain, but we do not yet understand even the physical mechanisms of thought or consciousness. The suggestion that thought has wave properties is thus based on analogy to nature.

In physics, resonance is the sympathetic vibration of an object exposed to oscillating energy waves. You may have observed resonance in certain objects (a table top for example) when music is loud and when specific pitches sound. The pitch that causes the object to vibrate is called the *resonant frequency*. Everyday objects have an acoustic resonant frequency associated with their shape, size, and physical properties. The energy of sound waves at a particular frequency causes physical vibration in the object that has the same resonant frequency. Microwave ovens cook by causing the chemical bonds in water molecules to vibrate and generate heat as they resonate with the microwaves. To properly broadcast and receive radio signals, antennas have to have lengths that are related to the wavelength of the broadcast signal. FM radio waves are around a meter in length, and so is the wire antenna you connect to a radio receiver.

Following this analogy, if thought, the aesthetic logos, or internal necessity are vibratory and have wave properties, then perhaps the form of the art work assumes an important role. Analogous to a radio antenna having a specific length to receive radio waves of a given wavelength, the form of the artwork needs to have certain geometric properties that enable resonance with the thought waves of internal necessity. If the artist creates a form harmonious with the idea (consonantia), then the art work will resonate with the aesthetic logos, and can potentially *transmit* the idea. A person viewing the artwork in a suitably receptive mind state – *attuned*, so to speak, to the resonant frequency of the artwork – might then experience the idea through aesthetic arrest. In this model, the form of an art work can function as a transceiver of aesthetic thought. As Plotinus (204–270) noted (my emphasis):

*I think, therefore, that those ancient sages, who sought to secure the presence of divine beings by the creation of shrines and statues, showed insight into the nature of the All; they perceived that, though this Soul is everywhere tractable, its presence will be secured all the more readily when an **appropriate receptacle** is elaborated, a place especially capable of receiving some portion or phase of it, something **reproducing or representing** it and serving like a mirror to catch an image of it. (Plotinus, 1991, p. 264)*

State of Mind, Improvisation, and Inner Necessity

The final element of my aesthetics involves the state of mind appropriate to the creation of proper art. While I believe that art work should assume a form dictated by internal necessity, the expression of the idea can be limited by the nature and quality of my conscious state (which can impose distortion on the idea being manifested). I agree with Itten that a non-personal and meditative mind state is central to creativity.

At the core of my art making process is the simple fact that the repetitive nature of preparative artistic activities – like stretching canvas, or cutting out collage images – helps enable a meditative, nonpersonal state of mind. Practitioners of Zen call this *Beginner's Mind* (Suzuki, 1973) and a neurophysiologist would say that our brain's electroencephalograph was exhibiting delta waves. Someone exercising might call it an

endorphin high. As a working scientist, I found that entering and validating data, and preliminary analysis and graphing of data sets also produced this receptive state of mind. As a musician, I found that practicing scales and arpeggios creates a meditative state. Regardless of how the state is attained, the important point is that you are not thinking, judging, or analyzing. You are in a *receptive* state, ready to allow internal necessity to manifest an integrative idea or artistic form.

This emphasis on the meditative state of mind during the actual execution of the art work does not mean that intellectual or analytical modes of thinking are not a part of the overall activity of the artist. Artists, like scientists, must study and learn fundamental skills and the history of their vocation. They must also develop an understanding of the theories they apply and test. Manual skills and facility with the tools and methods of the creative endeavor must be learned and mastered. During art critique, the form and composition of an art work are often analyzed and discussed in relation to use of line, color, and space. This process is no different in spirit to peer review, where the insights and expertise of colleagues are solicited to improve the work of the scientist.

Assuming the proper state of mind, the last element of my creative process is the practice of improvisation, which I define as spontaneously creating forms while in a nonpersonal or meditative mental state. Musicians are usually more familiar with improvisation, but the process can be applied during any creative activity. However, with improvisation the idea of skill and experience must be noted. The artist's skills in drafting, color, and composition are as essential to the quality or success of an art work as a scientist's mastery of his or her field, mathematics, and experimental method. With slight paraphrasing, Louis Pasteur's comment "In the field of observation, chance favors only the mind which is prepared." (Holmes, 1961, p. 39) also applies to improvisation in the arts.

AESTHETICS APPLIED

"The Elements in Golden Ratio"

I have always been fascinated by images of nature that embody an abstract and fractal quality, and I often use these sorts of images as backgrounds for my figurative collages. When I started studying the Golden Ratio in the late 1990s, I developed an approach for collage creation that combined abstract and fractal-like images of nature from various size scales using sets of Golden proportional squares, GRs, √5 rectangles and other combinations of Golden polygons. The images were arranged in a manner more associated with flat pattern design, tiling, and quilting rather than my previous figurative collages, so I called this work process the *collage of backgrounds* (Craft, 2010b).

The formal aesthetics behind the collage of backgrounds is based upon the use of polygon forms that feature the Golden Ratio. These forms provide a frame and scaling that inherently embody universal natural proportion and form. The selection of a set of Golden forms for collages is a way of establishing formal boundaries that helps define integritas for the work. The cropping and placement of images within the Golden polygon forms is based upon traditional compositional methods (Arnheim, 1988), the use of centers, grids of thirds, and the dynamic symmetry (Hambidge, 1967) associated with the Golden sub divisions, diagonals, and power points (such as the Eyes of God) implied within the polygons. These additional elements of compositional design help enhance the harmony of form, ideally promoting consonantia.

The use of natural images from many size scales that embody fractal forms is another emulation of natural structure associated with self similarity and the holographic metaphor we see in nature. These formal elements, along with the dimensions and shapes of the collages, should function (according to my theory of aesthetics) as good antennas for

inner necessity. Assuming I do my job as an artist working in a nonpersonal meditative state, my work may have claritas and function as proper art.

The Classical Elements

While involved in the process of digitizing my photographic film and slide stock in 2002, I realized that my image selections had been unconsciously following the themes of the classical elements earth, air, fire, and water. This was the inspiration that led me to create a series of collages using the collage of backgrounds based on the classical elements called *The Elements in Golden Ratio* (the *Elements* series) (Craft 2010a).

I can remember being taught in the 1960s that the ancient concept of the elements was a silly or foolish idea, especially considering that we moderns have the scientific quantum model of the atom and the periodic table of the elements. This unfortunate bias ignores the powerful symbolic meanings associated with metaphor, and assumes the ancients defined science like we do today. The ancient elements were part of creation mythology and ontology and were considered attributes associated with matter, perception, and phenomenal causality. If anything, I think the ancients were more likely describing what science now calls the different states of matter: solid (earth), liquid (water), gas (air), and plasma (fire). So, perhaps our scholarly ancestors were not as ignorant as modern prejudice might suggest.

The elements represent an ancient idea that invokes the concept of 4 or 5 essences constituting matter in the physical universe, or as active forces that represent change and transformation. The Babylonian creation myth in the *Enûma Eliš* (c. 1700 – 1100 BC), describes 4 elements: the sea, earth, sky, and wind – likely the earliest written example of the concept (Campbell, 1991b).

Indian civilization developed concepts of the elements based on the Vedas, which originated as oral tradition c. 1500 BC to 1000 BC. Samkhya philosophy elaborated on the concept of the five great elements, *pancha mahabhuta*, in both their subtle and gross appearance as *kshiti* or *bhūmi* (earth), *ap* or *jala* (water), *tejas* or *agni* (fire), *marut* or *pavan* (air or wind), *byom* or *akasha* (aether or void). This scheme accounts for the perception of the world using the 5 senses. Samkhya describes how all phenomena and forms originate as cosmic matter, *prakṛiti*, that first manifests in the 3 *gunas* (*sattva* – serenity and calm, *rajas* – activity and emotion, and *tamas* – darkness or sorrow), which in turn generates the 5 elements (Zimmer, 1946).

The pre-Socratic philosopher Empedocles of Sicily (c. 490 – 430 BC) was the first Greek to write of the division of matter into 4 components that he called 'roots.' Citing Empedocles, Plato (c. 427 – 347 BC) first used the term 'elements' in *Timaeus* for this division of matter into four archetypes (Kalkavage, 2001). Aristotle discussed the elements in his *On Generation and Corruption*, and *Physics*, and suggested a 5th element he called quintessence or aether to denote non-materiality. Aristotle also discussed sense qualities associated with the elements (hot, cold, wet, and dry) (Lloyd, 1968; Waterfield, 2008).

My *Elements* series collages follow the tradition of choosing a metaphorical interpretation of the classical elements as a meditation on nature. This theme has been an inspiration to artists in the past. In 1737, the French baroque composer Jean-Fery Rebel (1666 – 1747) composed a ballet, *Les Elémens*, and Swiss composer Frank Martin (1890 – 1974) wrote a collection of symphonic etudes for orchestra called *The Four Elements* (1964). The French author Georges Bernanos (1888 – 1948) also frequently used the imagery of earth, air, fire and water in his novels (Morris, 1989).

Creating "The Elements in Golden Ratio"

All collages in the *Elements* series were created digitally using various versions of Adobe Photoshop on a Windows PC. The first step in creating the collages was to select four images from my own or an open source archive: one each of earth (E), air (A), fire (F), and water (W). I used images stored as uncompressed TIF files with dimensions of 3400 x 2100 pixels. These dimensions are based upon Fibonacci number multiples and approximated φ to 2 decimal places. An image resolution of 254 dots per inch (dpi, 100 dots per cm) will yield GR prints sized at 34 cm x 21 cm (13.4" x 8.27"). I selected four sets of elemental images that were used to create four sets of 21 collages each. Each set also used several additional images of life or living things (which can be thought of as a fifth element representing the combination and interaction of the other 4 elements) for selected collages in each set. The total for the series was 84 collages plus all the source images.

Figure 6 shows the Golden polygons I used for templates following the work process of the collage of backgrounds. The fundamental basis of this approach is the use of square images and proportional polygons that are in φ-ratio to each other. In the digital domain, the basic square used in my work is 2100 x 2100 pixels and these squares were compositionally cropped from each of the E-A-F-W source images in each set. Subsequent reductions in dimensions of squares were calculated using the $\sqrt{5}$-based value for φ to produce squares with dimensions 1298 x 1298, 802 x 802, and 496 x 496 pixels. These proportional squares and GRs are combined to create all of the forms seen in the *Elements* collages.

Each set of 21 collages in the *Elements* series included four GR coils (1-each for E-A-F-W), four $\sqrt{5}$ rectangles (1-each for E-A-F-W), four offset proportional squares (1-each for E-A-F-W), five overlapping GR mandalas (1-each for E-A-F-W plus a 5th combination mandala), and four $1 + 3(\varphi)$ rectangles (1-each for E-A-F-W). All collages presented here from the *Elements* series feature the element water in keeping with one of the suggested themes of this book. The collages are reproduced here in black and white, but color versions may viewed at http://www.dougcraft-fineart.com/frameElements.htm (Craft, 2010a).

Figure 6. Golden proportional polygons used for the collage of backgrounds and the Elements in Golden Ratio series. (© 2010, Doug Craft. Used with permission.).

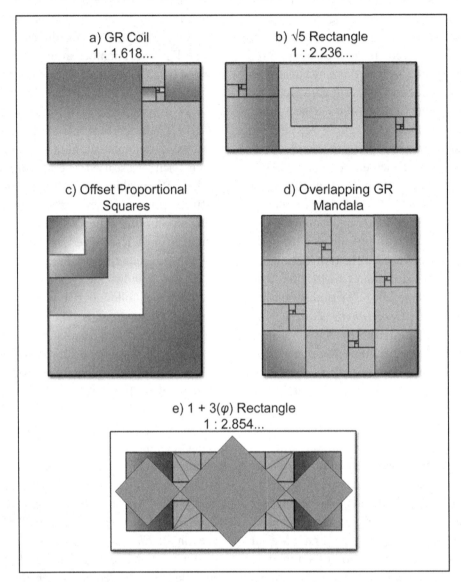

The elements themselves also imply a formal structure. Two sets of opposites are implied in the classical elements: water vs. fire, and earth vs. air. Two sets of elements also have associative relationships: earth with water, and fire with air. These themes provide an additional source for compositional form that refers to the structure of nature. The quaternary nature of the four elements also emulates the four-fold symmetry associated with the Golden Rectangle, thus reinforcing a formal relation between theme, geometry, form and composition.

Golden Rectangle Coils

Figure 6a shows the GR Coil created by the subdivision of the GR by short-side squares, seen previously in Figure 2. This form was used to create standalone GR coil collages, which were also used as collage components for other *Elements* series polygon forms. Dimensions of the GR coils are 3400 x 2100 pixels (13.4" x 8.3" @ 254 dpi). Each GR coil was named according to the element with the largest square and smaller squares were all sequenced according to the E-A-F-W order. For example, Figure 7 (upper image) shows *WATER: Elements Coil 2004-002*, from the *Elements* series second set of collages (denoted by *-002* in the name). Note the order of elements is W-E-A-F (a rotation of E-A-F-W). At each subdivision of the GR, the smaller square was also rotated 90° counter-clockwise to the previous square's orientation as a coiling movement suggestion of the logarithmic spiral converging on the Eye of God.

Square Root of Five Rectangles

Figure 6b shows the √5 rectangle also revealed in Figure 3. The √5 rectangle is formed by overlapping GRs that share a central square and include a GR life image in the center square of the collage with sides that are in √5 ratio to a 3400 x 2100 pixel GR. Dimensions of the √5 rectangles are 4700 x 2100 pixels (18.5" x 8.3" @ 254 dpi). The collage is named for the element appearing in the central square. The GRs to either side of the central square are identical GR coils that are rotated 180° relative to each other to suggest a circular movement. As seen in Figure 7 (middle image), *WATER – Elements Square Root of Five 2004-004*, the GR coils represent fire, the opposition element of water. The central GR √5 rectangle is an image of a leaf surface obtained using a high resolution flat bed scanner as a microscope.

Offset Proportional Squares

The offset proportional square (OPS) form, seen in Figure 6c is used as a standalone collage and as a collage component in other *Elements* forms. These collages are 2100 x 2100 pixels (8.3" x 8.3"

@ 254 dpi) and are usually presented diagonally rotated at 45° in a diamond arrangement. Naming convention for OPSs is the same as for the GR coils, using the largest square element and following the E-A-F-W sequence convention. These collages, however, do not rotate the smaller element squares and maintain a horizontal perspective for non-abstract images of the elements. Figure 7 (lower right image) shows *WATER – Elements Offset Square 2004-001*.

Mandalas

Mandalas are complex circular or symmetrical polygons with a dominant center that can serve as meditation objects. Overlapping GR mandalas (Figure 6d) were created using a life image as the center square with peripheral GRs forming a cross of four repeated source images of the element used to name the mandala. Dimensions of these mandalas are 4700 x 4700 pixels (18.5" x 18.5" @ 254 dpi), and I also usually present these collages diagonally at 45°. In the four corners of the mandalas are identical OPSs that are rotated to enhance the symmetry of the mandala. *WATER – Elements Mandala 2004-001*, seen in Figure 8 (upper image), shows the opposition element fire in the corner OPSs. The central life square is a microphoto of a Monarch butterfly wing from a series of similar images I took with a dissection microscope in 2002.

1 + 3(φ) Rectangles

The final form in the *Elements* series is seen in Figure 6e, the 1 + 3(φ) rectangle. This widest *Elements* form used a background composed of a central 3400 x 2100 pixel element source image GR plus two identical vertical proportional element source GRs. The background thus had an aspect ratio of 1: 2.854... The vertical GRs represent the opposition element to the central GR. In the center foreground is a 2100 x 2100 pixel OPS rotated 45° that establishes the elemental name for the collage.

Figure 7. Collages from the Elements series by the author. At the top is a GR Coil. In the middle is a √5 rectangle and below is an offset proportional square. Color versions of these collages may be viewed at http://www/dougcraftfineart.com. (© 2010, Doug Craft. Used with permission.).

a. WATER: Elements
Coil 2004-002

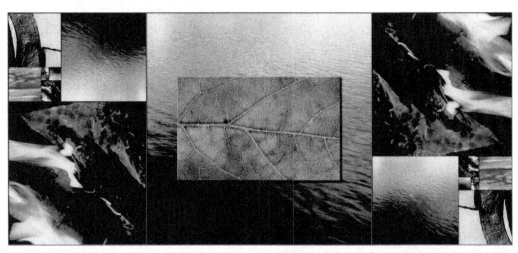

b. WATER - Elements Square Root
of Five 2004-004

c. WATER - Elements
Offset Square 2004-001

Figure 8. Collages from the Elements series by the author. At the top is a overlapping GR Mandala and below is a 1 + 3(φ) rectangle. Color versions of these collages may be viewed at http://www/dougcraft-fineart.com. (© 2010, Doug Craft. Used with permission.).

a. WATER - Elements Mandala
2004-001

b. WATER - Elements 1 + 3(φ)
2004-003

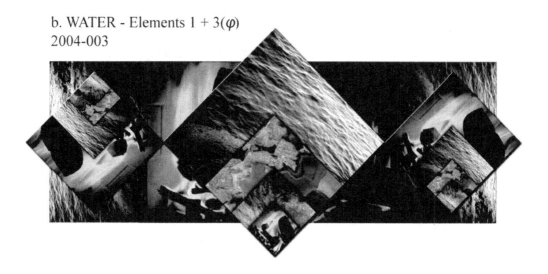

The opposition element is in the background. On the GR edges, proportionally smaller OPSs touch the central diamond in the foreground, with the background GRs consisting of the opposition element source image. In Figure 8 (lower image) we see *WATER – Elements 1 + 3(φ) 2004-003*. Note that opposition element fire is the background for the water OPS diamond, and peripheral fire OPS diamonds have water backgrounds. The OPSs on the periphery are rotated 180° to imply rotation about the center.

SOME PERSONAL CONCLUDING REMARKS

I have practiced art, music, and science for over 40 years, and all three activities have influenced each other. In college I studied chemistry but my electives were in art and spiritual philosophy, and all disciplines provided the inspiration to start painting and creating collage. I worked as a research environmental chemist for over 30 years, and during my career I continued to create art and play music as time and energy permitted.

The applied mathematics, experimental methods, and careful observation I used in my scientific research helped develop my understanding of and appreciation for the structure of nature. In fact, as my experience in science deepened, I was more in awe of the complex organization of nature and how little we truly know about the mystery of causality in the physical universe. Some of these realizations were almost spiritual experiences that have served as inspiration for my art work and my study of aesthetics and the Golden Ratio.

By the same token, my deepening understanding of form in art and musical improvisation carried over into my scientific work. Knowing the value of improvisation and meditative nonpersonal states of mind allowed me to develop and use creative strategies to intuit and understand the dynamic chemistry of a lake or watershed, or the secrets hidden in a complex data set. I found Edward Tufte's work on visual presentations a revelatory

experience: good data presentation could be a work of art and should also tell a story. I think that any practicing scientist could benefit from some knowledge and experience with creative strategies, aesthetics and the principles of composition.

I would hope that artists might seek greater knowledge of the science, geometry, and mathematics that can deepen their appreciation of how nature is so abundantly structured. We are not talking about understanding advanced calculus – just some simple geometry and high school algebra will do the trick. This kind of knowledge has its own mystical insights and I think the material in this chapter demonstrates that both science and math can have aesthetic implications.

Over time I have realized that conventional popular distinctions between science and art (science = objective, rational, reductionist, left brain; art = subjective, intuitive, wholistic, right brain) were simplistic and borne out of ignorance of what is involved in the actual creative practice of science and art. I found that being a scientist was a creative endeavor in many ways similar to art and music. Different methodologies and media to be sure, but all involve patience, serious study, routine chores, creative inspiration and intuition, proper application of form, storytelling, post hoc critique, the possibility of rejection, and communication to peers and the public. It's *all* art!

Form and beauty are of central importance to art, science, and life. And beauty revolves around resonance with the forms of nature that are the symbols and archetypes of the mystery of life.

ACKNOWLEDGMENT

I would like to acknowledge my art mentors, Duncan Stewart, University of West Florida, and Ralph Hunt, Pensacola State College, and my science mentors, Del Nimmo, University of Colorado Pueblo, and Ralph Birdwhistell, University of West Florida. I also thank Randa Tchelebi, Mike Vargas, and Henry Dempsey for manuscript review and comments.

REFERENCES

Arnheim, R. (1988). *The power of the center – A study of composition in the visual arts*. Berkeley, CA: University of California Press.

Bak, P. (1996). *How nature works – The science of self-organized criticality*. New York, NY: Copernicus.

Bak, P., Tang, C., & Wiesenfeld, K. (1987). Self-organized criticality: An explanation of 1/f noise. *Physical Review Letters*, *59*, 381–384. doi:10.1103/PhysRevLett.59.381

Ball, P. (1999). *The self-made tapestry - Pattern formation in nature*. Oxford, England: Oxford University Press.

Banks, R. B. (2010). *Growth and diffusion phenomena: Mathematical frameworks and applications*. Berlin, Germany: Springer-Verlag.

Barnsley, M. F., & Rising, H. (1993). *Fractals everywhere*. Boston, MA: Academic Press Professional.

Bohm, D. (1980). *Wholeness and the implicate order*. London, UK: Routledge.

Boles, M., & Newman, R. (1987). *The golden relationship - Art, math, nature* (2nd ed.). Bradford, MA: Pythagorean Press.

Briggs, J. (1992). *Fractals - The patterns of chaos - Discovering a new aesthetic of art, science, and nature*. New York, NY: Simon & Schuster.

Campbell, J. (1986). *The inner reaches of outer space – Metaphor as myth and as religion*. New York, NY: Harper & Row, Publishers.

Campbell, J. (1991a). *A Joseph Campbell companion*. New York, NY: HarperCollins Publishers.

Campbell, J. (1991b). The masks of God: *Vol. 3. Occidental mythology*. London, UK: Penguin Books.

Cohan, C. L., & Cole, S. W. (2002). Life course transitions and natural disaster: Marriage, birth, and divorce following Hurricane Hugo. *Journal of Family Psychology*, *16*(1), 14–25. doi:10.1037/0893-3200.16.1.14

Cook, T. A. (1979). *The curves of life*. Mineola, NY: Dover Publications, Inc.

Corbusier, L. (1996). *Le Modulor and Modulor 2*. Basel, Switzerland: Birkhäuser Architecture.

Craft, D. (2010a). The elements in golden ratio. *Doug Craft Fine Art*. Retrieved December 3, 2010, from http://www.dougcraftfineart.com/frameElements.htm

Craft, D. (2010b). Geometric forms for the collage of backgrounds. *Doug Craft Fine Art*, Retrieved December 3, 2010, from http://www.dougcraft-fineart.com/frameArtForms.htm

Critchlow, K. (1999). *Islamic patterns – An analytical and cosmological approach*. Rochester, VT: Inner Traditions.

Doczi, G. (1981). *The power of limits: Proportional harmonies in nature, art, and architecture*. Boston, MA: Shambhala.

Droste, M. (1998). *Bauhaus 1919 – 1933*. Berlin, Germany: Bauhaus-Archiv Museum für Gestaltung, (Benedikt Taschen).

Eco, U., & Bredin, H. (Trans. Eds.). (1988). *The aesthetics of Thomas Aquinas*. Cambridge, MA: Harvard University Press.

El Naschie, M. S. (1994). Is quantum space a random cantor set with a golden mean dimension at the core? *Chaos, Solitons, and Fractals*, *4*(2), 177–179. doi:10.1016/0960-0779(94)90141-4

Elam, K. (2001). *Geometry of design - Studies in proportion and composition*. New York, NY: Princeton Architectural Press.

Elenbogen, B., & Kaeding, T. (1989). A weak estimate of the fractal dimension of the Mandelbrot Boundary. *Physics Letters. [Part A]*, *136*(7-8), 358–362. doi:10.1016/0375-9601(89)90415-5

Gardner, M. (1989). *Penrose tiles to trapdoor ciphers*. Washington, DC: The Mathematical Association of America.

Gazalé, M. (1999). *Gnomon: From pharaohs to fractals*. Princeton, NJ: Princeton University Press.

Gell-Mann, M., & Ne'eman, Y. (2000). *The eightfold way*. Boulder, CO: Westview Press.

Ghyka, M. (1946). *The geometry of art and life*. Mineola, NY: Dover Publications, Inc.

Hambidge, J. (1967). *The elements of dynamic symmetry*. Mineola, NY: Dover Publications, Inc.

Herz-Fischler, R. (1987). *A mathematical history of the golden number*. Mineola, NY: Dover Publications, Inc.

Hoggett, V. E. Jr. (1969). *Fibonacci and Lucas numbers*. New York, NY: Houghton Mifflin Co.

Holmes, S. J. (1961). *Louis Pasteur*. New York, NY: Dover Publications, Inc.

Huntley, H. E. (1970). *The divine proportion – A study in mathematical beauty*. Mineola, NY: Dover Publications.

Itten, J. (1975). *Design and form* (rev. ed.). New York, NY: John Wiley & Sons, Inc.

Itten, J. (1997). *The art of color: The subjective experience and objective rationale of color* (rev. ed.). New York, NY: John Wiley & Sons.

Joyce, J. (2010). *A portrait of the artist as a young man*. New York, NY: SoHo Books.

Kalkavage, P. (Tr.) (2001). *Platos's Timaeus*. Newburyport, MA: Focus Publishing.

Kandinsky, W. (1977). *Concerning the spiritual in art*. Mineola, NY: Dover Publications, Inc.

Klee, P. (1966). *On modern art*. Boston, MA: Brill Academic Publishers.

Kock, W. E. (1981). *Lasers and holography – An introduction to coherent optics*. New York, NY: Dover Publications, Inc.

Lauwerier, H. (1991). *Fractals: Endlessly repeating geometrical figures*. Princeton, NJ: Princeton University Press.

Lawlor, R. (1982). *Sacred geometry – Philosophy and practice*. London, UK: Thames and Hudson, Ltd.

Livio, M. (2002). *The golden ratio - The story of Phi, the world's most astonishing number*. New York, NY: Broadway Books.

Lloyd, G. E. R. (1968). *Aristotle: The growth and structure of his thought*. Cambridge, UK: Cambridge University Press.

Mandelbrot, B. (1977). *The fractal geometry of nature* (rev. ed.). New York, NY: W.H. Freeman and Company.

Mandelbrot, B. (1998). *Multifractals and 1/f noise: Wild self-affinity in physics*. New York, NY: Springer.

Marder, M. P. (2010). *Condensed matter physics* (2nd ed.). New York, NY: John Wiley & Sons. Inc. doi:10.1002/9780470949955

Martineau, J. (2001). *A little book of coincidence*. New York, NY: Walker & Company.

Modis, T. (1992). *Predictions: Society's telltale signature reveals past & forecasts the future*. New York, NY: Simon & Schuster.

Morris, D. R. (1989). *From heaven to hell: Imagery of earth, air, water, and fire in the novels of Georges Bernanos*. New York, NY: Peter Lang Publishing, Inc.

Olsen, S. (2006). *The golden section – Nature's greatest secret*. New York, NY: Walker Publishing Company, Inc.

Pearsons, A. C. (Tr.). (2010). *The fragments of Zeno and Cleanthes: With introduction and explanatory notes by* A. C. Pearson. Saint Ansgar, IA: Forgotten Books.

Peitgen, H., & Saupe, D. (Eds.). (1988). *The science of fractal images*. New York, NY: Springer-Verlag.

Plotinus (1991). *The Enneads* (MacKenna, S., Trans.). London, UK: Penguin Books.

Pribram, K. (1991). *Brain and perception: Holonomy and structure in figural processing*. Hillsdale, NJ: Lawrence Erlbaum Associates.

Rhys Roberts, W., & Bywater, I. (Tr.) (1984). *The rhetoric and the poetics of Aristotle*. New York, NY: Random House.

Runion, G. E. (1990). *The golden section*. Palo Alto, CA: Dale Seymour Publications.

Sheldrake, R. (1981). *A new science of life: The hypothesis of morphic resonance*. Rochester, VT: Park Street Press.

Sheldrake, R. (1988). *The presence of the past: Morphic resonance and the habits of nature*. New York, NY: Times Books.

Slijkerman, F. (2010). *Ultra Fractal 5*. Retrieved January 3, 2011, from http://www.ultrafractal.com

Smith, P. (1997). *Seurat and the avant-garde*. New Haven, CT: Yale University Press.

Suzuki, S. (1973). *Zen mind, beginner's mind*. New York, NY: Weatherhill.

Talbot, M. (1991). *The holographic universe*. New York, NY: Harper Perennial.

Taylor, R. P. (2002). Order in Pollock's chaos. *Scientific American*, (December): 2002.

Taylor, R. P., Micolich, A. P., & Jonas, D. (1999). Fractal analysis of Pollock's drip paintings. *Nature*, *280*, 399–422.

Thompson, D. W. (1961). *On growth and form*. Cambridge, UK: The University Press.

Tufte, E. R. (1983). *The visual display of quantitative information*. Cheshire, CT: Graphics Press.

Tufte, E. R. (1990). *Envisioning information*. Cheshire, CT: Graphics Press.

Tufte, E. R. (1997). *Visual explanations: Images and quantities, evidence and narrative*. Cheshire, CT: Graphics Press.

Vivekananda. (1953). *Vivekananda: The yogas and other works*. New York, NY: Ramakrishna-Vivekananda Center.

Voss, R. F. (1988). Fractals in nature: From characterization to simulation. In Peitgen, H., & Saupe, D. (Eds.), *The science of fractal images* (pp. 21–70). New York, NY: Springer-Verlag. doi:10.1007/978-1-4612-3784-6_1

Voss, R. F., & Clarke, J. (1975). 1/f noise in music and speech. *Nature*, *258*, 317–318. doi:10.1038/258317a0

Walser, H. (2001). *The golden section*. Washington, DC: Mathematical Association of America.

Waterfield, R. (Tr.) (2008). *Aristotle – Physics*. Oxford, UK: Oxford University Press.

Wilbur, K. (Ed.). (1982). *The holographic paradigm and other paradoxes*. Boston, MA: Shambhala.

Wilbur, K. (1992). *A brief history of everything*. Boston, MA: Shambhala.

Zimmer, H. (1946). *Myths and symbols in Indian art and civilization* (Campbell, J., Ed.). Princeton, NJ: Princeton University Press.

KEY TERMS AND DEFINITIONS

Cantor Set: A basic fractal created from line segments, built by successively removing the middle thirds of a set of line segments.

Conjunction: A term used in positional astronomy and astrology. It means that two celestial bodies appear near one another in the sky as seen from the Earth.

Diffraction: The apparent bending of waves around small obstacles and the spreading out of waves past small openings.

Diffusion: The process whereby particles being acted on by random forces move from regions of higher concentration to regions of lower concentration. Diffusion can describe how a gas will fill an empty container or how salt or sugar molecules will mix through a liquid.

Exponent: Exponentiation is a mathematical operation, written as a^n, involving two numbers, the base a and the exponent (or power) n. When the exponent n is a positive integer, the base is multiplied by itself, or *raised*, n times. For example $2^5 = (2 \times 2 \times 2 \times 2 \times 2) = 32$ and $3^3 = (3 \times 3 \times 3) = 27$. Exponents may also be negative numbers and these numbers are reciprocals of the positive powers. For example $3^{-3} = 1 \div (3 \times 3 \times 3) = 0.03704$, or $1 \div 33$. Exponents may also be non-integers, such as $12^{3.567} = 7070.32$.

Irrational Number: A real number that cannot be expressed as a fraction a/b, where a and b are integers. Irrational numbers, like the square root of 2, φ, or π, are numbers that do not have terminating or repeating decimals and have infinite numbers of decimals.

Landsat: The Landsat Program is a series of Earth-observing satellite missions funded by the U.S. government. Since 1972, Landsat satellites have collected photographic and spectral information about Earth from space. This science, known as remote sensing, involves specialized digital photographs of Earth's continents and surrounding coastal regions that are used to evaluate changes in vegetation and land use.

Logarithm: The logarithm of a number is the *exponent* or power of a *base* number (base-10 is commonly used), needed to calculate the number. Logarithms of a number, x, are usually denoted with the base, n, as $\log_n(x)$. For example, $\log_{10}(1000) = 3$, because 10 (the base) must be "raised" to the 3rd power to calculate the number 1000 (x). Another example, $\log_{10}(546) = 2.737$, because $10^{2.737} = 546$. Logarithms were discovered by John Napier in the early 18th Century and were commonly used until the advent of computers as a computational shortcut to multiply and divide large numbers.

Nonlocality: A property of nature observed at the very small scale of subatomic particles whereby the behavior of a particle, such as an electron, causes a change in another physically separated particle. The change occurs instantaneously (faster than the speed of light), suggesting that the particles are connected at a deeper level or scale of causality.

Nonlinear: Characterized by curved lines. In mathematics, nonlinear equations usually have a variable that changes in an exponential manner, such as x^2 or x^3, or in a logarithmic manner, such as ex. Most processes in nature are nonlinear. Nonlinear equations often used in science include power, exponential, logarithmic, and logistic equations.

Ontology: The philosophical study of the nature of being, existence or reality, as well as the basic categories of being and their relations.

Polarizing Microscope: A microscope used by geologists to identify minerals in very thin rock specimens (called thin sections). This technique uses plane-polarized light filters that interact with crystalline materials to form vivid colors (pleochroism) that change as the microscope stage is rotated. Also called a petrographic microscope.

Polynomial: An algebraic equation containing *variables* (usually denoted as x, y, and z) and *constants* (usually denoted as a, b, and c), using only the operations of addition, subtraction, multiplication, and non-negative integer exponents.

For example, $3x^2 + 2x - 1 = 0$, where 3, 2, and 1 are constants and x is the variable.

Quadratic Formula: A formula used to calculate the roots or solutions to a polynomial equation of the form $ax2 + bx + c = 0$:

$$x = \frac{-b \pm \sqrt{(b^2 - 4ac)}}{2a}$$

Quantum: In this chapter this term generally refers to energetic phenomena associated with the atomic and subatomic size scales. The term comes from *quantum mechanics*, the theory that interactions at this scale involve discrete and specific exchanges of energy (quanta), and that the states associated with subatomic matter (electrons, protons, leptons, etc.) are *quantitized*, or restricted to discrete states associated with spin or other novel characteristics.

Reciprocal: The inverse of a number, x, equal to 1 divided by x. Also refers to a smaller and identically shaped proportional polygon created by sectioning of a larger polygon by a gnomon.

Standard Model: Is the name given to the current version of *quantum field theory*. This theory accounts for the strong and weak nuclear, and electromagnetic force interactions observed in all known subatomic particles. Predictions for the existence of particles such as quarks were an outgrowth of early versions of the Standard Model, and experimental confirmation of quarks led to widespread adoption of the theory. The Standard Model provides a common unified theory for three of the four universal forces observed by physics, but does not yet account for gravitation.

Synodic Cycle: A synodic cycle measures successive returns of a planet to its conjunction with the Sun, as seen from Earth. From the Greek *sýnodos* 'meeting'.

Chapter 18
Getting Closer to Nature:
Artists in the Lab

James Faure Walker
University of the Arts, London, UK

ABSTRACT

The term bio art has emerged in the past few years to cover the kind of art that seems to come from the biology lab, with simulations of life forms through generative processes, with data taken from organisms, or even through organisms themselves. This is often at the micro level, invisible to the naked eye, where seeing requires some degree of computer modeling. This could be a hybrid form, serving the interests of both art and science, but recent exhibitions have prompted some debate about the divergent roles of art and science. Rob Kesseler and Andrew Carnie are artists who have worked alongside biologists to produce visual works of extraordinary quality, in both their decorative and intellectual aspects. They follow in a long tradition of artists who have been fascinated by the close-up detail. Drawing manuals of a hundred years ago advocated the study of plant forms, sometimes as the basis for pattern design. The author describes his own use of scientific sources, arguing that there is also a place for art that evokes the wonders of nature without being tied to the visible facts.

INTRODUCTION

What happens when artists take images from the laboratory to the art gallery? Can the mesmerizing patterns seen through the lens of the microscope be looked at as art? Do they need to be modified in some way? Aren't they better if left just as they are? Or are these misleading questions? Artists have always been fascinated by the natural world. Science, nature and art have long been intertwined. Through botanical illustration, anatomical studies, visions of the cosmos, abstract analogies, artists have revealed nature's secrets – from Leonardo da Vinci, Albrecht Dürer, William Blake, John Ruskin, Ernst Haeckel, Paul Klee, and so on. Some are close-up, some speculative, some wide-screen. Some are blazingly mystical, some are romantic, and some are just plain and factual.

DOI: 10.4018/978-1-4666-0942-6.ch018

But 'bio art' is strikingly different: it appears to be a new hybrid form. As the term implies, the imagery is normally neither wholly natural, nor wholly synthetic; if based on 'data', this is presented in an aesthetic context. Sometimes this plays on our curiosity about the sheer weirdness of a magnified worm accessed through deep-sea photography; or the uncanny lifelike 'creatures' created in 3D animations from generative algorithms by artists such as William Latham and Yoichiro Kawaguchi. These examples blur the distinction between natural and artificial life. As non-specialists we cannot be sure what a living cell looks like, nor tell a simulation from the 'real thing'. Our ideas of DNA, or of black holes, rely on visualizations derived from reams of numbers, be they fuzzy bands of colour, or high fidelity animations. A printout of the methane on Titan does not convey the awesome distances and strangeness of that environment. We need another mode of imagery to move our souls. Our knowledge may have evolved far from the thinking of a hundred years ago, but artistically we haven't yet caught up, at least in representing what we know to be 'out there'. Bio Art resonates with Green politics, with anxieties about global warming, about ecosystems, about genetic engineering. It parallels the growth of 'info-tainment' in science museums, of wildlife features on TV that blend footage with computer simulation. In our ordinary lives we have shifted from paper-based information – newspapers, maps – to smart phones and car navigation systems. It should not come as a surprise that artists have been exploring how 'nature' might be represented. There are alternatives to drawings and photos. Add all this together and, yes, there is something in the air at the moment about art and science, a sense that we might be able to bring the visual games of contemporary art together with the Big Ideas of science, and provide approachable images for the non-specialist.

In this essay I shall first consider two projects where the collaboration between an artist and a biologist has produced images that are unmistak-ably – to use an overworked term – beautiful. Do these artists simply 'translate' data into art? That is putting it too simply, because whatever we now mean by data, it is not necessarily anything accessible to the naked eye. Being 'true to nature' is not as simple as it once seemed to be. We rely on 'visualization' to get close to a tiny cell, or to the planets of a neighbouring galaxy. A hundred years ago the natural world could be studied with little knowledge of these unreachable objects. Yet at that time 'nature walks' might have been more common in primary schools. In British art schools the detailed studies of plants - botanical drawing – had the practical purpose of providing a sound basis for the decorative arts, following on from the teachings of Ruskin and Morris.

Today, we can acquire images of unreachably small and exquisite patterns, and through abstract painting we have a rich vocabulary of forms. We can 'borrow' these glimpses of otherwise invisible worlds, compose some sort of picture, and perhaps for a moment bridge the gap between science and art. Visual art can explore the complexity of nature without adhering to the evidence. Artists invent, they improvise. In the final section I describe my own working method.

1. COMING TOGETHER

We have art/science exhibitions, collaborations between artists and scientists, organizations such as the Wellcome Trust. Some ventures are entirely positive about the science; others like the Arts Catalyst in the UK[1] are ambivalent, sometimes sceptical, presenting parodies of scientific endeavour. There is a growing list of publications, following the pioneering work of Stephen Wilson's (2002) 'Information Arts', featuring artists in the labs. This book is part of the same trend. 'Visualization' has become a discipline in its own right. NASA images, MRI images, movies of living cells[2], all are available as downloads. Artists do not have to pack up an easel and head out into the fields to paint the landscape. They download Hubble. If they are adventurous they arrange for their brains to be scanned. Colleges contemplate running courses called 'Art/Science.

What of the viewer's experience of sci/art? What will these pictures – or museum installations – offer that a non-science based work doesn't provide? Is it primarily an art experience or a science lesson? Or does the viewer have to puzzle over patterns and diagrams, which only make sense in the accompanying description? Shouldn't we expect a good work of art to engage us without the need for any explanation? And what of the integrity of the science itself? Can bad, or out of date science be the foundation for good art? Is a painting based on astrology to be trusted less than one based on astronomy? Will top class science lead to top class art?

Contemporary art has its own disputes. Generally speaking, artists who use the latest technology, keep in touch with the leading ideas in biology, are not thereby regarded as 'advanced'. It is worth pointing out that an advance in a science does not have its counterpart in art. There is no clear way of resolving what art is most 'advanced' at any one time. In one context, perhaps in a university art department, a category of work will be see as advanced because it chimes in with current philosophy, or is politically astute, or goes 'beyond' what is taken for granted; but in another context, in published art criticism, the same work will be seen as opportunist 'faculty art' and derided. There was a time when artists using computers - advanced technology - felt they were part of the technological revolution. Using digital gadgetry does not of course make you a revolutionary artist. The label 'advanced' may not be viable outside the orbit of its own practitioners. The art world has a variety of agendas, and by and large its mood has been anti-technology, anti-science, and 'post-modern'. As Graham Crowley (Brundrett & Crowley, 2010) pointed out we knew the idea of being 'ahead' had lost its grip "once 'avant-garde' had become a trim option of a mid-range Mercedes."

A botanical artist would not cause much of a stir either. In post-modernist thinking 'nature' has become an embarrassing term. Any photograph, or 'representation' is only interesting because of the way it 'mediates' the image. Artists may be fascinated by what they see down microscopes, and can be stunned by the beauty of nature's secret structures. But in this way of thinking they should be on their guard, and anyway, the decorative is a suspect category. In the 1970's there was a movement, Pattern Painting, celebrating extravagant colour. It arose in defiance of the Puritanism of minimal art. Today some argue against the 'purely visual', as being lightweight, and insufficiently challenging. Some code-based pieces by William Latham (2011), or Casey Reas (2011), that resemble exotic organisms, or indeed the Hubble images of remote galaxies, are undeniably radiantly beautiful. They required staggering feats of calculation in their production. But I have attended presentations by these and other artists and on every occasion the 'killer question' from the audience is invariably one about the work being just 'eye candy'. Within biology itself there are divisions. This is not my field, but some far out ideas, such as 'Bio Bricks-style synthetic biology' can be dismissed as 'Garage Biology' (Ellington, 2011). So when an artist joins forces with a biologist and comes up with a glorious array of colour, there could still be plenty to argue about.

Let me for a moment talk about the viewer's response. Let me suppose I am visiting a science/art exhibition. I shall speculate that I come across a cauliflower-like object on a plinth, rendered in transparent plastic. I assume it is a 3D rendering from a scan of a brain, most probably of the artist's brain. I am impressed; though this is something I have already come across several times before. I am mildly curious about the technical process, the patterns and ridges of the 'sculpture'. But, not being an expert, one brain looks much like another. I would not be able to identify it as this particular artist's brain. Alternatively, I might identify it as an anatomical model designed for medical students, one that comes apart to show the various regions of the brain working together. I have come across straightforward visual aids in art exhibitions. I feel some relief at finding a display that has the sole purpose of communicating information. It may have no pretensions as art, but it does its job. Of course the artist could be a lot smarter. Depending on the profile of the gallery, there could be another game afoot. The sculpture could be a tease, a cast of a cauliflower posing as a brain. I would appreciate this for the illusion, the little twist, fooling with my expectations. Do I feel at ease finding art holding hands with 'respectable' science? No, I have reservations; it could be a good target for satire.

2. EARLIER CONNECTIONS

We sometimes think of science as describing the world 'as it is' in terms of concrete facts, of data, of objects. We think of art as dealing with subjective responses, not verifiable proofs. Yet when it comes to describing what really is 'out there', we may find we are staring blankly at uncertainty. When it comes to visualizing the extraordinarily small, or the extraordinarily vast and distant, we have to use our imagination. We do not have a direct view. We have nothing in our experience that is comparable. We speculate and use analogies – a black hole might look like this, a chain of DNA like that. We create 3D 'walk-throughs' along nerve cells. Artists have the skill to create imaginary worlds, and can keep within the bounds of the verifiable 'data'. But a 3D animation in a TV science programme may look 'real' just because it is professionally produced. We feel we are 'seeing' data, but what we are looking at is texture mapping.

If you were designing a school building, you would keep the biology lab and the art studio separate: clean spaces for microscopes, natural light for the art room. Some artists might require lab conditions, and conduct research, in their own way.

But it is unlikely that the scientist would knock on the studio door to get the latest on neuroscience. Art historians remind us that in the renaissance science and art were not so far apart: in the pin-sharp detail of flowers and background vegetation in Van Eyck; in Stefan Lochner's 'Madonna of the Rose Bower', we have serious botany; Leonardo made accurate studies of the valves of the heart. In cosmology there were medieval paintings representing the universe as a series of rainbow circles. Visions of heaven or of hell were – in our terminology –visualizations. An exhibition featuring scientific visualizations made by artists throughout the ages would include phases of the moon, exotic animals, daguerreotypes of trees. There were photograms of snow crystals produced in the mid-nineteenth century, bacteria featured in Ozenfant's (1928) 'Foundations of Modern Art'. There is a rich history.

There was a time when art school lecturers claimed that the Cubists conception of a fractured 3D space was derived from Einstein's Theory of Relativity. In the 1960's the new 'hard-edge' painting was interpreted as being part of the technological revolution, driving us all forward, pushing at the limits of knowledge. That mood has passed. On the whole artists today do not keep up to speed with scientific literature, or even take much interest. The failure of digital art to take hold was in part because it was perceived to be as alien as genetically modified food (For an extended discussion of this see Faure Walker, 2006). If the art exhibits we come across in Science Museums do not engage the art world as much as they might, it is because they lack 'edge'; they are seen as corporate, initiated by institutions.

In looking at art that, so to speak, looks into the secrets of nature, we do need to keep the context in mind. This could on occasion be closer to entertainment or interior design than to the science academy. It is all too easy to get carried away with the idea that all of a sudden we have a new window into the laboratory, through the magical eye of computer graphics, with troops of present-day Leonardo's turning out visions of biological complexity. The artists I am considering here all express some degree of scepticism, frustrated that they are marginalized by an art world indifferent to science. Sometimes, too, frustrated that their colleagues in biology labs, or computer labs, are so naïve when it comes to contemporary art. What used to be termed 'computer art' initially only had a cult following, and was similarly brushed aside. So the status of these images – stranded between art and science - is very much at issue.

3. POLLEN AS ORNAMENT

Here is a picture of a pollen grain of a Seville orange, 'Citrus aurantia', to be precise (Figure 1). Or is it an illustration? A photograph? Or a self-conscious work of art? Does it even represent a real object? It is a work by the artist, Rob Kesseler, in his words: "realized with the power of scanning electron microscopy and the digital camera." Writing of the tension between the rationalist and romantic approach to nature, he points out the tensions that remain latent in our society, which "views nature with a contradictory mixture of voyeuristic sentiment and environmental responsibility." Along with scientists working with plants, artists "dissect, examine and analyze, modify and even transform their subjects" (Kesseler & Harley, 2006, p. 181).

He continues:

A detailed study of flower anatomy reveals unimaginable diversity. Moving below the surface, the minute and astonishing variety of form, structure and surface topology of pollen opens up yet another layer of visual and scientific complexity, a world invisible to most people. We may endlessly dissect but beauty, like infinity, is mercurial. That something as small as pollen is also so vital for the continued diversity of plant life is remarkable; that it is also beautiful adds immeasurably to its fascination (ibid, page 185).

Figure 1. Rob Kesseler, Citrus aurantia, Seville orange, pollen grain, from Kesseler, R. and Harley, M., (2009), Pollen: the Hidden Sexuality of Flowers, London: Papadakis Publishers. (© 2009, Rob Kesseler. Used with permission).

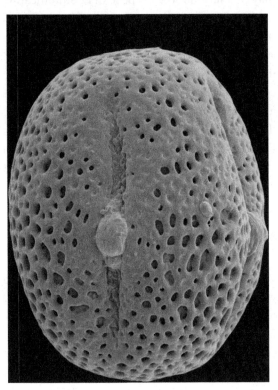

Kesseler collaborated with botanists at London's Kew Gardens. He describes his work as 'ornamental fantasy'.

I have attempted to create images that lie somewhere between science and symbolism, in which the many complexities of artistic representation of plants are concentrated into mesmeric visual statements, analogous morphologies with the power to burn themselves into the memory (ibid, page 257).

The development of abstract painting, Paul Klee's suggestion that painting should be less about imitating nature, and more about making nature visible, opened up a way of looking at diagrams, maps, x-rays, aerial photographs, and microscopic images in their own right. We take on trust that this is what the pollen might look like, though we could not verify this with the naked eye. In fact the colour does not correspond with its 'real' colour, but has been blended in by Kesseler in Photoshop. We accept the truth of the image, just as we innocently accept the truth of the Hubble images as photographs of what is 'out there'- again the colour is somewhat arbitrary and cosmetic, added to facilitate interpretation, even to dramatize vast clouds of pink gas. The actual data received by the gray-scale sensors would not – in its raw state – be so inspiring.

There is no contradiction in admiring these 'pictures' for what they are, while at the same time accepting that they are not literally 'true'. Artists tend to collect maps and diagrams of every kind, not because they need the information they contain, but because they value their graphic qualities, for what they suggest. They could be tangles of line, patterns, colour codes. As has been pointed out, Mondrian's last works have an affinity with the 1931 London Underground Map of Harry Beck, which was in turn prompted by electrical circuit diagrams. Mondrian lived in London from 1938 to 1940, and was fascinated by the Underground.

Similarly, artists who start from biological, or botanical data do not necessarily have a close interest in it as information. Yet it is not fair to say all they are doing is making pretty pictures. But this type of work is normally seen in science/art exhibitions, just as for many years digital art was only featured in computer conferences. It has been isolated from the broader art audience. It has been characterized as cold and 'scientific', without any connection to the world of humans and their emotions. But Kesseler's sumptuous coffee-table books have won awards as publications, and succeeded in finding a wide and appreciative audience.

Early computer artists, limited by what was available in the sixties and seventies - they had to be programmers, and used plotters - produced work that had the look of tangled diagrams. The 'drawings' they produced depended on a simple but maddeningly repetitive process – if done by hand – with tiny increments of curved forms. You can see this in the works of Roman Verostko (2011) or William Latham (2011). Viewers who saw these for the first time without any idea how they were made might mistake them for weird creatures living at the bottom of the sea, or exotically deformed seashells. Naum Gabo, whose sculptures of string and wire were in turn inspired by mathematics, influenced both these artists. One of the most influential publications for abstract artists was D'Arcy Thomson's 'On Growth and Form', originally published in 1917. (Frank Stella is one artist who has cited this as an influence). Its thesis is that there are geometric principles at work in organic forms, that similarities between related animals can be understood as mathematical transformations. When computer artists learned how to 'grow' forms from algorithms, they were mimicking a natural process. This notion was familiar to designers, who looked at foliage and flowers for their motifs. But before considering that use of 'nature' there is another work I must bring into this discussion.

4. BRAINS AS TREES

Andrew Carnie's 'Magic Forest' is essentially a slide show, using what are now obsolete slide projectors and multiple translucent gauze-like screens in a pitch-black room (Carnie, 2011). The viewer sees a 20-minute sequence of tree-like forms, which are derived from microscopic images of brain-cells, and these morph into images of the brain, the skull, the whole body, and photos of the naked Andrew Carnie. It is one of those mesmerizing works whose effect cannot easily be put into words, where the science and the art come effortlessly together.

In 2002 this work was featured in an exhibition at London's Science Museum entitled 'Head On'.

Figure 2. Andrew Carnie, a slide from Magic Forest

The eminent scientist Lewis Wolpert claimed in the Observer that the exhibition trivialized both art and science. Replying in the same paper Carnie (2002) wrote:

Art is too important to be left to artists - science too important to be left to scientists. Bringing the two together raises provocative and interesting ideas about fundamental issues on the nature of creativity, the role of education in shaping disciplines and the funding of culture… .

The practice of science is not isolated from the world we live in. Science has its politics, its economics, its fashions even. And anecdotally at least, some of the scientists involved in 'sci-art' collaborations report an intellectual engagement in them that goes further than personal enjoyment.

Figure 3. Andrew Carnie, a slide from Magic Forest (© 2002, Andrew Carnie. Used with permission)

It's not just that it allows them to get out of their labs a bit more; it also seems to offer a different way of looking at their own work as scientists. We have all experienced those moments of self-reflective insight brought on by the challenge of explaining to someone outside our natural sphere what it is we do and why.

As with Rob Kesseler's apparent 'photographs', immense care is taken with the way the work is presented. It is far more than just an illustration of lab data.

I think the difficulties are when you simply repeat the pretty pictures of science. I don't want to be doing that – I want to make something that's an artwork that's in a different kind of space. The science ideas that I've seen and explored are embedded in the work but they're not always what the piece of work is about (Chuter, 2010).

This leaves 'what the work is about' an open question. I don't come away from seeing this full of insights about how any brain works, or how it grows. I know that the connections he makes are more to do with the lateral thinking of a dream space than of demonstrable logical steps. I also realize that there is much more to this than a shuffling pack of vaguely associated brain, tree, and body slides.

5. FORGOTTEN TENDRILS

Some drawings occupy the no man's land between scientific curiosity and art. In the science and art debate we can lose sight of how important 'nature' was to artists and designers a hundred years ago as source material. Trees, plants, flowers, were not necessarily viewed as subjects that the artist should reproduce photographically, but as demonstrations of principles of growth, and thereby of principles of design. This is why a student might study botany.

In 1908 Lewis Day published 'Nature and Ornament: Nature, the Raw Material of Design'. Its special purpose was "to illustrate as fully as possible the decorative and ornamental character of natural growth, and its infinite suggestiveness, as the starting point in design" (Day, 1908).

It is out of facts that the fancies of the artist are woven. This being so, the most useful drawings have more in common with a botanical than with a pictorial representation; there is more to be got from an old herbal than from modern flower paintings; but, in making his own drawings, an ornamentist will naturally pass over points which have only scientific interest, and will emphasize others on which a scientist lays little or no stress (ibid, page 106).

This drawing of climbing plants is typical. But unlike Kesseler, Day did not draw the illustrations himself, but 'dictated' them. His purpose was to inspire students to draw plants more attentively. He had definite views. He was almost in despair at the neglect of tendrils. He described one plant as 'obnoxious':

The obnoxious calceolaria will, under favourable conditions, emancipate itself from thralldom (another condition being perhaps a reaction against the old order), and grow to something very different from the crude little clump of yellow, 'bedded out' with equally crude geraniums (ibid, page 99-100).

Though I could have picked any of the thirty odd illustrations, I should point out what an accomplished page this is, not only demonstrating the subtle twists and turns, but balancing dark against light, the whole seemingly all in one rhythmic movement. The illustrations are still vivid.

For some years I have been collecting how-to-draw books of this type, sometimes called drawing manuals, and I have a soft spot for those of the 1900 to 1940 period. To a browser this small book might be mistaken for a botany book. There are others like it, because drawing books at the time were specialized. A recent reviewer on Amazon

Figure 4. J. Foord, 1908, Nasturtium, Climbing Plants, Attaching themselves by the leaf stalk or by twining, from Day, Lewis (1908, republished 1929), Nature and Ornament: Nature, the Raw Material of Design, London: Batsford, preface, page 26.

described this book as 'cool' because he found it useful for designing wallpaper using Illustrator. The reviewer – who was using a reprinted edition - was apparently unaware that the text was a hundred years old. He complained that the language was archaic. When I came across this review it set me thinking about the basic operations of a paint program (copying, repeating, flipping, scaling, reversing). These were well understood generations ago. Those of us swayed by the euphoria of the 'new art' powered by digital processing sometimes forget this.

The thesis that runs through Lewis Day's book was shared by other authors writing on drawing:

before we could draw nature competently we needed to understand how plants, trees, flowers actually grew. This was part of a long-standing controversy: on the one side was the view that you first needed to learn geometry, perspective, anatomy, and only then would you be set the task of drawing from nature, eventually drawing from 'life' - the naked human form. And on the other side, the view that we were all innately able to draw as children, and this natural expression should not be 'corrected'. That would extinguish individuality and the creative impulse. There was a need for accurate representations – 'realistic' drawing – not only in fine art, but also in advertising, magazine illustration, medical and botanical illustration.

Day begins:

We all love nature: who could help it? And lovers of nature will maintain that the most beautiful forms are those taken from natural objects. They go so far as to say that forms not taken directly from natural objects must be ugly (ibid, page 1).

So his book takes the alternative approach. It is supplied with page after page of these exemplary line drawings. He demonstrates how the best ornament derives not from direct transcription, but from interpretation, from understanding the design principles nature displays. It went against the orthodox teaching of the time - the legacy of Ruskin - that was opposed to the 'idealization' and 'distortion' of nature.

6. LANDSCAPE AND IMAGINATION

There are many thousands of amateur artists who paint the landscape, or animals and flowers, who have little interest in the debates of contemporary art, and little interest in the deeper study of pollen, brains or tendrils. They are inspired by wonderful scenery. They paint it in order to capture it. Within contemporary art, as has already been mentioned, working uncritically 'from nature' has come to be seen as a questionable approach. Wildlife photography, nature documentaries on TV, fulfil that role. That does not mean that nature, in the broadest sense, is of no interest. Sophisticated artists – those engaged in contemporary debates, alert to the pitfalls - look at nature with an awareness of climate change, of fragile ecologies, of the complexity of the tiniest organism, of the vastness of the universe. The picture postcard version is hardly adequate.

Painting can reflect the complexity of the natural world without making any direct reference to it. Take how fascinating it is to watch animals competing for food: crabs and shrimps scuttling about in a rock pool; the aggressive ballet of the pecking order round a bird feeder; wasps returning to a nest; the kestrel gliding and hovering over its prey. I doubt that a literal picture of any of these would convey as much as the excitement of actually being the spectator. By absorbing these experiences, analyzing what is going on, making the odd diagram, a painter's work can become richer. A viewer need never know what went into a picture, but might sense something in its texture, its looping line. Or there could be just a feeling. To take the sensation of distance, such as watching the moons of Jupiter through a telescope; a circle with two or three dots around it would hardly convey the thrill of spying something so distant. Enthusiasm, curiosity, sympathy for the natural world, none of this could be measured in a lab; but they can be sensed in art.

7. DARK FILAMENT

Painting, as has been pointed out, does not advance collectively along a designated line of research, nor prove or disprove a hypothesis, with each new 'tendency' supplanting the previous 'theory'. Nor does poetry record its progress in scientific papers and conferences. Artists are not obliged to provide evidence and proof to back up their findings. At the same time, scientists – from neurology to computer science - are quick to point out that they have imagination, think 'laterally', and make discoveries by accident. Artists do not have a monopoly on intuition. But artists do not need teams of co-researchers. The painter normally works independently in a studio, furthering his or her work, keeping up the momentum. Undertaking a project set by someone else is a break in that routine. Some find that disruptive. They do not want to take on a set 'subject'. In my own case I have undertaken commissions, but I do find it hard to keep on track. I prefer to work on several themes at once. If required to go one way, I probably go off in the opposite direction.

Following on from the point that a visual work of art may refer only obliquely to the natural world, I should point out that the way a work comes together can be startlingly haphazard. It would be wrong to suggest - in a publication on how biology inspires art via the computer - that this happens like a school project: visit the lab, make drawings, test the results, construct the final piece. Sometimes the apparent source, or the theme upon which every other part depends, can only be found and slapped on at the last minute. If there ever was a 'research question', it will only become apparent a month or two after the answer has emerged (Figure 5).

If I recall the various ingredients that went into making the work illustrated here, 'Dark Filament', I shall make the process sound like I was following a script. But there wasn't a plan, and this picture is not 'based' on anything in particular. I just have routines of working with this or that motif, both by drawing on the computer – using a Wacom tablet and programs such as Painter, Illustrator, and Photoshop – and by drawing and painting. I already had a small collection of botanical illustrations, and I was studying floral motifs in Renaissance tapestries; I was also interested in astronomy. But this really began with a phone call. Out of the blue, I was asked to curate an exhibition of digital art at the London Print Studio. I had a day to think of a title, and to pick the other three artists I was to include. The

Figure 5. James Faure Walker, Dark Filament, 2006, archival Epson print 44" x 53" (exhibited in the Digital Pioneers exhibition, collection Victoria and Albert Museum). (© 2006, J. Faure Walker. Used with permission).

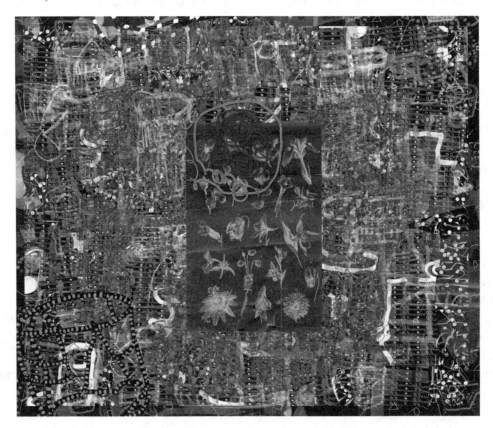

title I thought of was 'filament', a term used in electronics, astronomy and biology. At this time, July 2006, I was interested in all sorts of diagrams – early computers, optical devices, organic forms.

I had come across the 1928 'Introduction to Medical Protozoology' (Knowles, 1928), published in Calcutta, in an Oxfam bookshop in 2006. I debated with myself the point of buying this – it was not cheap - simply because of a handful of colour illustrations that fascinated me. They reminded me of those Miro biomorphs. The plate illustrated here shows the life cycle of the malarial mosquito, with the gentle swelling forms, the step-by-step development of the lethal disease. My first response was to paint some crude watercolour figure-of-eight studies. These I would photograph, and blend in with some designs I was already working on with complex digital 'pattern' brushes. One advantage of the 'Painter' program is that you can design a brush so that it paints with a streaming pattern, varied in several specified respects. It can be striped, dotted, wiggly, or even have sets of images (Figure 7).

I had moved to a new studio some months before in March 2006. I had pinned up rows of watercolour studies, and found I liked the arrangement they made in the photograph. I played around digitally with this composition, and the first work of this series, 'Studio Filament', was essentially a collage switched over into negative colour. I had begun by placing this botanical illustration of 'Corolla' over the top. I must have had it lying around for thirty years, and for some reason that I have now quite forgotten, I thought of scanning

Figure 6. James Faure Walker, study for Studio Filament, archival Epson print 44" x 53" (© 2006, J. Faure Walker. Used with permission).

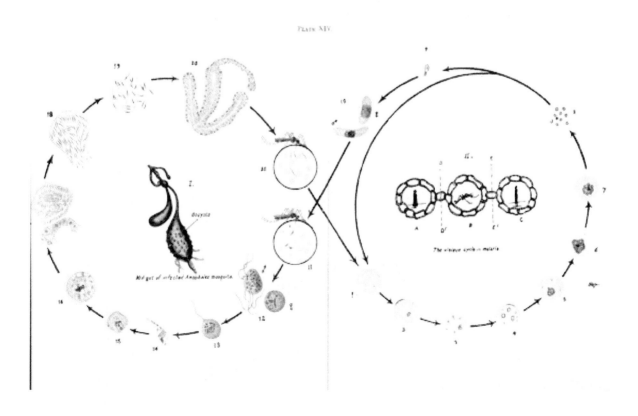

Figure 7. James Faure Walker, Studio Filament, archival Epson print 40" x 46", 101 x 113 cm (collection Victoria and Albert Museum).). (© 2006, J. Faure Walker. Used with permission).

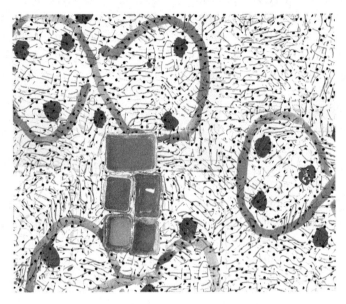

Figure 8. Source page for Dark Filament, Corolla, origin unknown. Author's Collection.

it, and placing it – digitally - over the watercolours. But it did not work, and instead I placed a photo of a palette, of the colours I had been using in making the watercolours.

The figure-of-eight idea, the life cycles of the mosquito, the flower drawings, the filigree motifs, all became enmeshed in the other drawings I was making. I extracted a circle of patterning from the design, and imposed it slightly rotated over what had by now become a complex pattern. I shuffled the layers around, putting some in negative, slipped in that botanical page, again in negative, and added a circular scribble on top. I called it 'Dark Filament', and like the other works in the series had it printed at the largish scale of about four feet across.

In the past five years this work has been shown in college galleries, in digital art shows, and at the Victoria and Albert Museum in the exhibition, 'Digital Pioneers' (Faure Walker, 2011). It has been reproduced in a how-to computer art book (where it was cropped) and in a book on patterns. I have heard comments about its colour and its composition, about the techniques involved. What no one has ever asked is why there is a panel of flower forms in the middle.

CONCLUSION

We know so much more than our predecessors of a hundred or so years ago when 'nature' more or less meant that postcard landscape. We know about the vast scale of the universe, that it is billions of years old; we know about evolution, about the weird lifeforms deep in the ocean, about bacteria, about the ecosystem of the planet. At the same time, the very idea of nature has an enduring appeal for the artist: the natural form that has grown of its own accord, adapting to a given environment. Artists – like novelists or composers – speak of the 'creative process', of making a 'world', populated with characters, motifs, forms. In the early abstract paintings of Joan Miro there were wiggly shapes, not identifiable as a particular

lifeform. These came to be called 'biomorphs', a term that, according to many, has no validity at all in science. What is the difference, then, between a made-up shape and one you transcribe, the 'real' natural form seen via an electron microscope?

REFERENCES

Britten, N. (2010, March 15). Artist uses live cells to create new form of design. *The Telegraph*. Retrieved June 28, 2011, from http://www.telegraph. co.uk/culture/art/art-news/8383363/ Artist-uses-live-cells-to-create-new-form-of-design.html

Brundrett, K., & Crowley, G. (2010). Graham Crowley, on the state of play for contemporary painting. *Artists Newsletter*, February 2010. Retrieved June 28, 2011, from http://www.a-n.co.uk/ jobs_and_opps/article/606719

Carnie, A. (2002, March 17). Scientists and artists must rub shoulders. *The Observer*. Retrieved June 28, 2011, from http://www.tram.ndo.co.uk/ afewwords.htm

Carnie, A. (2011). *Artist's website*. Retrieved June 28, 2011, from http://www.tram.ndo.co.uk/ magicforest2.htm

Chuter, J. (2010), Interview with Andrew Carnie. *ATTN: Magazine*, July. Retrieved June 28, 2011, from http://www.attnmagazine.co.uk/arts-literature/2452

Day, L. (1908). *Nature and ornament: Nature, the raw material of design* (p. vi). London, UK: Batsford. republished 1929

Ellington, A. (2011, March 5). On regulation. *Streamspace*. Retrieved June 28, 2011, from http:// streamspace.blogspot.com/2011/03/ ramblings-on-regulation-by-andrew.html

Faure Walker, J. (2006). *Painting the digital river: How an artist learned to love the computer*. Prentice Hall.

Faure Walker, J. (2011). *Works in Victoria and Albert Museum*. London. Retrieved June 28, 2011, from http://www.vam.ac.uk/contentapi/search/ ?q=faure+walker&search-submit=Go

Haeckel, E. H. P. A. (1899). *Art forms in nature*. New York, NY: Dover. reprinted 1974

Kesseler, R., & Harley, M. (2006). *Pollen: The hidden sexuality of flowers* (p. 181). London, UK: Papadakis Publishers.

Knowles, R. (1928). *Introduction to medical proto-zoology*. Calcutta, India: U. N. Dhur & Sons, Ltd.

Latham, W. (2011). *Artist's website*. Retrieved June 28, 2011, from http://www.doc.gold. ac.uk/~mas01whl/

Ozenfant, A. (1952). *1928). The foundations of modern art*. New York, NY: Dover.

Reas, C. (2011). *Artist's website*. Retrieved June 28, 2011, from http://reas.com/category. php?section=works

The Arts Catalyst. (2011). Retrieved June 28, 2011, from http://www.artscatalyst.org/

Verostko, R. (2011). *Artist's website*. Retrieved June 28, 2011, from http://www.verostko.com/

Walker, J. (2004). The reckless and the artless: practical research and digital painting. *Working Papers in Art and Design, 3*. Retrieved June 28, 2011 from http://sitem.herts.ac.uk/artdes_re-search/ papers/wpades/vol3/jfwfull.html

Wellcome Trust. (2011). Retrieved June 28, 2011, from http://www.wellcome.ac.uk/

Wilson, S. (2002). *Information arts: Intersections of art, science, and technology*. Cambridge, MA: The MIT Press.

ADDITIONAL READING

Blossfeldt, K., Bataille, G., & Mattenklott, G. (2004). *Art forms in nature*. Schirmer/Mosel.

Britten, N. (2010, March 15). Artist uses live cells to create new form of design. *The Telegraph*. Retrieved June 28, 2011, from http://www.telegraph. co.uk/culture/art/art-news/ 8383363/Artist-uses-live-cells-to-create-new-form-of-design.html

Hayes, B. (2010). Flights of fancy. *American Scientist*. Retrieved January 20, 2011, from http:// www.americanscientist.org/issues/ pub/2011/1/ flights-of-fancy/1

Hertz, P. (2009). Art, code, and the engine of change. *Art Journal*, 68.

Walker, J. (2004). The reckless and the artless: practical research and digital painting. *Working Papers in Art and Design, 3*. Retrieved June 28, 2011 from http://sitem.herts.ac.uk/artdes_re-search/ papers/wpades/vol3/jfwfull.html

KEY TERMS AND DEFINITIONS

Biomorph: A term used in art criticism to describe a shape that resembles a primitive life form.

Drawing manual: A type of publication popular in the early twentieth century providing guidance about drawing for the amateur, often specialising in subjects such as the figure, horses, trees, and so on.

Nature: A much-debated term, far from neutral, often used in debates about painting in the early twentieth century, often in arguments against science, technology.

Painter software: A sophisticated paint program that is modelled on artist's materials, and enables powerful image processing.

Sci-Art: A term used for exhibitions featuring art/science collaborations.

ENDNOTES

1   http://www.artscatalyst.org/
2   http://www.telegraph.co.uk/culture/art/ art-news/8383363/Artist-uses-live-cells-to-create-new-form-of-design.html

Chapter 19

drawing//digital//data:
A Phenomenological Approach to the Experience of Water

Deborah Harty
Nottingham Trent University, UK

ABSTRACT

In the context of contemporary fine art, the chapter discusses the translation (the finding of equivalences) of a phenomenological experience of water during the activity of swimming repetitive strokes in a swimming pool into drawing with both traditional drawing media and a tablet computer – an Apple iPad. Firstly, through the identification of various physical and psychological elements that appear to consciousness whilst swimming repetitive strokes, the chapter furthers understanding and gives insights into human interaction and relationship with water during this specific activity. Secondly, the research uses the data collected from personal experience of this activity in order to explore and discuss the premise that drawing is phenomenology, considering whether this premise is compromised when drawing with an Apple iPad rather than traditional drawing media. The text considers the phenomenological approach to the research through an engagement with both philosophy (including Merleau-Ponty 1964, 2002, 2004) and theoretical research (including Rosand 2002), to underpin and generate understanding of experiences of water during the activity of swimming and the process of translation of those experiences into drawing.

INTRODUCTION

The phenomenological experience of water during the activity of swimming repetitive strokes in a swimming pool serves as a means to investigate the premise that drawing is phenomenology. In recent years, there has been a growing interest in the relationship between drawing and phenomenology and the possibility of process of drawing to be considered phenomenology; this focused study intends to extend some of the thinking around this particular aspect of drawing. The specific experience of swimming identified here provided the opportunity to collect data through personal experience, which was subsequently translated into drawn marks with both traditional

DOI: 10.4018/978-1-4666-0942-6.ch019

drawing media (charcoal, graphite and paper) and an Apple iPad (Brushes and Sketchbook Pro apps). The chapter compares the data from both processes to uncover whether the introduction of the digital interface of the Apple iPad impacts on the premise that drawing is phenomenology.

Experience/Consciousness

Dewey (1934, p. 38) states, "An experience has a beginning and an end, 'experience' is ongoing, what we perceive every waking moment through consciousness." For clarification, the experience of swimming with repetitive strokes is considered to be 'an experience' as it has a clear beginning and end. Moran (2000, p.60) states, "... consciousness is the basis of all experience ..." This research adopts the position that an experience, such as the experience of swimming referred to here, consists of all that appears in consciousness during the time it is experienced. As Velmans (1996) states:

The "contents of consciousness" encompass all that we are conscious of, aware of, or experience. These include not only experiences that we commonly associate with ourselves, such as thoughts, feelings, images, dreams, body experiences and so on, but also the experienced three-dimensional world (the phenomenal world) beyond the body surface.

Working on this basis the translation of experiences of water into drawn marks considers the physical elements of the water – visual and tactile qualities for example, alongside the psychological affect the water has on the state of consciousness; what it feels like to experience water.

Drawing with Traditional Media

Currently, there is significant debate and disagreement concerned with answering the question, 'What is drawing?' It is not within the remit of this study to discuss or answer this question.

However, despite conflicting definitions most (including: Farthing 2005; Petherbridge 2008 *in* Garner 2008 & 2010; Fisher 2003 *in* Newman & De Zegher 2003) acknowledge both: the intimate and immediate manner of drawing with traditional media, as Marden (*in* Farthing 2005: 30) states there is, "Less between the hand and the paper than any other medium"; and the potential of drawing to record the trace of the draftsman in the marks created whilst drawing, to allow the viewer to become, "… as close to the action of an artist's thought as one can get" (Newman & De Zegher 2003: 70). Rosand (2002) furthers the debate of this attribute of trace by both: considering drawing's ability to record the trace of the draftsman; and by suggesting that drawing is a phenomenological process – recording its own making through the trace of the marks. Rosand (2002: 12) states, "… the line recalls the process of its becoming through the act of drawing, the gesture of the draftsman." The interest for this research is two-fold: firstly that drawing is phenomenology, capable of recording experience through the marks made whilst drawing; secondly, that drawing is a phenomenological process, capable of recording its own making through the trace of marks. Through discussion of the creative process of drawing during the translation of the identified experience, the chapter will attempt to make implicit aspects of the process of drawing explicit; considering if the intervention of the digital interface of the Apple iPad impacts or alters the potential of drawing to both document the specific identified experience and record its own making.

Drawing with an Apple iPad

Over the past few decades there has been a growing interest within contemporary fine art in drawing with technology. From drawing programmes, such as Adobe Illustrator and Photoshop, graphic tablets, moving image cameras, and the more recent use of Apple products: iPod Touch, iPhone and iPad, artists (for example, James Faure-Walker,

Angela Eames and John Roome) have embraced emerging technologies within their practices. Perhaps the artist most notable for his ability to embrace and incorporate new technologies into his work is David Hockney.

Over a career so far spanning over fifty years Hockney has worked with a range of technology, as it became available, including photography, photomontage, video projections and even embracing the potential of photocopiers and fax machines (Isenberg 2011). In 2009 the exhibition entitled 'Drawing in a Printing Machine' (Annely Juda Fine Art) featured a series of inkjet printed computer drawings Hockney created through collage and drawing on a graphic tablet with the program Photoshop. Hockney (Annely Juda Fine Art 2009) states, "Photoshop is a computer tool for picture making. In effect it allows you to draw directly into a printing machine, one of its many uses." It is perhaps not surprising then that Hockney has incorporated the latest Apple technology into his working processes.

In 2008 Hockney began to draw on his Apple iPhone using the Brushes App. Hockney would produce several drawings a day on his Apple iPhone emailing them instantly to a group of friends. Hockney has since progressed to the larger scale iPad, still working with the Brushes App. He has replaced the sketchbook he constantly carried in his jacket pocket with his Apple iPad. Hockney still paints with oils, however the Apple iPad drawings constitute a large part of his creative output at present. In 2010 the exhibition, 'Fleurs Fraiches' at Pierre Bergé – Yves Saint Laurent in Paris exhibited several of Hockney's digital drawings on installed Apple iPhones and iPads. This form of exhibition allowed the drawings to be seen in their original luminous state rather than as printed versions. A further exhibition of his works in Humlebaek, Denmark entitled 'Me Draw on iPad' saw Hockney email the entire exhibition to the gallery, regularly updating the exhibition through emailing new works (Juxtapoz 2011). Whilst Hockney uses an Apple iPad on a daily

basis, he has not left behind traditional drawing processes using the media alongside one another to, "… see and feel nature more clearly" (Hockney in Isenberg, 2011). Hockney sees the Apple iPad as, "… a serious tool …" which actually influences his other work due to its, "… boldness and speed" (Hockney in Isenberg, 2011). Hockney's ability to take advantage of the benefits of new media and his insistence on its ability to inform his engagement with traditional media inspired the use of the Apple iPad for this study. It is worth mentioning here that this study is focused on drawing with the Apple iPad; it is not within the remit of the research to discuss the vast range of digital technology available at present.

BACKGROUND: CONTEMPORARY FINE ART DRAWING

Drawing as a Phenomenological Process: First Person Research

Several researchers have carried out first-person research into the relationship between drawing and phenomenology concentrating on a specific aspect. Karen Wallis's (2003) research utilises drawing from life along with painting, adopting a methodology that incorporates a phenomenological approach. However, the inclusion of these two entities has a different emphasis to this research. Wallis incorporates phenomenology to influence how she approaches her drawings or paintings – Merleau-Ponty's (1964) suggestion that you are both seer and seen, (that is, not only are we, as human beings, seen by others, due to the position of our eyes we also have the ability to see ourselves in the world) influenced her decision to incorporate herself within the picture frame – unlike this research Wallis does not suggest that her process of making itself is phenomenological. Wallis (2003) is not suggesting drawing is particular to a phenomenological practice as the research here is but that by being both seer and seen the approach is phenomenological.

Prosser (2004) conducted phenomenological research, which included the production of several drawings and texts discussing themes such as Dasein, Ennui, Xenia, Notitia and Fantasia. The research included: a discussion of phenomenology; a phenomenological approach to the above themes; and phenomenological drawings. As with Wallis, Prosser's approach was phenomenological, although he did not discuss the process of drawing as phenomenological or relate the themes of the text to the drawings.

Cain's (2007) research through drawing focuses on drawing as a means of gaining understanding, which she entitles, "… drawing as coming to know …" Cain (2007) states, "I began to consider that drawing was perhaps a knowledge-constituting *process* involving a dialectic between knowing and not-knowing." Cain (2009) concludes that, "… the experience of making a drawing makes visible what are essentially tacit processes in activity through our ability to make sense of what we do." As a consequence, and in contrast to this research, Cain's research focused on, "… the evolution of the practitioner rather than the evolution of the drawing" (Cain 2009).

MacDonald's (2009) first-person research concentrates on a multi-sensory approach to observational drawing as a "form of enquiry … relating to the body and embodied experience." MacDonald used direct mark-making in response to perceptions. MacDonald's research also relates to Cain's in that it discusses drawing as a means of understanding perceptual processes. In contrast to MacDonald's research this research does not look at representational drawing per se but seeks to explore the experience of swimming repetitive strokes in a swimming pool through the most appropriate means.

Harty's (2010) practice-led research sought to answer the question: How is it possible, through *drawing*, to identify and translate the elements of a specific *experience* into drawings? The research

engaged with processes of drawing and phenomenology and/or psychoanalysis in order to address the question. One of the research considerations was that repetitive processes of drawing were phenomenological, recording the drawing process through the marks left on the paper. The research emphasis however, offered conclusions from a first person perspective furthering understanding of human experience and the documentation of implicit elements of processes of drawing offered insights into, and consequently, furthered understanding of a creative process. This premise is furthered in this research, which seeks to consider the hypothesis that drawing is phenomenology through the exploration of the identified experience.

Drawing as a Phenomenological Process: Third Person Research

In contrast to the first-person research of practitioners there are two theoreticians who discuss drawing and phenomenology from a third-person perspective.

Bailey's (1982) research presented a philosophical thesis, which sought to discuss drawing as implicitly connected with phenomenology; presenting the argument that the draughtsman, whilst drawing, is a phenomenologist. Bailey (1982: 3) states, "Within the scope of all the ways he [the draughtsman] makes his marks, through all their transmutations, he seeks routes for the interrogation of how things are." The thesis focuses on drawings, which are representational of the physical world but the author suggests that the same holds true for drawings, which seek to uncover the "how things are" of an internal thought. Bailey (1982: 339) relates the movement of the draughtsman's thought with the trace left upon the surface of the paper, as he suggests, "More deeply than any other form in the visual arts, drawing immediately betrays how the draughtsman thinks." Proceeding to state, "… drawing gives us insights into the pathways of the draughtsman's thought-in-action …" (1982: 340). Within the thesis Bailey (1982:

165) also states, "The draughtsman draws to give order to his thought, it is a process whereby he makes clear to himself what he is doing. It is a process that simultaneously orders and enlarges his experience."

Rosand (2002) writes from the perspective of a viewer of Masters' drawings (including, Leonardo da Vinci, Raphael and Michelangelo). He argues that drawing is a phenomenological process capable of both recording the movement of the draftsman's mind and the drawing's own making through the trace of marks on the paper's surface. Rosand (2002) suggests that viewing drawings can lead the viewer directly back to the draftsman. "Drawing is re(enactment). So too is our response to drawing. The line is a direct record of the draftsman's gesture. The gesture of drawing is, in essence, a projection of the body …" (Rosand, 2002: 16). The chapter refers to Rosand's research when discussing the process of drawing, however, this research concentrates on the process of drawing whilst discussing the experience of swimming repetitive strokes rather than on the viewing of drawings once completed.

DRAWING THROUGH WATER// WATER THROUGH DRAWING

Experiences of Water

"… water 'substantiates' links between the body and the material environment in which it is, equally, the substance of life for every organism" (Strong 2004: 62). As Schwenk & Schwenk (1989: p.5) state, "… water embraces everything, is in and all through everything; because it rises above the distinctions between plants and animals and human beings …" Water forms a large part of our existence from drinking, bathing, and travelling, we rely on water to support our existence. We experience water through all of the senses, whether breathing in the damp autumn morning air, listening to the sound of rain splashing against the window or watching the moonlight illuminate the sea, water appears to us as a fully sensuous experience. We experience water in a variety of means that are often contradictory: at its most obvious water is a means of survival – an adult human body is approximately 60% water; conversely, water potentially causes harm and death – through drowning etc.; water is also a means to establish political borders and as such also determines economies; water is a means of relaxation – through submersion and the calming effect of audible experiences of water. Our experiences of water are multifarious and in some instances individual.

Strong (2004) argues that water helps to develop a sense of self within the environment; our interaction with water builds and determines our communities. Strong (2004: 5) states that, "… engagement with the environment provides synaesthetic experiences that are integral to the generation of meaning and instrumental in the development of cultural values and practices." In agreement with this, Malpas (2006) discusses the potential of water to be constitutive of place; it ties us to our environment. Malpas (2006) states, "To think through the significance of water in human life […] involves more than just considerations of health or of economics – it touches on our very constitution as human, since it touches on our constitution in and through place."

There is a potential therefore to consider that experiences are culturally bound and to some extent individual; our relationship with water is constituted through our cultural environment and beliefs. However, Strong (2004) considers there are many experiences of water that we all share, for example its physical qualities and variations of temperature and as such, "Human sensory experience of these qualities is to some degree universal, and this commonality doubtless contributes to the recurrent themes of meaning encoded in water in many different contexts" (Strong 2004: 49). One experience of water that appears to generate comparable effects on consciousness whatever the cultural background or environment is that of being under water for example, immersion during the activity of swimming.

Immersion in Water

Immersion in water generates a feeling of weightlessness and ease of movement within the body. There appears to be a disconnection with the world and rather than alienation, a sense of calm and security. The muted world under water appears to allow a removal from the noise and chaos of the environment we exist in allowing a heighten sense of self and clarity of thought. As Valéry (*in* Sprawson 1992: 101) suggests, "It seems to me that I discover and recognise myself when I return to this universal element. My body becomes the direct instrument of my mind, the author of its ideas." The body is free from the usual pressures experienced and there is a sense of containment within one's self. As Sprawson (2004: 135) states, "Swimming [...] can cause a sense of detachment from ordinary life. Memories, especially those of childhood, can be evoked with startling strength and in vivid and precise detail." Swimming can induce states of consciousness that are close to the feeling of meditation as the body moves rhythmically through the water, emerging for air at regular intervals. This experience of repetitively submerging and surfacing was the inspiration and focus of the drawings discussed later within this chapter. The interest lies in understanding more about what effect this experience of repetitive action in water had on the state of consciousness and how this could be documented by drawing.

Immersion in water generates a particular state of consciousness as the changing environment challenges our senses and perceptions. Sounds are muted, vision distorted and there are contradictory perceptions of isolation from others around and conversely, a fusion with the environment that envelops the body. This fusion with the environment, where the boundaries of inner and outer experiences have become fused, means it is hard to determine where the body stops and the environment begins. There is an awareness of ourselves, as a part of, not separate to our surroundings (Harty 2010: 65). This state of fusion, Csikszentmihalyi and Csikszentmihalyi (1988: 38) refer to as flow suggesting that, "… the clearest sign of flow is the merging of action and awareness. A person in flow has no dualistic perspective: he is aware of his actions but not of the awareness itself." Bollas (1987) describes feelings of being joined with an environment as reminiscent of when we were infants and our every need was taken care of by our mothers. We saw her as what Bollas (1987) terms a 'transformative environment', we were aware of ourselves as a part of the environment however, not as a separate entity. Bollas (1987) suggests that these experiences happen before we have the ability for speech or thought and therefore the experiences are what he terms, 'unthought known' – we are familiar with the experience but we are not capable of remembering them through language or recalled thoughts.

Many people have identified this feeling of fusion with an environment when submerged in water and it is considered that these experiences may have resonance with the experiences of security of the womb, being suspended in and protected by the amniotic fluid. As Sprawson (2004: 143) states, "It is generally accepted that in the area of the unconscious, water in any form and immersion in it suggests a hidden desire for a return to the security and irresponsibility of the womb and its amniotic waters." This desire to return to the security of the womb could be compared with Bollas' (1987) 'unthought known' a feeling of familiarity without any conscious memory of the experience. There is also speculation that associations with the experiences of the womb are made in early life when being bathed or immersed in water and these experiences serve to affirm and potentially strengthen them throughout life (Strong 2004).

Rhythm in Repetitive Actions

Immersion however, is short lived before the impulse to breathe initiates resurfacing. The activity of swimming repetitive strokes necessitates a systematic resurfacing that develops a rhythmical action. The significance of rhythm within repetitive action on a generation of a state of fusion or flow is its resonance with the rhythm of existence; a series of rhythms - the changing of the seasons, the sequence of night and day, life and death, or the beating of the heart, for example - which regulate being. When we experience rhythm in any capacity it has the potential to resonate with the very core of existence and it is this factor that contributes to the generation of the state of fusion during repetitive actions (Harty 2010). Dewey states, (1934: 156) "Underneath the rhythm of every act […] there lies, as a substratum in the depths of subconsciousness, the basic pattern of the relations of the live creature to his environment." This again has resonance with the unthought known of the experience of the womb, the recalled connection with repetitive sounds of the mother's heartbeat experienced within the womb. "… water sounds replicate these 'heard' or 'felt' in the womb and […] consequently, humans associated rhythmical and circulatory sounds with prenatal security" (Strong 2004: 53). Therefore, swimming with repetitive strokes in a swimming pool has the potential to initiate a series of sensations and evoke long forgotten memories as the body is thrust through the water in a rhythmical pattern of submerging and surfacing. This potentially explains some of the reasoning behind why many become addicted and obsessive about swimming; it potentially fulfils a desire to return to the security of the womb.

Experiences of Drawing

When commencing the research through drawing consideration was given as to the appropriate means to draw. It was considered that if drawing commenced through direct observation there might be a tendency to concentrate only on the visual perceptions of water rather than the experience as it appeared to consciousness. The aim of the drawings was to research the experience of water phenomenologically; to uncover all that appears to consciousness, both physical and psychological elements of the experience. Drawing from observation was considered therefore to limit that experience to visual perceptions, as attention would be concentrated on the elements present – the physical not psychological qualities. As a consequence the decision to draw from memory appeared to be most pertinent approach as memory had the potential to contain all the significant elements as they appeared to consciousness.

Consideration was also given to the type of traditional media chosen to carry out the drawings to compare with the process of drawing with an Apple iPad. Pencil, charcoal and paper were selected as they were considered to represent a range of traditional media. Two apps were selected for the iPad, Sketchbook Pro, due to its range of drawing materials and mark making qualities and Brushes, due to its ability to 'play back' the drawing in creation and its publicized use by Hockney.

Before commencing drawing, memories of experiences of water during the repetitive activity of swimming were recalled and the phenomenological text detailed below generated by the author, to articulate and identify some elements of the experience to assist the process of drawing:

… breathe chaotic calm, dapple gushing fluidity, contemplate … breathe, bubble, repetitive weightlessness emerging, ripple blow, flashing, tiredness splash … breathe, surround, envisage, relax, bubble distortion, concentration, clarity contained, stretch, blow, hypnotic thrashing, stretch, muted flotation, cool, introspective absorption, reflection, deep transient light, mind and body … gasp ripple flow, thrashing meditative awareness, breath bubbles … gasp, breath bubbles … blow …

Drawing with Traditional Media

Drawing commenced with graphite and/or charcoal on paper, marks were created in response to the recalled memories of the identified experience. Initial drawings contained the presence of repetition, directional flow and light within the marks upon the surface. The media was applied to the surface using a variety of bodily movements, sweeping, rubbing and scoring the surface of the paper; an eraser removed areas of tone to draw the light back into the drawing (Figure 1).

Various parts of the hand and arm were initiated in the drawing process, altering the tone, depth and texture of the marks. These first series of drawings identified and addressed the physical qualities of light, reflecting and shimmering through the water. As the series progressed the sensation of movement and directional flow became part of the mark making, developing the sense of immersion and the hypnotic repetition that generates states of fusion and flow (Figure 2).

Part of the repetitive action experienced during the identified experience - alongside the movement of the limbs - is the rhythmical breath, systematically inhaling and exhaling in equilibrium with the movement of the body. The physical presence of this breath appears through bubbles in the water carrying the expelled air to the surface. The bubbles, created by the exhaling breath, have a tactile and sensory quality, they rush past tingling the sides of the face, leaving a distinctive and audible trace as they travel. The completion of this momentary event signals the necessity to surface and inhale. The breath bubbles have the potential to represent presence and life within the immersed world and for these reasons became a recurring motif in the drawings. Within the visual image of the breath bubble is contained a sense of weightlessness, light and freedom of movement, connecting the visual image with the sensory experience and recognition of its sound as it rushes through the water to the surface. These properties, it is suggested, are contained within this repeated motif.

Several drawings were created to explore the effect of multiple breath bubbles. Circular motions of varying pressure were created with the graphite onto the paper's surface engaging the rotation of the wrist or the entire arm to vary the size and density of the breath bubble. An eraser was vigorously rubbed across the surface creating its own marks through the smudges and revealing of the white surface. Traces of the breath bubbles' brief existence remained discernible in the indentations and residue graphite on the surface. Over this layer a further series of breath bubbles were created

Figure 1. Deborah Harty. Charcoal on paper. (© 2011, Harty. Used with permission).

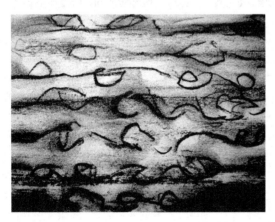

Figure 2. Deborah Harty. Charcoal on paper. (© 2011, Harty. Used with permission).

and erased again building a surface reminiscent of past and present exhalations. Experimentation with this process continued with consideration to the ephemeral nature of both the bubble and the breath; the drawing process replicating the continuous creation and expiry of the breath bubbles (Figure 3). The repetition of the flow of breath also has resonance with the sense of meditative calm and introspection generated through the repetitive action and focused awareness of self, experienced during the activity of swimming. Csikszentmihalyi and Csikszentmihalyi (1988: 43) states, "In some flow activities, perhaps in most, one becomes more intensely aware of internal processes."

The breath bubble motifs continued to be incorporated into the subsequent series of drawings alongside considerations of immersion, flow and transient light qualities experienced during the activity of swimming. Water is transient in both its fluidity and visual quality; it is affected and takes on both the shape and light quality of its environment. As Strong (2004: 51) states "… the eye is presented with a luminescent image it cannot 'hold'. Instead, it must simply absorb all of the rhythms of movement and the tiny shifts and changes." Whilst swimming these qualities are altered and manipulated by the movement of the body; the body to some degree therefore determines and becomes a part of the environment.

The bodily movement causes the water to ripple, affecting the light quality and directional flow of the water. In much the same way when drawing with graphite or charcoal the movement of the body also determines the appearance of the drawings. In response to this, in addition to the layers of graphite bubbles, tonal directional marks were vigorously drawn onto the surface to capture the flickering dappled light and gliding movement through the fluidity. Compressed charcoal was drawn into the surface, smudged and blurred with the fingertips, side and palm of both hands. Directional marks were added and erased to allude to directional flow and immersion. Pockets of light appeared through the revealed areas of the erased drawing. The breath bubbles appear to float in a light filled directional flow; there is a sense of flotation, calm and absorption. The directional marks are drawn out to the paper's edges suggesting expansion and continuation beyond the drawing, alluding to a continuous repetition of action (Figure 4).

Drawing with an Apple iPad

Using an Apple iPad and the apps Sketchbook Pro and Brushes, digital drawings were created alongside the drawings with traditional media. The drawings commenced with the same recalled

Figure 3. Deborah Harty. Charcoal on paper. (© 2011, Harty. Used with permission).

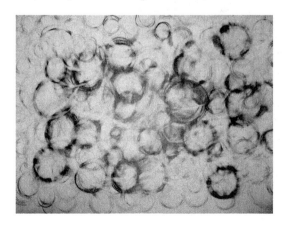

Figure 4. Deborah Harty. Graphite and charcoal on paper. (© 2011, Harty. Used with permission).

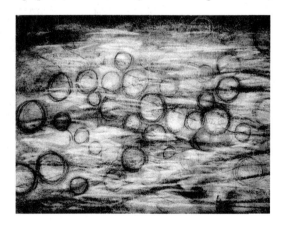

experiences of the activity of swimming repetitive strokes. Initially the same motifs appeared in the drawings, the use of light and flow and eventually the breath bubble (Figure 5). At these early stages rather than draw within the capabilities of the media attempts were made to replicate the process of drawing with traditional media. This was naturally not very successful; the device has two features, which make this particularly awkward. For a start if more than one pressure point is applied to the iPad's screen, then the drawing moves rather than creating two marks, there is also the potential to zoom in and out by using two points of pressure. So when attempting to engage the hands, arms etc in the process of drawing, rather than creating a variety of marks the drawing endlessly jumped around. Clearly this is due to tacit knowledge of drawing processes trying to be replicated rather than any fault with the Apple iPad. It was, however, challenging to override the natural instinct to immerse the body in the process of drawing.

Furthermore, when using Sketchbook Pro, to create marks of differing size, density, or texture, tools have to be selected from the menu. Several attempts were made to use different parts of the hand to make a mark and naturally the marks stayed constant and really highlighted the fact that whatever part of the body became involved, the mark would stay as programmed. It was interesting to consider why you would enter into this type of behaviour with a different medium to traditional drawing media; you do not pick up a piece of clay and expect it to move across a surface as a piece of charcoal. The point was, whilst the tactile quality of the medium differs from that of traditional drawing media – there is no gritty residue dust or chalky smell - the visual quality was such that at times if was difficult to remember you were working on a digital interface; the drawing apps gave a sense of drawing with traditional media. The tools you can draw with do have the resulting mark that can be found when using graphite for example. Using the Brushes app, Hockney (*in* Grant 2010) states, "… sometimes I get so carried away, I wipe my fingers at the end thinking I have got paint on them." The marks on screen become believable as charcoal, graphite or paint, whatever tool you have selected and therefore familiar visually but unknown behaviourally. The tactile nature of drawing with an Apple iPad is very different to that when drawing with traditional drawing media. The screen has the same tactile quality whether the tool chosen is charcoal or pen. This again interrupts with

Figure 5. Deborah Harty. Digital drawing. (© 2011, Harty. Used with permission).

the expectation of what is seen - a charcoal mark, and what is felt - a smooth screen.

To alter the qualities of a mark you have to think what kind of mark you wish to make and select the tool, width and density accordingly to suit. The process of drawing is altered as the thought processes and pre-selection of mark rather than an interaction of body, tool and surface determine the drawing. The completed drawings still have the potential to appear as a traditional drawing on the screen, however the process is quite different. The Brushes app does have the capability of responding to the speed and pressure of the movement across the screen. So there is a sense of response to bodily movement through the corresponding mark. This again, however is altered; it does not matter what you used to make the mark, speed reduces the thickness of the mark, pressure increases or decreases the transparency of the mark. Therefore whatever you chose to draw with does not affect the resulting mark. This was a disorientating experience; being use to utilising different parts of the body to vary the mark, it was hard to re-programme the self not to behave in this way.

After the production of several drawings discoveries of the possibilities and limitations of the apps began to affect the appearance of the drawings. One discovery was of a blur tool that in some

ways had a similar quality to smudging with the added benefit of the backlit screen, which alluded to luminosity. When the blur tool was used the drawing had the appearance of luminous fluidity reminiscent of the flickering changing environment experienced during the activity of swimming (Figure 6). Familiarity with the apps eased some of the earlier difficulties of bodily engagement and the process of drawing settled into a pattern of thought, choice of tool and movement of the middle finger.

Continuing to work within the capabilities of both the drawer and apps, several drawings were made that attempted to draw together the elements experienced during the activity of swimming. Similar marks and process to those created during drawing with traditional media were at times influencing the Apple iPad drawings, however the process became reciprocal. There was a point in time where discoveries made whilst drawing with the Apple iPad apps began to initiate approaches and experimentation when returning to draw with traditional media.

This is in evidence in Figures 4 and 7. Figure 7 was produced first as an experiment in combining the breath bubbles with the qualities of immersion, luminosity and directional flow. This influenced experimentation with the same qualities when drawing with traditional media. The appearance

Figure 6. Deborah Harty. Digital drawing. (© 2011, Harty. Used with permission).

Figure 7. Deborah Harty. Digital drawing. (© 2011, Harty. Used with permission).

of the drawings is distinct to the media used, however it is arguable that the drawing in Figure 4 would not have been made without the presence of the drawing in Figure 7.

A further capability of Sketchbook Pro app was the potential to incorporate text into drawing; in affect with this app you can use text to make a mark. Series of drawings were created to experiment with this potential. Words from the passage of phenomenological text, detailed earlier in the chapter, were incorporated into the drawings. Considering the text as marks with which to draw, the phrases and individual words were repeated, layered and inverted. The text suggestive of the physical and psychological elements experienced during the activity of swimming adding a further possibility to the drawings to incorporate phenomenological elements of the experience of the activity of swimming with repetitive strokes (Figure 8).

Drawing is Phenomenology

Drawing with traditional media is an immediate and intimate activity. The marks appearing on the paper directly respond to the thoughts and subsequent bodily movements through the trace on the paper's surface. When an eraser is used traces of the medium and indentations in the paper's surface remain leaving a residue of both the process of creation and the drawer's thoughts. Fisher (2002: 222 *in* Newman & De Zegher 2003) states,

… the act of drawing makes possible the magical identity between thought and action because to draw is the quickest medium and can therefore protect the intensity of thought. To draw is never a transcript of thought (in the sense of writing) but rather a formulation or elaboration of the thought itself at the very moment it translates itself into an image.

Drawing through response to the identified experience is made manifest in the marks upon the surface, as the memories are recalled and simultaneously translated into drawing. This process is immediate, thoughts and bodily movement working as one, recording the experience in the drawing. As Rosand (2002: 110) states, "Drawing records what has been seen and is known, but not after the fact – it is simultaneous with, and, for the draftsman, identical to perception."

Merleau-Ponty (1964, 2004) suggests the artist is able to communicate his specific mode

Figure 8. Deborah Harty. Digital drawing. (© 2011, Harty. Used with permission).

of being-in-the-world through his art, revealing the world through the trace left on the canvas or paper. "It is by lending his body to the world that the artist changes the world into paintings [...] that body which is an intertwining of vision and movement" (Merleau-Ponty 1964: 162). Merleau-Ponty (1964) suggests that the artist is able to recreate in his artwork the specific phenomena of the world, rather than a reproduction of how it is presumed to appear, through the mediation of his body. As Rosand (2002: 16) states, "The gesture of drawing is, in essence, a projection of the body ..." the body that is mediator between mind and world.

As discussed earlier the embodied process is somewhat altered when drawing with an Apple iPad. The process is immediate, in terms of the marks appearing in direct correlation to the movement of the finger. However, there is a pause in the process as media are selected from the menu. Consideration was given to how/whether this pause interrupted the relationship between thought and action and subsequently the phenomenological process. Initially, the pause to choose or alter the drawing tool appeared to interrupt the process as the usual spontaneity experienced during drawing with traditional media was diminished. As a consequence this affected the continuity of recall and embodiment of mind and body, thought, and action. Initial reflections then conceded that drawing with an Apple iPad could not be considered phenomenological as it interfered with the mind/body engagement and embodiment with the process.

However, as familiarity with the apps menus and the subsequent marks grew, so the pause to choose or alter the mark was reduced. As the tool selected made a mark determined by its settings, over time awareness of the vocabulary of marks enabled a more fluid and spontaneous process of drawing. Furthermore, as familiarity with the tactile nature of drawing on the interface increased the movement of the fingers became more sensitive to the capabilities and limitations of the device. Once this level of understanding of the device was reached, the process of drawing appeared to be spontaneous and immediate, attributes ascribed to drawing with traditional media. As Hockney (in Weschler 2009) states, "There's this wonderful impromptu quality, this freshness to the activity ..." Therefore, it could be argued that when the process of drawing with the Apple iPad became intuitive the process, whilst altered, became phenomenological and capable of recording the experience of the activity of swimming in the drawing.

When considering the potential of drawings created with the Apple iPad to be phenomenological, that is, to record their own making, once more the process differs from that when drawing with traditional media. As when drawing with charcoal or graphite, layers of marks can be built up and overlaid when drawing with the Apple iPad apps. Through the use of the transparency tool there is the potential to use the various chosen tools with greater transparency to reveal the under layers of the drawing. In this respect it is possible to create a drawing with the sense of its own history built into the surface. However, it is equally possible to erase marks, layers and even an entire drawing without a single trace or residue of its existence. In this respect, without the physicality of the indented paper to reveal the initial layers, the final drawing does not necessarily hold the essential information to reveal its own making. Therefore it is reasonable to assert that a drawing created with an Apple iPad is not phenomenological.

However, in contradiction with this statement, the Brushes programme has a 'playback' feature that enables you to view the whole process of drawing. When the playback feature is utilised, the screen goes blank and replays the marks as they were drawn, albeit at a greater speed. In this sense the drawing's entire history is revealed including anything erased and no longer discernible in the final drawing. Therefore rendering a drawing created in the Brushes app to be phenomenological.

CONCLUSION

The chapter has discussed experiences of water during the activity of swimming repetitive strokes in a swimming pool, highlighting the physical and psychological elements experienced. This included a feeling of weightlessness, fusion, transient light and meditative calm induced by the repetition of the action. It was suggested that the experience of swimming had resonance with feelings of immersion, fusion and security experienced whilst in the protection of the womb. The discovery of the mark of the breath bubble whilst drawing, aided understanding of the experience of transience, hypnotic repetition and directional flow experienced during the activity of swimming.

In conclusion, drawing with traditional media does have the potential to record the phenomenological experience of the identified activity of swimming in the marks on the surface. Also, due to the impossibility of complete erasure drawings created with traditional media do have the potential to record their own making, in this sense the drawings are phenomenological. With these considerations in mind, it is argued that drawing with traditional media is phenomenology.

In comparison, once the process of drawing with the Apple iPad apps becomes intuitive, the drawings also have the potential to record the phenomenological experience of the identified activity of swimming. The intuitive process, which allows for continuous drawing, is important in maintaining the embodiment of mind/body/drawing. This in turn initiates the same qualities of immediacy of mark, and intimacy between the mind, body and screen, as experienced during drawing with traditional media – a decision initiates the movement of the body, which in turn leaves a mark. Whilst the apps determine the mark made this did not restrict experimentation and discovery through the drawing. As discussed previously, there were discoveries made whilst drawing with the Apple iPad that influenced decisions when drawing with traditional media; drawing with the Apple iPad

therefore furthered knowledge and understanding of the identified experience.

It could be said that the process of drawing with the Apple iPad apps is not phenomenological as the completed drawing does not contain all the evidence of its making; the drawing can be erased and redrawn without trace – unlike drawing with charcoal or graphite, erasure is complete. However, the Brushes app has a playback option where you can watch the process of drawing from start to finish, revealing the process in detail through the virtual playback. Therefore, there is the potential to record and view the drawings own making albeit not present through visual indication in the final drawing.

With all these issues considered the conclusion is that drawing is phenomenology and whilst the use of the Apple iPad may alter the process of drawing, ultimately it is still pertinent to state that drawing with the Apple iPad apps is phenomenology. However, the final digital drawings as they appear on screen are not phenomenological – they do not reveal the marks of their own making – and this is arguably what is considered distinct about drawing, setting it apart from other creative processes.

FURTHER RESEARCH

The chapter has discussed a particular experience of the activity of swimming repetitive strokes in a swimming pool. It would be interesting to consider alternative experiences of swimming and water to gain further insight into the physical and psychological experiences of this life sustaining fluid.

The chapter has also discussed a particular device for drawing, the Apple iPad, and two apps – Sketchbook Pro and Brushes. Further research could be investigate other drawing interfaces and what affect they may have on the premise that drawing is phenomenology.

It was not within the remit of this chapter to discuss whether there was a benefit to the use of an Apple iPad over or alongside drawing with traditional media, therefore it would be interesting to carry out research that aims to discover the advantages and disadvantages of the use of both traditional and digital media for drawing.

REFERENCES

Annely Juda Fine Art, & Hockney, D. (2009). *David Hockney: Drawing in a printing machine.* London, UK: BAS Printers Ltd.

Bailey, G. H. (1982). *Drawing and the drawing activity: A phenomenological investigation.* Thesis (PhD), University of London.

Bollas, C. (1987). *The shadow of the object: Psychoanalysis of the unthought known.* London, UK: Free Association Books.

Cain, P. (2007). Drawing as coming to know. In *Ambiguity, Tracey Online Journal,* Loughborough University. Retrieved February 15, 2009, from http://www.lboro.ac.uk/departments/ac/tracey/somag/brien.html

Cain, P. (2009). *Abstract for thesis: Drawing as coming to know: How is it that I know I made sense of what I do?* Retrieved August 10, 2009, from http://www.patriciacain.com/research_statement.html.

Csikszentmihalyi, M., & Csikszentmihalyi, I. (Eds.). (1988). *Optimal experience: Psychological states of flow in consciousness.* Cambridge, UK: Cambridge University Press.

Dewey, J. (1934). *Art as experience.* London, UK: Penguin Books Ltd.

Farthing, S. (2005). *Dirtying the paper delicately.* In: University of the Arts, Inaugural Lecture, London, April 26th 2005.

Fisher, J. (2003). On drawing . In De Zegher, C. (Ed.), *The stage of drawing: Gesture and act, selected from the Tate Collection* (pp. 217–226). London, UK: Tate Publishing & The Drawing Center.

Garner, S. (2008). *Writing on drawing, essays on drawing practice and research.* Bristol, UK: Intellect Books.

Grant, C. (2010). *David Hockney.* Retrieved January 4, 2011, from www.bbc.co.uk/news/technology-11666162

Harty, D. (2010). *Drawing//experience: A process of translation.* Ph.D. thesis, Loughborough University.

Isenberg, B. (2011). *David Hockney's friends in art: The iPad and iPhone.* Retrieved July 4, 2011, from www.hockneypictures.com/current.php

Juxtapoz. (2011). *David Hockney: Me draw on iPad.* Retrieved August 3, 2011, from www.juxtapoz.com/Current/david-hockney-qme-draw-on-ipad-in-humlebaek-denmark

MacDonald, J. (2009). *Drawing around the body: The manual and visual practice of drawing and the embodiment of knowledge.* Ph.D. thesis, Leeds Metropolitan University.

Malpas, J. (2006). *The forms of water: In the land and the soul.* Retrieved January 4, 2011, from www.utas.edu.au/philosophy/staff_research/malpas/J.Malpas%20Articles/The%20of%20Water.pdf.

Merleau-Ponty, M. (1964). *1908-1961, The primacy of perception: And other essays on phenomenological psychology, the philosophy of art, history and politics.* Evanston, IL: Northwestern University Press.

Merleau-Ponty, M. (2002). *The phenomenology of perception.* London, UK: Routledge.

Merleau-Ponty, M. (2004). *The world of perception*. Oxford, UK: Routledge.

Moran, D. (2000). *Introduction to phenomenology*. London, UK: Routledge.

Newman, A., & De Zegher, C. (2003). Conversation. In C. De Zegher (Ed.), *The stage of drawing: Gesture and act, selected from the Tate Collection* (pp. 67-81, 165-173, 231-237). London, UK: Tate Publishing & The Drawing Center.

Petherbridge, D. (2008). Nailing the liminal: The difficulties of defining drawing . In Garner, S. (Ed.), *Writing on drawing: Essays on drawing practice and research* (pp. 27–42). Bristol, UK: Intellect.

Petherbridge, D. (2010). *The primacy of drawing: Histories and theories of practice*. New Haven, CT: Yale University Press.

Prosser, B. (2004). *An archetypal psychology of the ordinary: An investigation through drawing*. Thesis (PhD), University of the West of England.

Rosand, D. (2002). *Drawing acts – Studies in graphic expression and representation*. Cambridge, UK: Cambridge University Press.

Schwenk, T., & Schwenk, W. (1989). *Water – The element of life* (Spock, M., Trans.). Anthroposophic Press.

Sprawson, C. (1992). *Haunts of the black masseur: The swimmer as hero*. London, UK: Jonathon Cope.

Strong, V. (2004). *The meaning of water*. Oxford, UK: Berg.

Velmans, M. (1996). *Defining consciousness*. Retrieved January 5, 2005, from http://cogprints. org/395/0/Definingconsciousness.html

Wallis, K. (2003). *Painting and drawing the nude: A search for a realism of the body through phenomenology and fine art*. Thesis (PhD), University of the West of England.

Weschler, L. (2009). *David Hockney's iPhone passion*. Retrieved July 4, 2011, from www. hockneypictures.com/current.php

ADDITIONAL READING

Berger, J. (2005). *Berger on drawing*. Aghabullogue, Ireland: Occasional.

Block, N. (1990). Inverted Earth. *Philosophical Perspectives . Action Theory and Philosophy of the Mind*, *4*, 53–79.

Block, N. (2003). Mental paint . In Hahn, M., & Ramberg, B. (Eds.), *Reflections and replies – Essays on the philosophy of Tyler Burge* (pp. 165–200). Cambridge, MA: MIT Press.

Block, N. (2003). Philosophical issues about consciousness. In L. Nadel (Ed.), *The encyclopedia of cognitive science*. Nature Publishing Group. Retrieved December 28, 2009, from http://www. nyu.edu/gsas/dept/philo/faculty/block/papers/ecs.pdf.

Block, N. (2009). Consciousness. In T. Bayne, A. Cleermans, & P. Wilken (Eds.), *The Oxford companion to consciousness*. Retrieved January 5, 2010, from www.nyu.edu/gsas/dept/philo/faculty/block/papers/oxford.pdf

Brien, A. (n.d.). Thinking through mark and gesture. *Syntax of Mark and Gesture, Tracey Online Journal,* Loughborough University. Retrieved December 15, 2005, from http://www.lboro.ac.uk/departments/ac/tracey/somag/brien.html.

Butler, C. H. (1999). *Afterimage: Drawing through process* [exhibition catalogue]. Cambridge, MA: MIT Press.

Chalmers, D. J. (1995). Facing up to the problem of consciousness. [from http://www.imprint.co.uk/chalmers.html]. *Journal of Consciousness Studies*, *2*(3), 200–219. Retrieved February 2010

Chalmers, D. J. (1996). *The conscious mind: In search of a fundamental theory*. Oxford, UK: Oxford University Press.

Chalmers, D. J. (2004). *The representational character of experience*. Retrieved January 5, 2010, from http://consc.net/papers/representation.html

Craig-Martin, M. (1995). *Drawing the line, reappraising drawing past and present* [exhibition catalogue]. London, UK: The South Bank Centre.

Csikszentmihalyi, M., & Robinson, R. (1990). *The art of seeing – An interpretation of the aesthetic encounter*. California: Getty Publications.

De Zegher, C., & Newman, A. (Eds.). (2003). *The stage of drawing: Gesture and act, selected from the Tate Collection*. London, UK: Tate Publishing & The Drawing Center.

Dennett, D. (1991). Review of McGinn: The problem of consciousness. *The Times Literary*, (May), 10.

Dennett, D. (1995). The unimagined preposterousness of zombies. [from http://ase.tufts.edu/cogstud/papers/uzombie.html]. *Journal of Consciousness Studies, 2*(4), 322–326. Retrieved January 5, 2010

Dennett, D. (2001). Are we explaining consciousness yet? [from http://ase.tufts.edu/cogstud/papers/cognition.fin.html]. *Cognition, 79*(1), 221–237. Retrieved January 5, 2010 doi:10.1016/S0010-0277(00)00130-X

Derwent, C. (2009). *David Hockney: Drawing in a printing machine Annely Juda, London*. The Independent. Retrieved, July 4, 2011, from www.independent.co.uk/arts-entertainment/art/reviews/david-hockney-drawing-in-a-printing-machine-annely-juda-london1677831

Dexter, E. (Ed.). (2005). *Vitamin D – New perspectives in drawing*. London, UK: Phaidon.

Downs, S., Marshall, R., et al. (Eds.). (2007). *Drawing now between the lines of contemporary art*. London, NY: I.B.Tauris & Co Ltd.

Duff, L., & Davis, J. (Eds.). (2005). *Drawing – The process*. Bristol, UK: Intellect Books.

Eames, A. (1998). From drawing to computing and back again. In J. Mottram & G. Whale (Eds.), *Drawing Across the Boundaries, 17-18 September 2000, Loughborough*, Loughborough University.

Garner, S. (2008). *Writing on drawing, essays on drawing practice and research*. Bristol, UK: Intellect Books.

Garrells, G. (2005). *Drawing from the modern 1945-1975*. New York, NY: The Museum of Modern Art.

Glazebrook, M. (2009). *David Hockney on his so-called computer art*. The Sunday Times. Retrieved 4 July, 2011, from www.hockneypicture.com/current.php

Godfrey, T. (1990). *Drawing today, draughtsmen in the eighties*. Oxford, UK: Phaidon Press Ltd.

Greig, G. (2009). *David Hockney, iPriest of art*. London Evening Standard. Retrieved 4 July, 2011, from www.hockneypictures.com/current.php

Halliwell, L. (2007). *Going straight*. In Repeat Repeat Conference: Endurance and Repetition Stream, University of Chester. Retrieved April 6, 2008, from http://www.cpara.co.uk/events/repeatrepeat/labour/Haliwell.html

Harvard University Art Museums. (1997). *Drawing is another kind of language* [exhibition catalogue]. New York, NY: Woodstocker Books.

Hauptman, J. (2005). *Drawing from the modern 1880-1945*. New York, NY: The Museum of Modern Art.

Hoptman, L. (2003). *Drawing now, eight propositions*. New York, NY: The Museum of Modern Art.

Kantor, J. (2005). *Drawing from the modern 1975-2005*. New York, NY: The Museum of Modern Art.

Kivland, S. (2007). *Labour and wait*. Repeat Repeat Conference, Repetition & Embodiment Stream. Retrieved February 10, 2009, from http://www.cpara.co.uk/events/repeatrepeat/labour.html.

Kriegel, U. (2006). *Theories of consciousness*. Oxford, UK: Blackwell.

McGinn, C. (1991). *The problem of consciousness: Essays towards a resolution*. Oxford, UK: Blackwell Publishing.

Moran, D. (2000). *Introduction to phenomenology*. London, UK: Routledge.

Moran, D., & Mooney, T. (Eds.). (2002). *The phenomenology reader*. London, UK: Routledge.

Petherbridge, D. (1991). *The primacy of drawing an artist's view* [exhibition catalogue]. London, UK: The South Bank Centre.

Petherbridge, D. (1998). Drawing with the pencil and through the lens . In *J*. Mottram & G.

Petherbridge, D. (2006). Obsessive drawing. In *National Gallery Wednesday Lecture Series*. National Gallery 8th March 2006.

Rawson, P. (1969). *Drawing*. London, UK: Oxford University Press.

Rawson, P. (1979). *Seeing through drawing*. London, UK: British Broadcasting Corporation.

Rose, B. (1992) *Allegories of modernism: Contemporary drawing*. New York, NY: Museum of Modern Art.

Townsley, J. (2007). *Repetition and process in art production – A practitioner's account*. Repeat Repeat Conference, Repetition, Labour & Endurance Stream. Retrieved January 12, 2009, from http://www.cpara.co.uk/events/repeatrepeat/labour.html.

Turney, J. (2007). *Mindful knitting: escape, Catharsis and contemplation through repetitive craftwork*. Repeat Repeat Conference, Repetition, Labour & Endurance Stream. Retrieved January 12, 2009, from http://www.cpara.co.uk/events/repeatrepeat/labour.html.

Velmans, M. (1995). The relation of consciousness to the material world. *Journal of Consciousness Studies*, *2*(3), 255–265.

Velmans, M. (2001). *A natural account of phenomenal consciousness*. Retrieved December 18, 2009, http://cogprints.org/1813/.

Whale (Eds.), *Drawing Across the Boundaries, 17-18 September 2000, Loughborough*, Loughborough University.

Wright, K. (2010). Hockney retrospective – Brushes with Hockney. *Intelligent Life Magazine, The Economist*. Retrieved July 4, from, www.hockneypictures.com/current.php

KEY TERMS AND DEFINITIONS

Experience: An experience, as opposed to experiencing, is clearly defined by having a beginning and an end and contains all that appears to consciousness during the time of the experience – elements of both the physical attributes of the phenomenal world and what is experienced internally.

Fusion: Refers to a state of consciousness that generates a feeling of being part of, not separate to, the environment; a fusing of both internal and external elements in consciousness.

Immersion: Refers to the state of being fully immersed in water, in this context during the activity of swimming.

Phenomenal World: Relates to the world as it actually appears to us as human beings.

Phenomenological Process: The process can be two-fold: firstly, a process that aims to uncover the nature of a thing – in this case an experience – as it appears to consciousness in order to gain understanding; secondly, a process that has the potential to record the progression of the process – i.e. a drawing that records its own making.

Phenomenology: An approach that necessitates the study of experiences as they appear to consciousness, without the frame of social constructs and expectations.

Process of Translation: The process of drawing to gain understanding of the experience through reflecting on the finding of equivalences in drawn marks to elements of the experience.

Repetition: A repetitive action carried out with the body; the repetitive action initiating a rhythm due to the impossibility of absolute repetition generating variation in the repetitive action.

Swimming: The activity of repetitively moving through water; repeatedly submerging and surfacing in rhythm.

Traditional Drawing: Drawing with media considered to be part of traditional processes of drawing. In this instance, paper, charcoal and graphite.

Chapter 20
From Zero to Infinity:
A Story of Everything

Clayton S. Spada
Cypress College, USA

Victor Raphael
Independent artist, USA

ABSTRACT

Art, science, and spirituality comprise a triumvirate of conceptual and process-oriented contexts founded on different philosophical tenets, but all serving to help interpret human experience with the universe. This chapter examines the potential value in leveraging a generalist perspective as a counterbalance against deconstruction to perceived elemental units so as to avoid becoming bound by paradigm. Art and science are addressed as related observational methods that engage hand and mind to explore hypotheses about and represent the varied aspects of existence. A practicing artist and a practicing artist/scientist present examples of artworks that evolved from their collaborative project, entitled From Zero to Infinity, to illustrate the commonalities that art and science share with respect to pragmatic and creative processes, while not equating art with science as similar cognitive domains.

INTRODUCTION: MAKING SENSE OF REALITY

There is no science without fancy and no art without facts. (Vladimir Nabokov, from Appel, 1967:141)

What happens to us as human beings when we face the immense vastness and uncontrollable chaos of nature? In his *The Critique of Judgement* Kant (1790) wrote,

The mind feels itself set in motion in representation of the sublime in nature; whereas in the aesthetic judgement upon what is beautiful therein it is in restful contemplation. This movement may (especially in its beginnings) be compared to a vibration, i.e., with a rapidly alternating repulsion and attraction produced by one and the same object. (Kant, 1790: Section 27).

Since the beginning of human communication – first with drawing and speech, then followed much later by written language – humankind has tried to understand and represent the world and its

DOI: 10.4018/978-1-4666-0942-6.ch020

role in it (Botha & Knight, 2009). A concern with the nature of reality has been a central question that has compelled every culture to invent stories explaining the origins, structure, and eventual fate of the universe. These include oral histories and scriptures that describe the labors of a single omnipotent god or a pantheon of deities or the powers of ineffable forces in shaping the fabric of existence. Some traditions hold that nothing is real and everything is in constant flux through infinite space and time, while others envision a giant serpent floating in nothingness, swallowing its own tail to encircle the heavens and the world supported on the back of a giant creature, such as an elephant or turtle (Aveni, 1994; Barber & Barber, 2004). This quest for understanding continues unabated, as scientists hunt for elusive subatomic particles they hypothesize will tell them whether the universe will expand forever or continually cycle between expansion and contraction. There is even hope that science may be on the verge of bringing together the four principal forces (gravity, electromagnetism, the nuclear strong force, and the nuclear weak force) into a Grand Unified Theory that will reveal a more sublime level of causality (Gleiser, 1997).

The largest questions often lure the sharpest minds into the narrowest corridors. Faced with the ostensible starkness of simply being, some thinkers turn to the godly in search of a more remote explanation for why things are as they are. Confronted with the transience of their lives set within the context of an apparently indeterminate cosmos, they opt to invoke some model of a continued sentient existence as solace against the prospect of oblivion (Polyani, 1946). Others reject any arguments for a higher order of meaning or directed intent, pointing instead to pure chance as the prime driver. Challenged by evidence suggesting an overarching rational structure that governs even chaos (Gleick, 1987), these minds plumb ever deeper into reductive compartmentalization of the highly integrated system that comprises physical nature.

Despite the widely held perception that the science and spirituality are in opposition, scientific and metaphysical perspectives have integrated well throughout history. The ancient Egyptians directed their advanced architectural, medical and metallurgic technologies to theistic ends. Logic and mathematics flourished under Hinduism and Buddhism. Muslim *hakeems* (polymath scholars) contributed to many fields of both religious and secular learning during the Islamic Golden Age (circa 750 – 1258 CE), and 19th Century Christian communities welcomed scientists who claimed that they were not concerned with discovering and explaining the ultimate nature of reality (Habgood, 1964; Margenau & Varghese, 1991; Turner 1997). Given that science is deeply rooted in philosophy, it is ironic that the quarter between science and the spiritual continues to be widely perceived largely as an empty void, traversed here and there by lonely explorers navigating well outside the norms of either tradition.

Ancient Chinese, Greek, and Islamic thinkers clearly recognized that investigating 'how' and 'why' demanded distinctly different methodological approaches, but they did not discriminate these forms of reasoning as strictly segregated "fields" (Boorstin, 1983; Freely, 2010). From its roots in ancient Greece through the Enlightenment and Colonial periods, science was conducted as ontological investigation designed to reveal "truths" concerning physical reality. Indeed, even while the architects of the Age of Enlightenment attempted to avoid metaphysics, they were compelled to practice it to effectively counter the flaws and gaps in their explanations (Miller, 1996; Staguhn, 1992; Wilson, 1998). The decline of logical empiricism and the rise of linguistic and sociological conceptions in science during the early 20th Century led to a philosophical paradigm shift that de-emphasized the establishment of universal or ontological truth – relegated today by most modern scientists to the realm of philosophy – and more inclined towards pragmatic, functional modeling of physical systems (Devlin, 1997; Polyani, 1946).

Despite the impressive roster of leading scientific thinkers working in biology, chemistry, mathematics, and physics that have made excursions into metaphysical territory over the past two centuries, such efforts have met with mixed reactions from the modern scientific community at large. At best, such forays seem to have failed to set up fertile ground for dialog between science and philosophy, on the whole being dismissed as personal speculative journeys. At worst, oppositions have hardened. Physicist Charles Percy Snow, in his celebrated and influential 1959 Rede Lecture, *The Two Cultures*, claimed that a near-complete breakdown of communication had developed between the sciences and the humanities, and that this did not bode well for arriving at solutions to problems at the global scale (Snow, 1959). In his lecture, Snow essentially revisited the schism between scientists and "intellectuals" that the 18th Century British empiricists had promoted. A more recent exchange illustrates how caustic some parties have become: in a response to physicist Richard Feynman's quip that "philosophy of science is about as useful to scientists as ornithology is to birds" philosopher Craig Callender retorted in a webcast telephone conversation with philosopher Jonathan Schaffer that "it is likely that ornithological knowledge would be of great benefit to birds, were it possible for them to possess it." (Callender & Schaffer, 2010: 8 minutes 35 seconds - 9 minutes 41 seconds).

On the other hand, others have stepped forth in fulfillment of Snow's hope that a "third culture" would eventually emerge to bridge what is in effect an artificially constructed gap. Biologist Edward O. Wilson, widely acknowledged as the "father of sociobiology" and recognized for his secular outlook with respect to religious and ethical issues, wrote *Consilience: The Unity of Knowledge* to present how interdisciplinary approaches that have been used to unite the sciences might serve as models for bringing together the sciences with the humanities (Wilson, 1998). The term "consilience" was believed to have first

been coined by William Whewell in 1840 in his *The Philosophy of the Inductive Sciences*, but with roots extending back to the ancient Greek philosopher, Thales of Miletus (ca. 6 BCE), who believed that the material world is governed by an intrinsic order that is logically comprehensible (Wilson, 1998). Wilson is a prominent proponent of the modern viewpoint espousing the notion of scientific realism, that science describes the world as it really is, independent of what we may wish it to be, and that the various branches of science study compartments of reality that depend on and help in understanding factors studied in other branches. He defines human nature as a set of epigenetic rules — changes in gene expression mediated by mechanisms other than alteration in the underlying DNA base pair sequence — that constitute the genetic patterns of mental development. Ritual and culture, according to Wilson, are products, rather than parts of human nature, and interdisciplinary inquiry into psychological and sociological phenomena can be investigated with scientific methods. Wilson also makes the interesting claim that appreciation of art is part of human nature but art itself is not. So, science and the spiritual are thus sundered, but the longstanding relationship between science and art still endures.

The commonalities shared between art and science have been contemplated since antiquity. Beginning with the first philosophers of nature in the 6th Century BC and continuing through the next century, the ancient Greeks came to distinguish the knowledge of principles through "disinterested understanding" (*epistêmê*: knowledge, science) from the *implication* of the knowledge of principles within the context of a rational method involved in the production of something or the accomplishment of some objective (*techné*: craft, craftsmanship, art) (Zalta, 2010). This distinction extended to the structure of the ancient Greek polis in that the practice of the Mechanical Arts (*techné*, which included both medicine and music because these involved working with the hands) was generally relegated to the lower class while "free" men engaged in the Liberal Arts (*epistêmê*, which included ethics and philosophy, and also politics) (Dorter, 1973; Zalta, 2010). However, *epistêmê* could also imply knowledge of how to do something in a craft-like way (*technê*), such knowledge being most useful when reduced to practice, as opposed to consideration on purely theoretical or aesthetic grounds. The ancient Greeks thus tended to regard *techné* manifested as art for art's sake in a negative light, but assumed a positive view when it was employed in the practical application of a skill (Bloom, 1991; Zalta, 2010). Hence, the etymological derivation of *technique*, the term most commonly referenced to the methods artists employ, and *technology*, the directed use of scientific knowledge toward functional ends.

Both art and science are therefore rational methods for engaging the hand and the mind, under the guidance of careful observation, to investigate hypotheses and construct representations of our experience of the universe. Science works from specific instances of the contingent so as to establish more global relationships while art starts with generalities that are subsequently deconstructed to a personal level. The commonality of potentials and pitfalls shared by art and science suggests the prospect of improved progress toward maximizing our knowledge of the world when these disciplines converse. Like scientists, artists query culture and history, mythology and science, nature and mind, and even the materials with which they work, and then analyze and organize their observations into the scaffold of a coherent proposition that is then put forth in a public forum for independent evaluation and discussion. Scientists also share with artists a long-standing reliance on visual communication in order to effectively *describe* as well as *depict* their representations of what lies beyond superficial perceptions (Kemp, 2000; Miller, 1996; Robin, 1992).

In the cognitive sciences, there is no firm consensus on the degree to which reasoning can be explained as the mental manipulation of symbols, or, by extension, how abstract ideas come to be visualized (Elgin, 1997). Cognitive scientists suggest that the mind draws upon two sorts of representations: description and depiction. Descriptions arise from propositions – irreducible logical constituents from which "true" or "false" may be determined – while depictions are image-like representations created through the arrangement of object-oriented elements "borrowed" from experience with the tangible world (Miller, 1996; Mithen, 1996).

The issue of how information is stored and processed in the functional architecture of the mind has been addressed by revisiting the ancient Greek model of knowledge with the presumption that there are two kinds of knowing: declarative and procedural. Declarative knowledge functions as an intrinsic framework that is constructed within the arena of fact-like representation, while procedural knowledge refers to knowing a process for accomplishing an objective (Barber & Barber, 2004; Miller, 1996; Mithen, 1996). As with the ancient Greek scheme in which epistemological and technical knowledge can sometimes be indeterminate, the distinction between declarative and procedural knowledge can sometimes become quite ambiguous.

Many artists (and scientists) have come to regard the *terra incognita* between the indefinably metaphysical and the strictly analytical as fruitful territory from which to launch their investigations. We have done just that in *From Zero to Infinity*, an ongoing creative collaborative project that weaves the biggest of questions and the smallest of details into poignant arguments for discovering fresh ways of uncovering the untold unconventional riches and unexpected complexity that the universe has to offer. In this sense, a principal aim of our collaboration is to encourage a more unfettered cross-examination between two crucial requisites for conducting good science and making good art: curiosity and imagination.

PROCESS: THE "MAGIC ZONE"

In a society where tradition and deeply-held belief systems are in short supply, having a broad overview can help clear the path toward meaningful work. (Orland, 2006:105)

There is a "magic zone" in any creative process that is difficult and maybe even impossible to reduce to objective description. It is perhaps helpful to imagine this concept more as a space or state of being that encourages the collision of unconscious free association with conscious predilection. The "magic zone" grants equal standing to banality and profundity, and an intercourse between rationality and whimsy. This state is at once quite fragile and easily disrupted by attempts to mediate it, yet definitive enough to permit a full awareness of involvement with it. To put it in simpler terms: the magic of creativity typically fares best with a willingness to become totally immersed in paradox.

Collaboration might be fundamentally defined as bringing two or more "magic zones" into confluence to facilitate growth of knowledge and experience, which in turn increases the degree of complexity, and thus of paradox. Paradox provides the prospect of fashioning a host of conceptual and phenomenological arguments into new aggregate experiences that embrace a greater depth of meaning (Wagner, 2009). In fact, increased collaboration and interdisciplinary interaction has been the rule rather than the exception in both contemporary art and science.

Our working process was reshaped and enriched when we were granted access to the rare manuscripts and books held in Special Collections Department at the Doheny Memorial Libraries, University of Southern California. The experience of being granted access to and handling centuries-old volumes under the expert guidance of dedicated librarians bolstered a reverence for the knowledge of the past and its profound relationship to the present-day intellectual and spiritual climate. The institution's digital imaging laboratory provided high-resolution digital image files from which visual elements were extracted and incorporated into new artworks. The success of this association has led the authors to seek out additional cooperative prospects with specialists, institutions, and laboratories that span a variety of disciplines from the so-called "hard" sciences to psychology, sociology, and theology.

We have long been fascinated with the hidden interrelationships of all things and have been beguiled into the impossible attempt to tell a Story of Everything. Our collaborative work takes as its territory that space between science and art, where reason and emotion, *ego* and *id*, consciousness and instinct, fuse into novel constructs that might help us better appreciate the grand schematic we call reality and our place within this system. For almost a decade we have been engaged in a creative journey to trace the threads that inform how the mind relates to the contingent, finding visual inspiration in myriad sources, including works on classical philosophy, Newtonian optics, the Spanish Inquisition, Darwin's voyage on the *Beagle*, mythical creatures, electromagnetism, Leonardo da Vinci's notebooks, Native American religious rites, molecular biology, quantum physics, and the *Pioneer 10* spacecraft. Such diverse sources have exerted their own distinctive pull on our intellectual and creative processes as we try to coax our free associations from the realm of the inexpressible into the theater of the explicable.

The production of our visual statements is a complex undertaking — yielding multilayered images that conjure ideas of disciplines that do not yet exist: allegorical astrophysics, cartographic cave art, mythological microbiology, and cabbalistic quantum mechanics. Our working process can best be visualized as an old-style railroad handcar that is propelled down the track by two people alternately pushing down on their side of a pivoting rocker arm. Take that model of operation. Make it high tech. Then take away the track. That's the paradigm for our project. Specifically, we bounce high-resolution layered digital files back and forth between our Southern California studios with no preconceptions about what may happen to them on the "other side." Some works have been pushed along in this back-and-forth fashion for up to two years before reaching their final form as 24 x 30-inch archival pigment-based inkjet prints. In adopting this iterative approach, we have reaffirmed the basic conceptual arena of our operations by shaping art in the space between two minds.

Starting with abstracted images of the cosmos previously captured onto Polaroid 600 or Spectra "instant" integral print film, gold and various other metal leafs are applied by hand to the surface of the photographs, and these unique artworks in their own right are subsequently rephotographed with a high-resolution digital scanning camera back to create image files that serve as the basis for more extensive experimentation within the virtual domain. Objective technical processes and intuitive leaps of faith are joined into a work-flow that can best be characterized as a kind of latter-day alchemical methodology: layers from digitized images of woodcuts, engravings, litho-graphs, etchings, and other visual media, as well as artwork redrawn or created de novo with vector graphic software, are modified and intertwined into complex composite images often comprising scores of separate layers and masks and file sizes sometimes exceeding several gigabytes. Process-ing variables such as blend modes, channel mix-ing, opacity settings, and tone remapping more often than not result in serendipitous synergistic interactions between visual elements that supplant any pre-visualized expectations we may harbor. While intuition cannot be forced into action on demand in a workflow, it can be accommodated if we recognize when it springs into action. The creation of these works is therefore akin to con-ducting an experiment, in that specific outcomes are rarely certain.

Given our operating territory between science and metaphysics, it is hardly surprising that photo-based technologies were selected as the foundation for our collaborative effort. Photography has had a remarkably parallel science/art duality from its inception. The ability to capture and preserve shadows was made possible by the invention of photosensitive emulsions concurrently and separately developed by an artist and a scientist during the 19th Century. Louis-Jacques-Mandé Daguerre was a French theatrical impresario and panorama painter seeking a practical way to speed up the creation of realistic color images for his new popular entertainment, the Diorama (Newhall, 1982). William Henry Fox Talbot was an English scientist and mathematician who happened upon "photogenic drawing" while pursuing optical re-search, his invention motivated by romance (here defined as the space between love and frustration). While honeymooning in the Italian Alps, his self-acknowledged botched attempts to make souvenir drawings of the Lake Como scenery, even with the use of a *camera lucida* drawing aid, led him to seek a means of capturing and preserving the interaction of light – arguably the most ephemeral of natural phenomena – with the tangible (Gre-enough et al., 1989; Newhall, 1982).

Our creative process thus employs a fusion of technologies and artistic techniques that date back through centuries, starting as far back as 4 BC when the Chinese philosopher Mo Tzu first formally described the formation of images through a small hole in the wall of a darkened space (Hammond, 1981). Historical and concep-tual strata are thereby added to the open-ended inquiries posed by the resulting artworks. Themes of creation and destruction, harmony and strife, infinity and emptiness, resonate from the amal-gamation of inspiration and tangible constituents drawn from works by Newton, Einstein, Coleridge, Da Vinci, Paracelsus, Dame Rose Macaulay, and from among many other written works such as *The Divine Comedy, Hamlet,* and *Paradise Lost.* We have also mined personal and public archives for imagery obtained through optical and electron microscopes, earth-bound and orbiting telescopes, deep-space probes, and linear accelerator experiments. We do not presume that the associations we devise represent a working path toward objectively defined answers, but rather that our exercises might perhaps suggest another means by which the structure of the universe itself can be made more evident in the threads – or questions – that unify mankind's many attempts to understand it.

OUTCOMES: TOWARD THE INVENTION OF NEW POSTULATES

We used to think that if we knew one, we knew two, because one and one are two. We are finding that we must learn a great deal more about 'and'. (Sir Arthur Eddington, from Mackay & Ebison, 1969:89)

Much advanced scientific work in the past few decades has been focused on "big picture" questions about the underlying structure of the universe, such as how it all came into being and what its ultimate fate might be. While the three-dimensional world we can observe seems governed by the mechanical laws of classical Newtonian physics, such behaviors break down in the face of infinitesimally small objects like quarks or infinitely powerful ones like black holes. Indeed, theoretical physicists have recently put forth a hypothesis that our universe may actually reside within a wormhole that stretches between other universes (Than, 2010). This remarkable proposition bears metaphorical similarity to the lyrical Hindu model depicting the heavenly overlooking our world supported on the backs of elephants, which in turn are standing on the shell of a turtle, this entire scheme surrounded by an ouroboros – a recurring symbol from ancient times signifying birth and rebirth. *Problema X* frames the supreme uncertainty concerning how much we really know about the universe and how reliable our perceptions are (Figure 1).

Science is a system of knowledge concerning the physical world and its phenomena. It is based on empirical observations of the contingent and the conclusions drawn from those observations. Despite this rigorous process of questioning and analysis most seek answers to questions that are beyond rationality or scientific understanding. Because science cannot provide answers to inquiries of a purely philosophical nature, the quest for existential truth sometimes assumes sublime and sometimes ridiculous proportions. A reliance on prosaic descriptions of the directly perceivable electromagnetic spectrum or of some deity that sheer faith has turned into reality frequently impairs, even discourages, efforts to reach out for larger truths. *Above Reason* speaks to this need to know, in some form or another (Figure 2). Discovery often springs forth in the most surprising of ways from a fragile intersection between the metaphysically ineffable and the factually sterile.

The purpose of the earliest illustrations by humans on cave walls is still under debate. Their characteristics and locations have suggested to some investigators that the paintings may have been created to invoke magic for the hunt (Breuil, 1952) or as shamanistic devices to draw power from the cave walls or to evoke/represent trance states (Lewis-Williams, 2002; Morris, 2006). Others cite the broad range of quality of the paintings as evidence for their function as a means of communication or storytelling (Guthrie, 2006). A common characteristic of cave painting visual elements – including the so-called "entoptic" geometric representations – is their reference to observable objects or phenomena (Lewis-Williams, 2002; Lewis-Williams & Dowson, 1998). However, cave art "was not intended to mirror the surrounding world but to transcribe reality through filters of belief, tradition and ritual" (Clottes, 2002:96). The Egyptians made a conceptual leap with their ability to artistically represent abstract ideas, such as their pantheon of gods. Before the scientific revolution began around

Figure 1. Problema X. (©2006, Victor Raphael and Clayton Spada. Used with permission. Original in color.)

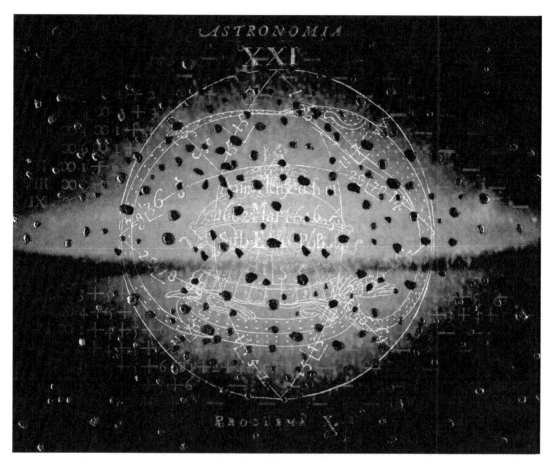

1500 AD, priests, astrologers, alchemists, and philosophers all claimed to have the answers to the workings of the universe. One might argue that in illustrations of real or imagined experiences one can find a broader understanding of the natural world and the *Final Causes* of all things (Figure 3).

In *Genesis*, the images from research into particle physics are coupled with the story of the creation of the universe, matter and life as told in the Book of Genesis (Figure 4). Profoundly poetic in its expression, the biblically conveyed sequence of events (though not the timing) is rational and, in its broad generalities, supported by science. The diagram embedded in this work refers to the tracings of elemental sub-atomic particles, which have allowed us to probe the very nature of matter. Events at the quantum scale often challenge common sense developed from the perspective gained within the macroscopic context of lived experience and our personal sensory model of reality. Particles seemingly pop in and out of being, yet behave in statistically predictable ways that permit examination of their behavior. Because nature always holds surprises, there is plenty of room for rationality to peacefully coexist with unfettered awe.

Bubble Chamber directly engages the viewer within this frontier (Figure 5). Streams of protons accelerated to tremendous speeds along a huge underground conduit almost 700 feet in diameter smash into atomic targets placed in a chamber

Figure 2. Above reason (©2009, Victor Raphael and Clayton Spada. Used with permission. Original in color.)

filled with liquid hydrogen, leading to high-energy collisions that release smaller particles. Mesmerizing trails of microscopic bubbles transiently suspended across a sea of liquid hydrogen, captured by ultra high-speed photography, serve as the only visible evidence that these particles exist. Faster moving particles form straight trails, while slower moving particles create spiral trails as they are deflected by magnetic-field generators positioned around this so-called "bubble chamber". The "atom smasher" has afforded scientists a glimpse into the inner workings of atomic nuclei in a fashion akin to an astronomer using a telescope to study the cosmos. Scores of fundamental subatomic particles have been discovered through the use of this technology, increasing our understanding of the structure and nature of matter, and thus, of existence.

Devotees of astrology assert that our lives are governed by the positions of the planets and stars in relation to Earth. They also believe the precise location and time of our birth provides the key determination for many of our actions. While scientists reject such claims, there is evidence that implies our biology and psychology are connected to the broader environment in ways that might seem inscrutable or illogical to our rational senses (Tarnas, 2007). *Beneath the Surface* suggests that perhaps there is some truth to both viewpoints, though not for reasons we can readily apprehend (Figure 6). The malleability of what can appeal to logic as factual is further exempli-

Figure 3. Final causes (©2009, Victor Raphael and Clayton Spada. Used with permission. Original in color.)

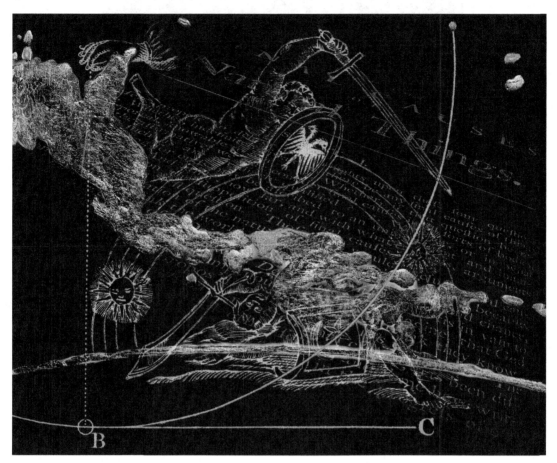

fied by the recent revival of a centuries-old debate over the number of star constellation signs comprising the astrological zodiac that began with the decision by ancient Babylonian astronomers to exclude Ophiuchus as a thirteenth group, consequentially setting the stage for unresolved confusion through the ages engendered by reference to either a seasonal or a sidereal calendar (Praetorius, 2011).

Against the backdrop of planet Earth and the sliver of atmosphere that protects life from the void of deep space, a diagram of Gavin de Beer's classic phylogenetic tree of the animal kingdom serves as a starkly graphic reminder of the common ground that humankind shares with all life on the planet (Figure 7). It is unrealistic to hope

that our activities as a species will have no impact on the integrated ecosystem within which we must survive, but this does not mean that we are absolved of the responsibility to mediate clearly unsustainable technological behaviors. In *Common Ground*, the image of Einstein's handprints do not merely underline humanity's ownership of this quandary, but also give hope that we have the capacity to solve the problems we have created.

Pioneer Greeting is a visual elaboration of our drive to be understood and acknowledged at a holistic level (Figure 8). A 6 x 9-inch gold anodized plaque was bolted to the Pioneer 10 spacecraft, which was sent out into deep space in 1972. It was designed to inform other intelligent life in the universe about who we are and where we come

Figure 4. Genesis (©2006, Victor Raphael and Clayton Spada. Used with permission. Original in color.)

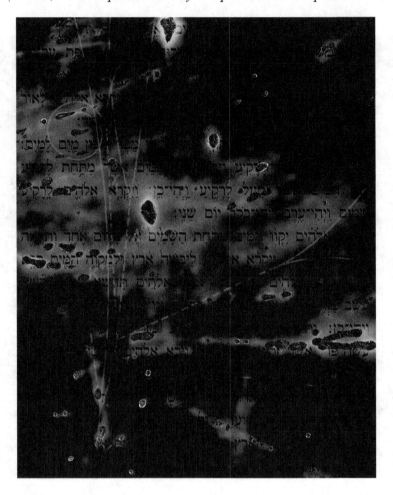

from. Male and female figures stand before an outline of the spacecraft. At the top left is a symbol of the hydrogen atom, the most common element in the universe. Below it, 14 lines radiate from a point representing the sun. Each line indicates the direction from the sun to a pulsar, a cosmic source of radio energy that should be known and understood by any civilization whose technology has advanced to the point of space travel. At the bottom of the plaque is a model of our solar system. The sun is at the left, followed by Mercury in sequence to Pluto. The background linear elements are derived from a radio astronomy map of a small sector of distant space, oriented so that radio signal strengths are displayed as contour lines, similar to the way a topological map shows elevations. Could signals generated by other intelligence be embedded in the tremendous background noise of the universe? Will another intelligence ever see this plaque? Will it ever be deciphered? The chance of either happening is infinitesimally small, but not impossible.

CONVERSATION: A UNIVERSE OF QUESTIONS

...neither the scientific system of mental development, nor the traditional, is adequate for our potentialities, for the work we have in front of us, for the world in which we ought to begin to live. (Snow, 1964:63 - 64)

Figure 5. Bubble Chamber (©2006, Victor Raphael and Clayton Spada. Used with permission. Original in color.)

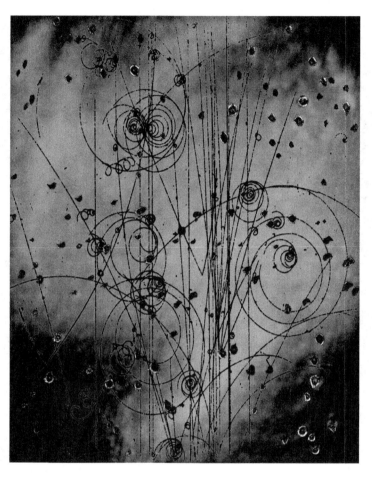

Friedrich August Kekulé von Stradonitz was a German theoretical chemist and principal formulator of the theory of chemical structure most known for his work on the structure and chemistry of benzene. He claimed to have realized the molecule's ring-like shape after day-dreaming of a snake seizing its own tail (Benfey, 1958). George Pierre Seurat's studies of the physics of color as an art student at the Academy of Fine Arts in Paris led to his invention of Pointillism, but it was the development of premixed synthetic pigments by French chemists in the late 19th Century that actually enabled him to create the paintings in which discrete dots and dashes of complementary colors placed adjacent to one

another could, when viewed at a distance, be fused by the eye into vibrant blended colors and coherent whole forms (Schlain, 1991). American optical scientist Edwin Herbert Land, an expert in the physical and chemical properties of color, paved the way towards new means of creative expression in film making and photography with his inventions of the Polaroid lens and instant photography (Newhall, 1982; Jaccard, 2007). Harold Eugene "Doc" Edgerton, an American electrical engineer credited with transforming the stroboscope from an obscure laboratory instrument into the high-speed electronic flash technology widely employed in photography, spent most of his career presenting the beauty of fleeting events

Figure 6. Beneath the Surface (©2009, Victor Raphael and Clayton Spada. Used with permission. Original in color.)

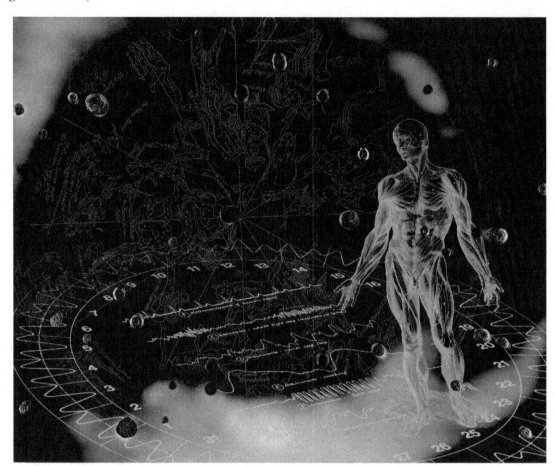

(Newhall, 1982; Orland, 2006). The histories of science and of art are replete with such examples of prepared minds seizing opportunities for the exchange of serendipity into design, and of the transformation of the pragmatic into the expressive. The histories of science and of art are also replete with examples of prepared minds doing just the opposite.

There is a large body of literature dating back thousands of years that has dealt with the confluence of the analytical, the creative and the spiritual facets of human cognition, generally resting on the presumption of some form of opposing dualism in attempting to elucidate how concept is translated through process into a result (Bloom, 1991; Bronowski, 1989; Jaccard, 2007; Leshan and Margenau, 1982; Kubler, 1962; Wilson, 1998; Wolff, 1999; Zalta, 2010). More recent expositions on creativity (Koestler, 1964; Kubler, 1962), the neurology and psychology of cognition and perception (Arnheim, 1969, 1974; Baltrusaitis, 1989; Doczi, 1981; Freedberg, 1989; Gombrich, 1989; Kappraff, 1991), and the applied organization of visual information (Hemenway, 2005; Huntley, 1970; Kemp, 2000; Tufte, 1990, 1997, 2001) also serve as excellent references that could lead to greater insight regarding how these aspects and mediators of real-world processes may function in relation to one another. However, the precision that may be afforded by teasing apart

Figure 7. Common Ground (©2008, Victor Raphael and Clayton Spada. Used with permission. Original in color.)

these constituents through reductionism does not satisfactorily resolve into comprehension of the cumulative experience.

It should be stressed here that this chapter is not intended as an in-depth reexamination of the common misconception that art and science are mutually opposing and dissimilar cultures, nor is there a desire on the authors' part to conflate art with science as equivalent states of knowledge so as to "rectify" their polarization. After all, scientists cannot be expected to conduct science from a similar perspective that artists handle art, nor should artists be compelled to justify their practice in the same way that scientists must pragmatically relate their conclusions to the methodology by which results were obtained. Science must remain science and art must remain art if they are to continue to fulfill their respective missions of inquiry. Still, we are compelled

to join the league of historical and contemporary predecessors working in the arts and the sciences who have expressed their belief that there is great value in encouraging open-ended dialog between these worldviews as a means of defining a deeper individual relationship with the cosmos.

Conducting science and making art are by nature different "attitudes of approach" toward solving problems. Perhaps the principal distinction between scientific and artistic workflows is that reproducibility defines success in the former, while the latter strives to achieve different outcomes from repeated inquiries. It may also be that conducting science and making art requires the management of a curious sort of tension between hubris and humility. Hubris because staying the course when striding forth into the unknown demands a great deal of confidence; humility because remaining engaged with a sense of awe helps to promote the

Figure 8. Pioneer Greeting (©2006, Victor Raphael and Clayton Spada. Used with permission. Original in color.)

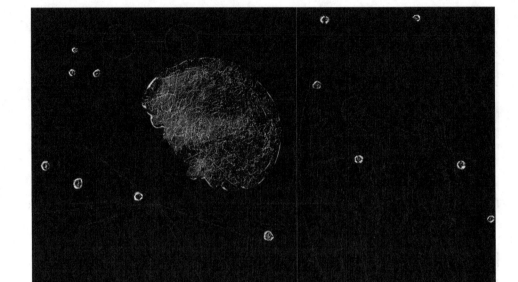

next question. An artist can employ processes with as much methodological tenacity as a scientist would bring to bear in an experimental inquiry. Similarly, a scientist can and should remain open to the unexpected or unwanted result. This is the "magic zone" where the overlap between art and science and spirituality can come to life. In art as well as in science, what matters most to others is the conclusion, the product arising out of the process, but what often matters more to the artist and the scientist is the *experience* by which the conclusion was shaped from the process. As a consequence, the result assumes greater significance as a springboard for further questions than as a definitive resolution.

Millennia after Pythagoras of Samos suggested that planets and stars moved in uniform circular paths within crystalline spherical orbits arranged in proportion to one another, and that points at which these orbits rubbed against one another produced vibrations he termed the "music of the spheres," NASA's Voyager deep-space probes transmitted telemetry back to earth of planetary and solar sound emissions in the audible spectrum (Jaccard, 2007). Leonardo di ser Piero da Vinci, the quintessential Renaissance Man, used rigorous scientific investigation and meticulous observation to inform his artworks believing that it was a moral responsibility to accurately represent the perfection of Nature (Richter, 1970). In developing his conceptions of archetypes and the collective unconscious, Carl Jung sought a deeper understanding of matter and energy by engaging in numerous discussions with Albert Einstein, an accomplished violinist as well as the theoretical physicist who catalyzed a revolution in physics with his discovery of the Theory of General Relativity (Jung, 1968, 1981). Indeed, Einstein apparently perceived no chasm separating art and science when he is claimed to have said: "After a certain high level of technical skill is achieved, science and art tend to coalesce in esthetics, plasticity and form. The greatest scientists are artists as well." (Jaccard, 2007:4). And the list of examples goes on (Benvenuti, 2006; Gleiser, 1997; Schrödinger, 1964; Staguhn, 1994).

In an expression of his desire to unify the factual with the ineffable, Henry David Thoreau made this journal entry on February 18, 1852:

I have a commonplace book for facts and another for poetry, but I find it difficult always to preserve the vague distinctions which I had in mind, for the most and interesting and beautiful are so much more poetry and that is their success. They are translated from earth to heaven. I see that if my facts were sufficiently vital and significant — perhaps transmuted more into the substance of the human mind — I should need but one book of poetry to contain them all. (Thoreau, 1852:356)

We prefer to follow Thoreau's dictate. Although we exploit the iconographic freight and specific concerns of both science and the spiritual, we are not bound by the doctrinaire constraints of either. Until Thoreau's time it was a common assumption that the observation of nature was inherently a spiritual enterprise that did not conflict with the tasks of science. Operating between two rich traditions, we draw on the vital and varied specifics of both – their symbols, suggestions, and substance – with the aim of making art that "contains them all." So, here we are, confronted by unabashed artistic license professing some inside track to distilling every aspect of existence and human rationalization of existence into a 'story of everything'. This may seem on the surface to be quite impudent. Be that as it may, expect no apologies for such hubris. It is an indispensable component in the equation that permits us to impartially question and examine everything and how we place ourselves within the context of everything else. We definitely do not have answers to anything, let alone a lock on a "story of everything". The real joy actually lies in coming up with the questions.

REFERENCES

Appel, A. Jr. (1967). An interview with Nabokov. *Wisconsin Studies in Contemporary Literature, 8,* 127–152. doi:10.2307/1207097

Arnheim, R. (1969). *Visual thinking.* Berkeley, CA: University of California Press.

Arnheim, R. (1974). *Art and visual perception. A psychology of the creative eye.* Berkeley, CA: University of California Press.

Aveni, A. (1994). *Conversing with the planets. How science and myth invented the cosmos.* New York, NY: Kodansha International Ltd.

Baltrusaitis, J. (1989). *Aberrations. An essay on the legend of forms.* Cambridge, MA: The MIT Press.

Barber, E. W., & Barber, P. T. (2004). *When they severed earth from sky. How the human mind shapes myth.* Princeton, NJ: Princeton University Press.

Benfey, O. T. (1958). August Kekulé and the birth of the structural theory of organic chemistry in 1858. *Journal of Chemical Education, 35,* 21–23. doi:10.1021/ed035p21

Benvenuti, A. (2006). A beautiful confluence: Science and religion as modes of human participation in the cosmos. *The Forum on Public Policy: A Journal of the Oxford Round Table, 2*(4), 758-774.

Bloom, A. (1991). *The republic of Plato* (2nd ed.). New York, NY: Basic Books.

Boorstin, D. (1983). *The discoverers. A History of man's search to know his world and himself.* New York, NY: Vintage Books.

Botha, R., & Knight, C. (2009). *The prehistory of language.* Oxford, UK: Oxford University Press. doi:10.1093/acprof:oso/9780199545872.001.0001

Breuil, H. (1952). *Four hundred centuries of cave art* (Boyle, M. E., Trans.). London, UK: Zwemmer.

Bronowski, J. (1978). *The origins of knowledge and imagination.* New Haven, CT: Yale University Press.

Callender, C., & Schaffer, J. (2010). *Do mereological sums constitute objects? Questions like this are hotly debated in contemporary metaphysics — Yet such questions seem utterly disconnected from science. Has metaphysics gone in the wrong direction?* Online video discussion, posted on September 8, 2010. Retrieved July 22, 2011, from http://www.philostv.com/craig-callender-and-jonathan-schaffer

Clottes, J. (2002). *World rock art.* Los Angeles, CA: Getty Publications.

Devlin, K. (1997). *Goodbye Descartes. The end of logic and the search for a new cosmology of the mind.* New York, NY: John Wiley & Sons, Inc.

Doczi, G. (1981). *The power of limits. Proportional harmonies in nature, art, and architecture.* Boston, MA: Shambala Publications, Inc.

Dorter, K. (1973). The ion: Plato's characterization of art. *The Journal of Aesthetics and Art Criticism, 32*(1), 65–78. doi:10.2307/428704

Elgin, C. Z. (1997). *Between the absolute and the arbitrary.* Ithaca, NY: Cornell University Press.

Freedberg, D. (1989). *The power of images. Studies in the history and theory of response.* Chicago, IL: The University of Chicago Press.

Freely, J. (2010). *Aladdin's lamp. How Greek science came to Europe through the Islamic world.* New York, NY: Vintage Books.

Gleick, J. (1987). *Chaos: Making a new science.* London, UK: Penguin Books Ltd.

Gleiser, M. (1997). *The dancing universe. From creation myths to the Big Bang.* Hanover, NH: Dartmouth College Press, University Press of New England.

Gombrich, E. H. (1989). *Art and illusion. A study in the psychology of pictorial representation.* Princeton, NJ: Princeton University Press.

Greenough, S., Snyder, J., Travis, D., & Westerbeck, C. (1989). *On the art of fixing a shadow. One hundred and fifty years of photography.* Washington, DC: National Gallery of Art, in conjunction with The Art Institute of Chicago.

Guthrie, R. D. (2006). *The nature of paleolithic art.* Chicago, IL: University of Chicago Press.

Habgood, J. S. (1964). *Religion and science.* London, UK: Mills & Boon.

Hammond, J. H. (1981). *The camera obscura. A chronicle.* Bristol, UK: Adam Hilger Ltd.

Hemenway, P. (2005). *Divine proportion. □ (Phi) In art, nature, and science.* New York, NY: Sterling Publishing Co., Inc.

Huntley, H. H. (1970). *The divine proportion. A study in mathematical beauty.* New York, NY: Dover Publications, Inc.

Jaccard, J.-L. (2007). Minding the gap: Artists as scientists, scientists as artists: Some solutions to Snow's dilemma. *The Forum on Public Policy Online,* Vol. 2007, No. 1 (Winter). Retrieved January 25, 2011, from http://www.forumonpublicpolicy.com/archive07/jaccard.pdf

Jung, C. G. (1968). *Man and his symbols.* New York, NY: Random House, Inc.

Jung, C. G. (1981). *The archetypes and the collective unconscious. Collected works of C. G. Jung* (2nd ed., *Vol. 9*). Princeton, NJ: Princeton University Press.

Kant, I. (1790). *The critique of judgment.* (J. C. Meredith, Trans.). Retrieved January 22, 2011, from http://philosophy.eserver.org/kant/critique-of-judgment.txt

Kappraff, J. (1991). *Connections. The geometric bridge between art and science.* New York, NY: McGraw-Hill, Inc.

Kemp, M. (2000). *Visualizations. The nature book of art and science.* Berkeley, CA: The University of California Press, by arrangement with Oxford University Press.

Koestler, A. (1964). *The act of creation.* London, UK: Arkana, Penguin Books.

Kubler, G. (1962). *The shape of time. Remarks on the history of things.* New Haven, CT: Yale University Press.

Leshan, L., & Margenau, H. (1982). *Einstein's space & Van Gogh's sky. Physical reality and beyond.* New York, NY: Collier Books, Macmillan Publishing Company.

Lewis-Williams, J. D. (2002). *The mind in the cave.* London, UK: Thames & Hudson.

Lewis-Williams, J. D., & Dowson, T. A. (1998). The signs of all times: Entoptic phenomena in upper paleolithic art. *Current Anthropology, 29*(2), 201–245. doi:10.1086/203629

Mackay, A. L., & Ebison, M. (Eds.). (1969). *The harvest of a quiet eye. A selection of scientific quotations.* London, UK: Taylor & Francis Group.

Margenau, H., & Varghese, R. A. (Eds.). (1991). *Cosmos, bios, theos: Scientists reflect on science, god, and the origins of the universe, life, and homo sapiens.* Chicago, IL: Open Court Publishing Company.

Miller, A. I. (1996). *Insights of genius. Imagery and creativity in science and art.* New York, NY: Copernicus, Springer-Verlag.

Mithen, S. (1996). *The prehistory of the mind. The cognitive origins of art, religion and science.* London, UK: Thames and Hudson Ltd.

Morris, B. (2006). *Religion and anthropology: A critical introduction.* Cambridge, UK: Cambridge University Press.

Newhall, B. (1982). *The history of photography.* Boston, MA: Little, Brown and Company.

Orland, T. (2006). *The view from the studio door. How artists find their way in an uncertain world.* Santa Cruz, CA: Image Continuum Press.

Polyani, M. (1946). *Science, faith and society.* Chicago, IL: The University of Chicago Press.

Praetorius, D. (2011). New zodiac sign dates: Ophiuchus the 13th sign? *The Huffington Post.* Retrieved on January 30, 2011, from http://www.huffingtonpost.com/2011/01/13/new-zodiac-sign-dates-oph_n_808567.html

Richter, J. P. (1970). *The notebooks of Leonardo Da Vinci* (*Vol. 1*). New York, NY: Dover Publications.

Robin, H. (1992). *The scientific image. From cave to computer.* New York, NY: W. H. Freeman and Company, by arrangement with Harry N. Abrams, Inc.

Schlain, L. (1991). *Art & physics. Parallel visions in space, time, and light.* New York, NY: William Morrow and Company, Inc.

Schrödinger, E. (1964). *My view of the world.* Cambridge, UK: Cambridge University Press.

Snow, C. P. (1959). The two cultures. *Leonardo, 23*(2/3), 169–173. doi:10.2307/1578601

Snow, C. P. (1964). *The two cultures: And a second look.* Cambridge, UK: Cambridge University Press.

Staguhn, G. (1994). *God's laughter. Physics, religion and the cosmos*. New York, NY: Kodansha International Ltd.

Tarnas, R. (2007). *Cosmos and psyche. Intimations of a new world view*. London, UK: Plume, Penguin Group.

Than, K. (2010). Every black hole contains another universe? *National Geographic News*. Retrieved December 14, 2010, from http://news.nationalgeographic.com/news/2010/04/100409-black-holes-alternate-universe- multiverse-einstein-wormholes/

Thoreau, H. D. (1852). [Princeton, NJ: Princeton University Press.]. *Journal, 4*, 356.

Tufte, E. (1990). *Envisioning information*. Cheshire, CT: Graphics Press.

Tufte, E. (1997). *Visual explanations*. Cheshire, CT: Graphics Press.

Tufte, E. (2001). *The visual display of quantitative information* (2nd ed.). Cheshire, CT: Graphics Press.

Turner, H. R. (1997). *Science in Medieval Islam*. Austin, TX: University of Texas Press.

Wagner, A. (2009). *Paradoxical life. Meaning, matter and the power of human choice*. New Haven, CT: Yale University Press.

Wilson, E. O. (1998). *Consilience. The unity of knowledge*. New York, NY: Vintage Books, Random House, Inc.

Wolf, F. A. (1999). *The spiritual universe. One physicist's vision of spirit, soul, matter, and self*. Needhan, MA: Moment Point Press, Inc.

Zalta, E. N. (Ed.). (2010). Epistêmê and Techné. *The Stanford Encyclopedia of Philosophy*. Retrieved January 10, 2011, from http://plato.stanford.edu

ADDITIONAL READING

Adamson, G. (2007). *Thinking through craft*. London, UK: Victoria and Albert Museum/Berg.

Batten, A. H. (1995). A most rare vision: Eddington's thinking on the relation between science and religion. *Journal of Scientific Exploration, 9*(2), 231–255.

Berger, J. (1972). *Ways of seeing*. London, UK: British Broadcasting Company/Penguin Books.

Boden, M. A. (2003). *The creative mind: Myths and mechanisms*. London, UK: Routledge.

Cartwright, N. (1983). *How the laws of physics lie*. Oxford, UK: Oxford University Press. doi:10.1093/0198247044.001.0001

Cartwright, N. (1994). Fundamentalism vs. the patchwork of laws. *Proceedings of the Aristotelian Society, 93*, 279–292.

Cassirer, E. (1946). *Language and myth*. New York, NY: Harper and Brothers.

Cushing, T. (1998). *Philosophical concepts in physics: The historical relation between philosophy and scientific theories*. Cambridge, UK: Cambridge University Press.

Dunne, J. (1997). *Back to the rough ground: 'Phronesis' and 'techne' in modern philosophy and in Aristotle*. Notre Dame, IN: University of Notre Dame Press.

Eco, U. (1999). *Serendipities. Language and lunacy*. New York, NY: Harcourt Brace & Company.

Elkins, J. (2000). *How to use your eyes*. New York, NY: Routledge.

Foucault, M. (1970). *The order of things: An archeology of the human sciences*. New York, NY: Pantheon Books.

Goodman, N. (1978). *Ways of worldmaking*. Indianpolis, IN: Hackett Publishing Company.

Gordon, C. (Ed.). (1980). *Power/knowledge. Selected interviews and other writings, 1972 - 1977.* New York, NY: Pantheon Books.

Highwater, J. (1981). *The primal mind. Vision and reality in Indian America.* New York, NY: Meridian.

Hoffman, D. D. (1998). *Visual intelligence: How we create what we see.* New York, NY: W. W. Norton.

Hofstadter, D. R. (1979). *Gödel, Escher, Bach. An eternal golden braid.* New York, NY: Basic Books.

Kandinsky, W. (1977). *Concerning the spiritual in art.* New York, NY: Dover Publications.

Knorr-Cetina, K. (1999). *Epistemic cultures: How the sciences make knowledge.* Cambridge, MA: Harvard University Press.

Kosuth, J. (1991). *Art after philosophy and after. Collected writings, 1966 – 1990.* Cambridge, MA: The MIT Press.

Lakoff, G., & Johnson, M. (1980). *Metaphors we live by.* Chicago, IL: University of Chicago Press.

Lavédrine, B. (2009). *Photographs of the past. Process and preservation.* Los Angeles, CA: Getty Publications.

Levi-Strauss, C. (1995). *Myth and meaning.* New York, NY: Schocken Books.

Maynard, P. (1997). *The engine of visualization. Thinking through photography.* Ithaca, NY: Cornell University Press.

Mayr, E. (1992). The idea of teleology . *Journal of the History of Ideas, 53,* 117–135. doi:10.2307/2709913

McManus, I. C. (2006). Measuring the culture of C. P. Snow's two cultures. *Empirical Studies of the Arts, 24*(2), 219–227. doi:10.2190/5NM6-FV42-X38A-F3VP

Nachmanovitch, S. (1990). *Free play. The power of improvisation in life and the arts.* New York, NY: Tarcher/Putnam.

Ouspensky, P. D. (1976). *In search of the miraculous.* San Diego, CA: Harcourt Brace Jovanovich, Publishers.

Rank, O. (1932). *Art and artist. Creative urge and personality development.* New York, NY: W. W. Norton & Company.

Scharfstein, B. (2009). *Art without borders. A philosophical exploration of art and humanity.* Chicago, IL: Chicago University Press.

Sennett, R. (2008). *The craftsman.* London, UK: Allen Lane.

Virilio, P. (2003). *Art and Fear.* London, UK: Continuum.

Zohar, D. (1990). *The quantum self: Human nature and consciousness defined by the new physics.* London, UK: Harper Collins.

KEY TERMS AND DEFINITIONS

Art: The particular human effort to imitate, represent, alter, counteract or supplement the natural through conscious arrangement, manipulation or production of colors, forms, movements, sounds, words or other material elements in a manner that affects aesthetic sensibilities.

Contingent: What is possible or incidental, and dependent on something that may or may not occur, or that is unknown. Contingency describes the status of propositions that are neither true nor false under every possible valuation, the "truth value" of a proposition being dependent upon the "truth values" of the parts that comprise it. Contingent propositions rely on facts, whereas analytic propositions are taken as true without regard to any facts about which they address. There are at least three other classes of propositions, some of which can overlap: tautological propositions, which are true no matter what the circumstances are or could be; contradictory propositions, which must be false no matter what the circumstances are or could be; and, possible propositions, which are true or could be true given certain circumstances. All necessarily true propositions and all contingent propositions are also possible propositions.

Cosmology: A branch of astronomy that deals with the study of the origins, structure and changes of the present universe. The National Aeronautics and Space Administration (NASA) distinguishes the study of the structure and changes in the present universe (cosmology) from the scientific inquiry into the origin and fate of the universe (cosmogony), but acknowledges the overlap of these scientific fields. Metaphysical cosmology encompasses the philosophical perspective that seeks to draw intuitive conclusions about the nature of the universe and its relationships with proposed supernatural factors drawn from the domains of religion and spiritual experience, and the placement of humanity in this broader context.

Episteme: Rooted in the Greek word for "knowledge" (or "science"), which in turn comes from the verb "to know", the more modern usage refers to paradigmatic practices and worldviews (particularly in science) and the grounding of knowledge in a necessary a priori framework (Foucault, 1970, Additional Reading Section). Episteme infers knowing through "disinterested understanding", in contrast to an intent to accomplish a task (see Techne, below).

Knowledge: The explicit (theoretical) and/or implicit (practical) *understanding* of a subject arising from familiarity with facts, descriptions, information or skills acquired through association, communication, intuition, learning, perception or reasoning (cognition).

Ontological Argument: The metaphysical *a priori* argument designed to prove that the real objective existence of God is necessarily involved in the existence of the very idea of God (i.e., if the existence of a supreme being can be imagined, then this supreme being must exist).

Paradox: A conceptual or situational contradiction that apparently defies intuition or logic, arising from an outwardly appearing truth or group of truths. In many cases, paradoxical conditions can be resolved by demonstrating that one or more of the underlying premises are not valid. In the arts, paradoxes are often used to describe situations that are ironic or surprising, with no implication of contradiction. However, paradoxical constructs have been presented that currently lack universally accepted solutions (e.g., Curry's Paradox, Gödel's Theorem; see Hofstadter, 1979 and Lakoff & Johnson, 1980, Additional Reading Section).

Philosophy: The critical and systematic study of general and fundamental problems, including those related to existence, knowledge, language, mind, morality, reason and values, employing rational argument. The term is etymologically rooted in the Greek word *philosophia*, literally meaning the "love of wisdom".

Polaroid Integral "Instant" Color Film: A self-contained, self-processing color photographic film process involving the diffusion and transfer of color dyes from multiple light-sensitive layers into a receiving layer. Polaroid integral films differed from the first "instant" film technologies in that they did not require the positive image receiving layer to be peeled away from the negative light-sensitive substrate, but rather were completely sealed, allowing the user to actually observe the progress of chemical development of the image under ambient illumination. The Polaroid Corporation was started in 1937 by physicist Edwin Land to manufacture polarizing filters and various other optical devices. Two years later the company introduced the first "instant" black-and-white photographic roll film, called Polaroid, and a specialized camera (the Land camera) to be used with that film. The first "instant" color material was released in 1963, but it took nine more years before introduction of the SX-70 system, incorporating the first integral print film technology. Polaroid 600 and Spectra integral "instant" integral color films became available in the early 1980s (see Lavédrine, 2009, Additional Reading Section).

Spirituality: An assumed immaterial reality or experience with the transcendent or immanent nature of the world. Although an integral component of religious experience, spirituality has come to be more broadly regarded as a personal orientation in life that can provide an "inner path" leading to the realization of the deepest meanings and values by which life should be lived, or the discovery of the essence of being (see Batten, 1995, Additional Reading Section). Spirituality is also often experienced as a source of inspiration.

Techne: Rooted in the Greek word that is often translated as "art", "craft" or "craftsmanship", techne refers to the rational method of producing an object or achieving an objective, as opposed to understanding for the sake of understanding (see Episteme, above).

378

Compilation of References

Aalkjaer, C., Heagerty, A. M., Petersen, K. K., Swales, J. D., & Mulvany, M. J. (1987). Evidence for increased media thickness, increased neuronal amine uptake, and depressed excitation-contraction coupling in isolated resistance vessels from essential hypertensives. *Circulation Research, 61*(2), 181.

Abbott, A. (2006). In search of the sixth sense. *Nature, 442*(7099), 125–127. doi:10.1038/442125a

Adamatzky, A. (2010). Physarum machines: Encapsulating reaction-diffusion to compute spanning tree. *Naturwissenschaften, 94*(12), 975–980. doi:10.1007/s00114-007-0276-5

Ahlquist, S., & Fleischmann, M. (2009). Computational spring systems: Open design processes for complex structural systems. *Architectural Design, 79*(2), 130–133. doi:10.1002/ad.870

Aish, R., Frankel, J. L., Frazer, J. H., & Patera, A. T. (2001). Computational construction kits for geometric modeling and design. In *Proceedings of the ACM Symposium on Interactive 3D Graphics, I3D 2001*, North Carolina, March 19-21, 2001. New York, NY: ACM Press.

Alcopley, L. (1994). Art, science and human being. *Leonardo, 27*(3), 183. doi:10.2307/1576049

Aliev, A. E., Oh, J., Kozlov, M. E., Kuznetsov, A. A., Fang, S., & Fonseca, A. F. (1575-1578). … Baughman, R. H. (2009). Giant-Stroke, superelastic carbon nanotube aerogel muscles. *Science, 323*(5921). doi:doi:10.1126/science.1168312

Alonso, M. P., Malone, E., Moon, F. C., & Lipson, H. (2009, August). *Reprinting the telegraph: Replicating the Vail register using multi-materials 3D printing.* Paper presented at Solid Freeform Fabrication Symposium (SFF'09). Austin, TX.

al-Rifaie, M. M., Bishop, M., & Blackwell, T. (2011). An investigation into the merger of stochastic diffusion search and particle swarm optimisation. In *Proceedings of the Genetic and Evolutionary Computation Conference GECCO'11* (pp. 37—44). Dublin, Ireland: ACM.

al-Rifaie, M. M., & Bishop, M. (2010). *The mining game: A brief introduction to the stochastic diffusion search metaheuristic.* AISB Quarterly.

Altenmüller, E. O., & Gerloff, C. (1999). Psychophysiology and the EEG . In Niedermeyer, E., & Lopes da Silva, F. H. (Eds.), *Electroencephalography: Basic principles, clinical applications and related fields* (pp. 637–655). Baltimore, MD: Williams and Wilkins.

Anderson, C. W. (1998). Multivariate autoregressive models for classification of spontaneous electroencephalographic signals during mental tasks. *IEEE Transactions on Bio-Medical Engineering, 45*(3), 277–286. doi:10.1109/10.661153

Animals in Medieval Art. (2011). *Heilbrun timeline of art history.* Department of Medieval Art and The Cloisters, The Metropolitan Museum of Art. Retrieved July 27, 2011, from http://www.metmuseum.org/toah/hd/best/hd_best.htm

Annely Juda Fine Art, & Hockney, D. (2009). *David Hockney: Drawing in a printing machine,* [Exhibition Catalogue]. London, UK: BAS Printers Ltd.

Appel, A. Jr. (1967). An interview with Nabokov. *Wisconsin Studies in Contemporary Literature, 8,* 127–152. doi:10.2307/1207097

Arduino . (2011). Retrieved August 14, 2011, from http://www.arduino.cc/, http://arduino.cc/en/Main/ArduinoBoardLilyPad

Arnheim, R. (1990). Language and the early cinema. *Leonardo, Digital Image Digital Cinema, Supplemental Issue*, 3-4.

Arnheim, R. (1969). *Visual thinking*. Berkeley, CA: University of California Press.

Arnheim, R. (1974). *Art and visual perception. A psychology of the creative eye*. Berkeley, CA: University of California Press.

Arnheim, R. (1988). *The power of the center: A study of composition in the visual arts*. Berkeley, CA: University of California Press.

Arnheim, R. (1997). *Visual thinking*. Berkeley, CA: University of California Press.

Arthus-Bertrand, Y. (2011). *The image of a deoiling basin at a water purification centre*. France: Marne.

Associated Press. (2008). *Early "leaf" photo could fetch fortune*. Retrieved January 31, 2011, from www.cbsnews.com/stories/2008/03/28/tech/main3977071.shtml

Audesirk, T., Audesirk, G., & Byers, B. E. (2001). Biology: Life on earth. *Benjamin Cummings., ISBN-10*, 0321598466.

Augoyard, J. F., & Torgue, H. (Eds.). (2005). *Sonic experience: A guide to everyday sounds*. Montreal, Canada: McGill-Queen's University Press.

Aupetit, S., Bordeau, V., Monmarche, N., Slimane, M., & Venturini, G. (2004). Interactive evolution of ant paintings. In *The 2003 Congress on Evolutionary Computation, CEC'03*, (Vol. 2, pp. 1376–1383).

Autodesk. (2004). *Maya*. Retrieved April 17, 2011, from http://usa.autodesk.com/maya/

Aveni, A. (1994). *Conversing with the planets. How science and myth invented the cosmos*. New York, NY: Kodansha International Ltd.

Badura, M. (2002). *Computerkunst/Computer Art 2.002 catalog*, (pp. 22–25). ISBN 3–923815–40–9

Badura, M. (2011). *Badura Museum*. Retrieved July 1, 2011, from http://www.baduramuseum.de/

Bailey, G. H. (1982). *Drawing and the drawing activity: A phenomenological investigation*. Thesis (PhD), University of London.

Bak, P. (1996). *How nature works – The science of self-organized criticality*. New York, NY: Copernicus.

Bak, P., Tang, C., & Wiesenfeld, K. (1987). Self-organized criticality: An explanation of 1/f noise. *Physical Review Letters, 59*, 381–384. doi:10.1103/PhysRevLett.59.381

Ball, P. (1999). *The self-made tapestry - Pattern formation in nature*. Oxford, England: Oxford University Press.

Baltrusaitis, J. (1989). *Aberrations. An essay on the legend of forms*. Cambridge, MA: The MIT Press.

Banks, R. B. (2010). *Growth and diffusion phenomena: Mathematical frameworks and applications*. Berlin, Germany: Springer-Verlag.

Barber, E. W., & Barber, P. T. (2004). *When they severed earth from sky. How the human mind shapes myth*. Princeton, NJ: Princeton University Press.

Barnsley, M. F., & Rising, H. (1993). *Fractals everywhere*. Boston, MA: Academic Press Professional.

Bartel, M. (2010). *Composition and design. Elements, principles, and visual effects*. Goshen College Art Department. Retrieved July 15, 2011 from http://www.goshen.edu/art

Baumbach, G. L., & Heistad, D. D. (1989). Remodeling of cerebral arterioles in chronic hypertension. *Hypertension, 13*(6), 968.

Bayazit, O. B., Lien, J. M., & Amato, N. M. (2002). Roadmap-based flocking for complex environments. In *PG '02: Proceedings of the 10th Pacific Conference on Computer Graphics and Applications* (p. 104). Washington, DC: IEEE Computer Society.

Bayliss, J. D., & Ballard, D. H. (2000). A virtual reality testbed for brain computer interface research. *IEEE Transactions on Rehabilitation Engineering, 8*(2), 188–190. doi:10.1109/86.847811

Becker, B. (2000). Cyborgs, agents, and transhumanists. *Leonardo, 33*(5), 363.

Beesley, P. (2010). *Hylozoic ground*. Ontario, Canada: Riverside Architectural Press. Also, retrieved August 14, 2011, from http://www.philipbeesleyarchitect.com/sculptures/0635hylozoic_soil/hylozoic.html and http://www.hylozoicground.com/

Bell, C. (2010). *Wild divine*. Retrieved January 4, 2011, from http://www.wilddivine.com/company_bios.html

Benfey, O. T. (1958). August Kekulé and the birth of the structural theory of organic chemistry in 1858. *Journal of Chemical Education, 35*, 21–23. doi:10.1021/ed035p21

Bennett, C., Ryall, J., Spalteholz, L., & Gooch, A. (2007). *The aesthetics of graph visualization. computational aesthetics in graphics, visualization, and imaging* (pp. 57–64). Eurographics Association.

Bentley, W. A. (1995). *1931). Snowflakes in photographs*. Mineola, NY: Dover Publications.

Benvenuti, A. (2006). A beautiful confluence: Science and religion as modes of human participation in the cosmos. *The Forum on Public Policy: A Journal of the Oxford Round Table, 2*(4), 758-774.

Berens, R. R. (1999). The role of artists in ship camouflage during World War I. *Leonardo, 32*(1), 53–59. doi:10.1162/002409499553000

Bergson, H. (1998). *Creative evolution* (New York, N. Y., Trans.). Dover: A. Mitchell. (Original work published 1911)

Biever, C. (2006). A good robot has personality but not looks. *New Scientist, 2561*. Retrieved January 9, 2011, from http://www.newscientist.com/article/mg19125616.400-a-good-robot-has-personality-but-not-looks.html

BioKino Collective. (2011). *The living screen: About*. Retrieved April 2, 2011, from http://www.biokino.net/about.html

Birkhoff, G. D. (2003, 1933). *Aesthetic measure*. Kessinger Publishing. ISBN 0766130940.

Bishop, J. (1989). Stochastic searching networks. In *Proceedings of the 1st IEE Conference on Artificial Neural Networks* (pp. 329–331). London, UK.

Blake, E. (2008). Letter from South Africa: Home of the modern mind. *Archeology, 61*(2). Retrieved August 8, 2011, from http://www.archaeology.org/0803/abstracts/letter.html

Blobel, W. (Ed.). (1987). *Computerkunst in Deutschland*. Munich, Germany: Barke-Verlag.

Bloom, A. (1991). *The republic of Plato* (2nd ed.). New York, NY: Basic Books.

Blue Brain Project. (2011). *Ecole Polytechnique Fédérale de Lausanne*. Lausanne, Switzerland. Retrieved July 16, 2011, from http://bluebrain.epfl.ch/

Boden, M. (2007). Creativity in a nutshell. *Think, 5*(15), 83–96. doi:10.1017/S147717560000230X

Boden, M. (2010). *Creativity and art: Three roads to surprise*. Oxford University Press.

Boettger, S. (2002). *Earthworks: Art and the landscape of the sixties* (pp. 23–27). Berkeley, CA: University of California Press.

Bohm, D. (1980). *Wholeness and the implicate order*. London, UK: Routledge.

Bohr, N. (1935). Can quantum-mechanical description of physical reality be considered complete? *Physical Review, 48*, 696–702. doi:10.1103/PhysRev.48.696

Bois, Y. (2000). Review of force fields: Phases of the kinetic. *Artforum*. New York. Retrieved on April 4, 2011, from http://findarticles.com/p/articles/mi_m0268/is_3_39/ai_67935450/

Boles, M., & Newman, R. (1987). *The golden relationship - Art, math, nature* (2nd ed.). Bradford, MA: Pythagorean Press.

Bolin, L. (2009). *Camouflage art*. Retrieved July 27, 2011, from http://www.toxel.com/inspiration/2009/10/04/camouflage-art-by-liu-bolin/

Bollas, C. (1987). *The shadow of the object: Psychoanalysis of the unthought known*. London, UK: Free Association Books.

Bonabeau, E., Corne, D., & Poli, R. (2010). Swarm intelligence: The state of the art special issue of natural computing. [Springer.]. *Natural Computing, 9*, 655–657. doi:10.1007/s11047-009-9172-6

Bonabeau, E., Dorigo, M., & Theraulaz, G. (2000). Inspiration for optimization from social insect behaviour. *Nature, 406,* 3942. doi:10.1038/35017500

Boorstin, D. (1983). *The discoverers. A History of man's search to know his world and himself.* New York, NY: Vintage Books.

Borgia, G. (1995). Complex male display and female choice in the spotted bowerbird: Specialized functions for different bower decorations. *Animal Behaviour, 49,* 1291–1301. doi:10.1006/anbe.1995.0161

Botha, R., & Knight, C. (2009). *The prehistory of language.* Oxford, UK: Oxford University Press. doi:10.1093/acprof:oso/9780199545872.001.0001

Bown, O. (2011). Generative and adaptive creativity . In McCormack, J., & d'Inverno, M. (Eds.), *Computers and creativity.* Berlin, Germany: Springer.

Bratton, D., & Kennedy, J. (2007). Defining a standard for particle swarm optimization. In *Proceedings of the Swarm Intelligence Symposium* (p. 120-127). Honolulu, HI: IEEE.

Brett, G. (2000). The century of kinesthesia. In S. Cotter & C. Douglas (Ed.), *Force fields: Phases of the kinetic* (pp. 9-68). Barcelona, Spain: Museu d'Art Contemporani de Barcelona and Actar. ASIN: B003U3Y7Z8.

Breuil, H. (1952). *Four hundred centuries of cave art* (Boyle, M. E., Trans.). London, UK: Zwemmer.

Briggs, J. (1992). *Fractals - The patterns of chaos - Discovering a new aesthetic of art, science, and nature.* New York, NY: Simon & Schuster.

Britten, N. (2010, March 15). Artist uses live cells to create new form of design. *The Telegraph.* Retrieved June 28, 2011, from http://www.telegraph.co.uk/culture/art/art-news/8383363/Artist-uses-live-cells-to-create-new-form-of-design.html

Britton, S. (April 2011). *GtkLife* (Version 5.1) [Software]. Retrieved from http://ironphoenix.org/tril/gtklife/

Bronowski, J. (1978). *The origins of knowledge and imagination.* New Haven, CT: Yale University Press.

Brown, P., Gere, C., Lambert, N., & Mason, C. (Eds.). (2009). *White heat cold logic, British computer art 1960-1980.* Cambridge, MA: MIT Press.

Brugge, D., Benally, T., & Yazzie-Lewis, E. (Eds.). (2006). *The Navajo people and uranium mining.* Albuquerque, NM: University of New Mexico Press.

Brundrett, K., & Crowley, G. (2010). Graham Crowley, on the state of play for contemporary painting. *Artists Newsletter,* February 2010. Retrieved June 28, 2011, from http://www.a-n.co.uk/jobs_and_opps/article/606719

Bubbles. (2011). Retrieved February 1, 2011, from http://bubbles.org/html/questions/color.htm

Buonarroti, M. (2011). *Deluge.* Retrieved January 27, 2011, from http://www.wga.hu/frames-e.html?/html/m/michelan/3sistina/1genesis/2flood/02_3ce2.html

Buonarroti, M. (2011). *Sistine Chapel.* Retrieved January 27, 2011, from http://www.wga.hu/frames-e.html?/html/m/michelan/3sistina/1genesis/2flood/02_3ce2.html%20and% 20http://www.wga.hu/tours/sistina/index3.html

CACHe. (n.d.). *Archive of pioneering British computer art.* Retrieved July 14, 2011 from http://www.e-x-p.org/cache/index.HTM

Cain, P. (2007). Drawing as coming to know. In *Ambiguity, Tracey Online Journal,* Loughborough University. Retrieved February 15, 2009, from http://www.lboro.ac.uk/departments/ac/tracey/somag/brien.html

Cain, P. (2009). *Abstract for thesis: Drawing as coming to know: How is it that I know I made sense of what I do?* Retrieved August 10, 2009, from http://www.patriciacain.com/research_statement.html.

Calder, A. (1937). Mobiles. In M. Evans & G. Howe (Ed.), *The painter's object.* Retrieved from http://calder.org/historicaltexts/text/9.html

Callender, C., & Schaffer, J. (2010). *Do mereological sums constitute objects? Questions like this are hotly debated in contemporary metaphysics — Yet such questions seem utterly disconnected from science. Has metaphysics gone in the wrong direction?* Online video discussion, posted on September 8, 2010. Retrieved July 22, 2011, from http://www.philostv.com/craig-callender-and-jonathan-schaffer

Calouste Gulbenkian Foundation. (2011). Retrieved July 18, 2011, from http://www.gulbenkian.org.uk/

Camouflage restaurants. (n.d.). Retrieved July 27, 2011, from http://www.toxel.com/inspiration/2009/06/20/10-unusual-and-creative-restaurants/

Campbell, J. (1986). *The inner reaches of outer space – Metaphor as myth and as religion*. New York, NY: Harper & Row, Publishers.

Campbell, J. (1991a). *A Joseph Campbell companion*. New York, NY: HarperCollins Publishers.

Campbell, J. (1991b). The masks of God: *Vol. 3. Occidental mythology*. London, UK: Penguin Books.

Carnie, A. (2002, March 17). Scientists and artists must rub shoulders. *The Observer*. Retrieved June 28, 2011, from http://www.tram.ndo.co.uk/afewwords.htm

Carnie, A. (2011). *Artist's website*. Retrieved June 28, 2011, from http://www.tram.ndo.co.uk/magicforest2.htm

Cavagna, A., Cimarelli, A., Giardina, I., Parisi, G., Santagati, R., Stefanini, F., & Viale, M. (2010). Scale-free correlations in starling flocks. *Proceedings of the National Academy of Sciences of the U.S.A.*

Cave of Altamira and Paleolithic Cave Art of Northern Spain . (2011). Retrieved August 8, 2011, from http://whc.unesco.org/en/list/310

Center for Disease Control. (2000). *Fernald risk assessment project*. Atlanta, GA: National Center for Environmental Health. Retrieved August 28, 2011, from http://www.cdc.gov/nceh/radiation/fernald/default.htm

Cézanne, P. (1885-87). *Mont Sainte Victoire*. Oil on canvas. Courtauld Institute of Art, London, England. Retrieved August 28, 2011, from http://www.ibiblio.org/wm/paint/auth/cezanne/st-victoire/1885/

Chan, W. C. (2007). Toxicity studies of fullerenes and derivatives. In *Bio-applications of nanoparticles*. New York, NY: Springer Science + Business Media. ISBN 0-387-76712-6

Change, G. (2010). *Human appropriation of the world's fresh water supply*. Retrieved December 11, 2010, from http://www.globalchange.umich.edu/globalchange2/current/lectures/freshwater_supply/freshwater.html

Chapin, J. K., Moxon, K. A., Markowitz, R. S., & Nicolelis, M. A. (1999). Real-time control of a robot arm using simultaneously recorded neurons in the motor cortex. *Nature Neuroscience, 2*(7), 664–670. doi:10.1038/10223

Charmi, S. (1990). *Computerkunst '90 catalog*. Gladbeck.

Cheetham, M. A. (2010). The crystal interface in contemporary art: Metaphors of the organic and inorganic. *Leonardo, 43*(3), 251–255. doi:10.1162/leon.2010.43.3.250

Choi, M., Stanton-Maxey, K., Stanley, J., Levin, C., Bardhan, R., & Akin, D. (2007). A cellular Trojan Horse for delivery of therapeutic nanoparticles into tumors. *Nano Letters, 7*(12), 3759–3765. doi:10.1021/nl072209h

Chuter, J. (2010), Interview with Andrew Carnie. *ATTN: Magazine*, July. Retrieved June 28, 2011, from http://www.attnmagazine.co.uk/arts-literature/2452

Ciurlionis, M. (2011). *Deluge*.

Clark, A. (2003). *Natural-born cyborgs: Minds, technologies, and the future of human intelligence*. Oxford University Press.

Clark, G. (1997). *The photograph*. Oxford, UK: Oxford University Press.

Cleland, T. M. (1921). *A practical description of the Munsell color system, with suggestions for its use*. London, UK: British Library Collection.

Cleveland Sculpture Center . (2011). Retrieved July 18, 2011 from http://www.sculpturecenter.org/

Clottes, J. (2002). *World rock art*. Los Angeles, CA: Getty Publications.

CNMM. (2010). *Computing for clean water project*. Center for Nano and Micro Mechanics. Retrieved December 11, 2010, from http://cnmm.tsinghua.edu.cn/channels/495.html

Cochran, R. D. (2009). Eve Andrée Laramée. *Sculpture Magazine, 28*(9).

Cockroach Controlled Mobile Robot. (n.d.). Retrieved July 15, 2011, from www.conceptlab.com/roachbot

Cohan, C. L., & Cole, S. W. (2002). Life course transitions and natural disaster: Marriage, birth, and divorce following Hurricane Hugo. *Journal of Family Psychology, 16*(1), 14–25. doi:10.1037/0893-3200.16.1.14

Cohen, H. (2001). *Biography of Aaron Cohen, creator of Aaron*. Retrieved September 29, 2011, from http://www.kurzweilcyberart.com/aaron/hi_cohenbio.html

Constant, J. (2011). *Wasan geometry*. Retrieved July 16, 2011, from http://www.hermay.org/jconstant/wasan/, http://hermay.org/jconstant/animation/animSangaku.html

Cook, T. A. (1979). *The curves of life*. Mineola, NY: Dover Publications, Inc.

Corbusier, L. (1996). *Le Modulor and Modulor 2*. Basel, Switzerland: Birkhäuser Architecture.

Corso, P., Kramer, M., Blair, K., Addiss, D., Davis, J., & Haddix, A. (2003). Cost of illness in the 1993 waterborne Cryptosporidium outbreak, Milwaukee, Wisconsin. *Emerging Infectious Diseases, 9*(4), 426–431.

Cottet, G.-H., & Koumoutsakos, P. (2000). *Vortex methods*. Cambridge, UK: Cambridge University Press. doi:10.1017/CBO9780511526442

Craft, D. (2010a). The elements in golden ratio. *Doug Craft Fine Art*. Retrieved December 3, 2010, from http://www.dougcraftfineart.com/frameElements.htm

Craft, D. (2010b). Geometric forms for the collage of backgrounds. *Doug Craft Fine Art*, Retrieved December 3, 2010, from http://www.dougcraftfineart.com/frame-ArtForms.htm

Creighton, T. (1969). *Building for modern man*. Manchester, NH: Ayer Publishing.

Crick, F. H. C. (1958). On protein synthesis. [from http://profiles.nlm.nih.gov/SC/B/B/Z/Y/_/scbbzy.pdf]. *Symposia of the Society for Experimental Biology, 12*, 138–163. Retrieved April 13, 2011

Critchlow, K. (1999). *Islamic patterns – An analytical and cosmological approach*. Rochester, VT: Inner Traditions.

Crow, D. (2006). *Left to right: The cultural shift from words to pictures*. Switzerland: AVA Publishing.

Csikszentmihalyi, M., & Csikszentmihalyi, I. (Eds.). (1988). *Optimal experience: Psychological states of flow in consciousness*. Cambridge, UK: Cambridge University Press.

Csuri, C. (2011). *Charles Csuri: Art & ideas*. Personal website. Retrieved September 29, 2011, from http://www.csuri.com/

CTR. (2010). *Center for Tardigrade Research*. Retrieved December 19, 2010, from http://www.tardires.ch/

CyberMed. (2002). *Medical software: Vworks*. Retrieved August 28, 2011, from http://www.cybermed.co.kr/e_pro_dental_vworks.html

Dalton, A. B., Collins, S., Muñoz, E., Razal, J. M., Von Ebron, H., & Ferraris, J. P. (2003). Super-tough carbon-nanotube fibres. *Nature, 423*, 703. doi:10.1038/423703a

Dalton, R. J. (1999). *Critical masses: Citizens, nuclear weapons production, and environmental destruction in the United States and Russia*. Cambridge, MA: MIT Press.

Damncoolpics. (2006). *Japanese manhole cover art*. Retrieved December 3, 2010, from http://damncoolpics.blogspot.com/2006/12/japanese-manhole-cover-art.html

Danh, B. (2006). *Chlorophyll prints*. Posted by David Pescovitz. Retrieved August 13, 2011, from http://boingboing.net/2006/10/23/binh-danhs-chlorophy.html

Danh, B. (2010). Retrieved April 25, 2011, from http://www.binhdanh.com

Davies, P. F. (1995). Flow-mediated endothelial mechanotransduction. *Physiological Reviews, 75*(3), 519.

Davies, P. F. (2008). Hemodynamic shear stress and the endothelium in cardiovascular pathophysiology. *Nature Clinical Practice. Cardiovascular Medicine, 6*(1), 16–26. doi:10.1038/ncpcardio1397

Davies, P. F., Civelek, M., Fang, Y., Guerraty, M. A., & Passerini, A. G. (2010). Endothelial heterogeneity associated with regional Athero-Susceptibility and adaptation to disturbed blood flow in vivo. *Seminars in Thrombosis and Hemostasis, 36*, 265–275. doi:10.1055/s-0030-1253449

Davson, H., & Perkins, E. S. (2009). *Eye anatomy*. Retrieved July 10, 2011, from http://www.britannica.com/EBchecked/topic/1688997/human-eye

Day, L. (1908). *Nature and ornament: Nature, the raw material of design* (p. vi). London, UK: Batsford. republished 1929 de Meyer, K., Bishop, J. M., & Nasuto, S. J. (2003). Stochastic diffusion: Using recruitment for search. In P. McOwan, K. Dautenhahn & C. L. Nehaniv (Eds.), *Evolvability and interaction: Evolutionary substrates of communication, signalling, and perception in the dynamics of social complexity*, (pp. 60–65). Technical Report.

de Meyer, K., Nasuto, S., & Bishop, J. (2006). Stochastic diffusion optimisation: the application of partial function evaluation and stochastic recruitment in swarm intelligence optimisation . In Abraham, A., Grosam, C., & Ramos, V. (Eds.), *Swarm intelligence and data mining*. Springer Verlag.

Dehlinger, H. (2002). *Instance and system: A figure and its 2^{18} variations.* Paper presented at the International Conference Generative Art 2002, Politecnico di Milano: Italy.

Dehlinger, H. (2005). *Programming generative drawings with small elements*. Paper presented at the International Conference Art+Math=X, Boulder, Colorado.

Dehlinger. (2004). *SIGGRAPH '04 catalog*. Digit@lkörper. (2002). Exhibition with Hobbytronic, Dortmund. In *Computer Art Faszination*, (p. 316).

Dehlinger, H. (2004). *Zeichnungen*. Kassel, Germany: Kassel University Press.

Dehlinger, H. E. (1981). Bildnerische Experimente mit der geplotteten Linie . In Bauer, H., Dehlinger, H. E., & Mathias, G. (Eds.), *Design Kunst Computer –Computer in den künstlerischen Bereichen* (pp. 81, 84, 85–87). Kassel, Germany: Jenior & Pressler.

Delamare, G., & Francois, B. (2000). *Colors: The story of dyes and pigments*. Harry N. Abrams.

Deleuze, G., & Guattari, F. (2004). *A thousand plateaus: Capitalism and schizophrenia* (Massumi, B., Trans.). London, UK: Continuum.

Denevan, J. (2011). *The art of Jim Denevan*. Personal website. Retrieved April 11, 2011, from http://www.jimdenevan.com/

Deruta Ceramics. (2011). *That's Arte.com: Fine Italian ceramics*. Retrieved August 8, 2011, from http://www.thatsarte.com/region/Deruta

Devlin, K. (1997). *Goodbye Descartes. The end of logic and the search for a new cosmology of the mind*. New York, NY: John Wiley & Sons, Inc.

Dewey, J. (1934). *Art as experience*. London, UK: Penguin Books Ltd.

DFG Research Center Matheon. (2011). *Mathematics for key technologies*. Berlin, Germany. Retrieved July 16, 2011, from http://www.matheon.de

Doczi, G. (1981). *The power of limits. Proportional harmonies in nature, art, and architecture*. Boston, MA: Shambala Publications, Inc.

Donchin, E. (1981). Presidential address, 1980. Surprise!... Surprise? *Psychophysiology, 18*(5), 493–513. doi:10.1111/j.1469-8986.1981.tb01815.x

Donchin, E., Spencer, K. M., & Wijesinghe, R. (2000). The mental prosthesis: Assessing the speed of a P300-based brain-computer interface. *IEEE Transactions on Rehabilitation Engineering, 8*(2), 174–179. doi:10.1109/86.847808

Doolittle, B. (2011). *Camouflage art*. Retrieved July 27, 2011, http://www.bnr-art.com/doolitt/

Doré, G. (2011). *The deluge*. Retrieved January 27, 2011, from http://en.wikipedia.org/wiki/File:Gustave_Doré_-_The_Holy_Bible_-_Plate_I,_The_Deluge.jpg

Dorin, A., & Korb, K. (2007). Building artificial ecosystems from artificial chemistry. *9th European Conference on Artificial Life* (pp. 103-112). Springer-Verlag.

Dorin, A., & Korb, K. (2011). Creativity refined . In McCormack, J., & d'Inverno, M. (Eds.), *Computers and creativity*. Berlin, Germany: Springer.

Dorter, K. (1973). The ion: Plato's characterization of art. *The Journal of Aesthetics and Art Criticism, 32*(1), 65–78. doi:10.2307/428704

Drmanac, R., Sparks, A. B., Callow, M. J., Halpern, A. L., et al. (5 November 2009). Human genome sequencing using unchained base reads on self-assembling DNA nanoarrays. *Science, 327*(5961), 78-81. Retrieved December 19, 2010, from http://www.sciencemag.org/content/327/5961/78.abstract

Droste, M. (1998). *Bauhaus 1919 – 1933*. Berlin, Germany: Bauhaus-Archiv Museum für Gestaltung, (Benedikt Taschen).

Dubinski, J. (2008). *Galaxy dynamics*. Retrieved from http://www.galaxydynamics.org/

Dubinsky, Y. D. (2006). *YDD Studio*. Retrieved April 25, 2011, from http://www.yddstudio.com

DW-World.DE Deutsche Welle. (17.08.2010). Retrieved December 15, 2010 from http://www.dw-world.de/dw/article/0,5918010,00.html

Dyson, F. (2011). The dramatic picture of Richard Feynman. *The New York Review of Books, LVIII*(12), 39–40.

Eberhart, R., & Kennedy, J. (1995). A new optimizer using particle swarm theory. In *Proceedings of the Sixth International Symposium on Micro Machine and Human Science* (Vol. 43).

Eco, U. (1984). *The role of the reader: Explorations in the semiotics of texts*. Bloomington, IN: Indiana University Press.

Eco, U. (1989). *1979). The open work*. Cambridge, MA: Harvard University Press.

Eco, U. (1994). *The limits of interpretation (advances in semiotics)*. Bloomington, IN: Indiana University Press.

Eco, U., & Bredin, H. (Trans. Eds.). (1988). *The aesthetics of Thomas Aquinas*. Cambridge, MA: Harvard University Press.

Ede, S. (2005). *Art & Science*. London, UK: I. B. Tauris. Retrieved August 5, 2011, from http://books.google.com/books?id=iiE3RsvK248C

Eichstaedt, P. (1994). *If you poison us: Uranium and native Americans*. Santa Fe, NM: Red Crane Books.

Einstein, A. (1916). *Relativity: The special and general theory*. Methuen & Co Ltd. Retrieved February 20, 2011, from http://www.gutenberg.org/ebooks/5001

Einstein, A., Podolsky, B., & Rosen, N. (1935). Can quantum-mechanical description of physical reality be considered complete? *Physical Review, 47*, 777–780. doi:10.1103/PhysRev.47.777

El Naschie, M. S. (1994). Is quantum space a random cantor set with a golden mean dimension at the core? *Chaos, Solitons, and Fractals, 4*(2), 177–179. doi:10.1016/0960-0779(94)90141-4

Elam, K. (2001). *Geometry of design - Studies in proportion and composition*. New York, NY: Princeton Architectural Press.

Elder, R. B. (1998). *The films of Stan Brakhage in the American tradition of Ezra Pound, Gertrude Stein, and Charles Olson*. Waterloo, Canada: Wilfrid Laurier University Press.

Elenbogen, B., & Kaeding, T. (1989). A weak estimate of the fractal dimension of the Mandelbrot Boundary. *Physics Letters. [Part A], 136*(7-8), 358–362. doi:10.1016/0375-9601(89)90415-5

Elgin, C. Z. (1997). *Between the absolute and the arbitrary*. Ithaca, NY: Cornell University Press.

Ellington, A. (2011, March 5). On regulation. *Streamspace*. Retrieved June 28, 2011, from http://streamspace.blogspot.com/2011/03/ramblings-on-regulation-by-andrew.html

Else, L. (2011, 15 March). What art can do for science (and vice versa). *New Scientist*. Retrieved March 11, 2011, from http://www.newscientist.com/blogs/culturelab/2011/03/where-science-and-art-collide.html

El-Sourani, N., Hauke, S., & Borschbach, M. (2010). An evolutionary approach for solving the Rubik's cube incorporating exact methods . In Di Chio, C. (Eds.), *Applications of evolutionary computing, LNCS 6024 EvoApplications 2010 Proceedings* (pp. 80–89). Berlin, Germany: Springer. doi:10.1007/978-3-642-12239-2_9

Emmitt, S., Olie, J., & Schmid, P. (2004). *Principles of architectural detailing*. Oxford, UK: Wiley-Blackwell.

Enchanted learning. (2011). Retrieved January 23, 2011, from http://www.enchantedlearning.com/biomes

Encyclopædia Britannica. (2011). *Holothurian*. Retrieved July 27, 2011, from http://www.britannica.com/EBchecked/topic/269645/holothurian

Encyclopædia Britannica. (2011). *Phenakistoscope*. Retrieved July 24, 2011, from http://www.britannica.com/EBchecked/topic/455469/phenakistoscope

Etzioni, A., Ben-Barak, A., Peron, S., & Durandy, A. (2007). Ataxia-telangiectasia in twins presenting as autosomal recessive hyper-immunoglobulin m syndrome. *The Israel Medical Association Journal*, 9(5), 406.

EvoMUSART. (2010). *Eighth European Event on Evolutionary and Bio-inspired Music, Sound, Art, and Design.* Retrieved January 9, 2011, from http://eden.dei.uc.pt/~machado/evomusart2010.pdf

Ewing, W. A. (1991). *Flora photographica: Masterpieces of flower photography.* London, UK: Thames & Hudson, Ltd.

Fabiani, M., Gratton, G., Karis, D., & Donchin, E. (1987). Definition, identification and reliability of the P300 component of the event-related brain potential. In P. K. Ackles, J. R. Jennings, & M. G. H. Coles (Eds.), *Advances in psychophysiology* (pp. 1-78). Greenwich, CT: JAI Press.

Farthing, S. (2005). *Dirtying the paper delicately.* In: University of the Arts, Inaugural Lecture, London, April 26th 2005.

Farwell, L. A., & Donchin, E. (1988). Talking off the top of your head: Toward a mental prothesis utilizing event-related brain potentials. *Electroencephalography and Clinical Neurophysiology*, 70(6), 510–523. doi:10.1016/0013-4694(88)90149-6

Faure Walker, J. (2011). *Works in Victoria and Albert Museum.* London. Retrieved June 28, 2011, from http://www.vam.ac.uk/contentapi/search/?q=faure+walker&searchsubmit=Go

Faure Walker, J. (2006). *Painting the digital river: How an artist learned to love the computer.* Prentice Hall.

Ferguson, C., & Ferguson, H. (1994). *Mathematics in stone and bronze.* Erie, PA: Meridian Creative Group.

Ferreira, R., Poteaux, C., Hubert, J., Delabie, C., Fresneau, D., & Rybak, F. (2010). Stridulations reveal cryptic speciation in neotropical sympatric ants. *PLoS ONE*, 5(12). doi:10.1371/journal.pone.0015363

Feynman, R. (1989). *The Feynman lectures on physics: Commemorative issue* (*Vol. 1*). Massachusetts: Addison-Wesley Publishing Co., Inc.

Feynman, R. P., Leighton, R., & Dyson, F. (2005). *All the adventures of a curious character. Collection of essays and lecture series.* W. W. Norton Publisher.

Fisher, J. (2003). On drawing. In De Zegher, C. (Ed.), *The stage of drawing: Gesture and act, selected from the Tate Collection* (pp. 217–226). London, UK: Tate Publishing & The Drawing Center.

Flake, G. W. (2000). *The computational beauty of nature: Computer explorations of fractals, chaos, complex systems, and adaptation.* Cambridge, MA: MIT Press. Retrieved January 14, 2011, from http://mitpress.mit.edu/books/FLAOH/cbnhtml/home.html

Flemming, A., Verolet, M., Goldstein, B., Hobgood, N., & Raines, G. (2008). *The most important microbe you've never heard of* [Video]. Retrieved October 10, 2011, from http://www.npr.org/templates/story/story.php?storyId=99800021

Fly Drawing Device. (n.d.). Retrieved July 15, 2011, from www.dwbowen.com/portfolio.html

Fox, M., & Kemp, M. (2009). *Interactive architecture.* New York, NY: Princeton Architectural Press.

Fractal Foundation. (2011). *Interconnections of natural systems and their essential nonlinearity.* Albuquerque, NM. Retrieved July 16, 2011, from http://fractalfoundation.org/

Frazier, I. (2011, September 5). The March of the Strandbeests: Theo Jansen's wind-powered sculpture. *New Yorker (New York, N.Y.)*, 54–61.

Freedberg, D. (1989). *The power of images. Studies in the history and theory of response.* Chicago, IL: The University of Chicago Press.

Freely, J. (2010). *Aladdin's lamp. How Greek science came to Europe through the Islamic world.* New York, NY: Vintage Books.

Freeman, M. H. (2003). *Optics* (11th ed.). London, UK: Butterworths-Heinemann.

Freestone, I., Meeks, N., Sax, M., & Higgitt, C. (2007). The Lycurgus Cup – A Roman nanotechnology. *Gold Bulletin*, 40(4), 270-277. Retrieved August 8, 2011, from http://www.goldbulletin.org/assets/file/goldbulletin/downloads/Lycurgus_4_40.pdf

Friedman, D., Leeb, R., Guger, C., Steed, A., Pfurtscheller, G., & Slater, M. (2007). Navigating virtual reality by thought: What is it like? *Presence (Cambridge, Mass.)*, *16*(1), 100–110. doi:10.1162/pres.16.1.100

Fry, B., & Reas, C. (2001). *Processing* [Software]. Retrieved from http://processing.org/

Fung, Y. (1997). *Biomechanics: Circulation*. Springer Verlag.

Furuyama, M. (1962). Histometrical investigations of arteries in reference to arterial hypertension. *The Tohoku Journal of Experimental Medicine*, *76*, 388–414. doi:10.1620/tjem.76.388

Galanter, P. (2011). Computational aesthetic evaluation: Past and future. In McCormack, J., & d'Inverno, M. (Eds.), *Computers and creativity*. Berlin, Germany: Springer.

Gao, X., & Jiang, L. (2004). Biophysics: Water-repellent legs of water striders. *Nature*, *432*(7013), 36. doi:10.1038/432036a

Gardner, M. (1970, October). Mathematical games: The fantastic combinations of John Conway's new solitaire game "life". *Scientific American*, *223*, 120–123. doi:10.1038/scientificamerican1070-120

Gardner, M. (1989). *Penrose tiles to trapdoor ciphers*. Washington, DC: The Mathematical Association of America.

Garner, S. (2008). *Writing on drawing, essays on drawing practice and research*. Bristol, UK: Intellect Books.

Gazalé, M. (1999). *Gnomon: From pharaohs to fractals*. Princeton, NJ: Princeton University Press.

Gell-Mann, M., & Ne'eman, Y. (2000). *The eightfold way*. Boulder, CO: Westview Press.

George, E. Palade EM Slide Collection. (2011). *Harvey Cushing/John Hay Whitney Medical Library*. Retrieved March 9, 2011, from http://cushing.med.yale.edu/gsdl/cgi-bin/library?p=about&c=palade

Georgopoulos, A. P., Schwartz, A. B., & Kettner, R. E. (1986). Neuronal population coding of movement direction. *Science*, *233*(4771), 1416–1419. doi:10.1126/science.3749885

Gericault, T. (2011). *Scene of the deluge*. Retrieved January 27, 2011, from http://www.wikigallery.org/wiki/painting_218864/Theodore-Gericault/Scene-of-the-Deluge

Ghyka, M. (1946). *The geometry of art and life*. Mineola, NY: Dover Publications, Inc.

Gibbons, G. H., & Dzau, V. J. (1994). The emerging concept of vascular remodeling. *The New England Journal of Medicine*, *330*(20), 1431. doi:10.1056/NEJM199405193302008

Gilchrist, B., Bradley, J., & Joelson, J. (1997). *Thought conductor #1*. Retrieved May 23, 2007, from http://www.artemergent.org.uk/tc/tc1.html

Girerd, X., London, G., Boutouyrie, P., Mourad, J. J., Safar, M., & Laurent, S. (1996). Remodeling of the radial artery in response to a chronic increase in shear stress. *Hypertension*, *27*(3), 799.

Gleick, J. (1987). *Chaos: Making a new science*. London, UK: Penguin Books Ltd.

Gleiser, M. (1997). *The dancing universe. From creation myths to the Big Bang*. Hanover, NH: Dartmouth College Press, University Press of New England.

Global Information Technology Report 2008-2009. (2009). *Mobility in a networked world*. Retrieved January 9, 2011, from https://members.weforum.org/pdf/gitr/2009/gitr09fullreport.pdf

Global Water Partnership. (2010). Retrieved January 4, 2011 from www.gwp.org

Glossary of Meteorology. (2010). Retrieved November 19, 2010, from http://amsglossary.allenpress.com/glossary/search?p=1&query=cloud+seeding&submit=Search

Golemboski, C. (2007). *Portfolio*. Retrieved April 25, 2011, from http://www.kevinlongino.com/portfolio.cfm?a=39&p=131&t=collector

Gombrich, E. H. (1989). *Art and illusion. A study in the psychology of pictorial representation*. Princeton, NJ: Princeton University Press.

Goodsell, D. S. (2006). Fact and fantasy in nanotech imagery. *Leonardo Journal, the International Society for the Arts . Sciences and Technology*, *42*(1), 52–57.

Google. (2011). *Google Earth.* Retrieved April 15, 2011, from http://www.google.com/earth/index.html

Gorbet, M. G., Orth, M., & Ishii, H. (1998). Triangles: Tangible interface for manipulation and exploration of digital information topography. In *Proceedings of the 4th International Conference on Human Factors in Computing Systems, ACM SIGCHI 1998,* Los Angeles, California, April 18-23, 1998. New York, NY: ACM Press.

Gordon, P. L. (1983). *The book of film care.* Rochester, NY: Eastman Kodak Company.

Gorman, M. J. (2001). Between the demonic and the miraculous: Athanasius Kircher and the baroque culture of machines. In D. Stolzenberg, (Ed.), *The great art of knowing: The baroque encyclopedia of Athanasius Kirche* (pp. 59-70). Stanford, CA: Stanford University Libraries. Retrieved August 10, 2011, from http://hotgates.stanford.edu/Eyes/machines/index.htm

Graf, W. (1994). *Plutonium and the Rio Grande: Environmental change and contamination in the nuclear age.* New York, NY: Oxford University Press.

Grant, C. (2010). *David Hockney.* Retrieved January 4, 2011, from www.bbc.co.uk/news/technology-11666162

Greenberg, C. (1971). *Art and culture: Critical essays.* Boston, MA: Beacon Press.

Greene, B. (2011). *An elegant multiverse? Professor Brian Greene considers the possibilities.* Retrieved March 22, 2011, from http://news.columbia.edu/briangreene

Greenfield, G. (2005). Evolutionary methods for ant colony paintings. *Applications of Evolutionary Computing . Proceedings, 3449,* 478–487.

Greenough, S., Snyder, J., Travis, D., & Westerbeck, C. (1989). *On the art of fixing a shadow. One hundred and fifty years of photography.* Washington, DC: National Gallery of Art, in conjunction with The Art Institute of Chicago.

Greenslade, T. B., Jr. (2011). *Instruments for natural philosophy.* Retrieved on 26 July, 2011, from http://physics.kenyon.edu/EarlyApparatus/Optical_Recreations/Praxinoscopes/Praxinoscopes.html

Grey, R. (2008, 5 October). Prehistoric cave paintings took up to 20,000 years to complete. *The Telegraph.* Retrieved August 8, 2011, from http://www.telegraph.co.uk/earth/3352850/Prehistoric-cave-paintings-took-up-to- 20000-years-to-complete.html

Groenendael, V. M. C. (1987). *Wayang Theatre in Indonesia.* Dordrecht, The Netherlands: Foris Publications.

Gross, L., Mohn, F., Moll, N., Liljeroth, P., & Meyer, G. (2009). The chemical structure of a molecule resolved by atomic force microscopy. *Science, 329*(5944), 1110–1114. doi:10.1126/science.1176210

Guthrie, R. D. (2006). *The nature of paleolithic art.* Chicago, IL: University of Chicago Press.

Gutzler, D. S., & Preston, J. W. (1997). Evidence for a relationship between spring snow cover in North America and summer rainfall in New Mexico. *Geophysical Research Letters, 24,* 2207–2210. doi:10.1029/97GL02099

Habgood, J. S. (1964). *Religion and science.* London, UK: Mills & Boon.

Haeckel, E. H. P. A. (1899). *Art forms in nature.* New York, NY: Dover. reprinted 1974

Haeckel, E., Breidbach, O., Hartman, R., & Eibl-Eibesfeldt, I. (1998). *Art forms in nature: The prints of Ernst Haeckel (monographs).* München, Germany: Prestel Publishing.

Hall, D. (2011). *Media installations: 1987-The terrible uncertainty of the thing described.* Retrieved from http://doughallstudio.com/1987-the-terrible-uncertainty/the-terrible-uncertainty-of-the-thing-described/3305605

Haloquadra . (2010). Retrieved January 27, 2011, from microbewiki.kenyon.edu/index.php/Haloquadra

Hambidge, J. (1967). *The elements of dynamic symmetry.* Mineola, NY: Dover Publications, Inc.

Hammond, J. H. (1981). *The camera obscura. A chronicle.* Bristol, UK: Adam Hilger Ltd.

Hansmeyer, M. (2011). *Computational architecture.* Personal website. Retrieved April 11, 2011, from http://www.michael-hansmeyer.com/html/

Haraway, D. J. (1991). *Simians, cyborgs, and women: The reinvention of nature*. New York, NY: Routledge. Retrieved August 5, 2011, from http://books.google.com/books?id=ejHWRgAACAAJ

Harris, J. (2008). *Beyond Flash*. Retrieved August 8, 2010, from http://www.number27.org/beyondflash.html

Hartman, N. W., & Bertoline, G. R. (2005). Spatial abilities and virtual technologies: Examining the computer graphics learning environment. *Proceedings of the Ninth International Conference on Information Visualisation*, (pp. 992-99). Washington, DC: IEEE Computer Society.

Harty, D. (2010). *Drawing//experience: A process of translation*. Ph.D. thesis, Loughborough University.

Hayes, B. (2010). Flights of fancy. *American Scientist*. Retrieved January 20, 2011, from http://www.american-scientist.org/issues/pub/2011/1/flights-of-fancy/1

Hayes, J. (2010). *Japanese pottery and lacquerware*. Retrieved August 5, 2011, from http://factsanddetails.com/japan.php?itemid=693&catid=20&subcatid=129jtt

Hébert, J.-P. (2011). *Website of the Artist*. Retrieved April 1, 2011, from http://jeanpierrehebert.com/

Hecht, E. (2001). *Optics* (4nd ed.). Reading, MA: Addison-Wesley Publishing. ISBN-10: 0805385665

Heetderks, W. J., & Schmidt, E. M. (1995). Chronic multiple unit recording of neural activity with micromachined silicon electrodes. In A. Lang (Ed.), *Proceedings of RESNA 95 Annual Conference* (pp. 649-653). Arlington, VA: RESNA Press.

Heller, D. (2004). *Manhole covers of the world*. Retrieved April 11, 2011, from http://www.danheller.com/manholes.html

Heller, E. (2011). *Personal website*. Retrieved April 11, 2011, from http://www.ericjhellergallery.com/index.pl?page=image;iid=68)

Helmcke, J. G., & Kull, U. (2004). *IL38 Diatoms II: Shells in nature and technics III*. Universität Stuttgart, Germany: Institut für Leichte Flächentragwerke.

Hematite Mineral Data. (2011). *Mineralogy database*. Retrieved August 8, 2011, from http://webmineral.com/data/Hematite.shtml

Hemenway, P. (2005). *Divine proportion. □ (Phi) In art, nature, and science*. New York, NY: Sterling Publishing Co., Inc.

Heon, L. S., Ackerman, J., & Massachusetts Museum of Contemporary Art. (2000). *Unnatural science: An exhibition, spring 2000 - spring 2001, MASS MoCA*. New York, NY: Te Neues Publishing Company. Retrieved August 5, 2011, from http://books.google.com/books?id=H7PpAAAAMAAJ

Hermentin, I. (2010). *Transcriptions decoded. Computerkunst/Computer Art 2.010 catalog*. Gladbeck.

Herz-Fischler, R. (1987). *A mathematical history of the golden number*. Mineola, NY: Dover Publications, Inc.

Herzogenrath, W., & Nierhoff-Wielk, B. (2007). *Ex machina - Frühe Computergrafik*. Berlin, Germany: Deutscher Kunstverlag.

Hevly, B. W., & Findlay, J. M. (1998). *The atomic west*. University of Washington Press. Retrieved August 5, 2011, from http://books.google.com/books?id=ugdHhzX3Fl8C

Hewlett-Packard Company. (1983). *HP7475A graphics plotter: Interfacing and programming manual*. San Diego, CA: Author.

Hidetoshi, F., & Rothman, T. (2008). *Sacred mathematics: Japanese temple geometry*. Princeton, NJ: Princeton University Press.

Hirsch, C. (1988). *Numerical computation of internal and external flows*. New York, NY: John Wiley & Sons.

Hirsch, R. (2000). *Seizing the light: A history of photography*. Boston, MA: McGraw-Hill Companies, Inc.

History of Nano Timeline. (2011). *Discover nano*. Northwestern University. Retrieved August 8, 2011, from http://www.discovernano.northwestern.edu/whatis/History/# Hopkins, C. (2008, 22 October). Prof George Palade: Nobel prize-winner whose work laid foundations for modern molecular cell biology. *The Independent*: *Obituaries*. Retrieved August 8, 2011, from http://www.independent.co.uk/news/obituaries/prof-george-palade-nobel-prizewinner-whose-work-laid-the- foundations-for-modern-molecular-cell-biology-968560.html

Hoberman, C. (2010). Expanding video screen for U2 360° tour. *Architecture and Urbanism, 2010*(2), 119-121.

Hochberg, J., & Brooks, V. (1996). *Movies in the mind's eye*. University of Wisconsin Press International Society for Mathematical Sciences. (2011). *Osaka, Japan.* Retrieved July 10, 2011, from http://www.jams.or.jp/

Hockney, D. (2011). *Personal website*. Retrieved April 11, 2011, from http://www.hockneypictures.com

Hoggett, V. E. Jr. (1969). *Fibonacci and Lucas numbers*. New York, NY: Houghton Mifflin Co.

Hölldobler, B., & Wilson, E. O. (1990). *The ants*. Cambridge, MA: The Belknap Press of Harvard University.

Hölldobler, B., & Wilson, E. O. (2009). *The superorganism: The beauty, elegance, and strangeness of insect societies*. New York, NY: W. W. Norton & Company.

Holmes, S. J. (1961). *Louis Pasteur*. New York, NY: Dover Publications, Inc.

Holtzman, S. (1998). *Digital mosaics: The aesthetics of cyberspace*. Touchstone.

Host. (n.d.). Retrieved July 15, 2011, from http://www.sonicobjects.com/index.php/projects/more/host

Huang, Q., & Balsys, R. J. (2009). Applying fractal and chaos theory to animation in the Chinese literati tradition. *CGIV, Sixth International Conference on Computer Graphics, Imaging and Visualization* (pp.112-122). Los Alamitos, CA: IEEE Computer Society.

Huang, S. C. C. (2009). MSOrgm (Motivational Sensitive Organism). *Leonardo/ISAST, 42*(4), 374-375.

Huang, S. C. C. (2011). *LBSkeleton (Listening Bio-Skeleton). Analogue is the new digital*. Retrieved August 10, 2011, from http://sonotonialand.org/siggraph2011/

Huber, F., Moore, T. E., & Loher, W. (1989). *Cricket behavior and neurobiology*. Cornell, NY: Cornell University Press.

Huhtamo, E. (2010). Media archaeology and media art . In Sommerer, C., & Jain, L. (Eds.), *The art and science of interface and interaction design* (*Vol. II*). New York, NY: Springer Verlag.

Huntley, H. E. (1970). *The divine proportion – A study in mathematical beauty*. Mineola, NY: Dover Publications.

ICAM-I2CAM. (2010). *The International Institute for Complex Adaptive Matter*. Retrieved December 11, 2010 from http://icam-i2cam.org/index.php/about/

Ida, S., Canup, R., & Stewart, G. (August 1997). *N-body simulation of moon accretion* [Abstract]. In Interactions between Planets and Small Bodies, 23rd Meeting of the IAU.

Ikeda, A., & Shibbasaki, H. (1992). Invasive recording of movement-related cortical potentials in humans. *Journal of Clinical Neurophysiology, 9*(4), 409–520. doi:10.1097/00004691-199210000-00005

IPCC. (2010). *Intergovernmental Panel on Climate Change*. Retrieved December 4, 2010, from http://www.ipcc.ch/index.htm

Isenberg, B. (2011). *David Hockney's friends in art: The iPad and iPhone*. Retrieved July 4, 2011, from www.hockneypictures.com/current.php

ISN. (2010). *Massachusetts Institute of Technology, Institute for Soldier Nanotechnologies*. Retrieved December 11, 2010, from http://web.mit.edu/isn/

It, P. (2009). *Traveller's language kit* (16th ed.).

Itten, J. (1970). *The elements of color: A treatise on the color system of Johannes Itten, based on his book The Art of Color by Johannes Itten*. Van Nostrand Reinhold Co.

Itten, J. (1975). *Design and form* (rev. ed.). New York, NY: John Wiley & Sons, Inc.

Itten, J. (1997). *The art of color: The subjective experience and objective rationale of color* (rev. ed.). New York, NY: John Wiley & Sons.

IUPAC. (2010). *Compendium of chemical terminology*, 2nd ed. Oxford, UK: Blackwell Scientific Publications. Retrieved October 2, 2011, from http://goldbook.iupac.org/C01058.html

Jaccard, J.-L. (2007). Minding the gap: Artists as scientists, scientists as artists: Some solutions to Snow's dilemma. *The Forum on Public Policy Online*, Vol. 2007, No. 1 (Winter). Retrieved January 25, 2011, from http://www.forumonpublicpolicy.com/archive07/jaccard.pdf

James, A. V., James, D. A., & Kalisperis, L. N. (2004). A unique art form: The friezes of Pirgi. *Leonardo, 37*(3), 234–242. doi:10.1162/0024094041139409

James, C. (2009). *The book of alternative photographic processes* (2nd ed.). Clifton Park, NY: Delmar, Cengage Learning.

Janson, C. H. (1998). Experimental evidence for spatial memory in foraging wild capuchin monkeys, *cebus apella. Animal Behaviour, 55*, 1229–1243. doi:10.1006/anbe.1997.0688

Japanese Temple Geometry Problem. (n.d.). *Sangaku*. Retrieved July 10, 2011, from http://www.wasan.jp/english/

Johnson, S. (2002). *Emergence: The connected lives of ants, brains, cities, and software*. New York, NY: Simon & Schuster.

Johnston, B. R., & School for Advanced Research. (2007). *Half-lives and half-truths: Confronting the radioactive legacies of the cold war*. School for Advanced Research Press. Retrieved August 5, 2011, from http://books.google.com/books?id=ReAeAQAAIAAJ

Johnston, J. (2008). *The allure of machinic life: Cybernetics, artificial life, and the new AI*. Cambridge, MA: MIT Press.

Jones, J. (2005). *Fractals & frequencies*. Retrieved July 28, 2011, from http://fractalsandfrequencies.blogspot.com/

Jones, O. (2001, 1856). *The grammar of ornament: Illustrated by examples from various styles of ornament*. London, UK A Dorling Kindersley Book, The Ivy Press, Limited. ISBN 0-7894-7646-0

Jones, J. (2010). Influences in the formation and evolution of *Physarum polycephalum* inspired emergent transport networks. *Natural Computing, 4*, 793–1006. doi:doi:10.1007/s11047-010-9223-z

Jones, R. (2008). *Nano nature*. New York, NY: Metro Books.

Jönsson, K. I., Rabbow, E., Schill, R. O., Harms-Ringdahl, M., & Rettberg, P. (2008). Tardigrades survive exposure to space in low Earth orbit. *Current Biology, 18* (17), R729-R731. Retrieved December 19, 2010, from http://www.cell.com/current-biology/abstract/S0960-9822(08)00805-1

Joyce, J. (2010). *A portrait of the artist as a young man*. New York, NY: SoHo Books.

Jung, C. G. (1968). *Man and his symbols*. New York, NY: Random House, Inc.

Jung, C. G. (1981). *The archetypes and the collective unconscious. Collected works of C. G. Jung* (2nd ed., *Vol. 9*). Princeton, NJ: Princeton University Press.

Juxtapoz. (2011). *David Hockney: Me draw on iPad*. Retrieved August 3, 2011, from www.juxtapoz.com/Current/david-hockney-qme- draw-on-ipad-in-humlebaek-denmark

Kac, E. (2011). *Website of Eduardo Kac*. Retrieved January 26, 2011, from http://ekac.org/

Kalkavage, P. (Tr.) (2001). *Platos's Timaeus*. Newburyport, MA: Focus Publishing.

Kamiya, A., Bukhari, R., & Togawa, T. (1984). Adaptive regulation of wall shear stress optimizing vascular tree function. *Bulletin of Mathematical Biology, 46*(1), 127–137.

Kamiya, A., & Togawa, T. (1980). Adaptive regulation of wall shear stress to flow change in the canine carotid artery. *American Journal of Physiology. Heart and Circulatory Physiology, 239*(1), H14.

Kandinsky, W. (1977). *Concerning the spiritual in art*. Mineola, NY: Dover Publications, Inc.

Kang, E. (2002). *Struldbrugg*. Retrieved August 28, 2011, from http://vimeo.com/26906691

Kang, E. (2005). *Siren III*. Retrieved April 15, 2011, from http://kangeunsu.com/siren3/

Kang, E. (2009). *Shin'm*. Retrieved April 15, 2011, from http://kangeunsu.com/shinm/index.htm

Kang, E. (2011). *Membranes*. Retrieved August 28, 2011, http://vimeo.com/26902851.

Kant, I. (1790). *The critique of judgment*. (J. C. Meredith, Trans.). Retrieved January 22, 2011, from http://philosophy.eserver.org/kant/critique-of-judgment.txt

Kappraff, J. (1991). *Connections. The geometric bridge between art and science*. New York, NY: McGraw-Hill, Inc.

Karniadakis, G. E., & Sherwin, S. J. (1999). *Spectral/hp element methods for CFD*. New York, NY: Oxford University Press.

Kastner, J. (1998). Preface . In *Land and environmental art*. London, UK: Phaidon.

Keirn, Z. A., & Aunon, J. I. (1990). A new mode of communication between man and his surroundings. *IEEE Transactions on Bio-Medical Engineering, 37*(12), 1209–1214. doi:10.1109/10.64464

Keller, R. (2009). Ant reconstruction one homology at a time. Homology Weekly: Stridulatory Organ. Retrieved March 26, 2011, from http://roberto.kellerperez.com/2009/02/homology-weekly-stridulatory-organ

Kelley, C., & Johanson, P. (2006). *Art and survival: Patricia Johanson's environmental projects.* Islands Institute. Retrieved August 5, 2011, from http://books.google.com/books?id=ghDqAAAAMAAJ

Kelley, C. (2006). *Art and survival: Patricia Johanson's environmental projects*. BC, Canada: Islands Institute.

Kemp, M. (2000). *Visualizations. The nature book of art and science*. Berkeley, CA: The University of California Press, by arrangement with Oxford University Press.

Kennedy, J., & Eberhart, R. C. (1995). Particle swarm optimization. In *Proceedings of the IEEE International Conference on Neural Networks* (Vol. IV, pp. 1942–1948). Piscataway, NJ: IEEE Service Center.

Kennedy, J. F., Eberhart, R. C., & Shi, Y. (2001). *Swarm intelligence*. San Francisco, CA: Morgan Kaufmann Publishers.

Kerber, C. W., Hecht, S. T., Knox, K., Buxton, R. B., & Meltzer, H. S. (1996). Flow dynamics in a fatal aneurysm of the basilar artery. *AJNR. American Journal of Neuroradiology, 17*(8), 1417.

Kesseler, R., & Harley, M. (2006). *Pollen: The hidden sexuality of flowers* (p. 181). London, UK: Papadakis Publishers.

Kettle, S. F. A. (2007). *Symmetry and structure: Readable group theory for chemists*, 3rd ed. Wile-Blackwell. ISBN-10: 0470060409

Kimball, J. W. (1983). *Biology*. Addison Wesley Publishing Company.

Kirby, W., & Spence, W. (2005). *An introduction to entomology; or elements of the natural history of insects*. London, UK: Elibron. (Original work published 1843)

Klee, P. (1966). *On modern art*. Boston, MA: Brill Academic Publishers.

Knowles, R. (1928). *Introduction to medical protozoology*. Calcutta, India: U. N. Dhur & Sons, Ltd.

Kock, W. E. (1981). *Lasers and holography – An introduction to coherent optics*. New York, NY: Dover Publications, Inc.

Kodama, S. (2008). Dynamic ferrofluid sculpture: Organic shape-changing art forms. *Communications of the ACM, 51*(6), 79–81. doi:10.1145/1349026.1349042

Koestler, A. (1964). *The act of creation*. London, UK: Arkana, Penguin Books.

Kolodziej, M. (2011). *Matthew Kolodziej - Home*. Retrieved August 5, 2011, from http://www.mattpaint.com

Korsgaard, N., Aalkjaer, C., Heagerty, A. M., Izzard, A. S., & Mulvany, M. J. (1993). Histology of subcutaneous small arteries from patients with essential hypertension. *Hypertension, 22*(4), 523.

Kraiss, L. W., Kirkman, T. R., Kohler, T. R., Zierler, B., & Clowes, A. W. (1991). Shear stress regulates smooth muscle proliferation and neointimal thickening in porous polytetrafluoroethylene grafts. *Arteriosclerosis, Thrombosis, and Vascular Biology, 11*(6), 1844. doi:10.1161/01.ATV.11.6.1844

Krasny, R. (1986). Desingularization of periodic vortex sheet roll-up. *Journal of Computational Physics, 65*, 292–313. doi:10.1016/0021-9991(86)90210-X

Kropotkin, P. (1987). *Mutual aid: A factor of evolution*. London, UK: Freedom Press. (Original work published 1902)

Krug, D. (2011). *Introduction*. Retrieved March 10, 2011, from http://www.greenmuseum.org/c/aen/Issues/intro.php

Kubler, G. (1962). *The shape of time. Remarks on the history of things*. New Haven, CT: Yale University Press.

Kuler. (2007). *Internet application.* http://kuler.adobe.com/

Kuletz, V. (1998). *The tainted desert: Environmental ruin in the American west.* New York, NY: Routledge.

Kurzweil, R. (1999). *The age of spiritual machines: When computers exceed human intelligence.* New York, NY: Viking Adult.

LaBarbera, M. (1990). Principles of design of fluid transport systems in zoology. *Science, 249*(4972), 992. doi:10.1126/science.2396104

Lang, W., Cheyne, D., Hollinger, P., Gerschlager, W., & Lindinger, G. (1996). Electric and magnetic fields of the brain accompanying internal simulation of movement. *Brain Research. Cognitive Brain Research, 3*(2), 125–129. doi:10.1016/0926-6410(95)00037-2

Laramée, E. A. & MIT List Visual Arts Center. (1999). *A permutational unfolding: Eve Andrée Laramée: MIT List Visual Arts Center, Cambridge (Mass.), 23.4.-27.6.1999.* MIT List Visual Arts Center. Retrieved August 5, 2011, from http://books.google.com/books?id=6AHVSAAACAAJ

Laramée, E. A. (2009). *Halfway to invisible.* New York, NY: Emory University. Retrieved August 28, 2011, from http://evelaramee.com/

Latham, W. (2011). *Artist's website.* Retrieved June 28, 2011, from http://www.doc.gold.ac.uk/~mas01whl/

Latham, W., Shaw, M., Todd, S., Leymarie, F. F., Jefferys, B., & Kelley, L. (2008). Using DNA to generate 3D organic art forms . In Giacobini, M. (Eds.), *Applications of Evolutionary Computing, LNCS 4974 2008 EvoWorkshops Proceedings* (pp. 433–442). Berlin, Germany: Springer. doi:10.1145/1276958.1277049

Lau, A., & Vande Moere, A. (2007). Towards a model of information aesthetics in information visualization. In *Proceedings of 11ᵗʰ International Conference on Information Visualisation* (pp. 87-92). Los Alamitos, CA: IEEE Computer Society.

Lauer, R., Peckham, P. H., Kilgore, K. L., & Heetderks, W. J. (2000). Applications of cortical signals to neuroprosthetic control: A critical review. *IEEE Transactions on Rehabilitation Engineering, 8*(2), 205–208. doi:10.1109/86.847817

Lausten, T. (2008). Datablik. *Computerkunst/Computer Art 2.008 Catalog.* ISBN 3-923815-44-1.

Lauwerier, H. (1991). *Fractals: Endlessly repeating geometrical figures.* Princeton, NJ: Princeton University Press.

Lawlor, R. (1982). *Sacred geometry – Philosophy and practice.* London, UK: Thames and Hudson, Ltd.

LeClerc, V., Parkes, A., & Ishii, H. (2007). Senspectra: A computationally augmented physical modeling toolkit for sensing and visualization of structural strain. In *Proceedings of the 13th International Conference on Human Factors in Computing Systems, ACM SIGCHI 2007*, San Jose, California, April 28–May 3, 2007. New York, NY: ACM Press.

Leeb, R., Scherer, R., Lee, F., Bischof, H., & Pfurtscheller, G. (2004). Navigation in virtual environments through motor imagery. *Proceedings of the 9th Computer Vision Winter Workshop* (pp. 99-108). Slovenian Pattern Recognition Society.

Lee, J., Bush, B., Maboudian, B., & Fearing, R. S. (2009). Gecko-inspired combined lamellar and nanofibrillar array for adhesion on nonplanar surface. *Langmuir, 25*(21), 12449–12453. doi:10.1021/la9029672

Leffingwell, J. C. (2003). Chirality and bioactivity I: Pharmacology. *Leffingwell Reports, 3*(1). Retrieved April 13, 2011, from http://www.leffingwell.com/download/chirality-phamacology.pdf

Leonard, A. (1975). Numerical simulation of interacting, three-dimensional vortex filaments. In *Proceedings of the IV International Conference on Numerical Methods of Fluid Dynamics, Lecture Notes in Physics, 35*, (pp. 245-250).

Leshan, L., & Margenau, H. (1982). *Einstein's space & Van Gogh's sky. Physical reality and beyond.* New York, NY: Collier Books, Macmillan Publishing Company.

Levine, S. P. (2000). A direct brain interface based on event-related potentials. *IEEE Transactions on Rehabilitation Engineering, 8*(2), 180–185. doi:10.1109/86.847809

Levine, S. P., & Huggins, J. E., BeMent, S. L., Kushwaha, R. K., Schuh, L. A., Passaro, E. A., ... Ross, D. A. (1999). Identification of electrocorticogram patterns as a basis for a direct brain interface. *Journal of Clinical Neurophysiology*, *16*(5), 439–447. doi:10.1097/00004691-199909000-00005

Lévi-Strauss, C. (1997). *Look, listen, learn* (B.C.J. Singer, Trans., pp. 83-87). Basic Books, a division of Harper-Collins Publishers. ISBN 0-465-06880-4

Levy, S. (2011, January). The AI revolution. *Wired*. Retrieved from http://www.wired.com/magazine/2010/12/ff_ai_essay_airevolution/

Levy, S. (1993). *Artificial life: A report from the frontier where computers meet biology*. New York, NY: Random House Inc.

Lewis-Williams, J. D. (2002). *The mind in the cave*. London, UK: Thames & Hudson.

Lewis-Williams, J. D., & Dowson, T. A. (1998). The signs of all times: Entoptic phenomena in upper paleolithic art. *Current Anthropology*, *29*(2), 201–245. doi:10.1086/203629

Leyton, M. (2006). The foundations of aesthetics . In Fishwick, P. A. (Ed.), *Aesthetic computing* (pp. 289–314).

Libbrecht, K. G. (2011). *Snow crystals*. Retrieved April 11, 2011, from http://www.its.caltech.edu/~atomic/snowcrystals/

Lifton, J., Broxton, M., & Paradiso, J. A. (2003). Distributed sensor networks as sensate skin. In *Proceedings of the 2th IEEE International Conference on Sensors, IEEE SENSORS 2007*, Atlanta, Georgia, October 22-24, 2003. Los Alamitos, CA: IEEE Computer Society.

Lifton, J., Seetharam, D., Broxton, M., & Paradiso, J. (2002). Pushpin computing system overview: A platform for distributed, embedded, ubiquitous sensor networks. In F. Mattern & M. Naghshineh (Ed.), *Pervasive Computing, First International Conference, Pervasive 2002* (pp. 139-151). Berlin, Germany: Springer

Lipkin, J. (2005). *Photography reborn: Image making in the digital era*. New York, NY: Abrams.

Lippard, L. R., Smith, S., & Revkin, A. Boulder Museum of Contemporary Art, & EcoArts. (2007). *Weather report: Art and climate change*. Boulder Museum of Contemporary Arts. Retrieved August 5, 2011, from http://books.google.com/books?id=p6JOGgAACAAJ

Liu, G. R., & Liu, M. B. (2003). *Smoothed particle hydrodynamics: A meshfree particle method*. Singapore: World Scientific Publishing Co. Pte. Ltd. doi:10.1142/9789812564405

Liu, Y. T., & Lim, C. K. (2009). *New tectonics: Towards a new theory of digital architecture: 7th FEIDAD award*. Basel, Switzerland: Birkhauser.

Livio, M. (2002). *The golden ratio - The story of Phi, the world's most astonishing number*. New York, NY: Broadway Books.

Lloyd, G. E. R. (1968). *Aristotle: The growth and structure of his thought*. Cambridge, UK: Cambridge University Press.

Loeb, A. L. (1993). *Concepts & images: Visual mathematics*. Boston, MA: Birkhäuser.

London National Gallery . (2010). Retrieved November 20, 2010, from http://www.nationalgallery.org.uk/server.php?show=ConConstituent.539

London, B. M., Jordan, L. R., Jackson, C. R., & Miller, L. E. (2008). Electrical stimulation of the proprioceptive cortex (area 3a) used to instruct a behaving monkey. *IEEE Transactions on Neural Systems and Rehabilitation Engineering*, *16*(1), 32–36. doi:10.1109/TNSRE.2007.907544

Loos, A. (1908/1998). *Ornament and crime. Selected essays*. (M. Mitchell, Trans.). Riverside, CA: Ariadne Press. (Original work written in 1908).

Lowell, B., & O'Donnell, F. (1986). Reductions in arterial diameter produced by chronic decreases in blood flow are endothelium-dependent. *Science*, *231*(4736), 405–407. doi:10.1126/science.3941904

Lugt, H. J. (1983). *Vortex flow in nature and technology*. New York, NY: John Wiley & Sons.

Lynch, M. (2010). *In her own lens: A look at Aida Laleian*. Retrieved April 1, 2011, from http://www.stockyardmagazine.com/galerie/in-her-own-lens-a-look-at-aida-laleian/

MacDonald, J. (2009). *Drawing around the body: The manual and visual practice of drawing and the embodiment of knowledge.* Ph.D. thesis, Leeds Metropolitan University.

Mackay, A. L., & Ebison, M. (Eds.). (1969). *The harvest of a quiet eye. A selection of scientific quotations.* London, UK: Taylor & Francis Group.

Majerus, T. (2011). *Eye of science.* Retrieved August 9, 2011, from http://nanoart21.org/nanoart-exhibitions/index.php.

Makhijani, A., Hu, H., & Yih, K. (2000). *Nuclear wastelands: A global guide to nuclear weapons production and its health and environmental effects.* MIT Press. Retrieved August 5, 2011, from http://books.google.com/books?id=0oa1vikB3KwC

Malpas, J. (2006). *The forms of water: In the land and the soul.* Retrieved January 4, 2011, from www.utas.edu.au/philosophy/staff_research/malpas/J.Malpas%20Articles/The%20of%20Water.pdf.

Mandelbrot, B. (1977). *The fractal geometry of nature* (rev. ed.). New York, NY: W.H. Freeman and Company.

Mandelbrot, B. (1982). *The fractal geometry of nature.* W. H. Freeman.

Mandelbrot, B. (1998). *Multifractals and 1/f noise: Wild self-affinity in physics.* New York, NY: Springer.

Mann, R. (2003). Yellowcake towns: Uranium mining communities in the American west. *The Journal of American History, 90*(3), 1082-1083. Boulder, CO: University Press of Colorado. doi:10.2307/3661002

Marder, M. P. (2010). *Condensed matter physics* (2nd ed.). New York, NY: John Wiley & Sons. Inc. doi:10.1002/9780470949955

Margenau, H., & Varghese, R. A. (Eds.). (1991). *Cosmos, bios, theos: Scientists reflect on science, god, and the origins of the universe, life, and homo sapiens.* Chicago, IL: Open Court Publishing Company.

Marien, M. W. (2002). *Photography: A cultural history.* Upper Saddle River, NJ: Prentice-Hall, Inc.

Markl, H. (1973). The evolution of stridulatory communication in ants. In *Proceedings IUSSI 7th International Congress* (pp. 258–265). Southampton, UK: University of Southampton.

Martineau, J. (2001). *A little book of coincidence.* New York, NY: Walker & Company.

Marvin, C. (1988). *When old technologies were new: Thinking about electric communication in the late nineteenth century.* New York, NY: Oxford University Press.

Masco, J. (2006). *The nuclear borderlands: The Manhattan project in post-cold war New Mexico.* Princeton, NJ: Princeton University Press.

Mataric, M. (1994). *Interaction and intelligent behavior.* Unpublished doctoral dissertation, Department of Electrical, Electronics and Computer Engineering, MIT, USA.

Mateo, J., & Sauter, F. (Eds.). (2007). *Natural metaphor: Architectural papers III, Zurich: The Millennium Development Goals Report.* United Nations. Retrieved December 11, 2010, from http://mdgs.un.org/unsd/mdg/Resources/Static/Products/Progress2008/MDG_Report_2008_En.pdf#page=44

Mathematics Museum. (2011). *Mathematical visualizations.* Tokyo, Japan. Retrieved July 10, 2011, from http://mathinfo.sci.ibaraki.ac.jp/open/mathmuse/

Maturana, H., & Varela, F. (1992). *The tree of knowledge.* Boston, MA: Shambhala.

McCorduck, P. (1991). *Aaron's code: Meta-art, artificial intelligence, and the work of Harold Cohen.* WH Freeman.

McCormack, J. (2003). Art and the mirror of nature. *Digital Creativity, 14*(1), 3. doi:10.1076/digc.14.1.3.8807

Mcfarland, D. J., Miner, L. A., Vaughan, T. M., & Wolpaw, J. R. (2000). Mu and beta rhythm topographies during motor imagery and actual movement. *Brain Topography, 12*(3), 177–186. doi:10.1023/A:1023437823106

Media Dirt. (n.d.). Retrieved July 15, 2011, from www.timo-kahlen.de/soundsc.htm

Merleau-Ponty, M. (1964). *1908-1961, The primacy of perception: And other essays on phenomenological psychology, the philosophy of art, history and politics.* Evanston, IL: Northwestern University Press.

Merleau-Ponty, M. (1964). *Sense and non-sense* (Dreyfus, H. L., & Dreyfus, P. A., Trans.). Northwestern University Press.

Merleau-Ponty, M. (2002). *The phenomenology of perception*. London, UK: Routledge.

Merleau-Ponty, M. (2004). *The world of perception*. Oxford, UK: Routledge.

Miller, A. I. (1996). *Insights of genius. Imagery and creativity in science and art*. New York, NY: Copernicus, Springer-Verlag.

Minerals Zone. (2011). *Industrial minerals, ochre*. Retrieved August 8, 2011, from http://www.mineralszone.com/minerals/ochre.html

Mitchell, K. (2011). *A celebration of beauty*. Digital Art Guild; Art through Technology. Retrieved July 28, 2011, from http://www.digitalartguild.com/content/view/56/26/

Mitchell, W. J. (1997). *The reconfigured eye: Visual truth in the post-photographic era*. Cambridge, MA: The MIT Press.

Mithen, S. (1996). *The prehistory of the mind. The cognitive origins of art, religion and science*. London, UK: Thames and Hudson Ltd.

Modis, T. (1992). *Predictions: Society's telltale signature reveals past & forecasts the future*. New York, NY: Simon & Schuster.

Moglich, M., Maschwitz, U., & Holldobler, B. (1974). Tandem calling: A new kind of signal in ant communication. *Science, 186*(4168), 1046–1047. doi:10.1126/science.186.4168.1046

Mogren, E. W. (2002). *Warm sands: Uranium mill tailings policy in the atomic west*. University of New Mexico Press. Retrieved August 5, 2011, from http://books.google.com/books?id=S3LbAAAAMAAJ

Moran, D. (2000). *Introduction to phenomenology*. London, UK: Routledge.

Morland, L. W., & Staroszczyk, R. (2009). Ice viscosity enhancement in simple shear and uni-axial compression due to crystal rotation. *International Journal of Engineering Science, 47*(11-12), 1297–1304. doi:10.1016/j.ijengsci.2008.09.011

Morris, B. (2006). *Religion and anthropology: A critical introduction*. Cambridge, UK: Cambridge University Press.

Morris, D. R. (1989). *From heaven to hell: Imagery of earth, air, water, and fire in the novels of Georges Bernanos*. New York, NY: Peter Lang Publishing, Inc.

Morris, R. (1998). Notes on sculpture part 4: Beyond objects . In Kastner, J. (Ed.), *Land and environmental art* (pp. 230–231). London, UK: Phaidon. (Original work published 1969)

Moura, L., & Ramos, V. (2007). *Swarm paintings–Nonhuman art*. Retrieved from http://www.leonelmoura.com/aswarm.html

Mulvany, M. J., Baumbachand, G. L., & Aalkjaer, C. (1996). Vascular remodelling. *Hypertension, 28*, 505–506.

Museo de Altamira . (2011). Retrieved July 3, 2011, from http://museodealtamira.mcu.es/ingles/index.html

Museum of the Moving Image. (2010). *Advances the public understanding and appreciation of the art, history, technique, and technology of film, television, and digital media*. New York. http://www.movingimage.us/education/teachers

Myatt, D. R., Bishop, J. M., & Nasuto, S. J. (2004). Minimum stable convergence criteria for stochastic diffusion search. *Electronics Letters, 40*(2), 112–113. doi:10.1049/el:20040096

Myrmecos. (n.d.). Retrieved July 14, 2011, from www.myrmecos.net

Mythology, (2008). *National Geographic essential visual history of world mythology*. Berlin, Germany: Peter Delius Verlag GmbH & Co KG. ISBN 978-1-4262-0373-2

Nagel, T. (1974). What is it like to be a bat? *The Philosophical Review, JSTOR, 83*(4), 435–450. doi:10.2307/2183914

Nake, F. (2007). Retrieved July 12, 2011, from http://viola.informatik.uni-bremen.de/typo/

Nake, F. (1989). Art in the time of the artificial [Editorial]. *Leonardo, 31*(3), 163–164.

NanoArt 21. (2011). *Art/science/technology*. Retrieved July 10, 2011, from http://www.nanoart21.org/

NanoArt Festival, Stuttgart, Germany. (2008). Retrieved August 8, 2011, from http://nanoartfestival-stuttgart.blogspot.com/

NanoArt21. (2011). *Art/science/technology.* Retrieved August 8, 2011, from http://www.nanoart21.org/

Nanotoxicology Conference. (2010). Retrieved April 13, 2011, from http://www.certh.gr/A806416C.el.aspx

Nasuto, S. J. (1999). *Resource allocation analysis of the stochastic diffusion search.* Unpublished doctoral dissertation, PhD Thesis, University of Reading, Reading, UK.

Nasuto, S. J., & Bishop, J. M. (1999). Convergence analysis of stochastic diffusion search. *Parallel Algorithms and Applications, 14*(2).

Nasuto, S. J., Bishop, J. M., & Lauria, S. (1998). Time complexity of stochastic diffusion search. *Neural Computation*, NC98.

Nees, G. (2006). *Generative Computergraphik.* Berlin, Germany: Vice Versa.

Neff, J. (2008). *Artist's statement.* Retrieved April 25, 2011, from http://artistregistry.artadia.org/registry/view_artist.php?aid=34

Nelson, W. T., Hettinger, L. J., Cunningham, J. A., Roe, M. M., Haas, M. W., & Dennis, L. B. (1997). Navigating through virtual flight environments using brain-body-actuated control. *Proceedings of the IEEE 1997 Virtual Reality Annual International Symposium* (pp. 30-37). Los Alamitos, CA: IEEE Computer Society Press.

Neville, A. C. (1977). Symmetry and asymmetry problems in animals . In Duncan, R., & Weston-Smith, M. (Eds.), *The encyclopedia of ignorance: Everything you ever wanted to know about the unknown* (pp. 331–338). Oxford, UK: Paragon Press.

Newhall, B. (1982). *The history of photography.* Boston, MA: Little, Brown and Company.

Newman, A., & De Zegher, C. (2003). Conversation. In C. De Zegher (Ed.), *The stage of drawing: Gesture and act, selected from the Tate Collection* (pp. 67-81, 165-173, 231-237). London, UK: Tate Publishing & The Drawing Center.

Niebrügge, S. (2010). *Computerkunst/Computer art 2.010 catalog.* Gladbeck.

Nieminski, E., Durrant, G. C., Hoyt, M. B., Owens, M. E., Peterson, L., & Peterson, S. (2010). Is *E. Coli* an appropriate surrogate for *Cryptosporidium* occurrence in water? *Journal - American Water Works Association, 102*(3), 65–78.

Noll, A. M. (1964). *Vertical- horizontal: Example of early computer art.* Retrieved 14 July, 2011 from http://www.citi.columbia.edu/amnoll/CompArtExamples.html

Nordborg, C., Ivarsson, H., Johansson, B. B., & Stage, L. (1983). Morphometric study of mesenteric and renal arteries in spontaneously hypertensive rats. *Journal of Hypertension, 1*(4), 333. doi:10.1097/00004872-198312000-00002

Northam, B. (2010). *Making future magic: Media surfaces.* Dentsu London. Retrieved November 11, 2010, from http://www.dentsulondon.com/blog/2010/11/03/mediasurfaces/

NSIDC. (2010). *National Snow and Ice Data Center.* Retrieved December 4, 2010, from http://nsidc.org/arcticmet/glossary/sublimation.html

Nuridsany, C., & Pérennou, M. (Directors), Barratier, C., Mallet, Y., & Perrin, J. (Producers). (1996). Microcosmos: Le peuple de l'herbe [DVD]. USA: Miramax.

NUS. (2011). *The National University of Singapore, Center for Research in Computing and the Arts.* Retrieved July 16, 2011, from http://amas.cz3.nus.edu.sg/art

Office of Legacy Management. (n.d.). *Department of energy geospatial environmental mapping system.* Retrieved April 1, 2011, from http://gems.lm.doe.gov/imf/ext/gems/jsp/launch.jsp?verify=true

Okubo, P. G., & Aki, K. (1987). Fractal geometry in the San Andreas Fault system. *Journal of Geophysical Research, 92*(B1), 345–355. doi:10.1029/JB092iB01p00345

Olsen, S. (2006). *The golden section – Nature's greatest secret.* New York, NY: Walker Publishing Company, Inc.

Oosterhuis, K., & Biloria, B. N. (2008). Interactions with proactive architectural spaces: The muscle projects. *Communications of the ACM, 51*(6). doi:10.1145/1349026.1349041

OpenGL . (2011). Retrieved April 15, 2011, from http://www.opengl.org

Oram, B. (2010). *Soils, infiltration, and on-site testing.* Wilkes University. Retrieved December 4, 2010, from www.water-research.net/powerpoint/soilinfiltration.ppt

Orfescu, C. (2007, November 27). NanoArt at the eye tricks show at Walsh Gallery – Interview with Jeanne Brasile. *Nanotechnology Now.* Retrieved August 9, 2011, from http://www.nanotech-now.com/columns/?article=138

Orfescu, C. (2008a, November 27). NanoArt pioneers - Interview with Hugh McGrory. *Nanotechnology Now.* Retrieved August 7, 2011, from http://www.nanotech-now.com/columns/?article=222

Orfescu, C. (2008b, February 8). NanoArt and nanotechnology - New frontiers. Nanotechnology Now. Retrieved August 9, 2011, from http://www.nanotech-now.com/columns/?article=169

Orfescu, C. (2008c, January 7). NanoArt pioneers - Interview with Jack Mason. *Nanotechnology Now.* Retrieved August 9, 2011, from http://www.nanotech-now.com/columns/?article=153. Also, http://www.nanotechno.biz

Orfescu, C. (2011). *NanoArt: Art/science/technology.* Retrieved August 8, 2011, from http://nanoart21.org/html/nanoart.html

Organisms, M. (2008). *The use of model organisms in instruction.* University of Wisconsin: Wisconsin Outreach Research Modules. Retrieved January 9, 2011, from http://wormclassroom.org/teaching-model-organisms

Orland, T. (2006). *The view from the studio door. How artists find their way in an uncertain world.* Santa Cruz, CA: Image Continuum Press.

Otsuki, T. (1999). *AIBO* (ERS-110). Japan Media Arts Plaza. Retrieved January 7, 2011, from http://plaza.bunka.go.jp/english/festival/1999/degital/000330/

Owen, E. (2009, March 14). After Altamira, all is decadence. *The Times.* Retrieved July 3, 2011, from http://www.timesonline.co.uk/tol/travel/specials/artistic_spain/article5904206.ece

Ozenfant, A. (1952). *1928). The foundations of modern art.* New York, NY: Dover.

Packard, A. (2001). A neural net that can be seen with the naked eye . In Backhaus, W. (Ed.), *Neuronal coding of perceptual systems* (pp. 397–402). Singapore: World Scientific.

Palais, R. S. (1999). The visualization of mathematics: Towards a mathematical exploratorium. *Notices of the American Mathematical Society, 46*(6), 647-658. Retrieved July 16, 2011, from http://3d-xplormath.org/DocumentationPages/VisOfMath.pdf

Palmer, J. (2009). *Single molecule's stunning image.* Retrieved August 20, 2011, from http://news.bbc.co.uk/2/hi/science/nature/8225491.stm

Parikka, J. (2010). *Insect media: An archeology of animals and technology.* Minneapolis, MN: University of Minnesota Press.

Pask, G. (1969). The architectural relevance of cybernetics . In Spiller, N. (Ed.), *Cyber reader: Critical writings for the digital era* (p. 78). London, UK: Phaidon Press.

Pask, G., & Von Foerster, H. (1961). A predictive model for self-organizing systems, Part 2. *Cybernetica, 4*(1), 20–55.

Pearsons, A. C. (Tr.). (2010). *The fragments of Zeno and Cleanthes: With introduction and explanatory notes by* A. C. Pearson. Saint Ansgar, IA: Forgotten Books.

Peitgen, H., & Saupe, D. (Eds.). (1988). *The science of fractal images.* New York, NY: Springer-Verlag.

PennState modules. (2009). *NACK educational resources.* The Pennsylvania State University. Retrieved December 11, 2010, from http://nano4me.live.subhub.com/categories/modules

Petherbridge, D. (2008). Nailing the liminal: The difficulties of defining drawing . In Garner, S. (Ed.), *Writing on drawing: Essays on drawing practice and research* (pp. 27–42). Bristol, UK: Intellect.

Petherbridge, D. (2010). *The primacy of drawing: Histories and theories of practice.* New Haven, CT: Yale University Press.

Pfurtscheller, G. (1997). EEG-based discrimination between imagination of right and left hand movement. *Electroencephalography and Clinical Neurophysiology, 103*(6), 642–651. doi:10.1016/S0013-4694(97)00080-1

Pfurtscheller, G., Guger, C., Müller, G., Krausz, G., & Neuper, C. (2000). Brain oscillations control hand orthosis in a tetraplegic. *Neuroscience Letters*, *292*(3), 211–214. doi:10.1016/S0304-3940(00)01471-3

Phaidon Books. (1996). *The 20ᵗʰ century art book*. San Francisco, CA: Author. ISBN: 0-71483542 0

Phaidon Press. (1994). *(The) art book*. London, UK: Author. ISBN # 07148 2984 6

Phaidon Press. (1999). *American art book*. London, UK: Author.

Picard, R. (1998). *Affective computing*. Cambridge, MA: MIT Press.

Pidwirny, M., & Jones, S. (2010). *Fundamentals of physical geography*. Retrieved December 4, 2010, from http://www.physicalgeography.net/fundamentals/chapter8.html

Plates to Pictures Gallery. (2007). Retrieved August 13, 2011, from (http://platestopixels.com/)

Plotinus, . (1991). *The Enneads* (MacKenna, S., Trans.). London, UK: Penguin Books.

Polich, J. (1999). P300 in clinical applications. In E. Niedermeyer, & F. H. Lopes da Silva (Eds.), *Electroencephalography: Basic principles, clinical applications and related fields* (pp. 1073-1091). Baltimore, MD: Williams and Wilkins.

Polyani, M. (1946). *Science, faith and society*. Chicago, IL: The University of Chicago Press.

Popper, F. (1968). *Origins and development of kinetic art*. (S. Bann, Trans., p. 121). London, UK: Studio Vista. *SBN, 28979592*, 3.

Posner, M. I. (1993). *Foundations of cognitive science*. Cambridge, MA: The MIT Press.

Posner, R. (1992). Origins and development of contemporary syntactics. *Languages of Design*, *1*(1), 37–504.

Praetorius, D. (2011). New zodiac sign dates: Ophiuchus the 13ᵗʰ sign? *The Huffington Post*. Retrieved on January 30, 2011, from http://www.huffingtonpost.com/2011/01/13/new-zodiac-sign-dates-oph_n_808567.html

Pribram, K. (1991). *Brain and perception: Holonomy and structure in figural processing*. Hillsdale, NJ: Lawrence Erlbaum Associates.

Prince, D. (2005). *Evolution of a creative vision in a digital environment*. Retrieved April 25, 2011, from http://www.douglasprince.com and http://www.douglasprince.com/statement-04-19-05.pdf

Processing. (2011). Retrieved August 14, 2011, from http://processing.org/

Prosser, B. (2004). *An archetypal psychology of the ordinary: An investigation through drawing*. Thesis (PhD), University of the West of England.

Purchase, H. (2010). Graph drawing aesthetics in user-sketched graph layouts. In *AUIC'10 Proceedings of the Eleventh Australasian Conference on User Interface*, Vol. 106. ISBN: 978-1-920682-87-3

Rainey, C. (2008). *One hundred miles from home: Nuclear contamination in the communities of the Ohio river valley: Mound, Paducah, Piketon, Fernald, Maxey Flats, and Jefferson proving ground*. Cincinnati, OH: Little Miami Press.

Ratner, B. D. (2004). Sustainability as a dialogue of values: Challenges to the sociology of development. *Sociological Inquiry*, *74*, 59–69. doi:10.1111/j.1475-682X.2004.00079.x

Read, J. (2010). *The digital camera, the cyanotype and grain*. Retrieved April 1, 2011, from http://www.alternativephotography.com/wp/cameras-film/the-digital-camera-the- cyanotype-and-grain

Reas, C. (2011). *Artist's website*. Retrieved June 28, 2011, from http://reas.com/category.php?section=works

Reas, C., & Fry, B. (2007). *Processing: A programming handbook for visual designers and artists*. Cambridge, MA: The MIT Press. Retrieved July 16, 2011, from http://processing.org/img/learning/Processing-Contents-070603.pdf

Reynolds, C. (2001). *Boids* (Flocks, herds, and schools: A distributed behavioral model). Retrieved from http://www.red3d.com/cwr/boids/

Reynolds, C. (2002). *Evolutionary computation and its application to art and design*. Retrieved January 9, 2011, from http://www.red3d.com/cwr/evolve.html

Reynolds, A. (1999). *Histories of science, histories of art*. Austin, TX: Austin Museum of Art.

Reynolds, C. W. (1987). Flocks, herds, and schools: A distributed behavioral model. *Computer Graphics, 21*(4), 25–34. doi:10.1145/37402.37406

Rhodes, R. (1986). *The making of the atomic bomb*. Simon & Schuster. Retrieved August 5, 2011, from http://books.google.com/books?id=aSgFMMNQ6G4C

Rhys Roberts, W., & Bywater, I. (Tr.) (1984). *The rhetoric and the poetics of Aristotle*. New York, NY: Random House.

Richter, J. P. (1970). *The notebooks of Leonardo Da Vinci (Vol. 1)*. New York, NY: Dover Publications.

Rizzoni, D., Porteri, E., Castellano, M., Bettoni, G., Muiesan, M. L., & Muiesan, P. (1996). Vascular hypertrophy and remodeling in secondary hypertension. *Hypertension, 28*(5), 785.

Robert, K. H., Daly, H., Hawken, P., & Holmberg, J. (1996). A compass for sustainable development. *International Journal of Sustainable Development And World Ecology, 4*, 79-92. ISSN: 13504509

Robin, H. (1992). *The scientific image. From cave to computer*. New York, NY: W. H. Freeman and Company, by arrangement with Harry N. Abrams, Inc.

Robinson, C. (2011). *NanoArt21 exhibitions*. Retrieved July 31, 2011, from http://nanoart21.org/nanoart-exhibitions/index.php

Rosand, D. (2002). *Drawing acts – Studies in graphic expression and representation*. Cambridge, UK: Cambridge University Press.

Rosenhead, L. (1931). The formation of vorticies from a surface of discontinuity. *Proceedings of the Royal Society of London. Series A, Containing Papers of a Mathematical and Physical Character, 134*, 170–192. doi:10.1098/rspa.1931.0189

Rosset, A., Spadola, L., & Ratib, O. (2004). OsiriX: An open-source software for navigating in multidimensional dicom images. *Journal of Digital Imaging, 17*(3), 205–216. doi:10.1007/s10278-004-1014-6

Rossitti, S., & Svendsen, P. (1995). Shear stress in cerebral arteries supplying arteriovenous malformations. *Acta Neurochirurgica, 137*(3), 138–145. doi:10.1007/BF02187185

Rothberg, A., & Hausman, C. (1976). *The creativity question*. Durham, NC: Duke University Press Books.

Royal Institution of Great Britain. (2011). Retrieved August 8, 2011, from http://www.rigb.org/registrationControl?action=home

Runion, G. E. (1990). *The golden section*. Palo Alto, CA: Dale Seymour Publications.

Ruttkay, Z. M. (2008). A *Sangaku* revived. *Bridges Mathematics, Music, Art, Architecture, & Culture Conference Proceedings*. EEMCS University of Twenet, Leeuwarden, the Netherlands.

Rykwert, J. (1973). Adolf Loos: The new vision. *Studio International, 186*, 957.

Saffman, P. G. (1992). *Vortex dynamics*. Cambridge, UK: Cambridge University Press.

Saxe, J. G., Lathen, D., & Chief, B. (1882). The blind man and the elephant. In *The poems of John Godfrey Saxe*.

Schermerhorn, P., & Scheutz, M. (2009). The impact of communication and memory in hive-based foraging agents. In *IEEE Symposium on Artificial life, ALife'09* (pp. 29-36).

Schilthuizen, M., & Gravendeel, B. (2011). *Evolution of chirality symposium*. The 13th Congress of the European Society for Evolutionary Biology, Tuebingen 20-25 August 2011. Retrieved August 26, 2011, from http://www.eseb2011.de/

Schlain, L. (1991). *Art & physics. Parallel visions in space, time, and light*. New York, NY: William Morrow and Company, Inc.

Schmidt, E. M. (1980). Single neuron recording from motor cortex as a possible source of signals for control of external devices. *Annual Review of Biomedical Engineering, 8*, 339–349. doi:10.1007/BF02363437

Schrödinger, E. (1964). *My view of the world.* Cambridge, UK: Cambridge University Press.

Schroeder, W. (2006). *The visualization toolkit: An object-oriented approach to 3D graphics.* Clifton Park, NY: Kitware.

Schwartz, A. B. (1993). Motor cortical activity during drawing movement: Population representation during sinusoid tracing. *Journal of Neurophysiology, 70*(1), 28–36.

Schwartz, A. B., Cui, X. T., Weber, D. J., & Moran, D. W. (2006). Brain-controlled interfaces: Movement Restoration with neural prosthetics. *Neuron, 52*(1), 205–220. doi:10.1016/j.neuron.2006.09.019

Schweikardt, E., & Gross, M. D. (2010). Experiments in design synthesis when behavior is determined by shape. *Personal and Ubiquitous Computing, 15*(2), 123–132. doi:10.1007/s00779-010-0310-z

Schwenk, T., & Schwenk, W. (1989). *Water – The element of life* (Spock, M., Trans.). Anthroposophic Press.

Sconce, J. (2000). *Haunted media: Electronic presence from telegraphy to television.* Durham, NC: Duke University Press.

Scott, S. H. (2006). Converting thoughts into action. *Nature, 442*(7099), 141–142. doi:10.1038/442141a

Shanken, E. A. (2009). *Art and electronic media.* Phaidon Press. Retrieved August 5, 2011, from http://books.google.com/books?id=qXpTAAAACAAJ

Sharp, W. (1998). Notes towards an understanding of earth art . In Kastner, J. (Ed.), *Land and environmental art* (pp. 199–200). London, UK: Phaidon. (Original work published 1970)

Sheldrake, R. (1981). *A new science of life: The hypothesis of morphic resonance.* Rochester, VT: Park Street Press.

Sheldrake, R. (1988). *The presence of the past: Morphic resonance and the habits of nature.* New York, NY: Times Books.

Shi, Y., & Eberhart, R. C. (1998). Parameter selection in particle swarm optimization. *Proceedings of Evolutionary Proramming,* (pp. 591–600).

Shinn, D. (2011, June 19). Summit ArtSpace showcases books as art. *Akron Beacon Journal,* p.1.

Shore, S. (2007). *The nature of photographs* (2nd ed.). London, UK: Phaidon Press Limited.

Short, D. (1966). The vascular fault in chronic hypertension with particular reference to the role of medial hypertrophy. *Lancet, 1*(7450), 1302. doi:10.1016/S0140-6736(66)91206-2

Shuey, C. (1992). *Contaminant loading on the Puerco river: A historical overview.* Albuquerque, NM: Southwest Research and Information Center.

Sims, K. (2009). *Karl Sims website.* Retrieved January 9, 2011, from http://www.karlsims.com/

Sims, K. (1991). Artificial evolution for computer graphics. *Computer Graphics, 25*(4), 319–328. doi:10.1145/127719.122752

Sims, K. (1994). Evolving 3D morphology and behavior by competition. [MIT Press.]. *Artificial Life, 1*(4), 353–372. doi:10.1162/artl.1994.1.4.353

Sitti, M., & Fearing, R. S. (2003). Synthetic gecko foot-hair micro/nano-structures as dry adhesives. *Journal of Adhesion Science and Technology, 18*(7), 1055–1074. doi:10.1163/156856103322113788

Skov, K., Fenger-Gron, J., & Mulvany, M. J. (1996). Effects of an angiotensin-converting enzyme inhibitor, a calcium antagonist, and an endothelin receptor antagonist on renal afferent arteriolar structure. *Hypertension, 28*(3), 464.

Sleigh, C. (2001). Empire of the ants: H.G. Wells and tropical entomology. *Science as Culture, 10*(1), 33–71. doi:10.1080/09505430020025492

Slijkerman, F. (2010). *Ultra Fractal 5.* Retrieved January 3, 2011, from http://www.ultrafractal.com

Small Work for Robots and Insects. (n.d.). Retrieved July 15, 2011, from hostprods.net/projects/small-work-for-robot-and-insects/

Smalley, R. (2011). *Resources.* Retrieved April 13, 2011, from http://4snk.info/links/richard-e-smalley.html

Smalyukh, I. I. (2010). *Intro to soft condensed matter physics*. Retrieved December 10, 2010, from http://www.colorado.edu/physics/SmalyukhLab/SoftMatter/

Smith, G. (1875). *Assyrian discoveries: An account of explorations and discoveries on the site of Nineveh, during 1873 and 1874.* Retrieved December 30, 2010, from http://books.google.com/books?vid=01cHWlP8ACrFcxC4bHx3bKB&id=1RudUM1WeQEC

Smith, P. (1997). *Seurat and the avant-garde*. New Haven, CT: Yale University Press.

Smithson, R. (1979). *Fragments of an Interview with Robert Smithson by P.A. Norvell, collected writings* (p. 194). New York, NY: New York University Press.

Smithson, R. (1998). A sedimentation of the mind: Earth projects . In Kastner, J. (Ed.), *Land and environmental art* (pp. 199–200). London, UK: Phaidon. (Original work published 1968)

Smithson, R., & Jack, D. F. (1996). *Robert Smithson, the collected writings*. Berkeley, CA: University of California Press.

Snow, C. P. (1959). The two cultures. *Leonardo, 23*(2/3), 169–173. doi:10.2307/1578601

Snow, C. P. (1964). *The two cultures: And a second look*. Cambridge, UK: Cambridge University Press.

Soddu, C. (2011). *Website of Celestino Soddu*. Retrieved January 26, 2011, from http://www.celestinosoddu.com/

Sommerer, C., & Mignonneau, L. (2010). *The value of art (Unruhige See)*. Retrieved January 9, 2011, from http://www.interface.ufg.ac.at/christa-laurent/WORKS/FRAMES/FrameSet.html

Sotheby's. (2008, April 7). *The Quillan collection of nineteenth and twentieth century photographs*. Auction catalog. New York, NY: Author.

Spencer, D. A. (1973). *The Focal dictionary of photographic technologies*. Focal Press.

Sprawson, C. (1992). *Haunts of the black masseur: The swimmer as hero*. London, UK: Jonathon Cope.

Staguhn, G. (1994). *God's laughter. Physics, religion and the cosmos*. New York, NY: Kodansha International Ltd.

Stanley, W. M. (1937). Crystalline tobacco-mosaic virus protein. *American Journal of Botany, 24*(2), 59–68. doi:10.2307/2436720

Sterk, T. D. (2003). Using actuated tensegrity structures to produce a responsive architecture. In *Proceedings of the 23th International Conference of the Association for Computer Aided Design in Architecture, ACADIA 2003*, Indianapolis, Indiana, October 24-27, 2003. Retrieved August 25, 2011, from Cumulative Index on CAD (CUMINCAD).

Sternberg, R. (Ed.). (1988). *The nature of creativity: Contemporary psychological perspectives*. Cambridge University Press.

Stock, M. J. (2006). *A regularized inviscid vortex sheet method for three dimensional flows with density interfaces.* Doctoral dissertation. Retrieved from http://markjstock.org/research/

Stock, M. (2012in press). Flow simulation with vortex elements . In Ursyn, A. (Ed.), *Biologically-inspired computing for the arts: Scientific data through graphics*. Hershey, PA: IGI Global.

Strandbeest. (n.d.). Retrieved July 15, 2011, from www.strandbeest.com

Strong, V. (2004). *The meaning of water*. Oxford, UK: Berg.

Struwe, G. (2011). *Bio gen art*. Retrieved July 1, 2011, from http://www.biogenart.de

Struwe, G. (1988). *Computerkunst '88 catalog*. Gladbeck.

Stubbe, A., & Lerner, M. (2007). *Outerspace: Reactive robotic creature*. Retrieved August 14, 2011, from http://www.andrestubbe.com/outerspace/

Sullivan, D. O., & Igoe, T. (2004). *Physical computing: Sensing and controlling the physical world with computers*. Boston, MA: Thomson Course Technology.

Sutter, J. D. (2011). Smart dust aims to monitor everything. Retrieved April 4, 2011, from http://edition.cnn.com/2010/TECH/05/03/smart.dust.sensors/index.html

Sutter, E. E. (1992). The brain response interface: Communication through visually induced electrical brain responses. *Journal of Microcomputer Applications*, *15*(1), 31–45. doi:10.1016/0745-7138(92)90045-7

Sutton, S., Braren, M., Zubin, J., & John, E. R. (1965). Evoked correlates of stimulus uncertainty. *Science*, *150*(3700), 1187–1188. doi:10.1126/science.150.3700.1187

Suwa, N., & Takahashi, T. (1971). *Morphological and morphometric analysis of circulation in hypertension and ischaemic kidney*. Munich, Germany: Urban and Schwarzenberg.

Suzuki, S. (1973). *Zen mind, beginner's mind*. New York, NY: Weatherhill.

Swift, J. (1726). *Gulliver's travels*. Retrieved April 17, 2011, from http://publicliterature.org/books/gullivers_travels/1

Synapse. (2005). Retrieved April 15, 2011, from http://www2.uakron.edu/phn/synapse.html

Szarkowski, J. (1966). *The photographer's eye*. New York, NY: The Museum of Modern Art.

Talbot, M. (1991). *The holographic universe*. New York, NY: Harper Perennial.

Tarnas, R. (2007). *Cosmos and psyche. Intimations of a new world view*. London, UK: Plume, Penguin Group.

Taylor, C. (1988). 4 various approaches to and definitions of creativity. In Stenberg, R. J. (Ed.), *The nature of creativity: Contemporary psychological perspectives* (p. 99).

Taylor, R. P. (2002). Order in Pollock's chaos. *Scientific American*, (December): 2002.

Taylor, R. P., Micolich, A. P., & Jonas, D. (1999). Fractal analysis of Pollock's drip paintings. *Nature*, *280*, 399–422.

Tegmark, M. (2007). *Shut up and calculate*. Retrieved March 3, 2011, from http://arxiv.org/PS_cache/arxiv/pdf/0709/0709.4024v1.pdf

Tegmark, M. (2008). The mathematical universe. *Foundations of Physics, 38*(2), 101–150. Retrieved March 3, 2011, from http://arxiv.org/PS_cache/arxiv/pdf/0704/0704.0646v2.pdf

Than, K. (2010). Every black hole contains another universe? *National Geographic News*. Retrieved December 14, 2010, from http://news.nationalgeographic.com/news/2010/04/100409-black-holes-alternate-universe-multiverse-einstein-wormholes/

The Arts Catalyst. (2011). Retrieved June 28, 2011, from http://www.artscatalyst.org/

The Nanoscale Science, Engineering, and Technology Subcommittee. (2004). *National nanotechnology initiative strategic plan*. Retrieved September 28, 2011, from http://www.nsf.gov/crssprgm/nano/reports/sp_report_nset_final.pdf

The Nobel Prize in Physiology or Medicine. (1974). Retrieved September 28, 2011, from http://www.nobelprize.org/nobel_prizes/medicine/laureates/1974/

Thompson D'Arcy, W. (1917, 1992). *On growth and form*, rev. ed. Dover Publications. ISBN-10: 048667135

Thompson, D. W. (1961). *On growth and form*. Cambridge, UK: The University Press.

Thoreau, H. D. (1852). [Princeton, NJ: Princeton University Press.]. *Journal*, *4*, 356.

Thybo, N. K., Stephens, N., Cooper, A., Aalkjaer, C., Heagerty, A. M., & Mulvany, M. J. (1995). Effect of antihypertensive treatment on small arteries of patients with previously untreated essential hypertension. *Hypertension*, *25*(4), 474.

Tiberghien, G. A. (1996). *Land art* (Green, C., Trans.). New York, NY: Princeton Architectural Press. (Original work published 1993)

Tilakasiri, J. (1968). *The puppet theatre of Asia*. Ceylon, MA: The Department of Cultural Affairs, Department of Government Printing.

Times, N. Y. (2009, August). Toxic waters. *New York Times*.

Tomasula, S. (1998). Bytes and zeitgeist. Digitizing the cultural landscape. Sixth Annual New York Digital Salon. *Leonardo*, *31*(5), 338.

Tufnell, B. (2006). *Land art* (pp. 15–17). London, UK: Tate Publishing.

Tufte, E. (1990). *Envisioning information*. Cheshire, CT: Graphics Press.

Tufte, E. (2001). *The visual display of quantitative information* (2nd ed.). Cheshire, CT: Graphics Press.

Tufte, E. R. (1983). *The visual display of quantitative information*. Cheshire, CT: Graphics Press.

Tufte, E. R. (1997). *Visual explanations: Images and quantities, evidence and narrative*. Cheshire, CT: Graphics Press.

Turner, W. (2011). *The morning after the deluge*. Retrieved January 27, 2011, from http://www.william-turner.org/The-Morning-after-the-Deluge-c.-1843.html

Turner, H. R. (1997). *Science in Medieval Islam*. Austin, TX: University of Texas Press.

Unverfehrt, G. (Ed.). (2000). *Zeichnungen von Meisterhand: Die Sammlung Uffenbach aus der Kunstsammlung der Universität Göttingen*. Göttingen, Germany: Vandenhoeck & Rupprecht.

Urbano, P. (2006). Consensual paintings. *Applications of Evolutionary Computing*, (pp. 622–632).

Urbano, P. (2005). *Playing in the pheromone playground: Experiences in swarm painting* (pp. 527–532). Applications on Evolutionary Computing.

van der Rohe, M. (1959, 28 June). A quotation, "God is in the details." Speaking about restraint in design. *New York Herald Tribune*. Retrieved September 26, 2011, from http://architecture.about.com/od/20thcenturytrends/a/Mies-Van-Der-Rohe-Quotes.htm

Van Meiss, P. (1990). *Elements of architecture*. London, UK: Taylor & Francis.

Vance, C. (2011). Japan earthquake a reminder about importance of groundwater. *News Hawk Review, News Update*. Retrieved July 13, 2011, from http://newshawksreview.com/japan-earthquake-a-reminder-about-importance- of-groundwater-protection/42305/

Velmans, M. (1996). *Defining consciousness*. Retrieved January 5, 2005, from http://cogprints.org/395/0/Definingconsciousness.html

Venter, J. C., Adams, M. D., Myers, E. W., Li, P. W., Mural, R. J., & Sutton, G. G. (2001). The sequence of the human genome. *Science*, *291*(5507), 1304–1351. doi:10.1126/science.1058040

Verostko, R. (2011). *Artist's website*. Retrieved June 28, 2011, from http://www.verostko.com/

Verostko, R. (2011). *Website of the artist*. Retrieved April 2011, from http://www.verostko.com

Verostko, R. (1988). Epigenetic painting - Software as genotype. [from http://www.verostko.com/epigenet.html]. *Leonardo*, *23*(1), 17–23. Retrieved July 1, 2011 doi:10.2307/1578459

Vesna, V., & Gimzewski, J. (2011). *At the intersection of art and science: NANO*. Los Angeles County Museum of Art. Retrieved August 8, 2011, from http://nano.arts.ucla.edu/files/nano_lacma_book.pdf

Vis, K.-M. (2010). *Chile – Protection of the Tamarugal Forest in the Atacama Desert*. Retrieved November 15, 2010, from http://www.suite101.com/content/chile--protection-of-the-tamarugal-forest-in-the- atacama-desert-a223618#ixzz15NUQxz2W

Vivekananda. (1953). *Vivekananda: The yogas and other works*. New York, NY: Ramakrishna-Vivekananda Center.

Von Uexküll, J. (2010). *A foray into the world of animals and humans*. Minneapolis, MN: University of Minnesota Press. (Original work published 1934)

Voss, R. F. (1988). Fractals in nature: From characterization to simulation . In Peitgen, H., & Saupe, D. (Eds.), *The science of fractal images* (pp. 21–70). New York, NY: Springer-Verlag. doi:10.1007/978-1-4612-3784-6_1

Voss, R. F., & Clarke, J. (1975). 1/f noise in music and speech. *Nature*, *258*, 317–318. doi:10.1038/258317a0

Wagner, A. (2009). *Paradoxical life. Meaning, matter and the power of human choice*. New Haven, CT: Yale University Press.

Walker, J. (2004). The reckless and the artless: practical research and digital painting. *Working Papers in Art and Design, 3*. Retrieved June 28, 2011 from http://sitem.herts.ac.uk/artdes_research/papers/wpades/vol3/jfwfull.html

Wallace, A. (2011a). *Home page*. Retrieved July 18, 2011, from http://www.amy-wallace.com/

Wallace, A. (2011b, July 9). Science to art, and vice versa. *New York Times*. Retrieved July 18, 2011, from http://www.nytimes.com/2011/07/10/business/science-to-art-and-vice-versa-prototype.html

Wallis, K. (2003). *Painting and drawing the nude: A search for a realism of the body through phenomenology and fine art*. Thesis (PhD), University of the West of England.

Walser, H. (2001). *The golden section*. Washington, DC: Mathematical Association of America.

Walters, J. (2003). *Blobitecture: Waveform architecture and digital design*. Boston, MA: Rockport Publishers, Inc.

Ware, C. (2004). *Information visualization: Perception for design*. Morgan Kaufman. Retrieved August 5, 2011, from http://books.google.com/books?id=ZmG_FiqqyqgC

Ware. M. (2011). *Alternative photography*. Retrieved August 8, 2011, from http://www.alternativephotography.com/artists/mike_ware.html

Ware, M. (1994). Photographic printing in colloidal gold. *The Journal of Photographic Science*, *42*(5), 157–161.

Warren, J. F. (2003). *Rickshaw coolie: A people's history of Singapore 1880-1940*. Singapore: Singapore University Press.

Wasserman, H., & Solomon, N. (1982). *Killing our own: The disaster of America's experience with atomic radiation*. Delacorte Press. Retrieved August 5, 2011, from http://books.google.com/books?id=Km0gAQAAIAAJ

Watanabe, S. (2009). Pigeons can discriminate âœgoodâ and âœbadâ paintings by children. *Animal Cognition*, *13*(1).

Water Bear. (2011). Retrieved October 10, 2011, from http://www.fcps.edu/islandcreekes/ecology/water_bear.htm

Waterfield, R. (Tr.) (2008). *Aristotle – Physics*. Oxford, UK: Oxford University Press.

Watson, J. D., & Crick, F. H. (1953). Molecular structure of nucleic acids: A structure for deoxyribose nucleic acid. *Nature*, *171*(4356), 737–738. doi:10.1038/171737a0

Waugh, M. (2011). *Liquid sculpture – Water drop art*. Retrieved April 11, 2011, from http://www.liquidsculpture.com/index.htm

Weaver, T. (1999). *Drip, blow, burn: Forces of nature in contemporary art*. Yonkers, NY . *The Hudson River Museum.*, *ISBN-10*, 094365128X.

Weesatchanam, A. M. (2006). *Are paintings by elephants really art?* The Elephant Art Gallery.

Weintraub, L. (2003). *In the making: Creative options for contemporary art*. D.A.P./Distributed Art Publishers. Retrieved August 5, 2011, from http://books.google.com/books?id=h6NPAAAAMAAJ

Weiss, P. (2004). *Wet 'n 'wild: Explaining water's weirdness*. Boston University, Center for Polymer Studies. Retrieved July 13, 2011, from http://www.phschool.com/science/science_news/articles/wet_n_wild.html

Wellcome Trust . (2011). Retrieved June 28, 2011, from http://www.wellcome.ac.uk/

Weller, M. P., Gross, M. D., & Goldstein, S. C. (2010). Hyperform specification: Designing and interacting with self-reconfiguring materials. *Personal and Ubiquitous Computing*, *15*(2), 133–149. doi:10.1007/s00779-010-0315-7

Weschler, L. (2009). *David Hockney's iPhone passion*. Retrieved July 4, 2011, from www.hockneypictures.com/current.php

Wessberg, J., Stambaugh, C. R., Kralik, J. D., Beck, P. D., Laubach, M., & Chapin, J. K. (2000). Real-time prediction of hand trajectory by ensemble of cortical neurons in primates. *Nature*, *408*(6810), 361–365. doi:10.1038/35042582

Wesseling, P. (2000). *Principles of computational fluid dynamics*. New York, NY: Springer-Verlag.

Wheeler, W. M. (1912). The ant colony as an organism. [Baltimore, MD: Waverly Press.]. *Journal of Morphology*, *22*, 307–325. doi:10.1002/jmor.1050220206

Whitaker, C. (2000). The vanishing human. [NY Digital Salon.]. *Leonardo*, *33*(5), 438–438. doi:10.1162/leon.2000.33.5.438b

White, C. (2011). *Liquids in motion*. Retrieved April 11, 2011, from http://www.liquiddropart.com/myliquiddropart/index.html

Wiener, N. (1948). *Cybernetics*. Cambridge, MA: MIT Press.

Wilbur, K. (1992). *A brief history of everything*. Boston, MA: Shambhala.

Wilbur, K. (Ed.). (1982). *The holographic paradigm and other paradoxes*. Boston, MA: Shambhala.

Wild, A. (2008). Breaking news: The atta phylogeny. Retrieved March 12, 2001, from http://myrmecos.net/2008/11/13/breaking-news-the-atta-phylogeny

Wilson, S. (2002). *Information arts: Intersections of art, science, and technology.* MIT Press. Retrieved July 13, 2011 from http://books.google.com/books?id=sHuXQtYrNPYC

Wilson, E. O. (1998). *Consilience. The unity of knowledge*. New York, NY: Vintage Books, Random House, Inc.

Wilson, J. (1977). *Physics: Concepts and applications*. Lexington, MA: D. C Heath and Co.

Wilson, S. (1989). Carbon and silicon playing a game of skill. *Leonardo, 22*, 1.

Wilson, S. (2002). *Information arts: Intersections of art, science, and technology*. Cambridge, MA: MIT Press.

Witcombe, C. (2011). *Water in art*. Retrieved April 11, 2011, from http://witcombe.sbc.edu/water/art.html

Wolf, F. A. (1999). *The spiritual universe. One physicist's vision of spirit, soul, matter, and self*. Needhan, MA: Moment Point Press, Inc.

Wolf-Gladrow, D. (2000). *Lattice-gas cellular automata and lattice Boltzmann models*. New York, NY: Springer-Verlag.

Wolfram, W. (2002). *A new kind of science*. Champaign, IL: Wolfram Media.

Wolpaw, J. R., & Birbaumer, N. (2002). Brain-computer interfaces for communication and control. *Clinical Neurophysiology, 113*(6), 767–791. doi:10.1016/S1388-2457(02)00057-3

Wolpaw, J. R., Birbaumer, N., Heetderks, W. J., McFarland, D. J., Peckham, P. H., & Schalk, G. (2000). Brain-computer interface technology: A review of the first international meeting. *IEEE Transactions on Rehabilitation Engineering, 8*(2), 164–173. doi:10.1109/TRE.2000.847807

World Community Grid . (2010). Retrieved December 17, 2010, from http://www.worldcommunitygrid.org/about_us/viewAboutUs.do

World, W. (2010). *Atacama desert NT 1303*. WWF Full Report. Retrieved November 15, 2010, from http://www.worldwildlife.org/wildworld/profiles/terrestrial/nt/nt1303_full.html

Yildiz, A., Forkey, J. N., McKinney, S. A., Ha, T., Goldman, Y. A., & Selvin, P. R. (2003). Myosin V walks hand-over-hand: Single fluorophore imaging with 1.5-nm localization. *Science, 300*(5628), 2061–2065. doi:10.1126/science.1084398

You, F., Dehlinger, H., & Wang, J.-M. (2010). *Generative art: Aesthetic events from experiments with lines and squares*. Guangzhou, China: Lingnan Art Publishing House.

Zalta, E. N. (Ed.). (2010). Epistêmê and Techné. *The Stanford Encyclopedia of Philosophy*. Retrieved January 10, 2011, from http://plato.stanford.edu

Zamir, M. (1976). The role of shear forces in arterial branching. *The Journal of General Physiology, 67*(2), 213. doi:10.1085/jgp.67.2.213

Zaretskii, Y. K., & Fish, A. M. (1996). Effect of temperature on the strength and viscosity of ice. *Soil Mechanics and Foundation Engineering, 33*(2), 46–52. doi:10.1007/BF02354293

Zarins, C. K., Giddens, D. P., Bharadvaj, B. K., Sottiurai, V. S., Mabon, R. F., & Glagov, S. (1983). Carotid bifurcation atherosclerosis. quantitative correlation of plaque localization with flow velocity profiles and wall shear stress. *Circulation Research, 53*(4), 502.

Zarins, C. K., Zatina, M. A., Giddens, D. P., Ku, D. N., & Glagov, S. (1987). Shear stress regulation of artery lumen diameter in experimental atherogenesis. *Journal of Vascular Surgery, 5*(3), 413.

Zeki, S. (1993). Vision of the brain. *Wiley-Blackwell.*, *ISBN-10*, 0632030542.

Zeki, S. (1999). Art and the brain. *Journal of Conscious Studies: Controversies in Science and the Humanities*, *6*(6/7), 76–96.

Zheng, J., Birktoft, J. J., Chen, Y., Wang, T., Sha, R., & Constantinou, P. E. (2009). From molecular to macroscopic via the rational design of a self-assembled 3D DNA crystal. *Nature*, *461*, 74–77. doi:10.1038/nature08274

Zimmer, H. (1946). *Myths and symbols in Indian art and civilization* (Campbell, J., Ed.). Princeton, NJ: Princeton University Press.

Zuanon, R., & Lima, G. C., Jr. (2008). *BioBodyGame*. Retrieved March 9, 2011, from http://www.rachelzuanon. com/biobodygame/

Zuanon, R., & Lima, G. C., Jr. (2010). *NeuroBodyGame*. Retrieved March 9, 2011, from http://www.rachelzuanon. com/neurobodygame/

About the Contributors

Anna Ursyn, PhD, is a Professor and Computer Graphics Area Head at the School of Art and Design, University of Northern Colorado. She combines programming with software and printmaking media, to unify computer generated and painted images, and mixed-media sculptures. Ursyn had over 30 single juried and invitational art shows, participated in over 100 fine art exhibitions, and published articles and artwork in books and journals. Research and pedagogy interests include integrated instruction in art, science, and computer art graphics. Since 1987 she serves as a Liaison, Organizing and Program Committee member of International IEEE Conferences on Information Visualization (iV) London, UK, and Computer Graphics, Imaging and Visualization Conferences (CGIV). She serves as Chair of the Symposium and Digital Art Gallery D-ART iV, 1997-2011.

* * *

Ahmed Aber is a Medical Doctor practising at the Luton and Dunstable Hospital. Ahmed received his Medical Degree from the Barts and The Royal London Medical School and his Bachelor's degree in Biomedical Engineering from Queen Mary University of London. He is currently undertaking his postgraduate training at the North Thames Central Foundation School. He is heavily involved in clinical and non-clinical research with a special interest in the use of nanotechnology, laser imaging, and artificial intelligence to enhance medical imaging. He is also responsible for teaching and organising courses for medical students at the University College London.

Mohammad Majid al-Rifaie is a PhD researcher at Goldsmiths, University of London. His background is in computing and journalism, and his artistic interests focus on the interconnections between artificial intelligence, swarm intelligence, robotics, and digital art. He has several publications in the field of swarm intelligence and biologically inspired algorithms (stochastic diffusion search, particle swarm optimisation, genetic and differential evolution algorithms), analysing their performance and providing possible integration strategies. Many of Mohammad's projects on the aforementioned fields have been well received and sponsored by external entities (i.e. Luz by VIDA Fundación Telefónica competition of art and artificial intelligence 13th edition, Swarms Go Dutch by the American University of Paris, and Mr. Confused Robotic Household by Goldsmiths Annual Fund, University of London).

Kuai Shen Auson was born in Guayaquil, Ecuador. He holds a BA in Digital Arts and an MA in Media Arts with honors from the Academy of Media Arts in Cologne. He has brought his work, exploring the cybernetic emergence of ants into new territories, from Quito to New York and now to Cologne. His artistic approach to self-organization and emergence is envisioned in four installations: ?Recurrent Ant Dream #1?, ?1.ant.ity?, ?The Cybernetic Emergence of Ants,? and ?0h!m1gas: biomimetic stridulation environment.? His current research focuses on game design and theory based on his interdisciplinary artistic/scientific work with ants at the University of Applied SciencesCologne.

Mark John Bishop is Professor of Cognitive Computing at Goldsmiths, University of London and Chair of the AISB. He has published over 120 articles in the field of Cognitive Computing: its theory - where his interests centre on the foundations of the swarm intelligence paradigm "Stochastic Diffusion Processes"; its application – he has worked on industrial problems in autonomous robotics, neural networks and colour; and its philosophical foundations - he has developed a novel argument against the possibility of machine consciousness. Together with John Preston, Mark has co-edited a critique of John Searle's arguments against machine intelligence, "Views into the Chinese Room" (OUP, 2002).

Jean Constant studied art at the Beaux Arts in Tours and at the San Francisco Art Institute. He worked as a muralist for the San Francisco Art Commission and a photographer for European agencies, which lead him to record the revival of the mural movement in California and throughout the country in the mid-seventies. Jean was a gallery director in Phoenix, AZ, the Arizona Artists Program, and later in Los Angeles. He worked as Public Art consultant and producer of several TV series on art, film, and culture. Jean taught film studies at the University of New Mexico and has been acting director of the NNMC Media and Visual Communication program. He is today Executive Secretary for the European Society for Mathematics and Art.

Doug Craft is a visual artist, scientist, and musician who creates collages, photographs, and paintings that incorporate the Golden Ratio, the fractal structure associated with nature. A member of Core New Art Space, he had numerous solo and group exhibitions, and was published in Math Horizons magazine and the journal Cybernetics and Human Knowing. His microphotography was recognized by the 2008 and 2009 Nikon *Small World* Competitions, and his website contains one of the largest collections of microphotos on the Internet. As an environmental research chemist Doug published numerous peer reviewed journal papers and research reports concerning natural water chemistry, water quality, toxicological chemistry, fate and transport of contaminants, acid precipitation, and the geochemistry. He is the CEO of Craft Geochemistry Consulting, LLC, http://www.craftgeochemistry.com, writes and lectures on Peak Oil, energy depletion issues, and relocalization. His art and music may be found on his website, http://www.dougcraftfineart.com.

Hans Dehlinger studied Architecture at the University of Stuttgart, graduated with a Dipl.Ing./ Architektur, and then at the University of California, Berkley (M.Arch., & Ph.D.). He worked as a chief designer in the design teams for the Olympic-Game-Buildings in Munich, a planning scientist for the "Studiengruppe für Systemforschung" in Heidelberg, and as a freelance architect and design scientist. He was a founder and director of the "Institut für Rechnergestuetztes Darstellen und Entwerfen." In 1980 he was appointed Professor of Industrial Design at the University of Kassel and started to explore computers artistically. Dehlinger's work received worldwide recognition, and was shown first in Europe, later in Canada, Russia, Australia, the USA, Armenia, and China. Drawings of Dehlinger are in private collections, in the Victoria and Albert Museum in London, and in the Mary and Leigh Block Museum of Art in Evanston.

Deborah Harty is an artist and researcher. She holds a PhD in Drawing from Loughborough University. Harty's ongoing research is practice-led and utilises drawing practice alongside theory to research aspects of phenomenology, perception, and experience. Harty has been involved in *TRACEY* - Loughborough University's online journal of drawing research - for several years, becoming a co-editor in 2010. In 2011 Harty's three-year long research project "drawing *is* phenomenology" will be launched within the new TRACEY Project Space. As a practitioner-researcher Harty has contributed to debates in drawing through both conference presentation and exhibition including a solo exhibition at C4RD and inclusion in the iNDA. Now she holds a post at Nottingham Trent University, UK.

Scott Hessels is filmmaker, sculptor, and media artist who mixes cinema with emerging technologies to explore new relationships between the moving image and the environment. His artworks span several different media including film, video, Web, music, broadcast, print, kinetic sculpture, and performance. His films have shown in numerous international film festivals, and his installations have been presented in exhibitions around the world including CiberArt in Bilbao, Ars Electronica, The Ford Presidential Museum, SIGGRAPH, ISEA, and Japan's Media Art Festival. His work is featured in several books on new media art as well as in magazines like *Wired* and *Discover*. His recent projects have mixed film with sensors, robotics, GPS systems, and alternative forms of interactivity and have included partnerships with NASA, The Federal Aviation Administration, and Nokia, among others. He is currently an Associate Professor at The School of Creative Media in City University of Hong Kong.

Collin Hover is a Master's of Fine Arts candidate at the University of Texas at Arlington, scheduled to complete his study in 2012. Currently his research focus is on virtual, interactive, and game-based visual communication applied to education and learning. His undergraduate study in Graphic Design was split between Virginia Tech and the University of South Dakota. Before attending university, Collin grew up in a nomadic family of (hyper)polyglots, travelling and living in the Middle East, Europe, eastern Asia, and the triangle of Polynesia to pursue a love of language.

Scottie Huang is an artist, designer, and researcher. He is interested in the use of interactive media into kinetic sculpture and architectural space. He was selected to participate in SIGGRAPH Biologic Juried Art Gallery, Prague Quadrennial of Performance Design and Space, recipient of the K. T. Creativity Award and Gold Award in Interactive Technology Art, and a Nomination of The 3rd Digital Art Award Taipei in Interactive Installation. His works has been published in a number of conferences, journals, and magazines including SIGGRAPH (ACM), Leonardo/ISAST (MIT Press), Ubiquitous, Autonomic, and Trusted Computing (IEEE Press), CAADFutures (Springer), Taiwan Reviews, RealTime Art, DeSForM, ASCAAD, etc. Scottie received a B.S. (architectural design) from National Taipei University of Technology; a M.S. (digital architecture) from National Chio-Tung University; and a Ph.D. in Architecture from National Taiwan University of Science and Technology.

Eunsu Kang is an international media artist from Korea. She creates audiovisual spaces interacting with people using interactive video, spatialized sound, site-specific installation and performance. Her work has been invited to numerous places around the world including Japan, China, Switzerland, Sweden, France, Germany and the US. All nine of her solo exhibitions, consisting of individual or collaborative projects, were invited or awarded. Her research has been presented at prestigious conferences such as

ACM, ICMC and ISEA. Kang earned her Ph.D. in Digital Arts and Experimental Media from DXARTS at the University of Washington. She received an MA in Media Arts and Technology from UCSB and an MFA from the Ewha Woman's University. She is currently an assistant professor of New Media Art at the University of Akron in Ohio, USA.

Matthew Kolodziej earned a BA in Economics from the University of Chicago in 1988 and an MFA in painting from Rhode Island School of Design in 1993. Interested in what people leave behind, Kolodziej worked on archaeological digs while in college. These formative experiences strengthened an interest in material culture. A Fulbright Scholar in 1995, Kolodziej traveled extensively in England to explore prehistoric ruins. In 2009, he was awarded a Pollock Krasner grant. His paintings have been featured in shows at the Rose Art Museum, The Akron Art Museum, and most recently in the exhibition There Goes the Neighborhood at The Museum of Contemporary Art Cleveland, the William Busta Gallery in Cleveland, and Pierogi in New York.

Eve Andrée Laramée is an interdisciplinary artist and researcher working at the confluence of art and science, specializing in the environmental and health impacts of Cold War atomic legacy sites. Laramée divides her time between Brooklyn, NY; Santa Fe, NM; and Baltimore, MD where she is Professor of Interdisciplinary Sculpture at the Maryland Institute College of Art. Her art has been exhibited throughout the United States, England, Germany, Italy, Switzerland, France, Holland, Israel, China, Japan, Poland, and the Czech Republic. Her work is included in the collections of the MacArthur Foundation; the Museum of Modern Art, New York; the Museum of Contemporary Art, Chicago; The Fogg Art Museum of Harvard University; MIT; and in numerous other public and private collections. Laramée has received grants from the Pollock-Krasner Foundation, Andy Warhol Foundation, New York Foundation for Arts, National Endowment for the Arts, and the Guggenheim Museum.

Liz Lee received a BFA from the University of Calgary in Calgary, Alberta Canada in 1990 and a MFA in Photography from the Savannah College of Art and Design in 1996. She is a Professor of Photography in the Department of Visual Arts and New Media at the State University of New York at Fredonia. Before this, she was an Assistant Professor at Missouri State University. Liz's work has appeared in numerous national and international exhibitions. Her work also appears in Robert Hirsch's text Light and Lens: Photography in the Digital Age and Exploring Color Photography: From Film to Pixels 5th edition. In 2007 she received a fellowship with Booksmart Studios in Rochester, NY to produce her series *Grassroots (the shun series)* as a limited edition fine-art book. She recently participated as an artist-in-resident at the Vermont Studio Center in Johnson, VT.

Peter H Niewiarowski is a professor of Biology and the interim director of the Integrated Bioscience Ph.D. program at the University of Akron. He has active research projects in amphibian population biology, and the ecology and evolution of geckos, particularly as they relate to adhesion. Through collaboration with material scientists, designers, and engineers, he has begun to explore biomimicry and biologically-inspired design. Biomimicry also provides an engaging platform for interaction with artists who are curious about the relationship between art and science, especially as it impacts our professional and personal lives.

Cris Orfescu was born in Bucharest, Romania, and has lived and worked in Los Angeles since 1991. He is a self-taught artist and also a degreed scientist who has been experimenting for over 40 years with different media and art forms including digital art, murals, acrylic and oil painting, mixed media, faux painting, trompe l'oeil, collage, graphics, animation, web design, video, and multimedia. For more than 25 years he has been experimenting and perfecting a new art form, NanoArt, which reflects the transition from science to art through technology. Orfescu was showing internationally his awarded works in USA, Italy, France, Finland, Korea, UK, Ireland, Spain, Germany, Colombia, Greece, Czech Republic, and Romania, in numerous solo and group exhibitions. His art was commissioned for public and private collectors.

Victor Raphael is an artist who works in several media—including painting, photography, digital art, printmaking, and video. Raphael explores the broad themes of time and space through his investigations of nature, deep space, art history, and metaphysics. Raphael's artwork is in many collections, including: Bibliotheque Nationale de France, Huan Tie Times Art Museum (Beijing), Los Angeles County Museum of Art, Sol LeWitt Collection, Polaroid Collection, the Skirball Museum, and Tokyo Metropolitan Museum of Photography. Raphael's work was included in the 50th anniversary exhibition *Polaroid 50: Art and Technology,* which toured European museums from 1996-98, as well as *American Perspectives: Photographs from the Polaroid Collection*, which toured Japanese museums from 2000-2001. Raphael has had two museum retrospectives of his artwork, a 20-year survey at the Frederick R. Weisman Museum of Art at Pepperdine University in 2000 and a 30-year survey at the USC Fisher Museum of Art.

Wolfgang Schneider (born in 1945) is a Natural Scientist. He completed studies in Geology, History, and History of the Arts (Universities of Cologne and Bochum, Germany). In 1977 – 2010 he served as a Director of the Museum der Stadt Gladbeck, Germany. He was a Co-Founder of the Gesellschaft fuer Elektronische Kunst (Electronic Art Society), and in 1986 – 2010 International Biennial Competitions for the 'Gladbeck Golden Plotter Award' and travelling exhibitions. He is also Editor of catalogs in history and cultural history.

Clayton S. Spada, artist, curator, writer, and adjunct faculty at Cypress College, works on applications in digital signal processing, still- and motion-based imaging. Clayton holds a PhD in Biology from Leicester University in England. He has been a Photoshop beta-tester and consultant for Adobe Software. Previously in charge of the Orange County Center for Contemporary Art, Spada was also co-founder and editor-in-chief of the art quarterly *NoMoPoMo: A Contemporary Artist's Resource*. Member of The Legacy Project, six Southern California photographers who document the decommissioned Marine Corps Air Station at El Toro, California, and its transition into the Orange County Great Park. Works exhibited and published in annuals, periodicals, and textbooks, and also featured in cable and network television spots in the US and abroad, held in institutional collections including the Fisher Gallery (University of Southern California), Digital Media Studio (University of California), and private collections in the US, UK, Germany, and China.

Shen-Guan Shih is Associate Professor in Department of Architecture at National Taiwan University of Science and Technology, Taiwan. His research interests are in computer-aided design in architecture, design theory, and artificial intelligence. He teaches architectural design, computer applications for architecture, as well as the methods and theory for architectural design.

Mark J. Stock is an artist, programmer, and scientist working in the space between visualization, computation, and new media art. His work depicts scenes from the hidden world of computational physics---the science of digitally simulating complex natural phenomena on supercomputers – and is created with custom software developed over the course of his scientific research. He has been producing art since 2000 and has had work in dozens of curated and juried exhibitions since 2002, including *Ars Electronica, ASPECT Magazine,* and six SIGGRAPH Art Gallery appearances. Mark finished his Ph.D. in Aerospace Engineering at the University of Michigan in 2006 for the study of vortex sheet methods, and he has worked for a small computational physics research company in Santa Ana, California since. He currently works and develops art in his studio in Newton, MA, where he lives with his wife and a pile of computers.

Kalyan Chakravarthy Thokala earned a Master of Science degree in Computer Science from the University of Akron. The title of his thesis was "Haptic-enabled Multi-dimensional Canvas." As part of the thesis work, he developed a virtual paint brush that allows artists to paint in multiple dimensions with gravity and force feedback. His interest in the arts motivated him to design and build innovative tools for artistic expressions. He has a particular interest in the mathematical theory of creating virtual flora and fauna and the relationship between such artwork and the nature of science behind it. Thokala also received a Bachelor of Engineering degree in Information Technology from Chaitanya Bharathi Institute of Technology affiliated with Osmania University in India.

James Faure Walker studied at St Martin's and the RCA. He has been integrating computer graphics in his painting since 1988. He co-founded *Artscribe magazine* in 1976. Recent one-person exhibitions include Galerie Wolf Lieser (2003); Galerie der Gegenwart, Wiesbaden (2000, 2001). Group exhibitions include Jerwood Drawing Prize (2010); Digital Pioneers Victoria and Albert Museum (2009); Imaging by Numbers, Block Museum, Illinois, USA (2008); Siggraph, USA (eight times 1995 -2007); DAM Gallery, Berlin (2003, 2005, 2009). In 1998 he won the Golden Plotter at Computerkunst, Gladbeck, Germany. In 2010 he produced a commissioned print for the 2010 South African World Cup. His book, "Painting the Digital River: How an Artist Learned to Love the Computer," (2006, Prentice Hall, USA), won a New England Book Show Award. He is Reader in Painting and the Computer at the CCW Graduate School, University of the Arts, London.

Donna Webb has been a Professor of Art at the Myers School of Art at the University of Akron since 1981. She teaches ceramics and the history of craft. She is also a studio artist. Her diverse work in ceramics includes vessels, sculpture, and tile installations. Her primary concentration has been in mixed media tile installations in public buildings throughout Ohio. Her work in glaze formulation has resulted in mosaics in which color is used in a painterly way. Her work has been published in "The Art of Mosaic Design" and in the "Penland Book of Crafts." Her studio and Gallery, Blue Sky, has been in operation since 1995.

Yingcai Xiao is an Associate Professor of Computer Science at the University of Akron. His research interests are in the applications of computer graphics and visualization. One area of particular interest to him is digital arts, where computer scientists can be inspired to develop tools for artists to expand their creativity in the virtual space. Xiao has been serving as the program chair of IADIS International Conference on Computer Graphics and Visualization since 2007. He received a Ph.D. in Physics and a Ph.D. in Computer Science, both from the University of Alabama in Huntsville. He was a computer scientist at Intergraph Corporation prior to joining the faculty of the University of Akron.

Hironori Yoshida was a visiting scholar at Carnegie Mellon University and researcher at dFAB and CoDe Lab. He organizes hy-ma.com, collecting new material experiences recently emerged due to computation, electronics, and advanced tooling process. His education in Material Engineering at Waseda University and Industrial Design at TU Delft crystallized to his recent work, Digitized Grain, presented at SIGGRAPH 2011. He worked as an interior designer in Tokyo and model maker at Vincent de Rijk Werkplaats. His current focus is hybridization of technology and materials, resulting in materiality augmented by technology such as advanced fabrication and sensing/actuating technology. The mediation of his focus is rooted in his multidisciplinary background among engineering, material science and interior design, and multi-national design activity in Europe, United States, and Japan.

Rachel Zuanon is media artist and designer. She is a researcher and Professor in the MA Design Program at the Anhembi Morumbi University, Brazil, coordinates the CNPq research group "Design: creation, language and technology, the "Sense Design Lab," the "TVDi Design Lab," and the study group "Design of Physical-Digital Interfaces." She holds a PhD in Communication and Semiotics (PUC-SP). She is partner-director of the Zuanon Integrated Solutions in Design, Interactivity, and Technology, a company focused in development of projects and interactive solutions for physical and digital environments. Her artwork "NeuroBodyGame" presented at File 2010 was finalist at FILE PRIX LUX 2010. Her artwork "BioBodyGame" was presented in 2009 at Itau Cultural. Her artwork "Biocybernetic Relational Object" won the prize Rumos Arte Cibernética granted by Itau Cultural. She has presented her research at several places, such as: ISEA 2011, 2008, and 2002; M-Connect 2010, among others.

Index